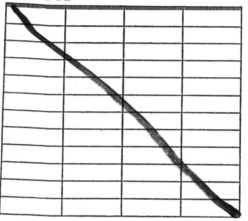

THE AMERICAN COMMUNIST PARTY

A Da Capo Press Reprint Series

FRANKLIN D. ROOSEVELT AND THE ERA OF THE NEW DEAL

GENERAL EDITOR: FRANK FREIDEL
Harvard University

THE AMERICAN COMMUNIST PARTY

A Critical History

by

Irving Howe

and

Lewis Coser

DA CAPO PRESS • NEW YORK • 1974

Library of Congress Cataloging in Publication Data

Howe, Irving.
  The American Communist Party; a critical history.

  (Franklin D. Roosevelt and the era of the New Deal)
  Reprint of the ed. published by Praeger, New York, which was
issued as no. PPS-64 of Praeger paperbacks.
  1. Communist Party of the United States of America.
2. Communism—United States—1917-   I. Coser, Lewis A.,
1913-   joint author. II. Title. III. Series.
[JK2391.C5H68 1974]   329'.82   73-22072
ISBN 0-306-70636-9

This Da Capo Press edition of *The American Communist Party* is
an unabridged republication of the second, corrected printing
containing a new Epilogue, published in New York in 1962.
It is reprinted with the permission of the authors
and Frederick A. Praeger, Inc.

Published by Da Capo Press, Inc.
A Subsidiary of Plenum Publishing Corporation
227 West 17th Street, New York, N.Y. 10011

Manufactured in the United States of America

THE AMERICAN COMMUNIST PARTY

THE AMERICAN COMMUNIST PARTY

A Critical History

by Irving Howe *and* Lewis Coser

with the assistance of Julius Jacobson

FREDERICK A. PRAEGER, *Publisher*

New York

BOOKS THAT MATTER

Published in the United States of America in 1962 by
Frederick A. Praeger, Inc., Publisher
64 University Place, New York 3, N.Y.

Second printing, 1962

The original edition of this book was published in 1957 by
Beacon Press. The present edition contains some corrections
and a new Epilogue.

Library of Congress Catalog Card Number: 62-10367

The poem on pages 291-292 is from *Selected Poems* by Bertolt Brecht,
translated by H. R. Hays, copyright, 1947, by Bertolt Brecht and
H. R. Hays. Reprinted by permission of Harcourt, Brace & World, Inc.

Manufactured in the United States of America

to

Ignazio Silone
and
Milovan Djilas

Contents

List of Abbreviations

AFL	American Federation of Labor
APM	American Peace Mobilization
AYC	American Youth Congress
AYD	American Youth for Democracy
CIO	Congress of Industrial Organizations
CLP	Communist Labor Party
CP	Communist Party
CPA	Communist Political Association
CPPA	Conference for Progressive Political Action
CPUSA	Communist Party, United States of America
FBI	Federal Bureau of Investigation
FFLP	Federated Farm Labor Party
FLP	Farmer-Labor Party
ILD	International Labor Defense
ILGWU	International Ladies Garment Workers Union
IWW	Industrial Workers of the World
NAACP	National Association for the Advancement of Colored People
NEP	New Economic Policy
NLRB	National Labor Relations Board
NMU	National Maritime Union
NYA	National Youth Administration
SP	Socialist Party
TUEL	Trade Union Educational League
TUUL	Trade Union Unity League
UAW	United Auto Workers
UCP	United Communist Party
UMW	United Mine Workers
UOPW	United Office and Professional Workers
WP	Workers Party
YCL	Young Communist League

Preface

This book is an effort to write a political, social, and cultural history of the American Communist Party from its inception in 1919 to its virtual demise in 1957. In the main, it is a public history, concerned with the relationship between American life and Communism as a political and intellectual current. We have used public sources and have not relied upon the personal testimony of Communists, ex-Communists, or anti-Communists. The statements in this book can be checked, just as the opinions can be debated.

Many matters concerning American Communism are not treated here. We are perfectly aware that certain underground operations were at times a significant part of Communist activity; that there have been secret transfers of funds; that Communist spy rings, whether in close association with the party or not, have been at work in the United States. Yet we have chosen not to deal with these matters, not because they are unimportant—they certainly deserve treatment by other writers—but because we have had to submit ourselves to the usual limitations of space, time, interest, and competence.

Even in these terms and despite its size, our book cannot pretend to be exhaustive. It does not present a detailed day-by-day or month-by-month chronicle of the inner workings and intrigues of the party. We have kept our main attention upon the public significance of the American Communist movement, and we deal with its institutional life primarily as it helps explain and relates to this public significance.

Within the bounds of our self-imposed limits there is more than enough, however, that requires presentation, ordering, analysis, and discussion. It would be disingenuous to pretend that we come to this subject without a point of view or strong predispositions—no writer worth reading could make such a pretense in regard to so vital and controversial a topic. But we have tried to keep statements of fact distinct from statements of opinion, and when we resort to surmise we say so. We have also tried to present all the relevant facts, including those that might jostle our opinions. The rest is for the reader to judge.

It should be remarked that we have devoted the largest portion of our space to that period—the 1930's—which is probably the most important in the history of American Communism and the smallest portion to that period—the last decade—which is likely to be most familiar to the reader.

To our regret, two excellent studies, *The Roots of American Communism* by Theodore Draper and *The Communist Party vs. the CIO* by Max Kampelman, appeared too late for us to take advantage of the material that each of these books presents.

To avoid spotting our pages, we have frequently bunched several references under one number.

We wish to say a few words of gratitude to those who have helped us with this book. Our first and largest debt is to Julius Jacobson, our endlessly patient and hard-working collaborator, who performed a large share of the research and submitted early drafts for several chapters. Despite his disagreement with a number of points in the book, Mr. Jacobson has worked with us in the closest and most loyal relationship, a co-author in all but name. To Michael Walzer, a former student of both authors, we are indebted for some excellent research in connection with Chapters IX and X. A grant from Brandeis University enabled Mr. Walzer to do this research and also made it possible for us to have the final manuscript typed. Finally, a word of thanks to our wives and children, who together with us suffered and waited and watched and hoped.

I. H.
L. C.

An Epilogue, written in September, 1961, has been added to this paperback edition to bring the story of the American Communist Party completely up to date.

Chapter I. Sources of American Radicalism

1. When the Communist Party of the United States was formed in 1919—formed, characteristically, as a movement split into hostile factions—it was generally regarded as an offshoot of American socialism. In the years to come it would deviate widely from the socialist ideal and would finally come to stand for its political and moral opposite. But to understand the beginnings of the Communist Party, if not quite its ending, we must turn for a moment to a neglected page of American history: the early years of American socialism.

Throughout the nineteenth century movements of social dissent, some serious and others bizarre, kept up a constant political clatter and intellectual vibration. Abolitionism, agrarian reform, the numerous utopian colonies, monetary tinkering and the single tax, Midwestern and Southern Populism, the young labor unions, and finally the isolated socialist sects of the 1880's and 1890's—these formed a loose community of revolt, each unique in quality and significance yet all indicating the capacity of nineteenth-century America to absorb and at times even tolerate political deviants. It is true, of course, that socialism in America never became a major political force. Whether this was, in some sense, inevitable or merely the result of failures that could have been avoided; whether the recuperative powers of American capitalism doomed the radical groups from birth or their own ineptness paralyzed them into their dotage—such questions, by their very nature, permit only speculative answers. But one thing can be stated with some assurance: socialism, far from being an exotic aberration or an imported disease like parrot fever, soon became an integral part of twentieth-century American life. It seemed part of the American readiness to cross European theory with native improvisations; part of that American yearning for utopia which had first shimmered into sight with the Atlantic settlements and may yet survive the atomic age.

2. When the Socialist Party was formed in 1901, it claimed a membership of 10,000. This figure, the Socialist leader Morris Hillquit was later to admit, "was born somewhat more of our enthusiasm than of actual fact." [1] During the next decade the party grew rapidly, reaching in 1912 a membership of 150,000 and polling a presidential vote of 897,000 or some 6 percent of the total. More than a thousand Socialists held public office, though the great majority of them in municipal governments—which would suggest that in getting votes the party's reform or good-government planks were at least as important as its Marxist ideology. The Socialist press mushroomed throughout the country: 5 English dailies (including 2 in such unlikely places as Belleville, Illinois, and Lead, South Dakota) and 8 foreign-language dailies; 262 English weeklies and 36 foreign-language weeklies; 10 English monthlies and 2 foreign-language monthlies.[2] A torrent of propaganda kept pouring out of the party office. The Socialist hall, where the bundles of "literature" lay stacked for distribution and the speaker's stand waited for the next street meeting, became a familiar landmark in hundreds of cities and towns. Socialist lyceums grew up as part of that urge to self-improvement which swept the country during the early years of the century. Socialist encampments, drawing farmers almost as if to revival meetings, were pitched in the Western states. Socialist Sunday schools, mixing a bit of simplified Marxism with a pinch of native agnosticism, passed on the message to the young. And in Eugene Victor Debs the Socialists had a leader who could stir the imagination of an American audience. Pouring out his call to brotherhood and revolt—the two were for him inseparable—Debs made the slogans of radicalism vibrate with truth and beauty and hope: the very slogans that in the mouths of others turned to the ashes of rhetoric.

It was a time of questioning and rejecting. The spoils of the Great Barbecue had been divided but not, millions of Americans were angrily discovering, according to the principles of Christian charity. The power of Big Business, ruthless and undisguised, had not yet been softened by paternalism or glossed by institutional advertising. The violent labor struggles that had made the last two decades of the nineteenth century a time of blood and bitterness still ached in the memories of American workers, so that without becoming revolutionaries or Marxists or, in the main, Socialists they began to think and act as a distinct social group with distinct social aims. Even so moderate a labor leader as John Mitchell of the United Mine Workers, who had never suffered a subversive thought in his life, declared in 1903 that "the average wage-earner has made up his mind that he must remain a wage-earner." [3]

A gifted platoon of muckrakers—Ida Tarbell, David Graham Phillips, Lincoln Steffens—charged through the country exposing theft, scandal, brutality. Directly behind them came the Socialists, pointing to the system that had created the abuses which the muckrakers exposed. As they capitalized on the work of the reformers, the Socialists were able to satisfy a variety of intellectual needs, from those of simple readers who learned from the Midwestern *Appeal to Reason* that the plutocrats were strangling the country to those of sophisticates who learned from Marxist theoreticians that the concentration of capital was inevitable in capitalist society.

Almost every young writer joined in the mood of rebellion. Upton Sinclair's *The Jungle* assaulted the sensibilities, and sometimes the conscience, of middle-class readers. The novelists set out to paint American life as it "really" was, which meant to paint it harshly and clumsily, as if the need to see things in their utter plainness made impossible anything but harshness and clumsiness. Jack London openly called himself a socialist, though his socialism was a rather messy affair, deficient in that sense of plebeian fraternity which made Debs' socialism so exalted an emotion. Theodore Dreiser thought of himself not as a socialist but as a dispassionate student of human fate, a moral scientist graphing the chart of desire and decline. Yet it hardly mattered in which role the writer cast himself. The appetite for social rebellion ran parallel to the infatuation with scientific metaphors, just as the famous "revolt against the village" in American literature ran parallel to the revolt within the town which had transformed thousands of Midwesterners into card-carrying Socialists.

Times change. In 1912 it was as fashionable to be optimistic about the fate of humanity as four decades later it was fashionable to be despairing. The young intellectual of the 1950's who believes that in the "tragic sense of life" he has discovered the root value of human experience would no doubt feel superior to his counterpart of 1912 who thought that the rising solidarity of the masses would soon blossom into the cooperative commonwealth. Yet both responses were organic to the life of their time, valid in their insights as in their limitations.

In 1912, as Gene Debs fired vast meetings throughout the country, thousands of Americans believed that the growth of "the party" would continue in a benevolent progression and that the formulas of their leaders provided a conclusive answer to the problems of society. Behind every word of the Socialists, though not of them alone, lay the unspoken assumption of Progress, the glow of certainty that the future was in hand. And a future, they knew, that would be bright, secure, and controlled.

In many ways it was a good time to be alive.

3. Whatever else it might do, the Socialist Party could never have satisfied Lenin's formula for a revolutionary party. It was neither compact nor centralized, and it certainly was not politically homogeneous. No one would have thought of calling it a "combat party," or of describing its leadership as a cadre of trained professional revolutionaries.

Had this party been required to face one of those revolutionary tests to which Lenin frequently referred, it would surely have crumbled into a thousand pieces; and when it did have to face a decisive, though not revolutionary, test during the First World War it proved to be lacking in that toughness and resilience which a party fundamentally opposed to the *status quo* must have. Yet it may well have been this very looseness of program and structure which made the Socialist Party of these early years so refreshing and lively a movement. By contrast to the Communist type of party it seemed to lack everything, the precise ideology, the trained leadership, the iron discipline—everything but a saving human warmth.

Except for a desire to protest obvious injustice, the political tendencies within the Socialist Party had little in common. There were impulses, like the Populist hatred of the railroads and trusts, that were lingering on from the past and impulses, like the class consciousness of factory workers, that might be matured only in the future. In its looseness and ranginess, the Socialist Party could gather to itself almost every kind of rebel and reformer. It won the support of farmers who simply hated Wall Street—turn the yellowed pages of the *International Socialist Review* and stop for a moment before the picture of Local Cloverdale, Indiana: the men, good solid farmers dressed in Sunday black; the women looking more like characters out of a Willa Cather novel than the radicals they called themselves.[4] Much of the party's fire and strength came from Jewish garment workers who dreamed of escaping from the blackness of the East Side sweatshops and finding a fraternity America had denied them. Millionaire converts—J. G. Phelps, William Bross Lloyd (later a founder of the Communist Labor Party), and Joseph Medill Patterson (later a publisher of the New York *Daily News*)—also joined the party, bringing the glamor of their names, disturbed consciences, and hard cash.

On the far right within the party were municipal reformers and tamed Social Democrats; on the left were the syndicalists, suspicious of intellectuals and politicians but gifted at organizing strikes. Brushing against each other, and sometimes raising sparks, were orthodox Marxist theoreticians like Louis Boudin, whose *Theoretical System of Karl Marx* is one of the few intellectual efforts of early American socialism that bears rereading, and such Christian ministers as the Reverend George Herron, for whom socialism was simply a latter-day version of Jesus' word. And in the ranks were thousands of ordinary Americans who collected dues, distributed leaflets, attended endless meetings.

In the Socialist press schematic lessons in Marxist economics jostled essays on popular science; reports of bloody strikes ran side by side with a feature on the Hawaiian pineapple; fierce calls to revolutionary action appeared next to bland humanitarian moralizing. Appealing to workers who were often breaking into literacy and to immigrants for whom the coming triumph of socialism was somehow related to their coming rise on the social ladder of the new world, the radical papers had regularly to print "self-help" articles. Sometimes these articles took dubious forms, as in the utilization of the Socialist press, particularly the west coast *Wilshire's Magazine,* for promoting get-rich-quick schemes.

In the *Appeal to Reason,* a weekly published in Kansas, American radicalism found its most indigenous voice. Supported by twenty-five-cent subscriptions and prize contests of the kind that would later be viewed as a special vice of the capitalist press, the *Appeal* expressed with equal vehemence the unspoiled idealism of American Socialists and their intellectual naïveté. It bubbled with ingenuous radical enthusiasm and spoke in rich homespun accents which immediately reached the ordinary American reader; but it was remarkable, as well, for its utter, simple certainty, its lack of political reflectiveness. At its best it serialized such worthy books as Upton Sinclair's *The Jungle* and Gustavus Myers' *History of the Great American Fortunes.* Somewhat later it tried, characteristically, to repeat its success by serializing *Tarzan of the Apes.*

The socialism of these early years may sometimes have verged on the nebulous; yet it would be a mistake to suppose, as some historians have, that it was merely progressivism or Populism with an overlay of left-wing rhetoric. For the bulk of the party members socialism implied a deep-going redefinition of human values, an effort to achieve a truly human existence such as could not be had within capitalist society. American Socialism, it is true, never attained a very high intellectual development in these early years, partly because it was so genuinely popular a movement; and of its vast journalistic output little remains except a few books by Morris Hillquit, William English Walling, Louis Boudin, and Jack London. But to make these qualifications is in no way to dismiss its political or human significance. What prompted thousands of Americans to become Socialists was, above all, an impulse to moral generosity, a readiness to stake their hopes on some goal beyond personal success. It was an impulse that drew its strength from an uncomplicated belief in freedom and fraternity; an impulse, to use an almost obsolete word, of *goodness.*[5]

Today, of course, it is hard not to feel that this socialism contained too large a quota of innocence, too great a readiness to let spirit do the work of mind. For the vision of the future which most early American Socialists held was remarkably unproblematic. The party would multiply its vote; Debs or some later reincarnation of Debs would be elected President; a certain amount of social violence might follow during the "transitional period," though on this there were (symptomatic) differences of opinion. But in the main, the Cooperative Commonwealth was felt to be within sight and its success virtually predestined. Problems that have since troubled

Socialists—the relation between the workers and the party that presumes to speak in their name, the difficulties of aligning economic planning with private freedom—were seldom discussed during the Debsian era, and then only by a few intellectuals. Socialism in the years before the First World War was untroubled in mind, familiar enough with struggle and defeat yet temperamentally alien to the idea of tragedy. In this respect, to be sure, the American Socialists were not so very different from their European comrades, who also felt that, somehow, the dialectic of History would dispose of the problems of men. But the lack of intellectual sophistication, of any sustained interest in examining themselves with the Marxist tools they were ready to apply to everyone else, was particularly striking among the American Socialists. Like most Americans of their day, they had little talent for self-doubt; like most Americans, they worked toward their goal with the cheerful assurance of a people that has not yet felt the blows of history.

This simplicity of vision, making as it did for an immense vigor of expression, proved temporarily advantageous to the Socialists. In Debs both the vision and the vigor were embodied with a raw purity. Debs felt the empathy with the downtrodden and exploited that other men talked about; Debs sensed the ritual uses of lonely anger and embodied in himself the need men have for a symbolic agent to bear the agonies of their time; Debs knew that the health of the state requires active opposition and that the health of the opposition requires dissidence within its own ranks. In a profoundly moral sense, he was a permanent revolutionist. He enjoyed that rare kind of power which does not depend upon exploiting followers but leaves them with a feeling of having been exalted and purified. There is a story that at one of his meetings Debs scrambled his papers and read the first half of his speech twice. That the audience nonetheless cheered him is not necessarily proof that it was being victimized; perhaps it had sensed the sly wisdom of the old Hasidic saying that what matters is not the words but the melody.

Like Lincoln, Debs was a shrewd man, and seldom more so than when he surrendered himself, and almost always with total sincerity, to the role of moral prophet. The notion that he was a sort of inspired naïf, a saintly figure deficient in gray matter, does

him an injustice. It is true that Debs never came close to being a
Socialist theoretician, and that when he lost himself in the rhapsodies
of his radical imagination he had a way of dismissing too lightly
specific political problems. He could never understand, for example,
that merely to reiterate the claim that socialism would erase discrimination was not yet to cope with the immediate problems of
the Negro in America. Too often, when faced with the complexities
of a given situation, he would fall back on a declaration of socialist
intransigence or declare that all subordinate problems would be
solved once the "labor problem" was solved. Perhaps so; but the
formula was inadequate to a country where the "labor problem" was
complicated by a great many other social problems. By comparison
with the best of the European Marxist leaders, Debs seemed inflexible and untutored; yet when he applied himself, he showed a
surprising gift for dealing with some of the difficulties that beset the
Socialist movement, particularly the vexing problem of its relations
to the trade unions. For Debs had one superb talent: far more than
any other Socialist leader he was in rapport with American life, he
knew what the people felt and thought, he could almost always
speak to them in terms they immediately grasped.

Debs' trouble as a political leader was hardly, as Daniel Bell
would have it, that his "romanticism . . . caused him to shun the
practical"; it was that he did not think through the implications of
his position in the movement. A little enchanted with his role as
moral nay-sayer, he veered away from the party's inner life, from
its routine work and factional disputes. He was less its leader than
its spokesman. If he seemed to rise above the pettiness and
scholasticism of radical bickering, he was actually—all too often—
flinching from his full and inescapable responsibilities. The "dirty
business" of party factionalism could be dirty enough, but often it
did involve genuine disagreements over genuine issues, and when
Debs stood aside, not attending party conventions or participating in
party discussions, he harmed both his movement and himself. His
stance of being "above" faction struggles had its bureaucratic aspect
as well, for it allowed him to cast an unsullied prestige on the side
he favored without having to assume the burden of leading it. It
may be, however, that this failure fully to participate in the movement to which he gave his life was a reflection of a deeper difficulty

in Debs' character: his disturbing impersonality, his failure to establish direct and spontaneous relations with more than a handful of persons. He came to life mainly on the platform, he communicated primarily with mass audiences, he seldom relaxed from the demands of his public image.[6]

Yet, so long as he spoke, his gaunt body arched with apostolic passion, the idea of socialism could never be quite dead in America; so long as he lived, it would always retain a militant and rebellious edge.

4. As it grew and prospered, the Socialist Party inevitably divided into hostile wings. By 1912 the party must often have seemed less a coherent organization than a turbulent forum in which various radical and near-radical opinions whirled about with bewildering freedom. That this ideological looseness brought advantages almost everyone agreed; but only now, as the movement began to acquire a paunch of success, did the disadvantages become clear. For precisely as the party gained a certain limited influence in American political life did the differences of opinion that had once seemed academic flame into intensity. The full story of the struggle between left and right wings does not fall within our range;[7] we need only stop for a few moments at the 1912 convention of the Socialist Party, where the struggle between the opposing groups came to climax and resolution.

Four years earlier, while interviewing Debs, the journalist Lincoln Steffens had asked: What will Socialists do with the trusts once you come to power? "Take them," answered Debs. "No you wouldn't," cut in Victor Berger, the right-wing Socialist leader who was present at the interview. "Not if I was there. And you shall not say it for the party. It is my party as much as yours, and I answer that we would offer to pay." [8]

Now in terms of doctrine this was not an expression of fundamental differences; if anything, it obscured those differences with the pedantic issue of "compensation vs. confiscation," once so beloved of radical kitchen-talk. But as an index of political temper the incident clearly revealed the two ways of thinking that had come to dominate the movement. Debs' remark, if lacking in finesse, was permeated with revolutionary spirit; Berger's reflected the attitude of those right-wing Socialists who had come to see the movement as an agency for reforming capitalism painlessly out of existence, and sometimes simply for reforming capitalism.

As it savored the fruits and responsibilities of electoral success, the right wing began to yearn for a patina of middle-class respectability. It wished to abandon the "revolutionary phrase mongering," which might have had its uses in the past but was no longer appropriate to its moment of maturity. With small but tangible successes came a new respect for the politics of parliamentary moderation, the wisdom of compromise and practicality. The power of the right-wing Socialists in the American Federation of Labor kept growing—almost as fast, remarked a critic, as within the Socialist Party itself. At the 1912 convention of the AFL Max Hayes, a well-known Socialist nominated as the opponent of Sam Gompers, received 30 percent of the vote, an astonishing figure when one remembers that by then the AFL was already the center of labor conservatism in America.

The Socialist Party was itself becoming an institution of substance, with its apparatus, its jobs and honors; and the more the right-wing leaders were impressed with the needs of institutional preservation, the more did they incline toward a reinterpretation of the Marxist doctrine of the class struggle so as to soften it into a method of electoral activity. Instead of being the most aggressive element within the working class, the party, as they now saw it, would become a force cutting across, or rising above, class lines and thereby winning to itself "men of good will" from all social levels.

Saying this, it is only fair to add that the focus of retrospect may prompt us to sharpen things a bit. Victor Berger and his Milwaukee colleagues, John Spargo, the most popular Socialist writer in the country, Job Harriman, the moderate leader of the party in California, had all edged their way to the calculated reformism of Social Democracy, though even Berger was capable—no one took him very seriously or grew excessively alarmed—of bursting into revolutionary bombast. But Eastern party leaders like Morris Hillquit, with a deeper tie to the Marxist tradition, still clung to the terminology, as occasionally the content, of earlier and more militant ideas. Language lags behind ideas.

Neither here nor later are "right" and "left" to be seen as fixed poles. People like Berger had certainly moved to the right, yet they sincerely believed that the Socialist Party was the sole political agency for realizing their ideas, and they would probably have been shocked at the position, common to their political descendants, of supporting the more liberal among the old party candidates. Shocked not so much from principle as from a feeling that they had at their command a movement of mounting resources which they did not intend to subordinate to any other.

In 1911, launching one of his rare interventions into party affairs, Eugene Debs printed a shrewd attack on the right wing.

> I cannot but feel [he wrote] that some of the votes placed to our credit this year were obtained by methods not consistent with the principles of a revolutionary party. . . . It may become permeated and corrupted with the spirit of bourgeois reform to an extent that will practically destroy its virility. . . . Voting for socialism is not socialism any more than a menu is a meal.[9]

If the right wing had not yet managed to align its theories with its practice, the left was in a far worse state. Though it enjoyed the support of an appreciable minority within the party, the left lacked a clear point of intellectual departure. It rumbled with militant fervor but did not know how to transform these rumblings into political policy. It exuded revolutionary intransigence but lacked a worked-out politics for the day.

Sporadically, during the previous several years, there had been outbursts from the left at what it called the party's gradual departure from socialist principles. The party had failed to take an unambiguous stand on the place of the Negro in America, contenting itself with a promise that under socialism he would have full economic equality but meanwhile doing little in behalf of his political and social rights. This the left declared to be a scandal. The party had for a time permitted the organization of segregated locals in the South and had never made a serious effort to appeal to Southern Negroes. This the left attacked as a concession to racial prejudice. The party had failed to take a forthright stand in favor of women's rights, a number of its leaders having indulged in Philistine musings about kitchens and nurseries. This the left decried as male chauvinism. The party had succumbed to the xenophobic fever of the time by supporting legislation to exclude Asiatics, some of its leaders justifying this with economic theories and others with quasi-racist appeals. This the left—but not, to its shame, all of it—denounced as the greatest scandal of all. Yet, even as the party's drift to reform proved galling to the left-wingers, they could do little to reverse the direction.

All of these were minor issues, however, by comparison with the problem that rocked the movement year after year, convention after convention. What attitude should Socialists take toward the AFL and its conservative leaders? Toward the revolutionary, anarcho-syndicalist IWW, which the AFL attacked as a dual union? The other issues generally involved matters of abstract principle, but this was immediately, oppressively real. Many Socialists were officials in the AFL, and party support of the IWW might seriously embarrass their standing and even their jobs; many Socialists were active in the IWW, and party support of the AFL seemed to them a downright betrayal of the revolution.

Yet it was on this central issue that the left enjoyed least clarity. Actually, there were two left wings within the party, one Marxist and the other anarcho-syndicalist. The Marxist wing, a forerunner of the Communist movement, was small, confined largely to Eastern intellectuals and without much influence in the party. Its most distinguished spokesman, Louis Boudin, was a gifted writer, but also a man blessed, or cursed, with a rare capacity for infusing the most revolutionary theories with the most pedantic tone. On paper, though mainly on paper, this left wing had a policy that seemed to combine radical motivation with realistic analysis. It described the AFL as "reactionary"; it stressed the need for industrial unionism, and, together with the IWW, insisted that the craft structure of the AFL made impossible the organization of the great masses of American workers. It proposed Socialist activity *within* the AFL in behalf of industrial unionism (which at the time, it must be remembered, meant not merely an organizational structure but also a militant temper), while advocating support of the IWW when it was actually engaged in strikes. As against the right, it insisted that electoral activity was not a primary end in itself but rather a means for spreading the socialist idea. As against the Wobblies (the popular name for the IWW), it insisted that political

activity was essential to the Socialist movement because it needed
to cope with the bourgeois state, and that trade-union struggles, no
matter how militant or violent, were not in themselves sufficient.

Far more influential, however, was that section of the Socialist
left composed of people active in the IWW or influenced by its
syndicalist outlook. Tough; hard-bitten yet buoyant; ready to give
battle at all times yet addicted to a verbal violence and infantile
brag which students of Western humor should not find hard to
identify; superbly gifted at stirring the unskilled transient workers
on the rim of the labor movement, but with only a faint capacity
for understanding the desire of the average American worker for
social stability; contemptuous, in the main, of politics and contemptuous, without exception, of reformers; a movement as lawless
as American capitalism itself in the era of company police and labor
spies; remarkably spontaneous, indeed, elevating spontaneous com-
bustion into a principle of social life, but really without an ideology
other than some *ad hoc* improvisations on the word "sabotage" which
few people understood but which, once having become a fetish,
caused endless grief—this was the IWW, the embodiment of the
fierce yet innocent radicalism of the American West, a radicalism
that had nothing to do with politics but expressed instead a sheer
explosive rejection of things as they were.

Time after time the IWW marched into the mining camps,
chanting its homely jingles, packing the jails till they burst, and by
sheer courage winning strikes. In Lawrence, Massachusetts, where
the textile industry maintained an almost feudal reign, the IWW
fought a bloody 1912 strike to a triumphant conclusion, slugging it
out with the police, springing mass picket lines, hurrying in its most
gifted leaders and organizers.

Little wonder, then, that to most left-wing Socialists the IWW
seemed the real thing, the revolution fleshed: Hillquit could quote
endlessly from Marx's *Capital* but Big Bill Haywood looked more
like the specter haunting the bourgeois world. Nor should it be
forgotten that the left Socialists, quite as much as the right, were
infatuated with success, sharing the American impatience with anything but quick returns. The left wing, which should have been
somewhat wary of IWW weaknesses, if only because it had the most
to lose from them, soon became little more than a political reflex of

the anti-political IWW. And whatever the prospects of the IWW itself might be, a reflex of syndicalism within a political party was not merely incongruous, it was doomed.

Even at the peak of its success the IWW was becoming obsolete, an anachronism in an industrial society. Immediately after the end of the Lawrence strike the Wobblies had some 14,000 members in the city; by the following year the number had fallen to 700.[10] The Wobbly organizers, footloose, eager for new excitements, indifferent to organizational routine, had been unable to create a lasting union: they had, in their own words, plenty of kindlin' power but very little stayin' power.

For all its courage and its color, the IWW failed to root itself in American life. It could not keep the workers it enrolled, it could not build stable industrial unions, it lost itself hopelessly in the trap of dual unionism. It helped corrode the faith of the more radical workers in political action, thereby dealing an unintentional blow at the Socialist left.* Failing to understand the significance of the machine process and the growth of the industrial city, the IWW simply could not grasp—it hardly wanted to—the fact that the psychology of the small section of American workers to which it appealed with such spectacular success was not at all the psychology of most American workers. It shattered itself on the reef of the average American worker's yearning for social stability; it was destroyed, as surely as the Western frontiersman had been destroyed, by the machine and the city.

Debs analyzed the Wobbly weaknesses with the same shrewdly empirical touch he had applied to the party's right wing. He began by quoting from a pamphlet in which Haywood had written that the worker "retains absolutely no respect for the property 'rights' of the profit-takers. . . . He knows that the present laws of property are made by and for the capitalists. Therefore he does not hesitate to break them." [11] Declaring that he too had "no respect for capitalist property laws"—he was not to be outflanked from the left!— Debs went on to say:

* A minority of the IWW, led by Haywood, who was also for a time a member of the Socialist Party's National Committee, did believe in political activity of a strictly limited kind; but its influence was meager in comparison with those Wobblies who stood for "direct action" and nothing else.

The American workers are law-abiding and no amount of sneering or derision will alter the fact. Direct action will never appeal to any considerable number of them while they have the ballot and the right of industrial and political organization.

Sabotage repels the American worker. He is ready for the industrial union but he is opposed to the "propaganda of the deed," and as long as the IWW adheres to its present tactics and ignores political action . . . he will regard it as an anarchist organization, and it will never be more than a small fraction of the labor movement.[12]

By 1912 the clash between right and left, Social Democrat and syndicalist, could no longer be evaded. Each wing of the party, fancying great opportunities before it, was impatient to go off on its own. Each felt the need for its own disciplined organization rather than the loose forum the Socialist Party had become. Each wanted an organization with a certain consistency in program and membership.

At the Socialist convention that took place in Indianapolis in 1912 the right wing, by far the cannier in faction sparring, sprang a coup. It proposed a new clause in the party constitution, the famous Article II, Section 6:

Any member of the party who opposes political action or advocates crime, sabotage or other methods of violence as a weapon of the working class to aid in its emancipation, shall be expelled from membership in the party. Political action shall be construed to mean participation in elections for public office and practical legislative and administrative work along the lines of the Socialist Party platform.[13]

The key word was "sabotage," and not the less so because hardly anyone could say what it meant. The left-wing speakers at the convention, foxed into a position where they seemed to be defending sin, came down heavily on the vagueness of the term, especially the vagueness in the minds of those quick to condemn it; but they met with no success, Victor Berger and his friends being temperamentally disinclined to semantic niceties. Sabotage might mean the slowdown, which had been practiced, openly or tacitly, by almost every union in America; it might mean the kind of sit-down strikes from which the CIO was later to spring to power; it might mean despoiling the product and wrecking the machinery of industrial plants. For all their ferocious talk, the Wobblies were rather vague about this, half from uncertainty and half from a somewhat adolescent, though hardly un-American, glee in mystifying and scarifying the enemy. And while the IWW, like every other union of that unpolished era, had engaged or been forced to engage in its share of violence, most of its talk about sabotage was just . . . talk. Which did not, of course, prevent the right wing from nailing the left to the cross of syndicalist vocabulary. As Lillian Symes and Travers Clement have shrewdly remarked in their history of American radicalism, the IWW was soon to reap the bitter fruit of its revolutionary braggadocio in the government's prosecutions during World War I, "while the AFL, which has undoubtedly practised more sabotage than the IWW ever talked about, was reaping the fruits of its discretion." [14]

Some of the left-wing spokesmen at the Indianapolis convention, like Marguerite Prevey of Ohio, tried to invoke memories of the Boston Tea Party, surely as neat a piece of sabotage as any syndicalist had ever talked about. But at a convention where Victor Berger was a dominant spirit this was hardly an argument calculated to win support. By a vote of 191 to 90 the convention accepted Section 6 and thereby brought to an end a chapter in the history of American radicalism—a chapter which in some important respects anticipates the later struggles from which the American Communist movement would emerge.

Curiously, Bill Haywood, though present at the convention, did not even join in the discussion of Section 6, perhaps because he thought it useless to argue with Berger, perhaps because he sensed how thoroughly the terms of the debate were stacked against him. Later, in his autobiography, Haywood would recall with vast contempt that "the class struggle meant nothing to many [of the delegates] who were there supposedly representing the working class. There were seventeen or more preachers who could scarcely disguise their sky-piloting proclivities." [15]

As it happens, he was echoing, perhaps unwittingly, one of the less attractive traditions of the radical movement by which contending factions wrap themselves in the flag of "proletarianism" and dismiss the other side as "petty bourgeois." More often than not, this is demagogy; but in 1912 there *was* a distinct clash of social interest and class psychology behind the struggle of factions. Not, to be sure, a clash simply between proletariat and petty bourgeois, for plenty of middle-class intellectuals supported the left and plenty of proletarians the right. Nonetheless, it is true that those sections of the party that were most heavily working class in composition did as a rule support the left, and that the syndicalist wing did speak for those unskilled workers, combative and transient, who had not yet been absorbed into American society—unskilled workers with whom the right wing could barely communicate. By accepting Section 6, the Socialist Party broke decisively from this stratum of the American workers and the rough-and-tumble improvisations of syndicalism through which it expressed itself. The echoes of this dispute, which mattered far less for the momentary issues than for the fundamental divergences of outlook it half revealed and half blurred, would reverberate in the radical world through 1916 and then through 1919.

The next few years bring a decline. Bill Haywood is recalled from the Socialist Party's National Committee in 1913. The average party membership drops from 118,000 in 1912 to 83,000 in 1916, most of those who resign being members of the left wing, people who either turn to the anti-political IWW or drift away entirely from radicalism. At the same time, the rightward swing of the Socialist Party does not really ease things for it, since as a mere reform movement it can hardly compete with Bull Moose, the Non-partisan League, and Wilsonism. Slowly, one of the basic rhythms of American radical life is again set in motion: the rhythm of internal dispute, violent split, and the dissipation of once dedicated energies.

5. Not until 1915 did a left wing within the Socialist Party manage to regain a certain coherence of expression, though even then it remained a minor factor in the party's internal life. The new, distinctively Marxist left that slowly began to arise was quite different from the syndicalist left of earlier years. It lacked the broad base of support among the unskilled transient workers which

the syndicalists had enjoyed. Where the syndicalists had tended to be insular in their concerns, the new left was oriented toward international affairs, much of its intellectual and emotional energy being derived from the bitter internecine struggle which the outbreak of the First World War had brought to European Socialism. If its leaders lacked the deep experience in the American class struggle that had characterized Haywood and his colleagues, some of them—such as Louis Boudin, Ludwig Lore, editor of the German Socialist paper in New York, and Louis Fraina (afterwards known as Lewis Corey), a fervent and gifted young intellectual in Boston—commanded, by way of compensation, at least a fraction of the theoretical equipment expected of Marxist leaders in Europe.

For a moment the outbreak of the war in Europe seemed to bring the tendencies within the Socialist Party closer together. Almost every American Socialist was shocked at the collapse of the European movement before the power of nationalism: the European Socialists, who had repeatedly declared at their international congresses that the threat of imperialist war would be met by revolutionary general strikes, were now rushing to vote war credits for their respective governments. Only a small minority of the European Socialists remained faithful to the anti-war program of the Second (Socialist) International, and at this point they were still a minority without power or influence.

Formally, the American party aligned itself with this minority. In 1915 it accepted, by overwhelming vote, a new section for its constitution which declared that "Any member of the Socialist Party, elected to an office, who shall in any way vote to appropriate moneys for military or naval purposes, or war, shall be expelled from the party." [16] Actually, however, its anti-war position was not held, and certainly was not felt, with the vigor that it was publicly expressed. The reasons for this apparent contradiction were several. Until very recently America's relation to world affairs had been such as to encourage many Americans in the feeling that the events in Europe, remote and alien, did not significantly impinge on their lives; hence, even the right-wing Socialists, moderate enough with regard to domestic affairs, where they were only too eager to proclaim the chastening pressures of reality, could keep on harmlessly repeating the traditional phrases opposing "imperialist war." In the party itself there was also a coloring of pacifist sentiment, which, though it had little in common with the revolutionary Marxist view on war, helped for a time to stiffen the party in its anti-war stand. And finally, it must be recognized, there was a distinct undertow of pro-German feeling among a minority of American Socialists, particularly in such party centers as Milwaukee, which could not be expressed openly but which manifested itself in an ambiguous accord with the party's formal position on the war.

Once, however, the United States entered the war, the discordant impulses within the movement *had* to crystallize into sharply opposed tendencies. Between the party's program and its practice, between Marxist doctrine and an increasingly moderate role in American politics, a conflict could no longer be suppressed. Most of the American Socialists who had been attracted in the 1916 election to Woodrow Wilson's "New Freedom" now left the party altogether. Such prominent party writers and speakers as William English Walling, Upton Sinclair, W. R. Gaylord, John Spargo, and A. M. Simons came out enthusiastically in support of the war, justifying their view by the theory that the Allies, being modern capitalist powers, were more progressive than "feudal" Germany.

Nor did the departure of the openly pro-war leaders really bring harmony to the Socialist Party—though for a time it brought a certain appearance, and indeed a possibility, of harmony. At its St. Louis convention in April, 1917, which opened a day after the US entered the war, the party took an unambiguous stand in behalf of its traditional opposition to imperialist war. The majority statement on the war question, brought in by Morris Hillquit, was supported by the mass of the delegates:

> The Socialist Party of the United States in the present grave crisis solemnly . . . proclaims its unalterable opposition to the war just declared by the government of the United States.
> The Socialist Party of the United States is unalterably opposed to the system of exploitation and class rule which is upheld and strengthened by military power. . . . We, therefore, call upon the workers of all countries to refuse support to their governments in their wars. . . . As against the false doctrine of national patriotism we uphold the ideal of international working class solidarity. . . .

In all modern history there has been no war more unjustifiable than the war in which we are about to engage. . . .

In harmony with these principles, the Socialist Party emphatically rejects the proposal that in times of war the workers should suspend their struggle for better conditions. On the contrary, the acute situation created by war calls for an even more vigorous prosecution of the class struggle. . . .[17]

From the left-wing point of view this declaration would appear to have been unexceptionable; it was certainly far more intransigent than anything that had been said by the European Socialist parties. Nonetheless, it was characteristic of the ingrained sectarianism of this left wing, a sectarianism it would bequeath to the Communist movement a few years later, that at the St. Louis convention it did not solidly align itself behind this declaration. Some left-wingers offered a statement of their own which, on the face of it, differed only in minor and rather academic details from Hillquit's. The consuming passion of the Communist sectarian for "differentiating" himself from everyone except those who accepted not merely his essential ideas but also his exact (or inexact) language was already at work.

This much said, it is only fair to add that some of the uneasiness and suspicion with which the left-wingers regarded the spectacle of people like Victor Berger voting for the St. Louis declaration was—again, given their political premises—quite justified. The left-wingers felt that the resolution, whatever the subjective sincerity of those who voted for it, did not reflect the day-to-day politics of the party leaders; that the opportunistic wing in the party, sensitive to a growing leftward sentiment in the ranks, had voted for the declaration "knowing that paper would be patient"; that the party was avoiding the full and inescapable condemnation of the Second International which political honesty and clarity required.[18] ("We do not presume to pass judgment upon the conduct of our brother parties in Europe," [19] the party executive had declared—which was precisely what the left wing wished to do.)

Soon enough the party leadership, of which the intellectual head was Morris Hillquit, provided the left with a sufficient warrant for its hostility. Meyer London, the Socialist Congressman from New York, failed to vote against war appropriations—which led the left-wing leader Ludwig Lore to charge that London was systematically neglecting "every opportunity of manifesting serious opposition to war—in direct violation of our St. Louis program." [20] The Socialist aldermen in New York City supported the third Liberty Loan in April, 1918, thereby violating at least the letter of the party's 1915 decision prohibiting such action. Hillquit himself, the main author of the St. Louis declaration, issued statements in which he kept qualifying and softening its blunt opposition to the war. As a historian sympathetic to the moderate Socialists has concluded: "By the middle of 1918 important sections of the party were no longer seriously, if at all, opposed to the war." [21] Unavoidably the result was that, despite the apparent agreement on the St. Louis declaration, factional bitterness increased day by day.

One of the specific, though muddled, ways in which the faction struggle manifested itself was over the question of the party's attitude toward the People's Council for Democracy and Peace, a liberal and quasi-pacifist movement which sprang up during the war and in which many Socialists were active. This now forgotten movement brought together all those—the People's Council claimed the support of organizations with a total membership of 2,000,000—who suspected the United States of having undertaken an imperialist adventure and who were disturbed by the severe repressions of civil rights that were occurring at home. The People's Council was not "against" the war, nor did it try to develop any fundamental view with regard to the social causes of the war. It merely proposed that the government set forth a series of democratic war aims, repudiate any claims for forcible annexations of territory or punitive indemnities, and, at home, defend "our constitutional rights of free speech, free assemblage," etc.[22] Despite this relatively mild program the People's Council suffered harsh attack, its first national conference in Chicago being dispersed by troops and its leading spokesman, Scott Nearing, being regularly denied the use of meeting halls.

For the Hillquit wing of the party there was no problem as to the political attitude to be taken toward the People's Council: it should be supported unconditionally. The left wing, however, insisted upon branding it as a "bourgeois pacifist" organization with which the Socialists had nothing in common, thereby committing the error of assuming that the act of giving a political phenomenon a name, even an accurate one, was to dispose of the problems it raised. Had the left confined itself to criticizing the Hillquit leadership for subordinating the Socialist anti-war program to the immediate demands of the People's Council, there might have been, from a Socialist point of view, a certain cogency to the criticism. But Boudin, Fraina, and Lore went further. They denounced the People's Council out of hand, which is to say that they failed to grasp that what mattered was not merely its program but its critical spirit and potential energy, the bringing together of almost every strand of resistance to President Wilson's war policy. Simply to denounce the People's Council was not yet to answer the question of what Socialists should do in or with it. And for that question the left had no answer but to splutter its revolutionary language—with the predictable result that it thereby blunted the edge of its more cogent criticisms.

6. Fully to understand the formation of the American Communist movement, we must now turn from the claustrophobic atmosphere of radical factionalism to the social conflicts, far greater in scope and significance, that were simultaneously taking place in the United States and Europe.

The official American ideology, now that the country was deep into the war, may have predicated a period of untroubled social peace and "national unity"; but the reality was different from the ideology. Throughout 1917 strikes—seldom large or dramatic, but massive in their sum—shook the country. Shook it not because anyone could suppose they were really a threat to the continued operation of the war machine or were inspired by radical sentiments, but because they demonstrated that the inner clashes and tensions of a modern industrial society, those clashes and tensions which the Marxist designated as "the class struggle," would persist through the war years. And to the Socialists, particularly those of the left, this was a fact both important and encouraging; it made them feel that their political analyses, even if not immediately usable, were intellectually relevant.

The radicals had pressing reasons for continuing to regard the government as their enemy. Attacks upon radical, pacifist, and at times even liberal groups, some government-inspired and others the result of mob outbursts, began directly after the declaration of war. But with the passage of the Espionage Act of June 15, 1917—a legislative net wide enough to catch almost any fish, from Wobbly sharks to pacifist minnows—the repression of dissident movements became an explicit policy of the Wilson administration. The official Socialist magazine, *The American Socialist,* was banned from the mails. So, by the end of the year, was almost every other radical publication. Party headquarters in Indiana and Ohio were raided; the national office in Chicago was occupied for three days by government agents; a party convention in Mitchell, South Dakota, was broken up by force; the directors of the Rand School in New York were fined $3,000 for publishing *The Great Madness,* a pamphlet by Scott Nearing; mobs of soldiers and sailors stormed the party office in Boston.

In July, 1917, 1,200 IWW strikers in Bisbee, Arizona, were herded into a ball park by armed deputies, packed into cattle cars, and dumped in the desert. In Tulsa, Oklahoma, seventeen IWW men were tarred, feathered, and abandoned half-dead. In Butte, Montana, a crippled IWW leader, Frank Little, was kidnapped by masked gunmen and hanged from a railway trestle. Simultaneous government raids were conducted against the major IWW halls throughout the country and 166 IWW leaders arrested on the charge of violating the Espionage Act.

Before the war's end, this charge would be brought against almost every Socialist and IWW leader. Bill Haywood, Adolph Germer, the SP national secretary, Victor Berger, Charles Ruthenberg, a leader of the Socialist left and later a founder of the Communist movement—these and many others (without distinction as to faction or program) were indicted and convicted. The editors of the irreverent *Masses*—Max Eastman, Floyd Dell, John Reed—were also considered a sufficient threat to the security of the government to be tried under the Espionage Act. The hysteria reached beyond a hunt for radicals. The Nonpartisan League, a Midwestern Populist organization, was harassed with a fury second only to that reserved for the IWW and the Socialists. Three professors at Columbia University were dismissed because they dared express criticisms, by no means fundamental, of the government's policy;

whereupon the historian Charles Beard, in a gesture of protest, re-signed his chair at Columbia. Numerous teachers were driven out of the public schools; German farmers in the Midwest were horse-whipped as a means of persuading them to greater patriotic feeling; meetings of the Friends of Irish Freedom were dispersed by mobs; a twenty-year-old girl, Mollie Steimer, was sentenced in the fall of 1918 to fifteen years in prison for distributing leaflets against Allied intervention in Russia. Religious pacifists, wrote Norman Thomas, were confined "in unsanitary guardhouses—sometimes in unheated cells during winter months, without blankets. . . . Men were forcibly clad in uniform, beaten, pricked or stabbed with bayonets, jerked about with ropes around their necks, threatened with summary execution, tortured by various forms of the 'water cure.' " [23]

Nonetheless, the radical movement grew. In the two months after its St. Louis declaration against the war, the Socialist Party gained 12,000 members. Morris Hillquit, running in 1917 for mayor of New York, conducted the most dramatic campaign in American radical history: night after night there were street meet-ings charged with a passion rare to American politics, and as a climax a series of packed rallies in Madison Square Garden. From the vantage point of historical distance, the Hillquit campaign may seem little more than one of the last outbursts of the idealism that had been fermenting among the garment workers ever since they had come to the New World and found sweatshops and slums; but at the time it naturally seemed a sign of the growth of American Socialism. Hillquit received nearly 150,000 votes, 22 percent of the total; ten party candidates were elected to the state assembly, seven to the municipal Board of Aldermen. Nationally, too, the Socialist vote rose sharply: in Chicago to 34 percent, in Toledo to 35 percent, in Cleveland to 19 percent. These substantial results of the party's continued vigor, as also of its role as critic of the war, came before it bent beneath the weight of the government's prosecutions; but they were sufficient evidence that no matter how greatly the left wing within the party allowed its revolutionary desire to blind it to the limitations confronting *any* socialist movement in America, it did have some sense of social reality, some feeling for political possibili-

SOURCES OF AMERICAN RADICALISM   25

ties when it insisted that during a period in which all critics were under attack only an intransigent radicalism would have the will and the spirit to survive.

No demonstration of socialist spirit could have been more intransigent, or any more inspiring to the left wing, than Gene Debs' famous Canton speech in the spring of 1918. At a time when many party leaders were edging away from the St. Louis declaration, Debs thundered his support of the party's anti-war position. Shortly afterward he was convicted of violating the Espionage Act and before being sentenced to ten years in prison he made the speech to the court which summed up the ethic of his life:

> Your Honor, years ago I recognized my kinship with all living beings, and I made up my mind that I was not one whit better than the meanest on earth. I said then, and I say now, that while there is a lower class I am in it, while there is a criminal element I am of it, and while there is a soul in prison I am not free.[24]

Yet nothing that was happening in American domestic life could mean so much as the sudden outbreak, first in February, 1917, and then in October, of the two Russian Revolutions. All the talk, the dreams, the theories—everything that to even the least doubting or least contemplative of socialist minds must sometimes have seemed dim and elusive now took on the force of reality. That a working-class state could be proclaimed in the most backward country of Europe, that the Lenin who yesterday had been a mere *émigré* lost in the fogs of factional dispute should today command the palace of the Czars—this seemed visible triumphant proof that the final victory of socialism was at hand. Until the formation of the Third (Communist) International in 1919 there was hardly a radical in America who did not support the Bolshevik Revolution, though some had already begun to dissociate themselves from one or another Bolshevik theory. Particularly among the intellectuals, who saw in the leaders of the new Russia not merely men of will but also men of ideas, there occurred a renewal of political hope. One reason, to be sure, was that for a while hardly anyone in America really knew what was happening in Russia: the reports in the daily press were so malicious as to discredit the possibility of more serious criticism of the Bolsheviks, and even the *Call,* the New York Socialist paper, knew so little about the differences among the Russian radical groups that in June, 1917, it could refer to Lenin as a Menshevik. Once, however, John Reed began filling the pages of the *Liberator* (successor to the *Masses*) with his detailed accounts of how the Bolsheviks had led the workers and soldiers and sailors to power— his articles seemed to blend the circumstantial richness of documentation with the commanding simplicity of myth—the American radicals found a source not merely of information but, far more important, of guiding inspiration: *this,* they could feel, *this was how it happened; this is how it's done.* Of doubts that it was worth the doing, or properly done, or done by the proper parties and leaders, there were very few. The fraternity of revolution—a blend of heroism and success—caught up the ranks of American radicalism; and to the left wing of the Socialist Party it gave a sense of authority and assurance it had hardly earned but was quite ready to exploit.

Nor was it merely a matter of Russia. All of Europe—this was partly exaggeration, but an exaggeration of a fact—seemed to be turning to Lenin's banner. In October, 1918, revolutions broke out in Hungary, Austria, and Bulgaria. A month later came the revolution in Germany which deposed the Kaiser and trembled on the edge of eliminating the Junkers. In Hungary, Finland, and parts of Germany soviets were declared, and while all went down to quick and bloody defeat no one could suppose that in any of these countries the impulse to revolt had been exhausted. Mutinies ravaged the French army; workers in the major Italian cities seized the factories; a radical shop-steward movement grew rapidly in England. Given this upsurge of the European working class, what reason was there to suppose—so the American radical might have reflected— that the blows suffered at home were anything but a momentary defeat, a sign of the inner panic felt by the American bourgeoisie as it looked fearfully across the ocean? What reason to suppose that America, for all its wealth and power, could long remain exempt from the pressures of revolution, pressures that in Socialist eyes often took on the aura of historical inevitability?

In retrospect one can see many reasons for supposing that

America would remain exempt; but let us remember that it is in retrospect. During the feverish months of 1918 and 1919 the hopes of the radicals with regard to Europe seemed to rest on solid reality, and nothing seemed so thoroughly to prove this as the equally intense fears of their opponents.

7. It was in this buoyant and heady atmosphere that the left wing, soon to be transformed into the early Communist movement, was born. Its distinctive traits—there is a temptation to mean by this its distinctive weaknesses—were largely due to its inability to distinguish sharply enough between its vision of the European revolution and the actualities of American life, or perhaps more accurately, to the deluded ease with which it assimilated the one to the other. Influenced more by European events than American conditions, the left wing found some of its most substantial support in the foreign-language federations affiliated with the Socialist Party, particularly the Russian Federation. Because the glamor of Bolshevism seemed to rub off on them, the Slavic Federations had quickly grown to the point where they claimed about one-fifth of the party membership. These foreign-language federations exerted a constricting political and intellectual effect upon the left wing. The leaders of the Russian Federation, more gifted at mimicking Lenin's postures than matching his sagacity, were narrow and dogmatic men, often ignorant of elementary facts concerning American life. In their relations with the native left-wingers, they behaved with an arrogance half apostolic and half imperialistic. A great deal in the early history of the American Communist movement that was sectarian to the point of stupidity, and much that was downright absurd, can be traced back to the "Russian fever" which beset the left-wingers.

If only in the interest of historical accuracy, however, it is necessary to deny the frequent assertion that the left wing consisted of little more than the foreign-language groups.[25] Actually, the left wing controlled the party in Ohio and Michigan, two major centers of working-class strength; it was very strong in New York, still the largest party branch; it had substantial support throughout the country. A reasonable estimate would be that the left wing, while enjoying the support of less than half the English-speaking members, did command a majority of the party.* Not the fact that it drew much of its support from the foreign-language federations but its tendency to shape itself, slavishly and mechanically, in the image of European Bolshevism crippled the left wing.

With its major source of inspiration the political events in Europe, and with the foreign-language federations dominant in prestige if not numbers, the left wing succumbed to a sectarian approach violently out of rhythm with social developments in America. Its ideology was put forward in weighty documents often reading like poorly translated versions of Bolshevik writings that had once, in their original context, made a kind of sense. Moreover, it was an ideology far better attuned to the needs of a large revolutionary party on the verge of power than to an embattled faction of a party still light-miles away from power and functioning in the one capitalist country that had emerged from the war strengthened.

In the first official documents of the left wing there can be found not merely rote-like mimicry of the Leninist line but formulations so crude and mechanical as to seem mere caricatures of that line. Parliamentary government is described simply as "the expression of bourgeois supremacy, the form of authority of the capitalist over the worker." The task of the radicals in America is said to be "to encourage the militant mass movements in the AFL to split the old unions. . . ." In "the Communist reconstruction of society," it is said, "the proletariat as a class alone counts." [26] Quite apart from their doubtful relevance to the American scene, these phrases were not even accurate repetitions—let alone intelligent applications—of Lenin's ideas.

Still more revealing was the unqualified assent which the American left wing gave in its program to the Bolshevik claim that a transition to socialism was possible only through a "dictatorship of the proletariat." This unfortunate phrase, the source and perhaps the symptom of profound moral ambiguities in the Marxist

---

* In any case, it should be remembered that we are concerned with a period that comes directly after one of the great waves of immigration to the United States. Most of these immigrants having come from eastern Europe, and most of them being forced to seek work in the lowest-paying industries, it stood to reason that the Slavic federations of the party would not merely grow but also lean toward the more radical wing of Socialism.

movement, first appeared in a few sentences of Marx's later writings
and was there used simply to indicate a society in which the political and social domination of the bourgeoisie is replaced by that of
the proletariat. The phrase, as Marx employed it, leaves open the
form which this domination is to take, but there is no reason to
suppose that he meant it to imply a totalitarian or authoritarian
dictatorship in the popular modern sense. With the Bolsheviks, however, the term had become a key political concept. The way in
which they used it, as well as their practice after seizing power, implied a radical break from the parliamentary institutions of "bourgeois democracy" and the creation of a "higher type of democracy"
based on soviets or workers' councils. The special emphasis the Bolsheviks gave to the "dictatorship of the proletariat" was closely
related to their belief that only one party, their own, could lead
the proletariat in fulfilling its "historic mission"—from which one
may wonder what is to happen to those parties which oppose this
mission or those which prove weak and vacillating in their support
of it. The key ambiguity in Bolshevik attitudes thus rests upon the
strong tendency to identify the "dictatorship of the proletariat"
with the dictatorship of a particular party.

To expect any critical attitude toward Bolshevik doctrine
among the American left-wingers in 1918 or 1919 may be to strain
the privilege of historical retrospect. But what is remarkable—and
helps prepare one for the later history of American Communism
—is the thoughtless assumption that the "dictatorship of the proletariat" could be a relevant and desirable concept in a country like
the United States with its long democratic and parliamentary tradition.

The left wing, to be sure, did try to justify its revolutionary
phrases by pointing to the serious labor struggles that swept the
country in 1919. And it is true that in this year the number of
workers who went on strike came to more than four million; that
the bitter steel strike led by William Z. Foster had been among
the first efforts, even if not a successful one, to crack the anti-union
resistance of the basic industries; that major strikes had also erupted
in coal, clothing, and textiles; that the general strike in Seattle
had brought the city, for a few days, under complete trade
union control. All true, and important. But what the left wing,

in the willfulness of its enthusiasm, failed to see was that these outbursts of labor unrest were taking place under the organizational control and within the ideological limits of an essentially conservative trade-union movement, and that the correlation it drew between labor unrest and political radicalism, whatever its long-range plausibility, was certainly nothing to be counted on at the immediate moment. The simple truth is that the left wing did not derive its talk about "soviets" and "proletarian dictatorship" from an examination of the actualities of American life, or even from an objective study of the 1919 strike wave; it seized upon the strike wave as confirmation of a revolutionary politics that derived mainly from Europe and partly from its desire to win the internal struggle within the Socialist Party.

In its estimate of the European situation, the left wing was more realistic than those who looked forward to social stability in the world made by Wilson, Clemenceau, and Lloyd George; but it failed to appraise with equal realism the enormous strength and resilience of American capitalism, as well as the deep-rooted attachment most American workers felt to the *status quo*. To employ a phrase that would figure in many later debates within the American Communist movement: the left-wingers in 1919 were insufficiently "exceptionalist" in their view of America, that is, they failed to give sufficient weight to those factors in American life which did make the political destiny of this country significantly different from that of Europe.

If, on the other hand, the revolution in Europe had succeeded, as Lenin was hoping and the American left assuming, then the talk about revolution in which the American radicals so easily indulged might not have seemed quite so bizarre as it now does. Could American capitalism have withstood the impact of a socialist or communist Europe? As a world power, America was now more deeply intertwined with Europe than ever before; and a Europe such as the left wing supposed to be in birth would have seriously threatened the economic stability and political assurance of American capitalism, not to mention that it would have proved a powerful political magnet for many American workers and intellectuals. None of this, speculative as it must be, can serve as justification for the sectarianism of the left wing: it is only to suggest that the left-wingers, because they held to an international perspective, were not quite as politically wild as they have generally been described. Which is not to deny that political intelligence would nonetheless have required the left wing to make the most drastic discounts in its estimate of radical possibilities in America.

An invariable mark of sectarianism in politics, especially in radical politics, is the inability to distinguish between fact and desire, from which there often follows an effort to force the will of the frustrated sect upon the rhythm of social developments; the sect, unable to make history, feels tempted to violate it. Certainly this was true of the American left-wingers during the years the revolution seemed to be flooding Europe. Eager to find in America evidence for a social crisis as intense as that of Europe, they soon lost themselves in willful fantasies. Strike actions which even a sophisticated Marxist analysis would have described as part of the "normal" functioning of capitalist society were seized upon by the nascent Communists as preludes to revolution. When the New York longshoremen and the Brooklyn trolley-car workers went out on strike in 1920, the Communists bombarded them with leaflets urging the overthrow of the government and the organization of soviets.[27] When local elections were held in New York City, the Communists, fearful of being contaminated by parliamentarism, urged the workers to boycott the polls—and offered as historical justification (how they loved Russian precedents!) the Bolshevik boycott of the Duma in 1906.

It was at this time that the intellectual leaders of the left wing developed a theory by which to justify their erratic course. The theory—one might more accurately speak of the mystique—of Mass Action was given its first major exposition in 1918 by Louis Fraina in a book called *Revolutionary Socialism,* and everything about it had a fatal attraction for the left-wingers. A rather heady Marxist home-brew spiked with a dash of syndicalist bitters, it challenged the assumption of the more conservative Social Democrats that socialism could be achieved through a gradual evolution within the framework of the existing state. But in addition to this orthodox Leninist dogma, Fraina and his colleagues had still to face the fact that there really was no revolutionary situation in the United States or anything approaching one; and so they announced that the American working class had entered the stage of Mass Action, in which there took place an extremely sharp and violent struggle between the classes but not yet a direct struggle for power. That this too was hardly an accurate description of what was happening in America forced Fraina to restrict his theory to a paradigmatic schema which had behind it little of the historical concreteness that characterized Lenin's descriptions of Russian social dynamics.

Wherever Fraina spun original embroideries on the Leninist pattern, the result was not felicitous. Having entered, according to his theory, the stage of Mass Action, the American workers and the American radical movement no longer needed to concern themselves with immediate reforms; political action was sharply subordinated to economic struggles in which industrial unionism (assumed by Fraina to be inherently revolutionary) was to be the main vehicle for the advancing proletariat.

In his own way Fraina tried to face one of the most troubling problems in the Leninist system: what is the relation between party and class, between the isolated "vanguard" secure in its political self and the masses bursting into occasional struggles but seldom reaching the desired level of political consciousness? How could the program of the party and the inchoate strivings of the class be brought into harmonious relations? Fraina's answer was a mixture of Lenin and Rosa Luxemburg, in which he tried to bring together the former's stress upon the activating powers of the disciplined party and the latter's belief in the "spontaneous" resources of the working class. In the passage that follows, one can see him stumbling from a version of Luxemburg to a version of Lenin:

> Mass action [wrote Fraina] is the *instinctive* action of the proletariat, gradually developing more conscious and organized forms. . . . It is extra-parliamentary in method, although political in purpose and result. . . .
>
> Mass action is the proletariat itself in action, dispensing with bureaucrats and intellectuals, acting through its own initiative; and it is precisely this circumstance that horrifies the soul of petty bourgeois Socialism. . . . It is the function of the revolutionary Socialist to provide the program and the course for this elemental action.[28]

Insofar as it had any significant relation to American politics, the theory of Mass Action teased the left-wingers into a series of tactical blunders: e.g., their indifference to immediate reforms, their misleading assumption that industrial unionism was by its nature incompatible with capitalist society, their undervaluation of electoral activity. Insofar as it provided them with a general theory of social action, it failed to encourage sufficiently precise and refined observations of the American scene. Whether the theory is to be seen as cause or consequence of the political ineptitude of the early Communist movement in America hardly matters. Either way, the result is the same.

8. Nothing in the immediate prospects of American radicalism, or in the relationship of factions within the Socialist Party, made it imperative or even tactically astute for the left wing to move toward organizing its own party. The radical movement as a whole, under the quickening impact of the Russian Revolution, had turned sharply to the left, so much so that Morris Hillquit, in an elegant polemic against the left-wingers called *Clear the Decks,* attacked none of the fundamental premises of Bolshevism but instead argued on a secondary, tactical level; e.g., he refused to accept the Communists' belief that a revolutionary situation was impending in the United States and that "underground" methods of work were necessary. Even after the split in 1919, the Socialist Party voted in referendum to apply for membership in the Communist International; Hillquit in a little book, *From Marx to Lenin,* defended the formula "dictatorship of the proletariat" as meaning a growth of democracy; and August Claessens, another right-wing leader, could say, "There is little real difference between the Socialist Party and the Communists." [29]

In reply the left-wingers claimed that the enthusiasm of people like Hillquit and Claessens for the Russian Revolution was far from complete. They argued that the SP leaders were shifting to the left, at least verbally, as a maneuver to retain a hold on the party membership. They charged that the SP leadership would never permit any left wing, even if it represented a majority of the members, to take control of its administration and press. And they concluded that, whatever their momentary and apparent closeness in America, Leninism and Social Democracy were so fundamentally at odds that they could not remain together in one organization. All of which had considerable truth, but not decisive relevance. For—

(a) The trend within the Socialist Party was clearly toward the left, and had the left wing kept a perspective of remaining inside the party it would have unquestionably accumulated still more support, even if formal control of the party might not have been within its immediate grasp.

(b) The actual, as distinct from the proclaimed, reason for working toward a separate left-wing (that is, Communist) party had little to do with anything happening either in the United States or in American radicalism; it was primarily the desire of the newly formed Communist International to create a disciplined, homogeneous, and world-wide movement which could serve as field general for the gathering forces of revolution.

(c) Less consequentially: those left-wingers such as Fraina, John Reed, and Benjamin Gitlow who were perceptive enough to favor remaining in the Socialist Party soon found themselves overwhelmed by the pressures of the Russian Federation, which, being largely indifferent to American conditions in any case, was quite as determined as were the beleaguered right-wing leaders of the SP to provoke a quick split.

So the intricate maneuvers, the fierce claims and counterclaims during the months before the split were of small consequence: everything had by then been decided; all that remained was a scramble for the party's resources and those few of its members who had not yet given their allegiance to either side.

The first formal organization of a left-wing faction took place in February, 1919, when a meeting was held in New York City at which a skeleton organization was created, plans for publishing a newspaper were made, and steps were taken to establish relations with left-wingers throughout the country. Soon a National Council of the left wing was organized, which included such later Communist leaders as Fraina, Charles Ruthenberg, Benjamin Gitlow, and Bertram Wolfe. Previously, there had been left-wing propaganda groups within various locals of the SP—the Communist Propaganda League of Chicago, the Socialist Propaganda League of

Boston—but these confined themselves to publishing journals and issuing statements; they did not proclaim themselves factions intent upon winning control of the party. Now the left wing explicitly stated as its aim the dislodgment of the party leadership and the transformation of the Socialist Party into a revolutionary Leninist organization. In April, 1919, it began publishing the *New York Communist,* edited by John Reed, and it issued a demand for an emergency convention of the party to settle the disputes that were tearing at its ranks.

The manifesto of the New York meeting was quickly endorsed by important state and city sections of the party: Michigan, Massachusetts, and Minnesota; Philadelphia, Cleveland, and Boston. By the spring of 1919 it was clear that the left wing had won a distinct majority of the party membership. Two tests, generally understood as tests, demonstrated the gathering strength of the left. A referendum on whether to participate in the conference called by Moscow for the formation of a new international was voted upon favorably by a majority of the party—though no practical result followed, partly because the party office delayed the referendum, announcing the returns two months after the Moscow conference. More decisive, a referendum held in April for the election of a new National Executive Committee gave a clear majority to the left wing, which won twelve out of the fifteen posts. Kate Richards O'Hare, a left-winger, defeated Morris Hillquit for International Secretary of the party by a vote of 13,262 to 4,775, while John Reed defeated Victor Berger by an even more decisive majority for the post of delegate to the Socialist International. Desperate, the incumbent national committee simply declared the vote to have been a fraud and set aside the results.

The SP leadership, for all its claim to be defending democracy against Bolsheviks and anarchists, now proceeded to expel or suspend numerous sections of the party that were led by the left wing. The Michigan branch with 6,000 members was expelled on the ground that its "One Plank Platform"—the unconditional abolition of capitalism!—violated the party's constitution, though the Michigan Socialists had been running campaigns since 1916 on this rather synoptic platform and had never before been molested by the National Committee. The Russian, Polish, South Slav, Hungarian,

Lithuanian, and Lettish federations were suspended. The Massachusetts and Ohio organizations were expelled without trial. By the time the party convention opened in August, 1919—admits Daniel Bell, a historian whose antipathy to the left wing is unveiled —"the right wing had saved its hold on the party name and machinery, but had lost two-thirds of its membership." [30]

Nonetheless, it is at least arguable that these dubious measures would have failed to save the party leadership had not the left itself been torn by internal disputes. Violent controversies broke out as to whether it was possible and/or desirable for the left wing to capture the Socialist Party—controversies which by their very existence settled the matter. At a national left-wing conference held in June in New York City, the majority of the ninety delegates voted to stay in the Socialist Party, at which point a minority, composed mainly of the Russian Federation and the Michigan Socialists,* who had

* Like many another political bloc, the alliance between the Russian Federation and the Michigan Socialists was rather weak on principle. The Russians were simply intent on clearing out of the "reformist swamp" of the Socialist Party, while the Michigan Socialists, having been expelled from the party, were looking for shelter. Politically, they were quite different. The Russians were intent upon proving themselves super-Bolsheviks, while the Michigan radicals, being rooted in an important area of American society, had developed into an interesting and rather individualized political tendency. The Socialists of Michigan had a genuine base in the labor movement. Distrusting all intellectuals and middle-class elements, no matter what their formal politics, the Michigan Socialists developed a syndrome which might be called proletarian fetishism. Yet this distrust was not so much a sign of anti-intellectualism as part of their belief that the workers could depend upon no one but themselves and therefore had themselves to acquire the political and intellectual heritage of society. Believing, that is, that the workers had to intellectualize themselves, the Michigan Socialists created a "proletarian university" in Detroit and several other cities, at which workers were educated in the intricacies of Marxist economics and similar subjects. Because of their stress on education, the Michigan Socialists were extremely critical of Fraina's theory of Mass Action with its reliance upon the spontaneous instincts of the workers. ("Instinct," wrote a leader of the Michigan Socialists in their magazine The Proletarian in October, 1919, "is an insufficient guide because it ignores the knowledge and ideas which promote reasoned action.")

Though they shared some of the sectarian traits of the other left-wingers —particularly in their reluctance to campaign for immediate reforms—the Michigan Socialists had, upon the whole, a far more authentic awareness of American society than most of their comrades. It followed, consequently, that their alliance with the Russian Federation could hardly last, and in 1920 they broke away entirely from the Communist movement to set up a small group of their own which exerted a certain local influence upon the Detroit labor movement through the 1930's.

been urging the immediate formation of a new Communist party, walked out. Most of the better-known leaders of the left wing—Fraina, Ruthenberg, Gitlow, Wolfe, Reed—remained with the majority group. Thus was the American Communist movement split before birth.

The minority group (the Russian-Michigan bloc) now proceeded mercilessly to pummel those left-wingers who desired to remain in the SP with a series of charges and denunciations which anticipated the polemical spirit that was to characterize the American Communist movement throughout its existence. Charging Fraina, Ruthenberg, and Gitlow with being "centrists," i.e., Marxists who vacillate between left and right, the Russian-Michigan bloc "raised" the immediate tactical problem to a matter of profound principle. In *Novy Mir*, the organ of the Russian Federation, Fraina, Ruthenberg, and Gitlow were castigated in no mild or comradely terms:

> The majority . . . meekly neglected to sever their connections with the reactionary National Executive Committee [of the Socialist Party]. Rendered impotent by the conflicting emotions and lack of understanding present, they continued to mark time as Centrists in the wake of the Right. Their policy is one of endeavor to capture the old party machinery and the stagnant elements who have been struggling for a false unity and who are only ready to abandon ship when it sinks beneath the wave of reaction.[31]

Before such rhetorical bombardments, coming as they did at a time when every left-winger wanted to be as "authentically" left as possible, the majority group could not long maintain its position. In late July, Fraina, Wolfe, and Ruthenberg broke under the pressure; and except for a few figures like John Reed and Ben Gitlow who still favored working within the Socialist Party, most left-wingers were now frankly committed to the speedy formation of an independent Communist party.

When the SP convention opened on August 30, the right wing was in full organizational control. A group of left-wing delegates led by Reed and Gitlow tried, rather forlornly, to take their seats but were met at the door by the right-wing manager, Julius Gerber. A brief scuffle between Gerber and Reed broke out (who, if anyone, punched whom is more difficult to discover than almost anything else in the buried history of American radicalism); with the help of the Chicago police, the left-wing delegates were prevented from entering the hall; and so ended the last important effort to transform the SP into a Leninist organization.

Meanwhile, as the Socialist Party was trying to regroup its battered ranks and insisting that, actually, it was as revolutionary as anyone else, two Communist conventions were being held. The Michigan-Russian Federation bloc, augmented by Fraina, Ruthenberg, and Wolfe, was meeting as the Communist Party, and the Gitlow-Reed group, augmented by many left-wingers throughout the country, as the Communist Labor Party. Exactly what now divided these two groups, other than their previous tactical differences with regard to staying in the Socialist Party, it would be hard to put in strictly doctrinal terms. Yet there *was* an important difference of tone and attitude. But at this point it might be best to turn to the testimony of Max Eastman, who wrote a long report for the *Liberator,* sympathetic to the left in general but shrewdly critical of both groups:

> Each of these groups [the CP and the CLP] would like to think that the rank and file of the American Communist movement was represented in its convention. But it is impossible to decide that question now. The rank and file never had time to consider and act upon the issue between them. It was a division among leaders, and a very vague and queer one too. Delegates were wandering from one convention to another under indefinite instructions, or no instructions at all, except the understanding that they were to form a party in accord with the Manifesto of the Third International. Out of this unhappy confusion almost everybody hoped and strove for a unity of the revolutionary elements, except the heads of the Slavic Federations, whose absolute control [of the CP] would have disappeared if unity had been achieved, and who maintained that their absolute control was necessary to the formation of a pure and perfect party of communism. . . .
>
> It was twilight when the Left Wing delegates (the CLP) convened. . . . But there was more life to be felt there—if life is spontaneous volition—than anywhere else during all the conventions. It seemed as though a thing with growth in it were being born in that place. In the other places [meaning the SP and

CP conventions] whatever came was engineered into being by the perceptible workings of an established machine. This may be —in cold reality—either a good or a bad sign for the Communist Labor Party. . . .

After sending a greeting to Debs and all class-war prisoners . . . the convention proceeded immediately to attempt to achieve unity with the "Communist Convention." C. E. Ruthenberg of Ohio, who had joined in the call for the Communist Convention, but nevertheless took his seat here for the time, introduced a motion that would have delayed the organization of a party here, until after a consultation could be had with those who were to organize the Communist Party the next day. It would have been a humble act on the part of these delegates, leading towards a possible submission to the control of the Slavic Federations. It was vigorously and at times violently opposed—especially by Jack Carney, who declared "before God," as irreligious Irishmen always do, that if this convention went over to the [foreign-language] Federations, he would go home and tell the workers of Duluth that there was no party of communism in existence. . . .

The Chicago police supplied the best of all arguments in favor of the Communist Convention. The Right Wing was protected by the police, the Left Wing was ignored, but the hall of the Communist convention was raided, photographs taken, decorations and revolutionary placards destroyed, and two men arrested. Perhaps the argument is a little crippled by the fact that one of the two men arrested was a lawyer, and the other was Dennis E. Batt of Detroit, one of the leaders of that Michigan group whose excessively political or educational brand of Communism is the chief weakness of the Convention.

My impression was that the heads of the Slavic Socialist Machine are in a mood for the organization of a Russian Bolshevik church, with more interest in expelling heretics than winning converts, and with a pretty fixed opinion that although Americans must perforce be admitted to the church they must not be admitted in such numbers as to endanger the machine's hold upon the dogmas and the collection box. . . . And it seems to me that what has compelled some at least of the American comrades to accept the dictation of this machine, and try to form an American proletarian party with so preposterous a handicap, is that inward dread of not proving sufficiently revolutionary which hounds us all. . . .

[The CLP] program is upon the whole a vital, simple and realistic application of the theories of Marx, and the policies of Lenin, to present conditions in America. It contrasts with the program of the Communist Convention in no point of principle, but it applies its principles more specifically to existing conditions, it is written in a more American idiom, it is written in the language of action rather than of historic theory. . . . In these respects it seems to me superior to the program of the Communist Party. . . .

It would be foolish to pretend that the Communist Labor Party, any more than the Communist Party, is a wholly satisfactory nucleus for the growth of Communism in America. Nothing that happened in Chicago was satisfactory. But the Communist Labor Party has a certain atmosphere of reality . . . a freedom from theological dogma on the one hand and machine politics on the other, which is new to American socialism, and hopeful. . . .[32]

History is endlessly strange. The author of the above passage—this is profoundly relevant to the whole experience of American radicalism—was later to become a Contributing Editor of *The Reader's Digest.*

Chapter II. Underground Communism: Disorder and Early Sorrows

It was characteristic of the early American Communist movement that it should be founded in factional strife and nurtured upon factional violence. Until the "Stalinization" of the party in the late twenties, when a pall of uniformity was lowered from above, it lurched and stumbled from one factional dispute to another. Wasteful and absurd as many of these may often have been, needlessly ferocious and vituperative as almost all of them were, they testified to the fact that in its own curious way the early Communist movement retained a measure of internal democracy. Many of these faction fights concerned problems that had no genuine relevance to America or American radicalism; others were little more than clique battles in which a barrage of ideology prepared the way for raids upon power; still others seized upon important political issues, though at times in distorted or pretentious ways. Small religious or political sects that suffer from an awareness of their own impotence will frequently turn their energies upon themselves, lashing deviants with the fury they would like to apply to enemies; and this is particularly true for those sects in which doctrine is seen as the bench mark of loyalty or in which the exegesis of an ideological system has a way of replacing the investigation of social reality. Nonetheless, every human enterprise has its own significance, value, and risks, so that, as part of our larger purpose in this book, we must turn back to these old disputes in order to disengage the essential meanings from the passing trivialities.

1. Though a split in the Socialist Party seemed inevitable by 1919, there was no clear view among the various left-wing tendencies as to their future perspective. Many delegates came to the 1919 Socialist convention merely with a general mandate for a "revolutionary" policy, and these tended to go along with the Left Wing group which did not participate in the founding of the Communist Party, though it had no major ideological differences from

it. The Left Wing group at its convention claimed 82 delegates, the Communist Party 128 regular and fraternal delegates; but soon the greater cohesiveness of the latter—it represented local branches that had already been expelled from or had themselves abandoned the Socialist Party—gave it an even greater advantage than the figures might suggest. The Left Wing tended to represent an unknown quantity, while the CP claim of 55,000 members, though extravagant, had behind it considerable strength.[1]

Both groups agreed upon political essentials. Both felt that the SP leadership was hopelessly reformist; both were passionate supporters of the Bolshevik Revolution; both desired the formation of an American revolutionary party. Bad faction blood notwithstanding, the question of unity—that reef upon which so many radical groups have foundered—could not be evaded.

Soon negotiations were opened between committees representing the Left Wing group and the newly proclaimed Communist Party. (The latter, it will be remembered, consisted largely of a bloc between the foreign-language groups, the Michigan branches, and a scattering of Easterners.) In its high-and-mighty fashion the CP committee invited the Left Wing comrades to sit in at the CP convention, "in a reserved section, as special guests," until a determination of the political worthiness of the Left Wing delegates could be made. Understandably, the Left Wing rejected this proposal for a Marxist loyalty test.

But before the problem of unity could be worried any further, one of the parties involved found itself badly in need of some unity within itself. The Russian Federation, led by Nicholas Hourwich and Alexander Stoklitsky, was the dominant force within the Communist convention; and with all the protective venom of an entrenched petty bureaucracy it fought against the idea of treating the Left Wing "centrists" as its political peers. In turn, this attitude was resisted by such English-speaking Communists as Louis Fraina and Isaac Ferguson, who represented the "softer"—which here meant simply the more sensible—group within the new Communist Party and who yearned to collaborate with the Left Wing in order to strengthen the English-speaking elements *vis-à-vis* the arrogant Russian Federation.

What was it, in any case, that separated the CP from the Left

Wing? Not clear-cut political issues; at least not as much as cultural and linguistic differences that were hard to specify but pointed to some deeper divergence. But since the Russian Federation realized that it could not very well organize an American Communist Party without *some* English-speaking delegates—a lamentable necessity, it sometimes seemed to feel—it reluctantly agreed to negotiate with the "centrists," who in the meantime were meeting at the Chicago IWW headquarters and organizing themselves into the Communist Labor Party (CLP) in order the better to be able to negotiate with the CP. Within a few days, then, there were two Communist organizations and the possibility, if only negotiations for unity continued long enough, of several more.

Hourwich and Stoklitsky might be forced to declare for Communist unity, but that did not mean they were going to surrender an inch of their ideological exclusivism. (It is a bit amusing that in a movement which claimed to dispense with all national prejudices the feeling of superiority among the Russian Federation leaders had little basis other than the fact that they happened to come from the same country as Lenin and Trotsky.) They launched broadside after broadside against the CLP for its "centrism," for the crime of using "revolutionary phrases" to conceal its "betrayal of the revolutionary class struggle." [2] They further attacked the CLP for being heterogeneous in its political composition, though this was sheer deceit since the CP itself, especially with the unassimilated Michigan group, was even more heterogeneous. And finally they issued an ultimatum that the CLP delegates be screened by a CP committee, those who met the test of political purity being admitted to a joint convention and those who flunked being banished from the gates.

Deciding to go the CP one better, the CLP gravely replied with a proposal that a *joint* screening operation be conducted to weed out "irreconcilable elements." In a further stroke of faction strategy, the CLP elected a "rank and file" committee of three which was to penetrate the bureaucratic barriers of the CP convention. But the CP generals were not to be taken in by such "miserable" tactics, and soon the unity negotiations broke down in an atmosphere charged with polemic and insult. Each group went its own way, confident in its possession of the future; each elected a national committee and a national secretary, Alfred Wagenknecht for the CLP and Charles Ruthenberg for the CP.

Though the formal programs of the two parties differed but little, they did reflect a divergence in political outlook as well as a variation in sensitivity toward American life. For all its self-proclaimed revolutionary purity, the CP leadership had only a foggy understanding of Leninist politics, and its program read more like a caricature than a faithful transcript of Bolshevism. Suffering unawares from a syndicalist hangover, the American CP saw in the process of capitalist development the source not merely of "mass action" but also of *"political* mass action." In other words, the tendency of the American CP—perhaps because of its great distance from the working class—was to assume that the rise of revolutionary consciousness was almost an inherent and spontaneous process within capitalist society, thereby in effect eliminating the Leninist stress upon the role of the revolutionary party. This view encouraged a progam keyed not to the realities of American society but to a faith in the "inevitable" end. For if the revolution were more or less predetermined, why dissipate one's energies in fighting for social reforms or in taking seriously electoral contests? Indeed, as the CP saw it, such activity was worse than useless, for it obscured the basic issue of power and postponed the inevitable showdown between the classes. "Parliamentary representatives of the Communist Party," declared the CP program, "shall not introduce or support reform measures." And what is more, any reform movement that did not accept the reading of history which was the monopoly of the Communist Party would be refused the privilege of its collaboration. Those excommunicated were "the Socialist Party, Labor Party, Non-Partisan League, People's Council, Municipal Ownership League," and to exclude any last-minute impulses toward fraternization, the list of organizations declared *non grata* was extended with a comprehensive *"etc."*

Perhaps the greatest disservice which the Communist Party inflicted upon itself—as upon the labor movement—was its virtual endorsement of dual unionism. After denouncing the entire American Federation of Labor as "reactionary and a bulwark of capitalism," [3] a typically naive and clumsy effort was made to justify the CP's dual-union perspective by citing the fact that it was meeting during the greatest strike wave in the country's history, a strike wave in which there were preliminary impulses toward breaking away from the limitations of AFL craft unionism; but a more careful analysis would have indicated that this ferment offered the Communists opportunities only if they functioned within the AFL. The CP could not distinguish between the urge toward industrial unionism, which had been at work within the labor movement for some time, and the urge toward revolutionary unionism, which was at work mainly in the remnants of the IWW. And even if some of its more knowledgeable American leaders such as Charles Ruthenberg and Isaac Ferguson had been inclined to challenge such policies, they did not yet command the factional resources to oppose the Russian Federation.

On the face of it, the CLP program was even more rigid than that of the CP, since, under pressure from John Reed and others, it went still further in rejecting electoral activity. But the language of the CLP was more accessible to American radicals, and its tone a bit more humane and friendly, as Max Eastman had noted in the *Liberator*. The CLP leaders—Wagenknecht, Ben Gitlow, John Reed, Ludwig Lore—enjoyed a somewhat better understanding (or say they had fewer misunderstandings) of American life than Hourwich and Stoklitsky. The CLP as a whole was possessed of a somewhat more reflective temper, and it contained a higher percentage of native-born members with a "feel" for American society. To insure its revolutionary credit rating, the CLP declared that in this period the "Communist platform . . . can contain only one demand—the establishment of the Dictatorship of the Proletariat"; in practice, however, it was capable of a more realistic and considered approach to the American scene.

2. Our focus, having been narrowed to factional strife, must now be widened beyond the scope of Communist organization itself; for to understand the character of early American Communism one must consider its seldom-noticed relationship to the fate of American progressivism.

There is a temptation—it should be neither wholly resisted nor embraced—to regard the story of early American Communism as low comedy, with the leading performers either naïve idealists or ambitious clowns. To do this is generally to forget the scope of social crisis that during these years afflicted not only Europe but also America. One writer, intent upon denying any basis for the Communists' revolutionary expectations, has described the America of 1919 as having had "a whiff of class warfare." [4] This whiff, as it happens, consisted of strikes by 25 percent of the industrial working class in the course of one year; long, hard, and bloody clashes between the unions and a variety of strikebreaking agencies; and the growth of social panic in leading governmental and industrial circles that shared, though with vastly different emotions, the belief of the Communists that Europe would be overcome by revolution. (In retrospect it is easy enough to see that this belief was mistaken; but historical hindsight ought to enable us to understand how and why such mistakes could be made at all.)

Still another reason for supposing in 1919 that class issues would be drawn with increasing sharpness was the decline of American progressivism. The prewar progressive movement had emerged, at least in part, as a deliberate strategy for offsetting the successes of the Socialists.[5] As long as an atmosphere of liberal optimism had continued to suffuse American life, the progressives were able to challenge and weaken the Socialists—particularly if the competition between the two was to be confined to their effectiveness as reformers. But now, in the immediate postwar years, the progressive movement lay stunned and broken, a casualty of the European war. As a political mood, progressivism had been overwhelmed by the militarist spirit of the war years; as a political program it had begun to seem pale, perhaps even irrelevant, in a world torn by revolution and counter-revolution. In 1919 the language of moderation was not likely to flourish.

When the news of the overthrow of the Czar had reached America, the response among intellectual spokesmen for progressivism had been entirely enthusiastic. So, for the moment, had been the response of the Wilson administration. The progressives had seen the revolution as a major advance for democracy; the administration had also been concerned with the possibility that it would give Russia a more efficient government and thereby improve the military position of the Allies. And for those forces within and without the Wilson administration that were straining toward direct participation in the war it made the job of propaganda much easier —the embarrassment of proposing a "crusade for democracy" in which the Czar would serve as a leading knight had now come to an end.

But as Russia continued to move toward the left, and the Bolshevik Revolution raised a threat to the continued stability of world capitalism, a major split took place between the Wilson administration and such leaders of intellectual progressivism as Herbert Croly, Robert Morss Lovett, and William Hard. The progressive intellectuals were friendly toward the "Russian experiment" in its own right, while the Wilson administration grew increasingly hostile toward the Russian revolutionaries. When President Wilson referred to the Bolsheviks as "men more cruel than the Czar," the *New Republic,* for whom he had so long been a hero, snapped back:

> Does anyone imagine that Woodrow Wilson ever made the least effort to ascertain the facts of either terms of his comparison? . . . Has he examined the relation between Czarist officialdom and such affairs as the massacre of Kishinev? No, he has been too busy. But, of course, he knows all about the spirit and the practise of the Soviet regime? No: he has been too busy to inform himself.[6]

Their political strength greatly diminished, their morale sapped by the disillusioning experience of the "war for democracy," and their sense of mission undermined by the rise of Communism throughout Europe, the progressive intellectuals were still further troubled by what they took to be Wilson's two-faced attitude toward the Russians. As Robert Morss Lovett was to write in retrospect:

> For liberals in the United States, as for the Allies in Europe, the acid test was, as Wilson defined it, the treatment of Russia. Here, again, the ambiguous course of our government was disconcerting. On the one hand the President was inviting the Soviet leaders to a conference at Prinkipo, while on the other hand he was making war on them on two fronts. . . . The excuse that our troops were sent to protect American supplies was too flimsy to bear repetition.[7]

During the war the progressive intellectuals had, by and large, transferred their energies from trying to curb the excesses of a newly industrialized society to helping save the world for democracy. When they began to suspect that the war was something less than a crusade in humanistic idealism, and when Wilson's Fourteen Points gave way to the intrigues of Versailles, many of these liberals, deprived of political moorings, began to drift further leftward. They sought in friendship toward the new Soviet republic an anchor for their idealism, a new outlet for their displaced political energies. Under the impact of war and revolution their very language took on a more radical flavor—a leftward turn made all the easier by the fact that they no longer represented a major political tendency in the United States but were now little more than helpless critics and spectators. An editorial in the *Nation,* which had passionately supported the war and celebrated Wilson's idealism, now denounced the President for his role in the "humiliation to every American that there should be such a thing as a political prisoner in America . . . What is wrong with Mr. Wilson that he appears so devoid of the magnanimity which should be inseparable from the just and truly great man?" [8] What mattered here was not so much the demand for an amnesty itself as a bitterness of language that would have been impossible two years earlier.

True, the charter Communists made no serious effort to win over, or even enter a dialogue with, these radicalized intellectuals. Both sides, trained in the perception of each other's weaknesses, looked upon the other with derision. The progressives felt that the Communists were hopelessly irrelevant to the American scene; the Communists, convinced that they would soon be in possession of the proletariat, thought it pointless to bother with vacillating petty-bourgeois intellectuals who did not even call themselves socialists. But whether they realized it or not, the Communists of 1919 were significantly affected by the increasing militancy of these intellectual remnants of progressivism which, in their disenchantment with their own past, now tended to look toward Russia as a possible source of hope. The mere fact that the progressive intellectuals were turning leftward gave the Communists greater confidence—to say nothing of arrogance—concerning their own prospects: it helped many intelligent Communists to convince themselves of things that they must have known to be extremely far-fetched.

But there was another and perhaps more important connection between the decline of progressivism and the formation of the early Communist movement. With progressivism dwarfed by the rising violence of revolutionary struggle in Europe, with political life tending to be polarized in the United States, there was eliminated—or at least seriously weakened—the middle group of reformers who before the war had been able to restrain the more violent impulses of the American industrial system. By 1919 most pretenses of refinement had been dropped from American politics. The dominant powers in the country, many of them former progressives like President Wilson, had backed up in the face of revolution in Europe and were now given to intermittent bursts of panic. Politics became harsh and unyielding; the red scares seemed further to decrease the possibility of a middle progressive way; the "polarization of social life" about which the Communists spoke so frequently began to appear an imminent reality, and not to Communists alone.

Given these facts about the nature of both American and European society in 1919, the Communist expectations of revolution become somewhat more understandable. Not correct, or very intelligent; but understandable. That the Communists fundamentally misread the nature and prospects of American society, if only because they never thought to examine it as an independent organism, and that even within the framework of their analysis they could have achieved a far more sensitive and resilient view of America— all this is true. But if the Communist resolutions of 1919 seem strange today, let it also be remembered that the year 1919 itself must seem hardly less strange.

3. The decline of the progressive tradition was accompanied during and shortly after the war by one of those orgies of political hysteria that have regularly stained American history. Not merely Communists or Socialists became suspect, but all nonconformists; and for some left-wingers life itself was occasionally endangered. During a wartime strike of oil workers in Tulsa, Oklahoma, a local newspaper wrote in its editorial columns:

. . . If the IWW or its twin brother, the Oil Workers Union, gets busy in your neighborhood, kindly take occasion to increase the supply of hemp. A knowledge of how to tie a knot that will stick might come in handy in a few days. It is not time to dally with the enemies of the country. . . . The first step in the whipping of Germany is to strangle the IWWs. Don't scotch 'em . . . Kill 'em dead. It is not time to waste money on trials. . . . All that is necessary is the evidence and a firing squad.[9]

Nor was this a mere isolated outburst of a benighted backwoodsman. What was threatened in Tulsa was nearly done in Tulsa and *was* done in many other American communities, from Bisbee, Arizona, to Butte, Montana to Centralia, Washington. The war-time repressions were matched in extent, and rivaled in physical brutality, by those that followed the war. The red scare of 1920 has gone down in history under the somewhat euphemistic title of the Palmer raids—after Attorney General A. Mitchell Palmer, the Quaker vigilante—but it ought to be remembered that these raids could hardly have taken place without the consent of the Wilson administration as a whole. Though opposition to Palmer's methods was registered within the administration, the mere fact that the raids took place on an extended scale must be regarded as adequate evidence that they met with the approval, or at least the toleration, of the President.

But where the wartime harassment of radicals had been inspired mainly by hysteria, the postwar repressions had a logic, perhaps even a realism, of their own. Mob actions during the war years had been more or less spontaneous, deriving from a popular fear and exaggeration of the strength of American radicalism; but the Palmer raids were a matter of calculated policy, based on the conviction that there was a genuine threat to the *status quo* stemming from the consolidation of Soviet power, the spread of revolution in Europe, and the immense strike waves at home.

In the 1917-18 round-ups the Wobblies had been the main victims; now it was the newly organized Communist groups. Yet, without accepting the facile assumption that any governmental persecution of radicals must necessarily be an attack on the unions, it is true that in 1919-20 the anti-red drive *did* sometimes serve as a convenient occasion for an attack upon the labor movement as a whole. An attempt was made, and with some success, to persuade "public opinion" that the lawless striker and the bloodthirsty Bolshevik, if not exactly twins, were close kin.*

The major attacks on the Communists came in the first week of January, 1920, though a preview of the Palmer raids had been released a few months earlier. On November 7, 1919, the second anniversary of the Bolshevik Revolution, agents of the Department of Justice raided the halls of the Union of Russian Workers, a fraternal organization including radicals of various convictions. Several hundred were jailed; in New York City a number of those arrested were taken to Ellis Island, "most of them with bandaged heads, black eyes or other marks of rough handling." The next day several agents led by New York Assemblyman Lusk, who was like Palmer in every significant respect except that of being a Quaker, swooped down upon the offices of the New York Communists; the assault was carried through with military precision and thoroughness. Out of these raids there followed on December 21, 1919, the deportation, authorized by the Department of Labor, of 249 real and alleged radicals, including the anarchists Emma Goldman and Alexander Berkman, who, as it happened, were hostile to the Bolsheviks.

On the night of January 2, 1920, the main blow was struck. As many as 5,000 people, it has been estimated, were arrested that night in simultaneous raids on radical meetings, offices, homes. Four hundred people were arrested in New York; 500 in New Jersey, where several "bombs" were picked up that turned out to be, prosaically, iron bowling balls; 700 in Detroit, where the "House of the Masses" was ransacked and boys in short pants picked up among the dangerous radicals. But it was in Boston that the Palmer raids as-

* Two examples: In January, 1920, the Kansas state legislature set up a Court of Industrial Relations, which was given jurisdiction over labor disputes and conditions in industries in which there was a "public interest," a term very broadly defined. In these industries, stated the law, workers "could not conspire with other persons to quit their employment." This arrangement was justified as part of a plan to thwart the schemes of the Communists.

Two years later, in an incident not at all unusual, Max Berger, an agent of the Justice Department, reported during the Railway Shopmen's strike that "there is a clear trail of evidence in the captured documents [from raids on Communist offices] leading from the Communist International to recent labor uprisings." [10] The possible uses of such statements are obvious.

sumed their ugliest form. There hundreds of captives, as if they were prisoners being marched through Rome by triumphant legions, were shackled together and paraded through the streets. In all these raids men were systematically beaten, property systematically destroyed. Few Americans cared or were able to protest at the time, and the newspapers were nearly unanimous in their appreciation of this master stroke against the forces of rebellion.[11]

While most of those arrested were soon released, the raids had their intended effect: they thoroughly disrupted the Communist Party. Shortly after the raids, Secretary of Labor Wilson ruled that mere membership in the Communist Party was sufficient ground for deporting an alien under the Deportation Act of October, 1918. And since the bulk of the CP was composed of aliens, it suffered severe losses, to the point where in January, 1920, it sold less than 2,000 dues stamps.[12] The CLP sustained similar attacks and similar losses.

For the two Communist groups there now seemed no alternative but to go underground. At first this was less a matter of a well-prepared policy than a simple effort to regroup the membership and protect it from the more violent persecutions. Public meetings under party auspices now became impossible in most cities, though meetings could still be held through a variety of sympathetic organizations. Except for the main Communist magazines, party publications continued to appear, though generally not under an official party imprint. To avoid too easy an identification between the "unofficial" Communist press and the underground groups that controlled it, the documents of the Communist International and even of the American Communist organizations would often be "reprinted" from conservative papers that had presented them to their readers as revealing scoops.

What was the nature, the quality of Communist organizational life during this underground period? Considerably less dramatic or conspiratorial than the word "underground" suggests. It is true that the internal organization of the Communist groups was necessarily transformed from large branches into small secret cells with a high degree of centralized control from above and a minimum of horizontal contact among the cells below; but except for a rather small minority that had had a certain experience with illegal political work in Europe, most of the members of the Communist groups, for all their bold talk and bolder writing, were thoroughly untrained and unequipped in the methods of conspiratorial work. Under the hammer blows of the Department of Justice and with party branches that had only recently been organized and had not yet had time in which to become cemented, it was not easy to create an underground apparatus that would function efficiently. The Department of Justice was not trying to liquidate or annihilate the Communist groups in the literal sense that fascist dictatorships later would; but it did everything in its power to prevent the Communists from surviving with any degree of political freedom or health. It harassed them, kept them off balance, frightened away potential members, prosecuted leaders, and kept a close check on those members who remained.

An underground Communist cell meeting, say, in Chicago would gather once a week in a private home and if it were properly trained in conspiratorial procedures would try to rotate the meeting places. Some of its members would conduct quasi-legal political activities through a Hungarian or Ukrainian or Jewish workers' club that continued to operate a headquarters though it had been raided by the police. Party speakers would sometimes be invited to talk at the meetings of such a workers' club, and party literature would be quietly distributed at the meeting—though it would have been risky to try to distribute any on the Loop. If the cell contained a student he could speak with some openness at the University, where tolerance of political deviants was greater than in the rest of the city. If the cell contained one or two union members, they could raise issues reflecting Communist policies when they went to their local meetings, though in the more conservative AFL unions it would be wiser to avoid explicit Communist identification. Some of the Communists, particularly those who had no "mass organization" in which to function, were certain to approach their former comrades of the Socialist Party, among whom they were known but generally safe, and there denounce the "betrayals" of the Social Democracy in Europe. At the cell meetings there would be reports from the upper party committee—provided the latter did not happen to be in jail at the moment; factional disputes, documenting the sins of the CLP or the stubbornness of the CP, were a standard item;

"socials" were frequently held as a relatively safe way to bring the
comrades together and perhaps invite some "contacts"; and all the
while there was the question, never quite brought into the open
yet never quite to be dismissed, as to which members of the cell
might happen to be stool pigeons.

It was a political life with intermittent risks for the members,
quite severe risks for the leaders, and very little possibility of
organizational growth. Necessarily it led to a rasping nervousness
in the inner relations of the party groups; and almost as predictably
it led to theories that made underground party life—which for all
its dangers also provided comforts of insulation—the appropriate
mode of Communist activity rather than an imposed handicap.
Meanwhile the danger of attack or arrest or deportation could not
be forgotten. Here is a credo circulated among underground Communists instructing them on how to conduct themselves:

1. Don't betray Party work and Party workers under any circumstances.
2. Don't carry or keep with you names and addresses, except in
   good code.
3. Don't keep in your rooms openly any incriminating documents or literature.
4. Don't take any unnecessary risks in Party work.
5. Don't shirk Party work because of the risk connected with it.
6. Don't boast of what you have to do or have done for the
   Party.
7. Don't divulge your membership in the Party without necessity.
8. Don't let any spies follow you to appointments or meetings.
9. Don't lose your nerve in danger.
10. Don't answer any question if arrested, either at preliminary
    hearings or in the court.[13]

As the Palmer raids gradually declined in frequency and viru-
lence, the scattered voices of American liberalism, at first almost
entirely silent, began to express their opposition. In May, 1920,
twelve prominent lawyers, including Felix Frankfurter, Zechariah
Chafee, Frank Walsh, and Swinburne Hale, denounced the government's action as a violation of constitutional procedures. That

same month Secretary of Labor Wilson ruled that the Communist Labor Party was a legal organization. Judge George W. Anderson, presiding over the trial of the Boston radicals, declared: "I can hardly sit on the bench and restrain my indignation at the tyrannous methods of the Department of Justice. . . . More lawless proceedings are hard to imagine." [14]

Though by the end of 1920 the national anti-red drive had somewhat subsided, state harassment and local vigilantism continued. Virtually the entire leadership of the two parties was indicted under state criminal syndicalism and anti-sedition statutes; leading Communists were embroiled in expensive court cases that reduced their effectiveness as party officials; major trials were held in New York, Chicago, and California.

4. In November, 1919, five Communist leaders, including Benjamin Gitlow and Charles Ruthenberg, were indicted for violating New York's criminal anarchy statutes. The first count charged that on July 5, 1919, the defendants had advocated "the violent overthrow of the government"; the second that they had "circulated the Manifesto of the June conference of the National Left Wing of the Socialist Party"; the third—and by far the most unconventional—that they were "evil-disposed and pernicious persons and of most wicked and turbulent dispositions" who tried "to excite discontent and disaffection." Had the state government persisted in prosecuting the Communist leaders on the ground of having "turbulent dispositions," the trial might have had a rare comic value; but the charge was soon dropped.

Defended by Clarence Darrow, who was kept busy these days traveling from one radical trial to another, the first Communist to be tried was Benjamin Gitlow. He came before Judge Barstow Weeks, who grew as proficient in dispatching radicals to jail as Darrow in pleading their cases. Gitlow took the novel position that the case was nothing but an act of political persecution and therefore refused to testify; but he was willing to make a final political speech in which he denounced his prosecutors, condemned capitalism, and extolled the Russian Revolution. Repeatedly interrupted and finally cut off by Judge Weeks, Gitlow never finished his oration.

Darrow, however, did put up a legal fight, claiming that the indictment was a violation of the constitutional guarantee of free speech. Bearing this in mind, Judge Weeks, who tended to combine his judicial role with a prosecutor's appetites, charged the jury, "You are not sitting here to determine any question of the rights of free speech." With Darrow's case thus undercut, the jury quickly returned a verdict of guilty and Judge Weeks congratulated the jury for a verdict of "distinct benefit to the country and the state." He then rebuked Gitlow for not accumulating property (on that count Gitlow certainly was guilty) and imposed a five- to ten-year sentence. of which Gitlow served nearly three years before being pardoned.

In the constitutional history of the United States, as well as in the long if intermittent legal effort to prosecute Communists strictly on the grounds of belief, the Gitlow case had a particular because precedent-making importance. It was argued in the higher courts for the next five years. The Appellate Supreme Court in 1921, the Court of Appeals in 1922, and the Supreme Court (with Brandeis and Holmes dissenting) in 1925 all affirmed the decision of the lower court. The argument of the Appellate Court was particularly striking as an example of the recurrent difficulties, not to say tenuousness, of the effort to convict radicals simply on the ground that they advocated force and violence:

> They do not expressly advocate the use of weapons or physical force in accomplishing these results; but they are chargeable with knowledge that their aims and ends cannot be accomplished without force, violence and bloodshed, and therefore it is reasonable to construe what they advocate as intending the use of all means essential to the success of their program.[15]

In other words, the conviction as here upheld rested not even upon the assertion that Gitlow advocated force or posed a clear and present danger to national security, but on the allegation that his "intent" as "construed" by the court was sufficient ground for declaring him to have violated the New York criminal anarchy statutes. With so permissive an interpretation of an already loose law, almost any radical could be put in jail, and for a time it seemed that most of them would be.

Nine months after the Gitlow trial, Charles Ruthenberg and

Isaac Ferguson—the latter a transitory but quite gifted leader of early Communism—came to trial, again before Judge Weeks, who had in the interim sentenced still another Communist leader, Harry Winitsky, to the standard five to ten years. Ferguson, arguing for both defendants, proved himself an able lawyer, particularly as a kind of legal "straight man" for Ruthenberg. The Communists had now decided that it was pointless to deny the jurisdiction of the court as Gitlow had tried to do, and that if they could hardly expect anything but conviction they might as well use the trial for propaganda. For days, as Ferguson fed him questions, Ruthenberg explained the Communist position on everything from general strikes to the Russian Revolution. Though hardly an intellectual titan, Ruthenberg was a cool and tough battler. Calmly, with an impudence that had its attractiveness, he denied membership in the underground Communist Party, and when District Attorney Rorke asked him whether he knew such leading Communists as Damon, Ruthenberg feigned total ignorance—though, as it happened, Damon was Ruthenberg's party name.

Ferguson's summary speech proved a better presentation of the Communist position than almost anything yet published in the dreary Communist press. But neither legal finesse nor political skill could affect the predictable outcome, and after three weeks of testimony the jury needed only two hours to declare Ruthenberg and Ferguson guilty. Before sentence was passed Ferguson openly denounced the judge:

> We have stood trial here before a judge who was challenged at the outset as unfit, by his prejudice, to sit in the trial of these defendants. That judge assumed to pass upon his own prejudice; that judge has acted as prosecutor in the case from beginning to end. . . .[16]

Which did not move Judge Weeks from his set pattern: five to ten years. Later the decision was revoked by the higher courts, not on the major constitutional issues involved, but for the technical reason that the state had not proved its claim that the defendants were owners of the *Revolutionary Age* when it published the Left Wing Manifesto.

Meanwhile a mass trial of twenty leading members of the Communist Labor Party was being held in Chicago with, again, Clarence Darrow as lawyer for the defense. The trial lasted from June until August, 1920, two months being taken up with the selection of a jury. As in New York, the prosecution rested upon the theory that merely to prove the defendants' membership in the CLP was sufficient evidence that they advocated the violent overthrow of the government. But this trial was more colorful and eccentric than the ones in New York. Here the evidence introduced by the state included a red flag; the text of the song "Red Flag"; a letter from Edgar Owens, Illinois secretary of the CLP, mentioning that he would like his son to grow up to be a rebel; the text of a speech made by one of the defendants, William Bross Lloyd, six months *before* the passage of the Illinois Sedition Act under which the CLP leaders were being tried (the state contended that this speech, while not evidence of conspiracy, was evidence of intent to violate a law that had not yet been passed); and, most damaging of all, a circular announcing a picnic to celebrate the second anniversary of the Russian Revolution, upon the introduction of which State's Attorney Barnhart tearfully cried out to the jury, "My God, can it be?" The state proved conclusively that it was.

One of the central points made by the prosecution was that the CLP advocated the kind of general strike that had recently taken place in Seattle, so that a great deal of time was spent in hearing witnesses, including ex-Mayor Hanson, detail the terrors of life in Seattle when the labor unions—mostly solid conservative AFL unions—had taken control of the city. The exact relevance of this was not clear, since the prosecution could not claim that the CLP leaders had been responsible for the Seattle general strike. But as was generally true in these cases, irrelevancies were themselves irrelevant to the manner in which they were conducted. Darrow brought in a mass of evidence to demonstrate that the Seattle general strike had been non-political in origin and peaceable and disciplined in conduct—though this, one might think, would more profitably have been a problem for a historian than a jury.

The Chicago trial reached a gory climax with the final speech of State's Attorney Frank Comerford, who cried out to the jury that if it reached a verdict of "not guilty," then

... Tear from your parks and your cemeteries the busts in marble and bronze of Lincoln and Washington, and put in their places the busts of Lenin and Trotsky; take from your churches the Christs on the cross and put Judas there ... destroy the monuments and mausoleums, build a new Arlington, and in it put the dust of the Haymarket anarchists, and find the resting place of Benedict Arnold. ...

In the same operatic vein:

When you leave to take up your deliberations tonight the flag will be flying over this court house and the people ... will wait, they will wait as they waited on another occasion. ...

That other occasion was when Francis Scott Key in the War of 1812 waited "with pain in his eyes" to see if the flag still waved over Baltimore after the town had been shelled by a British man-of-war. Comerford then concluded with a recitation of *all* the stanzas of the "Star-Spangled Banner." [17]

It requires no unusual insight into human or American nature to predict the outcome. The verdict was guilty, the sentence one to five years, and the flag was still there.

Though the whole drift of public emotion was against them, the Communists succeeded in putting additional obstacles in the way of their own defense. During the early wave of repressions the Communists had declared that the only proper means for defending political prisoners was "mass action." They objected to appeals, petitions, and legal action as reformist devices that would "sow illusions" in the minds of the workers. Wrote Louis Fraina:

Our comrades are languishing in prison: amnesty cannot reach them, and we don't want amnesty for them. *We want them released by the industrial might of the proletariat, by class conscious action.*[18]

The implication behind this ultra-left idea—that in the absence of mass action the convicted Communists would just have to put in their time—Fraina and his comrades did not draw; which was just as well, since no mass protest was in sight. Shortly thereafter Debs was freed by the Harding administration, which, uninhibited by any progressive Wilsonian past, declared an amnesty without having been subjected to mass pressure. The convicted Chicago CLP leaders were themselves pardoned by Governor Small on the eve of their departure to prison. No doubt mass pressure was from a Marxist point of view the most desirable way of coping with the imprisonment of the party leaders, but the refusal of the Communists to accommodate themselves to the fact that calling for mass pressure is not the same as getting it was a typical instance of their self-defeating ultimatism. Similarly rigid was their belief that any of the members who came into court should totally refuse to speak up:

> As to the idea that we can make propaganda through the court room,—it is impossible. . . . Bear in mind the appalling danger of betraying your comrades, betraying the Party—unconsciously, against your will, but opening them up to the attacks of our enemies just the same,—IF YOU ANSWER ANY QUESTIONS,—and you will resolve NOT TO ANSWER THEM. . . .[19]

The tactics of Ruthenberg and Ferguson at their trial indicate that, as in so many other respects, experience forced the Communists to abandon such ready-made notions; indeed, after a time it became conventional party doctrine that arrested Communists should use the courts as a forum for their views.

5. It is a moot point as to which did more to shatter the early Communist movement: the government's harassments or the furious inner squabbles of the Communist sects. Mass arrests, underground existence, and sustained sectarianism had completed their isolation from American life and turned the entire movement into an arena for political cannibalism.

The two Communist conventions were but a few months gone when a new split took place. The Michigan radicals, believers in socialism primarily through education, found life in the CP intolerable—it had all been a misunderstanding, they were far from being Bolsheviks. In June, 1920, they officially organized their own sect, the Proletarian Party. While continuing to declare its loyalty to the international Communist movement, the Michigan group devoted itself to violent polemics against the local Communist sects and to circulating long academic studies of Marxist economics by means of which it hoped to educate the working class.

Meanwhile civil war was ravaging the Communist world. The departure of the "Michiganers," as they were called, merely convinced the CP leadership of what it had long been certain: that it alone was the pure and certified representative of Communism in America. Another way of saying the same thing might be that the departure of the Michigan people left the Russian Federation more completely in control of the CP than ever. Nor did this split discourage the leaders of the Russian Federation, who positively thrived on splits and tended to think along the-worse-the-better lines: that is, the less contact the CP had with American life, the more immaculate would its revolutionary program be. The Russian Federation had seen to it that the CP would be structured very loosely, so that almost unlimited autonomy was permitted the foreign-language groups; by contrast, the CLP, reacting against the pressures of the foreign-language groups, had adopted a more centralized form of organization. In the "unity" negotiations that largely occupied the twenty months of their separate existence the two groups found that the role of the foreign-language federations—in truth, a real problem—was a major difficulty.

There were also political problems of a kind. Both Communist groups had taken the Socialists to task for their addiction to "parliamentary activity" and both formally adopted statements that, if taken literally, precluded electoral campaigns. But there the similarity ended. The Communist Party really believed that municipal campaigns were likely to contaminate revolutionaries (it believed that almost anything might contaminate revolutionaries), while the opposition of the Communist Labor Party to electioneering was more cant than conviction. In a sense the CP, particularly the Russian Federation that dominated it, did not really live in the United States, while the CLP, for all its revolutionary phrases, was led by indigenous radicals who realized that participation in elections was not merely imperative to any party wishing to root itself in American life but quite in harmony with the Marxist tradition.

The result of all this was often a comic situation, particularly in Ohio, where the bulk of the Socialists had moved either into one of the two Communist groups or out of active politics. Since Socialist nominations for local Ohio elections had occurred before the split-off of the two Communist groups, it was inevitable that a number of CLP members now found their names on the SP ballot. Disregarding the prohibitions of its own convention, the CLP decided to support those of its members who were on the SP ticket. For this descent into "opportunism" the CP denounced the CLP as "centrist" and "reformist," declaring that "a Communist party must have nothing to do with elections for judges and sheriffs, and for the executives of the capitalist state generally." This would have left the CP in a state of happy rectitude had it not been for the horrified discovery that some of *its* members were also, through no fault of their own, on the Socialist ticket. Whereupon the CP, with utter consistency, stuck to its theoretical guns and launched the most piquant election campaign in American history: it insisted that workers refrain from voting for its own members. An editorial in *The Communist,* the party's official weekly, announced that "The Communist Party comrades appearing on the Socialist Party ticket will make a campaign urging workers *not* to vote for them." [20]

Still another source of bitterness between the two Communist groups concerned an ugly subterranean struggle between the Russian Federation of the CP and the Soviet Bureau, then the unrecognized Soviet embassy in this country, at whose head stood Ludwig Martens, a German, and Santeri Nuorteva, a Finn. Partly this struggle reflected personal antipathies; partly it arose from the fact that the Soviet Bureau leaders seemed to favor the CLP rather than the CP; but in the main it had its source in the ambitions of the Russian Federation—ambitions that constituted a kind of inner Communist imperialism—to take control of the Bureau. Hourwich and his cronies cried out that Martens was hiring non-Bolsheviks for his staff, such as Morris Hillquit for the post of legal counsel, and that Martens was violating revolutionary principles by arranging necessary commercial deals for his government with American capitalists.[21] So fierce did the Russian Federation's vendetta against Martens become that the Communist International intervened to restrain Hourwich.

Though of faint interest in itself, this piece of intrigue led to an incident that reveals a great deal about the inner moral life of the early Communist movement. Nuorteva, testifying before a hostile Congressional Committee, declared that members of the CP were being prosecuted by the government for planks in the party platform that had been written by an agent of the Department of Justice. That government agents had infiltrated both Communist groups was not to be doubted; but that the very program of the party was the work of a provocateur was a charge so sensational and disturbing as to upset the balance of an already beleaguered movement, and still more disturbing because the platform had been written by Louis Fraina, a man of somewhat frail character but clearly one of the more gifted and intelligent figures in the party.

At a special party trial held just before Fraina was scheduled to leave for Europe as a delegate to the Third International, Nuorteva made his charge explicit. His evidence consisted mainly of a report given him by one Peterson, a former Department of Justice agent who had "reformed" and come to Nuorteva with the story that Fraina was a government spy. Peterson had testified that he had seen Fraina at the Department of Justice office and had glimpsed canceled government checks made out to Fraina for alleged service. When this testimony was largely ripped apart by Fraina's counsel, Dr. Jacob Nossovitsky, the trial committee not only exonerated Fraina but charged that Nuorteva, for motives of factional convenience, had engineered a "frame-up." [22]

The incident has never been entirely cleared up, though no evidence has thus far been presented to substantiate the charge that Fraina was a spy or that Nuorteva had committed a frame-up. Nor did the ugly barrage of charges and counter-charges quickly die down. At the second congress of the Communist International a trial committee was appointed to investigate the matter once more, with Fraina again being exonerated and Nuorteva sharply rebuked. But the rumors remained.

Two years after his trial Fraina was charged by the party with absconding with a sum of money entrusted to his care by the Communist International and intended for radical activity in the United States. (This, by the way, was one of the few times when there seemed some direct evidence of the presence of "Moscow gold" among American Communists.) And to provide a still more sinister conclusion, some years later it was revealed that the Dr. Nossovitsky who had so persuasively defended Fraina in his American trial and so subtly intimated that Nuorteva was perhaps a spy had all the while himself been an agent of the Department of Justice![23]

A final cause of the ugliness that characterized so much of the inner life of early American Communism was the moral and intellectual weakness of its leadership. Mostly young, almost always inexperienced in either American politics or trade-union activity, inordinately ambitious and self-admiring, the hordes of leaders all too frequently lived by a *Gauleiter* psychology: they thought of themselves, whether consciously or not, as men to whom power would *come,* and come mainly because they had so faithfully, if at times absurdly, tried to imitate the leaders of the Bolshevik Revolution. With its enormous stress on the "vanguard" role of the party and its leaders, Bolshevik doctrine could be a particularly heady brew for a group of men who had never gone through most of the experiences that had given rise to that doctrine. Few if any of the founding leaders of American Communism had even a fraction of Lenin's insight into the hidden workings of political life, Trotsky's brilliance of mind, Bukharin's taste for scholarship. With the unerring instinct of the epigone, they managed to absorb everything that was worst in the Bolshevik tradition, and sometimes to caricature it beyond recognition: the pose of toughness, the aura of certainty, the delight in annihilating factional opponents, the mechanical repetition of slogans, the appropriation of historical destiny.

Later Communist legend was to make Charles Ruthenberg, the first secretary of the CP, into a little-league Lenin; but there is no genuine warrant for this legend. After a career as a salesman and an office manager, Ruthenberg had joined the Socialist Party in 1909 and had rapidly risen to leadership. In 1912 he had polled 87,000 votes as the Socialist candidate for governor of Ohio; soon thereafter he became an SP functionary in Cleveland; in 1917 he drew more than a quarter of Cleveland's mayoralty vote; and the following year he was jailed for ten months on the charge of having violated the conscription law.

At most Ruthenberg was a competent administrator, the prototype of that dreary figure who would become so dominant in the American radical movement—the "organization man" who claimed no particular intellectual or political gifts but proceeded solidly to entrench himself as a party official. Colorless and conservative in manner, cold in his relations with other people, Ruthenberg was an odd but not untypical blend of the clerk's routinism with ferocious revolutionary fantasies. That he could consent to serve as party secretary at the time the Russian Federation was severely damaging the party indicates he was not of the stuff of independent men. Yet his organizational abilities were considerable; had the government been somewhat less ferocious in its attacks and the party line somewhat less preposterous in its sectarianism, Ruthenberg might have managed to build a solid organization.

At the opposite pole as leaders were men like Louis Fraina, who has already been discussed, and Isaac Ferguson, a Canadian who after graduating from the University of Chicago law school had divided his time between farming in Wyoming and a small law practice, had run for county attorney on the Republican ticket in Wyoming's Park County, and then in 1917 had returned to Chicago where he became friendly with the Socialists at the University and joined the SP in 1918. In less than two years, with no intellectual training in socialist thought or experience in the labor movement, Ferguson became a Communist leader; and even then, since he was a man of wit and intelligence, he proved more competent than most of his colleagues. In the early twenties he dropped out of the movement as casually as he had come into it and retired to the more sedate life of a lawyer.

Another example of the essentially casual way in which leadership was recruited for the Communist groups is the case of Robert Minor. A quite gifted cartoonist, Minor had been a sort of free-lance radical through the war years and had sent dispatches to the New York World from Russia in which he was sympathetic to the revolution but critical of the Bolsheviks. He soon abandoned this criticism, joined the Communists, and almost overnight became a top-rank leader. Though his personal background was richer than that of most party leaders, Minor was as mediocre a politician as he was gifted a cartoonist: he lacked the intellectual and moral qualities required of the independent leader, and in later years, together with men like Israel Amter and James W. Ford, he became the prototype of the pliable Stalinist functionary.

It would be an exaggeration to claim that none of the early Communist leaders had talents or personal qualities that distinguished them from the run-of-the-mill politician, or that most of them were as inflexible in their thinking and insufferable in their behavior as Nicholas Hourwich, the leader of the Russian Federation. But the exceptions were few and, perhaps just because they were exceptions, tended to be powerless within the movement. John Reed was a brilliant journalist and a remarkably attractive figure in his own right, but it cannot be said that his experience as a Communist leader was very distinguished—his were the kinds of talents that flourish in the open air of personal and intellectual life, not in the atmospheres of party committees. Ludwig Lore, who began in the CLP and remained in the Communist movement for several years thereafter, was a man of genuine thoughtfulness in his political writing; but his very independence, his distaste for the infantile radicalism of the early American Communists, doomed him to the role of party butt and scapegoat: every orthodox fool felt free to kick the heterodox Lore.

There is of course what Marxists would call a "dialectical relationship" between the weakness of the early Communist movement in America and the poor quality of its leadership. Not merely did the leaders hobble the movement but the isolation of the movement disabled the leaders and kept them from acquiring the experience and knowledge that might have matured them. Nonetheless, the unsavoriness of early American Communism, particularly in its internal life, was due less to the pressures of external attack than to the systematic mediocrity of its leadership—a mediocrity often rendered vicious by the arrogance of men who believed themselves to have been historically "ordained" and spent most of their time fighting for the symbols of ordination.

6. Everything that has just been said about the low quality of the early Communist leadership was soon to be demonstrated with a bizarre finality in what one historian has called the "Caligula period" of the party's existence.[24] Or perhaps, Caligula in the nursery.

From the time the two Communist groups had been organized, the CLP, with its greater political sensitiveness, had played the role of wooer, appealing to the members of the CP to force their leaders into unity. (At one point the CLP even pressed for economic sanctions, urging the CP ranks to withhold dues payments until unity was accepted by the leaders.) The cry for unity was soon taken up inside the CP: a month after the two groups were organized, the Boston local of the CP, claiming 2,000 members, passed a resolution urging unity.[25]

During late 1919 and early 1920 the two organizations engaged in elaborate "unity" maneuvers. Meetings were held between committees of the two parties, at which the CLP agreed to accept in advance the CP program and a minority status within the unified organization. But what kept the two groups apart was the problem of a constitution for the unified party, which meant, above all, the problem of how much autonomy to allow the foreign-language groups. The Russian Federation realized that in a united party its power would be shorn unless it made certain in advance that it had autonomous status.

For months the bickering, the bragging, the insults and counter-insults, the empty threats and emptier replies continued—months during which both groups were being heavily assaulted by the government. Membership dropped sharply in both parties, for many who might have been able to weather the Palmer raids alone could not bear the combination of external assault and internal disunity.[26]

Within the Communist Party there had arisen a considerable factional opposition to the doctrinal rigidity and the rule-or-ruin methods of the Russian Federation. This opposition, led by Ruthenberg, Ferguson, and Alexander Bittleman, the leader of the Jewish Federation, bridled at the quasi-religious tenor of the Russian Federation and began to yearn for unity with the CLP as a means of escaping the wardenship of Hourwich and his cronies. At one point Ruthenberg branded the majority of the CP, which is to say the Russian Federation, as a collection of phrasemongers who threw "a few undefined slogans around like hallelujahs at a revivalist meeting" and described the CP as having become "an institution for the holding of ritualistic incantations to the Russian Revolution." Ruthenberg also began to object to the ritualistic use of the phrase "mass action," claiming with some point that the task of the party was first to establish some "contact with the masses." But the Russian Federation people objected that "contact with the masses" would mean "dilution of Communist principles"—as perhaps it might—and that in order to gain contact with the masses it would be necessary to abandon illegal methods and thereby to modulate their public proclamations that force and violence were essential to the overthrow of capitalism. Spokesmen for the Russian Federation berated Ruthenberg's minority group within the CP for holding that "the use of *force* (armed revolution and civil war) may or may not be necessary in order to accomplish the overthrow of the capitalist state. . . ." [27]

At a conference of CP leaders held in April, 1920, the Ruthenberg minority pressed for immediate unity with the CLP. Defeated in the Central Executive Committee by a 5-4 vote, Ruthenberg and his friends abandoned the CP and prepared for a unity convention with the CLP, to be held a month later, in May.

"Sometime recently, somewhere between the Atlantic and Pacific, between the Gulf and the Great Lakes two groups of elected delegates assembled as the Unity Conference of the Communist Party and the Communist Labor Party. [That is, Ruthenberg was claiming to speak in the name of the Communist Party.] Of the former, 32; of the latter 25 . . . also a representative of the Executive Committee of the Communist International." [28]

So ran the opening paragraph of the account of the convention written by Y. F. (Isaac Ferguson) in the first issue of *The Communist,* organ of the newly merged organization, which called itself (somewhat prematurely) the United Communist Party.

Let it not be supposed, however, that there was very much unity at the first convention of this United Communist Party. Held at Bridgman, Michigan, its convention proved a seven-day marathon at which quarreling and doctrinal hair-splitting nearly provoked new splits. Some of Ruthenberg's friends, while eager to get away from the Russian Federation, still regarded the CLP as "centrists" and were determined that the platform of the new United Communist Party should be unambiguous in its advocacy of "force" as the sole method of overthrowing capitalism. The problem of force was then debated with a forcefulness that seems all the more mad when it is understood that no delegate objected to the commitment to force *per se* and that the only question at issue was how prominent this commitment should be. Some of the delegates, former members of the CP, wanted "force" to be plunked square into the first paragraph of the party's program, while the majority of the delegates maintained that it was no violation of Bolshevik rectitude to declare the party's ultimate reliance on force in subsequent paragraphs. But a number of delegates found this commitment to ultimate force pusillanimous, and to express their displeasure soon dropped out of the Communist movement entirely.[29]

During the election for a National Committee, the United Communist Party, having barely weathered the "force panic," as Ferguson sarcastically described it, was again almost ripped apart. The all-important question, crucial to the forthcoming American revolution, of power alignments on the National Committee was finally settled by making Ruthenberg secretary and giving each of the two tendencies equal representation.

The United Communist Party (even the name provoked a bitter fight at the unity convention) somehow managed to be still further removed from both the American scene and political intelligence than the groups that had gone to form it. The UCP rigidly committed itself to force as a political method; it moved closer to a dual-union position than the CLP had had; it repudiated the possibility of participating in municipal elections; it refused to endorse Eugene Debs, who was running for President on the Socialist Party ticket and instead called for a boycott of the elections; it denounced "laborism" even though the labor party movement (see p. 112) was beginning to show progress; it regarded its semi-underground status as a Communist virtue rather than an enforced necessity and refused to explore channels for legal activity. In short, it was committing itself to a political isolation ward. The only progress the new organization made was in establishing a firmer control over its foreign-language federations and in moving toward new linguistic habits. There is a certain pathos in Ferguson's report that at the convention many delegates with the barest grasp of English were "painfully struggling with the English language, no longer depending for expression on the artificial foreign-language

caucuses of prior conventions, but making themselves one with all
the other delegates in defiance of barriers of language or nationality." [30]

So again there were two—the newly formed United Communist Party and the Communist Party, the latter more firmly than ever
in the grip of the Russian Federation. And how violently, even
hysterically, the CP press fulminated against the UCP! In its
articles it invariably called the UCP the United "Centrist" Party—a
thrust well calculated to wound Marxist sensibilities. There were
more serious thrusts too, the CP charging that Ruthenberg, when
he left it, had walked off with the party treasury of $7,000. At first
Ruthenberg maintained a dignified silence about this rather considerable sum, but as the CP kept repeating the charge, he issued
the flimsy reply that his faction, because it had had a majority of
the members in the CP, was entitled to the entire treasury. Actually,
only about a third of the CP membership had gone with Ruthenberg.

In July, 1920, the depleted but not discouraged Communist
Party held its second convention, at which it declared that it was
"opposed to legal, cultural or educational organization," though it
did grudgingly concede that in special cases "Party committees, consisting of not more than fifteen in number . . . may use the legal
forms for special work." [31] Further than this it would not go in
contaminating its principles or risking contact with the masses. As
for unity with the UCP—"impossible." Charles Derba, a leader of
the Russian Federation, was elected executive secretary and then
the delegates left, determined to dig still deeper into the lonely caves
of underground existence.

It is very possible that if the two rival underground parties had
been left to their own resources they would now slowly have bled
to death. From the point of view of American radicalism this might
have had certain advantages. But the two parties were not left to
their own devices. Amazed at the antics of the American Communists, who were always regarded as the least talented in the world
movement, the Communist International, which had been organized
only about a year earlier, decisively intervened.

From the very beginning the Communist International had

fundamentally miscalculated with regard to the situation in America: it had believed that the US was on the verge of a profound social crisis that would reach its climax when the proletarian revolution triumphed in western Europe. What would have happened in this country had the proletarian revolution triumphed in western Europe is a matter for speculation; but in the meantime the Communist International (Comintern) obviously had its pressing reasons for desiring a unification of the two American groups.

Early in January, 1920, Gregory Zinoviev, chairman of the Comintern, had addressed an official communication to the central committees of the CP and CLP informing them that a special committee of the Comintern had agreed that the split

> . . . has rendered a heavy blow to the Communist movement in America . . . when . . . great possibilities and brilliant perspectives are opening up before the American proletariat. Insofar as both parties stand on the platform of the Communist International —and of this we have not the slightest doubt—a united party is not only possible but is absolutely necessary, and the [Comintern] categorically insists on this immediately being brought about.[32]

While Zinoviev had some kind words—probably spoken with tongue in cheek—for the theorizing talents of the foreign-language federations, he insisted that they play a subordinate role in a united party. Zinoviev's letter, as well as similar efforts, had little immediate effect, since it was followed, as we have already described, by the split in the CP and the formation of the UCP.

The Comintern kept pressing for unity. At the first meeting of the Executive Committee that had been elected at its Second Congress, the Comintern gave high priority to the "American question" and demanded unity from the warring American groups within two months. When this proved impossible, a new target date of January 1921 was set by Moscow. When even this deadline could not be met, the Comintern established in Moscow a special "American Agency" which was authorized to impose unity upon the American parties—somewhat like a nurse trying to establish friendship between children enormously enjoying a battle.

The creation of this "American Agency" was in effect a step toward placing the entire American Communist movement into receivership—an example, by no means the last one, of how little confidence Moscow felt in its American friends. On April 2, 1921 the "American Agency" sent instructions to its American wards: either unite by June 1, 1921 or "the whole movement would be reorganized without regard to the existing parties." [33]

Forced to the wall, the contending American factions finally agreed to unity, though with no great show of grace. Between the agreement and the realization, however, fell the shadow of exacerbated personal relations, of fantastically magnified doctrinal disputes, and above all of endless murky maneuvers for power status in a unified movement.

In May, 1921, after months of frenetic negotiations, unity was finally established between the United Communist Party and the Communist Party. The new organization was now to be known as the Communist Party of America. Actually it was something of a shotgun wedding. Until the month of the ceremonies, the inflamed mates kept tossing such love notes as "literary prostitute" and "liar" at each other—portents for a lively honeymoon.

As specified by the Comintern, there were thirty delegates each from the CP and the UCP at the unity convention. Charles Ruthenberg, who had a gift for elbowing his way to the top in unifications quite as well as in splits, became national secretary. A new program, departing radically from earlier Communist formulas on such matters as trade unionism and electoral activity, was adopted; but of this we shall treat in a later section. Only on the question of force did the newly and this time perhaps truly unified American Communist movement remain faithful to the notions of its infancy: "Mass action culminates in armed insurrection and civil war." [34]

7. Even as it was struggling to cope with government attacks and its own self-destructive factionalism, the early Communist movement was torn by a problem that had at least the merit of being related to social actuality: the problem of trade-union policy. For a good part of its infancy, the movement had absorbed the dual-union tradition of American syndicalism (IWW) and of its

sympathizers within the American Socialist movement. The strike wave of 1919 had further encouraged the Communists in their drift toward dual-union policies, since it seemed to them that these strikes would burst the bonds of AFL conservatism and leap forward spontaneously into new revolutionary forms. "Every big strike is a potential revolution, though it may in its first stages be merely a revolt against the price of bacon and eggs," declared a CLP publication—and it was this false estimate of American strike actions that repeatedly drove Communist trade-union policy into a blind alley. The CP wrote similarly about the 1919 steel strike: "The gigantic struggle may become the turning point of the American working class movement; the forces of capitalism may convert the strike into the 1905 of the American proletarian revolution. Who knows?" [35] And as a result of the theory that strike actions would lead the workers far beyond their conscious intentions, the Communists could both justify their separation from the American workers and look with disdain upon those trade-union struggles that involved nothing more than immediate demands.

So ultimatistic were both Communist sects in their attitude toward the unions that they attacked not merely the old-line Gompers leadership (which was understandable) but also the very left-wing and militant unionists whom they might more profitably have been wooing. In the first month of the steel strike William Z. Foster was denounced by the CP: "The old unionism is in decay. . . . But here, in the steel industry, the AFL is imposing this reactionary system upon the workers—assisted by the Syndicalist E. [sic] Z. Foster." [36] John Fitzpatrick, a leading militant unionist, chairman of the Chicago Federation of Labor and also of the 1919 steel Strike Committee, was blasted for suggesting that the steel strikers' demands might be submitted to arbitration. "Nothing permanent," intoned the Communists, "is secured from arbitration, which is always determined by fundamental capitalist interests. Arbitration invariably betrays. The value of the strike is not in the immediate concessions secured, but in the reserves developed for action in days to come." [37] Perhaps this was the value of strikes for the party leaders, but surely not for workers who were striving toward better living conditions. And besides—to touch upon a sore spot in the Communist attitude toward strikes—did not all strikes, so long as capitalist society continued, have to be settled and did that not mean, in turn, that one way or another they had all to be submitted to the authority and limitations of the *status quo?*

At the first convention of the United Communist Party the impulse toward dual unionism was openly expressed. The UCP program roared:

> A Communist who belongs to the AFL should seize every opportunity to voice his hostility to this organization, not to reform it but to destroy it.[38]

A few months later the UCP advised workers:

> You must direct your strikes against the government and must overthrow the capitalist government. When the final struggle to overthrow the government comes you must have guns in your hands. . . .[39]

What made this kind of talk particularly empty was its timing. It was now the middle of 1920. The steel workers had just been defeated. A strike of 500,000 coal miners had just been nipped by a court injunction. In Mingo County, West Virginia, miners had to fight a small-scale civil war simply to defend their right to organize an AFL union. The open-shop movement had made enormous headway. The labor movement was on the defensive. Where the American workers had engaged in large-scale strikes in 1919 to advance their interests, they were now, only a year later, fighting with their backs against the wall. To speak now of destroying the AFL, let alone overthrowing the capitalist government, was not merely a gigantic miscalculation; it showed that the labor movement and the Communists were moving along fundamentally divergent paths, the former battling to preserve itself and the latter taking this very occasion to assault it from the sidelines.

In 1919, when the Communist groups had not yet suffered the blow of the Palmer raids, when they included in their ranks some thousands of foreign-born workers who reflected the predominantly foreign-born composition of the industrial labor force, when workers were struggling aggressively and might have been receptive not to socialist doctrine but to concrete labor issues raised from the left—then the Communists had had their opportunity. But with the noose of dual unionism around their necks, and their snobbish condescension to the forms of the class struggle in America which they might have been expected to welcome, they missed this opportunity. By 1920 they had cut themselves off even from those elements in the unions that might have been willing to work with them.

Eventually the Comintern would intervene to change the trade-union policy, but in the period immediately after the founding conventions of the American Communist groups it was often responsible for encouraging them in their suicidal union tactics. One reason for this was that the Comintern, misinformed by such Americans as Big Bill Haywood, Louis Fraina, and John Reed, vastly overestimated the importance of the IWW, mistaking its present weakness for its past strength and trying very hard to win the Wobblies to its ranks. As a result, it had to look with some kindliness at the IWW's insistence upon building revolutionary unions outside the AFL. In a letter from the Comintern Executive Committee to the IWW sent in January, 1920, it was proposed that "the IWW take the initiative in seeking a basis for the unification of all unions with a class-conscious, revolutionary character. . . ." [40] And in a letter sent simultaneously to the American Communists, Zinoviev urged them "to establish a close contact with those economic organizations of the working class in which there is a tendency toward industrial unionism, the IWW . . . etc." How profoundly Zinoviev and his colleagues misunderstood the American situation, to say nothing of the American temper, can be seen in the additional advice he gave the local Communists:

> The party must as far as possible support the formation in the factories . . . of shop committees, which serve, on the one hand, as a basis for the economic struggles, and on the other hand, as a school for the preparation of the vanguard of the working class for the administration of the industries after the Dictatorship of the Proletariat has been established.[41]

Naturally, this sort of directive could only encourage the American Communists to assume a dual-union perspective.* And as for strike committees, which had indeed played a major role in recent revolutionary developments in Germany, Russia, and England, it was all very well to call for them; but as Hotspur had said in a somewhat different connection, "But will they come when you do call for them?"

There was perhaps some excuse for Zinoviev's misconceptions regarding the American scene: he was in the position of the modern head of a state who is systematically misinformed by a diplomatic corps which sends consoling rather than accurate information. In one issue of the *Communist International* Big Bill Haywood made the preposterous claim that the IWW "had been engaged in more serious struggles than all political and so-called labor organizations of the U.S. combined." Another article by a Russian trade-union "expert," V. Lossief, was similarly dotted with inaccuracies: the IWW was credited with 100,000 members at its founding (the truth: less than 40,000) and the AFL was declared "always most unfavorable to strikes." At the time Lossief was writing, the IWW had been reduced to not more than 20,000 members and its prospects were dim. Even A. Lozovsky, head of the All-Russian Central Council of Trade Unions, a man who might have been expected to find out the facts, could write:

> The powerful AFL is entirely in the hands of Gompers and Co. . . . The IWW is undoubtedly a revolutionary organization but its theory and tactics suffer from many serious defects, as a result of which it embraces only *some hundreds of thousands* of the millions of the American proletariat. . . . The unions are nevertheless becoming revolutionized.[43] [emphasis added]

* As if in response to the appeal for the "speedy split of the AFL," there was organized in New York in July, 1920, the United Labor Council, in which the Communists played the central role. Headed by Joseph Zack, a Communist trade-union "expert" whose later career was to run the gamut of idolatry from Joseph Stalin to Joseph McCarthy, this Council claimed 25 local unions with a membership of 50,000 in the clothing, shoe, textile, hotel, and automobile industries. Its constitution required that "Any union accepted to membership . . . must, within a period of three months, sever all connections with the AFL."[42] It came to a predictable and rapid demise.

By mid-1920, however, the Comintern had gained a more realistic and accurate sense of the American situation and it began to promote a change in the trade-union line of its American affiliates. This turn was complicated, however, by a conflict within the world Communist movement as to trade-union and other policies, so that a brief diversion becomes necessary at this point.

By August, 1919, the International Federation of Free Trade Unions, led by the European Social Democrats, had been reorganized at a conference in Amsterdam. To counter this move the Executive Committee of the Comintern publicly urged the formation of "a genuinely proletarian *red* international of trade unions" that would act "in opposition to the yellow international of unions which the bourgeois agents are trying to create in Amsterdam. . . ." [44] Now in a sense this was a call for an international revolutionary dual union. But it was not based on the tactic of trying to split the existing "reformist" unions primarily; it proposed a consolidation of mass revolutionary unions that were assumed already to exist. What did, however, lend a dual-union coloring to this ambiguous policy was that in addition to the American Communists there were large sections of the German, Dutch, and British Communist parties that favored dual unionism. It took a very powerful polemic by Lenin called *Left Wing Communism: An Infantile Disorder* to curb the dual-union tendencies of the international Communist movement. While favoring an international federation of revolutionary unions, Lenin sharply criticized the policy of provoking splits in the existing mass unions in order to create paper revolutionary competitors—a policy, he wrote, that could only isolate the Communists. What had to be done was to function in whichever unions the workers were to be found.

Lenin's pamphlet was written in preparation for the Second Congress of the Communist International, held in Moscow, July-August, 1920. At this Congress a position on trade-union policy was adopted which, while less forthright than Lenin's, reflected his basic view. This position boiled down to the common-sense directive: if the workers were in the "reformist" unions, that is where the Communists had to be. But at the Congress John Reed, representing the United Communist Party, vigorously argued against

the majority position presented by Karl Radek. Reed claimed that
it was necessary to enter the conservative unions in America so as
to hasten their destruction.* The workers, he argued, were already
beginning to move in a revolutionary direction, and this development would be speeded if the craft unions were destroyed, leaving
a vacuum that would be filled by new revolutionary industrial
unions. Neither Lenin nor Radek was much impressed, though
Reed personally won the affection of many Communist leaders. In
the debate Radek made a telling point against the American Communist policy:

> They urge their membership to work within the trade unions,
> not for the purpose of improving them, but in order to destroy
> them. . . . Our attitude on this question will not decide the fate
> of the AFL, but the whole future of the Communist movement
> in America depends upon it.[45]

Radek was correct: the Polish-born Bolshevik revealed a clearer
understanding of American society than Reed, the native American.

The authority of the Comintern soon proved overwhelming, and
at its July, 1920, convention the Communist Party came out, rather
flat-footedly, against dual unionism. Flat-footedly, because it declared that "Wherever the workers are, whether in the AFL or
similar organizations, or in the IWW, there the CP must constantly agitate, not for industrial unionism, but for Communism." [46]
It had certainly not been Lenin's intention that in abandoning dual
unionism the American Communist also cease agitating for industrial
unions—but dull pupils have a way of distorting instruction even
as they repeat it.

In the livelier press of the United Communist Party, James P.
Cannon, one of its few leaders with some trade-union background,
supported the new line by declaring that "we will be compelled to
make use of such organizations as are on the ground. . . ." [47] The
UCP, not above a little self-deceit, announced that its new line on

* While Reed spoke forthrightly for his opinion, his fellow delegate
Louis Fraina did not. Fraina was at least as committed as Reed to the policy
of trying to split the AFL but lacked Reed's courage in standing up against
the leaders of the Comintern. For that matter, few of the leaders of early
American Communism displayed the independence of Reed.

unionism, though in actuality the result of Comintern pressure, had been worked out through "dialectical reasoning." But as everyone familiar with the American Communists knew, it took a force greater than the philosophical talents of Cannon or the other leaders to break the party from dual unionism.

By the time the two groups came together to form the Communist Party of America, in May, 1921, relations with the IWW had become strained and some of the more heated fantasies of the Communists had begun to fizzle out. "The Communists," declared the CP, "shall not foster artificial division in the labor movement, nor deliberately bring it about." [48] So it seemed finally that the ghost of dual unionism had been cast out; but it was to prove a lively ghost, with endless capacities for mischief.

In the short run, the new and sensible trade-union policy made little difference, since the damage had already been done. But it did bring the party one important gain: it helped win over a major trade-union leader, William Z. Foster. The Socialists had had Debs, the IWW Haywood; but the Communists could claim no comparable figure. Fraina was smart; Ruthenberg canny; Reed colorful; Cannon experienced in trade-union work; Gitlow, Lovestone, Ferguson were bright young men. But Foster was the only one who approached the stature of a national figure.

Born of working-class parents, largely self-educated, and sent to earn his living while a boy, Foster had begun his political career as a Populist, switched to the Bryan wing of the Democrats, become a Socialist and then an active member of the IWW. In 1911 he had gone as an IWW delegate to an international labor conference in Budapest, and in the course of his year in Europe had studied the various labor movements and come back to reject the revolutionary dual unionism of the IWW. But he remained convinced of the need for industrial or "vertical" unions, and his subsequent career in the AFL was partly that of a spokesman for what then seemed a revolutionary departure in labor organization.

Foster was more than an industrial unionist. He was a syndicalist who regarded the future industrial unions as vehicles of social revolution. Back home in 1912, he organized the Syndicalist League, which flourished briefly in the Midwest, and then became organizer, successively, for the AFL railway carmen and packing-house unions. Throughout his career—which he himself was to describe as a journey from Bryan to Stalin—he was to prove inept and primitive as a Marxist theoretician; but there could be no question that Foster was an enormously skillful union organizer. Even his most bitter political enemies had to admit that he knew how to speak to workers, to build solid union locals and run dramatic strikes. As a revolutionary, however, he found his employment by the AFL somewhat complicating, for it was during this period that he sold Liberty Bonds, an act which his critics within the radical world and his factional opponents were never to allow him to forget.

It was on Foster's initiative that in 1918 the National Committee for Organizing the Iron and Steel Workers was formed, with representatives from AFL unions that claimed two million members. The drive to organize steel, long violently anti-union, was amazingly successful. When the Steel Trust refused to consider the new union's demands, a strike call was issued, in September, 1919, and was answered by 365,000 men. For four long and bitter months the strike was carried on, with Foster as the central leader—a strike that brought together the unevenly matched forces of an improvised union hindered by craft jealousies and a Steel Trust that had at its disposal the equivalent of two divisions of hired thugs. The strike was lost, the union broken.

During the steel strike Foster had been repeatedly attacked because of his revolutionary past and radical present. With the anti-red campaign mounting to hysterical proportions toward the end of 1919, and with the simultaneous effort to weaken if not destroy the unions, the AFL leadership regarded Foster as much too controversial a figure to keep on its payroll. Suddenly, after having led the organization of half a million workers in packing house and steel, Foster found himself isolated. But his reputation pursued him. He was blamed for provoking strikes even at a time when he had gone into seclusion to write his book on the history of the great steel strike.

As was true of a number of labor leaders, Foster found himself caught up in the enthusiasm for the Russian Revolution; but collaboration between the Communists and himself was excluded by their dual unionism and nagging criticism. Once, however, the Communists turned toward a somewhat more realistic trade-union line and discovered that their need for a prominent public figure coincided with Foster's own sense that his career in the labor movement had been blocked, his formal conversion became possible.

In November, 1920, Foster organized the Trade Union Educational League (TUEL), a propaganda group that was to fight for industrial unionism within the AFL. For about a year the organization lay dormant, but toward the end of 1921 it began to show signs of vitality and to offer new prospects for the Communists in the labor movement. Foster had, in the meantime, joined the American Communist Party while attending a conference of revolutionary unions in Moscow; but this fact was kept secret since it was felt that he could put his talents to better use in organizing the TUEL if he were not openly identified with the CP.

Upon Foster's return to the United States, he found that the CP militants were now entering the unions with all the zeal of the newly converted, and with their help, particularly in the daily routine work that all organizations require in order to survive, the TUEL began to move forward. Its 1922 membership drive, which brought in union leaders and members other than Communists, was a limited success. Chapters of the TUEL were established in the major unions; pamphlets appeared regularly; and in March, 1922, the first issue of the *Labor Herald,* its monthly magazine, came off the press. In August of that year a national conference was held in Chicago at which significant gains could be recorded. A dynamic mine-union leader, Alexander Howat, joined its ranks; Eugene Debs sent it word of praise; several important figures in the Chicago Federation of Labor—Jay Fox, Joseph Manley, Jack Johnstone— were its allies and later were recruited to the Communist movement. The TUEL was particularly successful in the railway industry, where the maze of craft unions was utterly bewildering, and its railroad conference, held in December, 1922, was attended by scores of delegates who could not be dismissed as Communists or Communist dupes.

But this early success could not become a lasting one. Gompers wheeled his powerful AFL machine into action against the young and still feeble TUEL; the economic upswing of the early twenties dissolved the militancy of many left-wing unionists; and the political programs regularly adopted by the TUEL were so closely geared to those of the Communists that its pretense to being a non-political group became something of a farce.

Yet for a time it seemed that with hard work, a certain minimum of realism, and skillful leadership the Communists could make small but significant gains in the unions. Their isolation, though largely the result of circumstances over which they had no control, was to some extent their own doing, a consequence of their systematic addiction to a grandiose rhetoric that prevented them from seeing what was actually happening in the labor movement. About the best that can be said for the trade-union work of the Communists during the early twenties is that they did help keep alive the idea of industrial unionism at a time when almost everyone else had conveniently put it aside.

8. Early American Communism was shaped by three major, related factors: the quality of its inner life and values; the attacks of the government and hostility of the bulk of the population; and the directives and pressures that came from the Communist International in Moscow. Our discussion of trade-union work should have indicated that the common view is false when it assumes that the influence of the Comintern was always directed toward pulling the American Communists away from a consideration of indigenous needs. There were some matters, though almost always those concerning strategy and tactics, on which the Comintern leaders had a keener appreciation of American realities than the Communists on the scene. And when it came to the fundamental nature of the movement itself, the American Communists were habitually subservient, accepting without criticism dogmas and directives from the Comintern that could only do them great harm. Even more, the status of political subordinate, whatever temporary advantage it might bring in such a matter as trade-union work, was bad in itself: it kept the American leadership from developing ideas of its own and prepared the way for still greater catastrophes.

At its Second Congress the Communist International had adopted its famous 21 Conditions of Admission.* The justification

---

* The most important of these conditions were: the propaganda of national Communist parties should correspond to the program and decisions of the Communist International"; reformist Socialists were not to be per-

for these 21 points, at least in terms of European conditions, was that a revolutionary situation was approaching in which everything would depend on the ideological clarity, the organizational firmness, and the disciplined striking power of the Communist parties. What was needed, the Communists kept repeating, was not debating societies but parties prepared to take power, parties that could act with the force and unity of armies.

Now in part the 21 points represented an effort by a revolutionary movement to create self-defining boundaries within a situation that led it to believe that the decisive moment of modern history was at hand. But even within this assumption the 21 points had a damaging effect on European radicalism: they made decisive, perhaps irrevocable, the great splits of 1920-22; they repelled from the ranks of the Communists most of the wavering independent Socialists who might have brought with them some divergence of opinion and independence of spirit; they tended to transform the Communist International from an association of more or less equal parties into a taskmaster of pliant affiliates; they helped strengthen the notion that the Communist movement had been "ordained" by history, thereby intensifying the contempt of the Communists for all those outside the chosen circle; and they assumed that the course of socialist revolution in Europe had necessarily to repeat the main steps of the Russian Revolution, so that parties were to be built in the Western democracies upon the model of the Bolsheviks. But however one may estimate the impact of the 21 points upon the European Marxist movement, it can at least be granted that within the terms of the Communist perspective they made sense. Right or wrong, damaging or not, they were relevant to European politics. In the United States, however, they neither made sense nor had any relevance.

During the fall of 1920, when the 21 points were proclaimed,

mitted to hold leading posts in any of the Communist parties; wherever required "because of a state of siege or of emergency laws" Communists should organize an underground apparatus and "combine legal with illegal work"; a number of "avowed opportunists" including Morris Hillquit were in advance denied membership; working in conditions of "acute civil war" the Comintern was to be highly centralized and its authority decisive; party members who rejected "on principle" the conditions for membership were to be expelled.[49]

the United States was in a particularly advantageous position *vis-à-vis* the other countries of the West. In Europe the war had brought defeat and suffering to every nation; the threat of internal revolution was real in most of them. In the United States, which had emerged from the war more powerful and wealthy than ever, there was nothing resembling a revolutionary situation despite the economic struggles of the workers, and the greatest menace to the *status quo* came not from within but from the possible repercussions of a socialist revolution in Europe. The 21 points disregarded the difference between continents, most crucially so in point 3: "In practically every country of Europe *and America* the class struggle is entering the phase of civil war" (emphasis added). This was simply not true, yet it carried far greater weight with the American Communists than the reality surrounding them. It encouraged them in the remoteness of their propaganda; it provided a rationale for their absurd chatter about "preparing" for the American revolution; it dragged them further into contempt for democratic forms and values.

Pitifully weak and harassed as they were, the American Communists took a kind of perverse pride—it had very little to do with preserving their principles—in proclaiming their support for the most far-fetched of the 21 points. Thus point 4 declared that Communists were "obliged to carry on systematic and energetic propaganda in the army. Where such agitation is prevented by emergency laws, it must be carried on illegally." This may have had its relevance to the postwar situation in Germany; but what possible point could it have in the United States, where the Communists had no significant support among the workers, let alone the soldiers and sailors? Yet at the second convention of the United Communist Party in December, 1920, the following item was inserted in the party platform:

> The United Communist Party will issue special appeals to the soldiers and sailors, which will be distributed among them and will create communist groups in the army and navy, which shall be closely connected in order to establish a unified revolutionary body within the armed forces of the state.[50]

What was this but empty bombast? A kind of play-acting at revolution which, by the very tense of its statements, revealed a condition of impotence? For as everyone in the radical movement then knew, the UCP was much more concerned with penetrating the CP than the armed forces.

The enthusiasm with which the American Communists embraced the 21 points encouraged a further retreat among them from the democratic stress of earlier left-wing Socialism. Thus in a widely publicized debate with James O'Neal, a Socialist Party leader, Robert Minor could speak in the following terms, so profoundly revealing of the way most American Communists were thinking:

> Now he [O'Neal] gave an illustration about how [Louis] Fraina advocated the rights of free speech until he learned from Moscow that was a petty-bourgeois thing to say. Let me set you right. If a man is a moralist of a theological type, he will do things that he thinks are idealistic. But if he is a modern materialistic revolutionary he will do the things not that are metaphysically moral, but the things that work, and he will take a position for free speech when it is the bourgeois dictatorship that is on top, and he will take a position against free speech when it is the workers that are on top. [Great applause] You see, that is a little dialectics. [Hearty applause] [51]

Such manifestations of the dialectic reflected not only the inner quality of the American Communist leadership but also a major difference in status between the American and European parties. Among the more important European Communist parties there was, during this early period, a relative independence with regard to Moscow. Leaders, factions, and individuals in the European parties often spoke out against policies and directives of the Comintern, and the minutes of the first few Comintern congresses are filled with debates and counter-proposals reflecting the views of minority groups within the German, French, and Italian parties. But with the exception of John Reed, who died shortly after the Second Comintern Congress, one could find no comparable spirit of independence or dissidence in the American movement. Each time the

Comintern made a major demand upon the American party, whether for a reversal on trade-union policy or for a unification of factions or for an end to the "underground" hibernation, it crossed the convictions of many, perhaps the majority, of the American Communists. There would follow resistance, reluctance, a dragging of feet—but no outspoken opposition, which alone could have made for a healthy discussion. No American Communist leader dared speak up to the Comintern—perhaps none saw the need to—and tell it that the 21 points were preposterous in relation to the United States, that its talk about "civil war" was still more so, and that it was not in the interests of either American or world Communism to attempt to launch (even if only in writing) cells in the American army.

The difference in attitude between the European and American Communist parties was a difference between parties with roots, prestige, and power in their native lands and an unpopular sect. A mistaken directive from the Comintern could cost the German party dearly; in the United States it was likely to do no more than pile absurdity on top of irrelevance. The support, honor, prestige, and solace that the American Communists could not find in the working class at home they sought in the Comintern, eagerly submitting to its wishes even when these clashed sharply with their own views.

Handicapped and harassed in so many ways, the American Communist movement might have faded into total insignificance had it not been refreshed by new recruits from the Socialist Party. Even after the August, 1919 split convention, the Socialist Party still retained a considerable number of left-wingers who, while hesitating to surrender themselves to the Communist sects or critical of their tactics, were yet closer in political spirit to Leninism than to traditional Social Democracy. It was in the nature of the amorphous Socialist Party that it should constantly be undergoing the agony of an internal polarization, with right wings splitting off to one or another kind of liberalism and left wings gravitating toward one or another kind of Communism.

Even after the Communists had gone, the American SP remained friendly to the Russian Revolution. A membership referendum held in early 1920 went so far as to favor overwhelmingly affiliation with the Communist International. (Which showed how vulgar was the charge of the Communists that the SP was merely a party of "bourgeois socialism.") On March 4, 1920, the Socialist Party accordingly applied to Moscow for affiliation. For some months the Comintern did not answer, while a debate continued within the ranks of the SP. In May the Socialists voted in convention to continue pressing for affiliation while declaring themselves opposed to the imposition of "the dictatorship of the proletariat . . . or any other special formula . . . as condition for affiliation with the Third International." [52]

The problem was settled a few months later when the Comintern issued its 21 Conditions for Affiliation. These conditions, which particularly aroused the resentment of Debs, were declared by the Executive Committee of the SP a sufficient ground for withdrawing the previous request to join the Third International. Whatever doubts the Socialist leadership may still have had were laid to rest when the Comintern sent an arrogant public letter to the Socialist Party ridiculing its "reservations" and appealing to its membership: "Workers! Leave the Socialist Party. It is your enemy and ours." [53]

Nonetheless, leftward impulses kept appearing within the Socialist Party during 1920 and 1921. A "Committee for the Third International," in which such prominent Socialists as Louis Engdahl, J. B. Salutsky, Benjamin Glassberg, and Alexander Trachtenberg were active, tried to establish a common political ground with the American Communists while severely criticizing them on tactical matters. In 1921 this group, by far the most independent and intelligent of any that moved within the Communist orbit, reorganized itself as the "Workers Council," left the Socialist Party, and began to negotiate for unity with the Communists, while not, however, abandoning its critical views. It stressed the need for a legal movement; it attacked dual unionism and the fetish of "violence"; it did not believe the United States was anywhere near civil war; and it mocked the Communist Party for having acted "as if the Russian Revolution had been bodily transplanted upon American soil." [54]

Still more significant numerically was the split of the Finnish Socialist Federation from the SP. Though its claim to 10,000 members was surely an exaggeration, the Finnish Federation was a solidly organized, predominantly proletarian group, and it would soon provide a very large portion of the Communist membership.

Equally important was the decision of a majority of the Jewish Socialist Federation to disaffiliate from the SP. Here again the Communists made significant gains, providing the basis for the strong support they would later find among the Jewish garment workers.

9. Left to their own devices, the American Communists could never have attracted these revolutionary Socialists; very likely they would have taken special pains to repel them. What won the new recruits to the Communist movement were the achievements of the Russians, the prestige of the Communist International (then at its height), and the fact that a new tactical turn was being introduced by the Comintern leaders which promised a more flexible and intelligent policy.

At the Third Congress of the Communist International, held in the spring of 1921, its leading spokesmen were forced—though against considerable opposition from various delegates—to make a painful reevaluation in their estimate of world politics. Trotsky's major report to the Congress described this reevaluation with characteristic frankness:

> In 1919 the European bourgeoisie was in a state of extreme confusion. Those were the days of panic, the days of a truly insane fear of Bolshevism, which then loomed as an extremely misty and therefore all the more terrifying apparition and which used to be portrayed on Parisian posters as a killer clenching a knife in his teeth. . . . In 1920 and 1921 we observe a gradual influx of self-assurance among the bourgeoisie and along with this an undeniable consolidation of its state apparatus, which immediately following the war had been on the verge of disintegration in various countries.

In a word, the "consolidation" of bourgeois society was forcing ᵗhe Comintern to retreat from both the policy of constant attack and the expectation of immediate revolution. The main task of the Communists, declared Zinoviev, was now to work "steadily, energetically and stubbornly to win the majority of the workers in all unions . . . by the most active participation in their day-to-day struggles." [55] What obviously followed from all this was a turn to the policy of the united front, a policy that tacitly acknowledged the increased stability of the *status quo*. The extent of this turn was indicated by the Comintern's agreement to participate in a joint conference with the Second and the "Two-and-a-Half" (Left Socialist) internationals and the appearance of Russian delegates at the January, 1922, conference called by the Western powers to discuss European economic reconstruction.

Together with the united-front policy went a demand from the Comintern that wherever possible the Communist parties operate openly and legally, and participate in parliamentary activities. In actuality, then, the new Comintern policy was closer to that of the left-wing Socialists who had just left the SP than to that of the American CP. Many American Communists grumbled—they did not want to abandon the dark comforts of underground existence—but the party complied.

The first public demonstration of this compliance came in July with a hastily put-together legal organization, the American Labor Alliance. It included such sympathetic groups as the Ukrainian Workers Clubs, the Associated Toilers Clubs and the National Defense Committee, composed for the most part of people already in the CP. For public effect Caleb Harrison, a non-Communist radical, was chosen as chairman of the American Labor Alliance, though he was well flanked on its executive board by several CP trustees. In its program the Alliance conspicuously omitted CP language and ultra-left politics: there was no commitment to force and instead of the Dictatorship of the Proletariat it proclaimed as its goal a "Workers Republic." The very act of forming this legal front met with opposition inside the CP, and when the relatively mild program of the Alliance was made public, thousands of die-hard underground Communists began to grumble. The Comintern, for its part, was also dissatisfied, though for a different reason: it felt that the Alliance was neither broad nor substantial enough to serve as the agency that might bring Communism into American public life.

In the fall of 1921 the CP took another step toward organizing a legal antenna. At a New York conference attended by a variety of radical groups ranging from the African Blood Brotherhood to the Irish

American Labor League and the Left Paole Zion, there was organized the Workers' League, which was to serve as the legal face of the party in its first venture into the New York elections. A municipal platform was adopted with a heavy barrage of immediate demands. Ben Gitlow was nominated for mayor and Harry Winitsky for president of the Board of Aldermen—a choice that immediately provoked a legal battle, since both men were still in jail at the time. At first their names were removed from the ballot by the Board of Elections because, among other reasons, they were declared to be residents of Sing Sing, not New York. But when the issue was taken to the courts—a step that must have struck some of the more intransigent Communists as a retreat to reformism—the judge ruled in favor of the Workers' League. Finally, the decision was amended by a higher court to permit the Workers' League to remain on the ballot, but without the names of its two major candidates. Appearing before the electorate in this emasculated form, the Workers' League polled between two and three thousand votes for its candidates. While many of the Communist supporters were among the non-voting foreign born, this meager vote nonetheless provided a graphic demonstration of how low the party's standing had fallen in the first two years of its existence. Other radical parties had also suffered severly, but the much-scorned Socialists still polled 90,000 votes in New York City, 35 times more than the Communists.

The painful process continued of coming up for air—or being dragged up by the Comintern. In December, 1921, at a conference attended by many left-wing groups including the Jewish Socialist Federation, the Workers Council, which had recently left the SP, and the American Labor Alliance, there was formed the Workers Party, which would now serve as the legal voice of American Communism. Its program contained none of the ultra-revolutionary idiom of the earlier Communist groups; it made no muscular predictions of violence; it anticipated electoral campaigns; it committed itself to working within the existing unions; and it placed a heavy stress upon immediate and local issues. The previous Communist talk about a dictatorship of the proletariat was replaced by a pledge to "work for the establishment of a Workers Republic." [56] Shortly after the convention the Workers Party began to publish a weekly, *The Worker*.

The formation of the American Communist movement at the two conventions in September, 1919, was a premature birth. Everything about it, from its poor organization to its inexperienced leadership, from its political abstractness to its factional ferocity, marked it as a movement that had crashed its way out of the shell before the necessary period of incubation.

In 1919 the Communists in America had deluded themselves with a large claimed book membership. The combined boasts of the two groups totaled nearly 90,000, the CP claiming 58,000 and the more modest CLP 30,000. Both figures were much too high, though according to Benjamin Gitlow the actual total was about 60,000 to 70,000. Immediately thereafter the movement began to shrivel. The CLP admitted that "Thousands of members, true revolutionaries as any who remain in either party, are dropped out, discouraged and disheartened because of the schism. . . ."

In October, 1919, the CLP reported a sale of monthly dues stamps of 14,879. The CP had an average dues sale for October through December of 23,744. Within two months, then, the combined membership dropped by three-fifths, indicating either that the loyalty of the Communist followers was extraordinarily weak and fluid or that the exaggeration of membership was even greater than anyone has supposed.

As schism was followed by repression, the membership figures fell even faster. For the month of January, 1920, the CP sold only 1714 stamps, though undoubtedly it could count upon more actual adherents who for one or another reason had not bought stamps during the height of the repression. When the CP reorganized itself as an underground group, its membership rose to about 8,000 in April, and even this figure is open to suspicion. Of these 8,000 about a third split in order to unite with the CLP into the United Communist Party, though as is always the case many of these defectors dropped out entirely. The Russian Federation, the backbone of the CP, had 7,000 members before the Palmer raids; by the spring of 1920 it had been reduced, by repression and schism, to about 2,000.

When the United Communist Party was organized in May, 1920, it claimed 11,000 members. It admitted, however, that within a short time almost half the membership dropped out. By its

December convention it was down to 5,700 members in 667 underground groups.

By the unity convention of the two parties in May, 1921, the membership had been cut to the bone. The unified Communist movement began in this country with a claimed membership of less than 11,000, and when a die-hard sectarian group, later called the United Toilers, refused to abandon its underground existence the figure was again sharply cut. At the Fourth Congress of the Communist International, in November, 1922, the American CP was credited with 8,000 members. The actual membership was probably no more than 5,000.

As for the Workers Party, the legal agency of the American Communists, its claimed membership in mid-1922 was 12,000, nearly a third of whom were not in the CP. If one were to go through the membership figures of all the Communist groups formed in 1919 and 1920, making rough allowances for duplication and exaggeration, one could legitimately conclude that of those who joined these groups some 60,000 quickly abandoned them.[57] This remarkable figure not merely points to an enormous loss of energy and resources for American radicalism; it sharply calls into question the usual portrayal of early American Communism as a tightly disciplined and conspiratorial movement.

Benjamin Gitlow, writing some years after he had abandoned any trace of radicalism, was to say:

> The raids helped the Communist party separate the wheat from the chaff. The Communists who did not have the courage to withstand the dangers accompanying membership in the Communist party went to the sidelines. The 16,000 Communist party members who remained in the two communist parties, after the raids, voluntarily undertook the perils of membership. They constituted the men and women who were willing to put up with the rigors of communist life, its regimentation and strict discipline. They put their personal lives at the disposal of the party, the party to do with them whatever was thought fit and proper. The small communist residue of the 1920's formed an intransigent, fanatical body of zealots—the human element that went into the building of a monolithic organization, an organization of one will and mind.[58]

Gitlow's description is vivid, plausible, almost lurid. But it has one fault: it is not accurate. For of the 16,000 claimed members of the two Communist parties after the Palmer raids, approximately 10,000 dropped out within the next two years. This is hardly the stuff of which "an intransigent, fantical body of zealots" is made.

The early Communist movement had its fair share of zealots and fanatics, but the truth is that the leadership failed completely to hold the firm loyalty of the vast majority of the rank-and-file members. Not only was the leadership unable to "do with them whatever was thought fit and proper"; it could not even get the members to undertake such routine organizational tasks as distributing leaflets or engaging in electoral activity for Communist candidates. Looking back at this period, many delegates at the 1922 Communist convention noted in a resolution: "Comrades distributed the leaflets (*if they did*) without participating in the [1921] campaign" (emphasis added). No doubt there were reasons for this rank-and-file attitude, ranging all the way from fear of arrest to contempt for legal activity to a general indifference to what was happening in the United States. But whatever the reasons, such an attitude among the members hardly made for the tight and monolithic party which subsequent political legend would take the early Communists to be.

This organizational looseness was characteristic of the early Communist movement at all its levels. Meetings of party units were few and desultory. The basic unit was supposed to be a group of about ten, but these groups seldom met to discuss politics or strategy. In theory the party was rigid, highly centralized, disciplined—and later, in writing for cold-war audiences, it became fashionable to assume that the early Communist movement actually was rigid, highly centralized, disciplined. But the truth is otherwise. At the 1922 convention, three years after the formation of the Communist movement and when the legal repressions had been considerably reduced, a resolution declared it an *aim* that the basic "groups of the Communist party must meet regularly at least once a month." [59] Which suggests that in earlier years meetings were often held even less frequently. And which is hardly what one expects from a disciplined revolutionary party.

The membership was not so much demoralized as indifferent

to American events. Living in America but with their hearts and minds in Europe, often finding it difficult even to communicate in English, they proved extremely reluctant to engage in the day-to-day activities—leaflet distribution, unit meetings, election campaigns—upon which the party could be built.

And of course there was a correlation between this lack of rank-and-file party activity and the spread of party factionalism. The animus of the competing factions and sects tended to grow in proportion to the decline of the membership's participation and interest. It was a vicious circle from which the Communist movement could not extricate itself—at least as long as it remained underground. The comrades grew bored with factionalism as they grew frightened of government assault, and when they left the movement this simply seemed proof to one faction that the policies of the other were "bankrupt."

We do not wish, in reaction to Gitlow's fantasy, to overstress this point. There were some party activities. Leaflets were distributed, the party press was mailed out. Occasionally an important debate would be held, as the one between Minor and O'Neal. There was some routine rank-and-file activity, if not directly in the party, then in several front organizations: the Friends of Soviet Russia, established to collect funds for famine-ridden Russia, and the Technical Aid Society, which recruited skilled labor for Russia. But even in the trade unions, despite some TUEL successes, Communist work was negligible.

Membership in the party during these early years was likely to be dreary. No effort was made to keep or entice members with promises of culture and romance; Hollywood stars and college-bred folk singers were not to appear in the Communist world for at least another fifteen years; the Bohemianism that was to crop up toward the late twenties was barely in evidence.

Why so many members dropped out of the party has been suggested in previous sections of this chapter. But there remains still another factor: the kind of expectations roused in the minds of the rank-and-file Communists during the years from 1919 to 1921.

A large portion of the early Communist membership was undoubtedly recruited on the basis of a promise that was not to be fulfilled, the promise of world revolution.* It could be held together, in an amorphous way, as a left wing within the Socialist Party where the "enemy" was convenient and the battle not too hazardous. But once the left wing had to strike out on its own, as an independent movement, it was soon forced to face at least some of the realities of American life, and its super-revolutionary slogans proved singularly irrelevant. The "get-rich-quick" attitude that so many early American Communists had toward the idea of socialist revolution simply could not sustain an organization having to function in the atmosphere of America during 1920 or 1921. Had the Communist rank and file been politically sophisticated, had it been educated to the fact that whatever hopes the Communist movement might have in America could certainly not be of an immediate kind, the party's reverses might have been less extreme than they were. But then, if the Communist leadership had tried to educate its following in this way, it might never have been able to win them away from the Socialist Party in the first place. As it was, after the most melodramatic factional antics and the most fantastically optimistic predictions, the American Communist movement found itself in 1922 a tiny and isolated sect, insignificant in the socio-political life of the nation as a whole and far from healthy in its own inner life. Thousands of people had quickly passed through its ranks, by far the majority of them inspired by motives of idealism: immigrant workers for whom the dream of America had not come true, young people who blazed with hopes for a better world, intellectuals who found in the Russian Revolution a symbol of aspiration. But between the motives of the anonymous ranks and the character of the movement itself the discrepancy was nothing less than startling.

* An interesting sign of this was the large number of Communists who voluntarily left for Russia in these early years, hopeful that they would there help build the future of humanity. In the first four months of 1921 the Communist Party records showed that 1,300 members left for Russia, approxi mately 15 to 20 percent of the membership.[60]

Chapter III.   A Plunge into American Politics

The formation of the Workers Party as a legal periscope for the underground Communists brought with it a few opportunities and a good many problems. The mere fact of trying to involve themselves in domestic political life meant a severe test for the organizational talents and political preconceptions of the Communists—a test they had to face under public scrutiny, not in the private world of theses and faction fights. Precisely this initial exposure to American political life, which took the form of working within the burgeoning farmer-labor movements of the twenties, will provide the dominant theme of this chapter; but as always, one cannot understand the public behavior of the Communists without a preliminary glance at the ideological disputes that helped shape it.

1. For many months after the Workers Party was founded, the underground Communist movement was ripped apart by splits, expulsions, and intrigues. Only a small minority of American Communists shared the Comintern's enthusiasm for the new public organization; most of them had sunk too deeply into the crevices of underground existence to want or be able to face daylight. If the majority of American Communists finally accepted the "legal strategy," it was with reluctance and only because the Comintern applied relentless pressure. And some did not accept this strategy at all.

In late 1921 the Comintern had drawn up a formidable document on "The Next Tasks of the Communist Party in America," which for several years was to serve as the major guide for instructions from Moscow.[1] Not only did the Comintern order a legal party; it also proposed a quite moderate platform of domestic reforms in striking contrast to the earlier "unconditional demand" for the dictatorship of the proletariat. If this "suggested" program was modest in its realism, the Comintern, with equal realism, insisted that those American Communists who refused to found a legal movement would "as a rule" have to leave the party.

And "as a rule" they either left or were thrown out. In 1923

Jay Lovestone, who had been a national secretary of the underground party, conceded that 2,000 members, refusing to "go legal," had dropped out in disgust. According to this low estimate, the cost of legality came to 25 percent of the party; actually, the loss was closer to 40 percent.[2] The opponents of legality, for whom the mere thought of a public party reeked with bourgeois corruption, were mainly members of the Lettish, Lithuanian, and Polish language groups, utterly sincere and hopelessly isolated immigrants who found in their attachment to the underground a "principle" by which to rationalize their embarrassment before American life. In February, 1922, with a fierce declaration that nothing could make *them* dip into the fleshpots of legalism and with an extravagant claim to 5,000 members, they formed the United Toilers, a bizarre sect that in its less than one year of existence contributed mightily toward burning out the energies of the early American Communists.*

The United Toilers episode was merely a somewhat weird reflection of deeper problems that festered in the early Communist movement. What, for example, was to be the exact relationship between the illegal Communist Party and the legal Workers Party, or as the comrades cryptically called them, Number One and Number Two? (An order of priority that reflected a relative valuation.) Upon this issue, which had some relation to political reality, new factions speedily sprang into being, and soon the polemicists were gleefully sharpening their knives. For where the previous disputes had taken place between two or more organized Communist parties, they now raged within a presumably unified party; and it is an Iron Law of Factional Disturbance that the closer the contenders, the warmer the contention.

---

* Its one claim to distinction was an exotic violence of language that put all other radical polemicists to shame. The editor of its paper wrote, for example, that the legal Workers Party was "an amalgamation of all the reformist, centrist pie-card artists and careerists that the old decrepit Socialist Party had spawned in all its years of vegetation as a diseased growth upon the body of the working class in America."[3] Imagery of disease, corruption, and mutilation runs obsessively through much of the early Communist polemics.

Soon, however, the United Toilers simmered down. When it became clear that Moscow would grant no indulgence to its underground vagaries, the leaders of the sect—they could not imagine an independent existence—crept back into the official Communist movement. Predictably, they brought back fewer members than they took out.

A majority of the American Communists—led by Israel Amter, Abraham Jakira, L. E. Katterfeld, and, upon his first release from prison, Benjamin Gitlow—held in effect that the Workers Party was a mere necessary nuisance, a concession to the Comintern. The legal party, they felt, could be used for recruiting members to the pure underground party, but it would be an error to allow legal work to monopolize the primary loyalties or energies of the true believers. This sectarian wing of the party came to be known— it is one of the few flashes of poetry in the history of American Communism—as the Goose faction.*

On the other side of the party's barricades were the Liquidators, led by Ruthenberg, Lovestone, Max Bedacht, and James P. Cannon, who paid lip service to the idea of an underground apparatus (as distinct from an underground party) but were really intent upon making the Workers Party the essential arm of American Communism. The term "Liquidators" had been Lenin's contemptuous label for those Russian Marxists who in 1905 had wanted to set up a politically diffuse organization that would conform to the legal requirements of Czarism—a situation that had of course nothing to do with the one in the United States, though mimicking it gave the forlorn demons of American Communism the pleasure of reenacting the drama of the Bolshevik past.

The primary difference between the two factions—it was an archetypal difference that would reappear again and again in radical history—was that between a group infatuated with its ideological sanctity and a group that wanted to participate in the life of the labor movement even if that meant collaboration with "centrists" and other uncertified American radicals. At first the Comintern, which certainly did not want its American supporters to commit themselves in principle to parliamentary politics, was rather cool toward the Liquidators, warning against "the tendency to become legal in fact as well as in outward appearance." [5] But Ruthenberg,

---

* But not because they were so adept at factional pecking. According to Gitlow, when Abraham Jakira, who stuttered badly, was heckled during a faction debate for "cackling like a goose," Amter rose to his defense by declaring that "the geese saved Rome and we shall yet save the Party." Lovestone, a bench-jockey for the opposing faction, thereupon shouted back: "All right then, from now on you're the Goose Caucus." [4] And so it was.

who was shrewd enough to realize that without legality American Communism would simply succumb to its inner cannibalism, kept insisting that there was no inherent political virtue in being underground. A simple enough idea, but hard for all the Communists to learn.

Even as this battle was being fought out in the party halls, the political factors that had helped drive the Communists underground were rapidly disappearing. The postwar hysteria, which had reached a climax during the Palmer raids, began to abate by the beginning of 1921. A year or so later the atmosphere in the country was both calmer and more rational than during the fiercely illiberal months that concluded Woodrow Wilson's administration. It was symptomatic that when William Z. Foster was deported from Colorado in 1922, only to be refused the right to detrain upon the sacred soil of Wyoming, the politicians and state troopers who had carried out this coup were not hailed as saviors of the republic. Quite the contrary; the treatment of Foster became a political issue in the 1922 Colorado election that contributed to the victory of a somewhat liberal administration.

Slowly the Liquidators overtook the Geese. By the time of the party's "secret convention"—held in Bridgman, Michigan, during August, 1922—the two factions were about equal in strength. That this "secret convention" proved to be a fiasco would soon serve to convince almost all of the Communists that the underground party was not merely an anachronism but a nuisance.

Solemnly playing the game of Cops and Revolutionists, the forty-five delegates—who included a certain number of both—made their way to designated spots, where they were met by couriers who led them to the convention site near the scraggly village of Bridgman. (The choice of Bridgman was itself a gross miscalculation: for the Communists could have lost themselves more easily in a Manhattan cafeteria than in a village where the appearance of a stranger constituted news.) Sessions were held in the open, on the shores of Lake Michigan. Proletarian watches stood ready to sound the alarm; credentials were carefully checked; guards feigning drunkenness lolled about the outskirts of the convention area to ward off intruders. Most of the delegates slept in the home and barns of a farmer named Karl Wulfskeel, who had been told he was accommodating a singing society—obviously one devoted to choral atonality.

Of the forty-five delegates, twenty-three were Geese prepared to cackle to the end for illegal work and twenty-two had been prevailed upon to vote for a version of the line taken by the legal Liquidators. Debates spun deep into the night; deals were closed and repudiated; but finally a "Thesis on the Relation of One and Two" was passed which tried to balance the claims of both factions:

> The underground machinery of the Communist Party is not merely a temporary device, to be liquidated as soon as the CP with its full program can be announced in the open. . . . The CP will never cease to maintain its underground machinery until after the establishment of the dictatorship of the proletariat.

And the legal party

> . . . must also serve as an instrument in the complete control of the CP, for getting public contact with the masses.[6]

The debates might be long and tedious, but one delegate whose attention never strayed was Francis A. Morrow, notorious as a fiery radical in the Camden-Philadelphia area but secretly a government agent—K-97—who had begun his service at a dollar a day and, upon demonstrating unusual talents, had worked himself up to $5 a day plus $4 for expenses. As soon as Morrow discovered that the secret site was in Michigan he managed to slip a message to William J. Burns, formerly head of the union-busting International Detective Agency and now chief of the FBI, who in turn notified his Chicago agent Jacob Spolansky, a former radical sympathizer who had become expert in hunting down old acquaintances. Spolansky hurried to Michigan, located the convention, and accidentally caught a glimpse of Robert Minor and William Z. Foster, the latter a secret member of the underground party. But even as he saw Foster, Foster saw him. The alarm went out; the delegates prepared to flee. First went the Comintern "reps"—H. H. Valetski, Boris Reinstein, and Joseph Pogany (Pepper); then those delegates lacking citizenship or under indictment; and finally the rest. The government agents trapped only seventeen delegates, including Morrow, who proved his true identity, and informed them where two barrels of secret documents had been buried. A few days later Foster and Browder were picked up in Chicago and extradited to Michigan.

Though meant as a death-blow to the Communists, the Bridgman raid unexpectedly helped them recover morale and gain new support. Unions, liberals, even conservatives who had previously been helpless or indifferent now began a national campaign protesting these violations of democratic rights. The radicals set up a Labor Defense Council which received the support of such men as Eugene Debs, Roger Baldwin, and Father John A. Ryan, director of the National Catholic Welfare Fund.

Foster was the first to stand trial for "assembling with persons who advocated the overthrow of the government." Two years earlier the verdict would have been entirely predictable; now it was not. During the trial, held in the spring of 1923, Special Agent K-97 declared himself to have been a consistent supporter of the Goose faction; indeed his vote at the convention had assured formal control of the CP to those who favored placing the main stress upon underground work.[7] And now, with all due righteousness, the government tried to offer as evidence against the party a decision that its own agent had been instrumental in having passed! The result was a hung jury, and a major victory for the Communists.*

Superficially the Bridgman raid appeared to bear out the warnings of the Goose faction against trying to work within the repressive atmosphere of capitalist America. Actually, the publicity the party received after the raid and the significant precedent set by the failure to convict Foster helped bring American Communism into

* The leading juryman to resist conviction was Mrs. Minerva Olson, a housewife whose family line went back to pre-revolutionary America. "My great-grandfather," she explained, "was an officer in the Revolutionary War. Perhaps for that reason I have some of the revolutionary spirit." Nor were the theoreticians of American Communism slow to note the significance of this declaration. Mrs. Olson's statement, wrote Jay Lovestone, "truly reflected the role of the farmers in the class struggle today."[8]

Such nonsense apart, the Communists proved skillful in organizing support for the defendants. According to Mother Bloor, the Labor Defense Council raised $30,000 for Foster's trial from the miners alone—which indicated that if a legal Communist Party could not count on a sympathetic political response from the masses it could expect some support for its right to public existence.[9]

the open. Party membership lists, secret instructions from Moscow, financial reports, almost all the precious but not really very sensational documents of the underground party were now plastered across the front pages of the newspapers. What then remained to be kept underground? Even the Communists, yearning to prove themselves in the rites of conspiracy, fell foul of the American passion for publicity: it was almost as hard to avoid the reporters as the police. And besides, how could any future decision to remain underground be taken seriously when it might well be made with the joyous connivance of still other government agents?

But rattled Geese can be very obstinate: they refused to accept the legal orientation. It was left to the Comintern, acting in the dual role of annoyed uncle and indulgent superarbiter, to force through a final decision. At its Fourth Congress in December 1922 approximately twenty-five American pilgrims came to plead for the various factions and sub-factions. By now the fight within the American party had declined into clique warfare, resembling somewhat a compulsive family argument which neither side can or wants to stop. A special American Commission was created, which took "testimony" from both factions and solemnly deliberated upon the shape of the revolutionary movement in a country most of its members had never seen. The verdict was entirely in favor of the Liquidators. "Unless all signs are misleading . . . a legal party is now possible," read a Comintern communiqué to the American party. "Illegality for the sake of illegality," it went on, "must cease. The main efforts must be devoted to work on the legal field." [10]

Formally the Comintern remained opposed to scrapping the "underground machinery," but it soon became clear that this was mainly a ceremonial stand. Except to make it easier for the government to put Communists in jail, the "illegal machinery" neither functioned well nor served any purpose. Chastened and perhaps a bit exhausted, the Central Committee "unanimously" and "without reservations" assented to the Comintern order.[11]

The Geese were liquidated. Like the United Toilers before them, they were unable to withstand the moral and political pressures of Moscow, and though for a time some front-rank Geese— Katterfeld, Jakira, Rose Pastor Stokes—continued to occupy roles of formal importance in the movement, most of them had been so badly mauled in the faction disputes that they lacked the energy and self-confidence to continue as leaders. Faction decorum within the Communist movement called not merely for the political defeat of one's opponent but for his utter moral and psychological destruction: one had to crush the heretic in order to demonstrate how "bankrupt" were his views. Many of the once high-spirited Geese soon dropped out of sight, joining the army of prematurely aged and disillusioned ex-Communists.

In April, 1923, the underground Communist Party held its third and last convention, a mere ghost of a convention of a mere ghost of a party, called primarily for the purpose of self-dissolution. Not much was left to dissolve. Even Ruthenberg could claim no more than 5,000 members. And since the bulk of the Communists were already in the Workers Party, little was added to its tangible assets. Still, by its belated self-immolation the CP contributed something to the future of American Communism, if only because it removed itself from the path of the legal Workers Party.

Though shaken by the reverberations of the Communist faction fights, the Workers Party still managed to hold public meetings, issue a few pamphlets, and publish an English weekly, *The Worker,* and nine foreign-language dailies. In 1922 it dipped a toe into democratic waters by running a token election campaign in a few states. Its membership was then about 13,000, and for a brief moment in late 1922, when it adopted a moderate public platform and came out for a labor party in America, it seemed relatively free from factionalism.

Only by comparison with the shattered underground CP, however, could one speak of the Workers Party as anything but a feeble sect. What handicapped it as a party on the American scene, quite apart from the ineptitude of its leaders, was an extremely heterogeneous membership. Organized into thirteen semi-autonomous federations, with the English-speaking section containing only about 1,200 members, the party resembled a political bazaar more than a disciplined movement. That such a party could attract very few native-born workers is obvious; but even in relation to the foreign-born it suffered from severe limitations. Although a great many American workers during the twenties were still of foreign birth, their dominant orientation was toward the life of their new and chosen country. The Jewish garment workers, the Polish mill hands, the Italian miners would surely have felt ill at ease in a party that made no allowance at all for their difficulties with the English language; but as they struggled to gain acceptance and status in American life, they could not be attracted in large numbers to a party which in its totality served as a constant reminder of their foreign birth and mannerisms. What is more, in the years directly after the war the ratio of foreign-born to native workers was changing. Mass immigration was now a thing of the past; many immigrants who had come at the turn of the century were now quite "Americanized"; and large numbers of native-born Americans were pouring into the shops, particularly those who moved from Southern rural areas to Northern cities. At the very time, then, that the American working class was beginning to emerge as a social group more homogeneous in composition than ever before, the Workers Party, which presumed to speak for it, was little more than a society of immigrant workers conspicuously divided into national groups.

To become an influential force on the American scene, the Workers Party had to solve the difficult problem of "Americanizing" itself.* It had to learn to speak the American idiom, to subordinate the language federations to a respected native leadership, and to break out of the *gemütlich* but constricting atmosphere of the immigrant *Verein* which characterized so many of its branches. Even if there had been a unified will toward achieving these ends, which there was not, it could hardly have been done in a year or two.

2. Such problems as the social composition or the alien quality of the Workers Party cannot be considered apart from its internal political life. Two kinds of political orientation could be distinguished among the members at this point—and in turning to this fact we leave behind the petty squabbles of Communist factionalism and approach one of the most persistent and difficult problems of radical (as perhaps any other kind of) political action: the relationship between doctrine and conduct, between eventual ends

---

* "If we were to read the nine dailies and twenty-one weeklies of the Workers Party carefully," wrote John Pepper, "one would get the complete picture of all European countries, but a very incomplete picture of the political life in America." [12]

and immediate methods, between the pressure for ideological exclusivism and the pressure of political actuality.

In the Workers Party, which by 1922 was still far from being a
Leninist organization, there were first the confirmed Communists
and second those radicals who had recently come from the Socialist
Party and whom the Communists sneeringly called "centrists."
Between these two tendencies, whose ultimate incompatibility lay
equally in politics and temperament, there was at best an uneasy
alliance.

The "centrists"—a good many of whom, by a curious twist of
politics, would subside into faithful Stalinists in a few years—had
their strongholds in the Jewish, German, and Finnish federations.
Among their leaders were men like Moissaye Olgin, editor of the Yid-
dish *Freiheit*; Alexander Trachtenberg, later to become head of the
Stalinist publishing house; and J. B. Salutsky (also known as J. B.
Hardman), educational director of the Amalgamated Clothing
Workers. In any precise sense, these people were not Communists.
They had been critical, though friendly, in their response to the
Bolshevik Revolution, and they did not accept the entirety of Bolshevik ideology. They wanted a radical propaganda group rather
than a tightly disciplined party; they looked with distrust upon the
discipline claimed by the Comintern; and while they found the
Socialist Party excessively tame they could not learn to regard it as
a deadly enemy. Within the Workers Party they felt bitter over
the existence of an underground CP which, working as a faction,
decided in advance how its members would behave and in effect
held the "centrists" captive in their own house. But perhaps most
important, "centrists" like Salutsky enjoyed a genuine prestige and
influence in the trade unions, which aroused a mixture of envy and
hostility among the more rigid Communists.*

* Many of the "centrists" were American equivalents of the left Socialists who in Europe had formed the Two-and-a-Half International, which
briefly brought together those radicals who found the Socialist International
too conservative and the Communist International too doctrinaire. In April,
1922, a conference was held in Berlin by the three internationals, but predictably it broke up in futility and recriminations. The Comintern thereupon
launched a brief experiment with the disastrous slogan of "the united front
from below," a maneuver designed to reach the Socialist ranks while by-
passing and creating hostility toward the leaders.

Within the Workers Party the "hard Bolsheviks," as they thought of

Some Communists, particularly a few remaining Geese, were intent upon "purifying" the Workers Party of its non-Communist elements. At the Bridgman convention of the CP a resolution had been passed virtually declaring war on the "centrists":

> Especially dangerous are the positions of power of the centrists . . . in the daily papers [of the Workers Party]. This condition must be remedied immediately . . . by organizational measures to get this press absolutely into our control . . . and by the open criticism of their mistakes in the official organ of the WP.[13]

Both these ends were speedily achieved, for in campaigns of this sort the early Communists were far more successful than in their sporadic efforts to influence American life. Soon they had taken over the Finnish daily *Elore* and the Yiddish daily *Freiheit* and were publicly denouncing the "centrists." Eventually most of the latter were either to make their peace with the Communists or drop out of radical politics entirely. By the middle of 1923 there was no longer a coherent "centrist" group within the Workers Party.

Symptomatically, this was an important turning point in the history of the movement. The inability or unwillingness of the Communists and "centrists" to live together in the same movement marked a significant step toward the creation of a Communist Party in which internal disputes would continue for a few years but within which non-Leninist radicals could not survive. Nor was this primarily a matter of ill will. The Communist leaders of the Workers Party hesitated to break irrevocably with people like Salutsky because he was one of the few members with standing in the labor movement; but between his conception of a radical party and theirs no compromise was really possible. Thus, when he began publishing in 1923 a radical journal called *American Labor Monthly* in which he presumed to criticize the Workers Party to which he him-

themselves, now felt confirmed in their view that it was necessary to maintain at all costs a Communist movement ideologically pure, organizationally centralized, and selective in its membership. The "centrists," for their part, considered the "united front from below" an absurdity and felt increasingly uncomfortable with their Bolshevik allies.

self belonged, the Communists regarded this as a major breach of discipline. Salutsky, however, felt that no American party should expect the kind of discipline that had been customary among the Russian Bolsheviks. In July, 1923, after much bickering, he was expelled.

But the political problems that he raised could not be expelled. Even before his expulsion a number of Communist leaders tried to make a turn toward American political and trade-union life which, in a sense, represented an adaptation of his views.

Though not uncritical of the official trade-union leaders, Salutsky managed to work with them; he had nothing but contempt for dual unionism, he neither publicly announced nor desired to wage a death struggle against the trade-union leaders, and he saw as his modest task the education of workers to socialist ideas. Obviously this was a concept of trade-union work sharply at variance with that of the Communists. Yet it is important to note that the more flexible Communist leaders, even while formally attacking the politics of the "centrists," found it necessary to adopt—or at least adapt—some of their tactics in the unions. Quite unwittingly, the "centrists" thus came to symbolize the problems that almost all radicals, but especially the Communists, would face when they tried to penetrate and influence the American labor movement.

For by 1923 there was no other choice: the Communists *had* to turn their faces toward public life. Genuine opportunities presented themselves in the farmer-labor movement; the Comintern kept nudging them to quit their sectarian shell; and their own ideological preconceptions also required that they try their hand in American politics. The whole underground experience, it now became clear, had been a kind of psychological luxury. As long as the Red Army kept winning spectacular victories in the Russian civil war and the sweep of revolution through Europe seemed a genuine possibility, the American Communists could count on being "rescued" by the European proletariat and, meanwhile, could rest emotionally secure in their underground retreats. Factions could be formed on abstruse topics unrelated to American life; devoted Communists could afford to be contemptuous of American working-class traditions; and meanwhile what did it matter, what point was there in rooting themselves in American experience, even in learning the English language, if tomorrow the tide of revolution would sweep across the Atlantic?

But now, in the gray morning of what the Comintern called "capitalist stabilization," it was necessary to reckon the consequences of the decline of the European revolution. That meant, for the first time, an effort to take seriously the domestic political life of the United States.

3. The problem of a labor party had always troubled the American left: would such a party be a threat, a competitor, or an opportunity? This question became particularly acute during the early twenties, when there arose one of those sporadic waves of third-party sentiment that have never quite managed to transform our political life but have frequently altered it.

In the past, when the trade unions had been relatively small and the Socialist Party had believed itself on the verge of becoming a mass organization, most radicals had been against forming a labor or farmer-labor party. At best, they felt, it would be a superfluous— and at worst, a dangerous—competitor. But now, by 1921, when the union movement numbered in the millions while the Socialists and Communists together came to a mere 25,000, the idea of a new party which would not be socialist in ideology yet would represent a decisive break from the two old parties had an obvious appeal to the radicals. It struck them as a possible way of quickly breaking out of their isolation; as a means for creating a leftward pressure in political life; and perhaps as a catalyst for speeding the growth of the American workers from political conservatism to a radical consciousness.

Significant changes had recently taken place in the character of the American working class that made the idea of such a party seem plausible. In 1900 a large proportion of the American workers was still employed in small enterprise; now they were increasingly concentrated in mass-production industries where common problems led to common action and an early form of industrial unionism was made possible. As immigrant quotas were restricted, wage differentials between skilled and unskilled workers reduced, and foreign-born workers increasingly absorbed into American life, there began to appear a socially compact industrial proletariat. This tendency toward concentration and homogeneity within the working class did not of course make its political independence inevitable; but it did make it increasingly possible. So reasoned some of the Communist theoreticians, and not without point.

More immediately, a number of socio-economic difficulties which did not quite add up to a full-scale depression but certainly helped to dispel the euphoria of Wilson's New Freedom and Harding's "normalcy" seemed to provide new political opportunities for the left.

The war had enormously stimulated the domestic and European demand for farm products, and to meet these demands the farmers had borrowed heavily, often to the point of overextending themselves. But with the end of the war and with an industrial crisis in 1921, agricultural prices dropped sharply. A Congressional Joint Commission reported that this price fall "had reduced the farmer to a condition worse than he had suffered under for 30 years." [14] In the spring of 1921, for example, the purchasing power of the farmer's dollar was less than half what it had been two years earlier.

Life on the farm became increasingly hazardous: in 1922 alone, 20 percent of American farms changed ownership from the previous year, and from 1920 to 1923 a million and a half people were forced off the farms. Bankruptcy, increased tenancy (from 25 percent in 1880 to 38 percent in 1920), and overloaded mortgages were the symptoms of a deep agricultural crisis. In the wheat-growing Northwest the situation was particularly severe.

This crisis came at a time when the memory of Populism, still strong and vivid, could move men to action; and if to this is added the lingering taste of wartime prosperity, it can be understood why many Midwestern farmers were in a combative mood. In general, both the farmer's vote and his political rhetoric tend to follow the curve of the market. High costs make him uneasy; add low prices, and he begins to get a bit radical; but threaten his property, and he is likely to become "revolutionary," though in a most un-Marxian way.

The workers too were restive. Once their strike offensive of 1919 had been crushed, it was followed by an open-shop counter-offensive, called by the publicity men "the American Plan." As

Perlman and Taft accurately remark, "The American Plan purported to abolish the 'un-American' closed shop, but as in previous open shop crusades, the destruction of unionism was the real objective." [15] This counter-offensive sometimes took the form, as in the packing industry, of provocative wage cuts which forced the unions to call premature strikes they were in no position to win. And because unemployment rose to five million during the winter of 1921 as a result of cutbacks in production and military demobilization, the unions found it harder still to fight back. Except for the garment workers and the typographers, almost no group of American workers escaped sizable wage cuts and attacks upon their unions in 1920 and 1921.

By 1922, however, a sharp turn occurred. Unemployment began to decrease as the result of a business upturn set off by a construction boom; the unions showed a greater capacity for fight; and some of the most massive labor battles in American history ensued. At one point during the year more than a million workers were on strike: 600,000 miners, 400,000 railroad men, 100,000 textile hands. In most of these strikes the unions were badly mauled, but the mere fact that they took place at all helped put a temporary stop to the open-shop drive. In this atmosphere of partial yet not paralyzing defeat, the more politically conscious unionists began to cast about for a new means of realizing their influence in American life; and as a result, genuine sentiment for a new party began to appear.

What gave particular edge to this sentiment was the belief held even by conservative unionists that the government was systematically working to help the open-shoppers and, indeed, the general interests of business. Under President Harding, charged the unionists, the US Shipping Board had openly helped defeat the 1921 maritime strike; the National Guard had been used to disorganize picket lines during the packing-house strike; the Railroad Labor Board had denounced the railroad strike of 1922 and encouraged the employers to form company unions; and Attorney General Harry Daugherty had used his power and influence to gain a sweeping injunction against the striking railway shopmen in September, 1922, declaring that "I will use the power of the government of the United States within my control to prevent the labor unions . . . from destroying the open shop." [16] All of these acts struck harsh blows at the unions and lent credibility to the claims of the radicals that during Harding's administration Big Business and government were in a state of virtual collusion. The Communists, for their part, were quick to develop theories about a new phenomenon in American life: the growth of a centralized, powerful government that paralleled and protected the increasing concentration of economic wealth.*

Many unions, simply to cope with this new situation, found themselves turning to ideas that a few years earlier would have been dismissed as socialist. The railroad brotherhoods, for example, proposed a scheme (the Plumb Plan) that would have prevented the return to private ownership of railroads taken over by the government during the war. A Nationalization Research Committee appointed at the 1921 convention of the United Mine Workers called for the nationalization of the mines with "a large area of control in the industry to all workers." John L. Lewis, as conservative politically as he was occasionally militant in trade-union matters, denounced the Plan as the work of "Greenwich Village radicals"— though its main sponsor was John Brophy, a leading official of the union.[18] That such ideas were floating about in the unions was itself extremely significant, for it indicated that even ordinary unionists, in their effort to relate themselves to a new industrial society, had to think in terms that went far beyond traditional pure-and-simple unionism.

With boldness here and timidity there, local third parties were being tried all through the early twenties. Some were large-scale efforts reflecting the needs of the labor movement; others, the result of discontent in the farm areas; and a number of them, artificially contrived by the radicals. One of the most significant of these parties had its origin and center in Chicago, where the Federation of Labor, led by a lively Irishman named John Fitzpatrick, was actively trying to create a new movement of grass-roots American radicalism.

Within the AFL the main opposition to the idea of a new party came from its president, the formidable Sam Gompers. A man of

* They could also push this idea to an absurd extreme: "The capitalist government of the United States has become just as centralized and as sinister as the former monarchy of the Czars." [17]

considerable skill and intelligence, Gompers was perhaps the only American labor leader capable of advancing a serious and effective argument against the radicals and other advocates of a labor party, certainly the only one who could raise the problem above transient pragmatic considerations. Labor parties, argued Gompers, might be necessary in Europe, where class lines had long been hardened and the constrictions of inefficient economies made strike action limited in value; but in the United States there was still enough social fluidity to warrant reliance on union organization and flexible maneuvering between the two major parties. Powerful though Gompers was in advancing this traditional AFL opinion, he could not entirely head off the growing sentiment among his followers for maverick politics.

In November, 1919, a number of local labor parties, very young and very confident, had coalesced into a nation-wide organization that was to call itself the Farmer-Labor Party. Somewhat rashly, the FLP presented a candidate in the 1920 presidential election who polled a mere 260,000 votes, about a quarter of what Debs received as the Socialist nominee. Mainly because it tried to by-pass the AFL and never won the support of the major trade unions, the Farmer-Labor Party, despite its considerable strength in such states as Illinois and Washington, never really got off the ground as a national organization. But under Fitzpatrick's vigorous leadership it remained a genuine potential in or near the American left, one that would have to be reckoned with in case a major turn occurred toward new political action—and one that was to be particularly important in the history of early American Communism.

4. Only in 1922, a troubled year in American history, did a major step occur toward independent political action by the labor movement. The embittered railroad unions, forced to think politically, took the lead in setting up a Conference for Progressive Political Action (CPPA). At its first meeting, held in Chicago in February, 1922, the United Mine Workers, the International Ladies Garment Workers, the Amalgamated Clothing Workers, as well as the Socialist and Farmer-Labor parties, were present. This meant that a substantial section of the labor movement, with a combined membership of nearly three million, was represented, but that many

of the big AFL unions, particularly those in the building trades, were still following Gompers. As for the Communists, who were anathema to the railroad unions, no official representatives from their party were admitted.

Formally the Chicago conference accomplished very little, since a major and indeed typical divergence quickly showed itself; yet in the history of American labor politics it was an important occasion. The railroad unions, strongly opposed to the immediate formation of a new party, wished to concentrate on the nomination of progressive candidates in the 1922 primaries—in effect, the tactic that would become almost universal among American trade unions. But the more radical unions, many of them under Socialist influence, felt this to be inadequate, and *Advance,* the newspaper of the Amalgamated Clothing Workers, while conceding that some purpose had been served by drawing "the attention of the American workers to the necessity of politicalization," felt that on the whole the conference had been little more than "a meaningless gesture." [19]

At least in retrospect, *Advance* appears to have been mistaken, for like most of the radical unionists it failed to see the potential of the CPPA. It failed to see that, no matter what the limited intentions of the railroad unions, the mere creation of a movement like the CPPA might constitute a step toward the labor party it desired. When the CPPA National Committee urged its affiliates to fight for progressive candidates in the primaries, it also added:

> When action within the old parties is futile, organize independently. It is often better to lose as independents with a square cut issue than to lose as you have lost in the past by wasting ballots on men who cannot be trusted.[20]

This, no doubt, was partly rhetoric for the occasion; but even the rhetoric that a political movement employs for self-adornment can reveal something about its purposes and possibilities.

The appearance of the CPPA raised some difficult questions for the Communists. During the "underground" period, when anyone neglecting to endorse the dictatorship of the proletariat was simply excommunicated, it would all have been quite simple: the CPPA would have been denounced as a "bourgeois labor party" deliberately ensnaring the workers. Now, however, as part of their effort to relate themselves to American politics, the Communists were enthusiastically for labor parties. Most historians have explained this shift by pointing to the new Comintern policy in favor of united fronts; and while such a mode of explanation always has some relevance when one is discussing American Communism, it seems a bit too simple in this case. For the Communists in America, or at least some of them, were responding not merely to Moscow but also to the social conditions that had galvanized the trade unionists and brought both the CPPA and the FLP into existence. Neither the Comintern nor any of its representatives were directly responsible for the specific attitude of the Workers Party toward the idea of a labor party. It is true that the new Comintern line made it easier for the Communists to deal realistically with domestic political life; but the application of this line could only be the work of the American party and for once—to give credit where it is so seldom due—the leadership was trying to approach the labor party problem with a measure of independence and flexibility.

In February, 1922, articles began appearing in *The Worker* under Jay Lovestone's signature that welcomed the formation of the CPPA. Instead of condemning the CPPA in advance as a "sellout," Lovestone soberly estimated its role as a step in the evolution of the American labor movement. He even proposed that the Workers Party try to send representatives to the conference—which was not, however, done.[21]

The Communists understood that from their point of view the Conference for Progressive Political Action was far more significant, both as the source of a potential movement and as an arena for immediate activity, than the Farmer-Labor Party. Militant and radical as the latter might be, its strength was confined to a few state and city federations of labor; it did not cut very deeply into the main unions of the AFL. Precisely those factors that made it attractive to the Communists also made it incapable of serving as a long-range organizer of political action in the labor movement. By contrast, the moderate CPPA, with its backing from major international unions, stood at the center of American labor politics: here, if anywhere, was the genuine beginning of a new political course. It is just conceivable that the Communists might have won for themselves a place as the acknowledged extreme left within the labor movement if they had been able to remain firm by this understanding. As soon as they decided to forget it, they came to grief.

In June, 1922, the Workers Party adopted a resolution that incorporated Lovestone's realistic views on the labor party movement. It remained, however, for a roving delegate from the Comintern—one of the most fantastic figures ever to thrust himself upon the American scene—to mastermind the details and compose a historical rationale for the new Communist approach to American labor politics. And this was only part of the supervisory role that Joseph Pogany (John Pepper) had cut out for himself since arriving in the United States a month before the Bridgman convention.*

No one could react mildly to John Pepper. The persuasive force of his public personality, his obvious intellectual superiority to the American leaders, his exotic political past, his close friendship with Zinoviev, and not least of all, his utter lack of moral scruples—these made him a man both idolized and feared among many leading American Communists.

The twentieth century has made us familiar with the political adventurer of inscrutable motives who in times of historical stress suddenly leaps to the forefront of a revolutionary movement. Of this type Pepper was a supreme example. In Trotsky's biting words, he was above all "the consummate type of man who knows how to adapt himself, a political parasite." [22]

Hungarian by birth, he had worked in prewar Budapest as editor of a boulevard sheet and then as Imperial correspondent during the war. He distinguished himself by a patriotic fervor that went so far as public praise for the censors who slashed his dispatches. When the Hungarian Revolution began, he quickly made his appearance as an ardent liberal in the government of Count Karolyi, where he was responsible for the arrest of a number of Communists, including his later colleague Bela Kun. During the Social Democratic interval of the revolution he again shifted allegiance, this time serving as head of the Soldiers Councils. When

* It is not clear whether Pepper had been sent by the Comintern as its "rep" to the American CP or just to the Hungarian Federation of the CP. He behaved, however, as if he were the "rep" to the party as a whole, and it was not until later that anyone thought to question his status.

the Communists seized power, Pepper transformed himself into a Communist and became—this political chameleon—People's Commissar for Military Affairs. Cabinets came, governments went; Pepper landed on his feet.*

Together with Bela Kun, Pepper shared responsibility for the collapse of the Communist regime. Because the Kun-Pepper leadership of the Hungarian Communists refused to divide the land among the peasants and insisted upon an immediate forced leap from semi-feudalism to state-owned collectives, the peasants quickly turned against them. The path for the Horthyite counter-revolution was cleared. Pepper, however, landed on his feet.

Together with Kun and Matyas Rakosi, he escaped the White Terror, made his way back to Moscow, and became a Comintern agent. It was at this moment that Stalin was beginning to build up his machine within the international Communist movement; and among the displaced, dependent, and often cynical Hungarian Communists he found men notable for their readiness to undertake almost any sort of job. Pepper was among those most ready, and the first job given him was to visit Germany together with Bela Kun, where they were to supervise the doomed Communist putsch of 1921 and at the same time drive out of the party Paul Levi, a gifted leader who opposed this adventure. Pepper and Kun saw to it that the putsch went off as scheduled; the German government, that the putsch was smashed. Levi was driven out of the party; Pepper and Kun returned to Moscow. There Pepper quickly aligned himself with the "left-wing Communists" who were resisting what they regarded as Lenin's retreat from direct revolutionary action during the NEP period—but, flexible man that he was, Pepper hurriedly scrambled back to the winning side and within a year was supervising the rightward course of the American party. Again, on his feet.

As a Moscow "rep" Pepper was unlike any that preceded or

* A political record of this kind required not merely cat-like agility but a generous portion of megalomania. Sigismund Kunfi, editor of the Hungarian Social Democratic paper *Az Ember,* was later to report that at a meeting of the Siofok Soviet Pepper declared: "There was a time when I could have been crowned king, and at one time I did have serious thoughts as to whether it would not be to the advantage of the revolution to have myself crowned." [23] No one who knew Pepper could dismiss such a remark as out of character.

followed him. A vain and arrogant man, dandyish in manner but ruthless in character, Pepper quickly became enmeshed in personal intrigues—he had a high opinion of rebel girls—and in the factional controversies of the Communist Party. Unlike the stolid Gussev ("P. Green") who succeeded him as Comintern "rep" in 1925, the well-named Pepper could not preserve ·the pose of a distant arbiter. He found the squalid atmosphere of American Communist factionalism exactly to his taste, and as a quasi-intellectual whose dialectical gifts lay in speed rather than depth he enjoyed complex political intrigues that did not involve risking one's neck.

In the United States Pepper's opportunities were limited: no matter what he did or failed to do, the stakes were far smaller than in Hungary or Germany. But this did not deter Pepper from throwing himself into his new task with energy and at the beginning, it must be said, with intelligence. He began to study English and to bone up on American history, neither of which he knew upon his arrival. Soon he had a keener comprehension of American politics than most of the party leaders who had spent their lives in this country.

It is a curious and revealing fact that the first major effort to bring an awareness of the United States to the American Communists was in some crucial respects the work of a Hungarian adventurer who had never before crossed the Atlantic. For the first six months of his stay in this country, before he became embroiled in factionalism, Pepper made a distinct contribution to the cause of American Communism. He learned from books what the leaders should have known through experience: that American society had a number of unique features sharply distinguishing it from European capitalism. In October, 1922, the Workers Party published his pamphlet, "For a Labor Party," in which he provided an analysis more interesting historically and more usable politically than any similar work done by an American Communist. With a flair for realism that sometimes went along with his erratic nature, Pepper wrote:

> A Labor Party should be launched only if it is created by the trade unions. A Labor Party of any other form would be a mere caricature, a political swindle, and a miscarriage.[24]

In later months, when he became the gray eminence for one of the factions, Pepper proved a disaster for the American Communists. But if they had been able to cleave to the conception of the labor party that he advanced in 1922, the history of their movement during the twenties might not have been quite the disaster it was.

5. In December, 1922, the Conference for Progressive Political Action called its second national meeting in Cleveland. The 250 delegates came in an elated mood, pleased that the progressives in both parties had done well in the recent primaries and elections, and confident that the political winds had finally begun to turn in their direction.

The dominant figure in the CPPA was William H. Johnstone, president of the machinists' union, former Socialist and still an insurgent union leader. For him, as for most of his AFL colleagues, the success of the liberal candidates in the 1922 election was proof that the CPPA, which had been active in the campaign, was correct in refusing to form a labor party immediately and in confining itself to non-partisan political work. But a minority of the more radical delegates saw the recent election, rather optimistically, as evidence of a leftward trend among the farmers and workers which made it worth risking a new party. In the forefront of this minority were the delegates from John Fitzpatrick's Farmer-Labor Party.

For both the Socialists inside the conference and the Communists on its sidelines a difficult choice had now to be made: whether to push ahead with Fitzpatrick's minority for a new party, which might well mean splitting the CPPA and losing touch with the major unions, or to seek a compromise formula by which unity could be preserved between Fitzpatrick's forces and the railroad unions. It was neither the first nor the last time that radicals in America have had to worry such a choice: indeed, this is the kind of problem that regularly bedevils small political groups.

When a vote was taken, the labor party people lost, 64-52; but the closeness of the vote was deceptive.[25] The fifty-two delegates represented mainly marginal organizations like the FLP and the Socialists, as well as a few garment unions under Socialist influence, while the bulk of the unions lined up with the majority. Even if the labor party people had carried the convention, they would have won a pyrrhic victory. An immediate split would have occurred, the railroad unions would have walked out, and almost no one would have been left to form a labor party that, in Pepper's memorable words, could be more than "a mere caricature."

An accurate gauge of the CPPA temper—more so than the vote on the labor party—was its refusal to seat representatives from the Workers Party; only a handful of delegates were ready to argue that the Communists represented a legitimate tendency within the labor movement that had a right to be heard. Despite this rebuff, the Communists were sensible enough to realize that the CPPA could not be discounted as the major arena for labor political activity.

But the less disciplined and more fiery leaders of the Farmer-Labor Party were convinced that the time had come to build a new movement. What was the point of maneuvering with the railroad "labor skates," asked Fitzpatrick. "We can't fiddle around with these liberals and their mushy third party," wrote the FLP paper, the *New Majority*.[26] The Chicago Farmer-Laborites withdrew from the CPPA and went ahead with plans to create a new national organization. With surprising astuteness, the Communists tried to keep Fitzpatrick from this rash course, and as late as March, 1923, a *Worker* editorial declared with blunt truth that the FLP ambition to become the rallying center for a new political movement was "a lost hope." The only possible basis for such a movement, wrote the *Worker*, "is laid in the activities" of the CPPA.[27]

But Fitzpatrick and his friends were not to be held back. They declared war on the CPPA—and presented the Communists with a genuine dilemma. To continue supporting the CPPA, correct course though some Communist leaders thought this to be, meant to antagonize the Chicago unionists, who were perhaps the most powerful friends the Communists had in the American labor movement. To collaborate with the FLP in its ill-prepared plunge into national politics meant for the Communists to alienate themselves still more from the major progressive trend in the labor movement. It was a real problem and a difficult problem.

Caught in this pincer, the Communists decided to hold on to

what they had (or thought they had) by going along with the FLP and the Chicago Federation of Labor.* The result was a disaster for everyone concerned, but most of all for the Communists themselves.

Yet it is not hard to understand their motives, or even to appreciate their problem. Fitzpatrick and his friends were aggressive and radical unionists who had broken the grip of the racketeers in the Chicago labor movement and had created an exemplary center of democratic unionism. Their paper, the *New Majority*, which frequently printed items such as a serialized version of John Dos Passos' *Three Soldiers* or a discussion by Franz Boas on "Are the Jews a Race?" was far superior in spirit and quality to most union publications. Fitzpatrick himself was a man to be respected—"one of the sturdy oaks of the labor movement," wrote William Z. Foster a short time before taking a saw to the tree.[29] Fitzpatrick was willing to cooperate with the Communists, whom he regarded simply as another variety of radicals; and if Arne Swabeck of the Painters local or Charles Krumbein of the Steamfitters were both delegates to the Central Labor Union and open Communists, that caused Fitzpatrick no dismay. Such men were his friends, and about certain things they seemed to talk sense. Whenever they brought up a labor defense case or a campaign to help famine-stricken Russia, Fitzpatrick was sure to help. It was symptomatic that, where the CPPA would not even allow the Communists to stand mutely near the door, the Farmer-Labor Party at its second convention, in May, 1922, had invited Jack Carney to bring official greetings from the Workers Party.

Given the fact that to the Communists the Chicago labor movement seemed like an oasis in the desert of American hostility, their decision to stick with Fitzpatrick, even while warning him against rupturing the CPPA, was understandable. To have parted from him at this point would have meant sacrificing a short-range tangible advantage for a possible long-range goal.

Once the break from the CPPA was decided upon, the Communists worked up a convenient theory that the CPPA was no

* Daniel Bell has written that this decision represented a reversal of the Communists' "sectarian tactics."[28] Perhaps, if one compares it with their earlier blanket denunciation of all labor parties; but not at all, if one sees it in the immediate context of choosing the FLP in preference to the CPPA.

longer the focus for an eventual new party. Now the honor was assigned to a "united front" of the Farmer-Laborites and the Workers Party. Soon, in a fine fury of sectarianism, it would be the Workers Party alone. For if the Communists' decision to go along with Fitzpatrick may have been a mistake, their treatment of him as an ally was a scandal.

Hell-bent for a new party, the Farmer-Laborites invited hundreds of organizations to a conference to be held in Chicago during July, 1923. The preparations for this conference formed a climax of sorts in the career of the Workers Party during the twenties. Enjoying close access to the Fitzpatrick group, they were soon deep into the plans for the conference; and as visions of a burgeoning mass party began to possess them—for Fitzpatrick's naïve enthusiasm was contagious—they felt that if the future of the Workers Party were not entirely assured, it certainly had greater possibilities for growth than ever before. They were in close relations with men like Fitzpatrick, men who had a certain amount of power; they saw the beginnings of a new organizational apparatus come into being, an apparatus they might be able to control; they had pleasant fantasies of sending in glowing reports to the Comintern, reports that for once would speak of progress; they lost their heads.

In a June issue of the *Worker* they wrote that the convention called by the Farmer-Laborites could "realize the demands of . . . *millions of workers* for the formation of the Labor Party" [30] (emphasis added). John Pepper, perhaps convinced that the role of a secret mover in an American labor party was as desirable as that of king in Hungary, was still more enthusiastic:

> The Labor Party movement is a political earthquake of the first magnitude. . . . The day of the Declaration of Independence of the American working class will be the day of the founding of its independent political party.[31]

With their own rhetoric pealing in their ears and undoubtedly deceived by at least some of it, the Communists began to wonder why they should share with the Fitzpatrick people the forthcoming triumph—a triumph that would surely provide them with a gleaming short cut to the masses! Better to brush aside the raw and untutored radicals of the Farmer-Labor Party, these Midwestern nativists who knew nothing about Marxism! Better to take over the whole thing themselves and thereby capture the labor party movement! As these visions danced before Pepper's eyes it became clear that a new theory would be needed to justify this new tactic. And as soon as Pepper had a minute he would provide one.

There was only one sour note. As the enthusiasm of the Communists rose, the spirits of the Farmer-Laborites drooped. The response from legitimate labor organizations to the Chicago conference was proving to be negligible; the Socialists refused to participate on the reasonable ground that a genuine labor party (had they been reading the Pepper of six months ago?) required "the active support of at least a majority of the great trade unions"; and meanwhile the intentions of the Communists were becoming all too obvious. Too late, Fitzpatrick discovered that he had been deluded by his expectations and boxed in by his allies. A militant left-winger but far from a Communist, he had been ready to collaborate with the Workers Party in Chicago provided it was one tendency among others; but to be their sole and subordinate mate— that, he was quick to see, meant political suicide.

Fitzpatrick tried to maneuver by suggesting that not an actual new party but an "organizing committee" be set up for one. The Communist smiled. To have gone along with him against their better judgment and now to be cheated out of the spoils—they were too shrewd to be taken in by so transparent a proposal.

Still, they did want to keep Fitzpatrick as an ally, and to show their reasonableness Ruthenberg suggested a compromise: if representatives of more than 500,000 workers and farmers declared their intention of starting a new party in Chicago, then both groups would agree to go ahead. Later Fitzpatrick denied that the Farmer-Laborites had accepted this scheme, but in a way it hardly mattered: the Communists were wildly, furiously, joyously at work concocting a pile of paper organizations which would send pliant cardboard delegates to the Chicago convention. If the magic number was 500,000 they could easily arrange it. Two days before the convention, relations between the Communists and Fitzpatrick were entirely severed. But the Communists went serenely ahead. Gloating over the anticipated spoils, the elated Pepper wrote that the Communists would fight against anyone hesitating to form a new party: "CHICAGO WILL BE A FIELD OF BATTLE FOR US." [32] And indeed it was.

When John Fitzpatrick surveyed the 500-odd delegates, he must have been aghast. Over half were members of the Workers Party. Later, even Ruthenberg admitted that there were 200 WP members among the delegates from local unions (not necessarily elected by the membership), party-front groups, and fraternal societies. Among the latter, the "Improvement Benefit Club" of Rosedale, Illinois, had its delegate representing sixty members. The United Farmers Education League put in a fighting appearance. And the Lithuanians! The Lithuanians were swarming all over the place: the American Lithuanian Literary Association of Brooklyn, the Lithuanian Joint Conference of Milwaukee, the Lithuanian Improvement Club of Chicago, the Lithuanian Workers Progressive Alliance of Brooklyn, the Lithuanian Workers Organization of Greater New York, and, not least of all, the Joint Conference of Lithuanian Societies. Had the problem of the convention been to seize power in Lithuania, its task would have been relatively simple.

Hardly a match for such wily operators as Lovestone, Pepper, and Ruthenberg, and inexperienced at the whole game of political maneuver, Fitzpatrick was at a loss. Not only was the block of hidden and half-hidden Communists enormous, but a number of the delegates from legitimate farmers' organizations, sore and desperate because of bad economic conditions, were ready to vote for the immediate organization of a new party and thus play into the hands of the Communists. Though he had behind him whatever fraction of "the masses" could honestly be said to be represented at the convention, Fitzpatrick lacked the votes. Yet he was too stubborn a man simply to walk out. As a result, and like many later mistreated allies of the Communists, he panicked and resorted to a kind of redbaiting. He introduced a resolution declaring "it would be suicide for us" to unite "with any organization which advocated other than lawful means to bring about a political change. . . ." [33] For a man who had been cooperating with the Communists during the past several years, this was a somewhat belated discovery; but Fitzpatrick was caught up in his own desperation. Once his motion was smothered by a vote of 500-40, he and his supporters left the hall.[34] The Communists pretended to be indifferent; but whether they knew it or not, the moment Fitzpatrick walked out there came to an end whatever possibility had remained for them to cooperate with the more progressive elements in the American labor movement.*

Left happily to themselves, the Communists, with their Lithuanian and agricultural allies, organized a new party—the Federated Farmer Labor Party—in which one of Fitzpatrick's former followers, William Bouck, was chairman and Joseph Manley, a son-in-law of Foster, was secretary. The Communist press rhapsodized over this first major front organization of American Communism, claiming that "conservatively" there were between six and seven hundred thousand workers represented at Chicago. Pepper, whose imagination was finally beginning to find adequate scope in this country, thundered that *"Never before in American history did a political party of workers and farmers have such mighty masses behind it"* [36] (italics in original). And how many might these "mighty masses" be? Pepper knew exactly: 616,000.

A few months later a somewhat sobered Ruthenberg reported that 155,000 people belonged to the organizations affiliated with the Federated Farmer Labor Party (FFLP). And even this figure was several times too high.

As they prepared to march forward under the FFLP banner, the Communists stopped for a moment to shed a tear over their battered ally. Wrote Pepper:

> It is really a pity about Fitzpatrick. He . . . was a good leader. The old saying is, that the road to hell is paved with good intentions. And we can say that the road to revolution is paved with the political corpses of well-intentioned leaders.[37]

The author of an unproduced play about Napoleon, Pepper was addicted to images of battle and blood: he was a fierce man with a typewriter. As an obituary of Fitzpatrick, his remarks were decidedly

---

* His pride wounded, Fitzpatrick quickly made a political turn to the right and in a little while was announcing the decision of the Chicago Federation of Labor "to cast our lot [in politics] with the AFL." [35] Fitzpatrick turned to supporting old party candidates, and his Farmer-Labor Party quietly faded away. Not for the last time, but with a lethal effectiveness they would seldom surpass, the Communists had done their job.

premature, but as a forecast of his own political fate—for he would be swallowed up some years later in the great Russian purges—they were uncannily exact.

One immediate result of the Chicago fiasco was that the local Communists, until yesterday acting with a freedom in the Federation of Labor they could enjoy in no other American city, now began to find themselves squeezed. Their resolutions, which had usually passed with large majorities, were regularly defeated. Far more deeply involved in the labor movement than the New York party functionaries, the Chicago Communists grew alarmed, for they realized that their influence depended on the sufferance of Fitzpatrick. Even before the July 3 convention they tried to dissuade the party from a head-on clash with Fitzpatrick. (Here, incidentally, were sown the seeds of a major faction fight within the Workers Party: the "Politicals," led by Pepper and Ruthenberg and centering mainly in New York, against the "Industrials," led by Foster and Cannon, with their stronghold in Chicago.)

For a time the Chicago Communists, trying to salvage what they could, were inclined to avoid any steps that would inflame Fitzpatrick against them. In a circular distributed to its membership the Chicago Workers Party declared: "We will not encourage any immediate conflict either with officials of the old [Fitzpatrick] Farmer Labor Party or in the unions that have been until now affiliated with that party." [38] But this sensible policy was too much for the New York Communist leadership, and soon Pepper and Ruthenberg were instructing the Chicago branch to "carry on an aggressive campaign to secure the affiliation of all unions in Chicago with the [Communist-led] Federated Farmer Labor Party, irrespective of any previous affiliation." [39] Reluctantly, the Chicago Communists made a stab at carrying out these instructions, not to the point of satisfying Ruthenberg but enough to seal the break between themselves and Fitzpatrick. Thus was lost one of the few significant footholds in the labor movement that the Communists could claim during the twenties.

The debacle in Chicago caused the Communists harm on the entire trade-union front. It was perhaps inevitable that they would soon be subjected to a full-scale assault by the Gompers leadership in the AFL, but this assault was both eased and hastened by the refusal of the Fitzpatrick group to continue protecting the Communists as a legitimate tendency within the labor movement. In the United Mine Workers, John L. Lewis began a lurid anti-Communist campaign, designed to preserve his autocratic rule against an opposition in which the Communists played an important part. *Labor,* the newspaper of the railroad unions, wrote, with more violence than intelligence, that "the majority of the leaders of the Communists are hired men of private detective agencies." [40] And at the 1923 AFL convention, William Dunne, a regularly elected delegate from Butte, Montana, was refused his seat on the ground that he was an acknowledged member of the Workers Party. (The motion to unseat him was made by Philip Murray, who years later, as president of the CIO, would find it possible to collaborate with Stalinist union leaders.) When Dunne was given a chance to be heard, he launched a withering and, in some respects, quite telling denunciation of the AFL leaders. But again no one from the Chicago Federation of Labor rose to defend him.*

For William Z. Foster the split with Fitzpatrick was a particularly bitter dose. Little in Foster's history suggests that he was the kind of man in whom spontaneous sentiments or passions would frequently overcome calculation, but for Fitzpatrick he undoubtedly felt a certain respect. Foster's ideal type was the radical labor leader, not the party functionary or the radical intellectual who tries to work his way into the union movement. He knew better than to call a man like Fitzpatrick a "political corpse." He realized that the Communists were now committing the very mistake against which he had always warned: they were antagonizing the most militant

* Realizing that he was doomed to expulsion, Dunne spoke without restraint and with a sharpness that must surely have struck home:

"I make a distinction between you, international officers, and the membership. . . . Drawing the same salaries as the employers, living in the same hotels, eating the same food, belonging to the same fraternal orders, hobnobbing with them in their clubs! What do you know or care about the eternal struggle of the wage-earners. . . .

"Sam Gompers, head and shoulders above 90 percent of you intellectually, also despises you, yet he is more to blame than any of you for the present pitiable situation in which American labor finds itself—forced to beg for favors. . . . Gompers understands you: he knows your prejudices and your ignorances, your preferences and your idiosyncracies, and he plays upon them as a violinist does upon his instrument. He wants no intelligent leadership and he sees that none develops." [41]

unionists. And he could see that once Fitzpatrick was alienated, his own ambition to become a national labor leader—the Gompers of the left—was hopelessly destroyed. Only after some prodding from the other party leaders did he finally declare war against Fitzpatrick, announcing at a tense AFL meeting in Chicago that henceforth his old friend and partner in militant unionism was an enemy. A month later, in November, 1923, he published an open letter excommunicating Fitzpatrick and adding, with a touch of wistfulness, an aside that revealed a frustrated ambition:

> It was my aim to propose, if the steel strike had been a success, the formation of a great organization committee . . . to sweep the masses into the unions. We were in a position to insist that such a committee be formed. Inevitably it must have been under our direction *in the usual combination with you as chairman and I as secretary.*[42] [emphasis added]

The note of vanity in this passage need hardly be stressed. What is perhaps more interesting is that in 1923 it was still possible for a party leader like Foster to speak publicly in these personal accents: the triumph of the machine was not yet complete.

6. Pepper might describe what had happened at Chicago as a triumphant marshaling of the "mighty masses"; but the reality, as some Communists began to see, was closer to a disaster. Triumph or disaster, it was clear that the Communists needed a new rationale for having abandoned their earlier view that if a labor party was to be more than a "political swindle" it would have to be based on the major trade unions. Pepper was exactly the man to contrive such a rationale, and under his bustling tutelage the party leaders worked up a document that in radical circles became known as the "August Thesis." Even in a party notorious for its intellectual and tactical instability, this was a remarkable innovation. Six months earlier the Communists had been pointing to the British Labor Party as the prototype of what they wanted in America; now it was scorned as a mere bureaucratic tool of the conservative union leaders. In the United States, by contrast, the labor party would come through the spontaneous pressures of the ranks who were supposed to be "permeated with communism." As

proof, the August Thesis cited the Chicago convention where the international unions had been conspicuous by their absence but the FFLP had nonetheless been formed. Because the FFLP had been created from "below," its "revolutionary spirit" was guaranteed. Thus the greatest single weakness of the Chicago convention was transformed, by a stroke of Pepper's pen, into its paramount virtue.

The militant rank and file, said the August Thesis, would create the *best* kind of labor party; but this was not to deny that there might be other kinds, ranging in political coloration from Northwestern agrarianism to Socialist reformism. Yet this was no cause for disturbance: let everyone on the left have his own labor party! And then all would compete for the support of the masses, a competition in which the Communists' FFLP would surely emerge the victor. Pepper seemed to be imagining a sort of left-wing tournament in which each jouster would appear with his own dummy shield labeled "labor party."

But suppose the Communist entry in this tournament—the FFLP—did not win the "mighty masses"? Again, no cause for alarm; for in that case the FFLP would be transformed into a strong party of American Communism. Either way the Communists could not lose: the FFLP as a labor party of millions or as a Communist vanguard of hundreds of thousands. Could anyone but Pepper have invented so comforting a fantasy?

It was a fantasy that aroused a certain amount of disquiet within the Workers Party, but no one ventured a fundamental critique. A bit later some reflections were added to the August Thesis on the role of "third" bourgeois parties, such as the LaFollette movement. These third parties might temporarily win a great deal of popular support, but ultimately their failure would become clear and their followers would shift to the best of all possible labor parties, the FFLP.[43]

Meanwhile, who was to staff and lead this genuine labor party? Not the middle-class progressives; nor the trade-union leaders; nor the CPPA; nor the Socialists. Not even Fitzpatrick. Everyone (that is, all the Communists) could see how "bankrupt" these people were. No political force but the Communists could create the true-blue labor party: hence they had to control it from the very beginning. The labor-party tactic that had originally been designed to break the Communists from their isolation now was transformed into a means for confirming them in their isolation. And thereby the party leadership also managed to justify every mistake and stupidity of the past few months. Only one trace of realism slipped past these theories: the genuine labor party (that is, the FFLP) which the Communists had blown into being might under certain circumstances be allowed to support third-party candidates.

In modified form, the August Thesis became the major issue at the third convention of the Workers Party, held in December, 1923-January, 1924. The Pepper-Ruthenberg "Politicals" supported this regression to sectarianism, while the Foster-Cannon "Industrials" uneasily and hesitantly criticized it. Everyone paid lip service to the "achievements" of the Federated Farmer Labor Party (this skeleton rattling in the common closet), but the Foster group allowed itself to release a certain bitterness over the way Fitzpatrick had been alienated.

As for the FFLP itself, six months of existence had demonstrated that, as usual, the Communists had captured almost no one but themselves. In New York the FFLP claimed the support of 60,000 unionists, but in the November, 1923 election for state assemblymen it had been able to muster the grand total of 1,500 votes in six districts. Nationally it began by claiming 616,000 adherents, but several months went by before it could even issue a paper (something that the tiniest left-wing group has almost always been able to do)—and that it managed only because the organ of the Chicago Communists was donated to it. By now the FFLP had become so discredited that Communists found it impossible to urge their local unions to affiliate with it. Trapped with this red elephant, the Pepper-Ruthenberg leadership faltered at the Workers Party convention and not even a letter from the Comintern could save it from being removed.*

A new Central Executive Committee was chosen by the Communists in which the Foster-Cannon group won a firm majority.

---

* In a letter dated December 7, 1923, the Executive Committee of the Comintern endorsed the formation of the FFLP and the split with Fitzpatrick, going so far as to describe the latter as a means for "creating the best bases for the united front policy. . . ."⁴⁴ Which indicates that if the Comintern leaders understood abstractly the need for an adaptation to American conditions, they certainly did not understand how this was to be done concretely.

But while the leadership changed, the policies remained essentially the same. The Foster-Cannon group had failed to raise or fight on the central question: could the Communists substitute themselves by *fiat* for the entire labor movement in the area of political action? The party having already embarked on a course that was symbolized by the FFLP and approved by the Comintern, the new Foster leadership lacked either the capacity or the courage to press for a sharp turn.

Still, it would be misleading to suggest that the "Industrials," once in control of the party, merely reverted *in toto* to Pepper's delusionary tactics. They were unable to break out of the erratic course that Pepper had charted, but they did try to use a certain discretion in following it. Instinctively Foster was more sensitive to the realities of American labor politics than were his factional opponents, and in his hesitant way—for he always kept a nervous eye cocked toward Moscow—he tried to undo some of the recent damage. One respect in which this came through concerned the party's attitude toward an "electoral alliance." At the WP convention most of the delegates, perhaps in reaction to Pepper, had refused to endorse the idea of giving support to third-party candidates. So acrimonious had this debate become that the convention decided to refer it "to the Communist International for decision." [45] In practice, however, the Foster leadership found that the question could not be postponed, and soon the party was functioning as if support for candidates like LaFollette were sanctioned. To avoid the total isolation that now threatened the Communists, Foster and his group were ready to compromise with labor leaders, third-party groups, and Farmer Laborites.

As a showpiece of sorts, but mainly to save face, the Federated Farmer Labor Party was allowed to linger on. But the Communists now realized they would have to turn elsewhere if they were to achieve any living relationship with the Farmer-Labor movements erupting in certain parts of the country. The natural place to turn was toward the Northwest, where the farmers remained discontented, the unions kept displaying their aggressiveness, LaFollette's political following was very large, and the Nonpartisan League, though in decline, still served as an outlet for agrarian radicalism. All Communist eyes now turned to Minnesota.

7. In 1923 the Minnesota Farmer-Labor Party was the most powerful movement of its kind in the United States. It had recently elected Henrik Shipstead to the U.S. Senate by an 80,000 plurality and had sent another successful candidate to the House of Representatives. Perhaps because of these victories, the various political tendencies within the Farmer-Labor Party began to cast suspicious glances at one another. Political leaders like Shipstead were contented with a loose electoral machine that could be oiled up once a year, while many trade unionists wanted an insurgent party committed to a grass-roots American radicalism, organized on a local level and active on a day-to-day basis. William Mahoney, the vigorous leader of these radical unionists, had first received his political training in the Socialist Party, had then plunged into the St. Paul unions, and now occupied a role in Minnesota similar to that of Fitzpatrick in Chicago.

It all looked promising for the Communists. Here was a left-wing party that rested upon firm popular support; that had rebuffed the CPPA proposal for a retreat to non-partisan work in the old parties; that was constantly being stirred up by a group of tough and indigenous unionists who campaigned for a new political alignment and were ready to do so together with the Communists. And under Clarence Hathaway's leadership, the local Communists, some of whom had rooted themselves in the unions, were inclined to co-operate with Mahoney.

Unfortunately for them, their inclinations counted for very little. The New York leadership of the Workers Party, which then meant Pepper and Ruthenberg, was determined to "differentiate" the American Communists not merely from all possible opponents but from every conceivable friend. Pepper had first led the comrades to the promised land of farmer-laborism, but under his guidance it was turning into a desert of political isolation. (As a political alchemist, Pepper was gifted at turning gold into dust.) Had the Minnesota Communists been able to work on their own, they might have registered modest achievements; but masterminded as they were by emissaries from Ruthenberg and Pepper, their task was almost hopeless.*

* Here is a typical example. The Communist delegates to a conference of Minnesota Farmer-Laborites, held in the fall of 1923, proposed that it

Meanwhile, there was every reason for expecting that the 1924 national election would be one of the most remarkable in the nation's history. The Harding administration, badly soiled by the Teapot Dome scandals, was distasteful to almost everyone in the labor movement. The Democrats were being subjected to strong conservative pressures. For the leaders of the Conference for Progressive Political Action—still, it should be remembered, the most important progressive tendency within the labor movement— the remaining hope was William McAdoo, who as a member of Woodrow Wilson's war-time cabinet had helped the railroad unions during the war. But when McAdoo was also splattered by the Teapot Dome scandal and his chances for the Democratic nomination thereby lessened, a large part of the CPPA began turning toward Senator Robert LaFollette, the traditional spokesman for American progressivism. LaFollette, however, stood little chance of winning the Republican nomination—and as a result the railroad unions dominating the CPPA found themselves in a quandary. They hesitated to form a new party yet felt there was hardly an alternative. An editorial in *Labor* noted: "It may be that in 1924 both old parties will select reactionaries. . . . *In that event a great new party will be organized overnight*" [47] (emphasis in original). Any American who, for whatever reasons, wanted a new political movement on the national scene now had cause for optimism and hope.

LaFollette's influence in the Northwest was so enormous and his moral standing throughout the country so high that he alone could serve as the candidate of a major new party. Not only did

---

affiliate with the Federated Farmer Labor Party, by now universally recognized as a feeble Communist front. They did this with a notable lack of enthusiasm, and only after much prodding from Harry Wicks, the commissar sent by the Workers Party national office.

Mahoney was willing to cooperate with Hathaway, but not to become his captive. The farmer delegates, for all their militancy, would not come into the FFLP. When the debate grew tense, most of the local Communists (experienced unionists and supporters of Foster's "Industrial" faction) were inclined toward a strategic retreat; but Wicks kept peppering them with the insistence that "they split the goddamned thing wide open." [46] Having learned something from the Chicago events, the Minnesota Communists refused to split the goddamned thing wide open. As a result Mahoney continued to work with them and brushed aside Fitzpatrick's advice to have nothing to do with Communists: he would have to go through his own experience before learning the lesson Fitzpatrick had.

the Communists recognize this fact; for the moment they even accepted it. They realized that both the anti-Communist farm organizations and the non-Communist elements in the Farmer-Labor parties which they themselves had organized were under LaFollette's spell. The new Farmer-Labor Party in South Dakota, though friendly to the Communists, was strongly in favor of LaFollette. The Progressive Party of Nebraska, though it had gone so far as to endorse the FFLP under Communist prodding, was equally committed to LaFollette. Many Minnesota Farmer-Laborites, though working with the Communists, looked upon LaFollette as the indispensable man. To attack LaFollette head-on meant immediate and total isolation in the left and progressive circles of the Midwest. With these facts in mind Pepper wrote:

> We can't assume the responsibility for LaFollette's Republican past, his present hesitations and his petty-bourgeois program. . . . But if you [Farmer-Laborites] nominate him nevertheless, we do not want to scab on the action of the workers and exploited farmers; we will vote for him. . . .[48]

Such a relatively sensible explanation could not content Pepper; he soon unfurled a fabulous new theory to justify his support of LaFollette:

> The coming third revolution will not be a proletarian revolution. It will be a revolution of well-to-do and exploited farmers, small businessmen and workers. This revolution . . . will come through rebellion within the old parties, through third parties, farmer-labor parties. . . . In its ideology it will have elements of Jeffersonianism, Danish cooperatives, Ku Klux Klan and Bolshevism. The proletariat *as a class* will not play an independent role in this revolution. . . . After the victory of this LaFollette revolution, there will begin the *independent* role of the workers . . . — the period of the *fourth* American revolution.* [49]

* Those familiar with the complexities of Communist doctrine will recognize in Pepper's "third revolution" a distorted echo of Lenin's theory, advanced during the early part of this century, that in Czarist Russia the workers could not achieve power in their own right but had to lead a bourgeois revolution. Lenin had proposed this because of his conviction that the Russian bourgeoisie was too weak and timid to brush aside the monarchy—hardly a case analogous to America in 1923.

In any case, when a call went out for a convention of Farmer-Labor groups in St. Paul just before the nominating conventions of the major parties, the Communists again swung into action, prepared to repeat both their whirlwind blitz and their spectacular errors of Chicago. The St. Paul meeting would nominate LaFollette as a Farmer-Labor candidate, the "third revolution" would begin—and all under the auspices of the Workers Party! But in trying to realize these heady ambitions, the Workers Party had to face at least four impediments: the CPPA, LaFollette, the Farmer-Laborites and, not least of all, the Comintern. Any two of these could have blocked it completely. But the four together . . .

The CPPA, as it prepared itself for the role of mainstay in the LaFollette campaign, realized that more than trade-union support would be necessary for a candidate traditionally associated with trust busting and the defense of the small farmers. Its leaders therefore began to make friendly gestures toward the Minnesota Farmer-Laborites, first to achieve an alliance with the farmers' organizations during the campaign and second to drive a wedge between Mahoney and the Communists.

Mahoney was in a difficult spot. The CPPA, Senator Shipstead, LaFollette himself were all urging him to postpone the St. Paul Farmer-Labor convention until after the two major parties had met and chosen their candidates. Clearly it would be embarrassing for LaFollette if he were nominated at St. Paul before having tried to gain the Republican nomination. But for the Communists May 30, the date originally chosen for the St. Paul meeting, became a "sacred" day, since to meet before the two major parties was symbolic, they argued, of the political break that was to be proclaimed from "bourgeois politics." Mahoney pleaded with the Communists not to rule out cooperation with the CPPA; the Communists replied that the CPPA had already ruled out cooperation with them. Finally, a compromise date, June 17, was set—one that would occur after the Republican but before the Democratic convention.

Pressured from all sides, Mahoney grew increasingly irritable. It became clear to him that he was now being given the "Fitzpatrick treatment" with a vengeance. In the spring, under instructions from the Workers Party national office, the Minnesota Communists had committed the folly of entering the Farmer-Labor primaries with a

slate of candidates instructed by Ruthenberg to "publicly announce
themselves as Communists. . . . They must publicly support the
full Communist program, stating . . . that they stand for a proletarian revolution, the establishment of a Soviet government, and the
Dictatorship of the Proletariat." [50] Ruthenberg had issued these
instructions because he believed the Communists had to function
as a clearly "differentiated" vanguard within the farmer-labor movements; but if he had been deliberately trying to help those who
wanted to root the Communists out of these movements he could
not have devised a better scheme. When these instructions arrived,
the Minnesota Communists groaned but, like good Communists,
obeyed. They entered a large slate in the primaries and prepared
to brace themselves for Mahoney's fury.

As the St. Paul convention drew nearer and plans were laid for
nominating LaFollette on the Farmer-Labor ticket, the Communists
became increasingly reckless—there was something about these large
conferences, perhaps some suggestion of a sudden overwhelming
triumph, that went completely to their heads. Fifty thousand in-
vitations went out for the St. Paul meeting; enormous publicity was
received in the papers; the Communist managers began to think
they might really snare LaFollette for their Farmer-Labor maneuver.
But they had made a fatal mistake. LaFollette was neither a
Mahoney nor a Fitzpatrick; he had not worked with them in the
trade unions or admired their courage in strikes, he felt no interest
in cooperating with them to build a strong labor political movement,
he thought of them only as disrupters threatening to strangle him
in their embrace. And from his point of view he was right. To
have tolerated support of the Communists by accepting the St. Paul
nomination would have meant sudden political death.

LaFollette moved fast. Shortly before the St. Paul meeting, he
made public a letter he had recently written urging that "all Progressives should refuse to participate in any movement which makes
common cause with any Communist organization." [51] With one
press release LaFollette undercut the grandiose hopes the Communists had had for the St. Paul convention. (Hathaway had pre-
dicted that between five and ten thousand people would attend.)
Yet by persuading most of the legitimate delegates to stay home,
LaFollette also insured that the St. Paul convention, no longer of

much importance, would be completely controlled by the Communists.

Mahoney now found himself in an impossible position, trapped between his increasing irritation over Communist tactics and his belief that they should not be quarantined in the labor movement. A single issue of his *Minnesota Union Advocate* graphically displayed the dilemma of his group: one article said that "the charge that the Communists will dominate the convention is a gross misrepresentation," while an editorial complained that "the thing that causes most irritation and distrust is the existence of a small group carrying on their intrigues and plots to control. . . . We are inclined to think that the attitude and activity of the Communists will eventually make their organized presence intolerable. . . ."[52]

Even if the CPPA, LaFollette, and the Farmer-Laborites had not, in effect, cooperated to spike the Communist plans, everything would have come to nought for a reason that had nothing to do with American politics at all: the Comintern.

At a meeting of the Comintern Executive Committee in May, the problem of the Communist attitude toward the LaFollette campaign was on the agenda. Pleading as supplicants were representatives of three American factions: Pepper for the "Politicals," Foster for the "Industrials," and Moissaye Olgin for a small group in the Workers Party that was headed by Ludwig Lore. The first two factions agreed on the necessity for endorsing LaFollette, but Foster complained that under Pepper's guidance the Workers Party was needlessly antagonizing and isolating itself from the more radical unionists. The Lore-Olgin group tended to reject the concept of a third-party alliance or the possibility of voting for LaFollette. Lore, to whose symptomatic fate we shall return in a later chapter, was one of the few genuinely independent American Communists, though on this particular matter he took a most dogmatic view, which at the meeting of the Comintern Executive Committee found support from Trotsky.

At this point the struggle between Trotsky and the *troika* or trio (Stalin, Zinoviev, Kamenev) was beginning to flare up in Russia. By 1924 world capitalism had clearly reestablished its authority throughout most of the world; hopes for immediate revolution were dim; the Comintern leadership had to find a way of adjusting itself to new and difficult conditions. Floundering about, it began to shift its focus of attention from the working class to the peasantry and ascribed to the latter an autonomous revolutionary impulse that was novel in Communist doctrine. The activities of Pepper in the United States, to the extent that they did not follow from personal megalomania, could be explained as part of this new turn toward the peasants—who, in America, were quaintly identified with the Midwestern small and tenant farmers. But while Trotsky's rejection of this new "peasant look" could easily be justified in terms of traditional Marxist experience, the opposition that both he and the Lore-Olgin group expressed to supporting LaFollette disregarded the specific conditions of American life that made both this country and its working class truly "exceptional." They failed to see that the LaFollette movement, far from being confined to farmers, was an expression of political discontent that touched both the labor movement and the middle class. Indeed, it would be the CPPA, not the farmers' organizations, that would provide the main organizational backbone for LaFollette's campaign.

Trotsky won his point. The Stalinists in control of the Comintern were ready to grant him this concession, since only the American party, not a very important one, was involved, and since, in withdrawing permission to endorse LaFollette, they also were shedding responsibility for the errors, stupidities, and absurdities that had characterized Pepper's third-party adventures.

A dejected Foster beat his retreat from Moscow. He bore with him instructions that at the St. Paul convention, originally called to push LaFollette, the Communists were to repudiate LaFollette— *but not before!* [53] The instructions were to be held secret, since it was clear that if the Communists denounced LaFollette before June 17 no one but Communists would trouble to come to St. Paul. (Foster's only satisfaction, as he brought these grim directives back to America, was that the Comintern had agreed to keep Pepper in Moscow.) It must have been a strange sensation—it was also a preliminary training in the methods of Stalinism—for the leading Communists to continue functioning as if nothing had changed; though not nearly so strange as the surprise of the rank-and-file Communists who came to St. Paul prepared to cheer for LaFollette and stayed to hiss and hoot at each mention of his name.

On June 17, 542 delegates from 29 states converged on St. Paul, a frail shadow of the promised thousands. Among the delegates were the entire corps of Workers Party leaders: Bedacht, Foster, Browder, Ballam, Ruthenberg, Lore, Poyntz, Anita Whitney, Benjamin Gitlow. The Lithuanians were not quite as prominent as they had been in Chicago, but a whole new array of curious "mass organizations" had sprung up: the Red Eye Farmers Club, the Illinois Self-Advancement Club, the Woman's Shelley Club, the People's Voice Culture Club, each with its pliant delegate. There also came a smattering of non-Communists and native radicals whose presence must have inflamed the frustrated WP leaders by giving them a slight taste of what they had hoped to bite off before the LaFollette denunciation and the Comintern prohibition. There was Tom Ayres, an old South Dakota cattle rancher who had long been active in the Farmers' Nonpartisan League; there was Alice Daly, who had been fired as a schoolteacher for speaking her heretical mind and had then polled 50,000 votes, just a few short of victory, as Farmer-Labor candidate for governor of South Dakota; there was John C. Kennedy, a former Chicago Socialist alderman who now led the Washington Farmer-Labor movement. And others: "Dad" Walker of the North Dakota Farmer-Labor Party, the Reverend Mr. Beebe of the Nebraska Progressive Party, the legitimate Farmer-Laborites of Minnesota.[54] Before the convention ended, as the Communists must have known, almost all of these delegates would be alienated by the sudden switch against LaFollette. But instructions were instructions.

When the moment arrived for presidential nominations, Benjamin Gitlow, an ardent Pepperite, led off with a prolonged and bilious denunciation of LaFollette. Many rank-and-file Communists must have gasped even while dutifully applauding Gitlow; the genuine Farmer-Labor people were stunned. To keep the latter from bolting immediately, the Communists offered a "concession": they would agree to nominate LaFollette if he endorsed the St. Paul convention and accepted its control over his campaign financing.

Knowing that LaFollette would no more accept such terms than Coolidge would agree to run on the Communist ticket, the convention proceeded to nominate Duncan Macdonald, former leader of the Illinois miners, for President and William Bouck, head of the

Western Progressive Miners, for Vice-President. It was agreed that if LaFollette did accept the convention terms, its slate would be withdrawn and he would become its candidate. A National Committee was elected on which William Mahoney refused a post and the Communists took an absolute majority, one reason being that there were so few others willing to serve.

A few weeks later, at a convention called by the CPPA, LaFollette was nominated for the presidency as an independent candidate. The isolation of the Communists was now complete: they had cut themselves off from the progressive unions, from the Farmer-Labor movement, and from the political structure set up for the LaFollette campaign.

8. Naturally, this reversal of fortunes kindled new tensions and disputes within the party, but before the Communists could turn upon one another they had to go through the motions of participating in the elections. Whatever their previous views of the LaFollette episode, almost all of them now felt a common need to "do a job" on the Wisconsin progressive that would presumably serve a political function but, perhaps more important, would release some of their pent-up frustration. In Jay Lovestone, only yesterday the most ardent spokesman for the LaFollette boom within the party, the right man was found for this assignment. In a pamphlet on LaFollette that is surely one of the intellectual atrocities of early American Communism, Lovestone "proved" through innuendo, guilt by association, and pure distortion that LaFollette was barely distinguishable from Coolidge or some cheap rural demagogue. The comrades felt better, and no one else paid much attention.

There remained, however, the matter of the campaign. Macdonald and Bouck, who had been persuaded to stand as candidates, were bewildered from the outset as to what they were supposed to do, or with whom they were to do it. On July 2 they opened what was to be one of the briefest and oddest political campaigns in all American history. They spoke at a meeting arranged by the Chicago Communists, a sort of "Potemkin village" rally that was supposed to bring together the workers, and perhaps the peasants, of Chicago but attracted no one except a few hundred faithful party folk who cheered "their" candidates with an easygoing cynicism.

Just one week later, much to the relief of the candidates themselves, who were beginning to realize that they had been badly duped, the Communists decided to drop the whole "Farmer-Labor campaign" they had but yesterday manufactured. A hastily arranged conference of Communist leaders, meeting on July 8-9, agreed to withdraw the Macdonald-Bouck slate and to run candidates openly under the Workers Party label: Foster for President and Gitlow for Vice-President.[55] Whatever remnant could be gathered of the Farmer-Labor National Committee elected at St. Paul now agreed to abandoning its campaign and obligingly endorsed Foster and Gitlow. With this political whimper ended John Pepper's great plan to take over the American Farmer-Labor movement.

Characteristically, the Communists were soon officially asserting that "the campaign for a Farmer Labor Party was a correct estimation of the situation in the United States." [56] Exactly how correct the Communist estimation had been was shown two weeks later when the ghost of the old Federated Farmer Labor Party was put to rest, and the unexpired subscriptions to its paper were turned over to the *Daily Worker*. The Communists who had been engaged in the Farmer-Labor maneuvers felt a certain relief; they could now appear in their own right, without those wearying deceptions that ended by deceiving no one; and as one of them put it, they could also drop the pretense of friendliness with the "LaFollette bucolics." [57]

Foster and Gitlow, the Workers Party candidates, managed to get on the ballot in only thirteen states. A vigorous campaigner, Foster traveled 18,000 miles and made LaFollette the main butt of his attacks, describing the progressive movement as "the most dangerous enemy of the toiling masses of America today." [58] An observer untrained in the intricacies of Communist dialectics might have detected an odor of sour grapes.*

---

* Though the Communist campaign was of no importance in its own right, there occurred toward its end a curious incident that goes far toward revealing the inner quality of early American Communism. Because the Comintern had asked for a prediction of the likely Communist vote, a faction dispute broke out on the number of votes Foster and Gitlow could *expect*. Lovestone, who had opposed dropping the Macdonald-Bouck slate, wished to send a pessimistic cable predicting 20,000 votes; the Foster-Cannon group, which at the moment controlled the party, wired that the candidates would receive 100,000. When the vote was finally tallied, it came to 33,316—a figure that failed to give either group much satisfaction. But under direction

Once it became known that LaFollette had received slightly less than five million votes—a quite impressive number if seen in terms of preparing the foundation for a new party, but disappointing to those who expected more immediate victories—the whole third-party movement began to wither away. The AFL, which for the first time in its history had dropped the non-partisan tactic in order to support LaFollette, fell back into its conservative mold; the CPPA decided to confine itself to working within the established parties; and except in Minnesota the local Farmer-Labor parties vegetated or collapsed.

The American Communists, with both time and problems on their hands, now devoted themselves to a series of factional post-mortems in which everything from Pepper's original theories to the treatment of Fitzpatrick to the 1924 campaign itself was probed and dissected. In a public statement issued in the name of the Workers Party, the Foster-Cannon majority in effect reversed the stand of American Communism *vis-à-vis* the labor party movement. The failure of the LaFollette campaign, read this statement, "completely eliminated the immediate possibility for the growth of a mass farmer labor party. . . . Our chief task in the immediate future is not the building of such a farmer labor party but the strengthening and developing of the Workers Party itself as the practical leader of the masses. . . ." [60]

The Foster-Cannon and Ruthenberg-Lovestone factions lined up around two slogans—"Build the Workers Party" *vs.* "For a Class Farmer Labor Party"—but by 1925 neither of these meant very much. All the hopes and possibilities of the past few years had quickly vanished as the country settled into a soft and conservative prosperity.

A serious inquiry as to the recent political behavior of the American Communists would certainly now have been in order, and no one needed to engage in such an inquiry more than the Communists themselves. Begun so grandiloquently, the whole venture into Farmer-Labor politics—perhaps the first sustained effort by the Communists to penetrate American life—had turned into a fiasco.

from the Foster-Cannon group, the party immediately wired Moscow charging fraud and "citing incidents in which votes were stolen from us." [59] Incidents there no doubt were, but surely not 70,000 of them!

But an inquiry of this sort would have required a dispassionateness, a freedom from transient factional interests, and, above all, a readiness to question primary assumptions that only a very few Communists could summon.

Why had they made so many palpable and even outrageous errors? First, because they had been utterly inexperienced in American politics, and indeed in any politics whatever, except the peculiar forms of doctrinal disputation and clique maneuver that took place within the movement. The expectations they had brought to the American Farmer-Labor milieu, flowing from a political tradition so utterly at variance with the tradition of the people whom they meant to win over, constantly tempted them to raise impediments in their own path that were even greater than those they would have found there in any case. For another thing, the intervention of factional needs—to say nothing of the need almost all American Communists felt to conform to the wishes of the Comintern—had repeatedly proved disastrous in concrete political situations. Groups of local Communists, as in Minnesota, could probably have done effective work if they had been allowed a certain freedom for self-education and room for flexibility. For still another thing, the Communists were too rigidly bound by their ideological preconceptions; they were unable to gauge the local situation in America with anything like the necessary exactness and delicacy; they worked upon the assumptions they wanted to believe rather than those required by what actually was happening in the country. With visions of revolutionary apocalypse always before them, they could not understand the possibility or relevance of long-range parliamentary politics—and what else could the Farmer-Labor movement be but long-range parliamentary politics? They were always politicians in a hurry, convinced that if only the properly clever maneuver or the properly correct slogan could be found they would suddenly sweep to the leadership of a great mass movement. And finally, though far from least important, they simply lacked good faith in their dealings with other people. The indigenous radicals of the Farmer-Labor movement they looked upon mainly as material to be manipulated and exploited; convinced of their own political superiority, they were never really willing to *listen* to anyone outside their own ranks; it was always they, the vanguard, who would work upon everyone else, never other people and opinions that might shape or influence them.

Certain important facts had been demonstrated during the past two or three years. It had been shown that the Communists were skillful at corralling delegates at heterogeneous Farmer-Labor conventions, skillful at winning publicity from a sensation-hungry press, skillful at capturing organizations in which they formed only a small minority. In situations such as the one in Minnesota, where the Farmer-Labor movement reflected genuine mass sentiments, a few dozen Communists could manage this movement almost without check. The art of manipulation by which a small, disciplined, and quick-moving group can control larger and more sluggish political bodies—this art at which the Communists would later become the supreme masters of our time—here received one of its first American applications.

Still, in saying this a certain sense of historical limitation is necessary. The workings of the small Communist group in 1922-24 were not nearly so efficient or deadly as they would be ten to fifteen years later. The Communists had not yet learned how to keep themselves—or manage from—behind the scenes. In their assumption that if only they could capture a Farmer-Labor convention they would really inherit a mass movement, there was a touch of naïveté, even innocence, that would be burned out by the later and more expert tutors of Stalinism. The Communists seemed unable to learn that the tactic of the quick public raid had a way of being self-defeating, even of coming to nothing more than the capture of themselves. In all of its relations with the Farmer-Labor movement, the Workers Party, especially during those intervals when Pepper moved as master behind the scenes, displayed a certain *opéra bouffe* character which, if not exactly ingratiating, was certainly less machine-like, less sinister and effective than the later work of Communists in the unions and the front organizations. At this stage there is still to be observed a certain element of fantasy, even childishness, in the behavior of the American Communists. It would all be eradicated in a few years—but not before one last factional explosion.

Chapter IV. The Party Becomes Stalinized

1. On March 2, 1927, Charles E. Ruthenberg, general secretary of the American Communist Party, died. Even as his body lay in state in Chicago, an intense struggle for the succession was being waged among the leaders of the party. Ruthenberg's factional associates feared that his death might mark the end of their ascendancy; the Fosterites saw new opportunities. Observing the appearance of mourning, the chiefs of both factions rushed to Chicago to stand guard at the bier and—no less important—to contend for preferment. While a stream of genuinely moved party members slowly passed by the coffin, the factions fought it out in the back rooms. Even funeral arrangements became a cause for dispute. Foster and his followers sought to take over the arrangements, but Jay Lovestone, the new leader of the Ruthenberg caucus, rallied his forces to repel this assault. Would the Fosterites or Lovestoneites win a majority of the pallbearers? Finally the inevitable compromise was adopted: there would be equality of pallbearers. And so Charles E. Ruthenberg was carried to his eternal rest by three comrades from each group. Factional parity even unto death!

Yet the wily Lovestone held a trump card. Under his prompting, Anna David, who had been Ruthenberg's sweetheart, tearfully told the party of the leader's dying words: "Tell the comrades to close the ranks and build the party." At a Lovestone caucus meeting she was still more specific, announcing that it had been Ruthenberg's last wish that Lovestone succeed him as general secretary. The Lovestoneites wanted more parity than others.

This ghoulish incident symbolizes the condition of American Communism during the middle and late twenties. Other Comintern parties were also torn by factional strife, but in few of them had it assumed such ludicrous forms. Partly because the American party had been so unsuccessful in establishing any real rapport with the masses of American workers, it had for years turned its best energies inward. Factional struggle absorbed greater and greater portions of the time and energy of the leading cadres. If prestige could not be gained by political activity in the world at large, it might be won by establishing ascendancy over the ranks of the faithful. The pettiness, malice, and dishonesty which accompanied the factional contests of the late twenties cannot be explained solely in terms of the ideological issues at stake. The prevailing atmosphere of suspicion and deceit was largely the result of a fight for personal prestige among a small group of bitter, disappointed, and resentful men to whom leadership of the party—that is, preferment by Moscow—had become the supreme goal and almost the only source of satisfactions. So absorbed were the Communists in their internal feuds that the very desire to influence the outer world had begun to atrophy: the faction struggle replaced the class struggle.

Not that these feuds were devoid of political content. Each group had a distinct programmatic orientation, for ideology retained its uses even after it had lost much of its meaning. It had become the practice of Communists everywhere to clothe contests for power in cloaks of many ideological colors; yet in Russia, as in most Communist parties, theoretical issues had genuine relevance to political life. Whether the Chinese Communists should support the Kuomintang, whether the French Communists should form united fronts with the Socialists, whether the Communists in eastern Europe should cooperate with nationalist peasant groups—these were issues that had an immediate bearing on the activities and sometimes the fate of a great many people. But in the America of the midtwenties such questions were debated in a political vacuum where they degenerated into casuistic exercises or dialectical displays; and frequently the debates served merely as pretexts for faction raids. Ideas had a way of becoming weapons in the struggle for control, and the less there was to control the more ferocious became the struggle to control it.

Historians have often and justly been chided for treating ideological differences as mere expressions of unprincipled power struggles. But in regard to the American Communists such a procedure, though not finally adequate, can yield a sizable measure of truth. Any historian who took the ideological dross of the party "theoreticians" at face value could never hope to understand the CPUSA. When ideologies are formulated to defend a set of special interests, it is more illuminating to examine the strategies of the disputants than to probe the theoretical content of their argument. Yet ideologies are never *merely* weapons in the service of special interests; they always have some meaning in their own right and must always be granted the provisional privilege of being discussed autonomously.

Though the inner life of American Communism from 1924 to 1929 was particularly ugly and unprincipled, one should remember that at the very same time there was reaching its climax the fateful dispute between Trotsky and Stalin, a dispute that involved basic problems of politics and reflected a fundamental divergence of values. With whatever distortions and whatever alloy of power interest, the struggles among the Russian Bolshevik leaders raised matters of principle within the limits—and soon beyond the limits —of their common ideology. These disputes had their impact on the American Communists, but not, as one might reasonably expect, in the form of serious discussion and debate. The issues between Trotsky and Stalin, it should be stressed, were never presented in sober terms to the American comrades; but the objective significance of Stalin's triumph was vividly reflected in the American party. What in Russia had an element of high tragic action assumed in America the quality of cheap melodrama.

2. In a speech before the Third Congress of the Comintern (1921), Lenin succinctly expressed the assumption that had been common to all the leaders of the Bolshevik Revolution:

> It was clear to us that without aid from the international world revolution, a victory of the proletarian revolution is impossible. Even prior to the [Bolshevik] revolution, as well as after it, we thought that the revolution would also occur either immediately or at least very soon in other backward countries and in the more highly developed capitalist countries. Otherwise we would perish.[1]

Russia, Lenin kept insisting, was a backward peasant land that lacked technology, experience, and, above all, the accumulated culture required for surpassing the achievements of the advanced capitalist nations. The fate of the Russian Revolution consequently depended on the ability of the Communist movement abroad to achieve power in at least one major advanced country (it was Germany that Lenin usually had in mind), so that assistance could come for backward Russia. With the defeat of the 1919-21 revolutions in the West, there were already many signs that Lenin's prophecy—"otherwise we perish"—would be realized. But realized in ways that neither Lenin nor Trotsky had foreseen.

The Communist Party of Russia, which had proclaimed itself the vanguard of the world revolution, now remained in power after the world revolution had waned. It found that it could preserve itself as a beleaguered state within the limits of a shrunken Russia; but in doing so it underwent extreme transformations in political ideology, social character, and moral quality. In a country where all the means of production are owned by the state, and the state is totally in the grip of the only legal party, major changes in the nature of the party are equivalent to—indeed, can constitute—a social revolution involving new relations between rulers and ruled.

Both the Russian economy and the Russian people had been exhausted by years of suffering, hunger, civil war. The harsh policies of war Communism had brought military victory over the White armies, but had left the nation gasping from weariness and privation. To prevent economic collapse or social explosion, Lenin had instituted the New Economic Policy (NEP), which involved major concessions to an already hostile peasantry; but this in turn helped bring into existence and legitimate a whole new conservative stratum of "rich" and middle peasants in the countryside. When the mass of soldiers, demobilized after the civil war, came back drained of their patriotic or revolutionary fervor, the conservative tendencies within the villages were still further reinforced.

Similar tendencies were at work in the cities. The workers were sapped of their social strength, some of them having been killed in the civil war, others having lapsed into a sullen weariness, and still others having become disillusioned with the regime. Ex-officers trying to transfer wartime habits to the social life of the nation and seeking careers in the party or the economic institutions; thousands of former Czarist officials whom the Bolshevik government, because it lacked trained personnel, was forced to employ in important posts; former leaders and members of opposition parties who, as they gave up hope of displacing the Bolshevik regime, decided to make a private truce with it—all these, whether consciously or not, helped sap the revolutionary *élan* of early Bolshevism. Many of the most devoted Bolsheviks had died in the civil war; others had been worn out by years of strain; and still others, men lacking the iron will of Lenin, displayed the characteristics of officials everywhere, with vested interests of their own that set them into increasing opposition to the workers in whose name they ruled and spoke. Apart from massive economic help, what the country needed most was the ventilation of new ideas and controversy, a gust of freedom to bring new life and energy; but after 1921 the Bolsheviks refused to allow any party but their own to function legally and thus contributed heavily to their own degeneration, not least of all by lending formal sanction to the idea of a one-party regime. As a defender of the Bolshevik Revolution has admitted:

> What was undertaken as a defensive measure imposed by the not very normal circumstances of the civil war [i.e., the outlawing of all non-Bolshevik parties] became the permanent rule when peace was established, and undoubtedly contributed to the gradual decay of workers' democracy in the country.[2]

Ruling as a minority dictatorship, though at times with mass support, the Bolshevik regime had planted the seeds of counter-revolution at the very moment the revolution triumphed. Each repressive step taken by the dictatorship further undermined and violated the ideological claims to which so many of its supporters were devoted, and helped create within itself a cancerous growth flourishing upon crisis, cynicism, deprivation, and repression.

A new social stratum—but it too had appeared, as it were, the morning after the revolution—now began to consolidate itself: the party-state bureaucracy, narrow in outlook, provincial and boorish in tone, primitive in culture, committed essentially to a Russian nationalist perspective, and instinctively authoritarian in method. It looked upon the workers as material to be shaped and prodded, upon the intellectuals as propagandists to be exploited and supervised, upon the international Communist movement as a not very important ally to be used and chained, and upon Marxist ideology as a crude process for rationalizing its new needs and aspirations.

To speak of a party-state bureaucracy in a country where industry had been nationalized means, it should be remembered, to speak of a new ruling group which parasitically grasped every institution of Russian life: not merely the government but also the party, not merely the party but also the unions, not merely the unions but also the industries, the schools, the cultural establishments, the press, the cooperatives—indeed, every organism of social life. That many members of this new party-state bureaucracy were unaware of the significance of this process seems obvious; it was, in many respects, a historical novelty, and as a result consciousness lagged behind activity even more than it usually does.

What was the nature of this new ruling stratum? Trotsky, whose criticisms were so frequently sharp and pointed, made the mistake of supposing that, in alliance with the new conservative elements in the countryside (whose interests he thought were reflected in the "Right Communist" group led by Bukharin), the bureaucracy might constitute a nucleus for the restoration of private capitalism. Actually, because it was slowly gathering into its hands control of the party-state, which also meant control over the entire socio-economic life of the nation, this new ruling group had every interest in preventing a return to private capitalism, since that would have meant a fundamental challenge to its authority. The new bureaucracy appropriated power *within* the framework of the nationalized economy, preserving its forms while changing the social relations that determined the actual distribution of power and quality of life; it destroyed every element of the "workers democracy" that had existed under Lenin while accentuating the worst features of his rule; yet none of this had anything to do with a return to private property. Stalinism—the political label of the socio-economic trend we have been describing—was a counter-revolution within the limits of a nationalized economy.

Criticism of this bureaucratic tendency kept rising both within and without the Bolshevik Party. Various opposition groups struggled to express themselves in the party between 1921 and 1923, that is, before Trotsky became the main anti-Stalinist spokesman and, indeed, without his sorely needed help. All the issues that Trotsky raised in his struggle against Stalinism—problems of revolutionary strategy abroad, of economic development at home, and of

democracy within the party—were important, both for the mid-
twenties and for later years; but, at least in retrospect, it seems clear
that the central significance of *all* the opposition groups, both Trotskyist and non-Trotskyist, was as efforts to stop or slow the powerful
trend toward authoritarianism in both the party and the state. It
was for this reason that Trotsky's insistence upon keeping his struggle within the confines of the Bolshevik Party and his refusal to
call for the legalization of all democratic parties so fatally limited the
value and effectiveness of the movement he led.

The "conservatism" that arose in Russia was not primarily a
matter of shifting toward more discreet or cautious policies within
either the Communist International or the domestic economy. It
was a question of social motivation and perspective. It was an
evolution from the politics of internationalism to the politics of nationalism, from the politics of the world revolution to the politics of
preserving the Russian state at all costs. Stalin's theory of "socialism
in one country" was the major ideological expression of this new
Russian nationalism, a justification for present and future subordina-
tion of the interests of the national Communist parties to the Russian state bureaucracy. Shortly after the Fifth Comintern Congress
(1924) there was no longer any such curio as an "autonomous"
Communist Party, even to the limited extent that any of them ever
had been autonomous. All were subordinated to the Comintern,
and the Comintern to the Russian party. And within the Russian
party there had already been organized by Stalin, Zinoviev, and
Kamenev a secret "central committee" that controlled the life of the
party. In order to achieve "socialism in one country," which immediately meant to guarantee its continued authority, this leadership had
to subject both the Russian party and all the parties of the Comintern to its monolithic will.*

At the Fifth Comintern Congress, under the cry of "Bolshevization," the Stalinist leadership marshaled its forces to crush all those
Communist tendencies and individuals who looked either question-

* We would not pretend that the above few pages represent anything
more than the merest background sketch of a highly complex social development. Additional material on this theme will be found in the final chapter,
but the reader wishing a full treatment is advised to turn to the enormous
literature available on this topic.

ingly or with alarm at what had recently been happening in Russia. Stripped of all pretenses, the slogan meant that all parties were to adopt the views demanded by the Russian leadership. Dissidents were smashed; the reign of unanimity was begun.

For the United States the Fifth Comintern Congress gave its assurance that "the upward economic movement in America has undoubtedly reached its end—the crisis has come." Flying in the face of enormous evidence to the contrary, the Ruthenberg-Lovestone faction, always the most obeisant toward Moscow, greeted the Congress' dire predictions with enthusiasm. That an economic boom of unprecedented dimensions was beginning in America did not stop the Ruthenberg-Lovestone group from "proving"—particularly with statistics on car-loading—that the country was on the economic down-grade. The Foster group, refusing to be overwhelmed by car-loading statistics, rejected this notion, though Foster, with at least one ear cocked toward Moscow, insisted that the depression might well break out as late as the summer of 1925—a "rightist" heresy for which he was heartily abused. What is more, after the 1924 election, when the Comintern was predicting imminent crisis and collapse, the Foster-Cannon group made the tactical blunder of conceding the stabilization of world capitalism and the revival of "bourgeois illusions" among the masses. Neither Foster nor Cannon was particularly inclined toward heresy; it was simply that they were making, for the moment, bad factional guesses and that they were then a bit more responsive to the "feel" of American life than the Lovestone group, whose responsiveness was primarily to the "feel" of Comintern politics.

As in almost all the other internal disputes among the American Communists, what matters is no longer the issues themselves— these have long ago been buried or settled—but the way in which they were approached. Perhaps because few American Communists could help regarding themselves as poor cousins at the outer edge of the Comintern feast, almost every American faction fawned and maneuvered for Russian favor, trying to guess which group of Bolsheviks it was best to support and pay homage to. Independence was fast becoming a lost art among the Communists throughout the world, but among the Americans it was downright rare.

3. The process of "Stalinization" within the American party began considerably earlier than some of its historians suggest. By 1923 it was already in full swing and by 1925 it had almost reached its climax. Though it took many forms, perhaps the most interesting and symptomatic was the insistent campaign conducted both by the Comintern and by the two dominant factions to crush Ludwig Lore, a man who made the mistake of remaining in the Communist movement until the mid-twenties while trying to think for himself.

It would be foolhardy if not impossible to present the two main Communist factions as committed all through the twenties to distinct ideological platforms that were sharply demarcated from each other. Anyone examining the details of their struggle will notice that they frequently seemed to shift sides, at one point the Fosterites saying what the Lovestoneites had said a year or two earlier and the Lovestoneites repeating what the Fosterites had said. Still, certain dominant stresses can be noted. By and large, the Foster-Cannon group had a greater sensitivity and a closer relation to the American union movement than the Ruthenberg-Lovestone group. In general, the Foster-Cannon group, with much of its strength in the Midwest, was a bit more indigenous in its political style, while the Ruthenberg-Lovestone group was somewhat more faithful or at least alert to signals from Moscow. Yet exceptions to these categories are easy enough to find: Benjamin Gitlow, one of the most loyal of Lovestone's men, had been active in the New York trade-union movement, while Alexander Bittleman, who fed Foster his political formulas, was as scholastic in the employment of Marxist phrases as anyone else in the party. Principle and careerism became fatally mixed; the clarity for which the historian wistfully yearns is not available in life.

Charles E. Ruthenberg, the best administrator and one of the wiliest faction men in early American Communism, had won to his support a generation of clever young Communists whose experience in the class struggle was meager, at least by comparison with Foster's or Cannon's, but who were agile debaters and shrewd faction operators. The Fosterites labeled them "the City College boys," to suggest that they were brash young intellectuals with a cockiness that came mainly from book-learning. Jay Lovestone, William

Weinstone, Bertram D. Wolfe, all of them founding members of the party, were men of greater intellectual sophistication than the top Fosterites but quite without the rough-and-ready gift for labor leadership that characterized men like Foster, Cannon, and William F. Dunne. The schoolmasterly Wolfe could teach classes in Marxist economics, but it was difficult to imagine him leading an economic fight on the picket line. Weinstone (called "Wobbly" Weinstone because he was so shaky in his faction loyalties) felt most at home behind a desk in the party office. And Lovestone was happiest in the thick of party intrigue, for which, it may be said without exaggeration, he had a kind of genius.

In December, 1923, Foster and his friends had seized effective control of the party, and for the following six years, as factional fortunes veered and shifted, there was a constant tug-of-war between the two groups.

Serving both as a balance of power and, more frequently, as a scapegoat to be denounced by the Fosterites and Lovestoneites was a third faction, led by Ludwig Lore, which enjoyed support in the Finnish Federation and among the Jewish garment workers. The Lore group, which frequently tried to think things out for itself and thus made its own mistakes rather than those ordered by the Comintern, had been against both the break with Fitzpatrick in Chicago and the later LaFollette alliance. A man of considerable integrity and talent, Lore seemed untrustworthy to Moscow. It was in the nature of things that the Comintern should seek to create national party leaders in its own image: weak men, obedient men. And Lore did not satisfy these requirements nearly so well as Ruthenberg or Foster.

What most incurred the wrath of Moscow against Lore was the suspicion that he was a sort of Trotskyist. For this suspicion there was very little evidence, other than the fact that Lore's reasoning against support of LaFollette had paralleled Trotsky's and that he was by temperament an independent man. In any case. throughout the mid-twenties the Comintern kept urging a campaign against the heresies of "Loreism," and the two dominant factions, both of them eager to win preferment and neither inhibited about kicking a weaker opponent, rushed to stir passions against Lore and his supporters. For the Ruthenberg-Lovestone group the campaign against

"Loreism" came easily; for the Foster-Cannon group, because it had
made a temporary alliance with the heretic in 1923, it came somewhat harder; but in the competition to gain favor and advantage by
stamping on Lore, both groups showed a sizable talent for learning
from each other the tactics of ruthlessness.

In the history of the American party the drive to annihilate
Lore and his group served the same purpose as the drive to destroy
Trotsky in the Russian party: it was the crucial symptom of that
process by which inner-party democracy was being ripped to pieces
and the authoritarian regime of Stalinism prepared. Both major factions kept crying for more "Bolshevization" in the party, and the
fact that Lore's ideological deviations were quite minor did not prevent them from abusing him as a social democrat who was an alien
irritant in the otherwise healthy body of American Communism.
Both major factions had signed a resolution at the Fifth Comintern
Congress denouncing Trotskyism, though in truth neither of them
knew anything whatever about it. In 1924 and 1925 the Lovestoneites succeeded in making what might as well be called a "better
impression" in Moscow, but the Fosterites soon caught up in the
competition for "Bolshevization." James P. Cannon, for example,
made a speech in 1924 in which he declared his conception of a
Bolshevik party to be one "prohibiting factions, tendencies and
groups. It must be a monolithic party hewn of one piece." [3] Nor
was this anticipation of the Stalinist ethos unique to Cannon.
When the Comintern ordered that "no Party paper shall reprint
[Trotsky's] book 1917 or any chapter thereof in the party press," [4]
every American Communist leader but Lore accepted this humiliating decree of self-censorship. And when the Ruthenberg-Lovestone
group charged that the Fosterites had wavered in the lynch campaign
against Lore, Foster could answer:

> I am for the Comintern from start to finish . . . and if the
> Comintern finds itself criss-cross with my opinions, there is only
> one thing to do and that is to change my opinions to fit the policy
> of the Comintern. [5]

To this principle Foster would remain loyal throughout his life.
That in 1925 it should find general agreement and approval in the

party indicates that the triumph of Stalinism as a climate of repression came sooner and more easily in the American party, which held no police powers and could prevent no one from leaving it, than in the Russian party, where the use of intimidation and force was already far advanced.

In early 1925 a phalanx of Communist leaders—Foster, Cannon, Ruthenberg and Lovestone—undertook a pilgrimage to Moscow in order to plead their factional causes before a special American Commission created by the Comintern. Nikolai Bukharin, then an ally of Stalin and one of the most powerful men in Russia, Klara Zetkin, the veteran German Communist, and the Finnish exile Kuusinen, now secretary of the Comintern, all sat in judgment upon the quarrelsome Americans. The heads of each faction scurried around trying to round up support, and sometimes the Russians, harassed by more important troubles, proved a bit elusive. "These birds are hard to catch," wrote the disappointed Lovestone to his friends back home.[6] By March, however, the pilgrims cabled party headquarters that a bull could soon be expected, though whom it would favor no one yet knew. In Chicago, where the faithful leaders of the American party had gathered to await the word, the Central Executive Committee declared in advance its acceptance of the Moscow decision:

> Within a few days the decision of the Comintern will have settled *all* controversial questions. All factionalism . . . within the party must be immediately liquidated.[7] [emphasis added]

Here was "democratic centralism" with a vengeance: the party's total commitment to Moscow made free discussion as impossible before a decision was reached as its discipline did afterward.

The verdict of the "American Commission" proved somewhat indecisive, though it tended toward increasing the influence of the Ruthenberg-Lovestone group. Politically, the Ruthenberg-Lovestone group was declared to have been correct "in having confidence in the vitality and future of the labor movement," though it was judged to have put forward the labor party slogans "somewhat too narrowly." A concession was made to Foster (and reality) by acknowledging that "American capitalism temporarily overcame its crisis."

And both factions were instructed to sharpen the fight against Lore —which both were delighted to do.

No sooner did this declaration that was supposed to end "all factionalism" reach the American comrades than, predictably enough, the faction struggle grew more violent. The debate no longer concerned the academic topic of the labor party—all groups now favored it—but a problem in *Realpolitik:* which faction had done better in Moscow? Mimeograph machines groaned under the weight of endless documents; spies reported every move of opposing leaders; papers were stolen, letters opened, personal resources mobilized for the impending "final conflict."

Meanwhile, to avoid being accused of "softness" toward the heretic, no one dared let up the denunciations of Lore. Gradually most of his supporters in the Finnish Federation, as well as such former faction colleagues as Moissaye Olgin, Julia Stuart Poyntz, Charles Zimmerman, Ben Gold, and Rose Wortis (the last four important in trade-union work) were broken away from Lore. He alone remained firm.

In June the Comintern intervened once more. It ordered the party to call its fourth convention in the fall of 1925 and proposed a "Parity Commission," to be made up of three from each major faction and a special Moscow "rep" as chairman, in order (it said) to avoid a split.

For each faction the big problem now became to win the friendship of the Moscow "rep." But confusion, uncertainty, anxiety— his appearance was delayed. No one knew where he was . . . no one but Lovestone. While the unfortunate Fosterites were still in the dark as to the Great Man's whereabouts, he had in fact arrived in Chicago and been met by Lovestone, who quickly made arrangements for his personal needs and put in a few words for his faction's cause. A great victory! The Ruthenberg-Lovestone men had won the ear of the "rep" before the Fosterites so much as knew of his arrival. Gussev—whose ear had so triumphantly been captured— turned out to be a high-ranking officer of the Red Army, who in America christened himself P. Green.

Though Green came to the United States only three years after John Pepper, the differences between the two men symbolized the changes taking place both in the Soviet Union and in the

Communist movement. Where Pepper had soon become embroiled in party factionalism on all levels, Green preserved a chilly distance. Silent, wary, uncommunicative, and cultivating the stance of omnipotence, he gave the impression, not without reason, that he was a man to be feared. In his personal and political style he was a perfect example of the new "Stalin man"—the type that Arthur Koestler would later immortalize as Gletkin in *Darkness at Noon*. Behaving toward the Americans somewhat like a colonial administrator, he relied simply upon his delegated authority and made no effort, as Pepper had, to impress the American comrades with his dialectical skills. In fact, his contributions to the party discussion were so primitive that the inept American "theoreticians" shone by comparison. It is hard to resist an example.

During the factional exchange a branch of the Finnish Federation, located in Superior, Wisconsin, had been charged with the sin of "opportunism." The indignant Finns replied:

> The essential distinctive feature of opportunism is blind patriotism toward an organization, the setting of an organization even above the leading principles, currying favor with heterogeneously colored elements and the avoidance of self-criticism.

Such heresies were too much even for the stolid Green to bear, and so he in turn replied:

> Blind patriotism toward a good Communist organization is no opportunism. But patriotism toward an opportunistic organization is undoubtedly opportunism.

Pleased with this brilliant thrust, Green continued:

> The comrades of the Superior Finnish branch affirm that opportunists avoid self-criticism. Quite the contrary. Nobody talks so much about the freedom of criticism as the opportunists. . . . The whole question is only a question of what we are talking about, whether we are talking of an opportunistic criticism or a Communist criticism. A party or a section of a party which carries an opportunistic criticism and resists a Communist criticism is an opportunistic party. . . . Self-criticism is necessary for every Bolshevik party . . . Thus it is only a question of what

kind of criticism is necessary for the party, opportunistic or Communist criticism.

And with a triumphant flourish:

We see then that the definition of opportunism given by the Superior Finnish branch is good-for-nothing.[8]

This weird double-talk was later to become the standard rhetoric of Stalinism. It was appropriate that in the American party—which, for all its faults, had never quite sunk to such intellectual nullity—it should be introduced by the official representative of the emerging totalitarian type.

As it turned out, Green had been instructed to be sympathetic to the Ruthenberg-Lovestone group, but not to allow it immediate control of the party; the Kremlin was content, for the moment, to create a balance between the two factions. Hence Green insisted that both groups unite on the basis of an intensified struggle against Loreism. But Loreism had already been pulverized; it could no longer absorb the tremendous energy generated by the rival caucuses, and in a paroxysm of activity they naturally turned upon each other.

With the party machinery firmly in their hands, the Fosterites were able to assure themselves a majority of the delegates to the fourth national convention. The Parity Commission was flooded with appeals and petitions, but when the convention finally opened on August 21, 1925, the Fosterite leaders seated forty delegates of their own and allowed twenty-one to Ruthenberg-Lovestone. Actually, the minority was stronger than this division indicates. Foster held control of the Finnish Federation with its 7,000 members, virtually half the party membership, but the Ruthenberg-Lovestone group dominated such large districts as New York, Boston, Philadelphia, Cleveland, and Pittsburgh.

At the convention Green, the Comintern "rep," proposed that on the forthcoming Central Executive Committee the Ruthenberg-Lovestone minority be allowed 40 percent of the seats. The minority's credit rating was rising in Moscow. Foster and his friends grew somewhat uneasy but still felt confident of their strength within the party. They had barricaded the national headquarters in Chicago against sudden attack by the opposition and also kept a close watch over the party press. Both factions had muscle men at the convention to act as "defense guards." Thus the debates could occur in an appropriately fraternal atmosphere. But as it turned out the real decisions were not to be made by the convention at all.

For, apart from the convention and in a quieter, deadlier atmosphere, the Parity Commission (Foster, Cannon, Bittleman for the majority and Ruthenberg, Lovestone, Bedacht for the minority) was holding private meetings. Cool and deliberate, Green read a telegram from Moscow. In the authoritative language of an ultimatum, this Comintern cable repudiated the Foster leadership, announced "that the Ruthenberg group is more loyal to decisions of the Communist International," and instructed the American party to give both factions equal representation on the new Central Executive Committee. Green, as chairman of the Parity Commission, would act as a neutral member—that is, as a kind of Bonapartist arbiter. "Those who refuse to submit will be expelled." [9]

At the eleventh hour, simply by sending a telegram, Moscow had reversed the decision of the party membership. Foster stormed and raged, threatened disobedience, but when some of his supporters, particularly Cannon, refused to go along with this threat, he caved in.

This was not all, however. The humiliation of Foster was completed after the convention when Green rose at the first meeting of the new Executive Committee and stolidly recited his latest instructions:

> Of course, we now have a parity Central Committee, but it is not exactly a parity Central Committee. With the decisions of the Communist International . . . there go parallel instructions to the CI Representative to support the [Ruthenberg-Lovestone] group which was the former minority. [10]

No matter what the membership had desired, the party was now effectively delivered up to Ruthenberg-Lovestone. The post of party chairman, formerly held by Foster, was abolished and Ruthen-

berg elected to the new post of general secretary. Even in its titles
the American party was quickly learning to resemble the party of
Stalin.

On one issue alone had there been unity at the fourth convention.* A motion to expel Ludwig Lore from the party was passed
unanimously, without a murmur of protest. A bit later, in publicly
justifying this action, the Communist leader Max Bedacht wrote
with a frankness that he himself could hardly have estimated at its
full significance:

> The Catholic Church is and has been one of the strongest
> and most consistent counter-revolutionary forces in society. In
> [our] struggles we find this organization a formidable opponent.
> The reason for this is its ideological unity and its organizational
> centralization. If we revolutionists have not already learned these
> lessons in our experience, we could learn the value of ideological
> unity and organizational centralization from the Catholic
> Church.[11]

* One of the "achievements" which the party leadership proclaimed at
this convention was the recent Communist campaign to deny Raphael Abramovitch, the Russian Menshevik leader, his right to free speech when he came
to this country in 1925 to rally support for the growing number of political
prisoners in Russia.
    The Communists had been driven underground by the Palmer raids, they
had been persecuted since the moment of their birth, Benjamin Gitlow was
just about to return to jail for having advocated Communism; yet free speech
for political opponents remained for them a joke. When Abramovitch,
under Socialist and labor auspices, tried to speak at the Garrick theater in
Chicago, the Workers Party invaded the meeting and hurled insults at the
speaker and chairs at those who wanted to hear him. The same performance,
part of a well-planned campaign, was repeated in a number of cities. Only in
Boston did the Communists refuse to employ force to break up Abramovitch's
meeting, preferring instead to hold a counter-meeting on the same day. For
this deplorable lapse into democratic attitudes, the Boston comrades were
chided at the fourth convention.
    When the Civil Liberties Union protested the use of violence against
Abramovitch, Earl Browder berated the ACLU and put forward a novel version of civil libertarianism. Instead of defending "the right of workers to
protest against Abramovitch's lies," wrote Browder, "the Civil Liberties Union
was defending the right of Abramovitch to lie without interruption or
heckling." [12]
    With such arguments Browder was proving his claim to become the
leader of American Stalinism.

So it went until the spring of 1927, when Charles Ruthenberg died and the struggle for factional parity at his casket—conducted, it must be said, somewhat more fairly than the struggle for parity at the fourth convention—climaxed the ceremonies to honor the first leader of American Communism.

4. In 1927 the party headquarters was moved from Chicago to New York. Motives of political expediency were partly involved, but the move also represented the crowning victory of Lovestone's faction over the Fosterites. The Fosterites were out of power; Ruthenberg was dead; from now on the party was to be centered in the favorite milieu of the young careerists and intellectuals who made up its new leadership. Union Square became the center of American Stalinism.

It would serve no purpose to record here the innumerable battles between Fosterites and Lovestoneites—in the United States and Moscow—during the years of Lovestone's ascendancy. Outvoted and outmaneuvered each time they sought to regain leadership, the Fosterites nonetheless remained a power within the party. In Moscow they had won the support of Lozovsky, head of the Red Trade Union International and a prominent Stalin man. In the United States, Foster commanded the loyalty of many trade unionists for whom the leader of the TUEL was equal, if not superior, to the head of the Communist Party.

For another year the inner life of the party was taken up with the usual unsavory routine of factional accusations, mutual recriminations, quarrels over jobs, policies, and prestige. But in 1928 a significant new development occurred. Suddenly, as if out of nowhere, there appeared a Trotskyist heresy. Considering the efforts of the American party leaders to anticipate every Moscow decision, this event was strange indeed. It had no public history. During the years before 1928, Trotsky's heroic and pathetic effort to halt the bureaucratization of the Russian movement had had almost no repercussions in America. Perhaps the only Trotskyist in the United States, and he an unorthodox one, was Max Eastman, an independent intellectual whom the Communists hated without restraint. Since the expulsion of Lore the entire party had periodically participated in ceremonial condemnations of Trotskyism, but it had hardly been a living issue in the American party, one way or the other.

James P. Cannon's appearance at the head of a Trotskyist faction was apparently a complete surprise even to his close friends within the party. Cannon had always tried to preserve his own little grouplet within the folds of the larger Foster caucus, but, as several Trotskyist leaders were later to acknowledge, "this Cannon group stood upon the platform of international Stalinism, sometimes a little to the right . . . sometimes a little to the left. . . ."[13] If anything, Cannon was one of the least internationally minded of the American leaders and therefore, one would have supposed, least likely to be interested in Trotsky's theories.

Cannon was later to explain that he had been converted to Trotskyism during his 1928 stay in Russia, when he had the opportunity of studying key "Trotskyist documents."[14] But this is not entirely convincing. Cannon had been to Moscow several times before and had shown no interest in these documents, which had all the while been available. Nor was Cannon, a hard-bitten veteran of the Wobblies, the kind of man to be suddenly moved by the power of theoretical arguments. Some students have speculated that, because in 1928 the Trotskyists seemed to be making a certain amount of progress in the European Communist parties, Cannon attached himself to Trotsky in order to win similar victories in America; but this, at best, could have been a very slim hope, and Cannon was too astute a politician to risk his career—if he were thinking in terms of career—on such a possibility.

Whatever his motivation, Cannon's efforts to organize a Trotskyist faction upon his return from Moscow were quickly discovered, and both Fosterites and Lovestoneites joined in the heresy hunt. Foster had a special need to dissociate himself from Cannon, since the latter had but yesterday been his factional ally. Fearing that the Lovestoneites would try to implicate him in the Trotskyist defection, Foster himself betrayed his former friends to the Lovestone-controlled Central Executive Committee. Forced into the open, Cannon played for time. As late as October, 1928, he told the party leaders: "Not a single person . . . can truthfully say that I advocated or did anything in connection with the Trotsky question contrary to what had been decided by the party." [15]

It was too late. Both factions, feverish to prove their devotion to Moscow, moved to drive Cannon and his few friends out of the party. On October 27 the handful of Trotskyists—Cannon, Max Shachtman, Martin Abern, a few others—were expelled without even the formality of a meeting of the Central Committee. The following month the tiny group began printing its own organ *The Militant*, and thus began the life of the American Trotskyist movement, which in the thirties would have an influence disproportionate to its numbers among certain intellectuals and in a few trade unions.

If Trotskyism earned only abuse, there was another theoretical position in the party which for a while produced something like a genuine discussion. There had always been a few men among the American Communists who recognized that the slogans and theories originated in the Comintern frequently had little relevance to American events. The blindly obedient "militancy" of 1924 had only resulted in sectarian absurdities; the party needed somehow to relate itself to Coolidge's America. Such a view only awaited a moment of factional stabilization, or of Russian tolerance, to become a full-fledged theory, and that moment seemed to have arrived with Stalin's "right" turn of 1926-27 and with Bukharin's ascendancy in the Comintern. The Lovestone leadership, fairly secure in its position, now put forward the principle of "American Exceptionalism," around which there developed one of the very few significant theoretical discussions in the history of the American Communist movement. Inevitably, the theory ended as a heresy, and the discussion became a factional struggle. Surveying the whole field it is as difficult as ever to establish consistent intellectual positions. Again it was a question of timing, and the clock was Moscow's; the moment for "exceptions" passed more quickly than Lovestone realized.

By 1929 Stalin had established his complete control over the Russian party and the Comintern, but he had captured a world movement which for several years had known only defeat. Everywhere his timid and half-hearted turn toward a "right" line had been utterly unsuccessful. As before, Stalin now veered sharply toward an ultra-left course. The attempts to form alliances with the

Social Democrats were suddenly out of date; instead Communists the world over joined in denunciations of "social fascism." In Russia itself the policy of concessions to the peasants and of gradual industrialization was replaced by the first Five Year Plan: a program for forced collectivization and industrial expansion at any cost.

This new Stalinist policy was opposed by the major theoretician of the Russian party's right wing, the old Bolshevik Nicholai Bukharin, who had been Stalin's ally in the struggle against Trotsky and Zinoviev and had replaced the latter as president of the Comintern. Now, as Stalin drove for absolute dictatorship, Bukharin was also threatened. During 1928 the long-postponed Sixth World Congress of the Comintern had finally been convened, and though Bucharin still played a leading role, the Congress endorsed the turn to the left. For a few months after the meeting adjourned Bukharin was able to mitigate the impact of the new line with subtle interpretations and a careful balancing of words. But it was already apparent that a new purge was in the offing and that the victims this time would be the "rightist" leaders in the various national parties who had previously looked to Bukharin for protection.

In America the Lovestone faction had been close to the doomed Comintern leader, while Foster's support had come mainly from some of Stalin's men. Lovestone was now in an almost impossible position. He joined, of course, in the general castigation of right-wing sins that was *de rigeur* after the Sixth Congress, and he struggled to prove that rightist errors had been committed as often by Fosterites as by his own followers. But the minority pressed its advantage, pointing to the fact that, quite apart from the merely tactical "right" deviations of the Lovestoneites, their whole theoretical orientation was in sharp opposition to the new Comintern course.

Lovestone had claimed that there were certain exceptional features in the development of American economic, social, and political life which sharply distinguished it from the general trends in other capitalist countries. Writing at the very height of Coolidge prosperity, he and his intellectual co-workers had argued that Comintern statements about the decadence of world capitalism and the imminent revolutionary crisis did not apply to America. In planning the strategy of the American Communist movement, they insisted, it was necessary to take these exceptional circumstances into consideration. Wrote Lovestone:

> American capitalism is still on the upward grade, still in the ascendency. . . . [Its] peak has not yet been reached. . . . We must take into cognizance the tremendous reserve power of American capitalism. . . . The power of capitalism is today more firmly rooted than it ever was.[16]

Bertram D. Wolfe was even more emphatic:

> We cannot even speak of stabilization of capitalism in America, because American capitalism was not at any time so shaken as to be called unstable in the sense that tottering European capitalism was.[17]

The Lovestoneites did not deny that American capitalism faced crises and contradictions, but they claimed that its potentialities for growth had not yet been exhausted. And they concluded that political tactics applicable in Europe might have no relevance in America.

> . . . The basic task of the Communist Parties of Germany and France is to fight for the conquest of the majority of the working class. The Communist Party of America has not yet reached this stage of development. Our present task is still more moderate, more limited. Our basic task today is to entrench ourselves in the masses, to get a foothold.[18]

The Fosterites and their allies launched the usual bombardment upon this theory. It constituted "an underestimation of the leftward drive of the masses," a "lack of perspective of struggle," and an "overestimation of the reserve powers of American imperialism." Indeed the foresight of Foster in this dispute might require congratulation had it not been so predictable. Foster's arguments were not determined by his analysis of American conditions but by the factional alignment of the moment. During the struggles of 1924-25 the position of the two groups had been revealingly different. At that time the Ruthenberg-Lovestone faction had enthusiastically foreseen the imminent collapse of the American economy. The beginning of a boom unprecedented in American history did not then stop the Lovestoneite spokesman from dragging out a massive assortment of incidental "facts" to prove that "the upward movement in America has undoubtedly come to an end—the crisis has come." The Fosterite majority, on the other hand, had then been wary of ultra-revolutionary slogans; in fact, before the Comintern's new ideological requirements became clear, it had conceded the "world stabilization" of capitalism and the revival of "bourgeois illusions" among the masses.

Now, four years later, the Lovestone majority was defending a somewhat realistic analysis, while the Foster minority hurried to win Moscow's favor by supporting the new "left" line as fervently as it could. As the two factions alternated in office, they alternated in ideology.

American capitalism, the Fosterites claimed in 1928, "is about to reach the apex of growth. . . . Further expansion leads [it] to further and more drastic attacks upon the standards of life of the American masses. . . ." "A process of widespread and general radicalization is taking place among the most exploited sections of the workers." [19] One indication of this increasingly radical mood, the faction's leaders lamely suggested, was the big vote Al Smith got in the 1928 elections.

Lovestone ridiculed his opponents: "The policies leading to this conception of radicalization would lead the party to radical isolation." "You say," he continued with mild contempt, "that the big Smith vote proves the radicalization of the masses. Perhaps . . . you will tell us next that there would have been a still greater radical force let loose in the country if Smith were elected." [20] Such arguments, as it turned out, had little value; the dispute was to be decided not by an ideological exchange but in Moscow where the criteria had ceased to be theoretical. Had the discussion on American Exceptionalism been pursued, it might have led to a reevaluation of the relationship between the development of capitalism in Europe and America; it might even have resulted in a fundamental and independent revision of American Communist strategy. But it was not allowed to proceed unhampered by local feuds and international

Stalinization. A discussion which had started with a theoretical bang ended in the usual factional whimper.

By late 1928 Lovestone was hard pressed but by no means beaten. The Sixth Comintern Congress had already drastically shifted the general Communist line, but its formulations had been sufficiently vague to permit variant interpretations. And as long as Bukharin retained his prominent Comintern post he would surely not permit his friends to be sacrificed to Stalinists of stricter obedience. Nevertheless, as the Lovestoneites watched Stalin's inexorable rise to absolute power, they frantically sought means of strengthening their position.

All Communist parties had been urged in the directives of the Sixth Congress to hunt down the Right Danger. Mindful of past party history, when Moscow had overlooked the sins of both major factions in the interests of a unified struggle against Loreism, Lovestone now hoped to retain control of the party by a concentrated attack upon the newly expelled Trotskyists. There was, however, one difficulty. The Trotsky opposition had been considered, both within Russia and on the international scene, as a "left" tendency, while the American party had been ordered to confront a threat from the right. But with their usual blitheness the Lovestone leaders simply decided that the Trotskyists, all appearances to the contrary, were "objectively" a "right" faction. The party's Central Executive Committee laid down the new line: "Trotskyism is an organic part of the Right Danger." "In Russia," Bertram D. Wolfe claimed, "a victory for Trotsky would have led to a restoration of capitalism," and this proved that Trotsky was to the right of everyone. Wolfe challenged the skeptics with a delightful exercise in non-Euclidean geometry: "Whether one departs from Leninism to the right or to the 'left,' he cannot travel far without landing in the camp of the enemy. Extend both lines of deviation any distance and they coincide." [21]

If there had been no Trotskyists, Lovestone would have had to invent them. They were indispensable to his new tactic. The viciousness of the campaign which he developed against them surpassed anything before known in the American radical movement. Jack Stachel, chief assistant in Lovestone's less savory projects, planned and led a raid upon the private apartments of the Trotskyist leaders, rifled their files, and stole whatever was likely to burn well in the factional fires. Trotskyist newspaper vendors were attacked by party agents and savagely beaten; Cannon's meetings were disrupted and his women comrades publicly called whores. The ideologists among the Lovestoneites had little difficulty in justifying this ugly campaign. Bertram D. Wolfe linked the Russian Trotskyists with the White Guards—"objectively" of course.

> It is no accident that they soon found themselves entangled in a White Guard conspiracy also in spite of themselves. The counter-revolutionaries supported their efforts to set up illegal printing plants. The White Guards also needed underground printing plants. They used the opposition, in spite of any desire it may have had.[22]

With such tactics the Lovestoneites might have succeeded in riding out the storm, as they had done in the past; indeed it appeared that Moscow did not want to put Foster in charge of the party. But then the majority committed an unpardonable blunder; it failed to gauge the shifts on the Moscow scene fast enough; it lost the tempo.

At the Sixth Comintern Congress Bukharin had retained at least the appearance of power, but by 1929 Stalin was ready to display the full extent of his triumph by ousting Bukharin from the presidency of the Comintern. Lovestone, however, failed to grasp the new power situation within the Soviet Union. In December, 1928, he still felt it politic to say:

> For me comrade Bukharin represents the Communist line, the line of the Central Executive Committee of the Communist Party of the Soviet Union. Therefore comrade Bukharin is an authority of the Communist International. . . . For me he does not represent the Right Wing of the Communist International; although for some he does.[23]

This speech must have been interpreted in Moscow as a declaration of loyalty to Bukharin, and an affront to Stalin not to be forgotten.

Yet there is nothing to suggest that the pro-Bukharin line of the Lovestone faction was dictated by a loyalty to persons or principles. It was, once again, the result of a miscalculation. When the news of Bukharin's disgrace belatedly reached the American party, Lovestone rushed to repudiate him.* At the party convention in February, 1929, only a month after the speech quoted above had been published, the Lovestoneites introduced a resolution disowning the fallen leader and hailing the victor. But it was too late. Stalin had decided that they were Bukharin's men and they had to go.

The impending decision to drop Lovestone was foreshadowed in an open letter sent by the Comintern's Executive Committee to the American convention. Bluntly, and with considerable accuracy, the letter enumerated the party's major weaknesses.

> The Workers (Communist) Party of America has been for many years an organization of foreign workers not much connected with the political life of the country. Owing to this immigrant exclusiveness two leading groups arose. . . . For six years an almost uninterrupted struggle for supremacy in the party has been going on between them. The struggle was, in the main, not based on principles . . . principles served chiefly to camouflage the struggle for supremacy. . . .[25]

The letter reiterated the usual Comintern insistence that factional feuds must be "unconditionally stopped." It upbraided the leaders of both factions for their recent conduct: all this without losing its paternalistic tone. But a set of organizational proposals accompanying the letter was phrased more roughly. It was clear that the Lovestoneites had lost. Without even a reference to the convention, where 80 percent of the delegates were pledged to his support, the Comintern ordered Lovestone to leave the American party and report to Moscow for international work. Foster was to become the new general secretary; two Comintern representatives,

---

* Early in 1929, so a story has it, Robert Minor brought into the *Daily Worker* an article written in his own hand, headlined "Lovestone Backs Bukharin." Late the same night, as the paper was readied for the press, Minor rushed in, breathless and distressed, shouting, "Stop the press!" He had heard that this story was a grave mistake. So he took it back and, changing a word here and there, reversed its meaning. The next day it appeared under the headline, "Lovestone Denounces Bukharin."[26]

Harry Pollitt from the British party and Philip Dengal from the German, would make all further decisions.

The Lovestoneites appealed this verdict to Stalin himself; they held in reserve a threat to split the party and leave not even a mimeograph machine to the orthodox minority. Stalin's reply was prompt and conciliatory. There had been no intention on the part of the Comintern, he wrote, to impinge on the rights of the convention majority. He invited Lovestone to come to Moscow to talk things over. Foster was shocked and dismayed; again his hope of becoming party secretary seemed shattered. Yet in this case, as so often before and after, Stalin proved a far shrewder man than his American servants. The Comintern's original proposals would undoubtedly have been rejected by Lovestone; had that happened a purge of the "right deviationists" would have been extremely difficult, for they would have remained in control of the party machinery. Now the Lovestoneites felt that Stalin had had a change of heart. Accordingly they named Gitlow general secretary, elected a new Executive Committee—maintaining their majority—and decided that Lovestone, Gitlow, and Bedacht would lead a large "proletarian delegation" to carry their appeal to the Kremlin judges. Thus Stalin's immediate objective was achieved; the key members of the Lovestone caucus were removed from the American scene.

The Lovestoneites did not, of course, intend to rely on Stalin's good faith. Before leaving, they made Robert Minor, a man hardly noted for political steadfastness, acting secretary; the more astute Jack Stachel was to be his *spiritus rector*. Elaborate care was taken to secure the majority's hold on all party organizations and resources. If the news from Russia were bad, and a split appeared inevitable, Minor and Stachel were to act to guarantee Lovestone's majority status. Not until all these arrangements were made did the pilgrims feel safe. Even so, Gitlow later reported, he had been somewhat disturbed by the curiously jubilant spirits of Minor during their farewell; but that, after all, was probably only hindsight. . . .[26]

The Americans' caution was justified by events in Moscow. They arrived to learn that Bukharin had been replaced as head of the Comintern. Molotov, Stalin's closest collaborator, and now Bukharin's successor, was to head the American Commission, which would hear their case. Stalin, they were told, took a very special interest in the matter. An even more unhappy omen awaited them. Bertram D. Wolfe, the faction's Moscow representative, had just been advised that he was shortly to begin work for the Comintern in Korea—a well-known graveyard for Communists out of favor. Stalin was clearly determined to have his revenge. Only a total capitulation, Molotov informed the disappointed Americans, would save them now.*

At the meetings of the Comintern's Commission, Stalin lectured the Americans as if he were the very incarnation of Bolshevik purity, a man without guile, upset by the immorality of both the Foster and the Lovestone factions. The old schemer must have enjoyed himself thoroughly as he mocked his pitiful collection of American "revolutionaries."

> You know that both groups of the American Communist Party, competing with each other and chasing after each other like horses in a race, are feverishly speculating on existing and non-existing differences within the Communist Party of the Soviet Union. . . . The Foster group demonstrate their closeness to the Communist Party of the S.U. by declaring themselves "Stalinites." Lovestone perceives that his own faction thereby might lose some-

---

* John Pepper, who had returned to America in 1928, now also arrived in Moscow. He had sought in every possible way to avoid going back to Moscow. The others were partly protected by their American citizenship; he was at the mercy of his Kremlin masters. Only a year before he had been the majority's spokesman against the Trotskyists; he had presented the motion for their expulsion and had written all the theses and declarations against them. Anti-Trotskyism, as Trotsky once wrote, had become a profession for him "as others run a matrimonial agency or sell lottery tickets." [27] Yet his undoing began almost immediately after the day of his glory. Pepper was known in Moscow as a Bukharin man and early in 1929 he was ordered to return at once to Russia. But Pepper did not budge. Cable after cable was sent by the Comintern; he did not answer. Then he disappeared. A few months later a party man found him living quietly in a New York hotel. It was soon discovered that the "missing" Pepper had frequently met with Lovestone and others to discuss factional strategy. This was an uncomfortable moment for Pepper, and no less for the majority's leader. Yet the ever resourceful Lovestone immediately announced that he had expelled Pepper for violating discipline: "The political platform of comrade Pepper is no doubt the real cause of his cowardly disinclination to do his duty and go and place himself at the disposal of the Comintern." [28] A few days later the expulsion was rescinded, Pepper reinstated, and the whole matter referred to Moscow for adjudication. The unhappy Pepper now presented himself: a reluctant victim ready for the executioner.

thing. Therefore, in order not to be outdone, the Lovestone group suddenly performs a "hair-raising" feat and, at the American Party Congress, carries through a decision calling for the removal of comrade Bukharin from the Comintern. . . . The Lovestone group performs another "hair-raising" feat and expels comrade Pepper from the party. . . . Let the Fosterites try to beat that! Let them know over there in Moscow that we Americans know how to play the stock market.[29]

The American Commission's verdict was pronounced on May 12, 1929, in an address to the American party read before the assembled Lovestoneites. Stalin attended the meeting presumably to judge, for future reference, the relative submissiveness of the majority's leaders. The address struck out at the "right-wing" faction as "rotten diplomatists" and "opportunists," rejected the theory of American Exceptionalism, and generally condemned Lovestone's leadership of the party. The Fosterites did not escape blame, but they were criticized in terms far more gentle. Once again Moscow called for factional peace, but this time it had found a means to its end: the elimination of one of the factions. Lovestone, Gitlow, Wolfe, and Bedacht were ordered to surrender unconditionally and publicly endorse the address. All but the last refused. Bedacht asked for time to make his decision. Struggling with his loyalties, he was brought to a state of collapse; agonized and ill, he lay sobbing in his bed. Finally he made his submission to Stalin.* The others

---

* When Bedacht came to explain his shift of loyalties, he anticipated the mode of abject confession that would soon become a customary part of the Stalinist terrorization of the mind:

"I have just returned from Moscow. Spurred on by my factionally corrupt logic, I have there helped to embody . . . the monstrous idea that the Comintern plans to break up our Party because it is determined to 'break up' my faction."

But, wrote Bedacht, he had learned better once the Russians began exerting pressure during the meetings of the "American Commission":

"This discussion broke down in me my will to resistance. The feeling gradually grew in me that to pit my will against the will of my World Party is a presumption not growing out of revolutionary but out of petty-bourgeois logic. I gradually began to understand that my very approach to the whole problem was in itself a proof of the correctness of the criticism of our [i.e., the American party's] leadership by the Communist International." (*Daily Worker,* June 5, 1929)

stood firm. Gitlow, the most steadfast, rose in front of Stalin and declared: "Not only do I vote against this decision, but when I return to the United States, I will fight against it." [30] The Russian leader replied with a violent tirade of personal abuse; at the end of the outburst he exclaimed: "The only ones who will follow you will be your sweethearts and wives." The Lovestoneites thought differently. Weren't Minor and Stachel standing guard in New York? Wasn't the great majority of the party members on their side? Once again they had underestimated Stalin.

For while the Lovestone delegation chafed in Moscow, Stachel and Minor, Lovestone's trusted lieutenants, were organizing the party against them. Minor later boasted of his betrayal: "Now I want to say that I am proud of the fact . . . that we succeeded in turning an 85 percent majority of the party against Lovestone within a very few days. It was a good job and I have so little to boast of that I must be allowed to boast of that." [31] Immediately after receiving a telegram which foreshadowed the Kremlin's decision, the Lovestoneites in New York hastened to desert their chief.

Lovestone and his followers reached New York in June to find the party completely turned against them. One by one they were expelled; Stalin's boast proved essentially correct. The Lovestoneite leaders had enjoyed the support of thousands of party members when they left for Moscow; they were powerless when they returned. The elected heads of the party, its spokesmen for many years, were now reviled and ostracized. Deprived even of a hearing, the Lovestoneites formed their own organization, pathetically calling themselves The Communist Party, USA (Majority Group). Hardly 200 members joined in their secession. The bulk of the party was now securely in the hands of Fosterites and renegade Lovestoneites; the factional feuds were over. No group was ever again to challenge Stalin's leadership in the American party.

There is no need to describe in detail the campaign of vilification which was now directed against Lovestone and his "majority group." The form of such attacks was already well known; it had been perfected by the Lovestoneites themselves in their attacks upon Trotskyism. This rough irony was grasped by one of the young ideologists of the new leadership. Writing in *The Communist*, Leon

Platt explained the rejection of Lovestone's appeals for an understanding of his heterodox position.

> When Lovestone today pretends not to understand the reasons for the decisive and energetic action of the Party against him and his group, it will be of interest to recall some of the views expressed by one of the present leaders of the right-wing group. . . . In a speech made by [Bertram D.] Wolfe on Trotskyism in 1928 it is said: "We live in a changing world and those who are not capable of adjusting themselves . . . become misleaders and must be fought." [32]

Indeed, in his zeal as chief inquisitor against Trotskyism, Wolfe had gone farther than this. He had insisted that past services to the party could not be taken into consideration in judging present usefulness. Now Platt, with a great show of innocence, merely repeated Wolfe's fatal words: "The revolution has no respect for persons."

During the next two decades there were to come many more "purifications" of the Communist Party. But none of these assumed the character of a factional struggle. With the expulsion of the Lovestoneites, the party leadership was in the hands of such trusted agents of Stalin as Foster and Browder. Just as in Russia the final defeat of the Bukharin wing marked the end of any general debate in the party, so the expulsion of the Lovestoneites ended all free discussion in the American movement. Like the Russian state, the American party had become a totalitarian monolith no longer susceptible to those inner pressures which had once stirred the membershop to at least a modicum of independent thought. Stalin had won his American triumph.

Chapter V. Ultra-Leftism in the Early Thirties

1. The presidential campaign of 1928, coming at a time when many Americans felt prosperity to be a blessing both eternal and uniquely deserved, was not one of the more important political battles in American history; only Prohibition and the Catholicism of Al Smith aroused any keen public interest. But for the Communists the election came at a particularly irksome moment in that it forced them to turn from their faction fights and pay at least a minimum of attention to the country in which they lived. To improvise the appearance of a political campaign, they nominated William Z. Foster for President and Benjamin Gitlow for Vice-President. Foster, in his acceptance speech, took care to point out that the participation of the CP in the campaign implied no concession to "parliamentary illusions" or, for that matter, democratic values. "Today," he said, "our party is small and the parties of the capitalists are large and strong, but the day will surely come when the Communist Party will be the *only* party in the United States" [1] (emphasis added).

As the best-known Communist in the country, Foster was a logical choice; but Gitlow was named less for his gifts as a flamboyant public speaker than for his prominence in the Lovestone faction. Like other parties, if in less conventional ways, the CP also had to present a "balanced ticket."

Given its background and bias, the CP could not help regarding its participation in the campaign with some doubt and even suspicion. For all its inner arrogance, it had very little faith in itself as a force within the life of American politics. Its mind was elsewhere: in Moscow, where the great internecine struggles of Communism were raging. During the summer of 1928, at the very moment when the ordinary American parties were beginning to campaign, twenty Communist leaders, including the presidential candidate himself, abandoned America to spend two months in Moscow at the Sixth World Congress of the Communist International.

Nonetheless, the party did wrest some gains from the campaign. Its vote of 48,228, while some 15,000 more than it had received in 1924, was puny; but for the first time the party functioned on a more or less national scale, appearing on the ballot in thirty-four states, running more local candidates than ever in its history (even in Texas, where John Rust, the inventor of a cheap cotton picker, was its candidate for US Senator), penetrating areas that had never before heard a Communist speaker, and winning considerable publicity through the frequent arrest of its candidates and campaigners.

Squads of unemployed comrades, living on a few pennies a day, toured previously untouched sections of the country to collect the signatures needed for putting the party on the ballot. Three party members from Denver rounded up signatures in Arizona; a handful from Boston somehow managed to persuade 1,200 citizens in conservative New Hampshire to sign the Communist nominating petitions. In some states, particularly New Jersey and Pennsylvania, "labor parties" were suddenly manufactured to endorse Foster and, this ritual completed, allowed quickly to fade away. Most important of all, at least from the Communist point of view, was that the party held its first public meetings in such Southern towns as Louisville, New Orleans, Birmingham, Atlanta, Norfolk, and Richmond.

Because it did penetrate new areas, the Communist campaign met with sharp and frequently violent resistance. In towns where the tradition of political tolerance had never been deeply established and where a Communist seemed a bogeyman as greatly to be feared as he was little known, party spokesmen were often arrested and mistreated. The CP candidate for governor in Arizona, William O'Brien, was arrested and beaten in jail; Scott Nearing, the radical economist, was arrested and his meeting dispersed in Wheeling, West Virginia; and Foster was arrested in Wilmington, Delaware, on the charge that a leaflet advertising his meeting had proclaimed the "inflammatory" slogan "Abolish Lynching!"

The minuteness of the Communist vote can largely be explained by such general factors as the conservative temper of the American people during the late 1920's and the prolonged isolation of the party. But there were also other causes, reflecting the inner weakness of American Communism. The anti-parliamentary tradition within the party was still strong—"Have we freed ourselves from the sectarian policy of 'boycotting the elections?' " asked a party leader in a worried voice that showed him to be doubtful that the answer was affirmative.[2] Many members did not take the campaign very seriously; they felt that the factional struggle was more important than the election (as, given their assumptions, it was).*

Writing in *The Communist*, Scott Nearing was frank to portray the essential isolation of the American Communists during the late 1920's; "The people who came to Party campaign meetings were for the most part apathetic, indifferent, inquisitive, fearful or hostile." [3] Nonetheless, and despite its genius for systematically placing hurdles in its own path, the party inched forward. No one can say with certainty how much progress it might have made had it been left to its own devices, since one condition of the party's existence was that it not be left to its own devices. Almost immediately after the election, the CP began one of its periodic shifts —a dizzying turn to the left—caused not by any estimate, right or wrong, of the American situation but simply by a decision of the Communist International. The effects of this turn upon work in the trade unions and among intellectuals were so important that they require consideration in separate chapters; here we shall focus primarily upon the fate of the party and its attendant organizations during the years from 1928 to 1935.

2. The late 1920's were bleak and bewildering years for international Communism.

Not merely had the movement itself been fractured into three irreconcilable groups, with exile, expulsions, and persecutions replacing debate and polemic as the means for settling disagreements; but on almost every front the Communist parties suffered humiliating defeats, partly as a result of their weakness and inexperience

---

* The criss-crossing of public campaign and inner factionalism produced at least one bit of high comedy. At one point during his national tour Gitlow was in Los Angeles, scheduled to proceed to Phoenix, Arizona, where local authorities were threatening to break up his meeting. When the time came for his arrival in Phoenix, he did not appear; and the next morning the *Daily Worker*, temporarily in control of the Lovestone faction, printed a screaming headline, "Gitlow Kidnapped." This effort to gain factional advantage by "martyrizing" its candidate caused the Lovestoneites a certain embarrassment when it came out that Gitlow had merely missed his train.

but still more because of ill-considered policies dictated by the increasingly authoritarian and nationalistic regime in Moscow. Meeting during the summer of 1928, the Sixth World Congress of the Comintern could do little but pass formal resolutions, for with the Trotskyists eliminated, it was paralyzed by a momentary equilibrium between the Stalinist Center and the Bukharin Right. By now the real power was securely in Stalin's hands, but he was not yet prepared to launch a full-scale demolition of Bukharin; that would come a little later, as a major step in the transformation of Russia from an authoritarian dictatorship to a totalitarian state. So the Comintern drifted. The "right" policy that had been followed since 1924 was clearly exhausted, but no replacement had yet been worked out.

Not until the Tenth Plenum of the Comintern Executive Committee, held in Moscow a year later, did a new policy come into being. Here were proclaimed the famous "Third Period" of postwar capitalism, the theory of "social fascism," and the tactic of the "united front from below," all of which helped measurably to demoralize the working-class movements of Europe and to bring disaster to millions of people who knew little and cared less about the theoretical innovations of Stalinism.

The first period, according to Moscow, had lasted from 1917 to the end of 1924: it had been marked by revolutionary offensives. The second period, from early in 1924 to the end of 1927, was a time of the "relative, partial and temporary stabilization" of European capitalism, achieved mainly through the Young and Dawes plans and characterized politically by a defensive tactic on the part of the revolutionary movement. Now, proclaimed the Comintern, the precarious stabilization of capitalist economy was coming to an end, and a new, third period was beginning in which the workers would take the offensive in militant strikes and unemployment would create the most severe social crises, thus preparing the way for a "radicalization of the masses" upon an international scale. The Third Period would mark the final death-agony of capitalism, from which the Communist parties, armored in the steel of Stalinist orthodoxy, would emerge triumphant.

Stalin himself had already announced that "the era of capitalism's downfall has come." Molotov, a faithful repeater, wrote that "one must be a dull opportunist, one must be a sorry liberal, not to see that we have entered with both feet into the realm of the most tremendous revolutionary events of international significance." And the American party obediently declared a few months later that the American working class too was entering a period of radicalization "as a result of all the antagonisms of capitalism." [4]

How is this sudden turn toward the offensive to be explained, particularly since it came at a time when, as the historian Franz Borkenau writes, the Communists were reeling from defeats:

> There had been defeat in Germany in 1923, defeat again in 1924-5, from which the German party had scarcely recovered. The year 1926 had brought defeat in Britain; a few days later, defeat in Poland. . . . In March 1927 came Shanghai, in June and July, Wu-han [both severe defeats for the Chinese Communists]. . . . The new turn to the right, timidly and inconsistently effected on the European continent, carried to great lengths in Britain, in the United States, in China, had led to catastrophe. Its continuation had become almost impossible. It was impossible to carry out a policy of alliance with any section of the Kuomintang, because all sections of the Kuomintang were equally severe in their persecution of the communists. It was impossible to cooperate with the British Trade Union Council, because the T.U.C. made a laughing-stock of the Anglo-Russian committee [set up together by British and Russian trade unionists]. . . . All hopes, all attempts were at an end.[5]

The catastrophic "right" policy of the Communist movement had coincided with Stalin's destruction of the Trotskyist opposition. Now that Stalin was preparing to annihilate the Bukharin tendency on the right perimeter of Communism, he suddenly veered far to the left, first to capitalize on the predictable revulsion within the Comintern against the policies of 1924-27, second to find an ideological rationale and an organizational base from which to launch a vendetta against the Bukharin tendency, and third to develop within the Communist movement an ideological equivalent to the widespread use of terror which his new domestic policy in

Russia would necessarily require.* At this point in its development, the Stalinist tendency, though it had almost completed its consolidation of power within the Russian party, had not yet reached its mature and final form. It had not yet emerged as the core of a new ruling class at the top of a totalitarian society, nor had it yet begun habitually to employ physical terror against factional opponents; and as a result it improvised its policies under the spur of immediate crises, wildly veering from one extreme to another in the domestic, foreign, and ideological spheres. Its major immediate goal was the destruction of all dissidents within the Communist movement, many of whom made the fatal error of not uniting with one another because they believed the formal terms of disagreement among the various factions to be more important than the ruthless drive of the Stalinist machine to destroy the very possibility of disagreement.

The usual justification of the Third Period concept was expressed some years later by William Z. Foster when he wrote that a year after its adoption "there developed the great world economic crisis" and that a few years later "fascism spread over most of Europe, and World War II broke out." [7] But this retrospective justification was, if anything, an unwitting condemnation. For one thing, the prediction of economic crises was common to all the Communist factions and indeed was not confined to Communists or even Marxists. For another thing, the Communists had been predicting crises with such unyielding regularity that, given the instability of the European economy after the First World War, one of these predictions had to prove correct. But most important was the fact that the concept of the Third Period consisted of a good deal more than a mere prediction of economic crises; it asserted that a stage justifying *revolutionary offensive* had been reached in the social development of world capitalism; and here it was hoped to be proved completely—even tragically—wrong. For during the next decade

---

* From the long-range point of view, the last of these was the most important factor. "The specific atmosphere of the first Five Year Plan, formed of a mixture of wild enthusiasm, cruel persecution, disregard for the suffering of countless victims, bureaucratic corruption and inefficiency—an atmosphere as un-Western as anything can be—transferred itself automatically to the leading 'Comintern men who were living in Moscow . . . and brought this atmosphere of civil war in the midst of peace to the European Communists." [8]

European radicalism was to suffer the most bloody and unprecedented defeats.

Trotsky, in these years at his most polemically caustic in criticizing the vagaries of Stalinism, pointed out that:

a. The Comintern had failed to distinguish between a cyclical crisis within capitalist economy and a revolutionary social crisis. The first could have severe consequences but need not call into question the very fate of a society, as by definition the second did. For the maturing of a revolutionary situation a whole series of political factors were essential, and these did not necessarily come into existence as by-products of economic depression.

b. The Comintern failed to take into account the immediate realities of European politics, such as the rise of fascism in Germany and the near-triumph of the semi-fascist Heimwehr in Austria. Such developments, far from signaling an opening for the revolutionary left, necessarily forced it into a defensive position.

c. Above all, the Comintern ignored the actual condition of its own parties—the fact, for example, that the French CP had dropped from 83,000 members in 1925 to 35,000 in 1929. And when the Comintern analysts wrote that this was due to a disproportion between party membership and party influence, Trotsky counterattacked by noting that such a disproportion could only suggest that the French party was slowly being transformed into a parliamentary institution—hardly the basis for an expected revolutionary upsurge.

That the Comintern did not take its ultra-left talk very seriously can be seen by the fact that at no point during the several years of the Third Period did it make any preparations for an actual seizure of power in Europe or anywhere else; it did not even try to mobilize its tens of thousands of members and its millions of followers in Germany to resist forcibly the triumph of Hitler, as the much-scorned Social Democrats resisted Dollfuss in Austria. The main function of Third Period ideology was to provide background noise for dismal events in Russia.

Nonetheless, as the depression burst across the world, it seemed for a time to the Communist followers in Europe and America that the ultra-leftism of the Comintern had been justified, for they assumed that the severity of the crisis would automatically lead to revolutionary consciousness among the masses. But as Borkenau has brilliantly observed:

> Depressions, and especially an economic depression of such a scope as that of 1929-33, do not create readiness for every sort of fight. The masses of unemployed, who determine, more and more, in such a situation the views and actions even of those who have remained at work, are little adapted to continual, methodical fights for determined aims. They waver between short, wild, desperate outbreaks and complete apathy. . . . They leave in millions their old organizations . . . mostly because they feel that these organizations are powerless to help them. Here, then, is the point where left-wing extremism of the type of 1929 meets admirably the mood of the workless. If the communist agitators tell the unemployed that the trade unions have betrayed him and are no good, he is ready to believe them. If they tell the worker who is still employed that the union—by betrayal, of course—cannot protect either his wages or his job, he feels that the communists are right—and leaves the union. Thus the turn of the Comintern to the left, which had originated in internal feuds rooted in its previous history, found an unexpected response among the workers as a result of the crisis.[8]

An unexpected response, yes; but a response confined to sporadic explosions of violence, bloody street demonstrations by men so desperate they could not be persuaded or trained into firm class loyalties. During the next few years the Communists—even those in America—would be able to evoke many such expressions of despair from the "bottom dogs," the millions of men left jobless and hopeless by the depression. At the time many Communists felt that the riots of the unemployed were releasing a total opposition to society, but in actuality these were far from providing the basis for that revolutionary offensive which had been posited by the theory of the Third Period. Perhaps because such outbursts had done little but confirm the sense of desperation that had first made them possible, they were ultimately to provide large sources of human material for the Nazis and fascists.

If the theory of the Third Period was proved false, the main political tactic that followed from it—the assault upon the Social

Democrats as "social fascist"—was simply a disaster. As early as 1924 this notion had already been put forward by Stalin:

> Fascism is a fighting organization of the bourgeoisie, an organization that rests on the active support of Social Democracy. Social Democracy is objectively the moderate wing of fascism. There exists no reason for supposing that the fighting organization of the bourgeoisie can achieve decisive successes in their struggles . . . without the active support of the Social Democracy. These organizations do not contradict each other, they complete each other. They are not antipodes but twins.[9]

In 1924 no one in the Communist world had taken these fulminations very seriously, since Stalin had not yet been elevated to the rank of universal genius and, in any case, the policy of the Comintern was directed toward collaborating with the Social Democrats. By 1929, however, "social fascism" was resurrected and declared essential doctrine by the Comintern. Seldom in history has so transparent an intellectual absurdity had so tragic an impact upon the lives of millions of people. Exactly what the Stalinists meant by "social fascism" it is hard to say, since they frequently assigned different uses to the term and even more frequently employed it as a mere epithet of abuse. In their extreme moments they simply declared that Socialists *were* fascists. Thus, Foster: "The socialist is a fascist." At other times they implied that fascism, apparently fearful of showing its true colors, was masquerading in the pink draperies of Social Democracy. Thus the Comintern Executive Committee: "In countries where there are strong Social Democratic parties, fascism assumes the particular form of Social Fascism. . . ." In their somewhat more lucid intervals the Communist theoreticians suggested that, as the process of statification proceeded in capitalist economy, there took place "a merging of the Social Democracy into an open instrument of imperialism."[10] By 1932, when the slogan was beginning to be abandoned, some Communists had diluted social fascism to mean no more than that the mistaken policies of Social Democracy had "objectively" helped pave the way for fascism.

Now it was one thing to say that the systematic timidities of European Socialism had created a condition that the fascists could successfully exploit. It was even possible to go so far as a then independent Marxist, Sidney Hook, went during a sharp polemic against the theory of social fascism: "It cannot be denied," he wrote, "that the historic function of Social Democracy since 1918 has been to suppress or abort all revolutionary movements throughout the world. . . ."[11] But even if, as Hook pointed out, all this were granted, there remained such basic facts as: (a) Social Democracy had as its premise of survival the existence of mass labor organizations; (b) fascism had as the premise for its conquest of power the suppression of mass labor organizations; (c) consequently between Social Democracy and fascism there was a necessary and irreconcilable conflict, which the theory of social fascism willfully obscured.

All this may appear so obvious—even to the reader untutored in Marxist polemics—as to raise the question: how could the many Communists whose intelligence is beyond dispute bring themselves to accept such fantastic doctrines as social fascism? It is an important question to ask, but a difficult one to answer. Perhaps the beginning of an answer is to note that the theory of social fascism was advanced at a time when the inner structure—indeed, the very nature—of the Communist movement was undergoing a profound change. As in all authoritarian movements, the crucial test of loyalty now became the capacity to repeat nonsense that no one in his heart quite believed. Thus Karl Radek, surely one of the cleverest of Communists, found it necessary to write: "Whoever attempts to oppose the general line of the Party . . . automatically places himself on the other side of the barricades"[12]—which is to say, whoever disagrees with the theory of social fascism is himself a social fascist.*

Fully to grasp how absurdities of doctrine can lead to human suffering it is necessary for a paragraph or two to shift our focus to Germany. All through the late twenties warning signs of disaster had kept multiplying. In September, 1930, the Nazis polled nearly

---

* A former Trotskyist who had capitulated to Stalin, Radek had to prove that he was ready, even eager, to repeat the official line. Demonstrating his loyalty Radek seems to have secretly exaggerated and thereby mocked the formulas he was required to repeat—as when he wrote that the Social Democrats were "for the carrying out of the fascist line, but in a *democratic* way."[13] This was the equivalent of saying that the only difference between life and death is that in the former condition man is alive.

six and a half million votes, an increase of more than five million since May, 1928. Terror took command in the streets; radical meetings were systematically broken up; the storm troopers displayed a new audacity; and the left, despite its total of twelve million votes, had clearly been pushed into a defensive posture. It was at this desperate moment, as if to defy reality itself, that the German Communists chose to press the doctrine of social fascism.

Directly after the Nazi electoral triumph in 1930, the *Rote Fahne,* organ of the German Communists, announced: "Last night was Hitler's greatest day, but the so-called election victory of the Nazis is the beginning of the end. . . . What comes after this can only be decline and fall." As the power of the Nazis nonetheless kept rising, the German Communists continued to direct their main fire not against the storm troop hoodlums but against the Social Democrats. The Communist youth paper advanced the slogan "Drive the Social Fascists out of the factories, out of the employment bureaus, out of the trade schools." Ernst Thaelmann, leader of the German Communists, justified his party's refusal to accept a Social Democratic suggestion for a united front: "This influence exercised over revolutionary workers by the treacherous ideology of the lying Social Democrats is . . . *the most serious danger that confronts the Communist Party.* How great that danger is, is shown . . . by the latest maneuvers of Social Fascism. . . . It is undertaking a new demagogic maneuver, it is 'threatening' to form a united front with the Communist Party." This threat at least Thaelmann knew how to ward off.

In the spring of 1932 Piatnitsky, secretary of the Comintern, denounced Trotsky for his stream of bitter pamphlets insisting upon a united front against the Nazis. "How is it possible," inquired the profound Piatnitsky, "to deduce . . . the necessity of establishing a 'bloc' with the German Social Democrats for the struggle against Fascism, when the Social Democrats are doing nothing but helping the Fascists?" Not only was a bloc ruled out; "even a temporary joint operation in individual actions between the Communist Party and the Social Democratic Party," wrote Muenzenberg, a German Communist leader, "would *forever* discredit the Communists among the broad masses of workers." As against the unity of party and party to resist Nazi terrorism, the Communists proposed a "united front from below," that is, a united front with the Social Democratic followers in order to combat the Social Democratic leaders.

This madness reached its height when *Der Propagandist,* a German CP publication, declared that a "Social Democratic coalition government, confronted with a non-combative, split-up, confused proletariat would be a thousand times greater evil than an open fascist dictatorship, against which would appear a class conscious proletariat. . . ."

Nor was social fascism merely a matter of abstract slogans. When the Nazis began to press for a referendum in 1931 to overthrow the Social Democratic government of Prussia, the first response of the German CP was to back the Social Democrats. But this policy was quickly vetoed by Moscow, which insisted that, to combat the "main danger" of Social Democracy, it was proper to support the Nazi campaign for a referendum. And the German Communists obeyed.

Not even the seizure of power by Hitler, with the brutalities it immediately entailed, could force a reversal of the Communist line. A few days after Hitler became Chancellor the *Daily Worker* printed a Comintern document which insisted that the "task of the Communist Party remains, as before—to direct the chief blow, at the present stage, against Social Democracy." In late 1933, after thousands of Communists and Social Democrats had been imprisoned, *Rundschau,* the German-language organ of the Comintern, wrote that "the ruthless suppression of the Social Democratic organizations and press does not change anything in the fact that now as ever they are the chief social support of the dictatorship of capital." [14] Such was the wisdom that culminated in Ernst Thaelmann's slogan of 1933: "After Hitler—Our Turn!"

That the tactics of the German Communists made Hitler's victory inevitable or that a more sensible policy could have prevented his victory is a matter for conjecture. What can be said with certainty is that the doctrine of social fascism, by dividing and demoralizing the German left, proved greatly to the advantage of the Nazis. And the cost that would be paid for this doctrine? A cost measured in mountains of bones and oceans of blood.

Politics that meant high tragedy in Europe often resulted in low comedy in America. "The bourgeoisie," declared Earl Browder in one of his less notable predictions, "is definitely building up the Socialist Party because it knows that in the coming great class struggles in America it is going to need the Socialist Party." If so, the bourgeoisie was doing a very bad job indeed: the Socialist Party had polled only a little more than 250,000 votes in 1928. Which did not prevent another Communist leader, Sam Darcy, from writing that in the 1928 electoral campaign the party had made a major error: it "had failed to direct our chief struggle against the most dangerous enemy of the workers, Norman Thomas and the Socialist Party." Its other "failures" the CP found rather difficult to cope with, but this one it proceeded quickly to correct.

From 1928 to early 1932 the *Daily Worker,* in attacking the American Socialists, printed some of the most fantastic vituperation that can be found in any political newspaper, vituperation which had it been even half-true would have branded Norman Thomas as not merely a reactionary but the very Devil himself. Here are a few characteristic *Daily Worker* headlines:

> Norman Thomas for Violence Against the Workers Under the Screen of Police Efficiency
> Socialists Are Brothers of the Gastonia Jailors
> Zaritsky [a Socialist trade-union leader] for Long Work Week
> Middle Class Liberals Join Socialists in Gastonia Frame-Up
> SP Competes with KKK for the Title of "American"
> Fascist White Terror Sought by Socialists
> Yellow "Socialist" *Forward* Is in Favor of Lynching Negroes.[15]

In relation to American politics as a whole, this may have had very little importance, but within the American radical world, isolated and confined as it then was, the tactic of social fascism created an utterly poisonous atmosphere. In previous years the Socialists had generally looked upon the Communists as reckless younger brothers, members of the family who had gone astray; but now they began to feel that the split between themselves and the Communists had come to reflect a fundamental divergence of moral and political views. That the Communists systematically raided and broke up Socialist meetings during these years—a favorite device was to shout demands at such meetings that a "workers' chairman" be elected—helped intensify this feeling among the Socialists and, indeed, the entire non-Communist left.

In America the importance of the doctrine of social fascism lay primarily within the life and development of the Communist movement itself. Social fascism was, so to speak, the ideological teething ring upon which the new Stalinist "cadre"—the core of devoted, militant, worshipful activists—emerged from infancy. Social fascism, to change the figure, was the ideological stiffening that helped create the peculiarly fanatical Third Period type of Communist. Those who could accept this doctrine and see in it proof of the wisdom and virtue of the Comintern were the ones who would be ready to accept everything, every twist and turn of Stalinist policy from the Popular Front to the Hitler-Stalin pact. The totalitarian party requires from its followers an acquiescence in some vast initial absurdity, which is to serve both as the link of faith and as proof of a readiness to surrender individual judgment. Seen in this way, the doctrine of social fascism was to have consequences that would reverberate through American life for at least two decades.

3. During the whole Third Period the American Communist Party was faced with an extremely difficult task: it had to align its picture of America with the ideological demands of the Comintern line. This meant systematically to write, and sometimes to behave, as if America were entering a pre-revolutionary situation. Politically, it meant to abandon the earlier Communist stand in favor of a labor party—which implied a belief that the growth of the American working class into radical consciousness would probably be slow—and to claim or pretend that the CP itself was on the way to becoming a mass revolutionary party. Organizationally, it meant a frantic campaign to toughen the CP into a tightly disciplined, quasi-military party (it had never been quite that before) in which every member would function as an obedient soldier at the disposal of the central committee. Factions were now formally prohibited, marking a major step in the transformation of the party into a totalitarian movement; the front groups were drawn sternly into the party's ideological orbit, which meant to abandon all pretense to independence and transform them into little more than

phantoms of the party; and the foreign-language federations, some of them lamentably open to "rightist deviations," were constantly being pressed into the Third Period mold.

From the dogma that the structural collapse of American capitalism was so severe as to permit neither recovery nor repair there followed a belief that the "final conflict" between a working class under Communist leadership and a bourgeoisie turned fascist would soon follow. But how was this expectation to be aligned with the fact that during the first two or three years of the depression the American workers proved, in the main, to be more fearful than militant, more shocked than aggressive? In several ways. First, by a systematic, often comic exaggeration of the revolutionary potential of strikes, unemployed demonstrations, and farm riots. Second, by a tacit belief in some cataclysmic and total change in American patterns of thought. Third, by resorting implicitly to one of the less happy notions hatched in the Bolshevik movement: Zinoviev's theory of "electrification," originally advanced with regard to Germany in 1921 and according to which the party had to embark upon offensive after offensive, bloody and painful as these might be, in order to shock a sluggish working class into a revolutionary mood.

The result was a curious mixture of deception and self-deception, a kind of systematic inducement of political hallucinations. For brief moments these could arouse enormous enthusiasm among the members of the party and persuade them to the most remarkable sacrifices in behalf of the revolution that seemed so close at hand; but in the long run, as hopes were frustrated and energies wasted, the demoralization of many followers was inevitable. In all things, big and small, the *Daily Worker* strove to create a picture of a capitalist world infinitely worse than it already was, though in 1930 and 1931 there could hardly be any point in exaggerating the sickness of American society. Simultaneously, the Communists tried to persuade their supporters that the movement was steadily marching forward to international victory. If, however, there *was* defeat at any point (Third Period theory made no allowance for defeat, but reality sometimes forced its recognition), this was due to the betrayals of the Socialist and other labor leaders who systematically misled a working class that, by its very nature, was constantly tensed for revolution. (Why then did so many workers continue to follow these misleaders? A difficult, even annoying question for the Communists.)

Day after day the party would call upon its members and sympathizers to demonstrate in the streets of the larger cities—nor was there ever a lack of occasion, from crises in unemployment relief to terror in Cuba, from denunciations of AFL sell-outs to defense of the Soviet Union against imperialist warmongers. These demonstrations, particularly since many of them led to bloody clashes with the police, created an aura of excitement and an illusion of achievement within the party. Providing a sense of constant and almost total engagement, such street actions helped preserve the belief that the ultimate decision was close at hand. And given this belief, everything could be taken as evidence for the mounting spiral of crisis, betrayal, and fated victory. The Third Period marked not merely the "totalitarianization" of the party but also the climax of the tendency within Communist thought—a tendency fundamentally terrifying, even if sometimes comic in its manifestations—to subsume every variety of experience under the monolith of ideology.

Did the streetcar workers of New Orleans go on strike in 1929 and engage in a few skirmishes with the police? The *Daily Worker* thundered that "again the workers of the South have, with elemental force, delivered heavy blows against the capitalist exploiters and defied the armed forces of the state." Did a few members of the Young Communist League publicly "graduate" into the party? They were, proclaimed the party secretary, the heroes who "will lead the Red Army in the United States." Did it happen that PS 109 of New York City required its pupils to eat their lunches only in the lunchroom? Two militant children, members of the Young Pioneers, were soon on hand to distribute leaflets denouncing this outrage. Did the Philadelphia YCL hold a meeting in praise of the Soviet Union? "Young Workers of Philadelphia Back Red Army," concluded a *Daily Worker* headline. Did the Seattle Boy Scouts arrange a jamboree? Again the YCL was ready, circulating a leaflet that denounced the Boy Scouts "as an organization of the bosses preparing the children of the workers for the next war." Did the Socialist Party go so far as to permit the "Star-Spangled Banner" to be sung at one of its meetings? "Unparalleled treachery," rang the judgment of the *Daily Worker*. And was spring, nonetheless, in the air? Baseball, cried the *Daily Worker* amid headlines calling for further demonstrations and still greater Bolshevization of the party, "baseball is a weapon against the workers." [16]

It was essential to the politics of the Third Period that the party feel itself both profoundly threatened and on the verge of triumph; beleaguered by enemies and, if only it could purify and steel itself, within reach of power. The politics of the Third Period, whether they made themselves felt in such deadly serious matters as dual unionism or in such trivia as the denunciation of baseball, had as their outcome the creation of a party in America such as had never been seen here before.

What kept the derangement of Third Period Communism from appearing even more weird than it did was that American society itself was grossly deranged. People *were* hungry, as the Communists said; men *did* feel themselves to be living without hope or purpose, as the Communists said; and in the early thirties there *was* a good deal of talk about forthcoming American revolutions, as the Communists said there should be. The sight of men without work, lounging in parks, idling around street corners, selling apples on the streets, shuffling in bread lines, had become not merely a familiar but virtually an accepted part of the social landscape. The CP, impatient with the fact that during these depression years it had not grown enough to allow it to emerge from sectarian isolation, now furiously lashed itself into efforts to organize what it regarded as the two crucial sectors of the population: the unskilled workers, into dual unions, and the jobless, into unemployed groups.*

The Communist efforts to organize the unemployed into stable organizations were to prove a critical test both for Third Period poli-

---

* The party leadership often betrayed a calloused inhumanity in the way it drove its followers. In 1934 the wretchedly underpaid textile workers went on strike. To its dismay, the party leadership was quite cut off from this important event. During the strike, as if to vent its pique upon its own followers, the *Daily Worker* printed a harsh attack on the Providence, Rhode Island, branch of the party for not distributing the paper among the strikers. Why no such effort had been made by the Providence branch became clear when the *Worker* correspondent in that city reported the next morning that "Every known Communist was picked up on sight today, and militant workers were taken into custody charged with being Communists. John Weber, CP organizer and 14 others have been in jail for the last 24 hours. . . ." [17] Nor did the editors publicly apologize to their Providence comrades. In "electrifying" the party, everything went.

tics and for the general capacity of the party for taking advantage of opportunities presented by the depression. As early as 1928 the party had begun making a few stabs at organizing the unemployed, though with no particular results. By the first few months of 1930, however, a major portion of party activity was devoted toward marshaling the unemployed into demonstrations and local organizations.

At first it seemed that the Communists had scored a major success. In city after city, during the winter of 1930, party-led committees organized demonstrations and marches upon city halls to demand adequate relief and to urge passage of unemployed insurance legislation. From the Communist point of view, these demonstrations came exactly at the right time. The shock of the sudden economic collapse was still acute; the apathy that would overwhelm millions of the jobless in the next few years had not yet set in; people were ready to pour into the streets to express their anger and frustration. On March 6, designated as International Unemployment Day by the Communists throughout the world, a series of quite impressive though frequently violent demonstrations were held in many American cities, almost entirely under party leadership. The next morning the *Daily Worker* claimed that 110,000 people had participated in New York City, 100,000 in Detroit, 40,000 in Milwaukee, 20,000 in Youngstown, 20,000 in Pittsburgh, 15,000 in Buffalo. Inflated though these figures were, they nonetheless reflected the fact that the party had managed to seize upon a highly explosive issue and to rally considerable numbers of non-Communist workers under its banner. In New York, where the demonstrators had tried to storm City Hall in order to present their demands directly to the mayor, William Z. Foster, Robert Minor, and Israel Amter were arrested, and later sentenced to jail for several months. This, however, did not hurt the CP effort to mobilize the unemployed; quite the contrary.

Trying to capitalize quickly on the success of the demonstrations, the party organized a conference in Pittsburgh for its leaders in unemployed work. Here plans were laid for creating a national unemployed organization in the summer of 1930, and Pat Devine, a CP functionary, was chosen secretary of the interim committee. But despite the aura of confidence that hung over this meeting, a critical observer might have noticed that the conditions were being set up for the eventual failure of the Communists to win over any significant portion of the American unemployed. In the preliminary program drawn up at Pittsburgh, immediate demands pertaining to the needs of the unemployed jostled political slogans reflecting Communist ideology. (One of the proposed planks for the unemployed program was: "Defense of the Soviet Union!") Here as elsewhere the Communists had to "politicize" each project they undertook, which in practice meant to saturate it with Third Period dogma.

About 1,200 delegates attended the convention held in Chicago during the summer of 1930 to establish a new organization called the Unemployed Councils, though the impressiveness of this figure is lessened when one learns that nearly 500 of the delegates came from Chicago itself. More important was the fact that the new organization was closely tied in with the Trade Union Unity League, the Communist dual-union center, thus fatally hindering it from becoming a mass unemployed organization and also cutting it off from whatever help it might have received from the regular trade unions. At this point, it is true, most AFL unions were so weak in their organization and so parochial in their outlook that they would have felt no great impulse to help any unemployed movement; but their indifference was reinforced and lent a needless plausibility when the Communists established the Unemployed Councils as part of the dual-union movement.

Late in 1930 the Unemployed Councils began calling the jobless into the streets once more. But to the surprise of the Communist leaders, the jobless did not come. The party leaders simply did not understand—or were prevented by the fetters of the Third Period from applying their understanding—that street demonstrations which lead only to more street demonstrations will generally result not in militancy but in demoralization. Even the tightly knit Communist "vanguard" could not be sustained by endless calls to battle in the streets. Initially the demonstrations had served a purpose in dramatizing the problem of unemployment; but the pattern of street actions that now followed had as its cause less the legitimate requirements of the frail unemployed groups than the impulse of the Communist leadership to create an atmosphere that would justify the politics—as it released the emotions—of the Third Period.

And the unemployed themselves? What was the Third Period to them or they to the Third Period? They were interested in finding jobs and, if that proved impossible, in getting adequate relief. As long as it seemed that the Communists could help in at least the second of these objectives, some of the unemployed would follow their leadership. But by the end of 1930 there had sprung up competing unemployed organizations, led by Socialists and independent radicals who did not "politicize" the work so crudely; and furthermore, the city administrations, though still unable to cope with the enormous crisis, had gained some experience in administering relief and handling complaints.

During the first crucial year or two of their existence, the Unemployed Councils failed to work out a satisfactory policy in regard to the people they claimed to represent. On the one hand, endless demonstrations that brought no immediate local results; on the other, a feeble effort at "community cooperation." Thus, in the spring of 1931 when it became clear that something other than demonstrations would be necessary, Earl Browder urged a policy of setting up local collection committees "to get food from the larger capitalists and corporations . . . particularly in those institutions where the unemployed were formerly at work." But when such committees are unable to get food "from the corporations and large capitalists, they shall then begin soliciting small merchants and petty bourgeois generally, calling upon these elements to join the Unemployed Councils in demanding relief from the government treasuries and in demanding unemployment insurance nationally." [18] This somewhat less than inspired substitution of communal charity for the class struggle was soon abandoned by the Communist leaders of the Unemployed Councils.

After the initial period of adventurism and confusion, the party did work out a sensible procedure for the Unemployed Councils. Nationally, they were to campaign for unemployment insurance; locally, they were to serve as grievance agencies representing the unemployed in their relations with relief bureaus. Whatever success the Councils finally had was the result of this decision to abandon the earlier "revolutionary" stress and to function as, in some rough sense, an equivalent of the trade unions.

Meanwhile there were several years of concentrated but not

very fruitful work in the unemployed field. A national "Hunger March" was held in early 1932; it drew 1,200 participants to Washington, many of them acknowledged Communists, and it stirred up a swirl of publicity; but the party leadership knew it had not been a success. Measuring the meager results of such actions, the CP leaders criticized the ranks for excesses that actually flowed from Third Period doctrine itself. Max Saltzman, CP leader in Connecticut, complained that at a meeting of the hunger marchers in Stamford a Communist speaker had described them as "the advance guard of the Red Army." This complaint echoed earlier warnings by Earl Browder that overzealous comrades should refrain at unemployed demonstrations from urging the seizure of city halls.[19]

Even with the best of programs and the most gifted of leaders it is always extremely difficult to organize the unemployed. In America, particularly, the unemployed worker was not prepared to think of himself as having been permanently removed from the labor force; for all that it caused him severe hardship he did not regard his condition of unemployment as the crucial determinant of his life. Only in such countries as Germany, where millions of jobless workers thought of themselves as men discarded by society, was it possible for the Communists to create mass organizations of the unemployed—and even these seldom remained stable for very long.

The life of the employed worker is given form and meaning by the time he spends in the factory, and his relationships with other workers are regulated both by their physical closeness and by their common interests on the job. The unemployed worker, however, tends to become a drifter, a demoralized and helpless solitary. At best, the unemployed worker can meet his fellows in the humiliating situation of waiting for relief in a government office, or in the idleness of time spent in the headquarters of an unemployed organization. Neither of these is likely to create the discipline necessary for sustained political activity; both stimulate moods of depression and dependence. And while the unemployed are capable of sudden outbursts of militancy and violence, it has always been difficult for any Marxist movement to lead them from such outbursts to regular and systematic activity. For where the employed worker knows or thinks he knows who his friends and enemies are, the unemployed

worker is either entirely bewildered by his condition or comes painfully to realize that he is the victim of a social collapse beyond
local remedy. In the factory the union is able to focus sentiment
upon specific issues and grievances; but the unemployed organization can at most try to represent its members in securing better
relief, a function that can seldom have the continuity or encourage
the sense of solidarity possible to union activity in the shop.

These difficulties were very real in the early thirties and would
have made the task of organizing the unemployed a back-breaking
one for even the most skillful and flexible leadership. But when
one remembers that the Stalinist campaign to organize the unemployed began under the curse of Third Period politics, the surprise
is not that by the middle of 1932 there were only 20,000 members in
the Unemployed Councils but that there were any at all.[20]

Throughout the early thirties the party press was filled with the
most bitter admissions of failure and ineptitude in unemployed work.
Writing in the spring of 1931, a year after the large street demonstrations, Browder admitted that "Weakest of all phases of the
[unemployed] movement has been its organization." At about the
same time, the organizational bulletin of District 2 of the party
(New York-New Jersey) complained: "Our Councils are too loose.
Thousands and thousands of workers join and leave. No membership meetings are held and, because of this, the Councils do not
have any elected officers. . . . The Party's guidance in the Unemployed Councils consists of nothing but one comrade bringing
down instructions of the CP to the unemployed workers." By the
fall of 1933, Israel Amter, the Communist leader in charge of New
York unemployed work, admitted: "Bureaucracy is widespread in
the unemployed movement. . . . There is direct appointment and
removals of Unemployed Council functionaries by the Party committees. These functionaries are responsible not to the masses but
to the Party committees." And as late as the spring of 1935, when
the Unemployed Councils claimed—it was a vast exaggeration—
300,000 members, Herbert Benjamin, one of the more talented Communist leaders in unemployed work, was still crying out: "If we
call a demonstration each time a grievance is brought to our attention, without first trying to get what we want by other means, the
workers will fall prey to the demagogic charge that we are merely

looking for an excuse to demonstrate." [21] It was like the boy who had cried "wolf" too often.

By 1936 the Unemployed Councils joined with the Socialist-led Workers Alliance and several independent groups to form a unified organization of the unemployed; and for a time thereafter the Communists reaped some profit from the domination they established over this new movement. Fundamentally, however, their opportunity in unemployed work had come and gone. Genuine difficulties such as anyone else would have faced in this work, together with their own crippling dogmatism, had deprived them of the chance to win the allegiance of any major section of the unemployed. Not merely intellectually, but also in the day-to-day party work within the "mass organizations," the Third Period exacted a heavy price. It was a price the party would keep paying long after the Third Period had been consigned to the "memory hole" of Communist history.

4. To chronicle the Communist adventures with front organizations during the Third Period—from committees in defense of the Chinese Revolution to committees in defense of American women, from the Freiheit Mandolin Ferein to the International Workers Order—would be beyond the scope of this book. It would also be very tedious. For the pattern of party domination, of wrenching each front group into a lifeless replica of the party itself, was essentially the same in all cases. Apart from unemployed work, however, there are two areas of Communist concentration so important that a few words should be said about them: youth and Negro.

During the late twenties the Communist youth organization, at no point numbering more than 3,000 members, was simply a duplicate of the party itself. Occasionally a few speeches would be made by leaders of the Young Workers (Communist) League urging that a distinctively "youth" atmosphere be created, but these were ceremonial gestures that had little effect on the life of the organization. The intense absorption in factional disputes (a YCL discussion meeting in April, 1929, was reported by the *Daily Worker* to have lasted eight hours—a saturnalia of juvenile polemic!); the highly demanding routine of a movement that expected each member to yield it his major energies and thereby come closer to the status of a professional revolutionist; the extreme "politicizing" of every area of discourse, so that an esoteric vocabulary was employed that deliberately cut off the unchosen—these traits of party life were also dominant among the youth. If anything, the YCL abandoned itself to the fantasies of the Third Period even more than the party did, since young people, generally not able or needing to earn their own livings, could afford to ignore daily experience more than could the adults. At YCL camps and schools catechistic exercises in doctrine were sometimes mixed with amateurish experiments in military drill—it was necessary, explained YCL leader Will Herberg, to root out "pacifist illusions." [22]   And while the learning of close order drill by a few Communist boys no more endangered the government than the rifle practice of National Guardsmen secured it, such things were indicative of the spirit to which the Third Period could lead.

In the late twenties most YCL branches were concentrated in the larger cities, and a good many YCL members were likely to be sons and daughters of old-time Jewish radicals who had brought with them the socialist tradition of Europe and for whom it continued to serve as the central principle of their lives. Ingrown and provincial, more of a club than a political movement, the Communist youth organization combined a mild Bohemianism (the revolt of its members against the puritan modesty of immigrant family life) with a rigid fanaticism (the desire of young converts to outshine the older Communists in the zeal of their attachment). For such members—there were other kinds, of course—the YCL could satisfy a mixture of seemingly contradictory needs: it helped maintain the intellectual heritage in which they had been raised, yet it also became a means of declaring their independence and, in a tortuous way, of establishing themselves in American life.

As the depression deepened, the idea of Communism began to strike fire in the minds of an important section of American youth. Those who joined or were influenced by the Young Communist League were never to comprise more than a very small minority of their generation—but a minority that, because of its devotion and energy, left its imprint upon many others. No matter how hostile one may be toward the politics of these young Communists, honesty requires the admission that some of them were among the best of their generation, among the most intelligent, selfless, and idealistic. No one was likely to join the YCL in 1932 out of ordinary careerism or because it was "the thing to do"; YCL membership could mean hardship and sacrifice. At the least, it brought young people into painful conflicts with their families—sometimes, by the way, with parents who were themselves radicals yet incongruously shared the immigrant dream of seeing their children become "successful" in the world. For others, joining the YCL meant a fundamental change in their lives that would leave them permanently shaken. This is not to deny that delusional motifs played a part in the revolutionary fervor to which the Young Communists drove themselves during the early thirties; but then, such motifs play a part in all public life, and it would be hazardous to suggest that they were necessarily or invariably stronger among Communists than among other people. Nor would we deny that a good many Young Communists were hopelessly narrow-minded and intolerant, pumped up with the pride of historical certainty and arrogant with the taste of future power. Perhaps the truth can at least be approached by saying that the Communists, while attracting some of the best American youth, frequently brought out some of their worst qualities.

By the early thirties the YCL began to make significant gains. It established strong units in a number of colleges that had always maintained a tradition of political life, even if only among the handful of students that would huddle into the Social Problems clubs; and these colleges, because they usually attracted many students from poor families, were particularly important to the burgeoning radical youth groups. City, Hunter, and Brooklyn colleges in New York, Temple in Philadelphia, the University of Chicago, Wayne in Detroit, UCLA, the University of Wisconsin—these were the schools in which the sparks of radicalism, having barely survived in the late twenties, now began to flicker. Some of them were free or almost free colleges, and many young people unable to find jobs became students for lack of anything else to do. Poverty was an immediate fact for many of these students; yet that alone might not have been enough to make them into Communists. What so strongly drove them leftward was their sense that American society seemed utterly adrift, that no large moral purpose animated the world of business and of work, that the *idea* of social crackup had become the common possession of millions of people who did not think of themselves as radicals.

Amid a mass of students who continued to move through the adolescent rituals of "football, frolics, and fraternities," or who simply attended classes with a dull slogging persistence, the young Communists sprang up as a purposeful minority. They were always ready to argue with all the appearances of knowledge and dialectic; they bubbled with conspicuous passion; they seemed endlessly energetic and astonishingly confident. In classrooms where professors droned on in the tones of academic caution, or revealed the genuine doubts that the depression had stirred in them, the YCLers were ready with their quick and monolithic answers: whatever else, no one denied that they were good talkers.* By comparison, even the young Socialists might seem tame and uncertain, never quite as "professional" in their politics as the young Communists.

For several years guerilla warfare tore up some of the American campuses. College administrators would be denounced as enemies of academic freedom; radical students as professional disrupters who behaved in the classroom as if they were leading a squad of strikers in pursuit of scabs. Both accusations touched upon the truth. Amid the clamor and hysteria of the crisis years, many college presidents grew fretful over the continued support of wealthy conservatives and behaved with little tolerance—sometimes with extreme harshness—toward dissident students. And in turn the Communists systematically employed their talents toward creating a permanent uproar on the campus.

Many college administrations, in their readiness to collapse before the pressures of trustees, right-wing community groups, and donors, unwittingly lent credence to the charges of the young Communists; the caricature of a college president drawn in *Student Review*, the Communist campus magazine, could be uncomfortably close to the reality of a man like Frederick B. Robinson, head of CCNY during the mid-thirties. On the other hand, the YCL and

---

* And not only in the colleges. They seemed to talk almost as well in kindergartens and grade schools. At the highly publicized 1930 Congressional hearings presided over by Representative Hamilton Fish, New York City principals testified that the Young Pioneers were generally bright students who could quote Marx "better than anyone in this room." [23]

its campus appendage, the National Student League, worked on the assumption that the class struggle raged as actively, if not quite as violently, in the classroom as in the factory. For many of the young Communists the idea of the university as a community of scholars investigating problems in a relatively disinterested way was an absurdity, a deception of the liberal mind. Starting with the plausible notion that the university could not be isolated from the major conflicts of society, they drove toward the dubious conclusion that ideas in the university were merely a reflex of events taking place beyond its walls.

Given this premise, it is understandable that, for the devoted young Communists, going to college did not necessarily mean being a student. Even if they had wished to, they could not genuinely respect the *idea* of the university. Secure in their possession of Historical Truth, they felt that their teachers—except for the occasional left-winger or technical specialist—had little or nothing to teach them. They went to college, or so they liked to tell themselves, in order to do political work. It was their "assignment," just as other comrades had assignments to the New York water front or the North Carolina textile mills. In practice, of course, few YCL members managed to live by so stringent a point of view; other pressures, ranging from family responsibilities to personal ambitions, came into play; and sometimes they could even be seduced by a brilliant "bourgeois" professor. But the attitude described here was the one toward which the more active YCL members aspired and that the YCL leaders encouraged.

Anti-intellectualism had long been traditional among American Communists, and until 1934 the student, no matter what his activity or zeal, was likely to be regarded as a dubious type by the older comrades. Desperately trying to "proletarianize" itself, the movement looked upon students as petty bourgeois, unreliable, and unstable by their very nature. At best, from the party's point of view, the students were to regard their college years as a period of training in which they would learn various secondary skills that, together with the primary knowledge available only in the class struggle, would prepare them for political leadership. With the skills and articulateness they acquired on the campus, the young Communists could then be tempered and hardened in the realities of social life even if, as frequently happened, this meant sacrificing their natural gifts and interests.

But as the Communists began to shake off the nightmare of the Third Period, they also changed their attitude toward students. Many of the college boys and girls who joined the YCL or one of its fronts in 1935 would clearly never break away from their middle-class style of life; and now the movement no longer badgered them to do so. It began to see that there were distinct advantages (potential middle-class following, financial support, intellectual allies) in cultivating the "student movement," even though it had previously been hostile to the notion that students form an independent social stratum with interests of their own. The YCL also began to see that the student movement had attained a measure of independent existence and was no longer *merely* the creature of the radicals. And then, the Popular Front line toward which the Communists were moving required a particularly tender cultivation of student liberalism.

Meanwhile, a widespread if superficial mood of pacifism had been growing up on the campus. This mood had little to do with pacifism as an ethic or ideology: it was an expression of uncertainty, a hesitant vote of "little confidence" in society; a symptom of discomfort rather than a flare of rebellion. Nonetheless, both Communist and Socialist student groups, which had been working together as uneasy allies, quickly sensed that if ever they were to root themselves in American campus life it could only be through taking advantage of this mood.

In the spring of 1934 there accordingly took place the first Student Anti-War Strike, a one-hour stoppage of classes in which 25,000 college students participated and at which the Oxford Pledge —a pledge, borrowed from England, not to support the government in any future war—was solemnly administered. The next year 150,000 students joined, and in 1936 the organizations sponsoring the strike claimed that 1,000,000 students participated while the *New York Times* granted 500,000. Even if the lower figure is taken as the more accurate one (which it was), there could be no doubt that the work of the campus radicals and, more particularly, of the campus Communists was yielding handsome returns. For while it would be absurd to claim that more than a tiny fraction of the student strikers consisted of Communists or their sympathizers, it would be unrealistic to deny that without the shaping and diligent hand of the Communists these strikes would at the most have remained local and sporadic.

By the proper application of the laws of leverage, a small power can be made to move one far greater than itself. The radical student groups, coming into existence in an atmosphere of fright and hope, thus created a student movement that would have a measurable influence upon American political and intellectual life during the next two decades. Though never approaching the social weight and seriousness of its equivalents in Europe and Asia, the American student movement was to be a training ground for liberals, intellectuals, and trade-union leaders—in short, for part of a new American elite, the articulate spokesmen and representative figures of postwar society. In a sense, then, the radical groups were too successful: what they helped bring to shape on the campus broke out of their grasp and became part of the larger rhythm of American life. By giving rise to that curious phenomenon, the American middle-class radical, the student movement paved the way for that familiar American phenomenon, the post-war version of the successful young man. No matter what the intentions of the Communist and Socialist founders of the student movement may have been, they helped—as, in general, the radical movement in this country has so frequently helped —young people to find their "place" in the very world against which they had first rebelled.

During the early thirties the young Communists and young Socialists on the campus had frequently quarreled and as frequently worked together. In neither respect did they have much choice. Though the quarrels concerned issues that were only too real (the nature of Russian society, for example), they were not immediately relevant to campus life. They were refracted quarrels. In the colleges the various radical groups necessarily found themselves drawn together, if only for warmth and protection—and somewhat closer to one another than were the adult movements to which they adhered in the outer world. There seemed to be common aims and interests particular to students, and as long as this was believed it helped knit the left-wing students into a temporary community—a fact that was itself a major victory for Communist strategy in the mid-thirties.

Against this centripetal tendency there was only one opposing force. The radical students, if only because they were students, often had a way of taking ideological disputes with a unique serious-ness: they could become as passionate about the Chinese Revolution as about the conditions of West Virginia miners. (They were hardly more distant from the one than the other.) And this capacity for ideological participation often worked to the disadvantage of the young Communists, who suffered repeated losses—numerically minor but involving some of their most gifted members—to the Socialists and Trotskyists. For if ideology *were* taken seriously, then the frequently unprincipled shifts of the Communist line and the vulnerability of Stalinism to attack from the left made it likely that a number of Communist students would be won away to some brand of independent Marxism.

Nonetheless, by the mid-thirties, the Communists had suc-ceeded in establishing themselves in a number of colleges as a significant minority force; they exerted an influence considerably beyond what their numbers might suggest; they had won to their ranks gifted young people, of whom some would become leaders in the Communist Party itself, others would work in front groups and trade unions, while those who broke from the faith would reappear as schooled anti-Communists in various liberal and radical move-ments. Not only did the student ferment of the early thirties matter in its own right; it served as a kind of prep school—though hardly the most fashionable one—for political leaders of the forties and fifties.*

5. At the sixth convention of the CP, in December, 1928, Jack Stachel, its "organizational specialist," reported that there were between 150 and 200 Negroes in the party. A year and a half later Earl Browder was claiming a thousand Negro members. Though some increase undoubtedly took place during this year and a half, neither figure need be taken too seriously.[24] Party statistics

* Nothing has been said about the non-student activities of the YCL during the early thirties. In the main, its work in the unions and neighbor-hoods duplicated that of the party and need not be detailed here.

were notoriously inaccurate, and the membership turnover was so rapid as to call into question the usefulness of any figure a few months after it had been released. These membership claims become even more dubious when one remembers that the party was not very rigorous in the standards of participation it demanded from Negroes, so that inactive Negro members would often be carried on the rolls long after inactive whites had been dropped.

By the late twenties, when the Third Period began, the party had made only the faintest progress in recruiting American Negroes or winning influence within the Negro community. In James W. Ford the party had found a Negro leader whose talents were modest but who could claim the advantage of quick obedience to the party line (among Negro intellectuals and liberals Ford became known as Earl's Uncle Tom); in Langston Hughes, almost the only Negro writer willing to grace its list of front organizations; in William L. Patterson and Benjamin Davis, Jr., two prominent Negroes who would later render important service. But neither in Harlem nor the South Side of Chicago—certainly not in the Southern states— could the CP claim any firm base among the Negroes.

Yet, as the depression kept weakening the fabric of American life, genuine possibilities seemed to appear for winning Negro recruits. If millions of people suffered economic deprivation, the Negroes suffered still more. The rate of unemployment in Harlem and the South Side was greater than in any other area of New York or Chicago; job discrimination against Negroes grew more severe than ever; and in the South millions of Negro sharecroppers lived on the edge of subsistence. None of this was lost upon the Communist leaders, and time after time they drove the party into Negro work. It was an area of activity that under the best of circumstances would have presented the Communists with many severe handicaps: the suspicion felt by many Negroes toward all white men, whatever their politics; the demoralization that had eaten into the lives of a good many unemployed Negroes; the hold that the old party machines retained upon the Negroes through petty patronage and handouts; and in the South the open terror that struck down anyone trying to organize Negroes. But for a long time it was the party itself— above all, the party's ideology—that proved to be its main enemy in Negro work.

Until the Sixth Comintern Congress in 1928 little attention had been paid by the Communists to *specific* Negro problems. Now, under the aegis of the Third Period, there was manufactured by one of Stalin's budding theoreticians—Otto Kuusinen, a Finn who had never been in the South or met more than a handful of Negroes —a theory less damaging than social Fascism only because it was so much more fantastic. The theses of the Comintern declared that the American Negroes constituted an oppressed *nation,* i.e., "an historically developed community of people with a common language, territory, economic life and an historic tradition reflecting itself in a common culture." [25] This oppressed nation was declared to exist primarily within the limits of the "Black Belt," a shifting block of Southern counties that contained a majority of Negroes. The main Communist slogan, concluded the Comintern,

> . . . must be: The right of self-determination of the Negroes in the Black Belt. . . . If the slogan of self-determination of the Negroes is to be put into force it is necessary wherever possible to bring together into one governmental unit all districts of the South where the majority of the settled population consists of Negroes. . . . Complete right of self-determination must include the right to governmental separation. . . . The Communist Party must stand . . . for the establishment of a Negro republic in the Black Belt.[26]

Directly after the Comintern Congress, the party leaders in America began providing embroideries of their own. John Pepper (who privately, however, considered the theory nonsensical) wrote that the Negroes constituted "a colony within the body of the United States," while the Negro party leader Harry Haywood declared that "to contend that the Negro question in the United States is a race question in contradistinction to a national question is to contend that the Negroes are oppressed because they are black" [27]—a view he would not tolerate for a moment. A little later, a corps of Communist "specialists" on the Negro question began searching through American history, geography, and sociology to find scholarly rationales for the theory of self-determination.

That the Negroes in the South, unlike, say, an oppressed Balkan nation, spoke the same language as the group that dominated them; that both Southern Negroes and whites were part of an indivisible economy and, increasingly, a unified culture; that the Southern Negroes had neither a distinct historical tradition of nationhood within the North American continent nor a memory of it elsewhere; that the Communist proposal tended to separate Southern whites and Negroes into frozen groups, suggesting at best segregation and at worst civil war; that the Negroes themselves showed not the faintest desire for creating a distinct national existence but wished only to be accepted upon terms of dignity and equality within American society—these utterly obvious facts were systematically ignored by the Communist theoreticians.

But why? How could anyone living in the United States fail to see that the scheme for a separate Negro republic was totally irrelevant to any kind of political reality? Valid as such questions may be, they are not easy to answer; inevitably they force us to the quicksands of speculation.*

In his study *The Negro and the Communist Party* Wilson Record suggests several reasons for the readiness with which the American delegates at the 1928 Comintern Congress accepted the slogan:

> First, a number of the delegates were top leaders of the party in the U.S. There was in process at the time a bitter internal fight. . . . Victory would come to the faction which could secure the nod of approval from leaders of the Russian section. . . . Each delegate was therefore reluctant to take exception to proposals which had been made by the [Comintern] Executive Committee. . . . Secondly, American leaders had been severely castigated for their failure to secure a following among Negroes and could point to no success with alternative programs. Finally, they had been much impressed with the growth of race and national feeling among Negroes during the 1920's and believed that such sentiment might be turned to account. . . .[29]

* Even some of the Communists resisted the Black Belt slogan. Thus in April, 1931, party leader Clarence Hathaway sharply criticized the Kansas district of the CP for omitting the slogan of "Self-Determination of the Black Belt" from its election program. (It is not hard to imagine the burning immediacy this slogan could have had for Communist work among the Kansas farmers.) And about the same time party leader William Weinstone was complaining that the slogan "has not at all been taken up by the party. There is opportunistic resistance to this slogan. . . ."[28]

Each of the reasons adduced by Mr. Record helps explain the genesis of the Black Belt theory in the American Communist movement; but to account for the persistence with which the party pushed this theory from 1928 to about 1934 other factors must be considered. Perhaps the difficulty lies in the assumption that the causes were all rational or calculated. Surely, it would be mistaken to suppose that ordinary motives of opportunism exhaust the reasons for the party position on the Negro question during these years: no intelligent Communist could have believed that this position would ease the party's quest for a Negro following. Nor are factional motives, relevant as these generally are, a sufficient explanation. What needs to be added to Mr. Record's analysis is some awareness of how tyrannical ideology can become once it captures the minds of men— ideology, that is, as a self-contained system of abstract assumptions. Ideology then has a way of spinning along from one dialectical web to another, leaving farther and farther behind the empirical moorings to which, presumably, it had once been tied. All of the Communist theoreticians on the Negro question, as they busily ground out their pamphlets and books, were concerned not with testing the theory against practice but with adjusting facts to the theory. In their writings the theory was the "given" that had unconditionally to be assumed.

This is not to charge that most of them consciously lied; not at all. Most of them did not consciously lie, and some were very intelligent men. But they were so caught up in the fever of ideology that they had no trouble in evading those simple blunt questions— what is the actual relationship between white and Negro communities in the South, what do American Negroes really want?— which, once posed, would have immediately shattered their theories. Understandably, it was more comfortable not to ask such questions, or to ask them only with the intention of confirming their premises.

The effort to advance the slogan of the Negro republic was accompanied within the party by a frenzied campaign to cleanse the membership of those "petty bourgeois" residues of prejudice which, the leaders claimed, were the main cause of resistance to the new line. That a residue of prejudice could be found among some party members, as among many Americans, was perhaps true; but the means that the party chose for removing it—public chastisement and humiliation—were no more effective, certainly no more humane, than the efforts of New England divines a few centuries earlier to purge sin from the hearts of men through rites of public abasement. The Negro party members were treated not as ordinary human beings, that is, as equals; they were looked upon as a special group requiring special "handling." Within the party Negroes found not an informal fraternity but a systematic and sentimentalized inversion of the values that moved the outer world. The phrase "white chauvinism" began to fall with dubious ease from the lips of party members who seemed not to realize that in guarding themselves against the stigmata of prejudice they might be guilty of another and perhaps graver fault: public condescension toward their Negro comrades.

Relations between white and Negro party members now became, by party decision, a matter for public display. Thus, in the spring of 1931 there occurred the Yokinen trial, one of the most remarkable though quite forgotten incidents in the history of American Communism. It was an incident that told more about the inner quality of party life than any number of documents and resolutions.

August Yokinen, an immigrant Finn who belonged to the Communist Party, earned his living as a janitor for the Finnish Workers Club in Harlem. One evening, at a dance sponsored by the club, three Negroes appeared and, apparently, were treated with a lack of courtesy. The party ordered an investigation, and when the club was taken to task all its members expressed regrets—"all except Comrade Yokinen." At this point, one might suppose that since Yokinen was poorly educated and neither spoke nor understood more than a few words of English, some Finnish comrades would have been assigned to educate him privately to the ethic of racial tolerance; but instead the party seized the occasion to stage a "public trial" as a means of publicizing its stand on the Negro question.

On March 1, 1931, a "Workers Court" was convened in Harlem which "1500 persons attended, including 211 elected delegates from 113 mass and fraternal organizations." Clarence Hathaway, for the New York District of the CP, was the prosecuting attorney; Richard Moore, head of the Negro department of the International Labor Defense, was the defense attorney; Alfred Wagenknecht, a veteran

Communist representing the Trade Union Unity League, served as judge; and a "workers jury" of fourteen was elected from the floor.

In a speech lasting almost an hour and a half, Hathaway charged that behavior such as Yokinen's could lead to the kind of bloody race riots that had seared Chicago in 1929; then proceeded to denunciations of the evils of capitalism, lynching, and white chauvinism; and ended by proposing that Yokinen, after being expelled from the party, "be given the task of calling a meeting of the Finnish Workers Club . . . and there make a report to the club itself on this trial, pointing out the basis for the jury's verdict of guilty. . . ." Yokinen himself, it should be noted, was not charged with abusive behavior toward the Negroes but, as Hathaway put it, with "failing to jump at the throats of those who would eject the Negro comrades" and with admitting, in later conversations, that he did not wish Negroes to use the baths of the Finnish Workers Club.

Defense Attorney Moore—it was a clever touch to have a Negro speak for Yokinen—granted all of Hathaway's charges but explained that "middle-class opportunism permeated the mind" of the poor and barely educated janitor. Moore then recommended clemency on the grounds that the Russians, models for all good Communists, were lenient in their treatment of deviationists, and that

> We must remember that a verdict of expulsion in disgrace from the Communist Party is considered by a class conscious worker as worse than death at the hands of the bourgeois oppressors. As for myself, I would rather have my head severed from my body by the capitalist lynchers than be expelled from the Communist International. (*Applause*)

Yokinen, who had meanwhile been sitting on the platform with head bowed, listening to denunciations that he could not understand, now rose—this pitiful anticipation of Van der Lubbe and certain defendants in the Moscow trials—to denounce himself in Finnish and to plead for mercy: "I refute and condemn my previous attitude." If permitted to remain in the party, he promised, he would prove his worthiness. But the "workers jury," unshaken by this plea, voted unanimously to expel Yokinen from the party, a decision that the audience upheld by hand vote, again unanimously.

Yokinen himself quietly accepted the verdict: even before the Russian trials a totalitarian movement had demonstrated its ability to persuade a chosen victim to volunteer for his role. With the fervent singing of the *Internationale,* the Harlem trial came to an end.

There remains, however, a bitter footnote to this grotesque episode. Yokinen's name having been brought to public attention (the trial was reported on the front page of the *New York Times*), the Department of Justice, as the CP report later put it, "jumped into action, arrested him and held him for deportation to Finland, where prison or death awaits a Communist." [30] The education of Comrade Yokinen had come to an end.

Despite the impediments it put in its own way, the CP made steady if modest gains in its Negro work between 1928 and 1934. It is worth noting a few of the reasons:

—The severity of the economic distress suffered by the Negroes set them apart as a uniquely underprivileged group and left at least a few of them receptive to radicalism.

—The enormous diligence with which Communist rank-and-filers worked in Negro neighborhoods enabled them to win a certain confidence among Negro workers and intellectuals.

—The party learned, by about 1932, to stress such immediate problems as housing, relief, and jobs rather than abstract slogans like "Self-Determination."

—Within the Negro community there was no organization sufficiently militant to be able to compete with the Communists in articulating sentiments of discontent.

—The Communists won respect among Negroes for their efforts to organize party branches in the South on a non-segregated basis.

—And, most important of all, the party seized upon a number of outrages against the Negroes, particularly the famous Scottsboro case, to present itself as the most intransigent defender of minority rights.

All through these bitter years the Communists stood almost alone in systematically wooing the American Negroes. The NAACP, primarily a legal defense agency, had not yet established itself as a mass organization within the Negro community; the Socialists were strikingly ineffectual in their approach to Negroes; and the major parties, not yet haunted by the national power of the Negro vote, paid only the most perfunctory attention (except on the ward level) to what was happening in Harlem or the South Side. Under the circumstances it is remarkable not that the Communists made some progress—a good deal in terms of influence, rather less in direct recruiting—but that they did not make more.

In the early thirties the party tried, against overwhelming odds, to penetrate the South. Its organizers were frequently subjected to physical brutality, and some of them, understandably enough, cracked under the strain. (During the fall of 1930 the police chief of Birmingham, Alabama, threatened that CP members would be driven out of town, dead or alive.) For a while, the Southern District of the party published a weekly, the *Southern Worker,* but it lacked the local resources and outlets to keep it going. For obvious reasons Negro party organizers were extremely difficult to secure, or keep, in the South. And even among its Southern followers, few and scattered as they were, the party met with a grudging, half-articulated resistance (a branch formed in Atlanta during the early thirties collapsed when the national office refused its request that the Communist stand on the Negro question be reconsidered).

Yet the party did not fail completely in the South. Branches were set up in Birmingham, Winston-Salem, and several other towns; party candidates participated openly in several local elections; and the party-led Sharecroppers Union, functioning in Alabama and Louisiana, claimed a membership of 3,000, mostly Negroes—about the same number that the Socialist-sponsored Southern Tenant Farmers Union had organized among the whites and Negroes in Arkansas. Necessarily, most of the Communist and Communist-led organizations functioned on a semi-underground basis; whatever else may be said about the party during the early thirties it would be ungenerous to deny that those of its members who "went South" often showed admirable courage.

The little that the Communists could do in the South itself had of course to be provisional and secretive, but when they succeeded in appropriating the Scottsboro case through their legal agency, the International Labor Defense, they acquired an "issue" that soon became an international *cause célèbre* only slightly less important than the cases of Tom Mooney and Sacco and Vanzetti. Here there could be no question, as with these others, of politically conscious rebels being punished for their chosen course in life; the Scottsboro boys were nine utterly bewildered Negroes who had been caught up, almost arbitrarily, in the injustice against their people that was part of the very fabric of the South. As the Communists soon proclaimed, the Scottsboro boys were simply victims—indeed, nothing but victims.

They had been charged with raping two white women on a freight train going south from Chattanooga to Alabama in the spring of 1931. Later, both of the women were shown to be of dubious virtue and one of them, Ruby Bates, recanted her damaging testimony and became a speaker at Scottsboro defense rallies. In their first trial the boys had been defended by NAACP lawyers, though with foredoomed failure; the murderous emotions aroused by the case made it less likely than ever that they could receive a fair trial in the state of Alabama. Eight of them were sentenced to the electric chair; a long series of appeals followed; and then the CP, which had been publicizing the case throughout the country, achieved its coup. The whole party and fellow-traveling propaganda machine directed its fire against the NAACP leadership, denouncing it for "legalistic" tactics and a failure to conduct a militant campaign in behalf of the boys.* But here let the Negro historian, Henry Lee Moon, take over the story:

> Stunned by the violence of this attack, not only upon the principles and policies of their organization, but also upon their personal integrity, the leaders of the NAACP . . . relinquished the defense to the ILD. The Communists maintained that legal defense had to be supplemented by international propaganda. American consulates, legations and embassies were picketed and stoned in many parts of the world. Mass meetings of protest were held in the capitals of Europe and Latin America. . . . This propaganda was effective in exposing the hypocrisy of American justice, but it did not gain the freedom of the boys. Only after it had ceased was a compromise effected which resulted in the release of four of the accused.[31]

* In June, 1933, the Political Bureau of the CP criticized the Communists in ILD for agreeing to cooperate with the NAACP on behalf of the Scottsboro boys. The party leaders insisted that the defense be run completely as a Communist project.

Finally, in 1935, after the defense had reached a legal impasse and the party line had changed toward cooperation with liberals, the ILD agreed to share the case with the NAACP and other liberal groups.

In the meantime, however, the Scottsboro case became an enormously effective propaganda theme for the American Communists. Appearing as local representatives of the Scottsboro Defense Committee, party members and sympathizers were guaranteed a warm hearing before numerous Negro (and white) organizations that had previously been hostile or inaccessible. In the unions, in the churches, on the streets, among the intellectuals, the party hammered at the Scottsboro case with a persistence that did the work of skill. Large mass meetings were held throughout the country at which the idea of justice for the Negro boys and the somewhat more special claims of the party had a way of becoming entangled. At these meetings some of the parents of the boys—shyly mounting the public platform for the first time in their lives—appeared as speakers: they had been worked upon by ILD representatives and persuaded to attack the NAACP in public as "a bunch of liars and fakers." [32] That these distraught parents knew little about the NAACP, certainly nothing that would render plausible the statements they signed attacking it in Communist jargon, signified very little to the Communist managers of the Scottsboro case. The Communists had their eyes turned in another direction: they saw, with an understandable sense of triumph, that the party was now in a position to claim that it was bearing the brunt of the Scottsboro defense and therefore deserved the bulk of the moral and political credit. And they saw that for the first time the party was becoming a power within the Negro community. Had anyone urged that between the idea of justice for the boys and the interests of any institution, be it Communist or not, there might be a clash, they would have regarded such a suggestion as either "petty bourgeois moralizing" or sheer naïveté.

This much can be said for the Communists: they did not hesitate to make public their insistence that the Scottsboro campaign be run according to party formula and party needs. The NAACP, wrote party leader Robert Minor in a particularly scurrilous article, was led mainly by middle-class agents of capitalism "engaged in soliciting a further consolidation of the white capitalist class for the perpetuation of this slavery of the Negro people"; and if this were true, what remained but party domination of the defense campaign? James S. Allen, a Communist theoretician on the Negro question, warned against the danger that the case might be taken over by "petty bourgeois Negro elements":

> History by no means guarantees in advance that the broad strata of the Negro population, holding varied and confused views, many dominated by ideas alien to the class-conscious proletariat, will simply fall into the organizations of the Communist movement. . . . Leibowitz [one of the defense attorneys] constitutes a danger to proletarian hegemony [that is, party control] in the Scottsboro movement because of the opportunity he offers for the retrenchment of the Negro reformist organizations and the capitalist political parties.[33]

In the years since the case reached its end there has been much discussion as to the validity of the Communist tactic of "mass pressure" as against the legal approach of the NAACP. To pose the problem in this way, however, may be to concede far too much to the Communists. The problem of the advisability of mass-pressure tactics in a given situation needs to be sharply differentiated from a judgment of the way in which the Communists utilized those tactics in the Scottsboro case. One may admit that merely legalistic measures might have led to a defeat that, without national publicity, would have constituted still another in the long list of silent injustices suffered by Southern Negroes. But to grant this is not necessarily to grant that the mass campaign for the Scottsboro boys should have been linked with vicious attacks upon the NAACP or with Communist propaganda in general.

Similar considerations pertain to another problem that arose in the Scottsboro case. One of the most frequent charges made against the party, both by its political opponents and by many of its ex-members, is that it cavalierly used funds collected for the Scottsboro boys to finance a variety of Communist institutions and causes. While such charges are extremely difficult to prove in specific instances, we have the word of no less an authority than T. Gussev, for a time the Comintern "rep" to the American party, that the "shortcomings of inner-party democracy stand out with increasing prominence in the attitude taken toward mass organizations. They are looked on and treated as a source of money. . . . The mass organizations have repeatedly protested against the free way in which the party organizations deal with their money. . . ."[34]

A good many years later Earl Browder, after he had ceased being a Communist, was to deny that the funds raised for the Scottsboro boys were used for any purpose other than their defense:

> Quite early in the defense, when its only funds were those contributed by the Communist party, I engaged in a discussion with a group of lawyers. . . . The issue discussed . . . was the relative importance of spending what money was available for a mass appeal to the moral and intellectual conscience of America or of spending it for high-priced lawyers. I took the position that conceding that the best lawyers possible must be secured at whatever fee current practise dictated, this alone would get the defense nowhere without previously arousing the nation's conscience. . . .[35]

Even if everything Browder says were taken at face value, a serious problem would still remain. To arouse "the moral and political conscience of America" may well have been as necessary as Browder says it was; but the problem is whether it was legitimate—and helpful to the Scottsboro boys themselves—to do this in Communist terms and through the employment of Communist agencies and personnel.

In any case, the Communists had by 1935 become a significant force in the Negro world. Though they may then have had no more than 2500 Negroes enrolled in the party, as Wilson Record estimates, this figure does not really suggest the extent of their influence among Negroes. Partly they had achieved this influence through their own hard work; partly through lack of scruples; partly through the default of others. But whatever the reason, their gains could not be disputed.

6. It is one of the distinguishing traits of the Stalinist movement, as well as a peculiar source of its strength, that each shift of political line has been accompanied by an extensive change

in the nature of its inner life. The Third Period was not merely a time of political adventurism and extreme leftism; it soon came to indicate a unique style of life. This was a style of life in which Bohemianism combined with quasi-military discipline; a righteous estrangement from the mores of American society with a grotesque mimicry of Bolshevik toughness; a furious effort to break past the barriers of hostility encountered by Communism at almost every point in American life with a solemn and consoling absorption in the rituals of the movement. Throughout these years the party remained a sect, that is, a compact assembly of the chosen, bound together by the faith that in their ideology alone resided Historical Truth; that all those who deviated from their path would soon be tumbling greedily into the arms of the Devil; that the test of their behavior lay in the growth of their power; that the freedom of the follower blossomed in his obedience to the apparatus; that the member had to yield the "whole of his life" if he were to be deemed worthy of membership at all. The style of the Stalinist sect regulated everything from belief to dress, from the ineluctable correctness of "socialism in one country" to the preference for caps and leather jackets in Union Square.

Furiously energetic, driving its members to both ecstasy and exhaustion, the party suffered from a hopeless contradiction during the early thirties. It repeatedly proclaimed that its goal was to break out of its isolation and become a rooted part of American life; it strained every nerve and muscle to achieve that end; but its ideology and ingrained habits of life were insuperable handicaps. Because the true nature of this contradiction could not be acknowledged—it would involve criticizing some fundamental assumptions of Stalinism—the party had to improvise a variety of bureaucratic deceits. Such as: the line is correct, always has been correct, but (somehow) is never properly carried out. Or: if the members drove themselves just a little harder, the magical union with the masses might be achieved and then the party, today so unloved and disshev-eled, would become the radiant bridegroom of history. The characteristic tone of party life during these years was a feverish straining, a willful sacrifice of human resources: revolution, revolution everywhere (cried the Comintern, the Theses, the Leaders) but in America hardly a revolt in sight.

The keynote for party work, declared the 14th Central Committee Plenum in 1932, is

> . . . to overcome the isolation of the party from the decisive masses of the American proletariat. . . . It must begin an *essential change* in the methods of mass work and above all root itself in the decisive industries. . . .*

Brave words! But the same words had been used at the 13th and 12th and, no doubt, the 11th plenums; and soon there would be a "Resolution on Carrying Out the Resolution of the 14th Plenum." Meanwhile, deadly admissions: the party, despite its strike leadership, had not one member in Gastonia; the circulation of the *Daily Worker* was suffering a "marked decline"; there was a "100 percent fluctuation in party membership"—and "an excessive number of paid functionaries" and "bureaucratic methods of work." In short, "the party appears before the masses as a party for the workers, but not the party of the workers."

An intolerable situation, and one that the 14th Plenum was determined to correct. A year later the *Daily Worker*, its editorial head spinning with plenums, was writing:

> The 15th Plenum of our Party clearly establishes that the resolution of the 14th Plenum of the Party remains the basic guide for examining the work of the Party in carrying out the line of the 12th Plenum of the E.C.C.I. The 16th Plenum of the Party established that since the 15th Plenum, the Party has begun to understand the line of the 14th Plenum. . . .

Applying within the party a home-made version (the parts came from Moscow) of Zinoviev's "theory of electrification," the leadership kept pressing the ranks unceasingly. The districts and sections of the party would pledge themselves to recruit a certain (generally an unrealistic) number of new members. By exhausting themselves in the effort and sometimes taking a liberal view of what constituted a new member, they might come near to fulfilling the

---

* To avoid cluttering with footnote numbers the numerous quotations that follow, references have been grouped together under one number at the end of this section.

quotas. But since the quotas, to begin with, had been based not on an honest assessment of local possibilities but on forced marches, the local units generally proved incapable of keeping and absorbing the new members. In 1928, for example, the party made a strenuous effort to establish itself in the mining districts of western Pennsylvania and managed to recruit 1500 miners. Within a year, however, only 300 of them remained in the party, and before much longer most of these had dropped out. The recruiting had served as inner-party display—it also looked good in reports to the Comintern—but it had not been based on solid preparation.

Like displeased schoolmasters, the leaders kept hectoring and harrying the ranks, insisting, as Browder put it, that the party's troubles were due to "the underestimation of the masses, of their readiness to struggle; rising out of this, doubts and hesitations about the party line. . . ."

In turn, when the leaders were engaged in assigned rituals of "self-criticism," they attacked the very methods they habitually employed. Here is Browder again, speaking at a conference of CP shop workers in Chicago and deploring

> . . . the tendency to explain all of our shortcomings in the shop work on the grounds that our Party workers are afraid to work in the shops . . . that they are not sufficiently ready to sacrifice themselves. This tendency tries to find the answer to our weaknesses by methods of shaming our Party members and *driving* them into more intense activities.

Most of the time, however, waves of pressure kept emanating from the New York headquarters, waves that could wash away district organizers, section organizers, unit organizers. And always the party commissars in New York knew just how things should be done. When the party fraction in Aberdeen, Washington, published a shop paper, *Grey's Harbor Worker,* the functionaries clucked that it lacked enough material on shop conditions. When the party fraction in the Schenectady General Electric plant published a shop paper, *Line Current,* the commissars clucked that it lacked enough material on world politics.

The one thing that had always to be assumed, however, was

that the masses were ready, taut with revolutionary desire; which is
to say, that the party line was correct. The masses were ready today,
they were ready everywhere:

> Austria! France! Spain! Europe on the barricades. The
> world is afire with revolutions. . . . It has begun! Today, to-
> morrow, or the next day, it will be Great Britain, or Germany,
> or Italy, or—yes, the United States.

And where there was a will to believe, there was also a way. A
"Communist soldier," Y. Y., wrote in the *Party Organizer:* "There
are great possibilities of creating a genuine revolutionary movement
among the soldiers . . . they are ripe for Communist influence."
And not the soldiers alone; letters received by the *Daily Worker,*
wrote a party functionary, "once again reaffirm the deep revolutionary ferment embracing large strata of the American workers." That
the letters received by the *Daily Worker* might not quite have constituted an adequate sample of what "large strata of American workers" felt did not seem to trouble this writer.

And where, meanwhile, was the party? Working hard, desperately hard; but also fantastically busy with its inner life. Seldom
have so few people held so many meetings. Here is how party
leader Clarence Hathaway described it in 1931:

> There are about 3,000 members of the Party in New York.
> Of this number . . . there are 700 direct Party functionaries, Dis-
> trict, Section and unit, not counting auxiliary functionaries which
> probably number several hundred more. The following is their
> schedule: Monday, unit bureau meetings; Tuesday, unit meetings;
> Wednesday, department meetings (Agit-prop, Negro etc.); Thurs-
> day, school, union meetings; Friday, section committee meetings,
> street meetings; Saturday, free; Sunday, weekend schools, "Red
> Sundays" (distribution of *Daily Worker* . . .).

The party leaders tended to be very solemn about the radical
curse of "meetingitis"; generally, what they did was to call another
meeting to discuss the problem of cutting down the number of meetings. But when rank-and-filers spoke up on this problem, they could
be rather touching:

Upon first joining [the YCL] I was willing to give a few nights a week to activities. However, now I am expected to give every night. I realize the necessity for giving all my time to unit activity, but since I am a student I find it impossible. . . . I have attended many demonstrations and also meetings and study circles regularly. I found it impossible to give any more time, and the other comrades began nagging. . . .

Or amusing:

The more meetings you have (it seems), the more active you are. . . . After getting through with a general functionaries meeting, the Organizational Secretary of our section ran around from comrade to comrade asking whether they had a meeting on Monday, as she had to get comrades for the Party's [social] affair committee. . . . Two comrades had meetings. The third comrade answered—no. "Good," said the Org Sec, "here's a meeting for you!"

The passion for meetings seems to arise in all movements and may be an unavoidable consequence of organization itself. During the Third Period, however, it was particularly strong in the CP because the party was completing a transformation toward bureaucratic authoritarianism as a mode of life—and the fungus of bureaucratism has a way of flourishing in a warm culture of meetings. But there was another, perhaps more immediately pertinent, reason for the multiplication of meetings: it served as a way of providing protection, solace, comfort for a band of dedicated people who, even as they intoned phrases about the forthcoming revolution, were often forcibly struck by the extent of their isolation. To attend a meeting, even a boring or interminable meeting, was more pleasant than trying to sell *Daily Workers* by knocking at doors that, more often than not, would be slammed in one's face. And the meeting was a way of helping to fill up the time, indeed the lives, of people who had deliberately emptied themselves of "outside interests" and therefore had to find cultural and personal sustenance within the party. The very elaborateness of the party structure—in 1934 the Kansas CP had 200 members and was divided into *ten* departments!—could be reassuring: the outer world might be a wolfish chaos but within the party things were neat and orderly.

True, the CP could hurl its members into violent demonstrations during the early thirties, but this was hardly the same thing as sustained contact with the outer world: in fact, it was the former that helped make the latter impossible. In a hostile world, particularly one in which many party members found themselves without jobs, the local Workers Club could become a kind of haven, a place to talk about important matters without being nagged by wife and children, a home away from home. The highly intense and inbred life of the party during the early thirties—with its innumerable "socials," its meetings to prepare for meetings, its endless and dreary reports of functionaries, its air of sodden messianism—was an implicit acknowledgment that the Third Period line about revolutionary upsurges lacked touch with reality.

It is when one goes beyond the formal resolutions and speeches that some sense is gained of the all-too-human atmosphere of party life during these days. Here, for example, is a sympathizer from Kentucky speaking about his problems:

> I agree with the principles of the party, I am ready to join it, but I must tell you beforehand that the belief in a Supreme Being is with both feet in my head, no one can knock it out.

Here a party functionary, reporting from Detroit, forgets for a moment the weight of abstraction that shadows his mind and talks about a problem that anyone can understand:

> Then there is the wife question. . . . When we already thought we had a member in our unit, suddenly the wife shows up and he says the wife does not allow him to read the *Daily Worker*. . . . The comrades must learn in the discussions in the units what to do on this question. . . .

What to do, as it happens, this functionary does not quite know; but surely his marvelous phrase "suddenly the wife shows up" is one to which even the non-believer can respond.

Here is a wry complaint about the bewilderment occasioned in the minds of new members by the multiplicity of party fronts:

When we bring a member into the party we immediately shove him into TUUL work, which would not be bad in itself, but then comes the ILD, the WIR, the LSNR and a half dozen other activities. . . . We send out an organizer into a new territory. He becomes the Party organizer, he becomes the TUUL organizer, the ILD organizer, the WIR organizer. . . . The result is that he is so confused he actually don't [sic] know where he stands.

Along similar lines, Si Gerson, one of the party's more gifted organizers, reports from the South in 1930 that workers who join one front group—say, the ILD—assume that their "ticket" will do for other groups—say, the CP, or LSNR, or the TUUL. After all, they see the same people at all the meetings. And then they become irritated, even angry, when told that one "ticket" doesn't serve as a general admission.

From the Bronx, though in a more high-spirited tone, comes a similar complaint:

At the entrance to the Bronx Coliseum, where the party is holding a mass meeting, are a squad of Red Builders, agents of the Friends of the Soviet Union, holding about 50 copies each of *Soviet Russia Today*. Others, agents from the *New Masses*. An army of agents with bundles of *Labor Defender* from various ILD branches come here to get rid of their "burden." A happy lot of young kids with the *New Pioneer* . . . are also at the door.

Here a Chicago functionary tells a story about the problems raised by the use of Marxist jargon:

We had not only to teach the principles of Communism, but we had to create a dictionary. The workers did not know what we were talking about. One worker asked our instructor, what is the bourgeoisie. He says that the only "burro" he knows is one that kicks.

This last raises a question of authenticity: is the Chicago functionary making up a clever story in order to score a point? In general, however, one gleans from these remarks a sense of how hard it was for the devoted rank-and-file member to mediate—as in practice he had to—between the demands of party ideology and the resistance of social reality. From the following passage—advice given by a Communist to his comrades on how to conduct shop work—one can learn a great deal about the nature and difficulties of party work during the early thirties:

> Step continually to the left in conversation a step at a time bringing the workers along. It will take time and patience. . . . They must see the perfect logic of your argument and you must speak not as a soap boxer or a seasoned Communist theoretician for they will not listen and you will be known too soon as a Communist before you have had the opportunity to get in all the necessary ground work. . . . Don't appear too insistent at first. Just be one of the workers, which indeed you are.

Sometimes, in such reports, touches of a deeper pathos would come through. In Chicago, reports an organizer, all the Negro members dropped out of a party unit though they did remain in the ILD. Why? Because at unit meetings the whites did all the talking, while they, the Negroes, sat and remained silent. In Philadelphia, writes a comrade, "Some members say they cannot speak English and therefore they cannot be useful in organizing block committees. . . . This is merely an excuse." But was it? And in Norfolk, Virginia, the party unit is "a Jewish-speaking one." A non-Jewish member stops coming to meetings because he can't understand what is being said. The Norfolk branch, reports a functionary, "has adopted a white chauvinist attitude. . . . The unit members cannot go about the task of organizing the Negro, conscientiously, because . . . they are now in the businesses, exploiting the Negro workers." Therefore, he concludes, the Norfolk unit must be completely reorganized. No doubt; but might not a little humaneness prompt one to add that these Yiddish-speaking members in Norfolk are old-time radicals who drifted South in order to earn their livings as tailors and grocerymen? Admittedly not ideal material for building the party—it is hard to forge the proletarian vanguard in Virginia from Yiddish-speaking cadres!—they might still have deserved some consideration as pioneers. That, however, would have been a kind of sentimentality for which the party, as it toughened into Stalinist monolithism, had little room.

No wonder then, as one bears in mind the above accumulation of testimony, that the party was troubled by an enormous turnover in membership, that at every plenum, convention, and meeting this turnover was declared to be its main problem. In September, 1931, the party reported that only 4 percent of its membership was organized in "shop nuclei" and that in the whole Pittsburgh District it had only five steel workers. During the first half of 1931 there had been a 77 percent fluctuation in membership; 4,000 new members had been recruited, but only 900 of them were still in the party by September of the same year.

At the 1934 convention, membership figures were broken down as follows:

1930	7,500
1931	9,257
1932	14,475
1933	19,165
1934	23,467

There had been one major improvement: by 1934, 9 percent of the membership was organized in "shop nuclei," partly the result of increased recruiting in the factories and partly the result of systematic "colonization" of New York party members into industrial towns. But the turnover had been enormous. Since 1930 the party had recruited 49,050 members and had lost about 33,000. In the four most severe years of the depression the party had made some significant gains, but only by a policy of adventurism and hysteria that had exhausted many of its most valuable members. The party had grown—from a tiny sect to a somewhat larger and more influential sect. During these years it had hardened and toughened the inner core that was to carry it through the next two decades; but it had also wasted some of its most precious human resources.

In one respect, however, the party did approach its objectives. The process begun in the mid-twenties of replacing inner democracy with an authoritarian regime reached its climax by about 1934. Thousands of Americans found it possible during these years to join a party whose basic position was determined neither by themselves nor by the formal leadership. It is this surrender of the will that finally forms the most troublesome aspect of the history of American Communism; for there is something more fearful about a totalitarian apparatus in which leaders and members participate voluntarily than one that rests upon the visible power of the state.

Year by year, the totalitarian symptoms grew more distinct. Other radical groups were regarded not merely as mistaken; their loyalties and intentions had systematically to be maligned. Not only were the meetings of dissident left-wing groups frequently broken up by force and rowdyism; such tactics were now openly sanctioned by the party. And with good reason too: they were a logical extension of the kind of political behavior that prevailed in Russia. "Why," asked the then Communist leader Will Herberg in 1929, "do we break up Trotskyist meetings? Because they are demonstrations against the Soviet Union of the same type as monarchist and socialist demonstrations." And most of the comrades believed this.

Baleful and absurd as the ferocious faction struggles among the Communists may have been during the twenties, they testified at least to a kind of inner democracy. Now, however, the right to form factions—that is, for party members to band together in order to urge their views upon their comrades—was officially forbidden. The forms of "democratic centralism"—discussion meetings, votes, self-criticism—were gravely maintained; but the content of democracy—which involves an acceptance of the right to organized disagreement—was increasingly absent. A pall of unanimity fell upon the party, a pall that was to last through the lifetime of Joseph Stalin.* Decisions were made, or at least transmitted, from on high. Thus, when the party began a major shift of line in 1935 toward favoring the formation of a labor party in America, this change was unknown to the membership until Earl Browder announced it at a National Congress for Unemployed Insurance. And when a reader asked the *Daily Worker* why there had been no discussion within the party of this change *before* Browder's speech, the editors answered:

* "For what is man that he should live out the lifetime of his God?" *Moby Dick.*

There was no violation of Party democracy. The widest discussion is being carried on within the Party on all phases of the question. Action and discussion is being carried on simultaneously.

The party leadership, in other words, felt no need even to consider the possibility that its proposed line on the labor party might be rejected by the members; the "discussion" was seen primarily as a way of soothing the change into the minds of the members.

Increasingly large areas of the members' lives were preempted by the party; like all authoritarian or totalitarian movements, it aspired to color, if not dominate, every aspect of the follower's existence. The party's heavy hand was felt in such comic trivia as the *Daily Worker's* denunciation of a comrade who had arranged a "Third Period dance,"

The comrade who is the originator of this brilliant idea . . . undoubtedly intended to aid our Party. . . . But the comrade's intentions are not decisive. The decisive thing is that he found no difficulties in stooping to such a vulgarization of a most serious political term as that of the Third Period.

And it could be felt in the formalized declaration by a party leader, Max Bedacht, of the Stalinist concept of organization:

The Party member who, after the nature and form of a contemplated action is once decided upon, continues his opposition to such action by agitation or counter-action, becomes an agent of the enemy in the ranks of the Party.

As it happened, this was precisely what Zinoviev and Kamenev had done a few days before the October Revolution in Russia; yet, under Lenin's leadership, they had been retained as members of the Bolshevik Central Committee. In the calculations of American Stalinism, however, such precedents counted for very little.

Not only was the organized expression of minority views forbidden within the party; individual members who stepped beyond

the ideological chalk line were quickly expelled. As a typical example, here are excerpts from a stenographic report of a hearing
held in Chicago on July 6, 1933, to try a CP member, L. Beidel,
who had questioned the Stalinist line in Germany:

> The comrade who had been brought up on charges was
> given, at 11 PM, after a long meeting, three minutes in which to
> explain her differences with the party. She began to speak about
> Germany, but was interrupted by Ferguson, a party leader, who
> shouted, "Germany is not under discussion."
> "Very well," said the unfortunate comrade, "I expected this.
> So I wrote my speech and here it is. "She proceeded to pass out
> three long sheets. . . .
> At this point the atmosphere was rent by shrieks from the
> District Agitprop, Shields. "What is this? Stop her! Stop her!
> She's passing out a document." Ferguson then said, "Comrades,
> we forbid you to read this statement. It's a counter-revolutionary
> document. It is a platform against the party. Hand every copy
> up here to me. You are forbidden to read it."

And thus was a dissident removed from the ranks.

In nothing, however, was the trend toward totalitarian party
life more fully revealed than in the systematic glorification of the
Stalinist leaders. The praise of Stalin that would become a disease
during the late thirties and forties was already far advanced in the
Daily Worker by 1933. Other leaders, especially the Russians,
received their portion of hosannahs. Karl Radek, on his fifty-third
birthday, was honored with twenty columns of celebration in the
Daily Worker. (That, a year later, he was being denounced as a
counter-revolutionist is another matter.) And not only did the
praise of the leadership *per se* become part of the Stalinist way of
life; a sharp differentiation was promoted within the leadership, so
that the general secretary, Browder, while subservient politically to
the Comintern, had considerable organizational power *vis-à-vis* the
other American leaders. When one of them, William Weinstone,
began to show signs of restiveness and ambition during the early
thirties—he had described the Washington Bonus March as an
"adventure" and had indicated the opinion that he was as handy a
man as Browder for the job of general secretary—the Polit Bureau

"exiled" him from the party center in New York to a Midwestern post.

The following account of the inner workings of the party leadership, though taken from a hostile source, is a knowledgeable one:

> The Political Bureau must not be made up of the leading, most experienced and most qualified members. That might be necessary if there were any policies to discuss, or political problems and disputes to thrash out collectively. But under Stalinism, the "line" is simply handed down from the Moscow secretariat to its agent in New York. He is directly responsible. He sits in the center of the Polit Bureau and, like a Delphic oracle, interprets the transmitted "line."
>
> . . . Polit Bureau meetings are positively weird affairs. The four [members in addition to Browder] are called into the Royal Presence, and summoned to give their reports. They do. Browder takes notes. Then he takes the floor and hands down the decisions. . . . And that is all. No questioning, no discussing, no disputing. That has been tried before, openly and covertly, and every venturesome soul came to a bad end.

The power that the general secretary could wield within the party rested ultimately upon his favor with Moscow, but it should be noted that he had also at his disposal a considerable bureaucratic apparatus. In early 1934, apart from the full-time functionaries employed in the CP national office, there were 86 full-time district functionaries, 67 full-time section functionaries, 36 other full-time local functionaries, and 231 full-time functionaries in the "mass organizations." This means that within a party of somewhat more than 20,000 members there were probably, if one includes secretarial and other help but excludes union jobs under CP control, about 600 people whose livelihood depended upon the party, which is to say, ultimately upon Browder. That these functionaries were paid extremely low and irregular salaries does not controvert the fact that, in a time of mass unemployment, they were dependent upon the party leadership and therefore likely to be its strongest support within the movement.

Only later, during the Popular Front period of the late thirties, would the apotheosis of Earl Browder reach its climax, but during the years that we are here discussing a preparatory sanctification had already begun. By 1935 it was possible for a Communist journalist, Moissaye Olgin, to write about Browder with only a shade less sycophancy than Russian journalists were habitually displaying toward Stalin:

> Now here he is. . . . This is the general staff which is to lead the working class. Browder is their acknowledged leader. What responsibility! What earnestness! [36]

In the world of American Stalinism all men were equal, but the general secretary was more equal than all the others.

7. Traces of Third Period politics and psychology could still be detected among American Communists as late as 1935, but most of the steam had evaporated from its ultra-leftism two or three years earlier. The frenzy to which the members had been whipped up could not be sustained indefinitely, so that after a while, and apart from whatever the leadership intended, there occurred a tapering off of sectarian hysteria. Paradoxically, the few achievements of the party during the Third Period, dearly bought as they were, forced a sobering of perspective: the need to assume responsibility in such areas of work as the unemployed movement and the Scottsboro defense prompted a somewhat more realistic policy. Finally, and in the long run most important, the Comintern by 1933 began fidgeting toward a change of line, though it took another two years for that change to be fully realized. It was in this interim period—1933-35—that the party had occasionally to work out its politics and tactics independently, if only because there was confusion as to what Moscow wanted. The results, while frequently contradictory in an amusing sort of way, were also comparatively sensible and brought distinct gains to the party.

Despite its previous theory of social fascism, the CP began to make sustained and serious overtures to the Socialist Party in 1934, partly because it hoped to chip off some of the new members that the Socialists were gaining (it did win over a sizable group in California, though most of these soon dropped out of the CP as well) and partly because, as the Socialists moved leftward under the impact of the depression and the Communists moved rightward under the impact of the Comintern, there *seemed* to be a temporary convergence of outlook. The new strategy of the united front had, of course, to be justified to party members who had been nurtured on the emotion of hatred and contempt for all Socialists, so that in 1933, when explaining why the CP was making friendly noises toward the "Musteites," a group of independent socialists led by A. J. Muste, Earl Browder whispered publicly to the comrades:

> Did you think we are making the united front with the Musteites because we have suddenly been convinced that they are good class-conscious fighters, good leaders of the working class? Have you forgotten that precisely the reason why we make the united front with them is because we have got to take their followers away from them?

But since the Socialists felt some well-justified suspicions as to the motives of the CP (the united front, wrote Norman Thomas to the *Daily Worker*, "cannot be achieved if your Party still regards it primarily as a weapon to destroy the Socialist Party"), a more persuasive approach was necessary. Clarence Hathaway, writing as if he had never heard of Earl Browder, told the party ranks:

> You cannot make an approach to the Young Socialists if you go to them and tell them that the purpose of the Young Communists is to smash their organization. . . .
> Sectarian   tendencies . . . have   shown   themselves   most clearly in a more or less openly expressed resistance to the united front . . . and in an ill-concealed tendency to get out of any united front at the earliest opportunity. . . . One frequently hears a sigh of relief after an action is finished; the comrades afflicted with these tendencies are always glad to crawl back into the quiet solitude of their own sectarian shells.[37]

Among the Socialist veterans—most of them Jewish trade unionists in New York—the united front campaign was doomed to fail. These people were well informed about Stalinist tactics in Germany and terror in Russia, they had suffered abuse as "social fascists" at home, they were deeply embittered by the way organized

Communist squads had broken up a Socialist meeting in early 1934 to honor the Viennese Socialists who had fought against the semi-fascist Dollfuss regime. Entrenched as they were in the garment and other unions, they had not the faintest revolutionary impulse that might lead them to regard the Communists in a fraternal spirit. Many times bitten, forever shy. But among the less experienced Socialists, particularly those in the West and South, there was neither such a concern with world politics nor such a habit of deadly feuding. To an earnest if not very knowledgeable Socialist who had joined his party a year or two ago in, say, Missouri or North Carolina, the united front appeals of the CP could seem reasonable; and as a result, the CP, now beginning to scrub its face and pants, made some progress between 1933 and 1935 in winning sympathy on the outskirts of American Socialism.

A more important issue that arose to trouble the Communists during this period of ideological flux was their attitude toward the New Deal. At the beginning, the Communists denounced the New Deal with an unremittent hostility. It was, wrote Earl Browder in the summer of 1933,

> . . . a policy of slashing the living standards at home and fight-ing for markets abroad for the single purpose of maintaining the profits of finance capital. . . . Roosevelt is carrying out more thoroughly and brutally than even Hoover the capitalist attack against the living standards of the masses. . . .

A few days later the *Daily Worker* printed a cartoon showing the blue eagle (the NRA symbol) whirling itself into a swastika. This line was formally restated at the party's eighth national convention in the spring of 1934: "The Roosevelt regime is not, as the liberals and Socialist Party leaders claim, a progressive regime, but a government serving the interests of finance capital and moving toward the fascist suppression of the workers' movement." A few months later Earl Browder insisted that the CP would never accept "the extension of the united front to include those who are part of the Roosevelt governmental machine."

On May 1, 1935, the *Daily Worker* went so far as to refer to the Wagner Act as an "anti-strike" measure. On June 5 it still spoke of the NRA as "a slave program." Yet three days later, in a report to the party's Central Committee, Browder noted

> . . . the growing discontent of the masses with Roosevelt, and the consequent failure of FDR to carry out his move to the right. . . . FDR will now attempt to again orientate to the left, to absorb again in the New Deal following those masses which have been following the various Third Party movement tendencies.[38]

If one remembers that Browder wrote this before the Supreme Court struck down most of the New Deal, his prediction seems rather shrewd. In any case, the ground was being prepared for enthusiastic Communist support of the New Deal.

A plausible case might be made out for saying that the CP shifted its attitude toward the New Deal not merely because of Moscow needs but because it was responding favorably to a sharp leftward turn that Roosevelt made in 1935. Even at their most blindly doctrinaire, when they were attacking the NRA as "fascist," the Communists did touch upon a reality: the trend exemplified in Roosevelt's early policy toward a "liberal garrison state," a trend that could also be noticed in the partiality the NRA showed toward big as against small business. So sympathetic a historian of the Roosevelt era as James MacGregor Burns has written of Roosevelt that "it probably never occurred to him that the NRA, with its functional representation of business and labor groups, and the AAA, dominated by the big farm groups, showed some likeness to the corporate state fashioned by Benito Mussolini." (The stress needs of course to fall upon the qualifying *some*.)

And then—so might continue a partial defense of Communist tactics—there took place during 1935 a major change in the character of the New Deal. The NRA, to quote Professor Burns again, had come "near administrative and political collapse";[39] the business community, elated by the Supreme Court decision, had launched a deadly attack upon the administration; short of total collapse, Roosevelt now had no alternative but to seek new sources of popular strength. The result was a leftward turn which won the allegiance of the unions and liberals and brought with it the most impressive legislation of the Roosevelt years: the Wagner Act, Social Security, etc. At this point, consequently, the Communists began to support the *new* New Deal.

Such a defense of the Communist change of line must, however, meet with severe difficulties. For one thing, it would seem improbable that, if the party leaders had really been free and flexible enough to respond on their own to Roosevelt's leftward turn, they would not have earlier been able to see some positive features in the New Deal worthy of their support. At the very least, they would then have refrained, between 1933 and 1935, from calling the New Deal "slave labor" and "fascist." Similarly, party leaders so sensitive to the complex problems of international capitalist development as to be able to see the inherent dangers of the trend toward statification in the early years of the New Deal would also have been able to notice similar trends at work during the later New Deal. And then party leaders capable of so delicate a response to American events as we have been assuming would also have publicly noticed (as in fact they did not) that toward the late thirties the New Deal once more shifted back to the right.

But the most important point to be stressed here is the way in which the party changed its line on the New Deal in 1935. As with all other major policy changes during the Stalinist epoch, there was neither discussion among the ranks nor open debate in the party press; all that was necessary to make a 180-degree turn was an announcement by the party leadership. That Roosevelt's leftward shift in 1935 made Browder's assigned task of negotiating a rightward shift much easier is true; but only when one places the CP change of attitude toward the New Deal in the tortuous context of Stalinist political zigzags can it be properly understood.

Meanwhile, the inner life of the party began slowly to take on a new quality. More than a year before completing its change of line, the CP had already announced that it "welcomes all white collar workers—*no special tests required*—they are accepted as part of the exploited working class" (emphasis added). Browder was soon adding that "we must abolish the sectarian nonsense which thinks that when a worker joins the party, he gives up his family life and devotes all his waking hours away from the job to party meetings and literature distribution." [40] From such "adaptations" to American life the party gained strength. Its vote in the 1932 presidential election, when it ran William Z. Foster and James Ford as its candidates, was disappointing: 103,000, despite the fact that its campaign was the most extensive it had ever conducted. But in many local elections it kept steadily increasing its vote, and in a state-wide California election one of its more popular candidates, Anita Whitney, polled some 80,000 votes.

Times were changing, quickly. On July 4, 1935, the *Daily Worker* carried a headline on page 1, "Toward a Soviet America," that would have been quite acceptable to the Third Period outlook. On page 2 there appeared pictures of Lenin and George Washington side by side, with a reprint of the Declaration of Independence. A phase in the history of American Communism had come to an end.

Chapter VI. The Dual Unions: Heroism and Disaster

In no other area of American life did "Third Period" Communism release such fanatical devotion or create such enormous havoc as in the trade unions. The effort to establish dual unions reached its climax during the early thirties, but the roots of this policy—at least some of them—go back to the origins of American Communism.

1. In 1920, after the defeat of the great steel strike, William Z. Foster and a scattering of followers organized the Trade Union Educational League. As they saw it, the TUEL would serve both as a left-wing educational society and as a focal point for militant unionists within the established labor movement. The early Communists, strongly tempted by the idea of "revolutionary unions," were at first contemptuous of Foster's plan for working inside the AFL; but as he drew closer to them politically, they began to realize that the TUEL could be put to profitable use.

For a while the new organization prospered. By 1922, though now completely under Communist control, it was exerting a measurable influence in a number of unions. Its claim to having won the support of unions with a total of two million members was an example of the Communist fondness for the mathematics of optimism; but there could be no doubt that in its campaign for industrial unionism—an explosive issue in those days—it was causing the stodgy Gompers leadership some uneasy moments. Politically the Communists might be impotent, yet it began to seem that the TUEL, by patiently "boring from within," could become a major force in the craft-oriented AFL.[1]

A year later everything had changed. The postwar depression had run its course by 1923, and with the return to "normalcy" the fervor of many TUEL sympathizers had evaporated and the confidence of the old-line AFL leaders returned. At the 1923 AFL convention, the TUEL was branded a dual-union tendency, William

F. Dunne denied his seat as a delegate, and formal war declared against Communists in the unions. Once it became known that Foster was a secret member of the Communist underground, progressive unionists such as the leaders of the Chicago Federation visibly cooled toward the TUEL. By the end of the year, it had lost a good part of its influence within the union movement.

Isolation led to desperation, and desperation to calamity. Many of the TUEL followers having been expelled from the AFL, and the efforts to form alliances with progressive unionists having failed, the TUEL now turned to an outright struggle for power in those few unions where it still retained any following. "The era of passing resolutions to have them thrown in the waste basket by sneering and stupid officials is passed," thundered Foster in 1924; "the era of action is at hand." [2] But little came from this "era of action," for as Foster was later to admit, "the TUEL was forced to take on more of a local or partial character than in its big sweeping movement of 1922-23." [3]

The TUEL soon aggravated its difficulties by openly identifying with the Workers (Communist) Party. Its program became little more than a blurred carbon of the party's, its shop nuclei little more than a reconstitution of the party fractions. A new paper, the *Workers Monthly,* was openly announced as the joint organ of the TUEL and the Communists.* Throughout the Coolidge administration, the TUEL remained a propaganda sect with little influence inside the AFL. [5]

One trouble led to another. The isolation of the party members in the unions provoked a few to sentiments favoring "revolutionary" dual unions; the more hopeless their immediate tasks seemed in the established unions, the more tempting it became to abandon them. Nonetheless, the TUEL remained fully committed to the tactic of working within the existing unions.

For this decision, credit must go largely to William Z. Foster, one of the very few Communist leaders with a genuine flair for American unionism. To the extent that there has been any con-

---

* The TUEL did not hesitate to declare that it "recognizes the futility of carrying on the trade union work merely for itself. The chief aim of all its efforts shall be the building of the revolutionary mass political organization of the working class, the Workers Party." [4]

sistency in Foster's career, it may be said to consist of nothing more than a rejection of dual unionism. As early as 1911, when he had been sent to an international union conference in Europe and had studied the fate of continental syndicalism, Foster concluded that the IWW policy of dual unionism was a fatal error.[6] This conviction he was to retain through all of his years in the Communist movement, even those in which he helped carry out a dual-union policy; indeed, the formal repudiation of dual unionism at the Second Comintern Congress, in 1920, had been an important factor in persuading him to join the party. All through the early and middle twenties he kept polemicizing against what he called "the American deviation" of dual unionism. In 1923 he wrote that it is "a malignant disease that sickens and devitalizes the whole labor movement";[7] in 1927, shortly before the CP began its catastrophic plunge into dual unionism, he wrote:

> The AFL and big independent unions are not hopeless. . . . It would be a basic error . . . to reject the existing trade unions altogether. . . . Under present conditions there is no room for a genuine dual union movement in the United States.[8]

Whether to work in the AFL or set up a parallel union center might seem a mere matter of expediency, but it soon had a way of involving the most crucial and perplexing problems of revolutionary politics. Against both his early syndicalist and later Communist opponents, Foster argued that the creation of dual unions violated the ethic of working-class solidarity. By digging into the established unions, he kept insisting, a left-wing minority might wrest control from the "misleaders of labor"—but only if it stayed close to the rank and file. A dual union, on the other hand, could attract only the "vanguard" elements, that is, those revolutionists and sympathizers who had already been convinced; which, in effect, would leave the majority of workers at the mercy of the conservative AFL. And if, concluded Foster, there were enough strength available for 'setting up dual unions, there would probably also be enough for taking over the old ones.

With some show of plausibility but with ultimately disastrous effects, the advocates of dual unionism argued that the AFL deliberately excluded and refused to organize the vast bulk of American workers. "Unskilled labor must become skilled before it can gain its rights," John P. Frey, an influential AFL leader, had once said.[9] And since most AFL leaders shared Frey's calloused outlook, it would be suicide, continued the dual unionists, to fritter away the energies of the radical "vanguard" in trying to keep a foothold in the corrupt and bureaucratic unions. Far better to organize the unorganized, and then return from the wilderness with enough strength to conquer the official labor movement.

Until 1928 the TUEL held fast to Foster's position, though with increasing difficulty. Whenever it did achieve a local success, emerging from obscurity to lead a militant strike or capture a local union, it quickly faced the threat of expulsion from the AFL. The official party line opposed dual unionism, but both the bitter hostility of the AFL leadership and the nature of Communist activity kept pushing the TUEL toward the organization of new unions.

In a period of general prosperity, when the labor movement as a whole was suffering a decline, it was almost inevitable that a Communist minority would totally isolate itself if it continued to flaunt its revolutionary purity, tried to "politicize" every humdrum bread-and-butter struggle, and promiscuously mixed immediate economic demands with rhetorical appeals to defend the Soviet Union. For several years now there had been a fundamental ambiguity in the CP line: it repudiated dual unionism in theory but pursued policies that could hardly lead anywhere else. The Communists in the unions were instructed to avoid the dual-union heresy, yet were told to press for something very close to a full-fledged Marxist program, which could lead only to isolation and the danger of expulsion. It is hardly surprising that under these conditions the Communists working in the unions either dissipated their energies in routine propaganda or were forced into flirting with the dual unionism they denied in theory. Nowhere was this dilemma more painfully revealed than in several dramatic strikes during the late twenties.

2. *Debacle in Passaic: 1926.* The first major strike led entirely by Communists began in the textile mills of Passaic, New Jersey, on January 25, 1926. For the past several years a

desperately sick industry had been suffering from "overproduction." In a time of general prosperity, the textile workers—always among the poorest paid in the country—were living in genuine want. There was a long history of frequent and bloody strikes in textile, for the effort to organize the depressed and inarticulate mill hands, while seldom arousing strong passions among the AFL leaders, had always appealed to the left-wing imagination. The IWW had tried several times and failed. The United Textile Workers, an AFL affiliate, was limited to a thin layer of skilled workers, a mere 30,000 out of a million people in the industry. For the Communists, or for anyone else who might trouble to pay some attention to the textile workers, there seemed to be genuine possibilities in Passaic.

At its fourth national convention, in August, 1925, the Workers (Communist) Party passed a resolution urging the unionization of the textile workers by "strengthening the existing organization and the creation of new unions where none exist. . . ." [10] This formula was ambiguous: its first half suggested support to the AFL union, its second half left the door open to dual unionism. And the ambiguity was to be characteristic of the entire Passaic adventure.

In 1926 the party moved into action. When the Botany Mills at Passaic announced a 10 percent wage cut in October, the party's Needle Trade Committee, headed by Benjamin Gitlow, decided that the time was ripe for a strike. [11] It is important to note that from the very beginning the party leadership was divided as to the advisability of having Communists openly lead a strike. The Foster group warned that to organize new unions might immediately raise the danger of sliding into dual unionism, and such party leaders as Cannon and Dunne expressed the fear that for Communists *publicly* to lead a strike in so difficult a situation as that in Passaic might doom the workers to defeat.

Brushing aside such doubts, the party leadership dispatched Albert Weisbord, a Harvard law student recently converted from the young Socialists, to prepare for a strike in Passaic. Like most Communist missionaries to the American working class, Weisbord was enormously articulate and had an unlimited fund of energy but knew very little about trade unionism in general or the textile workers in particular. Since he was to work under the close supervision of the party's Needle Trade Committee, the party felt that these handicaps would not prove too serious; what it wanted most from Weisbord was his flamboyant oratory.[12]

A United Front Textile Committee was quickly organized, consisting mainly of party members and sympathizers.* On January 23, 1926, a committee of forty-five workers presented Botany Mills with a demand that a wage cut be restored; the company replied by firing the entire committee; and immediately thereafter 5,000 Botany workers struck. The strike quickly spread to other Passaic mills, until 16,000 workers had walked out. But as was to happen repeatedly when the Communists took over strikes, a large proportion of the skilled workers remained on the job.[13]

The strike was bitter, bloody, merciless. Police and deputy sheriffs attacked strikers with clubs, fire hose, tear gas, guns. Injunctions were issued, picket lines broken, union halls closed. Nearly a thousand arrests were made during the strike. Mayors, magistrates, United States Senators, a local "Citizens Committee," the U.S. Secretary of Labor—the whole apparatus of "public opinion"—joined against the strikers.[15] But most harmful of all was the AFL denunciation. As *The Christian Century* wrote at the time, "It is within the truth to say that, if the strike is broken, the AFL will have borne a conspicuous part in breaking it." [16] The AFL United Textile Workers Union accepted, in the June, 1926, issue of its paper, large display ads from three firms that were being struck; about the men on the picket lines it said not a word.

Though aware that their leadership of the strike furnished the enemy with major ammunition, the Communists refused to relinquish control. Weisbord was unambiguously told by the Central Executive Committee of the party that neither he nor the general strike committee commanded decisive power in formulating strike policy; the real decisions were to be taken by the party. As Benjamin Gitlow has testified—and in this case there is every reason to credit his testimony: "The most intimate questions of strike policy were settled without even consulting the general strike committee, let alone the strikers." [17] Weisbord received enormous quantities of

* Despite occasional stabs at camouflage, the strike committee established its headquarters in the same building as the Passaic branch of the party—which may have made for speedy communications but was hardly a triumph of tactical discretion.[14]

national publicity and grew vain to the point where the local Passaic Communists protested against his dictatorial manner; but in actuality he was only a figurehead. The real decisions were taken in New York.

One thing the Communists did arrange with great efficiency: they set into motion an impressive machine for popularizing the strike and raising relief funds. Passaic was swamped with left-wing and liberal journalists who wrote passionate reports favorable to the strikers. Mary Heaton Vorse, Art Shields, Robert W. Dunn— either party members or sympathizers—held conferences, tried to influence public figures, congressmen, clergymen. Whenever strikers were clubbed, prominent liberals arrested simply for talking to pickets, parades organized of veterans and young girls, there quickly followed a barrage of stories and pictures favorable to the strikers. Simultaneously, the relief committee was raising sizable sums of money with which to support the destitute strikers—and, less honorably, to help pay the salaries of a number of party functionaries who had been "attached" to the strike organization.[18]

The strike dragged on for almost a year. Workers began to drift back to the mills or to leave Passaic entirely. In September— much too late—the Communist leadership finally decided that a settlement could not be reached and that the strike had reached the point of exhaustion. There seemed only one solution: to persuade the AFL Textile Workers Union to take over. It was a hard step for the Communists, but they took it. After much negotiating, the AFL union agreed to become a sort of receiver for the strikers, but at a heavy price: that the Communist leaders, particularly Weisbord, leave Passaic. The party winced, the leaders quarreled and hesitated, the strike committee succumbed to demoralization. Finally the Communists surrendered and Weisbord left.

The strike had been lost: completely, pitiably, and at enormous cost. Even after the AFL reached an agreement, many of the strikers were denied their old jobs. Within two years less than 100 Passaic textile workers remained in the AFL union. The Communists had managed to gain national publicity; they had been able to preen themselves as courageous leaders who did not fear to tackle enemies that the AFL avoided; but they failed to win a permanent foothold in the industry. The party's isolation in textile was now greater than ever, and the price the Passaic workers had paid for the party's insistence upon exploiting their needs was incalculable. Having hesitated between working through the AFL and creating a dual union in textile, the Communists had ended without the organizational benefits of either course. A sense of realism as to their own powers, to say nothing of a regard for the immediate interests of the workers, should have taught the Communists that when they led strikes openly, in the most violently anti-union industries and in blunt opposition to the AFL, the overwhelming likelihood was that they would lead the workers to grief.

3. *Debacle in New Bedford: 1928.* Less than two years later the Communists made a second major effort to crash textile. When the New Bedford mill owners announced a 10 percent wage cut in April, 1928 (the average weekly wage was $17), some 27,000 workers in the New Bedford mills fought a bitter strike that lasted into October. Several thousand New Bedford workers had been organized in a craft union for a number of years, the core of the local consisting of skilled Lancashire craftsmen. But most of the New Bedford textile workers were unorganized, and at the time of the strike only 20 percent paid dues. Having never been attracted to the craft-conscious AFL, the unskilled textile workers in New Bedford, most of them Portuguese, were ready for a more militant leadership.[19]

Fred Beal, a former textile worker who had been active in several Lawrence strikes, and William Murdoch, an experienced union organizer, now set up a Textile Mills Committee. This time the Communists seemed to have reached the conclusion that for organizing textile workers it was preferable to use men with a proletarian background rather than Harvard law students. Beal was not yet a member of the party but he was later to say: "In the interests of the strike it became necessary for me to join the Communist Party." A number of Communist leaders who had first become prominent in Passaic now journeyed to New Bedford and helped shape the Textile Mills Committee along lines similar to the Passaic United Front Committee. They organized mass meetings, soup kitchens, mass picket lines, demonstrations of the strikers' children. Local strike strategy was directed by Alex Bail, the Communist district organizer.

Once again the national headquarters of the party dispatched a flock of organizers representing not only the party itself but many of its subsidiary groups. Again the party ordered that its representatives be supported by contributions that had been sent for strike relief. Beal accepted this decree with misgivings; a woman comrade in charge of the relief drive objected violently and was "persuaded" to return to New York; Murdoch almost broke with the party after being taken aside by some Boston Communists who threatened, he said, "to beat the hell out of him" if he did not refrain from objecting to these arrangements.[20]

At first, things looked promising for the strike. The Textile Mills Committee succeeded in tying up the mills. The unskilled Portuguese workers felt that a deep social cleavage separated them from the French and British skilled workers, and they preferred the aggressive tactics of the Communist-led organization to the drowsy leadership of the local craft union, which by now had joined the AFL. Skillful at dramatizing the strike and getting headlines in the papers, the Communists understood the need for constant measures to sustain the morale of the workers. For a time it seemed that their leadership would be more intelligent in New Bedford than it had been in Passaic: they knew how to imbue the strike with the passions of a great cause, they learned how to bring out the pride of the Portuguese mill hands who had long suffered both as workers and as immigrants, they kept the town in a constant state of excitement and anxiety. But when they began to flood the area with copies of the *Daily Worker* and harshly attacked the local Citizens Relief Committee which had been set up by middle-class friends of the strikers, they badly undermined their own accomplishments. By June the strike was lagging. Police and National Guardsmen became increasingly violent; over 2,000 workers were arrested, including 275 of them in a single day. Mass picketing continued, but many of the strikers were savagely mauled by the police and then punished still further by severe penalties in court.

When a Citizens Mediation Committee proposed a compromise of a 5 percent wage cut, the AFL union agreed. But the Textile Mills Committee, spurred by the party's representatives, denounced this as a betrayal and demanded that the fight continue. It was too late, however. Nothing that the Communists might say or shout could disguise the fact that the 23-week-old strike was lost.

Meanwhile, as part of the Communist turn toward dual unionism, the battered Textile Mills Committee transformed itself into the New Bedford Textile Union. Perhaps because the estranged Portuguese workers felt a need for a place where they would be accepted, this new union did manage to preserve a following even after the strike was lost; later it became the nucleus of the party-controlled National Textile Workers Union.

By 1930 only two or three hundred of the original membership of 4,000 remained in the union; the New Bedford mills were still unorganized; wages were pitiably low. Though it had shown considerable ability at reaching some of the unskilled workers, the Communist leadership had failed to break through—it could not speak the language of—the skilled craftsmen. And partly because it had pushed its "revolutionary" line too hard, using the strike, though not quite so blatantly as in Passaic, as a means of self-aggrandizement, the party had been unable to register any lasting achievement or create any solid base. It had failed to realize that even the most militant strikes have to be settled, which meant that the economic component of a strike had always to be placed in the forefront—a difficult task for any revolutionary leadership in a trade union, but especially difficult for one that systematically subordinated the needs of the workers it led to the directives of the party it obeyed. At the end, when the Communist organizers retreated to Boston and New York they left behind them little but wasted energy and the bitter taste of defeat.

4. *Civil War in the Garment Center.* All through the twenties the Communist Party and its trade-union satellites found a major source of members and sympathizers in the New York garment industry. Traditionally the setting for the sweatshop, the garment industry paid wretchedly bad wages and, because of the seasonal nature of the work, subjected its workers to long periods of unemployment. It was an industry of small manufacturers and contractors, feverishly cutting corners and frequently on the verge of bankruptcy themselves. Here "the boss" was not some abstract,

unseen figure but a man who often worked in the shop himself, and between whom and the workers there was a constant struggle over wage rates and working conditions. The abstractions of the "class struggle" took on an immediate reality: the enemy could be seen and named.

The garment workers were men and women of a special type. Jewish immigrants from eastern Europe who were often more literate than the average American worker, they came to the shops not merely with feelings of personal desperation but with a tradition behind them of militant unionism and fervent radicalism. A great many figures of the old Socialist movement—men like Morris Hillquit, Meyer London, Abraham Cahan, Joseph Schlossberg—had been nurtured in the fiery and idealistic milieu of the Jewish garment unions. Each day "circles" of argumentative workers would form during lunch hours to discuss politics on the streets of the West Thirties in New York: here one could listen to Communists, Socialists, anarchists, DeLeonists, Zionists. Many of these workers had brought radical sympathies with them when they came to America; others discarded their religious orthodoxy in the New World and replaced it with the faith of socialism.

So frequent were the periodic slumps, long-drawn-out strikes, and union faction fights that it is hardly surprising that the Communists found the garment center a fertile field for activity. By the end of 1924 the TUEL had won majorities in the executive boards of the three largest New York locals of the International Ladies Garment Workers Union (ILGWU) and had also made sizable gains in Boston, Chicago, and Philadelphia. TUEL strength was then roughly equal to that of the old Social Democratic leadership headed by President Morris Sigman.[21]

Early the next year Sigman, alarmed by the growth of the TUEL, brought charges against its leaders for violating the union constitution—specifically, for having arranged a May Day meeting at which an over-enthused speaker shouted, "Long Live a Soviet America." The three TUEL-dominated locals were suspended; the headquarters of two were seized in the night by followers of Sigman; but the third local managed to repulse this raid and become the center of the Communist-led opposition in the ILGWU.

Contesting the legality of Sigman's action, the suspended locals organized a Joint Action Committee (JAC) which became the directing body for all left-wing work in the garment unions. Its leadership was unusually competent: Louis Hyman, a respected unionist, not a member of the CP but closely cooperating with it, served as chairman and Charles Zimmerman, a young and extremely able organizer, as secretary. Each day the struggle between the old-line officials and the left wing grew fiercer, and soon it took on a semi-military aspect. Scores of young Communists from the city colleges, Bronx housewives, party members from the entire city joined the left-wing garment workers in guarding their headquarters. In fact, if not name, there was civil war in the garment industry.

In fact, too, the JAC functioned as a union: it collected dues, serviced grievances, negotiated with employers. Yet, since the party was still opposed to dual unionism, it did not fall into the trap of setting up a full-fledged separate union. It carefully stressed as its main slogan the "full reinstatement" of the left-wing locals, meanwhile urging that as a gesture of protest the workers "stop paying dues" to Sigman's office.

That the Communist-dominated JAC commanded enormous influence among the garment workers during this struggle is admitted even by its most severe critics and enemies; it was able, for example, to call a mass demonstration at Yankee Stadium to which 40,000 cloak and dress makers came and to organize a work stoppage in which 30,000 workers left the shops and filled seventeen halls to listen to its speakers. A clear majority of the garment workers in New York City—certainly a majority of the active ILGWU members—supported the left-wing JAC, not necessarily because of its political line but because they felt the suspension of the three left-wing locals had been undemocratic.

The Sigman leadership had to retreat. It resumed negotiations with the left wing, agreed to reinstate the three suspended locals and to call a special convention of the international union. Still more important, it agreed to submit to the ILGWU membership a constitutional amendment providing for proportional representation of locals at the union convention. (The right-wing leadership had maintained itself in office partly through a system of voting that favored the small locals, which it controlled, at the expense of the big ones, where the Communists were strong.)

When the special convention met in Philadelphia on November 30, 1925, the two sides were evenly matched—and for a moment it seemed to the Communists that the enormous plum of the ILGWU might fall into its lap. The TUEL could count on 110 delegates representing the majority of the large and important locals, while the Sigman leadership outnumbered it by some 50 delegates, most of whom came from small and badly functioning locals. There could be no doubt that in terms of the key spots in the ILGWU the Communists now had the upper hand.[22] After fifteen days of wrangling, a convention committee recommended larger representation for the big locals, but not proportional representation. Zimmerman indignantly reminded the right wing of the earlier agreement for a referendum on this issue, but David Dubinsky, chairing the session, ruled that no previous agreement could be binding on a sovereign convention. The left wing had been outfoxed.

An extremely significant incident now occurred. Louis Hyman, the leader of the left-wing delegates, shouted, "Let's walk out," and the entire TUEL group left the hall. But this time the walkout was not part of Communist strategy—Hyman, an ally but not an agent, had impulsively acted on his own. The party steering committee, Gitlow and Dunne, immediately demanded that Hyman reverse his course, for dual unionism was not yet the order of the day. When Hyman refused to lead his delegation back to the convention hall, Dunne told him bluntly, "Then you will crawl back on your belly!" That evening the TUEL forces returned to the convention.[*]

A compromise was patched up, and the right wing kept control of the international by the unimpressive margin of 158 to 110. But again the TUEL won control of three big New York locals, and soon it added a fourth. The New York Joint Board of the ILGWU, the most important subdivision of the union, fell to the TUEL, Hyman becoming general manager and Zimmerman manager of the dress department. It seemed inevitable that within a short time the left wing would take over the whole international.

Yet a year later the power of the TUEL was shattered. In

---

[*] Hyman was helpless against the party fraction within the left wing. In an article he later wrote, William F. Dunne admitted that 52 of the 110 left-wing delegates were party members. Many of the other 58 were close sympathizers.[23]

1926 the left-wing leadership of the New York cloakmakers led a long, violent, and disastrous strike. Any strike in the garment center that year would have had to face enormous difficulties; but the Communists imposed additional difficulties that made defeat certain.

The strike grew out of a debate within the union over a report brought in by a special commission appointed by Governor Alfred E. Smith to consider ways of rationalizing the garment industry. So close did this commission come in a number of particulars to the previous ILGWU demands that President Sigman advised accepting the report as a basis for negotiations, particularly since the employers were themselves split in their attitude toward it. The TUEL group which ran the New York locals now faced a crucial decision. Hyman and Zimmerman, the leaders on the spot, were far from enthusiastic about calling a strike; as skillful leaders who knew the mood of the garment workers at the moment, they realized that the odds against success were very high; but behind them stood the Communist Party actively insisting on an immediate strike.

This pressure from the party leadership had little to do with any serious estimate of the situation in the garment industry; it was almost entirely the result of the violent faction fight that was being waged inside the party. The more experienced Communist leaders knew that there was little chance the strike would be successful, but neither of the two main factions was willing to accept the "onus" of opposing a militant strike since that might provide ammunition to the opposing faction.* From such motives of mutual cowardice and irresponsibility, the party pressured its people in the garment union to call a general strike in the cloak trade on July 1, 1926. The response of the workers was immediate; the shops were closed.

In the first months of the strike, the entire Jewish community and labor movement of New York supported the cloakmakers, despite the fact that the chairman of the strike committee was Louis Hyman rather than, as had previously been the custom, the president of the ILGWU. Had a settlement been negotiated within a reasonable time, the TUEL forces would have emerged with enormously increased prestige and the way would have been opened to-

---

* For his "opportunism" in hesitating to call a strike, Zimmerman was made to resign from the national committee of the needle trades section of the Communist Party.

ward taking over the entire union. But the strike was not settled in time. Hyman and Zimmerman negotiated informally with the larger employers and in the eighth week of the strike arrived at what seemed to them favorable terms. There remained one more barrier—approval of the party was necessary before they could enter formal negotiations. And again the factional interests that had led to calling the strike prevented its proper settlement. Neither the Lovestone nor the Foster group was willing to endorse a settlement that might make it seem insufficiently Bolshevik.[24]

The party decided to recommend a rejection of the terms of settlement and to urge an intensification of the strike. For this decision thousands of garment workers, who cared nothing for either Lovestone or Foster, would suffer for years to come.

Slowly the strike was being undermined by the appearance of goods produced in out-of-town shops and by settlements with the small employers. The ranks of the strikers held firm—these were people with a long training in disciplined struggle—but moods of discouragement could not be suppressed. The party leaders, especially Foster, added absurdity to mischief by insisting that the strike be "politicized"; and the TUEL activists in the union obediently began shouting for a labor party (hardly in the power of the employers to grant) and for amalgamation of all needle-trade unions (hardly an issue relevant to the immediate strike). Hyman would occasionally express some doubts, but the party whips soon prodded him into line.

Finally, on December 13 the international suspended the left-wing New York leadership and settled the strike. Lasting six months and costing three million dollars, the strike had brought misery and defeat to thousands of workers, largely because it had been prolonged for political reasons having nothing whatever to do with the union. Years would pass before the ILGWU could regain its power.

The Communists continued to fight, issuing bonds in a campaign to reinstate the suspended left-wing leaders and raising about $150,000 from sympathizers. But their moment had passed; the workers gradually drifted back to the right-wing leadership, and the bonds were never redeemed.

Though control of the ILGWU was now forever out of their

reach, the Communists were still able to launch guerilla raids. In the shops fights broke out regularly, sometimes with blackjacks and knives. The devotion of the left-wing garment workers, as blind as it was intense, made it possible to keep the union in a constant uproar.

By the time dual unionism did become party policy, most of the left-wing strength had been dissipated. A few years earlier it might have been possible to set up a strong revolutionary union in the garment industry; now it was too late. On New Year's Day, 1929, the Communists nonetheless organized the Needle Trades Workers Industrial Union. Only a few thousand workers joined it, mostly furriers, long to constitute one of the bulwarks of the party, and dressmakers, who had not participated in the 1926 strike and were therefore not yet disillusioned with TUEL leadership.

In a short time a number of the left-wing leaders, including Hyman and Zimmerman, broke with the Communists and returned to the ILGWU. Except among the furriers, the dual union in the garment center remained a negligible factor. The Communists who yesterday had seemed on the verge of gaining control of so important a union as the ILGWU retained a considerable following, but their capacity for challenging the official union leadership was broken. They reaped as they had sown.*

* The two other major garment unions differed sharply in their ability to resist Communist infiltration. In the Amalgamated Clothing Workers, Sidney Hillman's guile prevented the Communists from making any permanent inroads, though they did command a sizable influence during the mid-twenties.[25]

Among the furriers, however, the Communists established a strong and enduring base. Here the civil war between factions began to resemble a gang war. A contemporary account does not exaggerate:

"Vicious fights on the picket lines, in the shops and on the streets were a daily occurrence. Few weeks passed when workers, slashed with the knives of their trade or trampled by the boots of rival unionists, did not fill the emergency wards and night courts."

In the fur union the Communists had two remarkably gifted leaders, Aaron Gross and Ben Gold, while the right wing had no leaders of comparable stature. The furriers also had a strike in 1926, and it was fought with even greater violence, both sides using toughs and "gorillas"; but it ended with the first forty-hour week in the garment industry, as well as a 10 percent wage increase. When the AFL then accused the Gross-Gold leadership of being Soviet agents, of mismanaging union funds, and of bribing police and court officials, the majority of the workers paid little attention to these charges

5. These defeats, and others like them, were caused by the adventurism and irresponsibility of the Communists in the unions; but it would be unjust to ignore the objective circumstances that made *any* effort to organize American workers during the twenties both difficult and hazardous.

In 1919 there had been five million unionized workers in the United States; in 1929 there were less than four million. The twenties constituted the only period of prosperity in our century during which the unions lost ground. Even such formerly well-organized industries as coal became largely non-union. Blacklisting, the yellow-dog contract, the use of professional armed guards and labor spies, the injunction—all these were common in the twenties. The company union, partly as an adjunct of company "paternalism," made its appearance as a major phenomenon of industrial life. Before 1917 company unions had been virtually unknown, but by 1927 there were hundreds of them, with a membership of nearly a million and a half. Outmaneuvered on every front, the AFL clung to parochial craft concepts and made no headway whatever on the few occasions it tried to organize the mass industries. The number of strikes declined from 3,630 in 1917 to an average of 763 in the years between 1927 and 1931.[27]

No wonder the Communist minority in the unions, for all its devotion and doggedness, found itself blocked on every path. Its burden was heavy enough, but when the party leadership imposed ultra-revolutionary tactics upon it, the burden became insupportable. As A. J. Muste, a radical but anti-Communist labor leader, wrote at the time:

Amalgamation of craft into industrial unions, recognition of Soviet Russia, and affiliation of the AFL to the Red International of Labor Unions all figure in the [TUEL] program . . . though

—true though some of them were—and instead retained faith in the Communists.

During the Third Period the fur workers joined the Needle Trades Workers Industrial Union, and throughout the next two decades they remained the one indestructible source of Communist strength in the New York garment center. Even in the mid-fifties, when a variety of pressures forced Gold to resign and the fur union to seek shelter in the AFL, the Communists retained some strength among the fur workers.[26]

the first is on an entirely different footing from the other two as
a living, pressing issue for the American trade union movement.[28]

In December, 1927, at its third national conference, the TUEL
reaffirmed its opposition to dual unionism, directing those of its
members who had been expelled from the AFL to struggle for reinstatement. But then, with bewildering suddenness, a shift of
trade-union policy was announced in Moscow. Dual unionism was
the order of the day.

In early 1928 A. Lozovsky, a Communist trade-union "expert,"
charged the American party with "dancing quadrilles around the
AFL"—a charge that against the background of Passaic and New
Bedford was downright grotesque. The American Communists, he
wrote, had made a "fetish out of anti-dual unionism," and the TUEL
position had become one of deferring "to the leaders of the reformist
trade unions with requests to organize the unorganized, save the
unions, lead strikes etc." Instead, he concluded, the TUEL must
now "form unions in all those branches of industry where there is
either no organization or where what exists is practically negligible." [29]

A few days later the Red International of Labor Unions passed
a resolution stating:

> Further appeals to the [AFL] bureaucracy and dependence
> upon so-called progressives in the reactionary unions is useless and
> wrong. The TUEL must itself become the basis of organization
> for the . . . unorganized.[30]

Mining, steel, oil, auto, rubber, textile, marine, and transport were
singled out as the industries in which the TUEL should proceed on
its own.

The first response in the American party was simply bewilderment, for it was impossible to erase from the minds of its active
members the numerous statements of opposition to dual unionism
that the Communist movement had made. In 1921 the Comintern
had declared that Communists must learn "how to influence unions
without attempting to keep them in leading strings. Only the

Communist group is subject to the control of the party, not the labor union as a whole." [31] In 1924: "Leninism in the field of the trade union movement is the struggle against splitting in any form." In 1926: "The splitting up . . . of any trade union whatever is a blow to the entire trade union movement." [32]

But now, in the very throes of its weakness, the American party was being driven to a policy that meant deliberately splitting the unions.

In May, 1928, a hastily convened meeting of the party's Central Committee was held in an atmosphere of extreme agitation. James P. Cannon, soon to be expelled for Trotskyism, seemed rather enthusiastic about the new dual-union policy, but everyone else squirmed with discomfort. The Committee's resolution began, predictably, by expressing "full agreement with Comrade Lozovsky in laying the utmost stress upon the organization of the unorganized," and then it quickly moved to the heart of the trouble:

> But the Central Committee must disagree with a number of Comrade Lozovsky's criticisms. . . . Such added emphasis as may now be laid upon the formation of new unions is not a repudiation or rejection of our previous policy, but a development of it in accordance with a changed objective situation. . . . The combined unions still have a membership of approximately three million. These we cannot surrender to the leadership of the reactionary bureaucrats.[33]

Foster, who found the new line especially hard to take, could barely disguise his unhappiness:

> Our basic trade union policy remains the same. . . . It has nothing in common with traditional dual unionism. . . . The question at issue is one of emphasis. The objective situation demands that we put more emphasis on the establishment of new unions.[34]

These hesitations and scruples came to nothing. Moscow was inflexible, the Third Period had begun, and nothing that might be said by a mere American Central Committee—Moscow had seen them come and go—was able to change the line. William Z. Foster, lifelong opponent of dual unionism, was now put in charge of building the first major dual-union movement in America since the days of the IWW.[35]

Soon, at least in public, Foster was accepting the new line. "The pessimism," he wrote, "existing prior to the TUUL convention among active comrades, amounting to a certain degree of dragging behind the masses . . . must be drastically liquidated." [36] They ordered these things better in Russia, where the pessimists were liquidated along with the pessimism.

6. In September, 1928, the Communists set up the first of their dual unions: the National Miners Union. It was a particularly unfortunate choice. The miners were weary and de-moralized from a series of strike defeats, and the new organization, which claimed 15,000 members but never had that many, im-mediately antagonized the much larger group of non-Communists who were fighting against John L. Lewis's leadership in the United Mine Workers. A short while later came the National Textile Workers Union and then the Needle Trades Workers Industrial Union. The first claimed 5,000 members, the second 22,000—both exaggerations.

As a public display of "strength," the TUEL called its fourth convention for the fall of 1929. Held in Cleveland, this convention voted to change the name of the dual-union movement to Trade Union Unity League and to adopt as its slogan "Class Against Class"—though it was committed to organizing the workers, so to speak, behind their backs.* Even Foster would later admit that its claim to 57,000 members was inflated. The 690 delegates were mainly young Communists, their average age being only thirty-two, and more than a quarter of them were miners who had been loaded onto trucks and brought north to Cleveland for display. About 40 percent of the delegates were CP and TUEL officials. Once the

---

* To justify their dual-union course, the Communists improvised the clumsy theory that the AFL leaders had become fascists. Foster wrote: "The AFL leaders have become the chief strike-breaking agency of the employers. . . . Developing fascism in the United States has a main foundation in the leadership of the AFL." [37] Whether Foster really believed this sort of thing it is almost impossible to say.

various deductions are made, it becomes clear that few *bona-fide* unionists found their way to the dual unions.[38]

From its very inception, the TUUL was a puny hot-house product. A year after the Cleveland convention, the Needle Trades Workers Industrial Union had no more than 6,000 members in an industry employing 500,000. The National Textile Workers reported in June, 1930, that after a three-month organizational drive to recruit 5,000 new members it had barely managed to scrape up 500. The National Miners Union now had a mere 4,000 dues-paying members, the Independent Shoe Workers Union had dropped from 5,000 to 200 members, and the remaining TUUL affiliates were nothing but empty rattling shells.[39]

Like revolutionary unions in almost any period, the TUUL could come alive during dramatic strikes but it almost always collapsed immediately after the strikes were ended. The membership would rise suddenly and then fall as quickly. Even the leadership was remarkably unstable, the textile union having no less than seven national secretaries during its five years of existence. Foster warned against "a tendency to be attracted to the struggle and to make a fight only when the masses are all in motion, but a real union must learn how to conduct the fight in the trough between the waves of the strikes." [40] The diagnosis was accurate, but as long as Foster was confined to the policy of dual unionism that made the symptoms inevitable, he could offer no cure.

Communist publications during the Third Period were crammed with exhortations to organize the unorganized, with open letters from the Comintern, with self-criticism and breast-beatings by party leaders confessing their lack of success in the repeated campaigns to penetrate the mass industries—but all to no avail. Mainly because of the dual-union policy, the party and its trade-union shadow failed all through the years of the depression to win any substantial base in the mass-production industries. (In 1931, for example, the party had 652 street nuclei but only 75 shop nuclei, and these latter comprised a mere 4 percent of the total membership[41]—from the Communist point of view, a sign of deplorable weakness.)

There were times when the Communists managed to weaken or break up an established union; there were times when they could lead a violent strike; but only rarely could they organize a stable union. TUUL leaders and members often displayed a heroism and self-sacrifice which no amount of political disagreement should deter anyone from admiring; they were repeatedly beaten by the police, company agents, and vigilantes; they worked as volunteers or at subsistence wages; several of them were killed during strikes and demonstrations. But not all their passion and selflessness could prevent the increasing isolation of the Communists in the trade-union field.

7. *Tragedy in Gastonia: 1929*. When a series of spontaneous strikes—they bespoke an utter desperation among the workers —broke out in North and South Carolina mill towns early in 1929, the TUUL decided that a major effort had to be made to organize Southern textile. The Communist leaders knew well enough that nothing could be more difficult or risky for them, but they felt obliged to make the attempt.

Fred Beal, who had led the New Bedford strike, was sent down to North Carolina. He concentrated his activity at the huge Loray Mills in Gastonia, which seemed ripe for unionization. Wages at Loray averaged between $9 and $12 a week; work shifts between eleven and twelve hours a day. Simply to survive, whole families, including grandparents and children, had to sweat in the mills. The village was badly overcrowded, the houses were rickety and un-sanitary. Wages and working conditions had been deteriorating for the past several years; only a year earlier the stretch-out system and a wage cut had been introduced. If ever there was a situation that conformed to the classical Marxist vision of an exploited and suffer-ing proletariat in opposition to heartless capitalists, this was it.[42]

A skillful organizer, Beal went about his work in a methodical way, and soon had made considerable progress among the inexperi-enced men. But the company precipitated a strike when, in March, 1929, it fired twenty of the several hundred workers who had signed cards with the TUUL textile union. It was not the best moment to strike, but the TUUL had no alternative. At first it stressed the kind of economic demands that any union would have advanced: a $20 minimum weekly wage, abolition of piece work, the forty-hour week, repair of mill-owned houses, union recognition. Despite the moderation of these demands, the strike immediately aroused emotions of hysterical xenophobia among almost every segment of the Southern community: the press, business, ministers, judges, police officials. A red scare was whipped up. The papers denounced Northern agitators. William Green sent a letter to the nearest AFL unit urging it to oppose the strike.

Among the textile workers themselves the initial response to the Communist leadership was enthusiastic, for many of them were clearly unaware of the differences between the TUUL and any other kind of union, while the older ones remembered how dismally the AFL had failed in an organization drive a decade earlier.

The Communists began cautiously: they confined themselves to union issues. But in the very midst of the strike a quarrel broke out in the party's Central Committee over the proper strategy, some of the leaders favoring a straight union fight—hard enough in Gastonia!—but the majority believing that the strike should be "politicized." In the final phases of the strike, when everything was clearly lost except the political capital that could be squeezed out of the losses, the Communists allowed the trade-union issues to drop into the background and pictured the strike as a major incident in the struggle between American capitalism and a rising proletariat. Albert Weisbord, who was brought south for speech-making, declared at one of the strike meetings:

> This strike is the first shot in a battle which will be heard around the world. It will prove as important in transforming the social and political life of this country as the Civil War itself. . . . Don't listen to the poison of the bosses—extend the strike over the whole countryside. We need mass action.[43]

Soon a horde of Communist functionaries descended on Gastonia, and not only from the party itself but from the Young Communist League, the International Labor Defense, and the Workers International Relief. These organizers were young, bold, and inexperienced. They passed out copies of the *Daily Worker*, which contained wildly inaccurate "revolutionary" reports of the strike; sneered at the preachers (no doubt, to break the workers from the opium of religion); told highly colored stories about the treachery of the AFL (though the truth was bad enough). When the National Guard was turned loose against the strikers, the Communist phalanx distributed a revolutionary appeal to the Guardsmen:

> Workers in the National Guard: we, the striking workers, are your brothers. Our fight is your fight. Help us win the strike. . . . Refuse to shoot or bayonet your fathers or brothers. . . . Fight with your class, the striking workers.[44]

George Pershing, the YCL organizer, told the reporters:

> I am here for the purpose of organizing the YCL. The principal view of the Communists is control of the country by the workers. Under Communist control the Loray Mill and every other mill would be organized by a general committee made up of one representative worker from each department. . . .[45]

Does it require much imagination to see that such vain bragging was possible only if the Communists thought first of the political uses to which they could put the strike and second of the interests of the strikers themselves? Or how such statements could only serve to raise the already foaming hysteria of the conservative community to a boiling point? The day of revolution seemed at hand; it was time to take emergency steps; heavily armed special deputies and a vigilante gang calling itself the "Committee of 100" were organized to preserve "law and order." The South and the Communists brought out the worst in each other: both thought of the strike as a symbolic test in which fundamental issues would forever be settled. And meanwhile the strikers faced a reign of terror, and the demand for better wages was almost forgotten.

Yet none of this deterred the Communist strategists—experts in the art of world revolution—from "deepening" their campaign. From New York they bombarded the local strike leaders, already under unbearable pressures, with demands for extending the strike to other textile towns. In his autobiography Fred Beal, who later broke from the party, reports that he was ordered by the Central Committee to stress the Negro question in speeches at strike meetings. When he replied that there were only two Negro workers in the entire mill, both of whom had understandably fled the moment the strike began, Albert Weisbord, the bearer of political tidings, thundered at him: "We must prepare the workers for the coming revolution. We must look ahead and smash all feelings of inequality." [46]

What made the work of the local strike leaders impossible—apart, that is, from community terror, a hopeless strike strategy, and the inexperience of the workers—was that the party Central Committee allowed the Gastonia situation to become a factional football. Orders were given and countermanded, organizers sent and withdrawn in favor of men from the other faction. Yet the party did succeed, as in Passaic and New Bedford—but even more, for remember: *this was the South!*—in mobilizing an enormous publicity campaign in behalf of the strikers and in collecting huge sums of money for relief. As also in the past, some of this money was used to support the squad of organizers from the front organizations.

In April a band of masked vigilantes attacked the union office with axes and raided the store where the relief committee kept its supplies. In June, after the union had built a new headquarters and a tent colony for evicted strikers, the chief of police together with several cronies, some of them drunk, raided the tent colony. When asked to produce search warrants, they had none to show. The police chief tried to disarm a union guard; shots rang out; a striker was seriously hurt, two policemen were slightly wounded, the police chief was dead.

And now all the hysteria of the town broke loose. The Committee of 100 grew to thousands, who, deputized or not, hunted strikers in the woods to which they had tried to escape. Seventy strikers were charged with murder, assault with intent to kill, and conspiracy. The number was reduced to sixteen. When they were brought to trial, a juror went mad and a mistrial had to be declared.

Meanwhile a debate was raging among the party leaders in New York as to which strategy the defense should follow. The Lovestoneites proposed that the charges be fought as a "frame-up," while the Foster group favored a more aggressive defense based on the moral right of the strikers to protect their headquarters. The utter unwillingness or incapacity of the Communists to understand what was really happening in Gastonia came through in a pamphlet written by William F. Dunne after the terror had begun:

The struggle in Gastonia has reached a far higher stage—
that of armed struggle. . . . [This] furnishes irrefutable proof
of the process by which the inner contradictions of capitalism in
the imperialist period bring on economic struggles which speedily
take on a political character. . . . The strikers stood with arms
in their hands and exchanged shot for shot with the police. . . .[47]

While Dunne was marshaling his irrefutable proofs, an armed
mob was attacking a group of strikers on the way to a meeting. Ella
May Wiggins, a striker and mother of five children, was killed. Soon
the terror made further union activity impossible. At the second
trial four Northern organizers were given sentences of seventeen to
twenty years, and the three Southern organizers somewhat lighter
ones. The very day they were sentenced, a jury refused to indict
any of the men held for the murder of Mrs. Wiggins. Southern
justice was being dispensed; the higher stage of the Communists had
been reached.

Feeling they could not secure justice in North Carolina, the
convicted strikers skipped bail and several of them left for Russia.
"They are quite justified," wrote the *Daily Worker*, "in escaping
from the vicious sentences imposed upon them. . . . The working
class as a whole should glory in the fact that they got away. . . ."[48]
Later, when Beal returned to the United States, the party refused
to help him; a broken and disillusioned man, he was no longer
willing to obey its orders.

In Gastonia "law and order" reigned. The mill workers drifted
back to work, their conditions unimproved, their morale shattered.
The National Textile Workers Union remained a paper organization
staffed by Communist functionaries and representing a handful of
Northern workers and no Southern workers.

Could the strike have been won under *any* leadership? Probably not. In his brilliant book *The Mind of the South* W. J. Cash
has given persuasive reasons for believing that strikes like the one in
Gastonia were doomed from the outset:

For the quite simple reason . . . of the presence of the old
Southern reservoir of surplus labor. And not merely untrained
labor. There were those thousands who had been in the mills
at one time or another, and who were glad to grasp a chance to

escape from the status of sharecropper or even tenant and get
back to the mills by serving as strikebreakers—people who, in
their naïve individualism, were innocent of the notion in the word
"scab."

For the reason, also, that militant interest was arrayed against
these strikes. The masters of the mills were naturally terrified for
their profits, both present and future, which . . . they felt to be
dependent upon the maintenance of cheap labor and the *status
quo*. . . .

. . . The prevailing attitude toward the strikes was that they
were grossly disloyal toward the mill and then—if you listened
closely, you could sometimes hear it come out quite explicitly—
to the South as such. . . .

Yet Cash, writing as a Southerner whose disaffection stemmed
from love, believed that such strikes

. . . demonstrated beyond question that the level of dissatisfaction
was rising slowly in the mill workers in the South. And though
the unions promptly collapsed . . . yet the struggle left some
ponderable effect behind it. Looking back upon it today, it stands
out as a sort of—Lexington? Rather as a sort of Boston Massacre
—the point at which something which had been essentially unthinkable before suddenly began to be more thinkable. . . .
Hereafter the notion of labor unionism would distinctly be more
present to the mind of the Southern workers. . . .[49]

All this may be true, and for the historian of the South the
stress that Cash proposes is understandable, perhaps unavoidable.
But for the historian of American Communism the stress must be
placed upon the profound irresponsibility with which the Communists seized on the desperation of the Gastonia mill hands in
order to make political capital; the cynicism that lay hidden like a
canker in their idealistic readiness to suffer so long as it was "their"
strike; the indifference to the dignity and needs of the human beings
whom they involved and then manipulated in the interests of
ideology. In the Gastonia strike, as in so many other situations, the
Communists committed the greatest of all sins in their treatment of
the workers: they *used* them.

8. *Disruption in Coal*. Coal, like textile, seemed ready for TUUL penetration. In the late twenties it was a sick industry, suffering from overproduction, antiquated methods, and ferocious competition. One of the oldest unions in America, the United Mine Workers was also one of the sickest. Torn by internal factionalism, wildcat strikes, and sporadic revolts against John L. Lewis's autocratic reign, the UMW seemed an ideal target for Communist infiltration.

By the late twenties bituminous coal production was half what it had been during the First World War. Many owners, though operating at a loss, kept the mines open to prevent the still greater losses that might follow from flooding or caving in. Employment sagged, but since the mines operated intermittently, the miners remained in the villages. Besides, there was no place else to go. Daily wage rates were relatively high, yearly earnings low.

Though fighting vigorously, the union had lost district after district to the anti-union drives of the owners. John L. Lewis could force them to pay a daily wage of $7.50, but this meant that the operators in the North, where unionism more or less prevailed, had to compete against the Southern operators, who paid their unorganized workers $3 a day. And even in the North the union kept losing steadily.[50]

The inner life of the UMW reflected the chaos of the industry as a whole. Factional violence was greater than in any other American union, except perhaps the garment unions. When Lewis took over in 1920, the UMW was split into a number of autonomous districts often competing against and undercutting one another; from the beginning he tried to bind these districts into a highly centralized organization, arguing that only through centralization could the operators be prevented from setting one district into ruinous competition with another. Lewis was right; he achieved his ends; but in building a powerful machine he rode roughshod over dissident tendencies in the UMW and over democratic procedures as well.

The opposition was stubborn. Radicals of various shades could exercise some influence in the mines because the recurrent disputes between UMW districts and the desperate state of the industry as a whole made it plausible to inject larger political issues into economic struggles. During the twenties the CP was by no means the only radical group active in the coal union; there were a number of indigenous radical leaders, some of them both prominent and gifted, who collaborated with the Communists when they thought it necessary but refused to follow the party line unconditionally. So while the Communists maintained a certain influence in the miners' union throughout the twenties, they never managed to build up an independent group within the union or even a stable party fraction.

Time after time it seemed that the insurgents within the UMW, fighting for intra-union democracy and a more militant policy than Lewis then pursued, were close to ousting his regime. The Progressive International Committee, organized in 1923 and strongly influenced by the TUEL, brought together a number of Lewis's critics and advocated, among other things, nationalization of the mines as the only way to overcome the chronic crisis of the industry. But though the Committee was amazingly successful for a time, it found no way of coping with Lewis's counter-strategy, which was simply to expel his opponents.

In the December, 1924, union election the Committee ran as candidate for the UMW presidency George Voyzey, a Communist miner from Illinois. Although an obscure figure, Voyzey was credited by the UMW with 66,000 votes as against Lewis's 136,000; and the Committee produced evidence that the Lewis machine had systematically undercounted Voyzey's vote.

A few years later the Lewis machine faced a more serious threat. In 1926 John Brophy, son of a Lancashire miner and himself a miner since the age of twelve, became leader of the opposition. District president of the Pennsylvania soft-coal area in the UMW, Brophy was a man of stature and not a Communist tool. He had thought deeply about the problems of the industry and in 1922 had advanced a plan for the nationalization of coal that had been widely discussed.[51] Lewis could not dismiss him as an interloper or an alien agitator or radical. Brophy's lieutenant Powers Hapgood —Harvard 1920, mine laborer, skilled pickman, organizer for District Two—was one of the most gifted union leaders this country has produced.

When Brophy organized a "Save the Union Committee" with branches in many mining towns, the TUEL, still committed to working within the regular unions, came to his support. Foster personally spent five months on the road doing organizational work for the Committee, though it kept itself free from party domination.

In 1927 the Lewis machine defeated the opposition by a vote of 173,000 to 60,000, but the indications were that the Brophy group would keep growing. The UMW kept losing members. A desperate strike in 1927-28 was lost. Operators kept tearing up or ignoring contracts. As Lewis proved unable to cope with these problems, there was good reason to believe that the "Save the Union Committee," skillfully piloted by Brophy and Hapgood, would eventually take over the leadership.

Precisely at this point the Communists came out for dual unions and decided to build a separate union in coal. For Lewis it was a blessing, for the opposition a blow. Brophy and Hapgood, unwilling to abandon the UMW to Lewis, suddenly found themselves deprived of a sizable portion of their support, particularly of the kind of articulate people the Communists could provide in building up a union faction. Hapgood went to plead with Foster not to pull out of the UMW and thus cripple the progressive opposition group. Years later he would remember the following exchange:

Hapgood: "Look here, Bill . . . you denounced dual unionism and I agreed with you one hundred percent. I still feel the same way. Now I am told that you and the Communist Party have come out for dual unionism and frankly, Bill, I just don't understand it."

Foster: "Powers, the Communist Party decided that policy. As a good Communist, I just have to go along." [52]

Foster was as good as his word. Dutifully, he split the "Save the Union Committee," left Brophy and Hapgood behind, and created the National Miners Union,* which never managed to

* Perhaps uneasy at having to apply their new trade-union line to the coal industry, the Communists argued that the "new National Miners Union has nothing in common with the theory or practise of dual unionism. It is

organize more than small groups of workers in outlying districts. During the summer of 1931 the Communist miners' union led a violent strike in the western Pennslyvania coal fields and lost. In the same years the Kentucky miners, among the worst paid and most desperate, turned to the Communist leadership and another violent strike took place in Harlan County. Again it was lost. In Illinois another Communist-led miners' strike proved an absolute fiasco, and as Foster himself later admitted, "this ill-advised, poorly organized strike killed the National Miners Union in Illinois." [54]

After that, the Communist miners' union was little more than a paper organization. In 1930, meanwhile, the Brophy opposition came very close to winning the leadership of the United Mine Workers from John L. Lewis. Had the opposition within the UMW not been split by Communist directive, it is quite possible that Brophy would have been elected. Little had John L. Lewis realized that when A. Lozovsky in Moscow suddenly charged the Communists with "dancing quadrilles around the AFL" this would eventuate in a policy that, in effect, would save his head.

9. So self-destructive were the Communist policies in the trade unions during the Third Period that even the party press had occasionally to acknowledge the more glaring stupidities. Thus the Communist *Labor Unity* wrote in 1931: "The policy of our recent strikes was carried out in the most sectarian manner, by making it a condition that the workers join the TUUL union, in order to join the strike." [55] Another Communist writer reported in the same year that

In the single strike called in the Pittsburgh region, we found that the unions were told to fight for the 6 hour day and for a workers and farmers government, *while the grievances that led to the strike were either forgotten or put in the background.*[56] [emphasis added]

forming in an industry where the old union is either extinct or existing, through the policies of its reactionary leadership, as a company union." [53] For Brophy and his friends, as the rug was being pulled from beneath them, such apologias proved a dubious comfort.

The list of such gross errors and absurdities could be extended indefinitely, but at this point it might be more useful to turn to the *Party Organizer*, a sort of trade journal for Communist functionaries, where, because they were writing mainly for each other, the leaders could express themselves with unusual frankness:

> *Item:* "In our unit we have four new members who listened with interest to a speech about the new turn of the party. They heard the following: 'The party made very good progress in the IRD.' The eyes of the new members sparkled. One of them said, 'We make progress there too, we will lead the next big strike. . . . The subway workers are with us.' The speaker became very angry and said, 'How can anyone be so dumb. I said *I R D*, not IRT, and what I said means International Red Day. . . .' The four workers were very angry and at the next meeting they did not show up."

> *Item:* "It seems that some of our party leaders, especially on the local and district scale, take an aristocratic attitude toward the masses and single out workers here and there . . . and classify them as dumb-bells, unreliable and ignorant. . . . Then they wonder why once we start a movement, it starts with a bang and we cannot keep its mass character."

> *Item:* "In the small section of Library, not far from the center of the Pittsburgh district, where a few mine nuclei of the party and a few branch locals of the National Miners Union were built, for a long time we had the following fulltime function-aries: a section organizer of the party, a section organizer of the YCL, a sub-district organizer of the National Miners Union, an organizer of the unemployed movement, an organizer of women's auxiliary, a Negro work director and perhaps some others—prac-tically six or seven fulltime functionaries for a movement embrac-ing a few hundred workers in the Party, union and auxiliaries." [57]

In retrospect, it might seem possible to justify, or at least explain, Communist dual unionism as appropriate to the desperate mood of depression America. But nothing of the kind is true. The policy had been adopted before the crash of 1929 and for reasons that had nothing to do with the depression or any other aspect of American life. During the early thirties most American workers, fearful of losing their jobs, were not very receptive to strike calls—

certainly not to those coming from revolutionary unions. The party did achieve a few successes among the unemployed, but mainly because of the increasing social and psychological gap between employed and unemployed workers. Communist unions were able to call strikes among certain marginal and especially underpaid groups of workers, but the very reason that made this possible also cut them off from the bulk of the American working class. In 1932 a writer for the *Party Organizer* admitted that "a Chinese wall . . . stands between us and the decisive sections of the workers in the New York district"[58]—an admission both honest and rare.

With the election of Franklin Roosevelt and the beginning of the New Deal, the social temper of the country began to change. Most unions were enthusiastic about the NRA, particularly Section 7a, which recognized the rights of workers to organize, but the Communists, still mired in the Third Period, denounced the New Deal as "a program of fascization."

Yet reality has a way of imposing itself even upon those who systematically spurn it, and in this case the reality was a sudden and massive increase in the number of strikes, as well as in union organization, during the early thirties. In 1930 only 158,000 workers had struck in the United States; in 1934 the number was close to a million and a half. Nearly 500,000 textile workers struck along the Eastern seaboard in 1934, and there were important actions in almost every major industry. Both AFL and independent unions began to grow. Even the TUUL experienced a minor revival, increasing its membership to a claimed 125,000 and leading a number of strikes in 1933 and 1934. Nonetheless, it soon became clear to the party leadership that the TUUL had failed to establish any important relationship with the newly activated workers. Not the revolutionary TUUL but the old-line unions or improvised organizations helped by the old-line unions stood at the head of the big organizing drive. Writing in the *Communist International* in the fall of 1934, one "Kutnik" acknowledged this fact:

> In March 1934 . . . it was found that the TUUL organizations were pushed into the background by the unions belonging to the AFL. . . . The Red textile union did not participate in the leadership of the numerous strikes of this period. . . . At the present time it has only 1000 to 1200 members. . . . Among the

miners the revolutionary union led only one percent of the strikes.
. . . In the same way the revolutionary union succeeded only in
winning the leadership of two percent of the strikes in the automobile industry. The revolutionary miners union had only 1000
members now and the revolutionary automobile workers union
only a few hundred.[59]

To the party leadership it was utterly galling that at the very
time the American workers were beginning to move in large numbers
toward union organization it was the conservative AFL that, in the
main, won their allegiance, rather than the TUUL. Had the dual-
union policy been continued the Communists would have ended in
complete isolation from the burgeoning new unions, but what saved
them and gave them an opportunity to plunge back into the organizing work of the mid-thirties was that Moscow was slowly wheeling
into position for a change of line. In December, 1933, O. Piatnitsky,
a major Comintern spokesman, admitted that

> The Communists . . . in most countries surrendered the re-
> formist unions to the trade union bureaucrats almost without a
> fight and thus isolated themselves from the broad working
> masses. . . .[60]

More than a little duplicity went into this sort of observation,
for the problem that Piatnitsky was describing had largely been
created by the dual-union policy of the Comintern. Seven months
later he was still more explicit:

> In the United States there can be no question of the Com-
> munists building up a revolutionary trade union opposition . . .
> parallel to the existing unions of the AFL. There the task is to
> penetrate deeper into the AFL. . . . It was a complete mistake to
> try to build up a revolutionary trade union opposition in all coun-
> tries. . . .[61]

But the simple truth is that there had been more than a mere
"mistake"; there had been a deliberately worked-out policy imposed
upon the Communist parties throughout the world. Now, a year
later, after Hitler had come to power and the Russians were growing

frightened in their isolation, the "objective situation" had changed. Quickly, and with obvious relief, the American Communists fell into line. Jack Stachel, their trade-union specialist, wrote in the spring of 1934:

> Beginnings are being made to overcome the tendency to make out of the TUUL unions duplicates of the party. . . . A decisive turn toward work in the AFL, greater attention to work in the independent unions implies not a weakening but a strengthening of the work of the TUUL unions.[62]

Any observer experienced in the ways that Communists prepare for changes of line could have foretold that this disingenuous formulation was simply a preparatory step toward the dissolution of the TUUL. By November, Stachel was saying bluntly, "Now we are face to face with a new turn. The whole objective situation demands that the party establish its main policy today as one of work inside and building the opposition within the AFL unions." [63]

Suddenly, and for the first time, the party press had to admit that not only were the dual unions badly isolated but in the spontaneous upsurge of unionization they had had to go along with the old unions. Earl Browder was frank:

> After the establishment of the NRA, the reformist United Mine Workers Union swept through the coal fields with a broad recruitment campaign, and our Red Union members (*without even consulting us*) went along with the masses, and together with them organized the strike movement of July and thereafter the local unions of the United Mine Workers. We were slow in reorientating ourselves to work mainly through the reformist union, and therefore were weakened quite seriously for a period. . . .[64] [emphasis added]

For many party members, particularly those who had been devoting themselves to the dual unions, it was hard to accept the new line. Working in the AFL struck them as an outrage or an indignity, and in the process of persuading themselves to make the transition some amusing incidents occurred. Thus, during the west coast maritime strike of 1934 in which Harry Bridges—sympathetic, to say the least, to CP policies—gained control of the maritime workers, the Communists were so confused that instead of supporting Bridges, they violently denounced him and called upon the strikers "to resist the strike-breaking efforts of the International Longshoremen's Association." [65] With time, however, they learned to appreciate his contributions.

Slowly, clumsily, painfully, the change took place. In March, 1935, the TUUL was officially dissolved, its power and influence at its demise considerably smaller than at its birth.

It is sometimes hard to resist asking "History" the kind of question that by its very nature cannot be answered. What would have happened if the Communists had not blundered into the wilderness of dual unionism? Would their influence on the American labor movement during the years of the depression and New Deal have been greater than it actually was?

To be sure, the American party had no choice. As long as it remained a Stalinist party, it had to follow orders from Moscow, and these, rather than any domestic developments, brought on the catastrophe of dual unionism. Furthermore, the position of the Communists had already been so difficult in the unions that even before the formal inauguration of the dual-union policy they were being pushed in that direction. Their ingrained sectarian attitude frequently brought them to an impasse within the established unions and thereby tempted them to set up unions of their own. Yet it is hardly likely that without the general turn of the Communist International they would have taken so complete and so disastrous a plunge into dual unionism.

Did it necessarily have to be a disaster? Was not *any* revolutionary politics in the labor movement doomed to failure during these years of mass unemployment and depression? In the nature of things, no entirely certain answer can be given to such questions; yet in reviewing the material one has the strong impression that at least in some of the unions the Communists might have achieved major influence had they continued to work within them. Certainly this would seem to be true of the miners' union, where a strong indigenous rebellion of talented leaders came close to wresting control from the Lewis machine and would have come a great deal closer had not the CP divided the anti-Lewis forces by pulling its people out of the United Mine Workers. Similarly, it is at least arguable that in such unions as textile and garment the Communists could have come within striking distance of power had they pursued other tactics.

What impresses one most, however, is the enormous waste of human resources that followed from the sectarianism and obtuseness of the Communist leadership—to say nothing of the cynicism with which it utilized workers whose adherence it won in order to advance proposals and interests they could not even understand, let alone accept. The devotion, heroism, and selflessness of many Communist unionists during these years can hardly be overestimated: they burned themselves out in a senseless and irresponsible adventure. A few of them were killed, many more were beaten and imprisoned, but for most the damage took the form of emotional and intellectual scars that were never quite to heal. A considerable number of dedicated young intellectuals and workers, their social conscience aroused by the breakdown of American society, were transformed into disenchanted, cynical, and sometimes broken men; and this, more than any of the specific events or policies, is a measure of the havoc the Communist Party spread in the ranks of American radicalism.

Chapter VII. The Intellectuals Turn Left

1. The intellectual tradition of the old *Masses* and, to a lesser extent, of its short-lived successor, the *Liberator*—a tradition of wild-swinging, free-spirited radicalism—had been impossible to maintain during the mid-twenties. Infatuated with an image of "the proletariat" that had led it to regard intellectuals with suspicion or amused contempt, the Communist Party could count only a handful of them among its supporters. Nor were the American intellectuals particularly interested in Communism. These were years of billowing prosperity, when, as Granville Hicks would later remark, "our problem was a capitalism that was all too successful";[1] they were also years in which writers and artists, devoted to the impulse of private expression, showed little aptitude for any kind of collective effort.

When the monthly *New Masses* was founded in late 1927, it echoed—or seemed to echo—the voice of its predecessors. At first the party leaders, deep in the pleasures of factional cannibalism, showed only a mildly paternalistic interest in the magazine, for they had not yet realized how advantageous political work among intellectuals might be. The iron screws of party dogma, which would be turned so tightly during the later and more influential years of the *New Masses,* did not stand idle; but they were worked with a haphazardness that, from a distance, might create an illusory picture of freedom.

One major difference between the old and the *New Masses* was in cultural scope. Max Eastman, John Reed, Floyd Dell had been men of some cultural breadth and attainment—at least by comparison with most of the people who now wrote regularly for the *New Masses.* The older magazine had conveyed a quality of indigenous American speech and protest, while the *New Masses* could, at best, try to simulate that quality. Still, something of the old flavor remained: the process of "Stalinization," which would blot out every accent of individuality, was not yet complete. In 1929 the radicalism of the *New Masses* still kept a faint bloom of innocence, so that one might have associated it with the fresher and more generous radicalism of Reed and Eastman a decade earlier. But as the years went by it became clear that only the outer manner —the posture of windblown, rough-and-tumble camaraderie—had been retained, not the passion for freedom or the pleasure in eccentricity.

What gave the *New Masses* its focus of appeal during these early years—its "mass issue," as the party functionaries might say— was the indignation stirred in almost all American intellectuals by the Sacco and Vanzetti case. For many it came as a shock breaking into a daydream of literary detachment: "It is no longer possible," wrote Robert Morss Lovett in 1928, "to deny the existence of the Class War in the United States." [2] Unquestionably this was the feeling that led non-Communist writers like Lewis Mumford and Katherine Anne Porter to contribute occasionally to the *New Masses*. In one of its first numbers John Dos Passos, the only important writer to appear regularly in the magazine during its early un- fashionable phase, printed a poem that expressed the feelings of many non-Communist writers who turned to the *New Masses* be- cause it was one of the few places in which it was possible to cry out against the execution without fear or inhibition:

> The warden strapped these men into the electric chair
> the executioner threw the switch
> and set them free into the wind
> they are free of the dreams now
> free of the greasy prison denim
>
> their voices blow back in a thousand lingoes
>   singing one song
>
> to burst the eardrums of Massachusetts. [3]

The directing spirit of the *New Masses* at this time was Michael Gold, a writer endowed with a style of corrupt vividness and char- acterized by an astonishing incapacity for sustained thought. Gold was an inveterate low-brow who, if he had not turned radical, would have made a superb police reporter; he was a hater of refinements of thought, partly because he could not distinguish them from refinements of manners, which he *knew* to be a petty-bourgeois lure. He had learned once that there was a class struggle between workers and bosses, and that was all he knew or needed to know. He believed that the future of literature lay in the primitive propaganda sketches written by Communist workers or, more often, by young Communist quasi-intellectuals passing for workers. He wrote with a recklessness possible only to a man who could not even imagine that the possession of Marxism, key to all realities though it might be, did not exempt a writer from the need for knowledge and thought. ("Only Marxists," he thundered, "have the slightest clue to the social basis of fashion" [4]—though it might as easily have been the social basis of anthropology or Greek poetry or mountain climbing.) Actually, as some of his comrades would maliciously remark, Gold was not really much of a Marxist: he had no patience with the windings of Marxist (or any other) thought; he was a raw, totally sincere, simpleminded radical. His one virtue, if such it can be called, was a fatal steadiness of commitment, which may finally have come to no more than an incapacity to imagine any course but loyalty to the party machine. He was one of the few who stuck it out.

Under Gold's direction, the *New Masses* printed large quantities of "reportage," stories and poems that purported to come, and sometimes did come, from workers themselves. Fugitive though most of this work was, it had at least the modest virtue of not pretending to the status of literature; it spoke with the hoarse voice of bitter experience, and by 1930 and 1931 there was no lack of bitter experience. Much of this writing came from members of the John Reed clubs that had been set up throughout the country under the guidance of party branches, though they contained young writers who were not party members.

As they wrestled with the language, trying to discover the meaning of their experience and to whip their reports of suffering and humiliation into a positive claim for victory, the young radical writers seemed to be repeating the painful "struggle for realism" that had characterized American literature during the last two decades of the nineteenth and the first decade of the twentieth century. Like these earlier non-political writers, the *New Masses* contributors exhausted themselves in the effort simply to break into verbal expression, and in retrospect there is a genuine pathos in their straining toward articulation. Nor were they all untalented propagandists, as it has since become fashionable to suppose. The verses and stories of the young lumber-mill worker Joseph Kalar, though not his alone, were distinguished by a strength of language that testified to genuine talent. But what hurt the development of such young writers was, among other things, that it was never clear whether the main purpose of the *New Masses* was to print the work of accomplished writers who were turning leftward or to provide workers with an outlet for expression. If it was the former, Gold's editorship was a hopeless botch; if the latter, then the application of literary standards to the stories and poems he printed became not merely irrelevant but downright cruel.

In the main, however, the writing that Gold accepted and encouraged was notable for a naïve arrogance, a sweaty earnestness, an utter lack of literary awareness or modulation. The "proletarian" writers who appeared in the *New Masses* assumed that it was necessary—and even more naïvely, that it was possible—for them to start from scratch without caring or troubling about the literature of the past; in this respect too they remind one of the realistic novelists who had begun to write in America at the end of the nineteenth century, except that where the early realists worshipped experience the early Stalinists preferred ideology.

Proclaiming (and not for the first time) the birth of a glorious proletarian literature, Gold could say that when skeptics ask, "Where is your Shakespeare? . . . we answer: wait ten years more. He is on the way. . . . We promise you a hundred Shakespeares." [5] Horace Gregory, perhaps dizzied by the vision of the forthcoming Shakespeares, could dismiss Henry James as a writer "suffering from the disease of being a rich man's son." [6] And meanwhile the *New Masses* reviewers could write as Herman Spector did about a book of Alfred Kreymborg's poems:

> If Kreymborg is to expand he must cease being garrulous about trivialities, he must break with the rottenness of contemporaries like Pound and Williams. . . . A short course at the Workers School would certainly help this poet in the better organization of his material.[7]

It would be misleading to suggest that criticism of this sort, which was simply the literary equivalent of the Third Period in politics, frequently reached such extremes of silliness: Spector, being a worker with vague literary yearnings and a naïveté that partly excused his arrogance, was simply reducing the common practice to an absurdity. But in a "prose poem" written by the party functionary A. B. Magil on the suicide of the Russian poet Mayakovsky, one can hear the official brutality of the commissar berating "indecisive" intellectuals—in this case a dead one—as they were to be berate them all through the thirties:

> . . . You have committed a crime against us and against the Revolution, Mayakovsky. All your words thunder with a voice like Niagara Falls: MAYAKOVSKY, YOU HAVE BETRAYED US.[8]

A few Communist writers did try to dissociate themselves from this inquisitorial spirit. Joseph Freeman wrote with a surface reasonableness that not only set him apart from his colleagues but made him a far more effective spokesman for the party line. Slowly a conflict was shaping up between the veteran hacks like Gold, who loved to celebrate the simplicity of their commitment, and those radical intellectuals who were beginning to turn leftward. The complaint that appeared in the letter of one such intellectual was typical:

> What I do not like about the New Masses is the affectation of idealized proletarianism, the monotonous strumming on the hardboiled string . . . the contempt for modulated writing and criticism.[9]

At a meeting of the John Reed Club in New York there occurred a debate between Gold and Joshua Kunitz on the topic, "Can We Learn Anything from Bourgeois Writers?" That such a debate was even possible speaks powerfully for the cultural Know-Nothingism characteristic of the Communist intellectual world at this time; yet it did air issues that would persist into more sophisticated days:

Kunitz	*Gold*
Are we forever doomed to relish the flat grey stuff dished out to us by so many of our writers? We must learn from the bourgeoisie just as once it learned from the aristocracy.	[Kunitz's view is] nothing but academic banalism. . . . If a man has something to say, as *all* proletarian writers have, he will learn to say it clearly in time.[10] [emphasis added]

The mindless crudity of the *New Masses* in the years between 1928 and 1932—the left-wing regional magazines were even worse —is attributable not merely to the fact that Gold was a leading editor, or that much of American Marxism has always been half-baked, or that a great deal of what has passed for radical thought in America has been mere Populist *ressentiment*. It was also, and more immediately, a direct consequence of the international Stalinist line on cultural matters.

In 1930 an international conference was held in Kharkov, Russia—the "Second World Plenum of the International Bureau of Revolutionary Literature"—which was attended by six American delegates, headed by Gold and Magil. This conference, which marked a climax to the cultural "ultra-leftism" of the Stalinist epoch, was held under the leadership of Leopold Auerbach, a dismal Torquemada whom Stalin had assigned the task of suppressing cultural freedom in Russia during the late twenties. Between the perverse sectarianism of the Kharkov conference and the homespun "revolutionism" of Gold there was a rough-and-ready harmony. Thus, the conference demanded that left-wing writers no longer content themselves with "the struggle against war and fascism" but line up openly as partisans of the Soviet Union. And more: "you must fight not only against open fascism but also against concealed fascism which parades under the mask of 'socialism'—that more insidious type that has come to be known as social fascism." [11] And turning its attention to America, the Kharkov conference passed a special resolution criticizing the *New Masses* for a lack of political intransigence and urging it to "draw in new proletarian elements." This last was music to Gold's ears.

For the next several years, Communist work among American intellectuals fluctuated between the harsh, self-defeating line imposed at Kharkov and the need to exploit the growing leftward sentiment of American writers. At the national convention of the John Reed clubs, held in the spring of 1932, it was the Kharkov note that dominated; but soon, as it became clear that the party could anticipate gains among the intellectuals far greater than it had ever dreamed of, it became necessary to work out a more flexible tactic. Not very consistently or without serious lapses, an effort was made during the next few years to find intellectual spokesmen who could speak the language of serious writers and artists, even if in doing so they systematically abused it.

2. The stock market crash of 1929, wrote Edmund Wilson a few years later, "was to count for us almost like a rending of the earth in preparation for the Day of Judgment." When the slump began a month later,

. . . a darkness seemed to descend. Yet, to the writers and artists of my generation who had grown up in the Big Business era and had always resented its barbarism, its crowding-out of everything they cared about, these years were not depressing but stimulating. One couldn't help being exhilarated at the sudden unexpected collapse of that stupid gigantic fraud. It gave us a new sense of freedom. . . . With a businessman's president in the White House, who kept telling us, when he told us anything, that the system was perfectly sound . . . we wondered about the survival of republican American institutions; and we became more and more impressed by the achievements of the Soviet Union. . . .[12]

Shaken loose from traditional opinions, frequently forced to accept a sharp drop in income, and sometimes pushed into the ranks of the jobless, some American intellectuals may have welcomed the depression with the gaiety Wilson describes; but there can be no doubt that many of them were also stricken with a moral terror, a sudden feeling of desperation. And the cause of this feeling was not so much a lessening of circumstances as a disintegration of belief. Writers like Wilson, Sherwood Anderson, Erskine Caldwell broke away from the routines of literary life in order to travel across the country, measuring the human costs of the depression, the wastage of energy and hope; they talked to hungry men in New

York, they listened to strikers in North Carolina; and the vision of the United States that slowly began to emerge in their minds was surprisingly similar to that of John Dos Passos' *USA*: "We are two nations." Once a mere phrase, the class struggle had become the flesh and pain of life.

A very considerable number of American writers and artists turned left—and, as they were quick to declare, sharply left. Asked by the *Modern Quarterly,* an independent radical journal, to discuss the merits of the Communist and Socialist movements, some of these writers gave answers that were more revealing than they could possibly know. "Becoming a Socialist right now," wrote John Dos Passos, "would have just the same effect on anybody as drinking a bottle of near-beer." For Granville Hicks, "Being a socialist—like being a liberal—means that the writer is not really thinking and feeling in terms of the class struggle." The artist, added Sherwood Anderson, "would also like to think of himself as ready to die for what he believes." [13]

A little later Anderson, forever green to politics, would write in the *New Masses:*

> Among these fighting young Communists [he had been watching them make speeches on New York street corners] I found poverty, youth and no gloom. . . . If it be necessary, in order to bring about the end of a money civilization and set up something new, healthy and strong, [that] we of the so-called artist class have to be submerged, let us be submerged. Down with us. A little poverty and shaking down won't hurt us. . . . [14]

And at a New York meeting where Anderson had put to himself the question, what is the difference between a Socialist and a Communist, he answered: "I guess the Communists mean it." [15]

The Communists mean it! In its very ingenuousness, Anderson's remark was a classical contribution toward the understanding of Stalinism among the intellectuals. The belief in some ultimate Reality that the Communists alone had been able to penetrate; the implicit assumption that by adopting the pose of ruthlessness the party was proving its claim to a deeper seriousness; the impulse to self-abasement ("down with us") that so many intellectuals felt in the presence of the working class or, more frequently, a caricature of the working class in the person of a party functionary—all these are central to the experience of the thirties. For the truth is that not many intellectuals had been very careful in thinking out their new allegiance, let alone the organizational forms it might take, and fewer still troubled to read very deeply or critically in the Marx from whom it became fashionable to quote. The political involvements of the left-wing intellectuals may have spoken glowingly for their moral warmth and certainly testified to a flair for rhetorical abandon, but seldom did credit to their powers of analysis.

In any case, the turn was to the left. Between 1930 and 1936 a large company of gifted and distinguished writers appeared in the *New Masses*. Dreiser, Anderson, Dos Passos, Wilson, Caldwell, James Farrell, and (a bit later) Hemingway were only the more famous names.* Most of these writers would soon regret their brief flirtations with cultural Stalinism, for they were men of talent and integrity—though, since their contributions to the *New Masses* consisted mainly of depression journalism rather than political comment, they later had little reason to feel ashamed of what they had actually written. Wilson's powerful report of a Kentucky mining town, Caldwell's account of the misery he found among Southern sharecroppers, Hemingway's description of terrorized veterans in Florida—these were testimony concerning the hardship and struggle of the time. So much has happened since the early thirties, so many hopes have turned bitter and illusions been destroyed, that it is necessary to recall that, in the midst of their self-betrayals, many of the writers who accepted Communism did so out of a valid sense of social despair and a valid yearning for social betterment. A very great deal in the experience of left-wing intellectuals during the thirties cannot survive the glare of criticism; but this judgment takes on significance—it takes on full rigor—

* With the exception of Dreiser later in his career, none of these writers had any extended relations with the Communist Party. Most of them, like most of the other writers mentioned in this chapter, soon became anti-Communist. Throughout this chapter, it should be clear, we are concerned with the political outlooks and loyalties of the leftist intellectuals, not their organizational affiliations. Many of them had no organizational ties, and it would be erroneous to assume that because a writer contributed to a Communist literary magazine he was necessarily a member of the CP.

only if one recognizes that behind the mistakes lay authentic strivings and a pathos to be neither scorned nor dismissed.

An important sign of the leftward turn was the formation in
1932 of the League of Professional Groups for Foster and Ford.
Dos Passos, Anderson, Caldwell, Wilson, Sidney Howard, Malcolm Cowley, Sidney Hook, Granville Hicks, Matthew Josephson, Horace Gregory, Langston Hughes, Leonie Adams—these were
some of the writers who endorsed Foster for President. Two years
later, as a further indication of the growth of Communist influence
among intellectuals, the *New Masses* became a weekly with impressive additions to its list of contributors. Numerically the pro-Communist tendency among the intellectuals would never comprise more
than a small minority, but its aggressiveness, self-confidence, discipline, and capacity for hard work assured it a dominant position.

The sudden growth in the number and influence of the left-
wing literary magazines, theater groups, dance groups, and other
cultural appendages came as a surprise to the party leaders. "Sudden" may be a somewhat misleading word here, since in retrospect
it is clear that a number of intellectuals, morally and emotionally
stranded after the experience of the twenties, had been drifting
toward radicalism even before the Wall Street crash. But what
mattered was that to the party leadership, as to the editors of the
New Masses, it seemed sudden. And not only were writers and
artists contributing to party-sponsored magazines; some of them were
even joining the party itself. How many it would be impossible to
say; but it can safely be suggested that among the young and obscure
writers, who found in the Communist movement both an audience
and a brotherhood, it was relatively easy to win recruits, while the
more accomplished writers, who had sunk roots in other areas of
life, were inclined to guard their independence.

How then were these intellectual converts to be treated? What
steps might be taken to overcome the suspicion that some of them
still felt toward the party itself? Few sustained discussions were
held on this matter, but a study of the main cultural organs close
to the party suggests that in the early thirties a number of the more
gifted Communist intellectuals—which is something very different
from those party functionaries, like V. J. Jerome and A. B. Magil,
who had been assigned to supervise the intellectuals—were inclined

to favor a loosening of the chains of sectarianism, an abandonment of the more vulgar tones and mannerisms that had often made the *New Masses* embarrassing even to its friends. Yet no such change took place.

Gradually, it is true, Gold's influence declined.* The leading writers and editors during the thirties—Joseph Freeman, Granville Hicks, Isidor Schneider, Joshua Kunitz, Stanley Burnshaw, Joseph North—were more cultivated than Gold and could, if necessary, write in more moderate tones. Under their direction the *New Masses* became more "sophisticated," it tried to deal with a greater range of intellectual problems, it was less given to proletarian attitudinizing. But it also became more dogmatic.

Gold, a born sentimentalist, had never had much appetite for ideology: you either were "for the workers" (that is, the party) or against them, and that was that. For him Marxism was the justification of a posture, but for his successors it was primarily a closed and definite system of ideology clung to with ferocity and propagandized with arrogance. So while the magazine became a bit more worldly— it no longer resembled a revolutionary carnival run by a drunken revivalist—it also came to seem more stereotyped and flavorless. In his own dubious way Gold had managed to give off an aroma of individuality; now it was the gray and imperious spirit of ideology that took command.

Yet this, it seems, was exactly what many of the intellectuals wanted. The depression had done more than disturb their lives; it had ripped apart the fabric of their values and beliefs, leaving them cold and shivering in the winds of uncertainty. Intellectuals may deal professionally with ideas, that is, with problems, but like the rest of humanity they find it hard to refrain from the narcotic of certainty: not many are able to suffer a prolonged acceptance of a mode of life that is inherently problematic. The new converts, young and old, obscure and famous, came rushing in quest of a

---

* But never quite disappeared. The kind of blatant "let's-talk-the-workers'-language" approach for which he stood would always find support in the party, where intellectuals were habitually regarded with uneasiness. And it found even more support among some quasi-intellectuals who clung to the edges of the left-wing cultural world, identifying their lack of cultivation with revolutionary firmness, and the talent of the more experienced writers with petty-bourgeois vacillation.

system, like hungry geese to the trough; they wanted to feel that, at the very moment the world was being shattered, they had found the key to its meaning. Gold's ranting emotionalism they might regard with scorn, but a heavy dose of ideology was like sugar to their tongues. Many of them seemed to revel in the zeal with which the commissars tracked down heresies, for this meant that the new conceptual order they had embraced would be kept free of doubts and complications; and they themselves were ready to play, often simultaneously, the role of vest-pocket commissar and of the follower kept in line by the commissar.

Does all this seem in contradiction to what has been said about the moral idealism that often went with the intellectual's turn to radicalism? On the contrary. It is precisely this strange mixture of idealism and abasement, of a break from corrupt traditional authority and a surrender to corrupt untried authority, that goes far toward explaining the behavior of the Stalinist intellectuals.

What was wanted, both by the intellectuals turning to the party and by the party representatives assigned to recondition them, was nothing short of a total conversion, a transformation of personality such that the function of the intellectual would be exploitable but his spirit silenced. Like the institutions of mass culture in our society, the party learned to appreciate the uses to which intellectuals could be put, and it learned that to use them effectively it could allow them neither to remain nor entirely to cease being what they had been. The party wanted them *because* they were intellectuals, but it did not want them *as* intellectuals. It needed them for their knowledge, their talent, their inclinations and passions; it insisted that they retain a measure of these endowments, without which they would be of no use to it whatever. And what was still more astonishing in this grandiose deception: the party persuaded the intellectuals not merely that it was their duty to submit but that submission was good and joyful and spiritually renovating. Because it spoke in the name of the oppressed and because it claimed to have become one with the spirit and direction of history, the party could simultaneously tap the idealism and guilt of the intellectuals. They were to love Big Brother, and to love him not primarily in the flesh, for the flesh was notoriously wayward, but as an abstraction or an absolute. Every dubious turn in tactics dictated by the foreign policy of the Russian state could be rendered sacred by invoking the Working Class or the Party; and faced with these totems, how could the intellectuals—themselves, as they knew only too well, "unstable elements," mere puny novices in the steeled army of revolution—dare to speak their own minds or voice the doubts that sooner or later beset almost all of them? The kind of spiritual lobotomy the party demanded from its intellectual converts (except, of course, from the *famous* fellow travelers: they, it was shrewd enough to realize, should be left alone) was indicated by V. J. Jerome at the end of a bludgeoning polemic against a deviationist:

> The identification of the intellectuals with the revolutionary movement is dependent . . . on their complete rift with bourgeois ideology and liberalism. . . . The relationship of the intellectuals as a group with the working class is essentially an alliance. But that alliance can be established only on the . . . unadulterated principles of Marxism-Leninism. Not the workers to the intellectuals but the intellectuals to the workers is the historic course.[16]

The result was not merely an ideological debauch but a systematized indulgence in those appetites for domination which the party could not satisfy in its dealings with the bourgeois world and which, therefore, were all the more violently released in its dealings with writers and artists. The *New Masses* politicians knew exactly, at any given moment, what the true line on any event or problem was; and they saw it not only as their duty but as a therapeutic service to cram that line down the throats of believers, half-believers, and disbelievers. The *New Masses* ideologues, writing with the confidence possible only to those who have ceased to regard their own assumptions as an object of inquiry, were ready to claim the whole province of knowledge for their own, past, present, and future; nor did they hesitate to admit that the claim was made not on the ground of accumulated study but in the name of a general principle. The *New Masses* critics knew exactly what a good "proletarian novel" was—it was a novel that did not yet exist and could not yet exist, for no mere artist could reach their vision of purity; and they took a kind of fierce joy, not merely in puffing third-rate novels that followed the party line, but also in pointing, like stern schoolmasters, to the ideological deficiencies in those very novels. And of ideological deficiencies there was never any lack. As Alfred Kazin has remarked: "The left-wing critics, beginning with the commendable desire to show how firmly literature had always been planted in human experience, ended on the assumption that as scientific Marxists they alone understood the history of literature and knew the way to its possible salvation. . . . Wrapped in the vestments of his office, a Marxist critic could say *anything*. And he usually did. He had the norm, and the norm was everything." [17]

And it was everywhere, too. "No novel yet written," fretted Granville Hicks, the chief Keeper of the Norm, "perfectly conforms to our demands, [though] it is possible that a novel written by a member of the bourgeoisie might be better than a novel written by a member of or sympathizer with the proletariat." This generous admission out of the way, Hicks could proceed to improvise a critical method that might support his passion for dogma. The critic, he wrote, first determines the author's "attitude toward life" from a study of biographical, historical, and psychological materials and then "is prepared to examine the expression of that attitude in literature." An extraordinary view of the critical act—a view from which followed the worst dogmatics and most blatant ignorance of Communist writings on literature. Isidor Schneider, a not untalented writer who at times seems to have felt a vague guilt toward the muses, could justify the *New Masses* school of reviewing with the remark—at best a trivial half-truth—that he knew of "no writing which, upon analysis, will not yield some propaganda." On the same principle, though with greater unconscious humor, Obed Brooks wrote in praise of the criticism of Hicks and Malcolm Cowley: "In each case the critic is making *a diagnosis whose results he already knows*. He can thus work surely and quickly, without irrelevance or waste" (emphasis added).

So it was with the critics of the *New Masses*: surely and quickly. A. B. Magil could chastise the left-wing novelist Grace Lumpkin for succumbing to "bourgeois realism," which can "at best . . . produce only penetrating 'slices of life'" but which fails to present "the objective world as an evolving process." An anonymous *New Masses* reviewer, steaming with the Communist's fear of the untried and the ambiguous, could say of Gertrude Stein that her books "can be recommended to psychiatrists as an example of the final, paretic stage of bourgeois culture." Joseph Freeman, in praising the agit-prop verse of Edwin Rolfe, could elevate the Communist's distrust of individuality into a regnant historical principle: "Rolfe repudiates the cult of the ego inherited from the French Revolution, and gathers strength from the collective vision. . . ." V. J. Jerome, reviewing Fielding Burke's left-wing novel *Call Home the Heart,* could reveal with pride the total surrender that the party functionary demanded from the artist: "Fielding Burke has endorsed Communism in her novel. A writer of mystical poetry all her life, a 'mountain spirit,' she comes to Communism reverently, stands before it in adoration. She is a voyager gazing wonder-eyed at the shores of a newly-found universe." (Yet even she, "wonder-eyed," would be found wanting, for a few years later Granville Hicks was complaining of her novel *A Stone Came Rolling* that "her imagery sometimes seems too purely romantic. . . .") Robert Briffault, perhaps the most arrogant of all left-wing intellectuals, could write that "Bourgeois humor is bankrupt; it is mortgaged to Red radicalism. . . . Robert Forsythe [a *New Masses* writer] is the first master of humor in America . . . who has grounded his humor upon plain and narrowed Marxist foundations. There are, obviously, no other possible foundations for humor. . . . Marxism is the Gay Science." Edwin Berry Burgum, more inclined to classification, could write that the bourgeois novel is "either 1) a novel of escape written under the influence of idealistic philosophy or 2) a novel of despondency written under the influence of pragmatism or 3) a novel combining elements of both. An example of the first is Thornton Wilder's *The Bridge of San Luis Rey,* of the second William Faulkner's *Sanctuary,* and of the third Thomas Wolfe's *Of Time and the River.* . . . The first [type] tends to be supplemented by the second, and the third reflects the rise of fascism. . . ." And finally, with a frankness that is almost charming, Norman MacLeod could object to Albert Halper's radical fiction on the ground that "He relies upon emphasis rather than bias. And this is wrong."

As in literature, so in politics. "Anyone," wrote the *New Masses* editorially in the spring of 1934, "who can't see Hitlerism or Fascism written all over the NRA is either blind as a bat or Norman

Thomas." Archibald MacLeish, wrote a lady named Margaret Wright Mather, is "a dirty Nazi." The leaders of the radical though anti-Stalinist American Workers Party, screamed the *New Masses,* "those tailors, Salutsky-Hardman, Dr. Sidney Hook, the Rev. A. J. Muste . . . remind one of another party formed in Germany: the National Socialist Workers Party, the Nazis." And to round off this display of intellectual finesse, here, a few years later, is another Communist literary man rhapsodizing on Stalin's *The New Soviet Constitution:* "This is a document which for charm, frankness and simplicity can have few counterparts among the state papers in history. And just as it confirms socialism in the field of law, so it exemplifies the new regime in the character of its leadership." [18]

Though it would be easy enough to pile up passages of this kind, it is only fair to add that the left-wing cultural publications during the thirties did attract men of talent and intelligence. An anthologist systematically avoiding the typical could put together an impressive book of articles and stories from the left-wing magazines. Rolfe Humphries analyzing T. S. Eliot's poetry; Lewis Corey speculating on the role of the American middle class; Granville Hicks reviewing Kipling with an unusual warmth; Horace Gregory criticizing Auden's verse with intelligence and restraint; Milton Howard dissecting the nonsense of a book on Shakespeare by the Russian critic Smirnov; a reasonable minority of the strike reports from various parts of the country—all these read as well as most writings of their kinds. But they stand out precisely because they are so rare in their sensitiveness; the very possibility of noticing such exceptions serves finally to confirm the dreariness of the rule.

How then was it possible for writers of talent and training, men who would later do independent and distinguished work, to lend themselves to such intellectual buffoonery? Some of the possible answers have already been suggested: the mass infatuation with ideological formulas that afflicted intellectuals during the thirties and—so long as they believed themselves in possession of a total method for knowing history—led them to accept the dictation of the party as if it were a genuine intellectual source rather than an imposed institutional authority; the traditional callowness of American radicalism in general and American Communism in particular, which often tended to reduce Marxist thought in this country to a simple-minded caricature; the yearning for a monolithic system of ideas that could cope with a world that had come to seem terribly complex and problematic.

There were other, perhaps deeper, reasons. In 1932 a friend of Granville Hicks, apparently disturbed by the morality of the Communist movement to which he had pledged himself, wrote Hicks a letter that has, deservedly, been quoted many times as a key document for the study of the psychology of totalitarian affiliation. Here is the letter:

> It is a bad world in which we live, and so even the revolutionary movement is anything but what (poetically and philosophically speaking) it "ought" to be: God knows, I realize this, as you do, and God knows it makes my heart sick at times: from one angle, it seems nothing but grime and stink and sweat and obscene noises and the language of the beasts. But surely this is what *history* is. It just is not made by gentlemen and scholars, and "made" only in the bad sense by the Norman Thomases and the Devere Allens and the John Deweys. Lenin must have been (from a conceivable point of view) a dreadful man; so must John Brown, and Cromwell, and Marat, and Stenka Razin, and Mahomet, and all the others who have destroyed and built up. I believe we can spare ourselves a great deal of pain and disenchantment and even worse (treachery to ourselves) if we discipline ourselves to accept the proletarian and revolutionary leaders and even theorists for what they are and must be: grim fighters in about the most dreadful and desperate struggle in all history—*not* reasonable and "critically-minded" and forbearing and infinitely far-seeing men. My fundamental conviction about the whole thing, at this stage, is that everything gives way before the terrible social conflict itself: that the power of imperialism must be fought at every turn at every moment with any weapon and without quarter; that the consciousness of the proletariat—its sense of power and its anger—must be built up by every possible device; and that meanwhile the kinds of things we are interested in must take their place, where they belong, out of the thickest dust and along the rim of the arena. Let's salvage as much as we can of the rather abstract things we care for, but golly, let's realize that there are far more basic and primitive things that have to be

taken care of first (as long as men are starving and exploited), and do absolutely nothing, at any moment, to impede the work of the men who are fighting what is really our battle *for us.*[19]

In this document one finds almost all of the essential attitudes, expressed with remarkable bareness, that have gone into the history of political self-abasement among intellectuals. The result is somewhat terrifying, since the one thing that might redeem it in human terms—a pinch of uncertainty, even of insincerity—is nowhere in evidence. Our age has made us familiar enough with the phenomenon of political masochism,* but what makes it so powerful in this letter is that it has been elevated to the status of a morality and thereby accorded a sanction it could not claim in its own right. Almost every impulse that was at work in driving or luring intellectuals into the prison-house of Stalinism has here been rationalized with a rare eloquence: the initial idealism and disinterestedness; the decision of an obviously gentle person to take upon himself the alien role of the ruthless fighter and the vicarious joy he finds in imagining himself in the company of Marat and Stenka Razin; the readiness to surrender the intellectual's critical responsibility in the name of an assured apocalypse; the ease with which he evades the tortuous problems of political choice by appealing to a "historical necessity" that removes doubt and makes self-scrutiny a kind of treason; the eagerness with which he assigns the right of political decision to a False Collective (see Chapter XI, pp. 518-525); and at the same time, the urgency with which he speaks the truth, corrupted, twisted, yet the truth about the desperateness of modern life.

Though meant as a private communication, the letter bears a close resemblance to a poem by the German writer Berthold Brecht, in which the self-justification of the Stalinist intellectuals comes as close to moral seriousness as it possibly can. This poem, "To Posterity," is a superb work in its own right, much of what it says is deeply true, and only when one remembers the use to which Brecht

---

* Though we hesitate to employ the vocabulary of psychology in a political context, there hardly seems any alternative when dealing with a document of this sort.

means to put it does one realize—somewhat as with Hicks' friend, though of course in a far more profound way—the tragic corruption that lies behind it. Here are a few passages:

Indeed I live in the dark ages!
A guileless word is an absurdity. A smooth forehead betokens
A hard heart. He who laughs has not yet heard
The terrible tidings.

Ah, what an age it is
When to speak of trees is almost a crime
For it is a kind of silence about injustice!
And he who walks calmly across the street,
Is he not out of reach of his friends
In trouble? . . .

I came to the cities in a time of disorder
When hunger ruled.
I came among men in a time of uprising
And I revolted with them.
So the time passed away
Which on earth was given me.

I ate my food between massacres.
The shadow of murder lay upon my sleep.
And when I loved, I loved with indifference.
I looked upon my nature with impatience.
So the time passed away
Which on earth was given me. . . .

You, who shall emerge from the flood
In which we are sinking,
Think—
When you speak of our weaknesses,
Also of the dark time
That brought them forth.
For we went, changing our country more often than our shoes,
In the class war, despairing
When there was only injustice and no resistance.
For we knew only too well:
Even the hatred of squalor
Makes the brow grow stern.
Even anger against injustice

Makes the voice grow harsh. Alas, we
Who wished to lay the foundations of kindness
Could not ourselves be kind.

But you, when at last it comes to pass
That man can help his fellow man,
Do not judge us
Too harshly.

                              (translated by H. R. Hays)

Had the American Communist and fellow-traveling intellectuals possessed any serious capacity for self-examination, had they known the searing experiences suffered by their European comrades, had they been able to approximate the tragic vision that came spontaneously to Brecht despite his professional Communist optimism, they would have justified their lives in the terms of this poem. As it was, few of these intellectuals, for whom "the revolution" had a way of turning into a bloody carnival, could achieve the outlook of Brecht: they did not know or did not want to know that the "shadow of murder" lay upon their sleep. Still, Brecht's poem goes far toward explaining—or at least demonstrating—the motivations which, in a more primitive way, moved the leftist intellectuals in America.

For if they did not know about "the shadow of murder," they knew that, for all their complaints and even their suffering, life in America was still far easier than in Europe and that their kinship in the revolutionary cause had not been won through blood. Somehow—it seemed to them—they were to be judged for this, and found guilty. They felt guilty of saying more than they did or could do; guilty of not having transformed their lives as they had their vocabularies. Frequently proud and intransigent in their professional lives, they were nonetheless eager to humiliate themselves before the authority of "the movement," as if thereby to prove the loyalty they could not prove through sacrifice.

An astonishingly large part of the actual commitment of the Stalinist or fellow-traveling intellectual consisted of rituals of humiliation, willingly assumed, in which he pledged his faith anew and proclaimed his inadequacy, not primarily in terms of any personal faults but simply because he was an intellectual or a writer or an artist. The old self had constantly to be repudiated and a new one contrived, for it was assumed that the very calling of the intellectual made him politically unstable. Yet one could never be quite sure that the old self really had been destroyed, for just as the Christians preached the ineradicability of original sin so the Communists insisted upon the treachery of petty-bourgeois individualism. In one of her novels Fielding Burke had taken a step toward the working class, wrote V. J. Jerome, but she "is still not wholly of it." But could an intellectual *ever* be "wholly of it"? That was the question which troubled the left-wing writers, and that was the question the party never answered fully or decisively, for as long as the answer remained uncertain, the power of guilt was always at hand and the left-wing intellectuals—both those in the party and those who brushed against it—would stand ready to proclaim their essential unworthiness.

Michael Gold:

One half of me knew the proletarian. . . . The other half was full of the most extraordinary mystic hash. . . . Let me confess it now—I took Shelley, Byron and Whitman quite literally. They were my real guides to revolutionary action. But our great teacher Lenin clarified everything for me. . . .

It takes years to make a Marxist out of a bourgeois intellectual. He was fashioned in the womb of the middle class; his every fiber absorbed its traditional fears, loves and "eternal" values; to bring all these deeply hidden fears and dogmas to light, is almost the task of a psychoanalyst; and the relatively high percentage of renegades among intellectuals, as contrasted with workers, is only the ultimate demonstration of this truth.

Granville Hicks:

In lectures I have told how a young Italian once said to me, "It is only by study that an intellectual can raise himself to the level of the proletariat." This is no empty paradox. Of course proletarians have to study too, but the victim of exploitation undeniably has an advantage in understanding its nature.

Clifton Fadiman:

I have no illusions, I trust, about the importance of criticism in this period. . . . A person born in the middle class as I was, educated in bourgeois institutions, more or less professionally interested in literature, is poorly prepared to take a leading part [in revolutionary activity].

John Howard Lawson:

For a person with my particular equipment, a genuine acceptance of the proletarian revolution is a difficult task. . . . We all know that many intellectuals are so confused . . . that they waver idiotically between Communism and various manifestations of social fascism. . . . I am a fellow-traveller because I have not demonstrated any ability to serve the revolutionary working class either in my writing or my practical activity.

Waldo Frank:

The cause of Communism in the Soviet Union requires constant vigilance against counter-revolutionary forces, internal and external. . . . [I do not] arrogate . . . the capacity to judge the righteousness of all the Soviet Union's protective measures . . . [and am] reluctant to sit in judgment on Moscow's political decisions.

It is noteworthy that these lines were written at a time when Frank was proving not at all reluctant to sit in judgment on Washington's political decisions—an intellectual "double standard" that was deeply ingrained among all the fellow-traveling intellectuals.

Horace Gregory:

I have avoided party "splits." . . . I know of nothing sillier for us to do than to split our thinking into the divisions that are now part of the history of Communism in Russia. . . . I can't see that these divisions do more than complicate a course of political activity here in America. . . . The authority for party action is in the hands of a central committee of which Earl Browder is the spokesman. If we are politically active we can't call ourselves Communists without agreeing to follow its line of action and if we wish to see a successful culmination of our desires, we accept its terms of discipline. . . .

Ever since I left college, my political interests have been centered in the work of the Communist Party . . . my poetry has contained social implications that can be resolved only by the success of the Communist Party.

Gregory's intellectual self-denial, one might suppose, had gone far enough, but since he had concluded that, while a ready follower, he preferred not to become a member of the party, he was quickly attacked by another left-wing writer, Meridel Le Sueur, who wrote: "Every point Horace Gregory raises is extremely vital and indicates a middle-class malady . . . a sickness common to all of us nourished on rotten bourgeois soil."

It would be a mistake to suppose such confessions merely the psychic excess of young zealots. Confessions of heresy and inadequacy were an essential part of Stalinist political life throughout the world, an expression of that ideological anxiety which the totalitarian movement necessarily evokes in its followers. Potentially, though not of course at every given moment, the fellow-traveling intellectual had to be ready to act out a voluntary Moscow trial in which he himself would be judge, prosecutor, and defendant; whether he knew it or not, his adherence to the party made him an object of ideological terror in which, if he were well enough trained, he would learn to be his own persecutor.

Does this seem fanciful or exaggerated? Then consider once more the passages that have been quoted and compare them to the confessions exacted at the Moscow trials. Or consider the following passage from *The Judas Time*, a novel written by Isidor Schneider when he was still a fervent Stalinist, in which an intellectual named Schroeder is summoned to attend a party meeting to defend himself against charges of ideological deviation:

> At the mere summons to the hearing Schroeder collapsed. He arrived looking like a man who had left his sick bed. He offered no defense. He reviled himself as a "coward, vacillator" . . . he eulogised Calvin, his accuser, as a "monolith" of staunchness and fervently thanked him for not having spurned him as he deserved but, instead, having stretched out his strong and generous hand to pull him out in time from the quicksand of renegacy.
>
> On Calvin's motion the decision was that Schroeder should retain Party membership on a year's probation. For this decision

Schroeder was deliriously grateful. *Through sobs he thanked his comrades for their proletarian mercy; and the women and most of the men wept with him.*[20] [emphasis added]

Yet the pitch of fanaticism and self-destruction to which the fellow-traveling intellectuals drove themselves could not long be sustained in America. Where, as in some European countries, the party was a mass organization vitally participating in the social life of the nation, the process of rationalization—or the act of faith—by which the intellectuals sealed their loyalty to the party could find a certain grounding in reality. But in America, where the party had never been anything but sickly and the cultural arena was one of the few in which it could claim any significant influence, the process of illusion tended to take the form of a galloping fever that quickly reached a hysterical climax and broke. As a result, the turnover of intellectuals within the party was rapid, and the turnover among intellectual fellow travelers still more so.

In an amusing little study published in 1938, Herbert Solow reported on a check he had made of the contributors to the *New Masses* during the first year and a half of its existence. In 1926-27 there had appeared 268 articles by 150 writers. Seventeen of these writers, who had contributed fifty-three items, were now classified as "enemies of the people" (i.e., they had broken from Stalinism). Those writers who had contributed ten or more articles, Solow's figures proved, were far more likely to turn heretical than those who had contributed one or two. Of the five authors who had contributed ten or more pieces, three—Max Eastman, James Rorty, and John Dos Passos—had indeed become "enemies of the people." [21]

A decade later the turnover was at least as high. An effort to check the *New Masses* contributors for 1937 along lines similar to those of Solow's indicates that out of twenty-one editors and authors who were members of its staff or contributed five or more articles, eleven have since become "enemies of the people," two have remained in or with the party, one died in the Spanish Civil War, and seven (because of uncertainty regarding the use of pseudonyms) remain unaccounted for. It is clear, in any case, that the tendency toward defection has been a constant one, and that by the end of the decade almost every distinguished writer or editor connected with the *New Masses* had become an "enemy of the people." Many were called, but few remained chosen or chose to remain.

3. One reason for this rapid turnover was the susceptibility of intellectuals to criticism from the anti-Stalinist left. Though the Marxist sects that stood in opposition to the Communist Party had never counted for much in American trade-union or political life, they were able to launch damaging guerilla raids against the flanks of the Stalinist camp. And the party, for all its strenuous efforts to guard against the assaults of heretics, was simply unable to keep its intellectual sympathizers properly isolated.

When an intellectual in Germany during the late twenties or in France during the middle thirties attached himself to the Communists, he was at least choosing the "real thing." He found himself involved with and, in some respects, sustained by a powerful movement comprising millions of people—a movement so carefully organized and providing its followers with a life so nearly self-contained that it could guard its intellectuals from the stabs of left-wing criticism. But in America the party could provide no such "protective custody." And since all Marxist discussion in America had a way of seeming academic, it followed that some of the intellectuals who had been drawn to Stalinism as an ideology might also be open to the more rigorous and intelligent versions of Marxism that were being advanced by the splinter groups and the free-lance literary radicals. The difficulty thus presented to the party was aggravated by the fact that the leading intellectuals of the anti-Stalinist left—men like Sidney Hook, Max Eastman, and a few years later Philip Rahv—were unusually gifted both as writers and as political polemicists. At any given moment during the thirties the majority of left-wing intellectuals was likely to be sympathetic to Stalinism, yet the more independent minds among them were constantly drifting into one or another form of dissent.

So it was that the party in America found itself constantly threatened by the plague of deviation, a plague all the more troubling in that its carriers could not be isolated or destroyed. The Communists failed to understand—how could they?—that the very notion of a "monolithic" party necessarily implied a constant threat of heresy, that the trickle of "renegades" abandoning the *New*

Masses was a misfortune due not to the social instability of middle-class intellectuals but to the very nature of the Stalinist movement itself. Thus, even as Edmund Wilson was deciding to support William Z. Foster for President, he was also writing articles urging that Communism be "taken away" from the Communists—and the party was not sure whether to smile or to snarl. Foster seemed more intelligent to Wilson than the Republican politicians floundering about in the depression, but the Communist leader still lived constantly with "the awful eye of the Third International upon him—itself a secular church that rivals the sacred ones." [22]

Other heretics spoke up. Max Eastman, one of the first American radicals to support Trotsky, wrote *Artists in Uniform,* a pungent account of how cultural freedom had been suppressed in Russia during the late twenties; and though the *New Masses* worked itself up into a frightful rage against Eastman, the book clearly raised the most serious problems concerning the nature of Stalinism. Even for those who chose to remain loyal to the Soviet myth, *Artists in Uniform* was like a splinter lodged beneath the skin: it might be denied but could not be ignored. At about the same time Charles Yale Harrison, a regular *New Masses* contributor, struck at another sore point when he denounced the inhumanity of the Russian government in persecuting Trotsky's daughter despite her lack of interest in politics.

The notion of heresy has never been one to promote fine distinctions or precise measurements, and it was typical of the Stalinist movement that it tended to regard all heresies as equally threatening.* It could not distinguish between a personal variation upon common doctrine and a premeditated attack upon its ideas, perhaps because it worked on the assumption that the first, if clung to long enough, would lead to the second—and given its insistence upon a *total* ideology, this assumption had a point.

* With some exceptions, however. If the heresy were committed by a famous fellow traveler whose "name" was valuable, his chastisement would be light. Thus, when Theodore Dreiser was guilty of anti-Semitic remarks in the mid-thirties, he was rebuked in the *New Masses,* but since he continued to make his signature available to Communist "front" organizations he was not excommunicated. Had a small-fry intellectual made anti-Semitic remarks, or had Dreiser gone so far as to question the Moscow trials, the response of the *New Masses* would probably have been more severe. *The greatest, and least forgivable, heresies were those concerning intra-radical politics.*

And so the party theoreticians scourged the heretics, and the less power they had in American society the more imperious they were with those who adulterated the true doctrine.

In 1932 Philip Rahv, then a promising young critic, wrote an article called "The Literary Class War" in which he undertook the somewhat unlikely task of trying to reconcile Marxism with Aristotelian esthetics.

> Recognizing its present developmental stage as elementary, the critic who attempts to build a theoretical scaffold for proletarian literature [wrote Rahv] can but partially base his argument on what is actually being produced in capitalist countries at the present time. . . .
>
> The Greek idea of catharsis is one of the most fertile conceptions ever devised. However, its classic formulation by Aristotle as a process effecting a proper purgation of the emotions through pity and terror, is a static, passive conception quite in line with the needs of a slave-owning class endowed with cultural tastes. . . .
>
> Within proletarian literature one can discern the implicit form of a new catharsis, likewise a purgation of the emotions, a cleansing, but altogether of a different genus: *a cleansing through fire.*[23]

Rahv's article was clearly vulnerable, yet it had the merit of trying to lift the discussion about proletarian literature into the realm of serious critical discourse. In any case, it hardly presented a serious threat to the power of the Comintern. Nonetheless, the party apparatus, through A. B. Magil, then the doctrinal supervisor of the *New Masses,* launched a coarse and violent denunciation of Rahv which made it quite clear that orthodoxy was expected in esthetics no less than in politics.

A year and a half later the *New Masses* was confronted with a more serious heresy—in fact with the first major defection from the Stalinist intellectual camp. Immediately after the New York Communists had broken up a memorial meeting called by the Socialist Party and the trade unions to mourn the defeat of the Austrian Social Democrats (see p. 232), there appeared an "Open Letter," signed by Edmund Wilson, John Dos Passos, Lionel Trilling, James Rorty, John Chamberlain, Meyer Schapiro, Clifton Fadiman, Elliot Cohen, and Robert Morss Lovett, among others, which denounced "the culpability and shame of the Communists." While making it clear that they did "not approve the Socialist leadership in Austria or the United States," and in effect seconding the Communist criticism of Social Democratic politics, the signers charged that the "concerted booing and yelling [by the Communists at the meeting] was disorderly and provocative in the extreme. . . . The result was the disruption of working-class action in support of the Austrian workers." [24]

For the Communists this meant the loss of the most distinguished group of intellectuals that had ever approached the party orbit. A few years later these writers were to form the nucleus of an important anti-Stalinist group that tried to mobilize opinion against the Moscow trials and, for a time, seemed on the verge of creating an independent left within the intellectual world. Despite the later growth in numbers and influence of the Stalinist intellectual "front" groups, the Moscow trials actually marked a major step in the collapse of morale among radical American intellectuals, for the shock caused by the trials was a deep one, not only among peripheral sympathizers but also among many party intellectuals who kept pretending publicly that all was well in the "workers' fatherland." Much of the space and energy of the *New Masses* had now to be devoted to denunciations of those intellectuals, ranging from the liberal John Dewey to the radical Sidney Hook, who made the Moscow trials a touchstone for distinguishing between totalitarian Stalinism and democratic socialism.

The New York intellectual world was ripped into bitter factions. The anti-Stalinists sponsored a "Commission of Inquiry" headed by John Dewey, which declared Trotsky and the other defendants not guilty. The pro-Stalinists issued a statement, signed by 150 cultural figures and initiated by Malcolm Cowley, Stuart Davis, and Marc Blitzstein, which affirmed confidence in the trials. Those fellow travelers, like Waldo Frank, who questioned their validity or suggested an independent investigation, were summarily excommunicated. Steadily the feeling of bitterness kept growing, for it was sensed by everyone who argued about the trials that in some fundamental way the fate of radicalism—at least its moral fate—was involved. Many American intellectuals were of course totally indifferent to the issue, but in retrospect it may be useful to declare them mistaken: the trials, or the political problems behind the trials, were of immediate relevance to a far wider intellectual public than that which habitually concerned itself with Marxist polemic.

One significant result of these controversies was that the editors of the *Partisan Review,* a literary monthly published by the John Reed clubs, publicly broke from Stalinism and in 1937 began reissuing the magazine on an independent basis. Its immediate success, and the considerable prestige it gained during the late thirties, made the magazine a rallying point for those left-wing intellectuals who had turned away from Stalinism but, for a time at least, wished to remain Marxists. Devoted to *avant-garde* values in literature and to a quasi-Trotskyist position in politics, *Partisan Review* in its first several years provided a home for writers who could not be at ease with any of the established institutions that accepted or rejected society. By its sheer existence, the magazine came to symbolize the fact that the Communist Party had failed in its effort to appropriate the political energies of the radical intellectuals in America. And the party knew it.

4. All through the early thirties, amid apocalyptic expectations of revolt and the sodden excitements of faction polemics, the Stalinist intellectual world devoted a large part of its attention to the new "proletarian literature"—a school of writing, boasted two friendly critics in 1935, which shows the "bone and flesh of a revolutionary sensibility taking on literary form." [25] Though its formal life span was merely the first half of the thirties—actually it had begun somewhat before 1930 and was to linger a little beyond 1935—proletarian literature became a label, a catch phrase not only among radicals but in intellectual discussions, where it was often used as a term of contempt by people whose knowledge of it derived from contemptuous criticism. Indeed, the phrase has survived the reality, for the left-wing novels and poems of the thirties are no longer read. Yet there was somewhat more to the reality than to the phrase, somewhat more to the sensibility and achievement of the proletarian novelists than the formulas the party had stamped out for them.

In the late twenties, when Mike Gold was its directing spirit, the *New Masses* printed fiction, poetry, and reportage that described the life of the downtrodden and tried to arouse readers to rebellious emotion. Particularly if they were done as modest reports rather than as fiction, these writings had a certain documentary interest; but it is noteworthy that they show only the faintest evidence of having been inspired by any ideology of "proletarian literature." A few years earlier, it is true, the Russians had had a famous dispute in which the term "proletarian literature" had figured importantly. Bukharin and other Communist leaders had proclaimed the birth of a new Soviet culture, while Trotsky had insisted that since the proletariat is always a propertyless class whose historical function is to eliminate the causes of its social dependence and thereby "abolish" itself, there could be no such ephemeral being as a proletarian culture. Trotsky knew that the growth of a culture is necessarily slow and painful, and he concluded that a new culture would appear only after the proletariat had effected its own dissolution, that is, after a classless society had been built.

Now the terms of this dispute were not formally applicable to the United States, since it assumed a society where capitalism had already been destroyed; but the underlying assumptions were very relevant. Insofar as proletarian literature was not a mere political slogan for a moment's advantage, it flourished among earnest people who failed to understand how complex the whole idea of culture is, so that what now seems to have been the crude sloganeering of proletarian literature was also, and perhaps even more, an enormous naïveté concerning the sheer recalcitrance of the historical process.

As a formal dogma, proletarian literature did not come into its own until after the Kharkov conference in 1930. At meetings of the John Reed clubs and in the columns of the *New Masses* there were endless dreary probings into this new cultural wonder, yet the term itself remained elusive and ambiguous. At first it had been decreed by the Comintern, with characteristic arbitrariness, as the cultural slogan for the "Third Period," but after a while many critics were taking it seriously in its own right and studiously debating its intricacies. Was proletarian literature a literature written by proletarians? Then it might conceivably be objectionable in political content or without political relevance at all. Was it literature in which the life of the proletariat formed the main subject? Then like much writing of the past, it could provide friendly or even neutral social portraiture that led to no revolutionary climax whatever. Or was it a literature that prompted the reader toward a Marxist view of the world? But if so, it need not be written by or about proletarians.

It was puzzling. In the definitive anthology *Proletarian Literature in the United States* that appeared in 1935, several left-wing critics tried their hand at definition. Hicks spoke of "writers in alliance with the proletariat." [26] Joseph Freeman used the terms "revolutionary literature" and "proletarian literature" as if they came to the same thing. William Phillips and Philip Rahv studied "proletarian patterns of struggle" and "revolutionary themes." But none of this could be said to constitute or even promise a new culture, for what was new was not literary at all—it was political. Some years later, after he had adopted an anti-Stalinist position, Rahv wrote that the binding assumption behind proletarian literature had been that "the writer should ally himself with the working class and recognize the class struggle as the central fact of modern life." That, at least, was the formal assumption.

Yet even in its own terms the formula of proletarian literature, as Rahv later wrote,

. . . is empty of esthetic principles and advocates no particular esthetic direction; it establishes no defensible frontiers . . . between art and politics—it merges them; it draws no distinction between the politics of writing in *a generic and normative sense* and the politics of an individual writer in a particular historical period; and lastly, it fails to define in what way a writer's alliance with the working class is or is not an alliance with any particular party. . . . While the writer thought he was allying himself with the working class, in reality he was surrendering his independence to the Communist Party, which for its own convenience had fused the concepts of party and class. . . .

Whereas the literature of a class represents an enormous diversity of groupings and interests, the literature of a party is in its very nature limited by utilitarian objectives.[27]

These difficulties could be observed in almost any proletarian novel. Generally, it was set in a small industrial city, which provided a compact locale where class relations could manifest themselves with particular bareness; in an industry like textile or coal, which created a heavily oppressive atmosphere; and in the South or New England, which allowed for racial or regional complications. Its central action was a strike that had been forced upon the workers and in the course of which a variety of figures would be brought together, the backward workers discovering the value of unionism, the prejudiced ones the balm of solidarity, and the misled ones the wisdom of the Communists who, unobtrusively, were among the leaders of the strike. Almost always the strike was lost (a victory might create illusions about the value of mere trade unionism) and sometimes one of its leaders was killed. The shock of defeat, the education through struggle, which then came to a leading character would provide the novel with its political lilt—a lilt as essential and predictable in the proletarian novel as that which regularly occurs at the climax of a popular song.

The emotional falsification characteristic of so many proletarian novels was not of course confined to this prefabricated ending; but it was best epitomized by it. For the "conversion" ending, as the left-wing critics called it, was the result not of the writer's independent observation—the novel would then have been determined by the nature of his own experience—but of a generalized ideological expectation. It was, so to speak, the tithe the writer paid the party. As James T. Farrell put it, "Mere analysis, that is, the Party line, was . . . substituted for the raw, emergent movement of life itself. The psychology of human beings was deduced not directly from experience but from a set of political theses." [28]

As long as the radical writers worked upon the assumption that "art is a weapon" and that the political significance of a novel could or had to be compressed into a few synoptic phrases that reflected the party's current slogans, such endings were unavoidable. In one of his rare moments of intellectual sobriety Mike Gold wrote about this problem:

Anybody can write the first two acts of a revolutionary play. It is the last act, the act that resolves the conflicts, that has baffled almost every revolutionary playwright and novelist in the country. For you can't truthfully say in your last act or last chapter that there has been a victorious Communist revolution in this country.[29]

Inherently, there was no reason why good novels could not be written about the life of striking textile workers, and even today a reader with cultivated sympathies can be moved by parts of a book like Fielding Burke's *Call Home the Heart*. At the time they appeared, such novels were likely to evoke particularly strong emotions among sensitive readers who responded—as with anti-Nazi novels a few years later—more to their moral intention than to their artistic realization. Had the proletarian novelists of the thirties been left to themselves, free to work out their own needs and work through their own errors, it is quite possible that something valuable might have come from their efforts: some of them were genuinely talented men. But the demands of party dogma, and still more the demands of a party dogma that kept constantly shifting in the most erratic ways, forced them into a wrenching of the observed truth, a vast and programmatic oversimplification of the nature of human experience, and a contempt for those aspects of life that could not be contained by a narrow political utilitarianism. And these, in turn, led them not merely to literary failures but, far worse, to the moral deceit of passing off "the literature of a party disguised as the literature of a class."[30] When the ideological carpet was pulled out from beneath them and in 1935 the *New Masses* abandoned proletarian literature in favor of democratic or anti-fascist literature, most of the proletarian novelists were reduced to permanent silence.

It has since become fashionable to dismiss the radical fiction and verse of the thirties as hopelessly crude sloganeering. Much of it was exactly that; yet a blanket dismissal means judging literature in job lots, precisely the method that was so objectionable when used by Communist critics. Though our province here is not literary criticism, a sense of historical balance should be enough to persuade us that—as with all other literary or literary-political schools—the individual novels and poems that have been grouped under the rubric of proletarian literature are actually quite various in tone, meaning, and value. Almost always, those novels that were written out of a private feeling of rebellion or indignation yet were not chained to an explicit politics—James T. Farrell's *Studs Lonigan,* John Dos Passos' *USA,* Henry Roth's *Call It Sleep,* Nathanael West's *Day of the Locusts*—have survived far better as works of art than the books written close to the shadow of Stalinism. Few, if any, of the party-line novels now merit being read in their entirety, but there is a rugged social portraiture in Josephine Herbst's novels, a delicate sensibility in Robert Cantwell's, a concern with formal structure in William Rollins' that should command a certain respect. Even more than respect, however, these barely fulfilled qualities suggest how much talent was betrayed in the thirties, how high a price such writers paid for surrendering their gifts to the wardens of the party. In the long run, the damage wrought by the party in its passion to conquer or to destroy what it could not conquer was the same in literature as in the trade unions, the same in cultural matters as in politics. In the long run, that is, our story is a story of human waste.

As with literature, so with criticism. But since in criticism ideology tends to be more explicit and imperious, most of the criticism written in the thirties suffered particularly from an inquisitorial narrowness of spirit and from that form of intellectual presumption which has been described as taking upon oneself "the conceit of history." Earlier in this chapter a variety of examples was cited of the absurdities to which the left-wing critics were liable; what now concerns us is the general relationship between the Stalinist movement and left-wing criticism.

Like almost any other significant trend in modern thought, Marxism could prove useful to a literary critic, particularly if he allowed it to become an absorbed part of his thought, one of the numerous resources that came into play in his work, rather than trying programmatically to "wield" it as a technique of criticism. The power of Marxism as an analytic instrument for a critic dealing, say, with the nineteenth-century novel was clearly enormous—indeed, the trouble was likely to be that it was often too powerful a tool for the critic to control. Like vulgar Freudianism and other reductive schools of thought (those that say *Y,* despite all appearances to the contrary, *really* means X), vulgar Marxism could have a special fascination for the kind of critic who enjoyed the idea of ideological tidiness, whose dominant interest in the reading of literature was not to respond to the work of art in terms of its own quality but to provide systematic statements about its significance. All this was very well, provided the critic was aware of the risk he was taking, that is, provided he had sufficient literary sophistication or even craftiness to know that he should resist the very method to which he had pledged himself. Even during the years that the worst excesses of Communist criticism were being perpetrated, men like Edmund Wilson and, a little later, Philip Rahv were showing that in the hands of informed and sensitive writers Marxism could help, if not with the ultimate act of judgment, then certainly with the cognitive preliminaries to criticism.

Yet the truth is that, in regard to the experience of the thirties, discussions of the relationship between Marxism and literary criticism tend to be beside the point—for to discuss the problem in such abstract terms is to assume that in the Stalinist milieu it was possible for literary (or any other) ideas to flourish freely, undistorted by the demands of the party line. Actually, of course, ideas were regarded as convenient instruments to be employed or discarded upon political need. What really mattered was a relationship of power: the relationship between party ideology and a scattering of critics.

Given this fact, criticism as the cultivated and enormously difficult art of describing and evaluating—to say nothing of appreciating —works of literature could not be practiced by a person deeply involved in the Stalinist apparatus. This may seem an extreme statement and exceptions may quickly be noticed; but the most important exception, that of the fine European critic Lukacs, tends to support what has been said. For Lukacs, when he wrote of Stendhal or Balzac, was an independent and disinterested critic who happened to have a strong Marxist bent, and then he wrote excellently indeed; but when he turned to the work of Gorki, performing his task, perhaps even his assignment, as a member of the Stalinist apparatus, he wrote abominably. Nor were many Stalinist writers in a position to make the separation that Lukacs did between his intellectual self and his party role. Our statement, remember, was not that it was impossible for a Marxist or even a Stalinist to write good criticism, but that it was impossible for someone deeply involved in the Stalinist apparatus.*

Ideally, the critic should be able to give himself with love and devotion to the work before him; he must learn, if only for the moment, to see with the eyes of his subject, so that later he can judge how well his subject sees. But the Stalinist critic could allow himself no such luxury of disinterestedness; he had an entirely different set of obligations. The Stalinist critic was responding primarily not to a given work of art but to his feeling that the work could not satisfy the requirements of his dogma (and which work of art, if it were to remain one, could?) That is why the party-dominated critic —nor did domination have to take the form of "directives," the good Stalinist having long ago learned to anticipate directives—was not so much wrong as irrelevant: most of the time he was simply not talking about literature at all. His mind lacked the finesse, the patience, the delicacy, the passionate concern with problems of craft which are indispensable to the critic. Nor is it hard to understand why this should be so. Men with a deep conviction that they are on the verge of changing the world or saving humanity are seldom able to manage the fine observation upon which criticism rests; if one has, so to speak, the future in hand, it can easily seem unimportant whether this or the other little poem is good or bad—yet it is a fundamental premise of criticism that somehow it *is* important whether this or that little poem is good or bad.

In the prominence which Granville Hicks won as the leading Stalinist critic of the thirties one could see how paralyzing was the grip of the party on the critical mind. A completely selfless and serious man, far better informed than most of his comrades, never

---

* Consider the example of Michael Gold writing in the *Daily Worker* about John Dos Passos' *USA,* a novel of which many excerpts were published in the *New Masses* during Gold's editorship and which was repeatedly praised by the left-wing critics. Gold is writing, of course, after Dos Passos has attacked Stalinism: "On rereading *USA* one cannot help seeing how important the *merde* is in his psychology, and how after a brief futile effort, he has sunk back into it, as into a native element. . . ." [31]

Admittedly this is an extreme example, but it is an extreme example of a typical practice.

malicious out of personal motives, and genuinely dedicated to the idea that literature was valuable, Hicks succeeded in doing little more than to bring to the matter of Stalinist criticism some of the caution and solemnity of the academic manner. That so mediocre a book as his study of the American literary past, *The Great Tradition,* should have been hailed as a major work of Marxist or any other kind of literary criticism shows the complete lack of that devotion to standards which alone makes the critical act important in a civilized society. As it happens, V. F. Calverton had written a book of a similar kind, *The Liberation of American Literature,* which was considerably inferior to Hicks' book, being still cruder in its sociological assault upon literary values; yet Calverton's book was an individual performance, its failure due simply to his inadequacies of mind or training. *The Great Tradition,* however, was decisively shaped by the sectarian policies of the party's Third Period and its accompanying literary dogmas—so that a few years later, in response to another party turn, Hicks could drop the characteristic stress of his book and write a Popular Front tract called *I Like America.* By contrast Calverton retained his own way of looking at politics and literature to the end of his life: an unsatisfactory way perhaps, but his own.

Hicks would never have won as much notoriety as he did if the party had not realized that as an intelligent and scholarly native American he was a particularly valuable asset who could be promoted as the "representative man" of intellectual Stalinism. His reputation blown up in the party and left-wing press, Hicks was confirmed in his essentially conservative literary tastes and in his imaginative limitations. What Alfred Kazin has written about Hicks as a figure in the thirties may be harsh but it is true:

> He symbolized a race of young men, lost in the tides of change and vaguely hostile to traditional forms, who submitted to Marxism so hungrily that their ambition overreached itself in the spell of the absolute. They had found a new purpose for themselves in the light of the Marxist purpose; but in them one saw the working of that absolute on minds that were never supple or imaginative enough, never talented or sensitive enough, to write significant criticism.[32]

5. In any given "period" of Stalinist politics, particularly during intervals when the line seemed stable, the sympathetic intellectual could develop minor variations upon basic party themes without having to fear excommunication; and the more distant from politics his interests happened to be, the freer the variations. When the relationship between the party apparatus and the intellectual sympathizers could be assumed to be a settled and friendly one—in any case, it rested not upon physical force but upon ideology, a more binding and insidious kind of force—then a constrained freedom in regard to ideas was available to the Stalinist intellectuals. As it happened, not many cared to use it.

The Stalinist movement of the early thirties, it is true, was rapidly being transformed into a full-fledged totalitarian party; but this does not mean that in a country where it enjoyed neither power nor major influence it could exact the kind of total obedience that had become the rule in Russia. When Granville Hicks, in a later memoir about his Stalinist experience, wrote that no party commissar had ever told him what to say in his literary pieces for the *New Masses* he was unquestionably telling the truth.[33] The point is that in what the party regarded as trivial matters concerning taste there was no occasion to police the intellectuals and that in important political matters (such as defending the current line or attacking deviationists) there was no need to: they could be trusted to police themselves.

It was in moments of political transition, when the world Stalinist movement was lumbering through a major change of policy, that difficulties arose and the basic power relationship made itself felt. On the one hand, the party apparatus understood that considerable leeway of local expression and tempo was necessary during changes of the line, so that at the moment of change the movement always seemed to become somewhat looser and more "democratic" in tone. On the other hand, the result of such transitions was generally a stiffening of the new party line and a spewing out of dissidents. At such moments the hand of the "party rep" to the *New Masses*—it might be V. J. Jerome or A. B. Magil or Joe North—became more visible; and a check would show that such reliable party names had a way of suddenly creeping onto the masthead of the magazine at a time when the line had veered. These two processes of loosening for the turn and tightening after it might seem to be distinct in time, but in practice they often took place concurrently.*

For the fellow-traveling intellectuals in America these changes were particularly irksome: they had no mass movement that could shield them from the jeers of the liberals and the critical leftists, and they seemed to have a special knack for timing things badly.

In 1935, in order to replace the John Reed clubs with a more imposing structure and to consolidate the impressive gains the party had made on the intellectual front, there was convened in New York City a congress of American writers. A good many distinguished non-Stalinists were present, though, as usual, the control and direction of the congress lay in the hands of the party men.

The tone of this congress, though not quite as feverish as that of the *New Masses* a few years earlier, was still "revolutionary." Matthew Josephson, a year before the Moscow trials, assured the delegates that in a decaying capitalist world "Moscow has become an oasis of culture." Earl Browder, the only political leader invited to speak at the congress, solemnly announced that Marx and Engels were "the two most cultured men of history." A party-line trade-union official told the writers to stop fiddling with esthetic trivialities and

> . . . come down among the workers. . . . If they don't take the invitation, we'll give them an ultimatum. They can go on writing about the dead until finally we have to shove them into the grave and cover them up with dirt.

Jack Conroy, one of the few proletarian novelists who had ever been a proletarian, declared with a kind of impenetrable sincerity:

* As is revealed, particularly in the two italicized passages, in the following excerpt from Granville Hicks' 1939 statement of resignation from the party:

"The occasion of my resignation is the Soviet-German pact, but that does not mean that I am prepared to condemn the pact and its consequences. . . . If the party had left any room for doubt, I could go along with it. . . . But defense of the pact is *now an integral part of the line.* . . . Leaders of the party have generously urged me to *take all the time I wanted to make up my mind.* . . . But they have made it clear that, if I eventually found it impossible to defend the pact, and defend it in their terms, there was nothing for me to do but resign" [34] (emphasis added).

To me a strike bulletin or an impassioned leaflet are of more moment than three hundred prettily and faultlessly written pages about the private woes of a gigolo or the biological ferment of a society dame as useful to society as the buck brush that infects Missouri cow pastures and takes all the sustenance out of the soil.[35]

There were, to be sure, somewhat more considered and cultivated voices heard at the congress: Waldo Frank trying, with quixotic futility, to infuse a wider range of human concerns and philosophical interests into the minds of the delegates, and Kenneth Burke urging that the term "people" be substituted for "workers" as a matter of propagandistic strategy, a recommendation that brought down upon him a barrage of Marxistic sermons on the need for keeping class lines clear. No; the delegates to this first writers' congress, as they formed the League of American Writers to bring intellectuals into closer relationship with the working class and elected Waldo Frank as its first president, were not going to compromise the Marxian class outlook.

Three months later Dimitroff announced in Moscow the new People's Front line, and all the speeches, ideas, projects—even some of the officers—of the League of American Writers were summarily discarded.

In 1937 the League held another congress. Talk about socialism was now confined to a tiny and scorned minority of Trotskyist or near-Trotskyist participants; the class struggle and revolutionary action were replaced by "democracy" as the emotional binder of all anti-fascists. Where the call to the first congress, wrote an estranged left-wing critic, "summoned writers to the struggle against imperialist war and fascism, the second contented itself with a timorous meliorism designed not to offend well-paid scenario writers and ancient contributors to the *Saturday Evening Post*. In the past nothing short of the sovietization of 'the literature of the whole world' would do; today the gates of the dialectic have been thrown open to any successful money writer." [36] Big and respectable names from the bourgeois literary world that the Communists had but recently mocked—names like Thomas Mann, Ernest Hemingway, and Archibald MacLeish (in whom Mike Gold had once found traces of the

Fascist Unconscious)—were now invoked as the heroes and staunch friends of the "democratic front." Earl Browder, again the only political leader invited to speak at the congress, sneered at Waldo Frank as a dilettante who dared question the wisdom of the Communist movement—though this dilettante had a little while earlier been arrested in Terre Haute for speaking with Browder at a public meeting. Frank himself, still formally president of the League, did not even attend the congress.

Spain was now the emotional focus of the Stalinist intellectuals, as the slogan of the Popular Front was their political totem; at the congress there were "many dramatic descriptions of the heroism of the Spanish people, but no serious discussion of the fundamental politics of the Spanish situation as exemplified in the mutual relations of the social classes. . . ." [37] This lack of seriousness in the treatment of political and intellectual matters led Dwight Macdonald, who formed part of the left-wing opposition, to write that the congress was "one long pep talk reminiscent of the rallies I used to attend at Phillips Exeter Academy on the eve of the annual football game with Andover. In this case Andover was replaced by fascism." [38] The incantatory note that Macdonald detected in the congress speeches* was typical of Popular Front rhetoric: it betrayed the inner deceitfulness of Stalinist behavior during the whole period.

At the final session of the congress, Waldo Frank was replaced as president by the Hollywood comic writer Donald Ogden Stewart.[39] The first congress had ended with the singing of the *Internationale;* the second closed with Stewart's remark that it was hot and he for one was exceedingly thirsty. Symbolism need not always be planned.

The period of the Popular Front, extending from Dimitroff's pronouncement in 1935 to the Stalin-Hitler pact in 1939, was the most prosperous the Stalinist movement would ever enjoy in the intellectual world. True, it could no longer claim the devotion of such serious and independent writers as Wilson or Farrell or Dos Passos or Rahv; but it no longer cared to, for such people meant questions, discussions, all sorts of trouble. It now preferred to exploit

* Not in all of them, however. Kenneth Burke was present once more, to dazzle and mystify his listeners with a paper on "The Relation Between Literature and Science."

the formal patronage which men like Hemingway and MacLeish, who were not inclined to dialectic inquiries and for whom socialism had never been the passion of life, gave to the League of American Writers. Upon the famous writers who now fellow-traveled, so to speak, at several removes, generally meeting not the literary commissars but the genteel emissaries who had been trained by the commissars, the party never tried to impose any literary doctrine. The *New Masses* had badgered a whole generation of proletarian novelists, but Hemingway and Dreiser and Mann—these were too valuable to risk offending through mere literary criticism. All the party now cared about was that they be used as "stars" in the elaborate network of front organizations; it wanted names, signatures, faces, "prominent figures"; it wanted writers, not writing. And beneath the upper echelon of praised and petted celebrities there milled about a horde of second-rank intellectuals, Hollywood scripters, radio hacks, popular novelists, English professors, actors, dancers, newspapermen, and publicity agents for whom the *Schwärmerei* and political baby talk of the Popular Front were exactly right. "The poets were gone . . . the journalists remained." [40]

The Popular Front was popular: the party prospered. Stalinist influence during the late thirties (which is not quite the same as party influence) was very considerable in certain publishing houses, liberal journals like *The Nation* and *The New Republic,* and, most of all, the mushrooming industries of middle-brow culture. Nor was this primarily due to a Machiavellian conspiracy which planted cells in the powerhouses of intellect, as later journalistic accounts of the "Red Decade" would claim. (Though it should not be denied that the jobs at the disposal of the fellow-traveling fraternity in the communications and entertainment industries—as a few years earlier in the WPA writers' projects—played a role in attracting certain sympathizers.) The influence of Stalinism grew in the intellectual or quasi-intellectual world mainly because it was best able to provide the rudimentary ideology, the few threadbare slogans that corresponded to the yearnings of men of good will and not much political sophistication.

Nothing could have been more respectable than the *New Masses* of this period. The New Deal, once declared a prelude to fascism, was now celebrated; the death of so unradical a man as

Justice Cardozo evoked a piously cordial editorial; the savage cartoons for which the magazine had won a kind of fame were replaced
by warm drawings of celebrities ranging from Felix Frankfurter to
Wallie Simpson; a contest was organized for the best essay submitted
on the theme of "I Like America"; an anonymous author, writing
under the title "A Professor Joins the Communist Party," assured his
readers—shades of Lenin's professional revolutionaries!—that "my
own experience has been that the party demands no more time from
its members than they can reasonably spare from their other occupa-
tions"; the quoting of Earl Browder's "Message to Catholics" in St.
Patrick's Cathedral in 1938 brought forth the hope that "the perceptive minds of the Catholic Church, we feel sure, will recognize the
need for unity among all democratic Americans"; Hollywood, long
the symbol of everything serious writers had despised, now became
a reservoir of anti-fascist strength, and Joe North published solemn
researches on the "progressive" contents of the movies.[41] Only one
thing remained as before, one eternal verity: the denunciation of
writers who maintained a position of independent radicalism.

When the third American Writers Congress met in June, 1939,
the literary Popular Front seemed stronger than ever. Dreiser, Hemingway, and Kenneth Burke contributed papers; Thomas Mann, Dr.
Beneš, Vincent Sheean spoke; no dissenters appeared to disrupt the
proceedings. Somewhat later, in August, an impressive group of 300
intellectuals, many of them members or supporters of the League,
signed a statement denouncing the "fantastic falsehood that the
USSR and totalitarian states are basically alike." [42] Clifford Odets,
Matthew Josephson, Granville Hicks, Dashiell Hammett, Max
Lerner, Corliss Lamont, S. J. Perelman, Frederick Schuman, James
Thurber—these were but a few who spoke out against the "fantastic
falsehood."

One week later the Hitler-Stalin pact was announced.

The shock was immediate and its reverberations were deep. A
third of the officers of the League of American Writers, including
such an old stand-by as Malcolm Cowley, resigned; 100 of its 800
members formally left and many others drifted away. The party lost
heavily among its intellectuals, some like Granville Hicks openly
resigning and others quietly creeping out. As always in moments of
political stress, old hacks such as Magil and Gold began to appear

more frequently in the *New Masses,* Gold contributing a remarkable essay in which he boasted that the pact "throws Nazism to the mercy of its worst enemy, the Soviet Union" but that the Soviet Union, though it now enjoyed the balance of power, "will help neither imperialist cause, but will use their mighty power to establish some sort of democratic peace." [43] This tragi-comedy of mindless loyalty and bad timing came to a climax in the spring of 1941 when a fourth writers' congress was held at which the war in Europe was denounced as "a brutal, shameless struggle for the redivision of empires"—but this theme, too, was not long continued, for three months later, after Hitler's invasion of Russia, the League was calling for victory in the war. It hardly mattered any more, since by now the League, having outlived its usefulness, was allowed quietly to fade away.

An epoch in the history of American intellectuals had come to an end. In a few years the Stalinist movement would reestablish a certain strength among intellectuals, but they would not be the same ones—nor, more importantly, the same kind—as those of the early and even middle thirties.

A few remained faithful. One of those who did was a novelist named Albert Maltz, who had written a very fine story called "Man on the Road" portraying with economy and vividness the misery of a West Virginia miner stricken by silicosis, and who in the forties became a Hollywood script writer. The climax of his political career was to take place in the forties, but in tone and significance it really belongs to the thirties, as a sad footnote to everything that has here been described.

In 1946, during a discussion among party-line writers, Maltz published an astonishingly sharp article in the *New Masses* attacking the whole practice of Communist criticism:

> Much of left-wing artistic activity—both creative and critical —has been restricted, narrowed, turned away from life, sometimes made sterile. . . .
> Most writers on the left have been confused. The "conflict of conscience" [this phrase referred to a previous article by Isidor Schneider, who had described his conflict of conscience in choosing between propagandistic and artistic writing] resulting in wasted writing or bad art, *has been induced by the intellectual*

atmosphere of the left wing. The errors of individual writers or critics largely flow from a central source. . . . That source is the vulgarization of the theory of art which lies behind left-wing thinking: namely, "art is a weapon."

I have come to believe that the accepted understanding of art as a weapon is not a useful guide, but a straitjacket.[44]

Maltz then went ahead to object to the Communist practice of criticizing writers purely upon political grounds, pointing to the fact that Lillian Hellman's anti-Nazi play *Watch on the Rhine* had been attacked in the *New Masses* when it appeared on Broadway in 1940 but two years later, after the line had changed, was praised when it was made into a movie.

Within a week the counter-attack began. Howard Fast charged that Maltz's view was "in its final form, reactionary." [45] Joe North threw quotations from Marx at Maltz's head. Even William Z. Foster, never previously noted as an esthetician, joined the barrage. In Hollywood, at meetings of the Communist writers' group, Maltz was subjected to severe denunciations by John Howard Lawson, Samuel Sillen, and other comrades.

He held out for two months. And then in a *New Masses* article called "Moving Forward" Maltz submitted himself to the ritual of confession that had become part of the politics of Stalinism. "My critics were entirely right," he declared, "in writing that certain fundamental ideas in my article would, if pursued to their conclusion, result in the dissolution of the left-wing cultural movement." [46] The praise he had given to James Farrell was now replaced by a political denunciation. It was as if in the mid-forties the nightmares of the thirties had reappeared and Maltz, in his pitiful recantation, were living through once more the humiliations of men whose names had mercifully been forgotten.

But not many men of the thirties could bend themselves, could deny their own intelligence, as Maltz did. Most of them—the proletarian novelists, the Marxist critics, the flaming journalists, the actors and dancers, the poets, the professors—found the process of abandoning "the movement" an enormously painful experience, and some, scarred by the loss of faith, never could make a full recovery. For many of the party intellectuals and fellow travelers of the thirties, the radical plunge had been the one great adventure of their lives, and now, amid the rubble of their ideas and the bitterness of their betrayal, only a few brought themselves to ask and coherently answer: What had it all meant? Had all the talk and all the dreams, been in vain? In the decade of war that soon came such questions were likely to be forgotten, though in the memories of the more sensitive and conscientious radicals of the thirties they continued to stir self-doubt and anguish. For it is a terrible thing to commit one's hopes to a cause that turns out to be not a failure but a falsehood.

Chapter VIII. The Popular Front: Success and Respectability

1. The frequent and rapid changes of Communist policy during the past few decades have provided its opponents with the theme that the history of the Comintern can be traced in a fixed pattern of oscillations from left to right. Useful though it may be in certain contexts, this notion requires serious modification. For by taking the shifts of Communist policy during the forties or fifties as if they were equivalents to those of the twenties, such an approach sacrifices historical dynamism to formal neatness: it fails to consider the massive changes, whether for good or bad, that have occurred in both Russian society and the Communist movement. This is a way of regarding Communism that tends to remove it from the bruising context of history and thereby to endow it with an aura of invincibility that it very much desires but hardly deserves.

In the period between 1919 and 1923 the shifts in the party line were brought about by estimates—some correct, others not—of the political situation in Europe and Asia. The fierce debates among the European Communists had as their basis a common belief in the necessity of spreading the Russian Revolution to the West. By the early twenties, when the prospect of revolution had receded, a major change occurred: the Comintern still called itself the world party of revolution but it had begun to decline into a passive agent of whichever faction in the Russian party held the whip. It took only a few more years for the international movement to become a mere pawn of the Russian Foreign Office, to be manipulated and, if need be, sacrificed in the maneuvers of European power politics. As Franz Borkeneau has remarked, the new Popular Front policy announced at the Seventh World Congress of the Comintern in 1935 "implied a wholesale overthrow of the basic principles of communism. Instead of the class struggle, cooperation with the bourgeoisie. Instead of the Soviet system, eulogy of democracy. Instead of internationalism, nationalism." [1]

This was true enough; yet one may wonder whether such criti-

cism from the left was entirely correct in suggesting that the Comintern had replaced a Marxist revolutionary line with a reformist one.
What seems really to have been happening was the gradual removal
of Communist policy from the arena in which categories like "revolutionary" and "reformist" (both still implying a socialist bias) retained their point. The Popular Front policy represented neither a
conversion to liberal values, since for one thing it coincided with the
height of the Russian terror, nor a relapse into Social Democratic
"reformism," since at every crucial point the loyalty of the Communist parties resided not with the liberal bourgeois states but with
the new Russian ruling group.

Because the Stalinist movement, like the Stalinist state, constituted a historical novelty, its policy could be analyzed much more
profitably through terms such as "totalitarian" than the traditional
Marxist labels of "revolutionary" and "reformist." The left-right
oscillations of Stalinism continued, but within a new context: the
motions might seem the same but the meaning was different.

Given their premises, the left Socialists and dissident Communists clearly had a case when they attacked the Popular Front.
It was true, as they charged, that the Popular Front strangled the
revolutionary upsurge of the French workers in 1936. It was true,
as they charged, that during the Spanish Civil War the Popular
Front employed terror to pull the Loyalists back into the boundaries
of bourgeois liberalism. But whether such criticism penetrated to the
heart of the matter, to the deeper significance of the Popular Front,
now seems debatable. For the premise of this criticism was that the
Communists were still a section of the legitimate working-class movement and that it was therefore desirable to have them, or a coalition
of which they were part, take power in France and Spain.* Effective in detail and accurate in the short run, this kind of criticism
failed to consider what was historically novel in the rise of Stalinism:

---

* It is fair to add that Trotsky's view was somewhat more complicated.
He believed that if the parties of the French Popular Front were pressured
into something approaching revolution, the spontaneous momentum of the
workers would crack the bureaucratic shell of the French Communist Party.
This was an assumption based upon previous experiences involving the relations between insurgent workers and a *reformist* party. He failed to take into
account that the French CP was a party of a different type, a totalitarian
party with extraordinary resources for controlling and, if need be, suppressing
the popular energies that it set into motion.

that here was a movement which, in opposition to both capitalism and socialism, embodied a particular expression of the twentieth-century drift toward the total state. And if this was true, what point could there be in criticizing the Popular Front for its failure to seize power in western Europe?

The problems raised by such speculations would probably have seemed academic during the thirties, when the full meaning of Stalinism had yet to be grasped and other threats to human liberty seemed more immediate. In any case, for the Communists themselves the turn toward the Popular Front came as a pressing necessity. The politics of the Third Period lay shattered. In consolidating his rule, Hitler had shown a strength that made Communist predictions about his imminent collapse seem grotesque. In Vienna fascism had struck down the workers. In the Saar the Nazis had won a free plebiscite. In the Far East, Japan kept growing bolder. And the Kremlin leadership, no longer confident in the Third Period phrases it kept mumbling, now felt that its sole hope lay in a military-political bloc with the Western powers. The USSR joined the League of Nations and seemed decidedly untroubled by the earlier Comintern statement that the League was "an imperialist alliance in defense of the 'robber peace' of Versailles." On May 2, 1935, France and the USSR signed a mutual defense pact, pledging immediate assistance to one another in case of attack—a venture in *Realpolitik* which soon led to Stalin's famous declaration approving the military budget of Pierre Laval and thus to fundamental revisions of the Communist policy on war and political relations with bourgeois parties.

Traditionally the Communist movement had insisted, in accordance with Lenin's statements during the First World War, that wars fought by imperialist powers had to be regarded as reactionary and therefore undeserving of Communist support. Four months before the Franco-Soviet pact, the Communist theoretician R. Palme Dutt stated this view bluntly:

> The workers under capitalism have no fatherland. . . . The participation of the Soviet Union in the League of Nations no more transforms the character of the League of Nations than the participation of a Communist in parliament transforms the character of parliament. . . .

What then of the hypothetical argument of a possible war of "democratic defense" against a Fascist aggression? . . . Must we not "defend our country" against Fascism? . . . We do not for a moment exclude military defense against Fascism— on one condition, and one condition only, that we have a country to defend. . . . [But meanwhile] we shall not let ourselves be dragged into warring for one set of masters against another. . . .[2]

On May 11, 1935, a few days after the Franco-Soviet pact had been signed but still before the new line could be received, the traditional Leninist policy was reaffirmed in the *Daily Worker*:

Q.: In the event of war which would find both the Soviet Union and France fighting against Germany, what would the French Communists do?
A.: . . . The French Communist Party would continue to wage its relentless and unceasing struggle against French capitalism. . . . It would raise Lenin's slogan of turning the imperialist war into a revolutionary civil war. Under all circumstances the main task of the working class is the overthrow of the capitalists in its own country.[3]

Three months later and all was changed. Here is the German Stalinist leader Wilhelm Pieck reporting at the Seventh Comintern Congress:

If German fascism attacks the national independence and unity of small independent nations in Europe, a war waged by the national bourgeoisie of these countries will be a just war in which proletarians and communists cannot avoid taking part.[4]

For the Communists such a view involved a reversal of politics as fundamental in its way as if, for example, a liberal party were to declare itself in favor of dictatorship as a means of coping with a social crisis; and many followers, as well as a few leaders, found the new line very difficult to accept. It was a mark of how thoroughly the totalitarian ethos had seeped into the movement that this major change, whatever its merit or necessity, was announced at the

Seventh Comintern Congress in an atmosphere of mechanical unanimity and without any sign of hesitation.

The change involved here, it should be stressed, had nothing to do with the fact that the Soviet Union had signed a pact with a capitalist power; such temporary devices had been found necessary by Lenin and had always been sanctioned by the Communists. What was new and, from a Marxist point of view, a grave heresy was the readiness of the Communist parties to subordinate the class struggle at home to the strategic needs of the Soviet Union.

Many ideological justifications, some of them quite plausible, were found for the new Communist policy: the threat of Nazism, the campaign for "collective security" (an alliance among the "anti-fascist powers"), the need for unity on the left. Nor is there any reason to doubt that, even as some of the veteran Communists took such slogans to be part of a vast political maneuver, many of the new members accepted them at face value. It was possible to believe, as many liberals and Social Democrats did, that the rise of Nazism had created a political situation in which traditional policies, including the Marxist, had become obsolete and a new unity of anti-fascists necessary. But while this was a recurrent theme in the new Communist line, it was not the essential motive—as became clear three or four years later when Stalin signed still another pact.

A parallel change of Communist policy concerned relations with the democratic bourgeois parties. Not only were the Socialists to be wooed with appeals for a united front—there was nothing new about that, the Communists had tried it a number of times before. But now the Communist movement, which had begun with an attack on Social Democracy for its "class collaboration"—that is, for forming pacts and participating in cabinets with liberal bourgeois parties—entered into the same kind of pacts and with the same kind of liberal bourgeois parties. Again, it should be stressed that the innovation in Communist policy was not that an occasional electoral arrangement was worked out with a non-socialist party: that had sometimes been done by the European Communists during the early twenties, particularly in run-off elections. What was new was the formation of a sustained political bloc with a non-socialist party, a bloc clearly limiting itself to political goals within the framework of the *status quo*.

The rationale advanced by the Communists for this shift of line was, of course, the threat of fascism. This, to be sure, was a very real threat; but what the Stalinist theoreticians failed to explain was their violent rejection of anything resembling the Popular Front—or even a limited united front with the Social Democrats—during the whole previous decade, when fascism had first begun to accumulate its power. The orthodox Communist theory had been that fascism represented the open terroristic dictatorship of finance capital, and that the growth of fascism indicated how severe was the crisis of capitalist economy. Consequently—so ran the Communist argument—the only way to be rid of fascism was to eradicate the socio-economic system that bred it.

With characteristic zeal the Stalinist movement pushed its new "class collaboration" line to extremes that went far beyond the formulas of the Seventh World Congress. The impulse to drive each of its ideas to some ultimate limit seems inherent in any totalitarian movement; but at the moment there were substantial reasons of expediency for doing so. If what mattered most was finding strong new allies for the USSR in the arena of power politics, then there was no necessary reason for confining the search to liberals or liberal parties. In some countries the liberal parties lacked the strength to push foreign policy toward an *entente* with the USSR; hence the Stalinists had to look further to the right. And with time and experience they learned that a certain kind of conservative, untutored in the complexities of modern ideology and instinctively sympathetic to the authoritarian state wherever he found it, could prove a better partner—he might be less inclined to ask troublesome questions about concentration camps—than many liberals.

As a result, the *Front Populaire* had a way of expanding into a *Union Sacrée*. When Vailliant-Couturier, the editor of the French Communist paper *L'Humanité*, wrote about the Popular Front he could anticipate the rhetorical tone, though not the sincerity, of General De Gaulle:

> What is outstanding in [the Popular Front] is . . . the reconciliation of the opinions and religious beliefs, from the Communists and Socialists to the national volunteers [right-wing, semi-fascist veterans], from the Catholic to the unbeliever. . . .

A little later the Paris correspondent of the *Manchester Guardian* noted that

> The new Communist campaign . . . in favor of extending the Popular Front into a French Front, which would comprise not only the anti-fascists, but everybody, including the [fascist] Croix de Feu, has been unfavorably received by the Socialists. . . .

In Greece the Communist Party, which had been insisting upon the overthrow of the monarchy, now sent a delegation to King George and pledged itself to function "within the framework of the present regime." In Italy the Stalinists went still further, calling for a Popular Front to fulfill Mussolini's 1919 program and (it goes without saying) conclude a pact with the USSR. The Italian CP declared:

> Only the brotherly union of the people of Italy brought about by the reconciliation of fascists and non-fascists will be in a position to break down the power of the blood-suckers in our country.[5]

In the United States the situation was radically different from that of the European countries. Despite the depression, politics was not so fierce or ideological as in Europe; there was no serious immediate threat of fascism; and the Communist Party was very far from being a mass party. Yet in its modest way the Popular Front strategy, particularly through its appeal to the emotions of anti-fascist fraternity, was extremely successful in this country. It was the first approach the CP had found that enabled it to gain a measure of acceptance, respectability, and power within ordinary American life.

2. At first the Popular Front campaign in America got off to a rather modest start: the CP simply multiplied its overtures to the Socialists for united action. Hardly a Socialist meeting took place without there appearing a "friendly representative" from the CP with an armful of unity proposals. To break down the suspicion of the Socialists, Earl Browder went so far as to admit that his party had once been guilty of bad behavior:

When we were singing that song "On the Picket Line," the most popular of our whole movement, there was that line: "If you don't like thugs and Socialists and scabs, come picket on the picket line." We have stopped singing that line of the song . . . but it still has too much influence in our minds. . . .

We should speak openly and frankly. . . . Let us admit that we sang foolish songs about the Socialists, that it was a bad mistake and that we cut it out. . . .

So far (it might seem), so good. But within the velvet glove of the Popular Front there still lay a sharp Stalinist claw:

We want to build a strong left-wing in the Socialist Party. . . . We don't want to draw out from the SP individuals and small groups. . . . The most serious help we can get out of the SP is not in these individuals, but in the united front for which they could be of service if they remained in the SP. . . . Those drawn out of the SP (until now) are not the basic workers whom we want with us. Those basic elements have to be taken out *in great big chunks*. We can get them through the success of the united front.[6] [emphasis added]

To announce that what the CP wanted was not a stray convert but "great big chunks" may seem a curious way of winning the confidence of the Socialists. Yet it was not entirely a mistake: friendship can also thrive on aggression. The persistent flattery which the CP now thrust upon the Socialists ("I don't recognize myself any more when I read the *Daily Worker*," joked Norman Thomas), the feeling among some Socialists that unity on the left counted more than "bad manners," and the notion held by many radicals that within a united front it should still be possible to do some intensive undercover raiding—such factors brought the two parties together for a time. Thomas and other Socialists participated in the Scottsboro and Herndon defense campaigns; the CP lent its support to Socialist tickets in many municipal elections during 1935; and in reporting the results of these elections the *Daily Worker* would slyly write as if a pact had already been completed between the two parties: "The Communist gain was more than offset by the decline of the Socialist vote." So skillful were these

Pecksniffian gestures of friendship that within a short time Norman Thomas was saying that "The *Daily Worker* is certainly getting pretty good as a labor paper." [7]

Yet the moment when the two groups came closest to each other was actually the moment that revealed how quickly they would soon draw apart. In the fall of 1935 Browder and Thomas conducted a series of debates, the major one in Madison Square Garden before 20,000 people. For the *Daily Worker* the meeting represented "a milestone on the road to unity," but the speeches showed Browder moving rightward, Thomas leftward, and the two jarring one another as they crossed. Browder's calculated mildness confined him to appeals for unity, while Thomas, though favoring limited cooperation toward specific ends, took some sharp jabs at the more picturesque versions of the Popular Front:

> How can you have a people's front that will lead to the great cause of the emancipation of the workers if it is to include Democrats and Republicans? . . . Here is a leaflet from Pittsburgh, new style Communist propaganda. It has a picture of Joe Louis and I need not describe him to anybody, Lon Warnecke, the baseball player and in the middle the very attractive picture of Carolyn Hart, the twenty-three-year-old candidate on the Communist ticket for City Councillor of Pittsburgh, "who packs a mighty wallop." . . . I know what Communists would have said a little while ago if Socialists had issued such a leaflet. . . .
>
> I for one like to see you Communists reach out hands to the masses who follow Father Divine, but you have not convinced me that when you who are foes of religion, you, who most of you are convinced atheists, make common cause with God (for that is what Father Divine says he is)—that you advance understanding with colored workers. . . .[8]

By the spring of 1936 the Communists, with their eye on bigger political game, began once more to attack the Socialist Party. On the question of war the differences between the two groups became more acute, particularly as the CP fully absorbed the new Comintern line and the SP approximated a traditional Leninist view. The Moscow trials shocked many Socialists and created new grounds for hostility. In domestic politics the Communists were now again campaigning for a farmer-labor party, while the Socialists, rigid in their new leftism, tended to be hostile to the idea of a third party. And when the Socialists allowed the tiny sect of American Trotskyists to enter their organization, the CP grew still more irritated. Mournfully, Earl Browder told the Socialists: "Be careful, you are about to swallow a deadly poison, which we know from sad experience. Better prepare an emetic, for surely you will soon be in convulsions from severe internal political disturbances." [9]

The disagreement that mattered most, since it touched upon immediate American politics, was that concerning the 1936 election. Still a bit inexperienced and uneasy with their new line, the Communists worked out a curious strategy of not formally supporting Roosevelt but directing their main attack upon the Republican candidate, Landon; which meant, in effect, to steer voters toward Roosevelt. The Socialists for their part conducted a traditional though weak propaganda campaign for Norman Thomas. Browder, reverting from amiable didacticism to old-style polemic, wrote that "Our friend Thomas . . . cannot see the fascist direction of the Republican party. . . . He thus renders unwilling but nonetheless effective help to Hearst's demagogy." [10]

By 1937 the *Daily Worker* was regularly referring to the Socialist Party as Trotskyist or semi-Trotskyist, a label that virtually outlawed relations between members of the two parties;* by 1938 CP leader Jack Stachel was proposing a new version of the "united front from below." But as the Communists kept growing and the Socialists declining—for the one went with the political stream and the other against it—talk of a united front grew rare. The truth was that the Popular Front, if applied as promiscuously as the Communists now desired, made impossible the old-style united front between radical parties. And besides, the Communists were now

---

* It was an official procedure of the Stalinist movement to prohibit its followers from personal relations with Trotskyists. The New York party official, Charles Krumbein, spoke of this matter at a state CP convention in 1938 with the appropriate crudeness: "A few instances have come to our attention in which comrades showed tolerance and even social friendliness to some of these rats [Trotskyists]. Just as we turn away in disgust when we see a fascist, so must we do when we see these fascist agents." [11] Not until the Second World War, however, were the Socialists also treated as full-fledged "rats."

in pursuit of far bigger game: an alliance with the popular following of the New Deal.

Seen from a distance, each turn of Communist policy appears to have been made quickly and easily, as if someone were merely snapping an electric switch. But actually these turns were made with a certain difficulty, perhaps even a painful clumsiness. It was not easy for the Communists to transform themselves into uncritical defenders of the New Deal; old habits, old assumptions stood in the way; it took time. In 1935, when Popular Frontism was still an imported novelty and the flirtation with the Socialists at its warmest, the Communists directed their propaganda toward the need for a national farmer-labor party. Their hero of the moment, not at all a fellow traveler, was Francis Gorman, president of the textile workers' union, whose speech at the 1935 AFL convention in favor of a new party was rapturously greeted in the Communist press. And meanwhile the Communists continued to be critical of some aspects of the New Deal, particularly its mounting defense expenditures.

In the spring of 1936, as preparations for the presidential election began, the CP called for a farmer-labor slate. Though a certain sentiment could be found in limited trade-union and intellectual circles for such a new party, there was not enough to make it an immediate reality. Most of the trade unions were firmly committed to Roosevelt; the Socialists had decided to run their own ticket, partly because they saw no alternative and partly because they were going through a radical phase. In April, Alex Bittleman, a CP theoretician, was still arguing for a farmer-labor party: "The real and immediate problem is: to win away the masses from the capitalist parties." Failure to do this "means helping Roosevelt, helping the Republicans, helping reaction." [12]

Evidently, helping Roosevelt was bad. Two months later it was good. At the ninth national convention of the party Browder reported that "by May it had become clear that [a farmer-labor national ticket] was impossible. The great majority of organizations composing the farmer-labor movement . . . had decided to follow . . . the big progressive unions of the CIO in supporting Roosevelt for re-election." This was somewhat less than candid: it had been clear long before May that the unions were going to support

Roosevelt. Perhaps Browder really was saying that only by May did the CP work out its election strategy.

It was, to say the least, a two-faced strategy. Officially, the Communists maintained a "critical attitude" toward Roosevelt, though declaring themselves "fully prepared to continue and develop our united front relations with those who support Roosevelt." Unofficially, the CP helped the Roosevelt campaign. What other meaning can one attach to statements like this: "The CP declares without qualification that the Landon-Hearst-Wall Street ticket is the chief enemy of the liberties, peace and prosperity of the American people. Its victory would carry our country a long way on the road to fascism and war." [13]

What, however, was to be said about Roosevelt, the Roosevelt whom Browder had described as treading merely a "middle path" between fascism and democracy but who was nonetheless the implied favorite of the party? During the last months of the election campaign the *Daily Worker* solved this problem in a quite remarkable way: it said almost nothing about Roosevelt. Browder was quoted at great length; Thomas was sniped at; Landon was endlessly attacked as a sort of advance guard of fascism (a silly exaggeration, since he was merely a dull conservative); but Roosevelt, the desired candidate, the candidate who was to sweep the country, barely appears in the paper during the last weeks of the campaign. It was a case, perhaps, of preference through silence, and more probably of the difficulties met while negotiating a major shift of preference.

In the long run, the new policy saved the Communists from the isolation that would beset those American radicals who opposed the New Deal, for it permitted Communists in the unions to cooperate with the labor leaders, who by now were firmly tied to Roosevelt. In the short run, the party's disingenuous election policy resulted in minor organizational damage, creating disgust among a few old-timers who felt it was succumbing to "class collaboration" and confusion among some new members who, in the naïveté of their logic, wanted to support Roosevelt openly.

Once the magnitude of Roosevelt's victory was grasped, the CP dropped all restraints in applying the Popular Front line. Browder discovered a number of ideas that were commonplaces of American

liberalism but were hailed as profound thoughts by the comrades—
the difficulties of getting new parties on the ballot; the possibilities
of radicals and liberals working in old-party primaries; the gradual
differentiation of the old parties along class lines so that it no longer
made sense to dismiss them, in traditional Communist terms, as
capitalist Tweedledee and Tweedledum. Browder foresaw

> . . . a complete reconstruction in American politics. . . . This
> new party that is beginning to take shape before our eyes, involv-
> ing a majority of the population, is what we Communists have
> in mind when we speak of—the American expression of the
> People's Front. . . . What particular name the caprice of history
> may baptize it with, is immaterial to us.

In other words, the Popular Front now *was* the Democratic Party.
Which meant, as Clarence Hathaway soon made clear, that the
Communists in actuality were against the formation of a new party
in America:

> We can see now that the People's Front will not immediately
> and in a pure form express itself in a Farmer Labor Party. It
> will develop in the form of progressive movements inside and
> around the Democratic Party, and at the same time affect pro-
> gressive sections of the Republican Party.[14]

In Communist writings between 1937 and 1939 there remains
a slight element of criticism toward the New Deal—especially when
relief appropriations were cut and Loyalist Spain was subjected to a
damaging embargo—but to find many examples of such criticism
one must search very diligently. Once Roosevelt made his famous
"Quarantine the Aggressor" speech in Chicago, in October, 1937,
the Communists grew lyrical about the virtues of his administration,
for in advocating collective security he took the one path they most
desired him to take. Roosevelt's picture now appeared regularly on
the front page of the *Daily Worker*, which sometimes went so far
as to imply that he was as great a man as Browder. In early 1939
the CP began booming the President for a third term: he is a
leader, wrote the generous Browder, who stands "on the same plane

as Jefferson, Jackson and Lincoln." The Hollywood Communists contributed a ditty to the cause:

> Mister Roosevelt, won't you please run again?
> For we want you to do it
> You've got to go through it
> Again.

To make certain that no one could accuse the CP of hurting Roosevelt's chances, it declared against "launching artificial third parties, which can only split the people's ranks." In 1938, at the party's tenth national convention, the Popular Front had been face-lifted into the Democratic Front, a change calculated to suggest that between the 50,000 or so members then in the CP and the majority of the American population there could only be the most trivial of differences. A finger of peace was even extended to "the lesser leaders" of the Republican Party, those "who are closer to the masses." [15] Who then was doomed to remain outside the Democratic Front, which, as the Communists saw it, meant virtually to be excluded from the human race? Only a handful of malcontents, the isolationist Old Guard Republicans, and the isolated Trotskyists and Socialists.

Of the revolutionary struggle for socialism which the Communists had once proclaimed as their purpose, nothing seemed to remain.

3. The success of the Popular Front depended most of all on a wide diffusion of its political and cultural style: a few simple slogans, such as "democratic unity" and "anti-fascist struggle," were to be spread across the consciousness of large numbers of people who did not conceive of themselves as Communists or Communist sympathizers. That is why the Popular Front phase of American Communism thrived upon the "front organization" and the "front psychology": it required the creation of a mood of un-focused fraternity mixed with fretful alarm, or perhaps more accurately, it exploited among liberals and "men of good will" a mood of this kind that had arisen since the victories of fascism in Europe.

Yet—and here we reach the apparent paradox as also the inner mechanics of Popular Frontism—for this vague mood to crystallize into political action there also had to be, working unobtrusively in the wings, a leadership flexible enough to face the demands of opportunism with easy conscience and disciplined enough to fulfill them with maximum efficiency. Discipline the CP had in abundance, as a legacy of the early thirties; flexibility it now set about deliberately to acquire. For the leaders of the party understood that in order to carry out the Popular Front line a new type of party was necessary: neither the old revolutionary sect nor an amorphous reformist society, but a party in which a hard core of the former set about to create the appearance of the latter. It is a fact of first importance to the history of American Communism that the success of the Popular Front during the late thirties had for its prerequisite the building of a tight cadre during the Third Period. Comrades who had been able to swallow the theory of social fascism were not likely to gag on "Communism is Twentieth Century Americanism." Could any other movement in our time have achieved so remarkable a masquerade? Could any other movement have brought together the hidden belief of the inner party core that the Popular Front was a dazzling maneuver with the sincere belief of the outer membership that it was a genuine commitment?

Systematically, the party leadership went about the job of changing the language, the habits, the very appearance of the members. At this point it may be best to allow the comrades to speak for themselves. Here is a portrait of the old-style professional revolutionary as drawn by a Comintern "rep" to the American party:

> The professional revolutionist . . . gives his whole life to the fight for the interests of his class. A professional revolutionist is ready to go wherever and whenever the Party decides to send him. Today he may be working in a mine . . . tomorrow, if the Party so decides, in a steel mill; the day after tomorrow he may be a leader and organizer of the unemployed. . . . From these comrades the party demands everything . . . the matter of family associations and other personal problems are considered but are not decisive. If the class struggle demands it, he will leave his family for months, even years. The professional revolutionist

cannot be demoralized; he is steeled, stable. Nothing can shake him.

The new party member, by contrast, was to be distinguished by the fact that he was not supposed to be distinguishable from anyone else:

> To make our party a party of human beings who live and laugh just as everybody else does still remains a task before us. Our shop papers often tell the Communist position on this or that important problem, but seldom do we find an article on the kick one gets from doing party work. We always play up the gloomy side of life with hardly any relief in sight before the social revolution; yet our party has picnics, outings, affairs and such things.

No longer did the party demand from its members the whole of their lives:

> There is a widespread impression among non-party people that joining the party means complete subordination of the individual's life to the activities of the party. They think that if they join the party they will not have time for their families. . . . We must prove to these workers that this is not a true picture of our party.

Moreover, it was now necessary for Communists to find out something about the world and the country in which they lived:

> Communists are known as outsiders [in their communities] not because they are known as Communists and socially ostracized. Oh no, they are outsiders because they are not known in their neighborhoods at all—they merely come home to sleep. They never talk to their neighbors. They can't be bothered with children, so they never have time to get friendly with the kids playing in the street. They don't know the grocer and butcher because they never cook, and probably brag about their impatience with cooking and such things. . . . And even should they develop some friendship with their neighbors, it does little good because like gypsies, our comrades move from place to place, having no ties in any particular neighborhood to keep them there.

And it is because there is the basic difference between the lives our comrades lead and those of the average American family that our comrades find the territorial work unpleasant and strange.

No critic, certainly no enemy of American Communism, could have put it more harshly. But now, in the late thirties, not only was the good party member to play handball with the neighbors' kids, even if he suffered blisters afterward; he was to adapt his local branch meetings to the habits of those very neighbors:

Seasoned Communists can sit through the longest meeting and decide questions . . . without becoming bored. New members, however, will jump off the subject and begin to talk about the frill on the new green dress and why it should be taken off. . . . Women will exchange recipes or household hints even in a strategy meeting. . . . So we relax once in a while too.

Slowly, the whole structure of the party was being changed. Previously, its basic organizational form was supposed to be the shop unit, though more often than not it was a street branch. Now shop units were merged into larger industrial groups that paralleled the new industrial unions, and the street branches were succeeded by large area branches based on conventional political divisions, thus better preparing the party for electoral work and for joint projects with other groups similarly organized. By the 1938 convention of the New York State party, for example, it was reported that only 20 percent of the membership still belonged to shop units, and the implicit, though not formal, sentiment was for still further decreasing the percentage.

In a word, the party was to become like any other organization. "We have some organizational forms and practices," grumbled one leader, "which are not at all typical of any other American organization." (One would imagine that a Communist Party very well might.) Rapidly all distinctive modes of public organization were eliminated. Particularly important was the formal abolition at the 1938 New York State CP convention of the "party fraction" in the trade unions, that is, the organized caucus of Communists deciding which policy to pursue in their unions. "The trade unions, especially

336 THE AMERICAN COMMUNIST PARTY

those of the CIO, are progressive, as are also many of the AFL unions. Our party's line and policies are clear and understood by most of the comrades. . . ." In practice this generally meant not that the Communists in the unions ceased to function as a group but that the pretense of democratic consultation was no longer maintained. Party members at a union meeting were simply expected to follow the tips of the comrade acting as floor leader.

The stress was now upon neighborhood organization and penetration. Communist Voters clubs, and then clubs with more respectable names ranging from Patrick Henry to Abraham Lincoln, were organized—clubs "which will hold meetings—not too frequently— and which will serve as a center of social life and activity. . . ." At such meetings the old practice of "having half a dozen comrades pounce upon the unsuspecting person the moment he enters the building with the object of extracting money for various things from raffles to songbooks" would have to be stopped. Instead of the dingy, foul-smelling, half-lit hall which had traditionally been the party headquarters, the new one—well, let a lyrical comrade describe the branch headquarters of the Communist party in New York's 24th Assembly District:

> It might be a private evening school, or the offices of a nice neighborhood club. It is a respectable, modest, four-storey building of quiet firebrick with long, dignified French-type windows. . . . As you enter the large, clean lobby, you are immediately aware of a busy, smooth-running institution. . . . Bonnie Clark, a pretty smiling girl in Room 4—information—asks cheerily: "Yes, comrade?"

Only a few party members said, "No, comrade," those who felt, in the words of a horrified functionary, that "if the party follows the line of broad united fronts with 'everybody' this will lead the party far to the Right." A good many of these grumblers were members of the foreign-language federations who could not quite take to being "Americanized" with the glee that the American members did. Sometimes these barely articulate malcontents yearning for the days of revolutionary theses and street demonstrations got a guarded word of encouragement from such eclipsed leaders as William Z. Foster, who feared that the party was in danger of becoming too middle-class. But the drift was all the other way, so that in 1936 it was possible to read in a Communist organizational bulletin a warning to party members on WPA projects that they should be careful not to sound like "crazy Reds." [16]

Everywhere the branches pitched into the job of establishing the CP as a respectable American organization—not at all "crazy Reds"—which had the same interests and purposes as any other. In Bridgeport, Connecticut, for example, the CP dug itself in by organizing a "broad committee" to support the Roosevelt Recovery Program. AFL and CIO unions, the Democratic Party, "one Socialist alderman, ministers, representatives of small businessmen's associations . . . Young Democrats, the Democratic Women's Federation, the Veterans of Foreign Wars, the Disabled American Veterans"—all participated in a local popular front. "One of the most striking features of the whole movement," boasted the local CP leader, "is the acceptance of the Party by other groups, including the Catholics, and the absence of any Red-baiting."

In Sunnyside Gardens, a middle-class suburb of Queens, the party campaigned around issues like "sewage problems, mortgages and other ills of the small homeowner." Confessed a local Communist leader: "I never knew so many people were interested in sewage assessments before."

One branch issued a bulletin proclaiming its devotion to the great American sports: "When the football season came on, we had a football edition. When football was over, we used another game." Another branch, in the north Bronx, "worked actively with all organizations in the community sponsoring a Bronx Fair." [17] Other New York branches joined with Negro churches in celebrating the Marxist holiday known as Mother's Day.

Such activities may have contained a streak of the ludicrous, but they also brought palpable results, for the party, as a kind of secret sharer, was swimming with the tide of liberalism. That the Communists carried their decision to be "just folks" to fantastic extremes was proof they never were or could be "just folks"; but proof also of how considerable were the advantages of pretending. Naturally, a change of the dimensions that the party had begun could not be managed without an occasional disharmony. Behind the blue serge suit of the Popular Front there often grimaced the Old Stalinist of the Third Period. Here, for example, is Isidore Begun, the Bronx party leader, hectoring his charges on the need to keep informed about local issues:

> Now can you tell me what is the classification system [in regard to milk pricing in New York]? Can you explain "surplus"? . . . What is the Allen-Rogers bill? What is the McElroy-Young bill? You have to know these things if you're going to deal with the high cost of living.

But then, a few paragraphs later, Begun relapsed into an earlier self:

> Every time you go canvassing for housing, the best preparation is to read Engels on housing. There is no possibility of talking milk and high cost of living without reading Lenin on the agrarian problem in Russia. . . .

No small task: to know both the McElroy-Young bill and Lenin on the agrarian problem! But for a good Communist no obstacle was insurmountable. As the Young Communists at the University of Wisconsin explained:

> Some people have the idea that a YLCer is politically minded, that nothing outside of politics means anything. Gosh no. They have a few simple problems. There is the problem of getting good men on the baseball team this spring, of opposition from ping-pong teams, of dating girls etc. We go to shows, parties, dances and all that. In short, the YCL and its members are no different from other people except that we believe in dialectical materialism as a solution to all problems.

This incongruous blend of ping-pong and dialectical materialism as "the solution to all problems" was recurrent throughout the late thirties. It would be excessive to claim that it was always a planned incongruity, but there is good reason for seeing it as essential to the party's need for holding together old believers and new converts. At an inner party meeting two members could rise to speak, both with obvious sincerity yet in wildly different styles of political rhetoric:

The Old

The enemies of the working class say that our party . . . is opportunistic and is abandoning the struggle for socialism. I say emphatically, no! I say this as Marx, Engels, Lenin and Stalin would, no! The class struggle is deepening! The problems of the workers can be solved only under socialism. The Soviet Union is giving us the answer.

The New

Comrades, I am a new member of the Communist party, and I want to tell you that my heart is with it. A lot of people have asked me how I came into the party. . . . My answer is very simple. Communism to me means fundamental truth. . . . Take our public schools today . . . and in every one of them, through the politically controlled apparatus, they teach the children Communism—"Love thy neighbor as thyself." [18]

One reason the party could bring together such diverse minds and tempers was the utter brashness with which it embraced every absurdity of the Popular Front. It appropriated the slogans and paraphernalia of "Americanism" with so calculated a zest and so total a manipulative cynicism that its critics would find themselves disarmed in advance. For what could opponents of the left or right say when at every point the party cheerfully went further than they had thought to charge?

Communism became "Twentieth Century Americanism"; Washington and Lincoln, the progenitors of modern progressive sentiments; Jefferson, the ancestor of those "Americans who are fighting against the tyranny of Big Business with the revolutionary spirit and boldness with which he fought the Tories of that day." The American flag replaced the red flag at party parades and the "Star-Spangled Banner" became the official hymn at party meetings. In 1936 and 1938 violence was specifically repudiated at CP conventions. Speaking at a Boston meeting, Browder aligned himself with those who were concerned to prevent a proletarian dictatorship in America:

Proletarian dictatorship can become a practical order of the day in America only if President Roosevelt's promise of a higher standard of living under the present system is defeated or betrayed. We of the Communist Party are prepared to cooperate with everybody who will help win that higher standard of living. . . .

The party that had once spoken of turning imperialist war into civil war now proclaimed its patriotism and, like all patriotic organizations, announced its distaste for foreign "isms," as in the following circular of its Louisiana section:

May we remind you that this is Americanism Week. The Communist Party of Louisiana declares its steadfast loyalty to our Nation's democratic institutions, pledging ourselves in word and deed to fight any "ism" of any clique, group or minority from within our country or from abroad that would destroy or undermine our democratic institutions. . . .

Nor was Americanism merely a matter of ideas. The CP did not neglect genealogy, and since by happy chance Earl Browder could trace his line back to pre-Revolutionary Virginia, many were the descriptions in Communist literature of the covered wagons that had been ridden by his always forward-looking ancestors. A campaign biography by Moissaye Olgin, a leader of the Yiddish-speaking Communists, declared that "The Browders have a right to say that they are among the founders of America." More lyrical as well as historical was Robert Minor's saga of the Browders:

It was in the springtime of 1776 and Thomas Jefferson may well have been driving his one-horse shay . . . with a draft of the Declaration of Independence in his pocket, when a certain boy, just turned 21, stepped into a recruiting station in Dinwiddie County, Virginia. He gave his name as Littleberry Browder and was sworn in as a soldier of the Continental Army of General George Washington.

From Littleberry to Earl, intimated Minor, there occurred a development comparable to that of the nation itself. But since even the most skillful Communist pamphleteer might be troubled by the task of popularizing Littleberry, another ancestor was summarily appropriated for Earl, one not related by blood: John Brown. "John Brown of Osawatomie," they called Browder, and each time the *Daily Worker* reported a speech by "John Brown of Osawatomie" it made a point of noticing his "Kansas twang." "More Kansan than Alf Landon if it comes to a showdown," concluded Westbrook Pegler after an interview with Browder, and for once the Communists could not quarrel with him.

A kind of Machiavellian inspiration—the inventiveness that sometimes comes from total cynicism—characterized the Communist venture in patriotism. In the spring of 1937, for example, the New York chapter of the Daughters of the American Revolution was caught napping at the ramparts: it neglected to celebrate the 162nd anniversary of Paul Revere's ride. But the Young Communist League did not forget. It hired a horse and rider—dressed in Continental costume—to prance up and down Broadway with a sign proclaiming: "The DAR Forgets But the YCL Remembers." [19]

In its readiness to accept any new supporter of collective security, the party systematically canvassed every national and religious group. Among Protestant clergymen, many of them sincerely eager to build a more humane social order, it found a considerable number of indirect allies, particularly in such front organizations as the American League Against War and Fascism (see pp. 348-355). The problem of the Catholics was a thornier one, requiring either a head-on battle or major ideological concessions. In his report to the 1938 convention of the party, at which the Popular Front was stretched into the Democratic Front, Browder chose the path of ideological concession. (Not by his own initiative, of course; this was the era in which the French Communist paper *L'Humanité* printed a huge headline: *Le Pape Avec Nous!*) Attacks upon religion and the Church were to be stopped; even attacks upon the record of a number of Church dignitaries who supported fascist governments were to be muted. The "Catholic worker's deep religious feelings" must now be considered, for, as a CP leader said,

We feel that [the history of the Catholic Church in the eighteenth and nineteenth centuries] can become a powerful factor in winning the Catholic people to the united front. . . . The Catholics have faced bitter persecution from intolerant and bigoted groups. . . . Catholics have had to fight not only for religious freedom, but for political representation as well.

Directing attention to the role of the Church in Massachusetts during the eighteenth and nineteenth centuries was one way of forestalling those few comrades who might be churlish enough to remark upon its role in the twentieth century.

In France, Maurice Thorez, the Stalinist leader, wrote that "in both Catholic and Communist there is the same generous ardor to reply to the century-old aspirations of men for a better life." In America the party strategists told the members that "Our approach to [the Catholics] must be on the basis of urging them to carry into practice their own Catholic ideals and aspirations based on the concept of the brotherhood of man." [20] Cardinals now found themselves praised in the *Daily Worker*; the Catholic trade unionists, yesterday the object of fierce attacks, were courted as allies; and the irreconcilable conflict between Thomist scholasticism and Marxist materialism was dissolved in the syrupy formulas of the Popular Front. This campaign to win the Church to the Popular Front did not succeed in any major respect, but it certainly made things much easier for those Communists who worked in or led trade unions with a large Catholic membership, such as the Transport Workers Union in New York.

Similar and more successful efforts were made to penetrate Jewish communal life. Since the early twenties the Communists had enjoyed a strong following among the Jewish garment workers in New York, Chicago, and Los Angeles, but the fierce opposition of the party to Zionist sentiments had led to its being sealed off from the remainder of the Jewish community. (So virulent did this anti-Zionism become that in the late twenties the *Freiheit* printed cartoons bordering on the anti-Semitic.) For years bitter debates had been conducted in the Yiddish press and in the milling streets of the big-city "garment centers," with the Communists on one side and the Socialists and Zionists on the other: debates that focused on such affecting issues as the desirability of a Jewish National

Home, the problem of maintaining a distinct Jewish cultural life, and the character of the powerful needle-trade unions that were led by Jewish Socialists whom the Communists denounced as betrayers of the working class.

Now all was to be changed. The Communists found it possible to say a kind word for Palestine. They acknowledged that they were coming closer to the political outlook of those right-wing Socialists or ex-Socialists who controlled the Jewish labor movement. And they found, as if on demand, a host of virtues in Jewish cultural traditions for which they had previously shown little but contempt. Moissaye Olgin, leader of the Jewish Communists, declared that from now on they would be "the best sons and daughters of the Jewish people." In former years, he admitted,

> . . . We managed to alienate the Jewish masses. More than that, we managed to convey an idea that the Communists are hostile to the Jewish national aspirations. We fought Zionism, which was correct, but in fighting Zionism, we forgot that many progressive elements of the Jewish people were Zionistically inclined. We forgot also that the craving, the desire, for nationhood is not in itself reactionary, although Zionism is reactionary.

The earlier Communist attitude toward Zionism Olgin now repudiated as "national nihilism." To the somewhat bewildered Jewish Communists, for whom atheism had been a cry to battle, he declared that "we must learn not to scoff at religion." And he proposed as a road to the Jewish masses that the Communists establish themselves as "inheritors of the best in Jewish culture." [21]

In this area the Communists scored notable successes. A maze of organizations was thrown up in the Jewish neighborhoods of the big cities—some devoted to Yiddish folk singing, others to sick and death benefits, some to mandolin ensembles, others to propaganda for Biro-Bidjan, the Siberian province set aside by the Russian government for settlement by Jews already living in Russia. (Biro-Bidjan provided a not very persuasive reply to those critics who noted that Russia had done nothing to admit into its territory refugees from Nazi Germany.) In all these organizations the Communists played a leading and skillful role. Particularly successful in tapping the latent idealism and personal insecurities of immigrant Jewish workers were the many Workers Clubs established by the Communists. By creating a self-enclosed life that catered to the social, cultural, and political needs of Jewish workers, such organizations served as an important reservoir both for new recruits and for loyal supporters of party policy in the Jewish trade unions.

While all these shifts were taking place in Communist policy, in the tone of party life and discourse, and in the relationships established between the members and the outer world, the party keenly understood that everything now depended upon its ability to preserve an inner elite which, without the need for explicit directives, would defend its monolithic politics and total discipline. This goal was not always easy to achieve. By its very nature, the Popular Front policy made for a loosening of party organization. Many of the best militants had dropped out in the mid-thirties, some from political disagreement and more from exhaustion.* The rate of fluctuation in membership remained high. ("Half our membership spends its time keeping the other half in the party," reported the Bronx CP membership director.) Those party leaders, like William Z. Foster and Charles Krumbein, who felt a bit uneasy over the extremes to which Browder was driving the Popular Front, kept stressing the dangers of being washed away by waves of middle-class recruits. Wrote Foster:

> These middle-class professionals, when equipped with Leninist-Stalinist training, and a genuine Communist outlook, are of great service. . . . Their entry presents to the Party new problems and tasks. . . . [These] boil down to the issue of how to make use of the [professionals] to further our central objective of broadening and strengthening the proletarian base . . . of the CP.
>
> Especially now that our Party . . . is becoming an important political factor, we can expect that it will attract many opportunists and careerists.

* The behavior of the party veterans is indicated in the following report: "It was really humorous, if not tragic, to see a few of the old sectarian language comrades view the new workers joining the Party. Some in fact stayed away from branch meetings till they made 'sure' the newcomers were OK."

But such voices were as voices in the wind. Foster's carefully paced grumbling reflected a temperamental bias but no fundamental or considered criticism of the Popular Front. And the truth is that the party succeeded very well in keeping itself intact during the Popular Front period. Perhaps the best indication of this was the way it reacted to the Moscow trials. Among certain intellectual sympathizers the Communists lost a good deal of support, but the Popular Front mood was not significantly dispelled by the shock of the trials. That the Communist who could issue the democratic proclamations of the Popular Front could also defend the terror of the Russian purges was a stark contradiction, but precisely upon this contradiction rested the success of Communist policy. Given the esoteric faith of the inner party core, the party could circumscribe a wide arc of maneuver without risking its organizational distinctiveness.

A small incident—but one profoundly revealing of Stalinist psychology—illustrates the point. In 1937 a CP branch thought up a device for dramatizing the meaning of the Moscow trials for those who attended its meetings. "On the Trotskyist treason trials in the Soviet Union," ran its report, "actual testimony was selected and prepared. Members then read it and performed it as it occurred at the trial." [22] Whether the reading was followed by a mock execution of the defendants is not known.

As the party deepened its Popular Front involvements, a slow change took place among its leaders. Most of the old war horses remained on the Central Committee, but with their power reduced and their secondary status made explicit. Foster took the role of respected elder statesman, writing frequent but not major articles for *The Communist,* making the more militant speeches at conventions, and finding time to publish two autobiographies. For a while at least, he was a thoroughly shorn lion. Other leaders such as Minor, Hathaway, Ford, and Stachel, men long familiar with ideological roller-coasting, adapted themselves to the new line without much difficulty. More often than not, however, new figures were pushed to the head of the movement: Ben Davis, a talented lawyer with a following in the Negro world; Robert Thompson, a hero of the Spanish Civil War and a more conspicuously "clean-cut

American" than some of the older leaders; Eugene Dennis, who had helped build a strong party concentration in the Pacific Northwest. But the central and undisputed Communist leader during the Popular Front period, and the only one besides Foster to become nationally known, was Earl Browder.

A rather small, wizened man with the bearing of a small-town lawyer or politician, quite without the charm or wit of such contemporary political leaders as Franklin Roosevelt and Norman Thomas, Browder had grown up in a lower-middle-class Kansas family, left school at nine to work as a cash boy in a department store, and then moved from miscellaneous clerking to Socialist politics. During the First World War he had twice been sentenced to Leavenworth for opposing the war, and upon his release he had become active in the Communist movement.

Among the Communist leaders, none of them notable for intellectual independence, Browder had always been especially distinguished for the docility with which he obeyed Comintern orders. It was a gift that earned him the leadership of the American party. For a time he had worked in China as a Comintern agent and then, during the early thirties, had taken command of the American party in order—ironically, if one bears in mind his later career—to carry out the ultra-left policy of the Third Period. Foster, though clearly the most notable public figure in the American party, suffered the humiliation of seeing his former lieutenant placed above him, in part as punishment for having shown during the faction fights of the late twenties an occasional impulse toward independence such as Browder either never knew or had carefully suppressed. Though a drab speaker, a pedestrian writer, and a "theoretician" whose few ventures into Marxist casuistry fell painfully flat, Browder nonetheless proved the right man to lead the CP during the Popular Front period. He was shrewd. He had a sharp eye for the neat maneuver in a trade union, the clever "arrangement" in a front organization, the necessary pliancy and deceit in relations with sympathizers; and within the party he could play the role of stern mentor, pounding the table as an intransigent defender of the faith who did not hesitate to smash opponents and settle old faction scores on the sly. Under his leadership, the Popular Front policy of the Communists

acquired an importance in the United States that could never have
been surmised merely by checking statistics of party membership.

4. Though first conceived as a strategic maneuver, the Popular Front could succeed only if it became a climate of opinion.
The party had to be able to wield an influence—indirect and seldom
acknowledged—far greater than it could claim in its own right; and
for this the front organizations were indispensable. Not that the
technique of the front group was a new one: it had been used by
the Communists long before the Popular Front. But where it had
once made for a mere duplication of the faithful, it now succeeded
in widely diffusing the few slogans and notions that mattered most
to the party.

The innumerable front organizations with their inflated membership lists; with their rosters of "distinguished names" winding
across stationery like columns of Mexican generals; with their
swelling rhetoric of "unity, unity, unity" which made disagreement
seem a subtle version of disloyalty; with their assumption that all
political problems could usefully be lost in the rhetoric of progressivism; with their conscious exploitation of the yearning felt by so
many middle-class and semi-intellectual Americans to take their
stand on the "right" side—these front organizations now became a
prominent feature of American life, respectable in manner, expert
in technique, and certainly far more influential than their numbers
actually warranted.

> The corruption of the front technique [Daniel Bell has
> noted] was that many poor dupes, imagining that they were the
> leaders of the great causes, found themselves enslaved by the
> opium of publicity and became pliable tools of the communist
> manipulators behind the scenes. In other instances upper-class
> matrons and aspiring actresses found in the communist "causes" a
> cozy nonconformism to replace their passé conventions. The
> ultimate betrayal was of the masses of front members who gained
> a sense of participation which they sadly discovered to be spurious
> when the party line changed and they found that they themselves
> were victims of party manipulations.[23]

This is well put; yet one may question its picture of innocents who sadly discover they have been manipulated by the party machine. Some of the non-Communist members of the front groups were indeed naïfs who sincerely believed that the League Against War and Fascism was precisely what its name declared it to be. But a good many of the people who joined the front organizations were not deceived at all. These were the people who acquiesced in and winked at the process of deception that made them its apparent victims. They were people whose sympathies lay essentially with the Communists but whose personal situations or characters kept them from assuming the burdens of party membership, and who felt that the least they could do was to help the party build and smoothly control the front organizations. As their "contribution" they would often assume a variety of roles, from that of the professed near-Communist to that of the honest worker or utterly non-political citizen who simply wanted to lend his mite to the struggle against fascism. And it gave these people a vicarious delight to see the party spin its web of manipulation and to feel that, in however modest a way, they too helped with the spinning—that they too labored for a vast movement extending from Shanghai to Havana, from the Urals to Brooklyn Heights. Nor did the party have to coach these actors in the mock drama of the front organization: they came to each performance with their lines rehearsed and parts prepared. They were Good Volunteers.

By far the most important of the front organizations was the American League Against War and Fascism. This organization, which capitalized upon the deepest sentiments of the whole "progressive" sector of the American population, was formed in 1933, after an international Congress Against War that had been organized the previous year in Amsterdam by the Stalinist writers Romain Rolland and Henri Barbusse. Since the development of the American League was to be typical of that of most front organizations, it may be useful to glance briefly at its history.

At the very moment the American League was being formed, the heavy hand of Communist control had made itself felt. In an Arrangements Committee set up for the League's first congress, delegates from the Socialist Party proposed to "exclude from the Congress the [CP-controlled, dual union] Trade Union Unity

League, a proposal," scoffed Browder, "which was of course refused." [24] Feeling that the acceptance of TUUL delegates would automatically preclude any large-scale AFL participation, the Socialists withdrew, so that the only opposition to Communist control at the opening congress, held in the fall of 1933, came from a tiny bloc of delegates led by Jay Lovestone. When a proposal was made at this congress to add Lovestone to its Presiding Committee, the delegates broke out in a roar of opposition—a spontaneous response that might have been expected from an admittedly Communist meeting but was hardly in keeping with the pretense that the delegates were mainly "non-partisan" anti-fascists. In the rapturous words of the *Daily Worker,* Browder then rose to speak, "his first words . . . overwhelmed in a mighty storm of approving applause." "Comrades," he cried, apparently forgetting that he was not speaking at a party meeting, "we are not here to elevate into importance . . . little groups of renegades whose purpose in coming here is part of their moral preparation for intervention against the Soviet Union." That these words met with the wild approval of the delegates should have been enough to convince non-Communists as to who held the whip hand—had they really cared to know or had they not known all along. Browder himself did not hesitate to admit that, for all its 2,616 delegates, the congress "from the beginning was led by our Party quite openly but without infringing upon its broad non-Party character. . . ." [25]

The American League accepted both individual memberships and group affiliations—the latter a device which permitted it to claim an enormous number of adherents (at one point, seven and a half million!), though many members of the affiliated organizations probably knew nothing about it. In its first year the American League did not make any conspicuous progress. Its second congress, held in Chicago in 1934, was somewhat narrower in political composition than the first one.

> Over 70 percent of the total number of delegates [wrote a well-informed though hostile left-wing journal] represented the Communist Party or one of its numerous disguises—IWO, ILD, TUUL and other purely alphabetical combinations. . . . This of course was hardly enough for giving a "non-partisan" coloring to the Congress, so once again this coloring was supplied by our

well-known liberal friends [such as] Dr. Harry F. Ward (a professor of Christian ethics at the Union Theological Seminary). . . .*

A disenchanted party member gave a vivid impression of the inner mechanics of this second congress:

> The tremendous ovation every time the CP was mentioned, the ovations for Comrade Browder, were not signs of the strength of the Congress but of the weakness. . . . It is not enough for the credentials committee to report that there were 247 delegates from Defense and Civil Rights Organizations, 121 from Women's, 434 from Fraternal organizations etc. A true picture of the Congress' composition could only be gotten if the American League should publish the name of every organization that sent delegates, with the number of each. This they would not do, because we would see that the Fraternal delegates, numbering 434, were composed of about 430 from the IWO, Russian National Mutual Aid Society etc. . . .[26]

So it was that paper memberships were piled on top of paper memberships, creating a façade of paper strength so deceptive as to discourage any potential opposition from trying to dislodge the Communists from control. Fortified with paper outposts, defended by paper warriors, cheered by paper masses, and lodged fast in their paper stronghold, the Communists held the American League in their grip through unbreakable bonds of paper. And dissidents, who cared more for reality than for paper, either stayed home or dropped out.

In the nature of things, front organizations always limped a little behind the party in adjusting to changes of line. The process of rationalization in a front organization had to be a bit more cau-

---

* Dr. Ward was to remain a remarkably faithful leader of the American League, always ready to shift his steps when the Communist tune changed. The *Daily Worker* (October 24, 1939) recorded the following dialogue before a hearing of the Dies Committee: "When Rep. H. Jerry Voorhis maintained that there is a 'perpetual dictatorship' in the Soviet Union, Dr. Ward retorted: 'I know there isn't.'" There may be a sense in which it is still useful to say that someone like Dr. Ward was an innocent, but one would be hard pressed to specify exactly what that sense is.

tious and circumspect than in the party. *Sotto voce* cynicism would not quite do—especially if one's branch of the American League had a few genuinely innocent members—for explaining why collective security was replacing the traditional semi-pacifist, semi-Marxist stand on war. But by its third congress, in January, 1937, the American League had fully caught up with the Popular Front line. It was now close to being a "respectable" organization; it claimed affiliates with a total of more than two million members, of whom 460,000 were in trade unions; and, symptomatically, its congress was opened with a greeting from Mayor Harold Burton of Cleveland, who shared the platform with Dr. Ward and Browder. The personal memberships were still fewer than 10,000—and of these, according to an official party report, more than 10 percent were actual party members.[27] But the influence and power of the League was much greater than such figures might suggest.

Almost as if by design, there occurred at each of the American League's congresses an incident that neatly revealed the power of the Stalinist machine. At the trade union commission of the third congress, an old-time union leader, Max Hayes, who was not a fellow traveler, rose to express his indignation against the charge that the League was Communist-controlled. To put an end to such rumors once and for all, Hayes proposed a resolution that the League go on record against all dictatorships, including the Russian. Louis Weinstock, a Communist leader in the painters' union, quickly rose to suggest that the proposal be referred to the resolutions committee, where it could be buried quietly and without embarrassment. The only reference later made to Hayes' proposal came during the reading of resolutions to the congress, when it was remarked that "two resolutions submitted were not reported out by the committee because of their political character."[28] And then—how familiar was this tactic in the front organization!—there came the announcement that Max Hayes had been elected vice-chairman of the American League.

In opening the third congress Dr. Ward had made a point of stressing the anti-capitalist nature of the League:

Many times . . . those who come to our meetings ask us this: Is the American League anti-capitalist? Of course it is. How otherwise could it stop war? [Applause] How could we be against fascism without being against capitalism, seeing that fascism is an organized expression of capitalism in its declining period?

Though apparently one twist behind the comrades, Dr. Ward was the sort of friend who was eager to catch up. For a few months later, during his chairmanship, the American League published a Program Against War and Fascism which contained the following catechism:

> Is the American League an anti-capitalist organization? An anti-capitalist attitude is not a requirement for membership. Our only concern with capitalism is at the points where it breeds war and fascism. We are obliged to expose these points.[29]

By the League's fourth congress in 1937 these points had become invisible; not an anti-capitalist word remained in its program. To stress the extent of the shift engineered by the party, the name of the organization was changed to the American League for Peace and Democracy. (A movement pledged to collective security and its attendant risks did well not to declare itself "against war.") Also at this congress the Communist Party, with fanfares of self-congratulation, formally withdrew as a participating organization and Dr. Ward, in the true spirit of *noblesse oblige*, declared that "I have never worked with people who have played fairer or squarer than the Communist Party in dealing with the American League." [30] The claimed membership of the affiliated organizations was now over four million, and, perhaps more important, the CP-controlled unions in the CIO, particularly the National Maritime Union, contributed a solid bloc of delegates.

But the peak of influence exerted by the American League was reached at its fifth congress, in Washington, D. C., in January, 1939. A letter of welcome was received from Secretary of the Interior Harold Ickes: "The name of your organization must mean that you are committed to the policy of peace and the policy of democracy." (Did Ickes' verb suggest a veiled irony?) A few months earlier

Robert Jackson, another influential New Dealer, had wired the American League: "I am in full sympathy with your effort to demonstrate American peace sentiment." [31]

The fifth congress of the American League was an imposing, well-staged, and high-powered spectacle. No Communist (at least no publicly known Communist) gave an official speech of welcome, though greetings were delivered by Representative Walter Judd, Judith Epstein, National President of Hadassah, and J. Finley Wilson, Grand Exalted Ruler of the Improved Benevolent and Protective Order of the Elks. Two Congressmen were now on the National Committee of the American League: Jerry J. O'Connell of Montana and John T. Bernard of Minnesota. Delegates were present from the Young Judea, the YWCA, the Student Christian Movement, and the National Intercollegiate Christian Council. An impressive labor committee was set up, which, apart from the numerous Communist and fellow-traveling leaders of CIO unions, claimed such non-Communists as A. F. Whitney of the Trainmen's Brotherhood, Major Berry of the Pressmen, and A. Philip Randolph of the AFL Sleeping Car Porters. The membership of affiliated organizations was listed as being over seven million, with two million of these in trade unions; the personal membership was announced as slightly less than 20,000. [32]

Browder, it is true, was no longer listed as a vice-president of the American League, but surely this was a small price to pay for so enormously lucrative an investment as the American League had proved to be for the Communists. The American League spread the Popular Front line far more widely than the party itself could; it was a source of new recruits and sympathizers; and above all, it was a respectable agency through which to influence Congressmen, labor leaders, and public figures who could not be reached by open Communists. Throughout the late thirties the American League received an extraordinarily good press, sometimes even in the daily papers and almost always in the influential liberal journals. In the solar system of front organizations what mattered was not so much the influence that the party exerted upon Front Group A as the influence that Front Group A exerted upon the somewhat more distant Front Group B and Front Group B upon organizations outside the solar system entirely.*

No one can say how strong the American League might have become if the Hitler-Stalin pact had not destroyed the whole Popular Front myth. But once the pact was announced it became clear that the days of the League were numbered—and that the Communists, turning toward an entirely new tactic, would soon be impatient to get it out of the way. During the months immediately after the pact,

---

* It is worth noting, as an example of Popular Front diffusion, the consistently uncritical and sometimes deceptive coverage given the American League by the *New Republic*.

Item: ". . . The League has represented the most realistic attempt thus far to coordinate American anti-war sentiment. . . . Lately the door to such a 'united front' effort has been considerably widened, first by the intelligent shifts in Communist policy toward radical and trade-union leaders, second by the capable and honest direction furnished the League by such men as Dr. Harry F. Ward, and finally by the terrifying onrush of the war peril. . . .

"The Congress of the American League will be anxiously watched by hundreds of thousands who have heretofore remained aloof, but now recognize the importance of its mission." This encomium was written in 1936 by James Wechsler, then a close ally of the Communists in the student movement.

Item: "During the first two years of its life, the League was handicapped in its growth because of the suspicion held by some that it was merely an instrument of the Communist Party. But it now seems reasonable to say that these suspicions have proved groundless. . . . It is clear by now that the CP's interest in the League is only seeing that it becomes the largest and broadest front possible against the common menace of war and fascism." This disingenuous passage appeared in an article written by William Mangold, national treasurer of the American League, in 1936—though the *New Republic* failed to inform its readers that he held this post.

Item: "The Communists have given invaluable aid to the League in promoting peace and democracy and will doubtless continue, as individuals, to do so." This praise for the party came from Robert Morss Lovett in 1937. Lovett was a vice-chairman of the League but was not identified as such in the *New Republic*.

Only after the Russian invasion of Finland had completely cut the ground from under the Popular Front did the celebrations of the American League in the *New Republic* give way to candid reporting. In 1940 Alson Smith, the non-Communist director of religious work for the American League (this time the connection with the organization was not avoided), wrote with a certain naïveté but also with obvious honesty: "The League could have denounced Russia and run the risk of being gradually transformed into another Hoover Aid Committee [hardly a pressing danger!] or it could have refused to denounce Russia and become an out-and-out adjunct of the Communist Party. . . . From September 1939 the League lost an average of slightly more than 1000 members a month." [33]

almost no money came into the League's national office, so rapidly did its following melt away. An effort was made to avoid issuing foreign-policy statements, but this obvious evasion could not long be continued. In October, 1939, a special congress of the American League was hastily contrived, and here the Communists managed to maintain control, passing resolutions in support of the Soviet Union's "peace policy" and refusing to condemn the Hitler-Stalin pact. But when a farewell dinner was announced for the ineffable Dr. Ward in February, 1940, the end of a deception—a skillful and a profitable deception—had finally been reached. Not, however, before Dr. Ward could declare that there "is an increasing recognition in the League that the actions of the Soviet Union have given Hitler more of a check than a help." [34] Those whom ideology would destroy it first makes faithful.

5. No other front organization was nearly as important as the American League, but two or three should at least be mentioned.

In the area of Negro work the Communists found the turn toward Popular Frontism easier to make and more immediately advantageous than almost anywhere else. For a time, the fact that Soviet Russia kept selling oil to Italy even after Mussolini had invaded Ethiopia hindered the party's efforts to achieve a cozy relationship with the NAACP, the Negro ministers, and the Negro labor leaders. Explaining this behavior of the "Workers Fatherland" proved somewhat awkward for the dialecticians of the *Daily Worker,* and a number of Negro Communists left the party in disgust. But though Ethiopia could rouse passionate sympathies among a handful of Negro intellectuals and nationalists, it seemed terribly remote to most American Negroes, who were preoccupied with their own desperate economic and socio-political problems. This was not an issue upon which the Communists could be defeated in the Negro world.

It is therefore understandable that the new "reasonableness" of the Communists—in behalf of which they did not hesitate to sneer at their own immediate past—should have seemed persuasive to many American Negroes who felt that the common condition of having and suffering for a black skin was more important than any

fine shadings of doctrine. James W. Ford, Benjamin Davis, Jr.,
Angelo Herndon might be Communists; they might even be Communists whom many Negroes scoffed at for being subservient to the
white party leaders; but when Ford or Davis walked through the
streets of Harlem he was recognized as, in some sense, "one of us."
At times, when the pain of segregation grew intolerable, even the
most determined Negro anti-Communist could not help feeling that
the bond of common subjection bound him together with the Negro
Communist. It was a sentiment that had some basis in reality and
that no outsider had a right merely to dismiss. It was a sentiment
that the Communists deliberately exploited.

The National Negro Congress—the main front organization in
the Negro community during the Popular Front period—had
originally been set up by such prominent Negroes as Ralph Bunche,
A. Philip Randolph, and Lester Granger, who were neither party
members nor fellow travelers yet felt, at the time, that it was
possible to work with Communists. An aggressive movement speaking for the Negro community seemed a genuine need; the NAACP
did not answer this need; consequently, when the call for the new
organization went out, it met with an immediate response. It came
at a time when the Negro community enjoyed a greater self-confidence and a higher morale than it had had for some years, partly
because the New Deal had improved the life of the Negroes, partly
because thousands of Negro workers had gained a new awareness
and hope during the organization of the CIO.

When the National Negro Congress was created in 1936, it
was far less of a political dummy than most of the front organizations. Though the Negro Congress did not succeed in establishing
itself as a mass movement, the political spectrum among its leaders
was rather wide and included a majority of non-Communists.

At first the Communists stayed ostentatiously in the background, deliberately refraining from too obvious control. But from
the very beginning their ability to provide organizational forces,
experienced personnel, and a variety of skills assured them a powerful role. The non-Communists might show up for meetings and
congresses, *but the Communists were there every day.* That, indeed,
was half the secret of their ability to control all of the front groups.
And as long as they kept stressing the need for common action by all

Negroes, they were certain to win a hearing, if only because—on the face of things—what they said made a good deal of sense. To ask who was saying it, and why, took more sophistication in radical politics than many Negro leaders could command.

That the Congress remained essentially a paper organization during its first year or two of existence did not trouble the party too much. What mattered to it was that, through the Congress, Negro Communists were able to establish a whole network of friendly relations with important figures in both the white and Negro worlds. (In one of its aspects, the politics of the Popular Front was a politics of celebrities.) After a time local units of the NAACP and CIO were successfully wooed. At the 1937 meeting of the National Negro Congress such distinguished figures as Walter White, Philip Murray, and Norman Thomas spoke at the opening sessions. Through the Negro Congress' youth section, which was led by the Communist Edward Strong, preliminary contacts—very valuable to the party—were established with a number of Southern Negro youth leaders. In cities like Detroit and Chicago strong Congress branches were built up, providing the Communists with an excellent forum, recruiting ground, and political cover. When Gunnar Myrdal traveled through the country in 1938 and 1939 he noted that "the local councils of the National Negro Congress were the most important Negro organizations in some Western cities." [35] If Myrdal exaggerated, it was not by very much; there could be no question that in the Negro Congress the Communists had found an organization of great value to themselves.

By 1937 the Communists had firmly established their control over the Congress. Most of the non-Communist leaders had dropped out, though the proportion of "innocents" in the membership almost certainly remained higher than in other front groups. Yet, shortly after the Hitler-Stalin pact, it suddenly collapsed. Why, one may wonder, did the Negro front organizations have a way of tumbling apart even faster and more completely than the others? Perhaps for the very reason that they had been more substantial to begin with. A good many Negroes who belonged to or sympathized with the Congress took its manifest purpose with complete seriousness, so that when the moment of disillusion did come they were likely to leave with an abrupt bitterness. From the party's point of view, however, this was not an utter catastrophe, for the Communists worked on the principle: *unto each period its own front groups.* And the National Negro Congress had paid off.

Equally profitable, perhaps even more so, were the front groups in the student and youth areas. The American Student Union, formed in late 1935 out of a merger of Socialist and Communist student organizations, passed into the effective control of the young Communists within about a year. Against the bloc of Stalinists pretending to be liberals and liberals wondering whether it might not be interesting to become Stalinists, the Socialist opposition proved helpless. Though never claiming more than 20,000 members and never having nearly that many, the ASU became a significant institution on the American campus. The fiery young Communists of two or three years earlier now learned to dance the shag, comb their hair, speak in modulated accents, look determinedly pretty. Attractive new leaders, such as James Wechsler and Celeste Strack, were pushed into the forefront of the "student movement," while a handful of pliant young Socialists, led by Joseph P. Lash, remained within the ASU, deceived or flattered into collaborating with the Communists. Gradually the ASU dropped the more militant tokens of traditional student radicalism—the Marxist vocabulary, the anti-war strikes, the pacifist Oxford pledge—and became the very model of a junior Popular Front. Wechsler and Lash, widely advertised as authoritative spokesmen for the younger generation, even won the hearts of some New Dealers, while Miss Strack, a cool young woman, advised the few student radicals who found the new respectability oppressive to read Lenin's *Left Wing Communism: An Infantile Disorder.* Like most other front groups, the ASU appropriated the role of acknowledged representative of the "progressive" students simply because there was no coherent competition.

Its importance was never as a mass student movement, for except in a few colleges like the University of Chicago, CCNY, and Brooklyn College the ASU could never claim any large membership. Quite unintentionally, it became a training ground for the postwar political and intellectual elite. (American radicalism has always functioned as a kind of prep school for leaders of American capitalist society.) Here the liberal spokesmen of the fifties, the successful government, trade-union, and professional figures, could learn to make speeches, to maneuver and manipulate.[36] Had the Popular Front survived into the war years, the ASU would unquestionably have been its major source of new leadership; as it was, its most gifted figures drifted into liberalism, academic life, or anonymity, and the organization itself suffered the same fate as the other front groups of the thirties.

A more unusual sort of front organization was the American Youth Congress, which had been started by vague young liberals and was soon captured by specific young Communists. The AYC had no individual members at all but functioned strictly as a clearing house for other youth organizations. In 1939 it claimed the affiliation of groups with a total of almost five million members, and clearly, even after the usual discounts have been made for exaggeration, the number was both substantial and impressive. Nor could many of these organizations be dismissed as under Communist control. Yet the young Communists found it easier to manipulate an organization like the AYC, which was merely a vast hollow of affiliates, than a small-membership organization in which dissidents might confront them face to face.

The mechanics through which the Communists controlled the AYC are worth glancing at. Let us suppose that a local branch of a Methodist youth organization, numbering a thousand, affiliated with the AYC. Generally this would happen after one member—he might be a young Communist who had "colonized" or, better yet, a Methodist with "progressive" leanings—took the floor to propose affiliation to a Congress representing all of American youth. What, after all, could seem more reasonable? And naturally it would be the member who had made the proposal that would probably be sent as delegate to the AYC. Soon most of the other young Methodists turned back to their Methodism and forgot about the AYC, while their delegate continued to "represent" them. Thus, to control the bloc of votes he held, the AYC leadership needed to deal only with him and, more often than not, could ignore the members of his organization. It was neat.

Perhaps the major activity of the AYC was to work for the passage of the American Youth Act, which proposed that the government sponsor vocational training and employment on public enterprises at wages of $25 a week for unemployed youth between sixteen and twenty-five years old. This bill was never passed, but the agitation for it played a role in helping to improve the National Youth Administration, a sort of WPA for young people. Lobbying for the youth bill also enabled the AYC leaders to reach important New Dealers and especially Mrs. Eleanor Roosevelt, who soon developed a warm maternal-political interest in the AYC despite warnings that it was not quite the liberal assembly that she supposed. Years later she wrote that on one occasion she had asked the AYC leaders to tell her whether any of them were Communists and that "in every case they said they had no connection with the Communists, had never belonged to any Communist organization, and had no interest in Communist ideas. I decided to accept their word, realizing that sooner or later the truth would come out." [37] That it might come out too late, however, was a problem Mrs. Roosevelt did not discuss.

Through its Washington connections, the AYC established itself as a sort of self-appointed bargaining agent for American youth. AYC leaders such as Joseph Cadden, Abbot Simon, and William Hinckley were repeatedly consulted by the officials of the National Youth Administration. From 1936 through 1939 the only youth organization represented on the NYA Advisory Committee was the AYC—which gave it an unearned status almost like that of a "union" enjoying a closed shop. As late as June, 1940, when President Roosevelt wanted to "communicate with the young people," he arranged, upon his wife's suggestion, to bring the AYC leaders to the White House for an evening of discussion. A quarrel broke out between Roosevelt and Harry Hopkins, on the one side, and the AYC leaders, on the other; yet it is remarkable that a President who in his years at the White House had seldom given a similar hearing to any other single group thought it useful to argue with Cadden, Carl Ross, and Edward Strong. If important people could be deluded into treating the AYC as if it had real strength, then it would indeed have real strength.[38]

The ability of the AYC to ingratiate itself in Washington circles was only one of the ways by which the Communists worked themselves into the government apparatus during the Popular Front period. It lies beyond the scope of this book—nor is there yet enough reliable information—to measure the exact degree of Communist success in penetrating New Deal agencies. But it would be absurd to deny that the party and its friends did penetrate government agencies, and sometimes with telling effect. Under the supervision of Harold Ware, a son of Mother Bloor, these cells were devoted to influencing governmental policies, though some of their members were also drawn into an espionage network. Daniel Bell has written sensibly on this topic:

> At one time . . . the Communists exercised an influential voice in the National Labor Relations Board, where Nathan Witt was general counsel and Edwin S. Smith was one of the three-man board. The decisions of the NLRB . . . helped the nascent CIO considerably. . . . The extent of Communist influence, as revealed by the Mundt-Nixon-Wood-McCarthy exposures of 1950 is, I believe, somewhat exaggerated. Such influence was, however, *intensive* in the several agencies where Communist cells were able to gain a strategic position. . . . This was particularly true of the Department of Agriculture and the NLRB in the late thirties. . . .[39]

A particular difficulty in discussing this problem is that in the years after the Second World War it became an explosive and misused political issue. Conservative critics of the New Deal made severe and frequently exaggerated charges about the extent of Communist penetration; some of them were malicious in suggesting that New Dealers were characteristically receptive to secret agents from the left; and the few who claimed that the entire course of recent American history, from the social legislation of the New Deal to foreign policy in China, was the consequence of Communist infiltration were succumbing to a paranoid fantasy. On the other hand, those liberal apologists who tried to persuade us that there was no important Communist penetration at all were doing neither liberalism nor the truth a service.

What is politically important—we leave aside the problem of espionage—lies in the relation between the Popular Front temper and the attitudes of some New Dealers. To say, as have the more extreme right-wing critics, that something inherent in New Deal liberalism made it soft toward Communism, is irresponsible. Yet it seems beyond dispute that *some* New Dealers, with their vaguely

"progressive" social outlook, their floating sense of class identification, and their oppressive burden of class guilt, were prepared to be
particularly friendly toward Popular Front rhetoric and to look upon
Communists as somewhat impractical "progressives in a hurry." For
which liberals this was true, we need hardly specify; but that it *was*
true for some of them no student of the thirties is likely to deny.

Without the front organizations, the Popular Front atmosphere
would have been impossible and from the front organizations the
Communists recruited heavily; but in the long run it was the atmosphere that for them mattered most. To the degree that a significant
minority of Americans was induced to think in terms derived from
or harmonious with the Popular Front, the Communists could
claim success. We are not trying to suggest that such ideas as collective security were simply the product of a party conspiracy; surely
the proposal for a common front against the Nazis would have been
politically popular even if there had not been a single Communist
in the country. But the particular shape and tone that the Popular
Front movement took in the United States was largely the work of
the Communists. It was they who gave it coherence and expression,
who inspired its activities and formulated its slogans. Political moods
are always potentially available; it takes organized movements to
crystallize them and transform them into modes of power.

On the other hand, no amount of organizational effort could
have mattered very much unless the social climate had been favorable to the outlook and psychology of the Popular Front. During the
late thirties, when the acceptance of Popular Front ideas was most
pervasive in certain areas of American life, people were still living
with acute memories of the depression; the fear of fascism was deep
and genuine; many Americans had lost their earlier unquestioning
confidence in the *status quo* and, while not prepared to become its
intransigent critics, were certainly receptive to a number of schemes
for progressive social reform. The attachment to the symbols of an
undifferentiated political progressivism was widespread in the labor
movement, the universities, and the cultural and entertainment
worlds. If President Roosevelt gave the most significant national
expression to this social impulse, the Stalinists, in their more limited
way, succeeded in exploiting it for their own ends. Many of their
front activities may in retrospect seem absurd or transparent, but it

should be remembered that they were tapping genuine hopes and fears. Their tactics might be crude in the American League Against War and Fascism or in the National Negro Congress, but because these tactics took advantage of felt needs, the Communists kept making steady gains. And while the American party never became a mass organization like the French CP, not even its most violent enemies could deny that in both the labor movement and the cultural world it was jockeying itself into positions of genuine power. Its membership grew steadily, its influence increased, and its circle of effective sympathizers widened.

6. The Popular Front was not merely a political tactic; it was also, and in the United States even more importantly, a kind of culture. Some of its cultural expressions were little more than the mechanical improvisation of party hacks, applicable to almost any intellectual area because utterly without respect for the material it exploited. Under the promptings of the Popular Front there blossomed, for example, a school of "historiography" which transformed almost every figure in the American past into a progressive political ancestor. How Stalinist leaders were attached to the American past has already been noticed; even more curious was the assimilation of the American past to the needs of party strategy.

No iconography was too outrageous for the Communist historians. "The army Washington led," wrote one Communist, "was a true people's army. . . . He was no 'softy' in shooting Tory traitors, spies and cowards. . . . He had to fight counter-revolutionary treachery in his ranks" (as Stalin did too). Benjamin Franklin, that solid Philadelphia burgher, became another pre-Popular Front hero:

Those "pacifists" who are now playing the reactionary game by proposing non-resistance to fascist aggressions should learn from Franklin's life how an American revolutionary forefather defended the freedoms of our country. . . . Franklin was a true internationalist.

That Abraham Lincoln would be fair game in this heady remaking of the past was entirely predictable; but it was characteristic of the indifference to scruple with which the Communists went about this job that almost everyone in the national past, except Benedict Arnold, Aaron Burr, and Alexander Hamilton (said to have been friendly to banks), became a champion of "the people." And not only did they seize upon the country's revered heroes, they were also ready to appropriate its more attractive villains. A good word was found in the *Daily Worker* for Jesse James, who "while not a working class hero . . . belonged to that class, and it protected him."

Perhaps the supreme curiosity among Communist ventures into American history was Earl Browder's *Traitors in American History: Lessons of the Moscow Trial,* in which he noted that "like Burr, Trotsky relies mainly upon the extravagances of his plots to obtain non-belief in their exposure." With cheerful cynicism, Browder pursued his historical analogy:

> It took the US government 38 years before it finally suppressed the treasonable circles that had arisen in the first days of the revolution. . . . The Soviet Union has dug out and liquidated its treasonable sects in only half of that time. . . .[40]

It was characteristic of the Popular Front approach, whether toward the historical past or contemporary culture, that distinctions of intellectual quality tended to disappear before the overriding question of whether someone was or was not on the "side of the people." In 1938 the *Daily Worker* burst into praise for Whitford Kane, an actor who played the gravedigger to Maurice Evans' Hamlet, because he had managed to sneak in "the anti-fascist salute" during his scene. Said Kane to the *Worker:*

> Here's how I feel in my part. . . . The rich girl, Ophelia, drowns herself, and by all that is right a suicide is not allowed to have a Christian burial. When she gets one I resent it. "Shall great folk who drown or hang themselves get privileges not given a suicide of the poor class?" I ask. And there I raise my hand.

To dismiss this sort of thing as mere tomfoolery would be a total misunderstanding of the Popular Front psychology; for it was this outlook that, precisely through its vulgarity, helped smooth the way for fellow travelers on the stage, in Hollywood, and in radio.

Like modern advertising, with which it had deep spiritual affinities, the Popular Front outlook aimed at indiscriminate saturation of the audience rather than intellectual quality.

It was this outlook that motivated a good many WPA theater productions: right or wrong, faithful to the text or not, but raise your hand in the proper salute! This was the outlook that led the Brooklyn WPA theater to stage *Julius Caesar* so as "to emphasize the dictator angle and show Brutus as the defender of the rights of free men"—no doubt in imitation of Orson Welles, himself one of the cultural monuments of the Popular Front era. It led the *Daily Worker* to proclaim, with all due solemnity, that "Hollywood has become the West Coast center of progressivism," but also to complain, with equal solemnity, that in Western movies "the redman has not yet gotten the chance to tell his side of the story." It led a Popular Front poet, James Neugass, to declare, "When American writers learn how to be public figures, then they'll turn out good stuff." It led Martha Graham to stage a dance, "American Document," for a *New Masses* benefit which a party critic hailed because its imitation of events from the American past was as immediately recognizable as a Currier and Ives print. It led to the historical novels of Howard Fast, in which progressives and reactionaries replaced—but were certainly no improvement on—good and bad guys. It led the party to poll the delegates to its 1938 convention on their favorite movie stars and proudly announce that their taste was just like any other American's: "The favorite movie actress was Claudette Colbert while tall, dark and handsome Gary Cooper won the honors in the male division." But most typically and with a lovely sort of unconscious humor, it led the *Daily Worker* to exclaim in 1938, concerning the newest triumph of the Broadway front group, Theatre Arts Committee:

> It's gone and happened. People everywhere in the progressive, audacious and outspoken theatre have talked about it for so long. . . . But it's here—the social-minded night club.[41]

There, indeed, was the perfect symbol for at least one side of Popular Frontism: the social-minded night club.*

---

* This incomplete record of Popular Front achievements requires at least a word about sports. During the early thirties the *Daily Worker* had

Between the "progressive" sentiments of Popular Front politics and a certain kind of urban middle-brow cultural yearning there was a deep rapport—most of all, in a common anxiety and pathos—which the Communists brilliantly exploited. The phenomenon of mass culture is pervasive in modern industrial society, but there can be little doubt that at least part of its contemporary American flavor is a heritage of the Popular Front. Even after the Popular Front lay shattered, deep into the forties and fifties, the style of American mass culture retained many of its crucial elements: in the Hollywood and TV drama, where stress upon the amiable fumblings of "the little man" constituted a simple displacement of social consciousness; in musical comedies, where the exploitation of regional "folk" quaintness replaced social satire; in the historical novel; in the cult of city-made folk dancing and singing; and perhaps most important, in a quivering, folksy, and insinuating style—*vibrato intime*—which came to favor in the Popular Front press, reached a kind of apotheosis in the newspaper *PM*, and has since become a national affliction.

Finally, it was Spain—the Spain of civil war—that brought out the best and the worst in the Popular Front mind. The feeling that Spain was the test of a generation, that here, against the armies of Franco, Hitler, and Mussolini, men were making a last stand against fascism, rested upon truth. But in the world of the Popular Front this feeling was corrupted by a willful refusal to acknowledge —even to inquire into the possibility—that behind the Loyalist lines a new terror was being spread by the Stalinists. Only a few Americans were capable of George Orwell's double vision: that free men should passionately align themselves with the Loyalist side and yet recognize that within the republic terrible things were happening.

For the Popular Front in America, for the middle-class fellow travelers and the middle-brow progressives, Spain made possible a vicarious participation, a thrill over cocktails. Here is a report—it

---

given some space to union and YCL sport activities. By the time the Popular Front was established, the *Worker* put together a quite professional sports page, covering major league baseball, big-time boxing, and professional football. Apart from a worthy stress upon getting Negroes into baseball, there remained but one touch of the old Communist spirit: each year, as spring training began, the party's sports writers would take their place unambiguously on the side of the holdouts.

would be malicious to claim that this was typical of American attitudes toward Spain, but it would be preposterous to suppose that
it was unique—published by the North American Committee to Aid
Spanish Democracy:

Fiesta for Spain

A highly successful benefit for Spanish refugee children was
held on Saturday, August 14, at the New City estate of Adolph
Zukor, movie magnate, under the auspices of the Rockland
County Milk Fund, a branch of the North American Committee.
The Spanish Fiesta, which was sponsored by Mrs. Franklin D.
Roosevelt, Mrs. Caroline O'Day, and a group of stage and screen
notables, was estimated to have attracted 8,500 people from 24
states. . . .

The committee in charge was headed by Mrs. Henry Varnum
Poor, wife of the famous painter, and included a group of celebrities who make their summer residence in Rockland County. . . .

The wide publicity given the affair . . . resulted in the
formation of a Hollywood Fiesta Committee to raise funds for
Spanish refugee children.

Fund-raising affairs for Spain did so well that the Communists,
who were systematically nowhere in sight, issued a bulletin on how
to use them:

Have a "guest book" to register names and addresses. This
makes a mailing list afterwards. . . . Add refreshments, dancing,
mix well and dish out! . . . For beer parties, comrades, remember that pouring in the middle gives more foam and less liq-
uid. . . .[42]

There were a few, however, who gave more than foam: the
young Communists who left their homes to fight in Spain. Deluded
in the belief that Stalinism meant a better world, unable to distinguish between the radiant cause of Loyalist Spain and the totalitarian apparatus to which they were bound, they stood ready to die
in a doomed battle against the fascism of Franco. And some of them
died.

7. By far the most substantial achievement of the Popular Front period, perhaps the greatest single success of American Communism, was the penetration of the CIO. The full story of this penetration cannot be told here—it has, in any case, been told elsewhere; but a few dominant features need pointing up, if only to indicate how Stalinism did succeed in becoming a significant force in American life during the late thirties.

In 1934 and 1935, the years when the Communists were trying to make the extremely difficult and painful turn from dual unionism to working within the AFL, they found themselves badly off balance in the unions. Ingrained political attitudes that had arisen among the Communist unionists during the TUUL days could not be discarded overnight. No matter what the party leadership might say, it was hard for the average Communist worker in the garment or maritime industry to feel genuine enthusiasm for a return to the AFL. He knew, far better than the party leaders who kept showering him with "directives," how difficult it would now be to reestablish himself in the AFL unions, how the old-line union leaders would be waiting to mock and sneer at him.

Once the Communists did make the decision to turn back to the AFL, they were determined to do it with a vengeance and not to be deluded by any further chimeras outside the established unions. Even after John L. Lewis had declared himself in favor of industrial unionism at the 1935 AFL convention, the Communists kept minimizing the issue. All through 1934 and 1935 the party leadership hammered away at the need for the comrades to dig into the AFL. In August, 1934, the *Party Organizer* pointed out that 90 percent of the strikes in the spring of that year had been led by AFL unions: there was, it implied, no point in expecting any major unionization elsewhere. Communists were told to cease behaving as if they always had to constitute an "opposition group" within the unions; now, like good AFL patriots, they were "to convince the workers . . . that the Communists are responsible trade union leaders." Apart from its strong element of duplicity, this effort of the CP leadership to reeducate the ranks on the virtues of the AFL had more than a touch of humor:

> Some of our comrades think that the AFL leadership does nothing but sit around plotting how to sell out strikes. We

cannot place the problem in so simple a manner. . . . Recently a letter was received from one of our leading comrades in Cincinnati giving a report on a strike in Norwood, Ohio. The workers returned to work having gained some very important concessions . . . an increase in wages, recognition of a shop committee etc. Our comrades estimate this strike as a complete sell-out. Such an estimation of the strike will not convince anyone.* [43]

For a time, indeed, it was Communist policy to urge AFL units not to affiliate with the CIO, and until the spring of 1937 the CP-led unions refused to join with Lewis; the party strategists feared that his committee might prove to be still another fly-by-night operation and that if they succumbed to this one they would never be able to reestablish Communist strength in the unions. Jack Stachel, the party's "expert" in trade unionism, wrote in June, 1935:

The crisis within the AFL Executive Council, of course, is not over policies for and against the workers. . . . These labor lieutenants of capitalism are fighting over the question of how best to prevent strikes, how to keep the masses chained to the policies of class collaboration.[44]

Had Communist tactics in the trade unions been no more skillful than Stachel's analysis, both the fortunes of the party and the history of the CIO would have been very different from what in fact they were. Stachel's extreme position soon had to be abandoned, and the CP began to speak endearingly of the more "progressive" AFL unions that were committed to John L. Lewis. But when the big CIO drive began in 1936, the Communist-led unions in the AFL still did not join with the Lewis group. As late as December, 1936, Browder was talking of "unity" in the labor movement, apparently unable to realize how extraordinary a phenomenon the CIO was or how extraordinary were the opportunities it offered for political penetration. When waves of strikes swept the country in 1936 and 1937 the Communists responded not so much to the overwhelming drama

* One of the recurrent marvels in Communist life is the way party leaders will criticize their followers for doing what the party itself taught them to do until a short while before.

of what was happening in the factories as to their own recent traumatic experiences with dual unionism. They were, so to speak, on the wagon again and determined not to fall off; but as it happened, the wagon itself was beginning to fall apart. For just at the moment they had decided to get back into the AFL at all costs, massive new industrial unions were being formed outside the AFL.

In 1934 alone there had been the San Francisco general strike led by Harry Bridges, a shrewd and ruthless unionist whose policies were seldom distinguishable from those of the Communists; two violent teamsters' strikes in Minneapolis led by the Trotskyist Dunne brothers, which attracted national attention; and a spectacular strike at the Toledo Auto-lite plant, where workers, reinforced by thousands of unemployed, battled National Guardsmen for two days. All through 1935 wildcat strikes were bursting out in the auto plants. By May spontaneous strikes had occurred in the Toledo Chevrolet and in Cleveland Fisher Body. In November the first great sit-down was staged in the Akron Goodyear plants—a spontaneous outbreak marking the real start, on a factory level, of the CIO upsurge. From Akron the flames of industrial unionism spread to Flint, where another sit-down strike forced General Motors to recognize the CIO auto union. At the very moment that this major change in the patterns of American industrial life was taking place, Earl Browder kept mumbling that "very careful study" remained necessary in order to determine "the correct policy" *vis-à-vis* the dispute between the AFL and the CIO.[45]

What was all the more remarkable about the slowness of the CP in recognizing the significance of the CIO was that the 1936 strikes were almost always called not by union leaders but by the workers themselves. The Communists, whatever their miscalculations about the thought processes of union leaders, prided themselves on keeping expertly informed on the temper of the men in the shops; but the truth is that at this crucial moment the CP leadership simply failed to realize how ready the industrial workers were for everything the CIO represented. It was fortunate for the CP that the wave of spontaneous strikes caught many party members and sympathizers in its motion and swirled them into posts of influence in the new unions. Responding instinctively to the new and exciting events, many Communists in the industrial towns plunged into the organizing drive—which meant, in effect, that they tacitly ignored the caution signals of the party leadership.

By the spring of 1937 the CP finally realized that its interests lay in trying to win power within the CIO. The Pacific Maritime Federation led by Harry Bridges, the fur workers' union led by Ben Gold, the Transport Workers Union led by "Red Mike" Quill, and the radio telegraphists' union led by Mervyn Rathborne—these and other CP-dominated unions bolted the AFL and joined the CIO. But whatever their local importance, none of these unions, with the exception of the Pacific Maritime Federation, was to be a main source of the new Communist strength in the CIO. Most of the party's rising influence in the new labor federation came from the very nature and momentum of the CIO organizing drive itself.

When John L. Lewis resigned as AFL vice-president in the fall of 1935 and began to set up the Committee for Industrial Organization, he faced a curious problem. He could use his burly coal-mine organizers for the CIO—they would do for the rough stuff and the pack work; but he sensed that for many purposes they were inadequate. They would not be able to capture the feel of the problems faced by workers in industrial cities, which were decidedly different from those in coal towns; they would not be able to express the larger social motivations that would be essential if the CIO was to infuse an element of idealism into its work. The Lewis boys were a little weak on ideas and inspiration, and some of them were not very good at talking, either: they left all that to the boss. As a result, Lewis had to turn to the radicals whom he had previously driven out of the UMW because they had opposed his dictatorial regime and, unlike himself, had always championed industrial unionism. He called in such an unorthodox unionist as John Brophy to become his organizational chief of staff—which meant, as well, to call in such radical veterans as Powers Hapgood, Adolph Germer, Rose Pesotta, and Leo Krzycki, some of whom still had ties with the Socialist Party. At this time, it might be remembered, there was precious little glory and still less comfort in organizing for the CIO, and as a rule, only men moved by a conviction that unionization of mass-production industries was a step toward a larger social end were willing to take the risks that came with the job. Not many other people cared enough; the time-servers would buzz in later.[46]

But not only the free-lance radicals and Socialists found a place in the expanding ranks of the CIO staff. The Communists, who now outnumbered all other radical groups and had a much more efficient machine than any of them, streamed in by the scores. Lewis knew perfectly well that many Communists had joined the CIO staff; indeed, he must have known that Brophy, though not himself an ideological fellow traveler, would be ready to hire competent Communists. But at this stage Lewis felt entirely confident that he could control them—a mistake deriving from his (perhaps willful) failure to understand their unique discipline and ideological cohesiveness. When Sidney Hillman and David Dubinsky expressed concern over the large number of party-liners on the CIO staff, Lewis loftily replied, "Who gets caught? The hunter or the hunted?" [47] Lewis might have waited a few years before answering his question.

In public Lewis roared that those who accused the CIO of being Communist-dominated "lie in their beard and they lie in their bowels." Lewis was entirely correct, of course, in denying that the CIO had ever been dominated by the Communists; the only real question was the extent of their *influence*. In 1937 there were good strategic reasons for denying any Communist influence at all, since wherever the CIO tried to organize underpaid workers it met with the cry of "red." Lewis felt that the major problem was to get the steel, auto, and textile workers into industrial unions, and if the Communists helped with the job that was all right with him. "I do not turn my organizers or CIO members upside down and shake them to see what kind of literature falls out of their pockets," he would say.[48] And if the Communists made trouble, why, John L. Lewis was "man enough" to take care of that too.

There was another important reason for the systematic public underestimation by the CIO of the role of the Communists. This, we must remember, was the era of the Popular Front, and if its outlook did not seep into the union movement as deeply as into other groups, it undoubtedly affected a good many secondary union figures. Progressive unionists like John Brophy had been red-baited all their lives; they were accustomed to thinking of the Stalinists, not as manipulative totalitarians, but as reckless left-wingers. Attacking Communists, said Brophy, was generally "nothing more than a smokescreen for [attacking] the CIO." [49] The Communists themselves, expanding with well-advertised good will and ready to do whatever they were told in regard to organizational matters, naturally exerted themselves to encourage Brophy's view.

8. What was the basis for—and what were the techniques behind—the accumulation of Communist strength in the CIO? A number of factors can be noted separately, though in practice they frequently operated together:

For years the Communists had been trying to establish a grip on some of the very industries that the CIO now began to invade. Although their previous efforts had failed, the Communists still retained a kind of skeleton apparatus in such industries as transport, auto, electric, and shipping. There were experienced party-line organizers like Julius Emspak and James Matles in electric, Wyndham Mortimer in Michigan auto, John Santo in New York transport. Lewis saw that such an apparatus, though insignificant in its own right, could be immensely valuable to him. He therefore absorbed it into the CIO and for a time looked the other way when these organizers did a bit of discreet work for the party on the side. In this way, the Communists were able to begin functioning in the CIO with an embryonic structure of organizers who knew each other from "the old days" and, though assigned to different industries, could help one another with regard to both party interests and their own status.

At the same time, the CP-controlled unions that had come over from the AFL received a major boost from the CIO organizing drive. The fur workers' union, perhaps more closely tied to the Communists than any other American union, deepened and extended its power during the late thirties partly because it carried the prestige of the CIO label. The United Office and Professional Workers Union, led by party-liner Lewis Merrill, was merely a continuation of an old CP-dominated union, but it now received all kinds of help from other CIO units such as it had never had before. If none of these unions counted for very much individually, all together came to a significant minority within the CIO, though not a minority that could by itself have given the Communists the power they soon would have. Still, these unions served their purpose: they provided the party with jobs for organizers, they could be used as springboards from which to move into other and more important CIO unions, they were useful as sources of recruitment, and they helped pad the list of organizations signing the statements of front groups.

Also minor on the scale of CIO power, yet not without some strength, were those unions of semi-professional or professional workers who were particularly susceptible to the "progressive" political and cultural appeals of the Popular Front ideology. The Communists quickly took control of such unions as the Newspaper Guild, organized under the colorful leadership of Heywood Broun, who thought of them as gallant allies; major parts of the Teachers Union; the office workers; the Federation of Architects, Engineers, Chemists and Technicians, comprising at the outset mainly the technical staffs of the WPA; and the State, County and Municipal Workers, containing mostly employees of the New York Department of Welfare. The main value of such unions for the Communists was not so much the role they could play within the CIO itself but as a means for approaching various occupational groups and middle-class neighborhoods.

Meanwhile, and far more important, the CP was establishing a firm beachhead in the national office of the CIO. Brophy, until 1939 the national director of organization, was their closest contact among the top leaders and a man with whom they could talk on almost entirely open terms. A number of party members or close sympathizers wormed their way into major posts. Len DeCaux, a skillful journalist and faithful party-liner, became editor of the *CIO News*. Lee Pressman, an extremely shrewd lawyer, established himself in 1937 as chief counsel and informal adviser for John L. Lewis, a post of considerable power which he was to maintain deep into the presidency of Philip Murray. Serving as a not-quite-secret agent who pressed the claims of the Stalinist unions even as he sometimes seemed to be assuring Lewis and Murray that he would keep them in check, Pressman soon established himself as indispensable to the top CIO leadership. Lewis and Murray admired his cleverness at maneuver, negotiations, and publicity. Deluded into supposing he was merely their pliant tool, they winked at Pressman's politics or persuaded themselves he was merely a "progressive," while he kept meeting secretly with Roy Hudson, John Williamson, and other CP labor specialists.[50] It was Pressman who helped persuade John Brophy to appoint Harry Bridges as west coast director of the CIO, a major coup for the Stalinists. Similar recommendations helped place Donald Henderson, a Communist who had formerly taught at Columbia University, at the head of the CIO agricultural workers' union; Albert Stonkus in charge of the Utility Workers Organizing Committee; James Matles as chief organizer for the light metals industry. And each of these jobs meant many more beneath it.

But the main and new source of CP strength in the CIO was the participation of thousands of its members in the organizing drives of the late thirties. The Communists won power and trust by the traditional methods of winning power and trust in American unions: they became the organizers. If there was dirty work to do, they were ready. If leaflets had to be handed out on cold winter mornings before an Akron rubber plant or a New York subway station, the party could always find a few volunteers. If someone had to stick his neck out within the plants, a Communist was available. And the Communists were indefatigable meeting-goers, caucusing before each meeting, ready to sit out their opponents into the early hours of the morning, working together with a religious fervor. They knew little things, like parliamentary procedure, which quickly won them an advantage over ordinary trade unionists, and they knew other things too, things that for a while they kept to themselves.

The point should not be exaggerated. Never were the Communists more than a minority among the CIO organizers, and often a disruptive and distrusted minority. Plenty of other people, ranging from run-of-the-mill unionists to left-wing Socialists, worked hard and took chances. But the Communists were the best-organized political group within the CIO, despite—or perhaps because of— the fact that at the beginning the party national office provided very little guidance and the local comrades had to fend for themselves. The moral is that, even when a political movement is slow in reacting to major events, it can still capitalize on them if its membership has been trained and disciplined.

Here is the testimony of Zygmund Dobryzynski, who for a time had been national director of the UAW organizing drive at the Ford plants:

During the first organizational days, when the UAW was formed, and the men were beginning to recognize that unionism was the thing they needed, they came in by the hundreds; the automobile industry was made up of men, primarily, who had never been in any union before, and who were completely inexperienced, not knowing even how to make a motion on the floor. . . . [But] the members of the Communist Party knew how to speak; some of them had extensive soap-box experience. . . . It is very simple for a man who understands public speaking and parliamentary rules to control a meeting of uninitiated people. . . . By preparing motions ahead of time, having discussions ahead of time, and then by dividing up in various sections of the hall, [the CPers] would give the impression that the particular policy they were trying to have the meeting adopt was generally supported throughout the membership.[51]

The experience here described is quite typical, and once the party finally got around to taking advantage of the CIO drive it soon learned how to advance its personnel and its interests. In April, 1938, a Communist steelworker reported from western Pennsylvania:

Our party unit a few years ago had ten members, and it was the hardest job to get them to a meeting. Now, our party has grown to 43 members. How was this done? When the CIO started organization work in steel, there were four of us comrades who put ourselves in the front line to help build the union. I want to say as a Communist that, with my own signature, I have signed 800 members into the CIO. Through such activity we won the confidence of the men and were able to recruit. Our branch meeting now has a weekly attendance of more than 25.

All through 1937 and 1938 the party leaders, finally aware of the opportunities available to them in the CIO, kept pushing their followers to appear openly as Communists in the unions and no longer to fear public exposure. A report from a party organizer in a New York industrial town stresses this point:

The Communists in that plant do not yet see that they are living in a new period, that Communists are not feared or looked down on, that the Communists are recognized as among the best leaders in the plant. The comrades have not yet realized that in this new period the workers are thinking politically. . . . A lack of boldness and an absence of a realization that the door is open for the building of the Party in that town are the most serious obstacles facing us here.

From Seattle came another report stressing the same point and also indicating the new willingness of the party to cooperate with ordinary union leaders of the sort that only a few years earlier Foster and Stachel had been calling "labor lieutenants of capitalism":

> In our section in Seattle, which is the harbor section in the center of the lumber industry, we have succeeded in increasing our membership from 92 members to approximately 250 members. . . . This was possible because for the last two and a half years we have concentrated our main efforts on helping the trade unions in our section, mainly in the basic industries. We brought the Party forward in all of the struggles, correctly and boldly. . . .
> One of the methods we followed was to establish close relations with officials of unions, to meet them and discuss with them frankly and freely how our Party can cooperate to strengthen the unions. . . . We did not overlook the importance of greetings to the unions at Christmas time from the Communist Party.[52]

Yet the strength of the Communists in the CIO could never have been consolidated if it had depended merely on having comrades become organizers in the big drives (many of them, particularly in steel, were soon weeded out) or upon manipulations in the national CIO office or upon the intervention of party branches. What finally secured a number of unions for the CP and gave it a mass base in others was its capacity to bring in reinforcements on the lower levels who could provide a solid layer of support for its people on top. Many of these reinforcements came from the CP-dominated unemployed organizations, the members of which were frequently absorbed into the burgeoning new unions as the job market expanded in the late thirties; others came in response to a persistent CP campaign to "colonize" its big-city members in basic industries and in the smaller industrial towns. The success of the Communists in taking and keeping control of certain CIO unions depended most of all on their capacity for building strong party fractions around which clustered sympathizers and allies.

Hundreds of party members flocked into the electrical, auto, steel, machine, and maritime industries during the late thirties: the demand for unskilled labor kept growing, and Communist "colonizers" could be planted in strategic factories by sympathetic union officials. As a result, the party succeeded in molding strong rank-and-file groups to balance and support its influence on top. Wherever it had significant strength in the ranks, it could not easily be dislodged from a position of power within the CIO. Later, when it ran into serious trouble in the electrical and auto unions, it managed—precisely because of this strength in the ranks—to hold its grip on the electrical workers and for some time to preserve a substantial minority group in the auto union.

In the Transport Workers Union, by contrast, Communist influence depended mainly on a core of secondary leaders who worked closely with the union president Mike Quill, a man with a superb gift for sensing and exploiting the psychological needs of the Irish Catholic workers who formed the bulk of the membership. As long as the Communists and Quill kept the peace, they provided one another with useful services; but inside the union Quill remained the undisputed boss and the Stalinists could never create an independent following of much consequence among the rank and file. As a result, when Quill finally broke with the CP some years later, he found it quite easy to destroy its prestige within the union.

Still another relationship held between the Communists and non-Communists in the National Maritime Union. The water-front nucleus of the party, a remnant of its aborted effort to build a dual union in maritime, had never been very large; but it had been notable for its fervor and doggedness. Men like Jack Lawrenson, Charles Keith, Tom Ray, and Harry Alexander, all of them known, at one time or another, as open Communists, naturally became influential leaders of the new CIO union that was built up among the sailors in the late thirties. It was with their help that Joe Curran rose to the presidency of the NMU, and with their expert guidance that he established a cruelly repressive machine that repeatedly smashed dissidents and critics. Years later, when the party fraction in the NMU split wide open, partly because of political disagreements and partly because of personal quarrels, the way was prepared for Curran to destroy the Communists, who had by now become an impediment to his quest for respectability. Though their base in the NMU was larger than that in the Transport Workers Union, the Communists could not cope with the brutal Curran machine: they had done their work too well, and now were destroyed by their own creature.

What particularly helped the Communists to set up strong rank-and-file groups in a number of CIO unions was the appearance of a new kind of union man: the militant young leader with the sit-downs and organizing drives behind him, who identified with the CIO as few workers had been able to identify with the AFL, and who was vaguely radical in his political impulses. From the Communist point of view, these secondary young leaders were ideal material for recruiting and of crucial importance in union politics, since their friendship or at least neutrality was indispensable in the struggle for control. Systematically the CP union fractions would go to work on these people, trying a bit of quiet indoctrination but, even more important, laying claim to an identity of interest and outlook on union matters. Clayton Fountain, a local UAW leader who for a time belonged to the party, has remembered his experience accurately:

> Being responsible for educational activities in Local 235 made me a natural target for the Communists. . . . One bright and energetic party member working as an educational director or editor in a strong local union is worth a dozen members occupied with the lesser duties of settling grievances. . . . Such a spot gives the party member an outlet through which to pour a steady stream of Communist propaganda. For this reason I was high on the list of up-and-coming unionists on whom the party focussed its wiles in Detroit early in 1937.[53]

An equally important group upon whom the Communists in the CIO concentrated their attention—and at times with striking results —was the large number of Negroes who for the first time had been drawn into the world of unionism. The record of the CIO in regard to racial discrimination was obviously superior to that of the AFL, yet it could not, simply by passing resolutions or announcing its will, eradicate the numerous marks of Negro discrimination in the factories and the inherited attitudes of contempt still held by many white workers. Precisely because the Negroes in the auto, electrical, and maritime unions had gained a new sense of confidence upon being accepted as equals during the rise of the CIO, they now felt ready—and with good reason—to press on for their rights.

For the Stalinists this was a golden opportunity. Untroubled by any fears of engaging in condescension or exploitation, they appointed themselves the special defenders of the Negro unionists. In the unions they controlled, they kept hammering away at the "Negro question" with a manipulative insistence that could hardly fail to impress a good many inexperienced Negro unionists. And with mechanical regularity they kept pushing Negroes into the leadership of their unions or factions, quite regardless of whether these Negroes were competent. Men like Revel Cayton in the longshoremen's union, Sheldon Tapps in the UAW, Ferdinand Smith in the NMU, Henry Johnson in packing house—either party members or close associates—were prodded and wheedled into leadership. Cynical though such devices were, they paid off. During the early years of the CIO, the "Negro blocs" that functioned informally in many of the unions frequently supported the Stalinists when there were struggles for power.

There were other tactics which enabled the CP to extend its grip within the CIO. Incomparably skillful at applying the arts of mass flattery, the Stalinists developed to a fine point the technique of what Walter Reuther would later call "political valet service." (Reuther could speak with some authority on this matter, since for a brief time during the late thirties he himself was a recipient of this service.) Union leaders cooperating with the Communists suddenly found themselves praised not merely in the *Daily Worker* but in an astonishing variety of other publications; they were frequently invited to speak as honored guests at "important" meetings; the CP claque was always at hand to applaud them wildly; and most valuable at all, if any critics dared oppose them within their unions, the CP was ready to defend them as only it knew how. Being at least as human as anyone else, these leaders often succumbed to this flattery.

Perhaps the classical instance of such a deception occurred at the 1940 UAW convention, where John L. Lewis was greeted with a remarkably fervent forty-five-minute demonstration. Delegates marched through the aisles singing "Lewis Is Our Leader," and Lewis himself, abandoning for once his traditional pose of the Old Curmudgeon, put a UAW cap on his head while tears of emotion streamed down his cheeks. Lewis could hardly have realized at the time that this show, while undoubtedly expressing sincere feelings of many UAW people, had been staged by the two dominant factions in the union, the then anti-Roosevelt group led by the Stalinists taking the lead in the hope of aggrandizing some of Lewis' prestige and the pro-Roosevelt group hurriedly tagging along in the hope of minimizing the effects of this prestige.

Years later, long after the honeymoon had turned into a civil war, some of the CIO leaders cried innocence. Jim Carey, who had worked with the Communists in the electrical union, told a Congressional subcommittee:

> We made one mistake in the first flush of organizing ardor: we let the party-liners in. In those days the Communists talked like democrats. . . . We got along well enough until the Nazi-Stalin pact. . . . Then my leftist associates suddenly laid off Hitler and started ranting about the imperialist war. Not understanding the dialectical profundities, I didn't change my line— and I suddenly found myself isolated in my own union. It was now easy to spot the Communists because of their flip-flop on the war, and as months passed I discovered that they were in complete control of the national office; they dominated the executive committee, ran the union paper, and were strongly entrenched in the locals and districts. All the organizers were party-liners.[54]

Carey's testimony has the ring of truth, particularly in that revealing sentence "We got along well enough . . ."; yet it also seems a bit disingenuous, for surely so sophisticated a man did not have to wait until the Hitler-Stalin pact to discover who controlled his own union.

In any case, it would be an error to suppose that Communist strength in the CIO rested solely on the ability of the party fractions to manipulate leaders and members through their organizational skills. In some very important respects the Popular Front line fitted perfectly the temper of the time in which the major CIO drives took place. Unlike the ultra-revolutionary policies of the early thirties, the Popular Front line did not alienate the mass of unionists who had no particular interest in radical politics. Unlike the party's approach during the Second World War, it did not spin so far to the right as frequently to become indistinguishable from strikebreaking and thereby antagonize many unionists. Popular Frontism during the late thirties permitted the Communists to be combative enough to participate actively in the CIO drives, yet sufficiently moderate to accept and second its dominant New Deal sentiment. As long as the Stalinists could maintain this balance they were able to satisfy some of the more aggressive elements in the unions while staying on good terms with a number of the leaders.

In turn, many union leaders, who as a group have seldom been notable for their ideological awareness, were ready to play along with the Communists. Partly this derived from motives of convenience, partly from sheer laziness. As one acute observer has remarked about the liberal unionists:

> Many . . . are opportunists on the CP issue: they are caught between a lack of political ideas and a fear of big business. They become fellow-travellers by default, as it were, and only in a passive way. Given their dearth of political ideas, they think that to criticize the Communists is to play ball. But they are not merely opportunists, nor are they . . . naïve ideologically. They feel lost and homeless and are reduced to becoming ideological opportunists. Probably the shrill voice of the anti-Communist liberal helps to keep them in line.[55]

Though no longer true for the fifties, this description goes at least part of the way toward explaining CP strength in the unions during the late thirties and the years of the Second World War.

Wherever the Stalinists won control of a CIO union or local, they showed particular talents for harassing and disintegrating opposition groups. There had been no lack of undemocratic unions in the past, but where, for example, the carpenters' union under William Hutcheson was simply an old-fashioned oligarchy with barely a pretense at being anything else, the Communists specialized in distorting the very mechanisms of democracy in order to perpetuate their rule. Seldom has so meticulous an adherence to the outer forms of democracy so thoroughly violated its spirit and intent. By now the evidence on this matter has grown to enormous proportions, but a simple statement by a former Communist makes the point with exactness and economy:

> For one thing we had superior speakers. Our boys not only attended all the union educational classes . . . but also took lessons in speaking from party experts. We were also trained in the fine points of parliamentary trickery. . . . We raised points of order, points of information, divisions of the house, objections to consideration of the question, amendments to amendments, and appeals from the decision of the chair in endless and swift succession.[56]

To the more intelligent CIO leaders it soon became clear that the Communists could not be fought by the usual pork-chop or walking delegate techniques. Because they politicized issues, it was necessary to meet them on political grounds; because they manipulated democratic procedures, it was necessary to mobilize democratic sentiments against them. In some unions, such as steel, the Murray leadership managed to squash the Communists before they could settle into the ranks; but in unions like the UAW the struggle against Stalinism became a prolonged exercise in political education.

In some instances, however, such comparatively rational and orderly methods were rendered impossible by the Stalinists themselves. On the west coast, for example, the Bridges machine systematically knifed away at all opposition tendencies and openly kept violating the principles of union democracy. Though it could not touch established unions such as garment, auto, and rubber, the Bridges leadership unrestrainedly pounced upon anti-Communists—particularly anti-Communist leftists—in the weaker CIO unions.

From the yellowed files of labor journalism we extract a typical incident, perhaps unimportant in its own right but revealing the level to which the CIO was reduced whenever the Stalinists held complete power. The account is from the pen of Travers Clement, a veteran labor writer:

The office workers situation in San Francisco during the past six months has offered an almost perfect laboratory specimen of CP tactics in the labor movement. . . . Local 34 of the United Office and Professional Workers Union had been run by a CP fraction until January 1938, when it was defeated by a rank and file progressive group which . . . objected to having the union used as a political football.

Shortly after this happened, the anti-Communist group was denounced by Bridges and his friends as "Trotskyist" and "fascist" (it happened to be led by Socialists). In May, Bridges appeared at a Local 34 meeting with four "affidavits" charging the Local 34 leaders with being agents of the San Francisco Industrial Association and of the AFL. When one of the Local 34 leaders, Millie Goldberg, attacked Bridges for these accusations, a CP member took the floor to say—the sentence should be engraved as a classical contribution toward the understanding of Communist psychology—that he now appreciated the Moscow trials: "In Russia traitors like Goldberg are lined up against a wall and shot." Local 34, however, repudiated these "affidavits," reaffirmed its confidence in its leaders, and demanded that Leo Allen, the party-lining representative of the UOPW office, be recalled. Clement continues:

A letter written by Allen to the East several weeks before the "affidavits" were sprung on the membership then came to light. This letter revealed the whole CP strategy. Allen wrote of the affidavits which were being prepared, admitted that the CP move—which included the setting up of a CP-packed investigation committee—might prove to be a boomerang, and stated that in this case he, as international organizer, would step in and dissolve the investigating committee.[57]

Early in May the San Francisco CIO Council, dominated by Bridges, recommended the dismemberment of Local 34. Finally, the leaders of the local appealed to John L. Lewis, who listened in silence and told them there was nothing he could do. Discouraged and isolated, Local 34 then voted to shift to the AFL.

It was an accumulation of such incidents that in 1938 led to a virtual split in the west coast CIO. Locals from the auto workers, the ILGWU, and the rubber workers withdrew from the Los Angeles Industrial Union Council on the ground that it had become a tool of the CP. To gain a feeling for the situation, one item in the impressive bill of particulars drawn up by the "secessionists" needs to be quoted:

> Without consulting or reporting to the Council . . . a new business manager for the *Industrial Unionist* [the local CIO paper] was imported all the way from New York. The fact that the new manager, Rose Boyd, is . . . a functionary of the Communist Party evidently answers why the change of management was not explained to the Council.[58]

In only a few places, however, did the Communists meet such opposition. For the most part, they were allowed to consolidate their grasp over the unions in which they had won leadership—though there appears to have been a tacit understanding that they would not disturb the Lewis machine in coal or the Murray machine in steel. By the summer of 1939, just before the Hitler-Stalin pact, the Communists had established themselves as one of the important blocs within the CIO. Their agents were firmly planted in the CIO national office; they had taken full control over a number of important unions and had established strong bases in other unions.*

By the summer of 1939 the Communist Party had become an important, if not yet a major, force in American political life. At the tenth CP convention, in 1938, the membership was announced as 75,000. In 1939 the party claimed to have reached 100,000,

---

* By 1939 the following unions were under effective CP control: Maritime Federation of the Pacific; United Electrical, Radio and Machinists; State County and Municipal Workers; International Longshoremen and Warehouse; Mine, Mill and Smelter; Fur Workers; American Communications Association; United Cannery, Agricultural, Packing and Allied Workers. In the Transport Workers Union, the American Newspaper Guild, the Furniture Workers Union and the Teachers Union the CP shared control with cooperative fellow travelers. It also had control of strong sections of the auto and shoe workers' unions.

though there is internal evidence to suggest that this figure was exaggerated. It is possible, however, that between 80,000 and 90,000 people were in the party at one time or another during 1939. The core of moderately active members probably never went above 50,000, and the rate of turnover was enormous, one check-up of membership in a large New York branch indicating that its secretary did not even have the addresses of 45 percent of the members.[59] Yet there can be no doubt that the CP had taken some major steps toward becoming "a mass organization" and that it was now a powerful force in the CIO, the youth movement, the intellectual world, and in a few large cities. Political masquerade as it may have been, the Popular Front strategy had done its work.

Chapter IX. World War II: Are the Yanks Coming?

1. When Joachim von Ribbentrop and Vyacheslav Molotov shook hands over the Nazi-Soviet pact on August 24, 1939, the leaders of the American Communist Party were at least as surprised as anyone else. Stalin, contemptuous as always of the Comintern, had seen no need to give advance warning to his American—or European—followers. Years before he had labeled the Comintern a "gyp-joint," and so he treated it throughout his life. As a result, all through the summer of 1939 the American CP had kept denouncing reports of a Russo-German rapprochement as anti-Soviet slanders. "Reactionaries," warned Earl Browder, "openly speculate that the Soviet Union may try to beat Chamberlain at his own game by joining hands with Hitler. But even those who hate the land of socialism cannot believe it when they see the Soviet Union alone round up the traitorous agents of Hitler." A mere forty-five days before the pact, in another of his notable predictions, Browder was still more emphatic: "There is as much chance of [a Russo-German] agreement as of Earl Browder being elected President of the Chamber of Commerce." [1]

No wonder the party leaders were stunned into silence when the very event they had been declaring impossible suddenly occurred. For twenty-four hours after the radio reports of the pact, the *Daily Worker* kept a discreet silence. It was a test of the capacity of the American Communists to accept anything on faith, to applaud any move the Russians made. They passed the test. Haunted by reporters, Browder finally permitted an interview in which he came up with the reflection that *every* nation should sign a non-aggression pact with Russia and that, in any case, the pact was Stalin's "master stroke" for peace. The next day the *Daily Worker* put on a face of assurance: "The pact is a smashing blow at Munich treachery. . . . By compelling [!] Germany to sign a non-aggression pact, the Soviet Union tremendously limited the direction of Nazi war aims. . . ." [2] In a sense hardly intended by the American comrades, this statement proved to be true: the pact "tremendously limited" the Nazi war thrust—directly toward Poland.

For the party leaders these were not comfortable days. Apart from the usual praise for the Soviet Union, which now came as mechanically as the counting of beads to a believer, the Communists still seemed anxious to hang onto the Popular Front strategy: they foresaw that abandoning it would mean to lose much of the influence they had so tidily accumulated during the late thirties. Two days after England and France declared war against Germany, the National Committee of the CP was still trading in Popular Front slogans: "Embargo Japan and Germany for the defeat of fascist aggression" and "Demand full moral, diplomatic and economic help for the Polish people." Headlines in the *Daily Worker* still leaned on Popular Front rhetoric: "Unity Grows in France in Face of Conflict" and "British People Determined to Crush Fascism." The *Worker* congratulated the French Communist leader Maurice Thorez for entering the French army: he was, they wrote about the man who would soon desert the French army, "offering his life to defend the national security of France." Such phrases, headlines, and sentiments made sense only if the Communists were still in favor of supporting the West against Hitler.

It did not take very long, however, for the signals from Moscow to become clear. Here is a chart of how the party kept shifting and squirming through September, 1939, all the while moving closer to the new line:

> *September 7:* "The people of this country deeply sympathize with the struggle of the Polish people for the independence of their country." (*Worker* editorial)
>
> *September 12:* The war, declares Browder, is an "imperialist war in which the rulers of both sides are equally guilty."
>
> *September 15:* The *Daily Worker* reprints a *Pravda* editorial denouncing the Polish government as an oppressor of the people.
>
> *September 18:* The Polish government is now denounced as semi-fascist, and the Red Army hailed for marching into eastern Poland to "protect" innocent Poles and thereby "score another triumph for human freedom."
>
> *September 19:* The CP National Committee declares that "this war cannot be supported by the workers. It is not a war against fascism. . . ."

All through late September: The stress of the *Daily Worker* is increasingly anti-English, noticeably more than anti-German.[3]

But this was merely preparation for the major shift. From sympathy for the Polish people in their struggle against the Nazi invaders, to declaring both sides equally guilty in an imperialist war, the Communists soon turned to placing the main burden of guilt upon England. Wrote William Z. Foster:

As Stalin recently said: "It was not Germany who attacked France and England, but France and England which attacked Germany, *assuming responsibility for the present war.*" The imperialist Allies assumed further responsibility by rejecting the peace proposals of Germany, the Netherlands and the Soviet Union. [emphasis added]

A few months later the Communist view was put with authoritative bluntness in the magazine *Communist International.* An unsigned editorial entitled "England Drives to a New War" explained that since Germany had entered peaceful and friendly relations with the Soviet Union, and since England had "unleashed" the war, English imperialism "revealed itself to the whole world as *the chief enemy* of the international working class"[4] (emphasis added). At the very moment that Nazi totalitarianism was reaching the climax of its power, the Comintern found England "the chief enemy." *

While the CP now characterized the war as imperialist (with

* The party's difficulties at home were further aggravated when the Soviet Union attacked Finland in November, 1939. Finland was popular among those liberals whom the Communists wished to maintain as friends. Only a few years ago the *Daily Worker* had pictured Finland as a progressive country ruled by a coalition of Socialists and liberals; now, in trying to present Finland as "a counter-revolutionary outpost" ruled by White Guardists, William Z. Foster explained that Finnish democracy had always been a mere façade. He neglected to discuss, however, why the *Daily Worker* had been so naïve as to take this façade for the reality.[5]

At any rate, when Russia signed a peace with Finland on March 12, 1940, the "White Guard government" was quietly if slowly rehabilitated.

The Finns had ceded territories totaling some 16,000 square miles and a population of 450,000 persons to the Russians—which may have been enough to change the "objective character" of their government.

some imperialists being more imperialistic than others), it did not follow an orthodox Leninist mode of interpretation nor did it return to the Leninist policy of "revolutionary defeatism." As has been remarked earlier, it is a superficial view of Stalinist history which sees it as simply oscillating between "left" and "right" policies. The whole character of the party had changed since the Third Period: it would not and could not revert to the policies of the twenties or early thirties. Nor did the Russians even desire their American agents to assume a revolutionary posture. Given their alliance with Nazi Germany, the Russians were interested primarily in keeping America out of the war; and as a result, the CP now began to function as a pressure group borrowing sentiments and phrases from both pacifism and isolationism. In practice, the American party tried to create a *new kind* of Popular Front which—now that the anti-fascist and collective security slogans had become obsolete—would focus on the theme "Keep America Out of War." So deeply had the party dug itself into a number of important institutions that it could not revert, by mere decision, to the organizational techniques of the Third Period; it continued to think in terms of influencing a mass following and tried to surround itself with a new galaxy of fellow-traveling groups. (Some party leaders, however, anticipating that the party might be banned from legal politics, retired from public life into a sort of semi-underground existence.)

"Keep America Out of War" and "The Yanks Are Not Coming" —these were now the main Communist slogans. "The workers everywhere," wrote Louis Budenz, the *Daily Worker* editor, "do not want their sons to die, mangled scraps of flesh . . . in order to enrich Wall Street. America, keep out of this war!" "Our message to Europe," wrote Mike Quin, a folksy Communist pamphleteer, is "Lafayette, we are here—and we are going to stay here and solve mighty important problems in mathematics. . . . We're not in any danger of being invaded. As a matter of fact when both sides are finished with that war, and no matter who wins, they won't be in any condition to invade the island of Yap."

A calculated exploitation of pacifist sentiment became a major strategy in the CP press. For weeks the *Daily Worker* serialized Dalton Trumbo's novel *Johnny Got His Gun* and each day the reader was treated to a synopsis that began: "It took a long time for

Joe Bonham to get hold of himself after he woke up on a hospital cot behind the lines and found himself without legs or arms and with his entire face blown away." A woman CP leader wrote in a popular pamphlet: "I could think of plenty of things that could make a woman prouder and happier, after all that it takes to bring a son into the world and raise him to be a man, than a Gold Star. Grandchildren, for instance." [6] It was noteworthy that emotions about "mangled scraps of flesh" or soldiers with their faces shattered had not troubled the Communists for some years before August 24, 1939, and were certainly not to trouble them for some years after June 22, 1941.

Though occasionally remembering to intone that "capitalism is the root cause of the great evils of war, hunger and oppression," [7] the party leaders were primarily concerned with reshaping the political attitudes of the "progressives" whom the CP had attracted during the Popular Front days. But here they faced some difficult problems. The existing front groups—the American League for Peace and Democracy, the American Youth Congress, the American Student Union, the League of Women Shoppers, etc.—had as their very *raison d'être* the idea that collective security was the way to destroy fascism. At least some "innocent" members of these groups had taken their anti-fascist claims at face value; others had been faithful New Dealers yearning for the unity of all progressives. How could they now be persuaded to reverse themselves on every major political point; how could they be herded into the pen of anti-Roosevelt isolationism? For as soon as it adjusted itself to the changed needs of Moscow, the CP opposed the Roosevelt administration right down the line: it fought against lend-lease, against conscription, against the proposal to send fifty destroyers to England.* Unavoidably, a

* After years of tender flirtation with the New Deal, the Communists discovered that "not only the old division between the Republican and Democratic Parties, but also that between the New Deal and anti-New Deal camps, is losing its former significance. Both are parties of the bourgeoisie and seek in various ways to realize and promote the predatory interests of American imperialism."

After Browder had been prohibited by court order from touring the country during the 1940 presidential election, he said of the President whom only a few years ago he had ranked among the American titans: "Mr. Roosevelt has studied well the Hitlerian art and bids fair to outdo the record of his teacher." [8]

number of leading and previously dependable fellow travelers, such as David Lasser, head of the Workers Alliance, and Joseph P. Lash, a key figure in the American Student Union, now broke away from the whole milieu of front groups: they were people who had taken the Popular Front seriously. A. Philip Randolph, the Negro union leader, resigned from the National Negro Congress, Roger Baldwin from the League for Peace and Democracy. Some front groups, like the American Student Union and the American League for Peace and Democracy, simply collapsed; others, like the American Youth Congress, abandoned by almost all its church and liberal affiliates, survived as a mere shell. The Friends of the Soviet Union was discontinued and replaced by an American Committee for Friendship with the Soviet Union—nor was such a change merely a matter of labels; it involved some new people and a quite different political content. New committees for civil rights and peace were created in the larger cities, most of them improvised coverings for the faithful who had been left in the cold. The names of these new groups were as impressive as their existence was to be brief: the Miami League for Peace and Human Welfare, the Greater New York Conference on Inalienable Rights, the Pan-American Conference on Democratic Rights, the Los Angeles Yanks Are Not Coming Committee.

With some skill but more persistence, the Stalinists went about the job of contriving a political transubstantiation. Immediately after the American League for Peace and Democracy was dissolved, for example, its inner core of Stalinists contacted people on the membership and sympathizers lists and held local meetings to form new groups. A bit later they were loosely linked together in city-wide federations. At one such local meeting, in Greenwich Village, the main speaker told the audience that the American League had made the mistake of concerning itself with foreign affairs: "Let us now build a peace organization that will concern itself exclusively with domestic affairs. . . . We have nothing to do with Finland or

---

Perhaps more revealing than all such statements is a ditty that was popular among the party faithful during the years of the pact:
"Oh, Franklin Roosevelt told the people how he felt,
We almost believed him when he said:
'Oh, I hate war
And so does Eleanor
But we won't be safe till everybody's dead.'"

Russia or any other foreign country." At another meeting of the same group, a speaker declared: "I am in favor of a united front ranging from John L. Lewis' CIO to Father Coughlin. If I hate John L. Lewis and organized labor, and Lewis is for peace, then I am for Lewis on the question of peace. If I hate Father Coughlin and if Father Coughlin is for peace, then I am for Father Coughlin on the question of peace." [9] Now it is true that this speaker, probably not one of the more experienced hands, may have pushed the party line toward an embarrassing extreme; but he understood its general spirit perfectly. If keeping America out of the war was the central objective for Communists and their friends, then every other political issue and distinction became insignificant.

The Brooklyn section of the old American League now became the Brooklyn Community Peace Council; other sections transformed themselves into the Hollywood Peace Forum, the Peace Committee of the Medical Professions, the Mother's Day Peace Council, and even—let it be forever recorded in history!—the Milwaukee Indians' Peace Group. In Washington, D. C., the announcement of the new "peace group" reached members in the same envelope that carried a report on the death of the old one. With each change of line the comrades learned to be more economical about it.

Long ago the Communists had discovered that in these matters subtlety was of no particular value and could sometimes even prove a hindrance: they understood that fellow travelers and "progressives" responded, in the main, not to the manifest content of the front group's program, but to the emotions of fraternity which the front group promised to provide and, behind that, to the myth of Soviet progress which made everything else—slave camps, shifts of line, murders, pacts with Hitler—seem mere transient inconveniences or, at most, painful necessities. All the old and dependable propaganda tricks that had been developed during the Popular Front period were now put to new use—and if the slogans were precisely the opposite of those used a few months earlier, what did it matter? Who really cared?

"The downtown Brooklyn Peace Council will hold a rally Thursday night April 4," reported the *Daily Worker* in the spring of 1940, "and the Council for Peace and Civil Liberties distributed 1200 lollypops labeled *Don't be a sucker for war propaganda.*" In

Patterson, New Jersey, clergymen replaced lollypops. A joint AFL-CIO Committee to Keep America Out of War held "a mass peace rally" which requested "local clergymen of all denominations to devote their sermons for the weekend to the subject of peace." Predictably, "many ministers and rabbis signified their intention of doing so." [10]

Once again the wheels were turning, and if not quite with the old Popular Front smoothness, then with a bumpy sort of efficiency that more or less did the job. By late summer of 1940 the preparatory work was finished: 300 Emergency Committees for Peace had been formed on the east coast alone, countless "peace rallies" organized, and a surprisingly large number of liberals recaptured. Wherever the Stalinist wing of the CIO commanded influence, it did valuable work for the new campaign to set up a national "peace" organization. To speak in the name of the Transport Workers Union or the Los Angeles CIO Council or the electrical workers' union was, after all, more impressive than the obviously trumped-up —or even authentic—Lithuanian groups upon which the party had depended in its earlier, less expert days.

At a mass convention held in Chicago on September 2, 1940, the American Peace Mobilization was born. Officiating at the baptism were Vito Marcantonio, Paul Robeson, and, of all people, Dr. Francis Townsend. Having learned to appreciate the advantages of clerical blessings during the Popular Front period, the Communists found an obscure Oklahoma clergyman, the Reverend John B. Thompson, to serve as president. The list of remaining leaders included Joe Curran, Carl Sandburg, Richard Wright, Franz Boas, Frederick Vanderbilt Field, Theodore Dreiser, Father Smith of the Society of Catholic Commonwealth and Rabbi Moses Miller of the Jewish People's Committee.

For months the American Peace Mobilization, which never built up much of an organization but served as an effective apparatus, kept breaking into the front pages by a daring stunt: it kept a "perpetual peace vigil" in front of the White House. At one point Joe Curran's sailors joined the picket line with placards reading "No Convoys."

Though circumstances beyond its control kept the American Peace Mobilization from reaching the age of two, it kept hammering away, during its short and happy infancy, on the dangers presented by England to peace-loving humanity:

> All-out aid to the British Empire or any other such warring Empire means total war for the American people. . . . Men in high places are dragging us into a war 3,000 miles away. It is not a war to defend democracy.

On June 21, 1941, the APM issued a call for a National Peace Week. On June 22, Hitler's armies invaded Russia. Nothing was ever again heard about National Peace Week and very little about the APM. In July a *Daily Worker* item announced that the American Peace Mobilization would henceforth be known as the American People's Mobilization (an admirable economy in the utilization of scarce initials), and that its program would now feature "aid to Britain." [11] But the APM outlived its usefulness and was soon quietly dissolved. New times, new fronts.

The perpetual peace vigil? That too was never seen again.

2. It is a remarkable testimony to the resilience of the American CP, as well as to the power which the Soviet myth can exert upon its captives, that even during the years of the Hitler-Stalin pact—years in which Molotov was declaring that one's attitude toward fascism is "a matter of taste"—the party managed to keep its hard core intact. It suffered important losses among intellectuals and Jewish sympathizers, but in the CIO, which was now its most important area of activity, it preserved its essential strength.

Wherever the Communists have been able to transform sympathetic sentiments into a stable institutional structure, the changes in party line have been relatively easy to manage. In the CIO, for example, the Stalinist-led unions developed an inner life and momentum of their own, which often remained impervious to the shocks of European events. To the degree that Communist leaders satisfactorily performed routine union chores, they kept the support of many non-political members; and in some cases the impulse toward careerism that in one union might take the form of obedience to a Lewis or a Murray expressed itself in another union as a readiness to work with the Stalinists. The restraints of the Popular

Front period having been partly removed, some Communist officials
in the CIO even won new support among the more active unionists
by adopting an ultra-militant vocabulary and being ready to shout
"strike" at the drop of a grievance.

Some unionists broke from the party, particularly in the railroad
brotherhoods, but the bulk of the CIO "left wing" held firm. All
through late September, 1939, the *Daily Worker* kept proudly
ticking off the faithful as they swung into line: "Julius Empsak
Says US Has No Place in War," "ACA and Rathborne Resolve
Against War," "State, County and Municipal Workers Union Urges
US Maintain Neutrality." [12]

Directly after the November, 1939, CIO convention and as the
result of pressure from the right-wing CIO leaders, Harry Bridges
was demoted from West Coast to California director—a move that
somewhat restricted his operations but did not really challenge his
power. At the 1940 CIO convention the loss was compensated for
by the election of Joe Curran as a vice-president and the decision
to give each affiliate, small CP-controlled unions as well as the
gigantic steel and auto unions, representation on the CIO National
Board. Another important step in the consolidation of CP strength
occurred that same year when a CIO Council was formed in New
York City under Stalinist domination. Just as Bridges' office had
become a taking-off point for Communist organizers roaming about
the west coast, so this new Council gave the CP-led unions in New
York a valuable outlet for advancing their line.

In the fall of 1940 it did seem for a moment that the CP might
be facing serious trouble within the CIO. John L. Lewis, having
staked his prestige on Wendell Willkie in the national election,
resigned as CIO president, and the Communists, who owed him
most of their initial opportunities in the industrial unions, were
naturally fearful that his successor might not be as tacitly cooperative. But when Philip Murray became president, the Communist
bloc proved strong enough to keep its men in office: Lee Pressman
remained as general counsel and, if anything, widened his ambiguous influence, while Len DeCaux continued as editor of the *CIO
News*. During the first period of his administration, when he was
painfully conscious of being regarded as a larger man's replacement,
Murray neither had the power nor showed much desire to move

against the Communists: they were still being protected by Lewis, whose influence rested on more than possession of office. Personal factors also came into play. With Murray, the cagey Pressman could ingratiate himself more than he had ever been able to with Lewis. Murray could be softened by gestures of friendliness and deluded by signs of apparent loyalty; Lewis knew, most of the time, what he was doing and what was being done to him. In the long run—at least until the years of the "cold war"—the choice of Murray as Lewis' successor did no harm to the "left wing" bloc in the CIO.

During the time of the pact, however, it was Lewis whom the Communists elevated to the rank of national hero. "There can be nothing but contempt," growled Browder, "for the caviling against Lewis which came from the camp of the Roosevelt 'labor' lieutenants. Among these Lilliputians Lewis has stood forth as a giant." [13] Behind Browder's tenderness for the "giant" lay hard-headed political considerations. Since the CP now opposed all war preparations of the Roosevelt administration, it naturally backed Lewis in his refusal to accept the restraints that other labor leaders advocated. Lewis served the Communists as a massive boulder behind which they could take cover and direct their fire at "Roosevelt's labor lieutenants."

"The issue," wrote the *Daily Worker*, "is the Lewis program of winning [wage] increases versus the Hillman program of sacrifice." When Hillman helped set up the pro-administration Labor Policy Advisory Committee in 1940, the Communists charged him with "a sinister attempt to mobilize the entire labor movement behind the war-hunger program of the Roosevelt administration." William Z. Foster, stirring back to life as the party veered toward the "left," could now thunder in his accustomed style: "If [AFL leaders] Green, Woll, Hutcheson and Tobin have their way, the workers will be tied up with no-strike, no-wage-advance, no-organize restrictions as they were by Gompers during the first world war." [14] Had Foster waited a few months, he could have added his own name to the list.

Within the limits of their capacity, the Communists worked hard to pursue an aggressive trade-union policy during the period of the pact. They were too shrewd, of course, simply to call strikes indiscriminately, for they realized that such a tactic would merely endanger their position in the CIO. But whenever it seemed at all plausible, they were conspicuously eager to provoke strikes, particularly if war production were involved. In the Allis-Chalmers plant at Milwaukee, where tanks were produced, and the North American plant at Inglewood, California, where combat planes were built, the Communists led strikes that raised legitimate trade-union issues but in which their main interest was clearly political. When the 12,000 workers at North American were pulled off the job by a CP-led UAW local, negotiations were still in progress before the National Defense Mediation Board, and the UAW international office had not yet authorized the strike. But the leaders of the North American local eagerly jumped the gun, managing thereby to tie up for several days 20 percent of American combat plane production. Alarmed, the Roosevelt administration ordered the army to take over the plant, and on June 17, 1941, William Z. Foster was bitterly saying: "When President Roosevelt sent federal troops against the aviation workers and broke their strike, it was a taste of the Hitlerite terrorism that Wall Street capitalists have in mind for the working class."

Five days later the Soviet Union was invaded by Hitler, the cause of the North American workers was forgotten, and soon the CP, no longer troubled by Roosevelt's "Hitlerite terrorism," was insisting that "all disputes in industry must now . . . be solved without interruption of production." [15] And William Z. Foster was saying it too.

3. Though the CP held its own in the CIO during the time of the pact, it suffered losses elsewhere. Many of the intellectuals who had found no moral difficulties—or at least had shown none—in accepting the Moscow trials now abandoned the party, some, like Granville Hicks, issuing honest and forthright statements of resignation and others quietly slipping away. For the party ideologues, accustomed as they were to the fealty of pliant intellectual sympathizers, these desertions came as something of a shock; and they reacted with more than their usual violence. Look, sneered *The Communist* in December, 1939, look at the parade of "dubious hangers-on . . . ignoble . . . weaklings, the fair-weather friends . . . Ralph Bates, Louis Fischer, André Malraux, John

Strachey, Granville Hicks, Vincent Sheean, Jay Allen, Malcolm Cowley, Herman Reissig, James Waterman Wise. . . ." Ignoble or not, it was an impressive list, impressive enough to explain the spleen with which the party met the loss of such once valuable friends. And there were more lost friends, some fellow travelers of the party and others merely of the Popular Front: Richard Rovere, Archibald MacLeish, Waldo Frank, Moishe Nadir, a distinguished Yiddish writer, Ephraim Schwartzman, secretary of the Jewish People's Committee, George Wishniak, former business manager of the *Daily Worker*.

To pulverize the intellectual deserters, the party turned to its experienced hacks, who had been kept in the background during the happier days of the Popular Front but who were now ready with a full supply of gall and invective. Wrote V. J. Jerome in a booklet called *Intellectuals and the War*:

> Let the imperialists bring forth their Edna St. Vincent Millays to lure with Lorelei songs the people of our land into a war that is not our war—to chant the *leitmotif* of U.S. Steel and the House of Morgan. . . . Let their Librarians of Congress deplore the disillusioning books which have taught America's young men the nature of that first "spiritual" war to end war. Let the Mumfords and Cowleys, the Stracheys and Laskis and Malraux fawn when their imperialist masters crack the whip.
>
> When the war clouds burst and the imperialist line-up began to form against the Soviet Union, fairweather sailors could not face the storm. . . . To cover the tracks of their desertion, certain intellectuals charged that the Soviet Union and the Communist Party had "deserted" the fight against fascism. . . . [But actually] the Soviet Union's independent peace policy closed the door to the Chamberlain-Hitler complot. The Soviet-German Non-Aggression Pact drew an entire sixth of the earth out of the war. . . . It thus promoted the interests of all peace-loving peoples.

The vituperation is here so coarse and the logic of the last few sentences so obscure that one may doubt whether Jerome's attack served, or was meant to serve, any purpose other than to soothe the sensibilities of the still faithful. That, surely, was all Mike Gold managed to do in his book *The Hollow Men,* where he reflected upon the inherent vacillations of the intellectuals, weaklings caught between two warring classes and in moments of crisis subservient to the stronger one:

> So here are two psychological elements that go into the makeup of the renegade: his deep fear of proletarianization, from which he has never freed himself, and his lack of love for people, a trait arising out of the inhuman competitiveness of bourgeois society.

Those intellectuals who supported the Allies, wrote Gold, had turned to the service of fascism, since anyone "who is for America's entrance into the war must also demand an end to American democracy." And then in one of those orgies of venom that seemed a necessity of his soul:

> These Mumfords, MacLeishes and Franks may go on spouting endless torrents of "spirituality," all the large, facile, greasy, abstract words that bookmen, like confidence men, are so perfect in producing. But basic tendencies remain. Where are they going after rejecting liberalism? Not to Communism surely, but toward the other pole, toward fascism.[16]

The honeymoon of the Communist Party with the intellectuals thus seemed to have been nasty, brutish, and short.

Yet the party needed the intellectuals. It needed them because, apart from its anti-war activity, there was little it could now do in its own right except to campaign for civil liberties—the very problem that had traditionally most concerned the intellectuals.

Throughout 1940 the CP was subjected to a series of court actions instituted by the Roosevelt administration. In January, Browder was found guilty of a passport fraud committed years before—which during the Popular Front period the government had never gotten round to noticing—and sentenced to four years in prison and a $2,000 fine. In March, Communist leaders of the Fur Workers Union were indicted on anti-trust charges and an NMU leader was arrested on libel charges. In May, Clarence Hathaway was found guilty on a moldering libel charge. In June, Sam Darcy, a veteran party organizer, was extradited from Pennsylvania to California on a charge of false registration in 1934. During the same month charges were brought against the California party leader, William Schneiderman, to revoke a citizenship obtained in 1927. In September the state of Oklahoma revived a World War I criminal syndicalism law and a number of local Communists were accordingly sentenced to ten years in prison. These prosecutions, as the CP said, were clearly motivated by political needs, and whatever energy the party had left from its crusade for "peace" was spent in an effort to protect itself from governmental attack.

4. It was in the Jewish community that the Communists encountered their most serious troubles during the time of the Hitler-Stalin pact. CP members of Jewish descent who functioned in general political life may frequently have suffered some shock when they saw the picture of Ribbentrop and Molotov shaking hands; but those who presented themselves as *Jewish* Communists, writing and speaking in Yiddish and appealing to a distinctive Jewish consciousness, suffered the greatest emotional turmoil within themselves, met with the most violent criticism from the anti-Communist Yiddish press, and soon began to drop out of the movement in considerable numbers. Ever since the twenties the party had enjoyed a devoted following among the Jewish garment workers. During the thirties it had won the friendship of important Jewish intellectuals and established itself as a force within Yiddish cultural life. The fellow-traveling fraternal society, the International Workers Order, which was mainly Yiddish speaking, had served as a valuable source of financial and political support. Now all of these gains were threatened.

The first response to the pact among the Jewish Communists was sheer consternation. Heated meetings were held of the Yiddish-speaking branches and the sympathetic Jewish organizations, at some of which members announced their withdrawal and harassed leaders tried to justify the unjustifiable. A writer in the *Forward,* the Yiddish daily, described a Yiddish-speaking meeting in the Midwest where a prominent fellow traveler rose to say that he was not really concerned with Russia's betrayal of England and France but that he felt "all of us who put our trust in Stalin were exposed naked in front of the world as a pack of idiots." [17]

This, indeed, was the response of many Jewish sympathizers: a sense of having been betrayed politically, betrayed as Jews, and betrayed as people who had given their lives, frequently with a matchless devotion, to the radical movement.

At first the *Freiheit*, the Yiddish Communist daily, claimed there was nothing necessarily wrong with non-aggression pacts and that, in any case, they did not conflict with the anti-fascist Popular Front line. This justification quickly becoming obsolete, the Jewish Communists tried to console their followers—and themselves—with the legend that the pact contained a secret clause voiding all relations between Germany and Russia in case Germany attacked a third nation. Once Germany did attack Poland, the Jewish Communists used a "special" argument among their followers. The partition of Poland, wrote the *Freiheit*, was "good for the Jews." For while two million Polish Jews had fallen under Hitler's heel, another million had been "saved" by Russia.

The *Yiddisher Kempfer,* a labor Zionist weekly, attacked this argument by noting that it had been the pact which had first precipitated the war by freeing Hitler from the threat of an eastern front: "We reject with loathing the saving of a million Jews when it is bought at such a price." One Yiddish writer bitterly likened the Communist rationalization to the story of a man who starts a fire, burns down the house and its inhabitants, and then asks for a medal because he has saved one child.

The Yiddish-speaking Communists were clearly in a profound emotional panic. As *Der Yiddisher Kempfer* wrote: "Explanations [of the pact by the Jewish Communists] changed daily and new ones were offered that sometimes contradicted old ones. It was difficult not to form the impression that the faithful did not themselves believe in the arguments they were putting forward." [18]

A stream of desertions began from the Yiddish-speaking front groups: IKUF (a Yiddish cultural organization) and IKOR (an organization for Jewish resettlement) and the all-purpose Jewish People's Committee. Distinguished Yiddish writers like H. Leivik, Joseph Opatashu, Moishe Nadir, and Peretz Hirshbein, some of whom had contributed to the *Freiheit* and participated in the IKUF, now drifted away. Leading members of the *Freiheit* staff—Melech Epstein, Louis Hyman, and several others—resigned their posts. These Yiddish writers now formed an anti-Communist organization called the League Against Fascism and Dictatorship, composed mainly of former Jewish party members and sympathizers.[19]

In the Jewish labor movement, where Stalinist strength had been steadily whittled down since the late twenties, the pact brought frequent embarrassment and measurable losses to the Communists. By far the most important of these losses occurred in Local 22 of the International Ladies Garment Workers Union, which contained 20,000 Jewish dressmakers and had traditionally been a radical stronghold. Until the fall of 1939, the local had been run by a shaky coalition of Communists and Lovestoneites (see p. 152), though the latter were somewhat stronger because the extremely competent manager of the local, Charles Zimmerman, was a follower of Lovestone.

In the fall of 1939 a group of dressmakers presented a petition signed by 500 members of Local 22 calling upon its Executive Committee to pass a resolution denouncing the Hitler-Stalin pact. To prevent a split in the local's leadeship, the Executive Committee refused this request, but Zimmerman, aware of the strong feelings held by many Jewish workers, expressed his personal opposition to the pact in interviews with the Yiddish papers.

Ideological war broke out in the garment center. The *Daily Worker* began denouncing the leadership of Local 22, and CP leaflets were distributed in the dress market declaring that "The Trotskyists and Lovestoneites betray the workers and are attempting to force them into support of the present imperialist war." [20]

At the next meeting of Local 22, held on October 23, 1939, the issue came to a head in a way that was to be characteristic of many other Jewish unions. Sensing the angry mood of the meeting, the Stalinist leaders confined themselves to speaking about local matters and came down heavily on the bad conditions in the trade—an approach that would ordinarily have brought applause from the membership. This time, however, the ranks hissed and many obscure members, obviously agitated by the news from Europe, rose to denounce the pact. Fist fights broke out all through the hall and Zimmerman barely managed to control the meeting.

The final outcome was that in December six leading Communists, all members of the Executive Committee of Local 22, resigned from the party. Once they left, the CP lost its power and prestige in the local—a loss that reverberated throughout the Jewish labor movement.

Meanwhile, in the last months of 1939, the Yiddish press was filled with taunts and jibes, all focused on the question: were the Communists still in favor of the boycott of Nazi goods that had been conducted for some years by the entire Jewish community? Foster's answer for the CP had been a definite "No," but for weeks the *Freiheit* had avoided printing his statement and had tried to evade the topic. Finally, the *Freiheit* broke down and shamefacedly admitted that the Jewish Communists now favored abandoning the boycott against Nazi Germany. For a number of Jewish sympathizers, this was the final straw.[21]

Yet, despite these losses, the hard core of Yiddish-speaking Communists remained faithful, as the hard core of English-speaking Communists remained faithful. The will to believe, the necessity for faith, ran deep among them; the emotional investments of a lifetime could not so easily be abandoned; and always there remained the hope that somehow the Soviet Union would yet prove the land of socialism and freedom about which they had dreamed.

That the party as a whole was weakened during the years of the pact there can be no doubt. Membership figures are harder to find and less reliable with each passing year—particularly since party membership during the Popular Front era had been a very ambiguous thing indeed, not requiring regular activity or dues payment. The party acknowledged that it had sustained a 15 percent loss from 1939 to 1940, but such percentages tell us very little since no membership figures had been released for 1939. From various hints dropped by party functionaries, however, one may conclude that the registration in 1940 was probably below 50,000, as against a 1938 registration of 57,000 and a higher figure for 1939.

More revealing are the recruitment figures for 1940. Only 658 new members were taken into the party in February and 819 in March, as compared with a monthly average of 2,000 in 1937 and about 4,000 during most of 1938.[22] The party claimed, of course, that by shaking off the faint-hearted it had really strengthened itself, but such claims seldom amounted to more than bureaucratic whistling in the dark. Some of the front groups prospered, but the party as such found the political weather rough. (The total vote for the Browder-Ford ticket in 1940, despite a vigorous campaign, was only 46,251 as against 80,181 in 1936.)

That the CP was spared further difficulties was the result not of any efforts of its own but, as Communist jargon would have it, of a change in "objective circumstances." On June 22, 1941, Hitler, perhaps remembering that his pact with Stalin had "tremendously limited the direction of Nazi war aims," hurled his troops across the Russian border.

5. Being a Communist editor during these years was a notably thankless task. Consider, for example, the plight of the editor of *The Communist* who for his July, 1941 issue had set up an appropriately belligerent piece by William Z. Foster arguing that "the present war constitutes a violent division of the world among the great imperialist powers." Just as the number was going to press, news of war on the eastern front suddenly reached him, too late to pull out Foster's article and barely in time to insert a hasty editorial calling upon all mankind to support the Soviet Union "in its struggle against Hitlerism." [23] The issue of *The Communist*, with its contradictory positions on the war appearing side by side, became a minor collector's item.

Again, a complete shift of line was necessary. But this time the party leaders and members made the turn with far more ease and gusto than they had in 1939. For many of them, the "anti-war" policy had meant a rather severe break with habits of thought deeply ingrained during the Popular Front period. They had gone along with the pact out of loyalty to the movement, but some had felt vague discomfort and others acute pain. Even if at its beginning the Popular Front had been a mere tactic, in the course of time it acquired an autonomy of its own. Dropping the rhetoric of anti-fascism during the days of the pact had not been easy: many Communists, particularly those who had reached maturity during the mid-thirties, had a genuine emotional stake in the political outlook and style of the Popular Front.

Now, by contrast, there were neither difficulties nor hesitations.

The party leaders seemed happy to cast aside their pacifist pretensions and give unambiguous support to the war. For many Communists, in fact, the years of the war were to provide their most satisfying political experience. Two strong needs that in the past had frequently clashed could now be brought together. The Communists were able to reestablish close bonds with those "broad strata of American progressives" with whom they felt so much in common but from whom they had been somewhat cut off during the past two years. And without alienating themselves on the home front they were also able to appear as the fiercest defenders of the Soviet Union. They could be Russian patriots and American patriots at the same time; they could be agents of the Russian national interest while marching in warm fraternity with the Western liberals, indeed with Westerners of any political complexion. For a movement appealing simultaneously to impulses of fraternity and a worship of power, nothing could be more convenient.

There was hardly another period in the history of the American CP during which its essential status as a "foreign national party" was as difficult—not to detect, but to demonstrate. Even such veteran Stalinists as Foster, who had never been too happy with the Popular Front, could now relax in the knowledge that by helping defend the West they were fulfilling their main and passionate task: to defend the Russian fatherland.

During the first few months after the Nazi invasion of Russia, the American Communists were obsessed by the fear that the West would make an alliance with Hitler to carve up the Soviet Union. Old visions of a capitalist encirclement of Russia acquired a new urgency. "The first hour," wrote Mike Gold in one of his more sober moments, "was awful. I shall never forget it. Now it has come—the thing we so feared for five, ten, twenty years. At last the capitalist world was invading the workers republic." And the one sure way of preventing a rapprochement between Hitler and the West, as the Communists soon realized, was for America to enter the shooting war. "To the question of how far we should go in the struggle against Hitler," wrote Foster, "the answer must be an emphatic ALL THE WAY." [24] A year or two after having drawn fearful pictures of mangled flesh, shattered faces, and Gold Star mothers as the inevitable consequence of a new war, the party became the most outspoken interventionist force in American life.

As the Wehrmacht sped across the Russian plains—on September 9 it besieged Leningrad, on November 12 it approached the suburbs of Moscow—the cries of the party for immediate American entry into the war grew more frantic each day. And understandably so. The Russian fatherland seemed on the edge of collapse, yet the British could do little to open a Second Front and the Americans contented themselves with sending old destroyers. The nightmare of a negotiated peace with Germany kept haunting the Communists, and haunting them with a magnified intensity as the Nazi armies knifed into the heartland of Russia.

Pearl Harbor therefore came to them almost as a relief. Emotionally at war since June 22, they felt that the Japanese attack had done what no force in our domestic life had been able or courageous enough to do: it had put an end to America's hesitations and driven it into war. "This tremendous event," observed Foster, "does not change the basic line of our party. It merely swiftly matures our analysis." [25]

For the next several years the party's slogans seemed barely distinguishable from those of non-Communists also desiring a speedy and forceful prosecution of the war effort. The CP might be more shrill than other political groups, the neophytes of patriotism more zealous than the seasoned patriots; but on the face of things, the Communists now said exactly what many other Americans were saying.

Yet this appearance was delusive. Beneath the surface of agreement there continued to be major disagreements of view and clashes of interest. The Communists had committed themselves to the war only on June 22, 1941, while most Americans had become emotionally involved either in September, 1939, or on the day Pearl Harbor was bombed. In the early months of the war, when the Japanese overwhelmed large areas of the Pacific, this difference might appear unimportant; but within a few years it was to prove decisive.

Even in regard to immediate domestic policies the differences were very real. Driven by the idea that *anything* was justified that helped Russia, the American CP agitated for total mobilization on the home front, indeed, for a kind of total state. Other groups that had been radical, Socialist, or pacifist in prewar years also supported the war effort, yet most of them still felt a need to safeguard democratic rights at home, to watch against reactionaries who might try to exploit the war crisis in order to enact repressive measures. Only the CP was willing not merely to subordinate all other ends to the war but to abandon those ends entirely. It was supremely characteristic of the Stalinists that, in throwing themselves into what they now proclaimed as a democratic crusade, they did so in a thoroughly totalitarian manner.

The party whose election platform in 1940 had read, "No armaments or American soldiers for imperialist wars and adventures," now proposed universal military service. In accents not very different from those of the Army and Navy League, John Gates wrote in *The Communist*: "The people of America must master the military art. Military training must become an essential everyday part of our life, like the right to vote and compulsory education." [26]

The party which had so recently been instigating strikes in defense industries now demanded all-out mobilization in "the battle of production." Such a mobilization, it said, involved opposition to strikes in defense industries, and since, as Foster logically remarked, "there is no hard and fast line between defense and non-defense industries," the CP soon opposed all strikes. "Any strike," declared the *Daily Worker*, "is bound to prove a hindrance to the war effort." [27] Conservative groups may also have believed this, but at least some of them felt it wise or expedient not to say so. Ordinary labor leaders were more than hesitant about calling strikes during the war years, but they realized that a total pledge not to strike gave the employers an extremely powerful weapon and they felt there were times when it really was in the national and their members' interest to call a strike. Such scruples, perhaps unavoidable to any genuine democrat, struck the Stalinists as either absurd or defeatist.

Quite understandably, business spokesmen were at first taken aback to discover that the Communists now stood at the extreme right wing of the labor movement—indeed, that they were now one of the most right-wing groups in the country as a whole. With a mixture of glee and bewilderment, *Business Week* noted that unions "identified as Communist-dominated" have "the best no-strike record," are "the most vigorous proponents of labor-management cooperation," "the only serious advocates of incentive wages and the only unions which support the President's call for a national service act." * [28] It soon became a common practice for employers to point, with or without malice, to Stalinist-led unions as models that other labor leaders should emulate. And when Earl Browder was accused by the Trotskyists of being "a strikebreaker," he replied:

> As regards the fomenting of the strike movements that threaten America at this time, I consider it the greatest honor to be a breaker of this movement.[30]

No one could accuse the Communists of doing things by halves.

It proved particularly infuriating for them that the one labor leader who spoke most forcefully in favor of the continued right to strike was their hero and semi-patron of yesterday, John L. Lewis.

* Shortly before the *Business Week* story, the labor columnist Victor Riesel, who at the time had close connections with the top CIO leadership, wrote the following report:

"A bitter feud between President Roosevelt and CIO leader Philip Murray is embarrassing Sidney Hillman, CIO political boss, and his new left-wing allies. Murray's fight with the President began the morning after Mr. Roosevelt called for a labor draft law. William Green, AFL head, and Murray were in the President's study listening to him complain vehemently about labor's attitude toward the national service proposal.

"The President, according to reports, sharply attacked Murray for calling the proposal 'quack medicine.' . . .

"Murray then asked Mr. Roosevelt, 'Do you expect to get a realistic tax program?'

"The President said no.

" 'Do you expect to get a good subsidy program?'

"Mr. Roosevelt said no.

" 'In such a case,' Murray asked, 'would you sign a national service bill if Congress passed it?'

"The President said he would sign it.

"Murray grew red-faced while Bill Green fidgeted.

" 'Suppose Congress were to pass a severe Smith anti-strike bill instead of a national service law . . . ,' Murray queried.

"The President said he would sign that, too.

"Murray then said he would tour the country and speak in opposition to the President's proposal. Mr. Roosevelt declared that Murray did not speak for the CIO. The President then waved a telegram which endorsed his views.

"It was signed by a prominent left-wing CIO leader. Murray saw red in more ways than one—and left shortly after." [29]

His call for a miners' strike in 1943 brought from the CP reactions at least as violent as those from management or the government. Before the strike had begun, the *Daily Worker* warned: "A strike cannot be tolerated under any circumstances for it would be a stab at our armed might." (The very language was of a kind to be found in the writings of such conservative columnists as Westbrook Pegler and George Sokolsky.) In a special radio appeal to the miners, Charles Spencer, CP leader in the anthracite district, urged them not to obey the union's "treasonable" strike call. Once the strike began, Browder pictured Lewis as an accomplice of the Nazis whose "every effort to break down the no-strike policy is a blow for Hitler . . . and is treason to the people." In a report to the CP National Committee, Browder spoke of "the Lewis insurrection against the war" and charged that a pro-Nazi conspiracy was trying to elevate Lewis to the rank of Hitler's American Gauleiter. In July Browder, who was now beginning to resemble Attorney General Palmer of some twenty-odd years before, went so far as to say that

> There is not the slightest doubt that Lewis is working and has worked *during the past two years at least* as an integral part of the pro-Nazi fifth column, aiming at a negotiated peace with Hitler, and at the Nazi subjugation of the United States itself. . . . This is treason.[31]

What is most notable in this statement, which appeared in *The Communist* in July, 1943, and could therefore not have been written later than about the middle of June, is the phrase we have italicized. Did Browder mean to suggest that Lewis was a Nazi accomplice even before June 22, 1941 ("during the past two years *at least*"), working for "the Nazi subjugation of the United States" at the very time the Communists had been praising him as "a giant among Lilliputians"? Or had Browder, by a not uncommon act of projection, revealed some obscure feeling of guilt about the private views he had held during the time of the Hitler-Stalin pact?

In any case, Lewis was far from being the only target of Communist ultra-patriotism. Any labor leader who maintained the mildest sort of militancy in relation to employers, even if he were also an unconditional supporter of the war, might now be attacked as a saboteur or fifth columnist. When Walter Reuther came out in support of the miners' strike, the CP denounced him as a defeatist playing the game of the "pro-Nazi" Lewis. "If you think," fumed Browder, "that grievances are more important than the war, then your place is with John L. Lewis, Walter Reuther and all other advocates of a negotiated peace." Going farther than all but a few of the most extreme right-wingers desired or dared to go, Browder charged that the AFL and CIO strikes in 1943 formed "a well-developed conspiracy against the war." [32] It would seem plausible to conclude that one reason there was so much less conventional anti-labor activity during the Second than the First World War was that the CP did the job better than any reactionaries or conservatives possibly could. For the Communists were the most reliable and devoted strikebreakers the labor movement had ever seen: they were strikebreakers with a good conscience.*

Toward the end of the war, the CP union leaders and fellow travelers went a step further: they now declared that strikes should be outlawed not only during but even after the war. Speaking at a meeting of his Warehousemen's Local 6 in San Francisco on May 25, 1944, Harry Bridges said that "the strike weapon is overboard, not

---

* As always with the Communists—and as may be endemic to the totalitarian mind—they seemed to gain a kind of pleasure in pushing their current line to the uttermost extreme. Thus, when the CIO retail clerks' union, led by Samuel Wolchok, called a strike against Montgomery Ward, Harry Bridges instructed the members of the Longshoremen's and Warehousemen's Union to ignore its sister CIO union's picket line. Bridges' union declared: "No matter what the motive of the employer, any strike aimed at him is in physical fact a strike against ourselves and our country. No matter if he claims or seems to be in non-essential production, no strike is proper, for strikes are infectious and damaging to morale."

Sewell Avery, the antediluvian reactionary heading Montgomery Ward, could hardly have found another defender to put the case for him on so exalted a moral plane.

Later the Communists issued a defense of their role in this strike that is worth quoting. "The perfect team," wrote George Morris, a CP labor expert, "is where an employer is of the most rabid reactionary type, like the America Firster Sewell Avery, head of Montgomery Ward, while the union is under Trotskyist control. . . . In such a case the employer and the union officials have far more in common than in dispute. . . . Trotskyites, of course, made the most of the opportunity to advertise themselves as champions against a reactionary like Avery. But the fact remains that the reactionaries exploited the dispute to arouse middle class and rural fervor against the administration. . . ." [33]

Wolchok, a quite routine labor official, was no more a Trotskyist than George Morris himself, as Morris knew perfectly well.

THE AMERICAN COMMUNIST PARTY

only for the duration of the war, but after the war too," and urged employers to "refuse to give consideration to the demands of any section of labor" that went on strike not merely during the war but "indefinitely thereafter." The *Pilot,* organ of the National Maritime Union and at the time edited by Stalinists, wrote in February, 1944: "Among the great industrialists there are many who believe in and will fight just as sincerely and effectively as ourselves, for enduring peace. These are our allies and we must learn to work with them honestly and whole-heartedly." [34] Is it any wonder that *Business Week* rubbed its eyes when examining the Communists' record in the unions?

The NMU, once among the most militant unions in the country, now set up a "leadership school" which taught sailors the virtues of not striking. Two awed correspondents from *Collier's,* in an article slyly called "Readin', Writin', and No Strikin'," described this school in detail:

> Perhaps the most remarkable thing about the school is that it really works. Nearly four hundred men have graduated from it, according to NMU educational director Leo Huberman, who also set up similar schools in Detroit and St. Louis. While not all graduates have returned from trips yet, those who have, have brought in "good" ships on which there was excellent cooperation between the crew and [the officers].

Student seamen would raise questions like: "What the hell is this? Are [the NMU leaders] working for us or for the shipowners? These lousy shipowners are making millions and we are getting our melons knocked in. Sure I'm for winning the war. But by the jumpin' Holy, the minute this war is over we gotta hit the bricks." Such sentiments, which were surely those of a great many American union men, were intolerable to the Communists. The party-line "teacher" replied with the stock phrases used against the labor movement during wartime: "Sure, we know conditions are lousy. . . . But soldiers are taking that and worse, day in and day out. We gotta back them up."

After a talk in favor of extending the no-strike pledge into the postwar period, "teacher" took a poll of the class to see how it felt about this proposal. The vote being about 50-50, "teacher" felt it necessary to explain the party line a bit more:

> Now here is our program: Unity at the top and unity at the bottom. Unity at the top means unity of the Soviet Union, Great Britain and the US. Now if these three wholly different countries are able to agree . . . surely we should be able to sit down with the shipowners and do it at home.[35]

Nor was this merely an over-zealous aberration of a seaman Stalinist. Roy Hudson, the CP leader in charge of labor policy during the war, reported to the party's National Committee in 1945 that

> Strikes in the post-war period will not solve the problem of providing sixty million jobs. . . . [This] will be brought about by the more effective organization of labor's political strength to maintain unity and cooperation of all those who support President Roosevelt's program and the decisions of Teheran and Crimea. But this unity and cooperation cannot be secured if labor places its reliance on the strike weapon. . . .[36]

Only "national unity" could achieve sixty million jobs, said Hudson; and where, amidst all this, the old Marxist doctrine of class struggle came in, neither he nor the other "Browderites" at the head of the party troubled to explain.

Communist wartime policy in the unions was not limited to agitating against strikes and enthusiastically breaking those that occurred. Alone in the labor movement, the Communists spoke out for "incentive pay" schemes and piece-work formulas which the unions had traditionally rejected as vicious forms of the speedup creating dissension among workers. The CP justified this policy, which made it decidedly unpopular in such militant unions as the UAW, by generalized and emotional references to the war effort; but more often than not, such references were either consciously demagogic or psychologically compulsive; for there was nothing inherent in support of the war that required an "incentive pay" scheme in the factories. It could even be argued, as most unionists did, that the speedup which the Communists were advocating would lead to fatigue, demoralization, and decreased production.

Earl Browder added a piquant note by claiming, as one reason for proposing "incentive pay," that it was now the duty of the workers "to force better profits on unwilling employers"—though most legitimate unionists felt that the profits were good enough and the employers not at all unwilling. When President Roosevelt sponsored a National Service Bill in 1944, which almost every non-Communist section of the union movement bitterly attacked as a labor draft, the Communists in the CIO came out for it. Harry Bridges wrote: "It is hard for me to see why we should fight for the preservation of such so-called rights ["an individual's right to work or not to work"] as against the President's proposal." [37] There was logic of a kind, it must be granted, in the Communist position: having never been troubled by the denial of "such so-called rights" in Russia they could declare there was no reason to preserve them in America.

Toward the end of the war Eric Johnston, William Green, and Philip Murray offered their "New Charter for Labor and Management," a scheme for industrial peace that the Communists in the past would automatically have rejected as "class collaboration." Now the *Daily Worker* praised it as "a step which grew out of wartime unity and . . . will help continue this unity in the post-war period." Browder, a master of wartime one-upmanship, added his solemn regret that the National Association of Manufacturers refused to join the pact, since its participation, he felt, would have deepened "national unity." [38]

Ruthless in its fanaticism, the CP was ready to sacrifice not only the interests of the workers but also those of the Negroes. Here the war line of the party was carried to an extreme that surely could not be explained in terms of immediate political interests—for it clearly alienated important sections of the Negro community—but did make sense for a "foreign national party" totally dedicated to the Russian state.

The morale of many Negroes was understandably low during the war years. Illiterate Southern sharecroppers as well as sophisticated Northern intellectuals could see that a war proclaimed as a democratic crusade was being fought on Jim Crow assumptions, with segregation in the armed forces and discrimination in war-production industries. Liberal and even conservative Negro leaders kept insisting that the one way to tap the full energies of American Negroes for the war effort was to make dramatic improvements in their political and social status. (A few intransigent souls continued to urge such improvements not on the ground of wartime expediency but simply as a matter of justice.) Major Negro newspapers began a "Double V" campaign: Victory over Hitler abroad and Victory over Jim Crow at home. This apparently sensible and certainly just proposal—made, it should be stressed, by Negro leaders committed to the war—was harshly denounced by the Communists. At a 1942 meeting of the Southern Negro Youth Congress, which the Communists controlled, Double V was labeled "disruptive." [39]

Those Negro leaders who felt that the struggle for the rights of their people could not be suspended in the name of the war were ferociously attacked by the Communists. The very organizations that James W. Ford had previously scorned for deluding Negroes into support of "the imperialist war" were now found to be "sabotaging the war effort," "aiding the Axis camp," and endangering "the unity of the American people." In Stalinist eyes the most dangerous of these organizations (because most intelligently led) was the March on Washington Movement headed by A. Philip Randolph. This group, wrote Ford, was creating "confusion and dangerous moods in the rank and file of the Negro people and utilizing their justified grievances as a weapon of opposition to the Administration's war program." [40] Ford neglected to add, however, that the March on Washington Movement, through constant public pressure and threats of assembling a vast pilgrimage of angered Negroes in the nation's capital, was mainly responsible for President Roosevelt's Executive Order No. 8802 (FEPC) and for still another executive order which put some teeth into FEPC.*

Throughout the war, the Communists were the main force within the Negro community in favor of muting—and often prevent-

---

* As for Randolph himself, he was given the full *Daily Worker* treatment. "A fascist helping defeatism," a saboteur who "guaranteed the triumph of fascism," were among the phrases repeatedly applied to him. [41] That he was a lifelong Socialist who had given all his energies to the cause of Negro rights and the interests of Negro railroad workers—such details could also be sacrificed to the "needs of the war effort."

ing—the campaign for equal rights. In September, 1941, Benjamin Davis, Jr., soon to become the most prominent Negro Communist, wrote that "the CP is *disturbed* by the increasing struggle of Negroes for jobs in defense plants" (emphasis added). A genuine liberal or radical, one might suppose, would have been delighted rather than disturbed. Instead Davis went on to say that "many of the Negro groups and newspapers are not clear on the international situation" —by which he meant that they believed the war should not be used as the occasion or pretext for giving up entirely the struggle against Jim Crow.

The following year, in a symposium appearing in a Negro magazine, a Communist spokesman wrote: "Hitler is the main enemy. . . . Foes of Negro rights in this country should be considered secondary." [42] Had the Communists worked even by this policy, their enmity to the campaign for Negro rights would not have been as total as it was; but the truth is that they believed the struggle for Negro rights should be suspended entirely during the war. To show that they really meant this, and to offer a hand of peace to the Dixiecrat wing of the Democratic Party, the CP dissolved its branches in the South. At least during the war years, no one could accuse it of stirring up "dissension" either in the North or in the South.

In 1945 there occurred one of those peculiarly symptomatic incidents that reveal more than any number of party documents. A group of wounded Negro soldiers had been left unattended and without medical care at Fort Devens early in 1945. Four Negro WACs who chanced to come upon the wounded men complained to the camp authorities. The answer of the army was to court-martial the WACs. Protests from churches, unions, and civil rights organizations were so widespread that the army reversed its decision. All ranges of authentic Negro opinion naturally felt this to be a victory; only Benjamin Davis, Jr., thought otherwise. Instead of supporting the WACs, Davis reprimanded them in a fashion that made Uncle Tom seem like a reckless revolutionary:

> The U.S. general staff has on many occasions . . . proved that they deserve the full confidence of the Negro people. . . . We cannot temporarily stop the war until all questions of discrimination are ironed out.[43]

The leaders of the NAACP and the March on Washington Movement might have replied that they were trying to stop not the war but the court-martial of four girls; by now, however, they were so embittered at the behavior of the Negro Communists that they usually felt it useless to reply. Yet it is important to observe that despite its loss of prestige within the Negro community, the party persisted in its policies. One can even describe its behavior toward the Negroes as "principled": no temptations of political advantage or emotions of sympathy for abused Negroes* could deflect the Communists from their main task.

"To us," wrote Willard S. Townsend, the first Negro to become president of a CIO union, "the present line of the Communist carpetbaggers on the Negro question . . . is indistinguishable from that of many of our southern poll-taxers and Uncle Toms." As soon as the war was over, the Communists themselves hastened to say almost the same thing. During the ritual condemnations of "Browderism" (see pp. 437-449), Doxey Wilkerson, a leading Negro comrade, wrote that "A critical examination of Communist practice [in regard to Negroes during the war] can but reveal a striking gap between ideological profession and actual performance." [45] No critic could or needed to say more.

If Negro rights were now expendable, so were civil liberties. The first major test of the Communists came when the Smith Act was used late in 1941 as the basis of government charges against a group of Trotskyists in Minneapolis. Passed in June, 1940, aimed primarily against the Communists, and criticized both by the CP and by liberals as lending itself much too easily to punitive use against unpopular minorities, the Smith Act defined it as a crime

* Individual Communists undoubtedly continued to feel such emotions, but the party line prevented their unencumbered expression. When in 1942 a Mississippi Negro, Cleo Wright, was lynched in an indescribably horrible way, the *Daily Worker* wrote that the crime "must be judged in an entirely new light—in light of the requirements for military victory against the Axis enemy. It is a conscious deed of sabotage and interference with a domestic phase of the military program to defeat the enemy." [44]

As a factual description, this was utterly inaccurate: the Mississippi mob, far from plotting "a conscious deed of sabotage" against the war effort, was simply concerned with torturing and mutilating a Negro boy. Morally, "protests" of the kind expressed by the *Daily Worker* were almost as bad as silence or approval, since they reduced matters of human dignity and justice to a mere function of political or military expediency.

"to teach and advocate the overthrow of the United States government by force and violence." During the years of the cold war, the Smith Act would serve as the legal basis for sending many Communists to jail. Yet when the Trotskyists were brought to trial in 1941 on the very same charges that would later be used against the Communists, the *Daily Worker* supported the prosecution:

> The American people [wrote CP journalist Milton Howard] can find no objection to the destruction of the Fifth Column in this country. On the contrary, they must insist on it. The leaders of the Trotskyist organization which operates under the false name of "Socialist Workers Party" deserve no more support from labor . . . than do the Nazis who camouflage their party under the false name of "National Socialist Workers Party."

Anyone during the war years who disagreed with the Communists from the left could expect to be called an "agent of Hitler." Frequently informing to government agencies against left-wing dissidents, the Communists contributed to the corrosion of civil liberties from which they themselves were to suffer in postwar America.

As a kind of kangaroo loyalty board, the CP repeatedly declared Norman Thomas to be an accomplice of fascism and a fifth-columnist, though his sin consisted of nothing but a belief that, while a military victory over the Axis powers was necessary, American radicals and liberals should continue to fight for the needs of labor and the Negroes. Here is Israel Amter, a top CP leader, writing about Thomas in 1942:

> Mussolini was a "socialist"; Laval was a "socialist"; Norman Thomas, too, is a "socialist." He offers the world only one kind of peace—the peace of a Hitler, a Mussolini, a Laval. . . . The Socialist Party realizes that its anti-war position is unacceptable to the American people; nevertheless to perform its service to Hitler, it must raise questions that will keep it before the public eye. Hence Thomas and the Socialist Party become the stalwart "champions" of civil liberties. . . . It is the function of Thomas and the Socialist Party to appear as revolutionary leaders, to obstruct the war effort. . . . This is nothing but downright Fifth Column activity—activity that must be stifled. . . . Norman

Thomas, Fifth Columnist and spearhead of fascism, still has access to the radio and spews forth his traitorous program. It is a distinct disservice to our country to allow this worker for fascism to use the air in order to spread disunity and hatred for our allies. . . . Let us rather adopt the methods of the Soviet Union. . . . [The government] must proceed against such people as Fish, Nye, Reynolds, Norman Thomas and the whole Fifth Column, who are downright workers for fascism.[46]

It is true: heretics were handled more efficiently in Russia. Had Thomas been unfortunate enough to be born a Russian, he would long ago have received a bullet in the back of his neck. But since he happened to be living in America, he remained alive to defend in the late forties and fifties the Communists suffering prosecution under the Smith Act.

6. Party membership rose rapidly during the war years, approximately doubling from 1941 to 1944 and reaching 80,000 by mid-1944. Because the Communists now held such a strong grip on sections of the CIO, they managed to recruit heavily among industrial workers. In 1943 alone, CP membership in the auto industry increased by 100 percent, in steel by 50 percent, and in shipbuilding by 60 percent.[47] If some of the CIO veterans were repelled by the Stalinist line during the war years, there were others, usually without any radical or militant labor traditions to suppress, who accepted it at face value.

Maneuvering with an unprecedented assurance and basking in unprecedented public acceptance, the Communists piled up major organizational gains. On the west coast they penetrated the Democratic Party, taking control of local units in California and Washington. In the November, 1941 elections for Brooklyn councilmen the CP candidate, Pete Cacchione, was elected with nearly 50,000 "final votes" in a complicated PR system. Two years later his vote rose to nearly 70,000, and a second CP candidate, Benjamin Davis, Jr., was also elected in Manhattan. Even in the conservative borough of Queens the party vote rose by 33 percent between 1941 and 1943.

Meanwhile, after a fierce battle with the Social Democratic

leaders of the garment unions, the Communists won control of the American Labor Party, which for a time became a genuine force in New York politics. In East Harlem, a dismal slum inhabited mainly by Puerto Ricans, the fellow-traveling demagogue Vito Marcantonio built up a tough political machine that kept returning him to Congress and yielding the New York Stalinists valuable fruits.

Yet it would not be very useful to compare the growth of the CP during the war years with its growth in other periods, since the meaning of party membership had now changed radically from what it had ever been before. Not only was the wartime recruit not expected to be a dedicated revolutionist or even a political activist; he now had only the vaguest of political responsibilities. An authoritative report by a party leader listed the following conditions for membership:

> Agreement with party platform in applying it where one is active. . . . Participation in some phase of war [N.B., not party] work. . . . Reading of the party press. . . . Payment of dues and membership in a branch, *but not compulsory regular attendance*.[48] [emphasis added]

Gone were the days when the members were bound by the closest fraternal and ideological bonds into a community of the elect (or as some almost seemed to feel, a consecrated family). No longer were there the old "rent parties" at which Communists would pool their quarters and half-dollars to help pay the rent of unemployed comrades. Instead, as a new-style Communist leader would recall from the vantage point of later disillusion:

> The rank and file were once again tasting the joy of being accepted by all groups. The party line made it possible during this period for ordinary members to be merely human beings and to act naturally, for their neighbors were now less frightened, and even listened to Communists explain that they were on the side of the American people.[49]

If the inner life of the party was now less intense and demanding than it had once been, the active Communists found new compensations. It was extraordinarily pleasant to be able once again to move into wide areas of American life, reaching more deeply than during the late thirties and gaining a popularity they had never before experienced. It was pleasant, and it brought immediate tangible results.

But with success came new problems. An interesting tension could now be observed between the centripetal pull which any organization (but especially a Communist one) must exert and the centrifugal looseness encouraged by the new line. There was clearly the possibility that if the Communists really became absorbed by the "outside world"—that misty province of ordinariness which for radicals had always been so tempting and so threatening—they would lose their sense of "difference" and thereby become less dependable politically.

What was true for the rank and file was equally true for the leaders. Communist union officials now began to command sizable treasuries, to batten off expense accounts like other labor bureaucrats, to wear expensive clothing, to frequent fashionable night clubs (particularly if, like Café Society, they mixed "progressive" skits with pretty girls). Communist lawyers and journalists, working for unions, community groups, publishing houses, and war relief committees, found themselves rubbing shoulders with Important People. Party leaders were sometimes seen in public wearing formal evening dress—imagine Lenin in a tuxedo!—required, they humorlessly explained, for the dinners held by the respectable committees it was expedient for them to cultivate. As all these pleasures of respectability ate into their Stalinist hearts, creating new expectations and styles of life, softening their sense of rectitude as only American comforts can, was there not a danger that they would slowly become estranged from the party? that their careers would gradually supplant their convictions? that they would forget which country it was to which they owed their *primary* allegiance? So at least felt some of the old-timers, Foster and a few disgruntled cronies, grumbling in secret, fearful to speak openly lest Browder, now puffed up with vanity and arrogance, should expel them.

But in the main they were wrong: the party core did not disintegrate. A few Communists did wander off into bourgeois pastures, and a good many were softened to the point where they could not resist the pressures that would come after the war years.

(For the thousands of new members this was hardly a problem at all, since they, having been recruited on the basis of "national unity," seldom became genuine Stalinists; they might pay their dues or attend an occasional meeting but essentially they were still men of the "outside world.") The party militants, however, were buoyed up by the mounting victories of the Russian army, thrilled by the heroism of Stalingrad, gratified by the sense that, no matter how far to the right the CP moved, they were still members of an invisible political army. And though on the face of it they seemed to have broken out of their isolation and become deeply involved in trade-union or community work, they were seldom really part of the "outside world." They might be in it, but only rarely were they of it. The very busy-ness of their schedules—party committees, Russian War Relief, CIO locals, Joint Anti-Fascist Refugee Committee, Jefferson School lectures, community war drives—became an anodyne lulling them into a mechanical acceptance of the party slogans. Reflection, which is the prerequisite of doubt, requires both time and privacy. Time and privacy were what the party militants lacked. Their bodies moved ceaselessly through a feverish grind of public activity, with the result that their minds, lying idle, remained the property of the party. Like men engaged in night work who form part of the productive process yet are cut off from the social life of the community, the party militants insulated themselves from the "outside world" precisely through their intense and successful activity within that world.

Local branches were now directed to become leaders in pushing the community war effort, and despite the resistance of a few old-timers the party assumed among its main neighborhood tasks the selling of war bonds, organizing blood donations, participating in civil defense—in other words, ceasing to function, or apparently ceasing to function, as a distinctive political movement with a distinctive political view. "We have some experiences," boasted John Williamson, the main organizational wheelhorse of the CP during the war years, "such as in Hartford, where the City Salvage Committee chose the CP branch to organize salvage collection in one ward just as it chose the American Legion or the Kiwanis or a church, for others. . . ." The *Daily Worker* listed as typical branch activities:

In the electrical industry . . . our party helped work out the beat-the-schedule plan for increased production; in connection with the shortage of scrap the Cleveland Communists in the steel industry in collaboration with others influenced the initiation of a mass scrap collection; and in Youngstown as a result of the initiative of the Communists thousands of school children, Boy Scouts and the people at large were involved in the collection of many tons of tin.

No longer did party meetings drag on endlessly, with one report droning into another. Now everything was slick and short, far closer in spirit to a high-powered fraternal lodge or a businessmen's lunch club than to a radical party. At a typical branch meeting the following was the agenda:

1) Talk by an American seaman just back from England . . . he spoke for ten minutes. 2) Entertainment: some songs and a short dramatic skit. 3) A brief report (20 minutes) on a branch program of work in the community followed by short discussion. Among the topics raised briefly were: branch campaign to get 100 pints of blood for the Red Cross; branch campaign to sell $1000 in stamps and bonds; anti-Nazi work in the community. . . . 4) Induction of new members. 5) Refreshments.[50]

Such changes did not take place by chance or drift: they were the result of careful discussion and planning. John Williamson, in one of his organizational articles, touched upon a real issue—even if he also displayed a notable lack of humor—when he chided one party group for leaving Communist literature in the toilets of a union hall. This, he claimed, was undignified: "Let them put it in the union reading room." The problem was, however, whether the CP could ultimately negotiate the turn from the toilet to the reading room, whether a dignified and respectable Communist Party could in the long run preserve its organizational coherence as a tightly bound elite.

By 1944 the problem became more acute when party spokesmen announced that it would be "un-Marxian and sectarian" to demand that CP members believe in Communism at all. "We can ask of new applicants to membership," wrote Williamson, "only loyalty to the principles already comprehensible to all workers." As for the Young Communist League, once the training school for future party organizers, by 1943 it had a sizable portion of members who did not even profess Communist beliefs. "It was quite inevitable," reported YCL leader Max Weiss, "that in its growth the YCL should more and more recruit young people who did not have a socialist outlook. . . . A substantial part of the YCL today is not socialist in its belief." When the YCL was dissolved in late 1943 and reconstituted as the American Youth for Democracy, the new constitution declared that the AYD "is a character-building organization dedicated to education of youth in the spirit of democracy and freedom." [51]

At times, of course, the party leadership showed signs of hesitation, remembering to warn that it was mistaken "that collaboration in the camp of national unity means losing the party's identity." [52] Had the process of organizational loosening and the deliberate blurring of boundaries between the party and the surrounding environment gone ahead unchecked, this problem might conceivably have taken on serious dimensions. But despite the conflict of pressures and counter-pressures we have sketched, the party's popularity would not last long enough to constitute a decisive test: there was not to be enough time.

7. On June 10, 1943, the Communist International was dissolved, a step, declared Stalin, which facilitated "the organization of all freedom-loving nations against the common enemy—Hitlerism. It exposes the lie of the Hitlerites that 'Moscow' allegedly intends to intervene in the life of other nations and to 'Bolshevize' them." In terms of *Realpolitik,* this move was made primarily as a gesture of reassurance to the West at a time when the Russians were pressing hard for a Second Front. That it did not mean the end of Moscow domination over the various Communist parties only the most naïve failed to see.

Yet the dissolution of the Comintern had perhaps unintended consequences for the American party. In 1940 the CP had already ended its formal affiliation with the Comintern, but this had been no more than a maneuver to comply with the Voorhis Act. The dissolution of the Comintern in 1943 was another matter.

During the early years of its existence, the CP had been marginal in American society; during the Popular Front, it had influenced important segments of the liberal public; but only during the war years, when it could fuse American and Russian patriotism and penetrate a great many wartime institutions, did it seriously begin to approach the centers of American political power. For a good many members the psychological boundary line between the inside and outside worlds, though never erased, grew increasingly blurred. Party militants might regard the wartime line as a maneuver, but many members began to believe—and some of the militants too—that a new era of mutual understanding and good feeling had arrived.

These feelings were most sharply expressed by Earl Browder, who in May, 1942, had been released from prison by special presidential pardon and had immediately resumed undisputed leadership of the party. When the Comintern was dissolved, Browder hailed it as a step providing "new and favorable conditions for the integration of the CPUSA into our own American democratic life and national unity." Was Browder merely parroting convenient formulas which he did not take seriously in his heart of hearts? Probably not. From 1942 on, Browder seems to have been groping toward a long-range policy that, while remaining essentially faithful to Russian interests, would place heavy stress upon absorbing the CP into the ordinary political life of the country: a postwar Popular Front extending into the indefinite future.

In his book *Victory and After*, published in 1942, Browder pushed this theme hard:

> The CP has completely subordinated its own ideas as to the best possible social and economic system for our own country . . . to the necessity of uniting the entire nation, *including the biggest* capitalist. . . . We will not raise *any* socialist proposals for the United States, in any form that can disturb this national unity. [emphasis added]

Browder then proceeded to outline a "state capitalist" program for the development of a centralized war economy in which profits as well as wages would be rigidly controlled by the government:

In the United States we have to win this war under the capitalist system. . . . Therefore we have to find out how to make the capitalist system work . . . we have to help the capitalists to learn how to run their own system under war conditions. . . . We will postpone until some indefinite postwar period the basic problem of capitalism.* [53]

These, of course, were all themes that the party had been developing to one or another extent since the Nazi attack upon Soviet Russia. What was new was that Browder formulated them with greater sharpness and boldness than anyone else had ever done before. Even at the height of the Popular Front in the late thirties it would have been hard to find a party leader willing to say that class collaboration rather than class struggle was the party goal for the indefinite future. National unity in the United States, Browder now wrote,

. . . is above all a problem of adjusting class interests without the severe struggle by which this has usually been accomplished. . . . In the United States national unity can be achieved only through compromise between the conflicting interests, demands and aspirations of various class groupings.

It is hard to see what the *New York Times* or even the *Wall Street Journal* could have found to disagree with in such a statement. Whether Moscow approved every detail in Browder's wartime approach is another question, and one that is probably pointless. The over-all orientation of the CP under Browder's leadership during these years was clearly in harmony with Moscow's policy; its detailed application probably Browder's alone. Certainly his own was Browder's tendency to believe in the surface meaning of what he said. If the Russians were even aware of this, it does not seem to have troubled them very much: they had far more important problems on their hands.

* Joe Curran, cruder but not brighter than Browder, went still further. Where Browder preached collaboration between the classes for an indefinite postwar period, Curran announced that "there are no economic classes in America. There is only one class, the American people." [54]

Browder's euphoria about the prospects for class collaboration and national unity in the United States reached its high point after the Teheran meeting of Roosevelt, Churchill, and Stalin in late 1943. Apparently sharing the widespread belief that the three major allies would collaborate after as closely as during the war, he concluded that

> Any plans for American postwar reconstruction which are based upon the introduction of socialism are in effect a repudiation of the aim to unite the majority of the nation behind the Teheran policies. . . . This requires from the Marxists the reaffirmation of our wartime policy that we will not raise the issue of socialism in such a form and manner as to endanger or weaken national unity.

But since it is obviously impossible to raise the issue of socialism without arousing disagreements, Browder was saying in effect that he would not raise it at all. In the months immediately before the 1944 election he made plain what the practical consequences of this policy were:

> Marxists will not help the reactionaries by opposing the slogan of "Free Enterprise" with any form of counter-slogan. . . . We frankly declare that we are ready to cooperate in making Capitalism work effectively in the post-war period with the least possible burden upon the people.[55]

As he worked out this approach, Browder seemed to take a perverse glee in *épater les gauches*. Late in 1944, during the course of an interview, a reporter from the fellow-traveling *PM* remarked that, given the Communists' support of men like Bernard Baruch, Edward Stettinius, and Cordell Hull, they were politically to the right of *PM*. Browder gravely agreed. At the end of the interview, the reporter joshingly told Browder: "I had a discussion with two friends of the National Association of Manufacturers and I must say that you would get along with them fine." Browder drawled back: "I'm awfully glad to hear that." A bit earlier he had written: "If J. P. Morgan supports this [Teheran] coalition . . . I as a Communist am prepared to clasp his hand on that." There was hardly a view on the right that Browder was not prepared to conciliate.* [56]

As a serious political leader, Browder was ready to face the consequences of his line. Having sacrificed the defense of labor, the Negroes, and civil liberties on the altar of the fatherland, he was now willing to sacrifice the Communist Party itself. Early in 1944 he wrote:

> The American working class shares very largely the general national opinion that the "two party system" provides adequate channels for the basic democratic rights.[58]

The conclusion Browder drew was that the CP had become obsolete, an impediment to "national unity." Under his guidance the National Committee sent a letter in early 1944 to all party districts recommending that the party be dissolved and replaced by a "political-education association." The proposal was endorsed almost unanimously by the subordinate bodies and in May, 1944, at the tenth convention of the CP, adopted without discussion. Immediately afterward, the body reconstituted itself as the Communist Political Association, taking Browder's Teheran thesis as its general program. With one significant exception, the leadership remained unchanged. William Z. Foster was dropped as national chairman, and Browder took over under the more "American" title of president.

The CPA now called itself "a non-partisan association of Americans" which "adheres to the principles of scientific socialism," but

---

* Even Mayor Frank ("I am the Law") Hague of Jersey City was now eligible for the "national unity" pact. Opposition to the "Jersey Hitler," as the Communists had called him for years, was declared by the Communists to be based on a misconception. "Such a misconception," wrote the *Daily Worker*, "continues to exist in regard to Frank Hague and so-called Hagueism. . . . [Continued opposition to Hagueism] is a convenient instrument serving the demagogic purposes of reaction. . . . The issue here is the unity of all forces who support the administration program for all-out war against the Hitler axis. That unity cannot be attained by perpetuation of past differences." [57]

If Molotov had been able to say that fascism was a matter of taste, there was no reason to regard "Hagueism" as anything but the same.

which did not necessarily compete with political parties. A few months later Browder proposed that the word "Communist" be dropped from the title of the CPA but was defeated by one vote in the Political Committee.

Reporting at the convention as an understudy for Browder, Robert Minor spoke in accents of complacence that reflected the sentiments of most Communists:

> We, the Communists of the 1940s, will say that history has given the role of "preachers in the wilderness" not to us but to such a gamut of political characters as Martin Dies and Norman Thomas, Mrs. Dilling, Hamilton Fish. . . . The role is not ours. We, who have never hesitated to "go against the stream," have never been fated by our historical role to be always in such a position. The character of the struggle has given us our place unreservedly with the masses of the American people. . . . Those who are opposed will cry in the wilderness.[59]

Minor spoke better than he knew: the wartime Stalinist, committed to the most powerful of both possible worlds, was indeed no preacher in the wilderness.

One immediate result of the change from Communist Party to Communist Political Association was the scrapping of what had passed for Marxist education among the loyal Stalinists. The New York Workers School, located at the party headquarters, was merged with the School for Democracy, which had been set up by the Teachers Union to provide jobs for teachers dismissed from the New York school system during the Rapp-Coudert inquiries into Communism in the schools. Alexander Trachtenberg, a wily old-timer who headed the Communist publishing firm, International Publishers, bought a large building on 16th Street and Sixth Avenue in New York with funds raised mainly from wealthy businessmen who were invited to intimate dinners at the homes of wealthy Communist supporters to hear chats by Earl Browder. The new school was named the Jefferson School, as similar ones were called the Abraham Lincoln School in Chicago, the Thomas Paine School in New Rochelle, and the Samuel Adams School in Boston. Had the CP been strong enough in the South, there would probably have been a John Calhoun School in South Carolina.*

For Browder, the dignified president of the Communist Political Association, there was only one fly in the ointment—a fly named Foster. When Browder first made his report on Teheran to the party's National Committee, Foster signified an intention of speaking against Browder's line. He was dissuaded from doing so upon the assurance that Browder's report would soon be discussed by the Political Committee (the resident group of the National Committee which made the day-to-day decisions for the party). No such discussion ensuing, Foster wrote a lengthy letter to the National Committee attacking the whole Browder line. "In this picture [as painted by Browder]," he complained, "American imperialism virtually disappears, there remains hardly a trace of class struggle, and socialism plays practically no role whatever." [61] The membership of the party knew nothing at all about this letter, which was not published until July, 1945.

At an enlarged Political Committee meeting in 1944 Foster's letter was discussed in private where it won the support of only one among some eighty leading Communists. Foster was then bluntly told by the Political Committee that if he dared carry his views to the membership he would be expelled. Not for the first time, Foster collapsed, writing in the *Daily Worker* that he had no disagreements with the new line.

For the next year and a half Foster criticized and fretted at meetings of the party's National Committee, but only the inner party circles were aware of this. By now Browder had become the undisputed boss, autocratic and arrogant in manner, ruthlessly impatient of disagreements or doubts. The first place to establish "national unity," he felt, was within the Communist movement itself.

Browder's "liquidationist" policies, as they would later be called, may well have gone somewhat further than the Kremlin strategists

---

* The "Americanization" of the party had its unplanned comic touches. The party's 12th Street headquarters in New York had always been terribly drab, the only pictures being those of Marx, Lenin, and Stalin, the only decorations red flags. Upon Browder's orders, a cleanup job was begun. The walls were freshly painted, but the result was curiously depressing: a ghastly cream with brown trim. An unsympathetic observer might have regarded this as an "objective correlative" of the whole new line. [60]

might have advised or desired, yet in the main they worked to the interest of the Soviet Union. The Kremlin had no need for political sects; it wanted a dependable mass of followers and friends who would speak within the labor movement and the Democratic Party* in order to insure a climate of accommodation to all things Russian. Undoubtedly the dissolution of the CP and its replacement by the CPA contributed to this end.

8. In September, 1944, a nation-wide poll asked a cross section of the American people: "Do you think the kind of government Russia has at the present time is about the same kind she had five years ago, or do you think it is different?" Thirty-six percent of the respondents said that Russia had "the same kind of government," but 30 percent replied that it had changed for the better. Another poll asked people whether they thought Russia had the kind of government which was "as good as she could have for her people." Only 28 percent replied in the negative, whereas 46 percent thought the answer was yes.

Such startling shifts in public opinion from the earlier antagonism toward the Russian dictatorship were even more vividly reflected in the nation's press—not merely, it should be stressed, in the liberal journals but also in the mass circulation magazines. When *Collier's* asked itself in December, 1943, "What kind of country is Russia anyway?" it concluded that it was neither Socialist nor Communist but rather a "modified capitalist set-up" evolving "toward something resembling our own and Great Britain's democracy." The entire March 29, 1943, issue of *Life* was devoted to the theme of "Soviet-American cooperation" and was climaxed by a paean of praise for Stalinist Russia. The Russians, wrote the Luce weekly, are "one hell of a people" who "look like Americans, dress like Americans and

---

* In the 1944 election the CPA moved into high gear to help reelect Roosevelt. The Independent Committee of Artists, Scientists and Professionals; the National Citizens Political Action Committee; the American Labor Party were all under CPA direction or influence and particularly useful in areas where the Democratic machine tended to become a bit sleepy. All the fellow-traveling resources in the New York mass communications industry were mobilized. The CIO Political Action Committee, in which Communist trade unionists made a special point of being active, helped mobilize the labor movement. While in no way decisive in Roosevelt's victory, the Communists contributed significant help.

think like Americans." The NKVD, *Life* solemnly assured its readers, was simply "a national police similar to the FBI" whose job was "tracking traitors." *Readers Digest* contributed its mite to an understanding of Stalinism by publishing a condensation of former U. S. Ambassador Joseph Davies' outright apologia for the Russians, *Mission to Moscow.* (Given Mr. Davies' style there was, for once, something to be said for capsulization.) Even magazines like the *Rotarian* printed highly sympathetic accounts of the Stalinist dictatorship. The blunt truth is that for realistic wartime descriptions of the Russian state one could turn neither to the popular American press nor even to most of the extreme right-wing papers, but to such obscure and harassed weeklies of the anti-Stalinist left as the *New Leader,* the *Socialist Call* and *Labor Action.*

Hollywood also contributed to what a critic would later describe as Operation Whitewash, its version of *Mission to Moscow* containing outright and grotesque historical falsifications more favorable to the Stalin dictatorship than the Davies book itself. The description of a contemporary critic, Meyer Schapiro, is worth nothing:

> At the very end [of the film], as Davies is about to leave the Soviet Union and is saying good-by to the dear little father, Kalinin, Stalin comes in unexpectedly—a veritable theophany, which is prolonged by the dictator with an affectionate bonhommie that convinces us of the double nature, divine and human, of the prime mover of the Russian sixth of the globe.

Everything Russian, from dances to folk songs to Shostakovitch's symphonies, became tremendously popular. Sympathy for Russia was now so widespread that there was hardly any need for Communist manipulation in order to attract "bourgeois" enthusiasts. At one meeting in Madison Square Garden, Donald Nelson, then head of the War Production Board, spoke from the same platform as such old dependables as Paul Robeson and Corliss Lamont and told a wildly cheering audience that "the Russians whom I met understand the meaning of a square deal and a firm agreement." Joseph Davies felt that to question Stalin's good faith was "bad Christianity, bad sportsmanship, bad sense."

When Wendell Willkie published his *One World,* an enormously popular book that contained a rather obvious glorification of the Russian regime, so acute a journalist as Walter Lippmann claimed in all earnestness that this book and Davies' were the two finest analyses of the Soviet Union in print. As late as 1945, when the public mood had already begun to shift, General Eisenhower told a House committee that "nothing guides Russian policy so much as a desire for friendship with the United States." That President Roosevelt shared this estimate is so widely known as to require no documentation here, but it may be worth recalling that even such extreme reactionaries as Captain Eddie Rickenbacker and Congressman Rankin of Mississippi were also enthusiastic about the Stalin regime. After a trip to Russia, Rickenbacker expressed his admiration for the "iron discipline" in Russian industry which prevented workers from going on strike, while Rankin announced in the halls of Congress that

> Stalin is a gentile and Trotsky was a Jew. Stalin was educated for the priesthood. The Bible says, teach a child the way he should go and when he is old he will not depart therefrom. It was but natural therefore that when Stalin got into power he should open the churches. . . . Stalin broke up the Comintern. . . . He restored rank and discipline in his army and introduced the incentive payment plan among the men who work in his factories.

Nor did Stalinist Russia lack ecclesiastical blessing. The number of rabbis and ministers who had a good word to say for the totalitarian state was legion, and even Monsignor Fulton Sheen could not restrain his admiration. Speaking of the conservative family legislation introduced in Russia in 1944, he exclaimed: "The family is higher in Russia than in the United States, and God, looking from heaven, may be more pleased with Russia than with us."

The errors and absurdities that have since been attributed solely to the liberal intellectuals could also be found on the extreme right. At the 1942 congress of the Daughters of the American Revolution, Mrs. Tryphosa Duncan Bates-Batchellor, a leading daughter, declared amid an obbligato of gasps from the other daughters: "Stalin is a university graduate and a man of great studies. He is a man who, when he sees a great mistake, admits it and corrects it. Today in Russia, Communism is practically nonexistent."

Given this atmosphere, the Communists and their friends naturally found it possible to penetrate government offices, publishers' offices, the union movement, and the press. But it should be remembered that this was easy for them primarily because they advanced an image of Russia that was in basic harmony with that held by a large part of the non-Communist public. Nor was this image confined to intellectuals, liberals, laborites, and "progressives." A *Fortune* poll in 1943 indicated that of all the occupational segments of the American population it was the "executives" who had the greatest confidence in Russian postwar intentions. Forty-eight percent of the executives, as against 31 percent of the entire population, was convinced that "after the war . . . Russia . . . will not try to bring about Communist governments in other countries." [62]

The imposing headquarters of the new Russian Institute on New York's Park Avenue now served as a sophisticated propaganda agency where Communists could mix with public officials, educators, and artists. Russian War Relief, despite its useful humanitarian work, served as another important vehicle for penetration. Its glittering affairs were attended by prominent society and government people who mingled freely with Communist leaders and fellow travelers: here Corliss Lamont and Thomas Lamont could, for once, meet on easy terms, and Frederick Vanderbilt Field need no longer feel estranged from the other Vanderbilts.

Since the days of Whittaker Chambers' confessions and Alger Hiss's trial much has been said and written about the infiltration of American Communists into the Roosevelt administration. Very probably the extent of that infiltration has been exaggerated, though there can be little doubt that Communist spies and agents found their way into the Office of War Information, the Office of Strategic Services, and the Treasury Department. What needs to be stressed, however, is that Stalinist access to government offices was immeasurably eased by the almost universal American infatuation with all things Russian.

Among some liberals this infatuation began to assume a novel and interesting form. In reading through the yellowed pages of *PM* or the *Nation,* in struggling with the tortured syntax of Henry

Wallace, one is struck by the fact that among many American liberals enthusiasm for the Soviet Union had a meaning quite different from that found among liberals in the twenties and thirties. The admiration once felt for the Soviet Union by men like Edmund Wilson or John Dos Passos had in part been a projection of their rebelliousness against what they perceived to be the injustice, the inequality, and the competitiveness of American society. The Russia they wrote about was largely an image of their desire, a symbol of their own revolt—even then, to be sure, a poorly chosen symbol but at least one that related to essentially libertarian impulses. But for the wartime admirers of the Soviet Union it frequently served less as a "counter-image" to American society then as the ultimate embodiment of values they admired in industrialism and capitalism.

What impressed these "totalitarian liberals," as Dwight Macdonald would later call them, was primarily the fact of power. Many of them were not really concerned with the question of whether Russia was a more humane or fraternal or just society than America; if pressed hard, they might often admit that it was not; but what they so admired was that Russia was efficient, a society in which "things got done." Often unwittingly, they applied to the Soviet Union the same criteria which an American corporation executive might use in appraising a rival company.

Just as American tourists sometimes indulge in conduct abroad that they would frown upon at home, so some of these liberal fellow travelers approved of brutalities in Russia that would have horrified them in the United States. Often this led to a kind of moral schizophrenia, staunch defenders of civil liberties at home finding no difficulty in accepting their suppression in the Soviet Union, lifelong defenders of the rights of labor overflowing with admiration for Stalin's militarization of labor.

Nor was this "One World" enthusiasm of the "totalitarian liberals" at all similar to the internationalist enthusiasm that swept the ranks of American liberals after Woodrow Wilson announced his Fourteen Points. The liberals of 1917 had dreamed—rightly or wrong, with reason or not—of a world in which free, coequal, and self-governing nations would live together under the rules of international law. The "totalitarian liberals" of 1944 envisaged a world split between two massive imperial law-givers, Russia and America.

A little while later Henry Wallace, who would soon become the oracle of this group, put the matter neatly:

> We do not like what Russia does in Eastern Europe. . . . On our part [however] we should recognize that we have no more business in the political affairs of Eastern Europe than Russia has in the political affairs of Latin America, Western Europe and the United States. But whether we like it or not, the Russians will try to socialize their sphere of influence, just as we try to democratize our sphere of influence. . . . By mutual agreement, this competition should be put on a friendly basis. . . . Today the world is bankrupt, and *the United States, Russia and England are the receivers.*[63] [emphasis added]

It would be foolish and unjust to deny that much generous idealism, much genuine revulsion against the horrors of Hitlerism, contributed toward the pro-Russian sentiments of the war years. Yet it would be foolish and unjust to refrain from observing that during these years there also occurred an atrophy of moral sensibility among many American liberals. For Stalinism this was an ideal culture in which to breed, and for the wartime Browderite policy it provided a persuasive rationale. Only when the realities of power began to emerge after the victory of the Allies did the whole structure of deception—sentimentality about Russia, political advantages won by the American Communists, Browder's perspective of "national unity"—crumble into dust.

Chapter X. The Cold War: Repression and Collapse

> We express what all of us so deeply feel about you, the beloved leader of our movement. Your bold, matured Marxist leadership has enabled our movement to make a lasting contribution to our nation and to world democracy. . . . And we have the highest confidence that under your firm guidance, we shall continue. . . .
>
> You are one of the great leaders of the people. . . .

These affectionate phrases came from the pen of John Williamson, organizational secretary of the Communist Political Association. Written on behalf of the *Daily Worker* staff and printed in the paper on May 20, 1945, they were addressed to Earl Browder on his fifty-fourth birthday.

Exactly one week later there began the vendetta against "Browderism." With a brusque and contemptuous gesture—a letter from the French Communist Jacques Duclos that was not even delivered to the American Communist press—the Moscow leadership gave the signal for toppling the man who for fifteen years had been hailed by the American comrades as the incarnation of wisdom, kindliness, and patriarchal sternness.

No leader of American Communism before or after Browder ever enjoyed a position of comparable power. Demanding from his followers the total obedience that he yielded to Moscow, Browder had become an unchallenged autocrat within the party. A systematic campaign of glorification had invested him with the necessary authority among the members: he had been endowed with a new history, a new face, a new profundity. Stronger and better men would have found it hard to withstand such accumulated flattery.

One of his biographers had described Browder as a man "deeply rooted in American soil. He is of the prairie and the woods, the mines and railroads, offices and country schools"—a sort of Stalinist Paul Bunyan. "His leadership is accepted, willingly, and with admiration. He is leader by dint of having the clearest judgment in the affairs of the Communist Party," and not only in the party but in "the nation as a whole." Joseph North presented Browder as "a mid-Westerner," fired with "an all-consuming love for the common people." A. B. Magil found in Browder's books "creative insight, devotion to the people, talent for the pungent phrase, a grasp in every situation of the essentials required to move forward to a given goal." [1] Seldom has so much been made of so little.

Yet the faithful believed. They believed that Browder's woolly prose was rich in pungent phrases, that his clubfoot drawl constituted a brilliant oratorical style, that his repetition of the Stalinist catechism produced "creative insight." Active and devoted membership in the party made such belief a psychological imperative: no rank-and-file Communist could survive without it. That Browder's reputation was actually a triumph of mass-produced folklore, an adaptation of Madison Avenue techniques to 12th Street uses, could not diminish the intensity of their desire to regard him as the chosen guide of the American proletariat.

And in a sense Browder had earned his position. Under his shrewd and ruthless guidance the party had proved increasingly useful to Russian Stalinism and become an important force in American life. No other leader in the American movement could touch him. When Sam Darcy, a veteran functionary, challenged Browder's line, he was expelled. When Foster almost challenged Browder's line, he was almost expelled. Browder held the American party in an iron grip, but the condition for his power in relation to the American Communists was an utter powerlessness in relation to Moscow. Whom Stalin could raise, Stalin could destroy.

Perhaps more than anyone else, Browder had been responsible for "Stalinizing" the American party. It had been Browder who had expelled dissidents, perfected the authoritarian regime, and worked mightily to cultivate the Soviet myth. No one in America deserved better from Moscow, but unfortunately for him gratitude was alien to Stalinist politics, as to any other totalitarian politics. By the spring of 1945 he had outlived his usefulness; but for an accident of geography, he might soon have been a corpse.

Moscow's decision to remove Browder came at about the time

of the Yalta conference, and between the two events there was almost surely an important connection. Held in February, 1945, the Yalta conference was the first occasion at which major differences concerning the postwar world broke past the surface of diplomatic cordiality among the Allied powers. It was now evident that the defeat of Germany would soon be completed; that France and England would emerge from the war badly weakened; that only two major powers would determine the nature of the peace: Russia and the United States. This changed relationship of forces alarmed Churchill, began to disturb Roosevelt, and encouraged Stalin. Even before Yalta, the Russians had made it clear that they intended to keep under their control those east European areas that had been seized by the red armies.

At Yalta the American spokesmen were prepared to surrender eastern Europe to Stalin but insisted that western Europe had to remain within the sphere of a new power bloc headed by the United States. Inevitably, even before the formal end of the war, all the repressed hostilities burst into the open: a clash between power blocs for a division of economic and political spoils, and a clash between two irreconcilable social systems. Aggravating this conflict was the fact that the Communist parties had come out of the war stronger than ever in western Europe; where all other political tendencies were fragmented and uncertain, the Communists functioned with iron discipline and fanatical self-confidence. For a time it seemed that what Stalin had won in Poland through bayonets might be won in Italy and France through the strength of his parties.

Anticipating that in the coming years its main enemy would be its wartime allies, the Kremlin began to prepare another change of line, this time a return to militant tactics as a means of threatening and perhaps destroying the strength of the Western capitalist powers. A political reconversion of such scope raised the possibility that some Communist leaders, too closely associated with the wartime slogans of "national unity," might have to be dismissed.

In America it was Browder who was chosen as the sacrificial lamb. But why Browder? Stalinist turns did not mean an automatic purging of leaders; neither Duclos nor Thorez nor Pollitt was removed in 1945. The answer might be summed up in a sentence: Browder was the leader of the *American* party, America was now the *main* enemy, and Browder had been the dominant spokesman for the view that the postwar years could bring indefinite harmony between America and Russia.

A year before Browder's dismissal, one of his most servile followers, Robert Minor, had written a passage more important than he could have realized at the time:

> The most decisive characteristic of the present century of world history is that a *socialist* state is the most powerful in Europe and Asia, and that it has become possible for the most modern of capitalist states to find a means of long-time cooperation with it.
> Most fundamental for our understanding is the fact that socialism became established *in a single country* while the rest of the advanced countries remained capitalist. . . .[2]

Now originally, during the Russian disputes of the twenties, the notion of "socialism in one country"—antipathetic to the whole Marxist tradition and repudiated specifically by Lenin—had been improvised by the Stalinists in order to justify the consolidation of their power. All through the twenties and thirties the Stalin dictatorship had been on the defensive, concerned above all with strengthening its position within Russia. During that period the theory of "socialism in one country" had served as an indispensable rationale; and if during the war years Browder and Minor adapted it to a vision—which they may have taken a bit too seriously—of a long-range *entente* between Russia and the West, this surely did no immediate damage to the interests of Moscow.

Now the situation was entirely different. Russia had moved into an active imperialist phase, one in which it was both compelled and inspired to expand. Compelled because it needed to repair its badly damaged economy by means of that direct aggrandizement which Marx, in speaking of early capitalism, had called "primitive accumulation"; inspired because for the first time it saw the possibility of smashing the power of the German state and thereby approaching complete control of Europe.

But even as this fundamental clash between Russia and the United States was beginning to take shape, the American Communists continued to write and dream of a happy postwar collaboration. From the point of view of Moscow, this was intolerable. It could not regard with pleasure Browder's failure to emphasize its "rights" in eastern—and western—Europe. It felt that the new role of the American party could not be adequately prepared for if Browder kept reiterating that "capitalism and socialism have begun to find the way to peaceful coexistence." It must have regarded as still more disturbing the way in which Minor developed Browderite notions to a point that seemed almost to clash with Russian interests:

> Events duplicating those that occurred in Russia in 1917 did *not* occur in the leading capitalist countries, and are not occurring and *are not expected to occur;* the orientation of the Communists is definitely that history will take a different course.
>
> If the spokesmen of the Communist parties of France, Italy and *Yugoslavia* today do not call for the setting up of Soviet states in those countries, but on the contrary say that this will not occur and that *all classes must participate in those democratic governments that will be set up*—this is due to the fact that for the first time in history there has come an assurance of orderly, democratic and peaceful progress *throughout* the continent.[3] [emphasis added]

Browder, Minor, and the other American party leaders had become a little too infatuated with their patriotic rhetoric, a little too enthralled with wartime political comforts; apparently some of them had even begun to believe what they had been saying. Here the Kremlin drew the line: it was one thing to help American capitalism during the war years, even if that meant breaking strikes and suspending the campaign for Negro rights. But after the war years? Who had given Browder permission to move so far ahead of himself, to behave as if he were an independent agent? Certainly not Moscow. Had Browder's assurance of a cozy marriage between Russian "socialism" and American capitalism come from a Communist chief in any other Western country, it might have been overlooked; but for an *American* Communist leader, one who would have to guide the followers in the land of the "main enemy," it was utterly impermissible. Elsewhere compromise was conceivable: Russia must still try to play off France and England against the United States. But if an atmosphere of violent antagonism toward American policy was now to be created, the Communists in this country would immediately and radically have to change their line. And for this, what could be more ill suited than Browder's scheme to make postwar capitalism work?

In early 1945 Stalin, who had always shown a special contempt for his American legions, met with Jacques Duclos. The political death sentence for "that man from Kansas" was not only to be delivered by a foreign Communist; it was not even to be delivered to Browder in his own language. Duclos's famous letter appeared in the French magazine *Cahiers du Communisme* in April, 1945, which means that it was probably written in February or March. Browder, then, was purged three months before he or his National Committee knew what was happening to him.

On May 25 the Duclos letter, having already been discussed in the New York press, was finally published in the *Daily Worker*. Blunt and direct, it came to the heart of the matter in its first pages:

> The Teheran agreements mean to Earl Browder that the greatest part of Europe, west of the Soviet Union, will probably be reconstituted on a bourgeois-democratic basis and not on a fascist-capitalist or Soviet basis.

This illusion cast aside, Duclos proceeded to note the other real grievance of the Kremlin against Browder:

> By transforming the Teheran declaration of the Allied governments, which is a document of a diplomatic character, into a political platform of class peace *in the postwar period*, the American Communists . . . are sowing dangerous opportunistic illusions.[4] [emphasis added]

Almost everything regarding the dismissal of Browder is explained by the key phrase, "in the postwar period." The other items mentioned by Duclos can be regarded as secondary, particularly his complaint that the American Communists had transformed their "party" into a "political association." Such a change of name was not at all unprecedented in the Communist movement, and in any case did not by itself lead to tactics significantly different from those pursued by Communists in countries where they continued to call themselves a party.

Not only did Duclos's letter signal the downfall of Browder; it pointed to his chosen successor, William Z. Foster. Gently, with a maddening sort of disingenuousness, Duclos chided Foster for not having openly opposed the dissolution of the CP, but in the main he had only praise for Foster's criticisms of the Browderite perspective. For a period in which the CP would return to "class struggle" policies Foster, both by temperament and training, was the appropriate leader. And with the years Foster had lost whatever slight impulses he once had shown toward independence: even his timidity in opposing Browder when the latter had been in favor now probably spoke well for him.*

Among the American Communists the immediate effect of the Duclos letter was consternation, bewilderment, fear. The first major signs of panic came from the leaders: they had been Browder's most slavish disciples, they had followed his orders unquestioningly, and now they feared humiliation and dismissal. Bella Dodd, at the time a member of the party's National Committee, would later provide a vivid memoir of the "palace revolution . . . taking place at Twelfth Street, with William Z. Foster leading the forces of Marxist fundamentalism":

> The large corps of jobholders in the party added to the confusion, for like horses in a burning stable they had lost all sense of discretion. Frightened at being caught in a state of "revisionism," even if they did not know what it meant, and feeling that the voice from overseas [Duclos] presaged a change in the line of world communism, they tried frantically to purge themselves of the error they did not understand but which they had evidently committed. They confessed in private and in public meetings that they had been remiss in their duty, that they had betrayed the workers by support of a program of class collabora-

* When Foster had expressed criticism of Browder's line, and particularly of its commitment to a no-strike pledge for the postwar period, only one other member of the CP National Committee had agreed with him: Sam Darcy. But where Foster retreated in face of Browder's threats, Darcy continued to express his critical views within the party. For this he was accused of "disruption," and a special commission of the CP leadership was chosen to try him on charges of factionalism. The commission voted to expel Darcy. That the chairman of the commission was William Z. Foster should surprise no one who has read this book with attention.

tion. There were some demonstrations of public self-flagellation that stirred in me feelings of disgust and pity.
. . . To me nothing made sense. Over and over I heard people say they had betrayed the workers. I saw members of the National Board look distraught and disclaim responsibility, plead that they had not known what was going on, or that they had been afraid to speak up when they saw errors. They cried that Browder had confused and terrorized them. . . .

Gil Green [a party leader] went about white-faced and distraught because he had been so closely identified with the chief— had, in fact, been known as Browder's boy.[5]

At a meeting of the party's National Committee, called for the first week in June, Browder debated Foster. Though now trying to prove that he was as radical as the next CP leader and emphasizing his "belief" that America was "imperialist," Browder did not recant; on the whole, he defended his views. Foster, suddenly returned to power from a condition of virtual exile, lashed out at Browderism with a violence he had never before dared to show.

And then, in an orgy of humiliation that is surely one of the most terrifying events in the whole history of American Communism, the confessions began. At the National Committee meeting, in the *Daily Worker,* in *Political Affairs,* at party meetings, grown-up men and women, none of them subject to physical compulsion and all of them free at any moment to walk forever out of the party headquarters, rose to beat their chests, to weep and grovel for having followed Earl Browder, "the beloved leader of our movement." *Mea culpa,* they cried from the depths of their arranged humiliation. At the June meeting of the National Committee, Browder, whose appearance at Communist rallies had traditionally been hailed by thousands of people springing to their feet and chanting *"Browder is our leader, we shall not be moved"*—Browder, suddenly broken and cast off, sat hunched alone in a corner of the room, ungreeted, barely spoken to, flanked by empty chairs.

The party leader Robert Thompson, a man whose physical courage had been tested in the Spanish Civil War and celebrated by two decorations for heroism in the Pacific theater of operations, spoke with tears in his voice, begging forgiveness for "his first big mistake" in accepting Browder's "opportunist line" after "a momentary hesitation and reluctance." Apparently, it was easier to risk one's life against Japanese guerillas than to behave like a free man on the Communist National Committee. Thompson confessed "a failure to appreciate the role of Comrade Foster, for 40 years the finest example of an American working-class leader." That made Foster America's greatest working-class leader since 1905. Thompson was placed on the next, Fosterite, National Committee: he had earned it. Robert Minor, chief theoretical aide-de-camp of Browder, rose to do penance,

> I am among those who must take a substantial share of the fault for many of the errors which are criticized in the first place as Comrade Browder's errors.

Elizabeth Gurley Flynn, who had never lacked courage in fighting cops when she had been a Wobbly years before, joined the rites of confession. But first she would not let Minor off so easily:

> Maybe I am naïve but it appeared to me that every time I heard Comrade Minor speak . . . he was out-Browdering Browder and that he was fastened to Browder's mental apronstrings, even to the extent of making Browder uncomfortable at times.

A hit! Would this old veteran of the class wars call a halt to the masochistic spectacle by speaking a word of truth? But no: she turned upon Browder, the man who had won her to the Communist movement, with that special venom friends reserved for each other in the Stalinist movement:

> Take a trip around the country, alone, unknown, unhonored and unsung, but *meet the people,* Earl, and learn to be one of them again.

No one could challenge this call to humility, yet if Browder had been able to reply he might have recalled words spoken by Elizabeth Gurley Flynn only a few years ago, shortly after he had gone to jail during the days of the Hitler-Stalin pact:

When the day of freedom dawns for Earl Browder, the struggle around the world will be stronger . . . by the restored voice and pen of the man from the heart of America.

Why a man coming from "the heart of America" had to take a journey of penance through the country in order to "meet the people" Elizabeth Gurley Flynn did not trouble to explain.

Came the turn of Eugene Dennis, the stolid Northwestern being groomed for the role of new national secretary. Three months earlier, in March, Dennis had delivered a major report to the party in which he proudly declared himself to be "following the leadership example of Earl Browder." Now Dennis admitted that he "participated in and contributed toward the main errors which our national leadership committed. . . . I wish to reemphasize that I submit this report with a profound sense of humility. . . ." After which he demonstrated what a profound sense of humility meant to him by a violent hour-long excoriation of Browder.

Roy Hudson, the Communist maritime leader, had at first abstained on the motion to denounce Browderism. His crimes compounded, he now had to confess to having been a Browderite and then having hesitated to join the mob against Browder. "Foster," he cried, "was far too lenient in his criticisms of the rest of the National Board members and especially of myself."

Ben Davis, hot with expectations of becoming Foster's right-hand man in the new leadership, rose to sneer at Browder for having disbanded the party in the South; but neglected to add that he, Davis, had recently joined a Tammany Hall club in New York so as to insure his reelection to the City Council. Morris Childs called for "a thorough scraping off of the bureaucratic crust." Doxey Wilkerson, Carl Winters, Gil Green added their voices to the chorus: self-flagellation, pleas of ignorance, claims to having been deceived or intimidated.

Looking back upon this extraordinary spectacle, it is impossible not to be struck by the comparison with the Moscow trials—except that in a way the American incident is worse. Many of those who confessed in Moscow had been shattered men, victims of years of persecution by a totalitarian state, years of imprisonment and, in some instances, months of physical torture; many of them confessed, it would now appear, in order to save their wives and children; and even a few of the Moscow defendants like Bukharin, when pressed too hard by Vyshinsky, burst out with a sudden impulse to dignity, a brief display of dialectical brilliance mocking their tormentors. As the occasion for the collapse of once proud and powerful men, the Moscow trials contained an element of tragedy; but here, at the Communst National Committee, there was no tragedy: it was all simply repugnant, an ultimate example of how a totalitarian creed can destroy man's will and dissolve his moral fiber.

Immediately after the National Committee meeting, the "discussion" percolated to the ranks. A few wistful letters in the *Daily Worker* came to Browder's defense, but most of rank-and-file Communists spoke in terms such as these:

> Browder . . . You've been torpedoed and sunk . . .
> Browder . . . You are suffering from political nervous shock . . .
> Browder, you have to change your position like I did. Because I an ordinary rank and filer and a simple worker tell you at this time, "Forget your formulations, systems of ideas and thinking. Forget your theories and listen to my feelings—listen to the working class instincts. You have to have, like me and the rest of us and the National Board, moral courage—guts. In that road lies your continued greatness.

For weeks the *Daily Worker* was filled with pleas of recantation. Here is James W. Ford, the Negro leader who for almost twenty years had been Browder's political shadow:

> I share fully in the responsibility for the opportunistic line which has led our organization into the swamp of revisionism. . . .
> My error here is grave, especially in regard to what I did to create illusions in my individual capacities, among the Negro people of expectation of democratic rights gratis from Roosevelt and the Democratic Party.[6]

Meanwhile, the movement was preparing to shift political gears. A special convention of the CPA was called for July, in preparation for which a commission of thirteen, headed by William Z. Foster, was selected to hear the personal testimony of each member of the outgoing National Committee and to determine exactly how trustworthy each sinner was in his penance. Bella Dodd, one of the thirteen judges, would later recall this spectacle:

> One by one the leaders appeared before this committee. We were silent and waited for them to speak. Men showed remorse for having offended or betrayed the working class. They tried desperately to prove that they themselves were of that working class . . . and were unspoiled by bourgeois education. They talked of Browder as if he were a sort of bourgeois Satan who had lured them into error. . . . Now they grieved over their mistakes and unctuously pledged that they would study Marx-Lenin-Stalin faithfully, and never betray the working class again. One by one they came before the committee and I began to feel like one of Robespierre's committees in the French Revolution.
>
> It was weird to see tall, rawboned Roy Hudson pick and choose his words with pathetic care, to hear him plead, as if it were a boast, that all he had was a third-grade education and that he came from a poverty-stricken background. . . . It was strange to hear Elizabeth Gurley Flynn beg forgiveness and offer in extenuation that she was of Revolutionary stock. . . .[7]

Browder's political career was at an end. At the special convention of the Communist Political Association held in late July, 1945, which reorganized itself as the Communist Party, the main resolution denouncing Browderism was passed unanimously. Foster was chosen as the new national chairman and Dennis as national secretary. Formally, Browder remained in the party another half-year, though he played no role whatever. On February 5, 1946, he was expelled as a "social imperialist."

In the years that followed, as the party lost thousands of members in the cold war and suffered decimation at the hands of the government, "Browderism" remained a convenient bogey, and though no flesh-and-blood specimen could be found within the ranks of the movement, it continued to be attacked with mounting violence. Thus John Gates, who in the mid-fifties would present himself as a "liberal Communist," declared at a CP convention in 1950:

Browder has become indistinguishable from Budenz [by now a government informer]. . . . [His recent writings] are degenerate . . . outpourings of filth. [Browder is] the troubadour of American imperialism . . . his recent writings . . . pour out of Browder like pus from gangrene.[8]

Balancing the witch-hunt against the "right-wing revisionism" of Browder was a witch-hunt against "left-wing sectarians," prominent party figures like Ruth McKenney, Bruce Minton, William F. Dunne, and Vern Smith, who were expelled, among other reasons, for advancing "the petty-bourgeois anarchistic slogan of 'freedom of criticism' to facilitate their propagation of views hostile to the party." Years later, after the Khrushchev revelations had driven the party into a prolonged trauma, a comrade writing in a Communist internal bulletin would recall the atmosphere of the late forties:

When [the government] attacks came, when the socalled "objective conditions" broke down upon us, we could see nothing but enemies on all sides. We could no longer even trust ourselves. We began our own type of heresy hunt. In a frenzy of fear and distrust we began to finish the job of decimation begun by the bourgeoisie. We used expulsion and vilification against our own loyal members and friends.[9]

Yet it would probably be an oversimplification to explain the atmosphere within the American party by ascribing it to the political needs of Stalinism during the cold war. An additional element, one in which corrupted idealism and psychopathology are inextricably mixed, came into play. What that was may be clarified by a curious incident which Browder would later describe in his post-Communist period.

At the very time that every party leader was unburdening himself of abject confessions, one of them, Gil Green, approached Browder and quietly suggested that the best reason he could offer for his behavior—and why Browder should also agree to confess his political sins—was to be found in a Russian novel entitled *Chocolate*. Since, as Green knew, most of the Communist leaders had read this

novel with intense interest upon its translation into English in
1933, this advice was both candid and sinister. Written in the late twenties by the Russian novelist Alexander
Tarasov-Rodionov, *Chocolate* is set in a small Russian town during
the civil war between red and white armies. Its hero is an Old
Bolshevik, Zudin, who is head of the local Cheka. Zudin anticipates
the two main figures in Arthur Koestler's *Darkness at Noon*: as a
human being and political leader he resembles Rubashov, as a
Chekist he resembles Gletkin.

A man of some feeling and compassion, Zudin is also capable of
extreme brutality. The village in which he is stationed is under
attack from "counter-revolutionaries." During the fighting a close
friend of Zudin is slain by the enemy. To avenge his friend and
strike fear into the "counter-revolutionary" bands, Zudin indiscriminately rounds up 100 townspeople and has them immediately
executed. When he is berated by an opponent within the Bolshevik
Party, Zudin replies in words that go far toward explaining the
course of twentieth-century history:

> I was right in shooting 100 prisoners without taking into
> consideration their guilt or innocence, because guilt or innocence
> in your philistine sense of the word does not exist for me—and
> that is all.[10]

In the context of the novel it is clear that Zudin speaks for the
author, Tarasov-Rodionov. To murder 100 innocent people is justifi-
able if it helps disarm the enemies of the revolution.

Soon, however, Zudin falls victim to his own morality. He has
befriended a young woman, a ballerina under the Czarist regime,
who was slated for execution but whom he has allowed to work in
his office. As a sign of gratitude, she brings his wife a few pieces
of chocolate, which are given to his children. In the besieged town
where the people are close to starvation, chocolate is the rarest of
luxuries; and as the townspeople learn that Zudin's children have
been eating chocolate while their own are starving, they begin to
mutter in resentment. The situation becomes dangerous for the
Bolsheviks. The party committee, forced to intervene, elects a commission to try Zudin for accepting bribes and consorting with a

bourgeois woman—charges that are palpably false and that the accusers know to be false. But the only way to appease the restless townspeople and save the town for the revolutionary army is to punish Zudin, guilty or not. Zudin is sentenced to death.

In a moment of final revelation, Zudin admits to one of his friends who had voted for the sentence that it is both just and necessary. Did not he, Zudin, send 100 innocent people to their deaths in the interests of the revolution? And is it not true that his children did eat chocolate while other children starved?

The novel ends on a note of exaltation. Zudin the Old Bolshevik, innocent of the charges, devoted to the revolution, knowing that his name will forever be stained, calmly awaits his death, rewarded by a sense that in his way he is helping the Communist cause.

There is a fitting epilogue to *Chocolate*: its author, Alexander Tarasov-Rodionov, disappeared during the Great Purges. An enemy of the people.

Communist functionaries like Gil Green, fortified by a conviction that Russia embodied the imperatives of History and that in the name of History everything could be condoned, thought of themselves as miniature Zudins. And so, in a sense, they were. Prepared to adulate Browder one day and trample him the next, they believed that the question of whether he personally merited such treatment was merely a moralistic abstraction quite unrelated to the immediate needs of political struggle. And this is what Green was hinting at when he quietly mentioned *Chocolate* to Browder.

But what of Browder himself? Four years after his expulsion he would recall Green's reference to the Russian novel and add:

> I *always* judged and still do that this is one of the most poisonous books ever written. It is intellectual, moral and political corruption, distilled into its deadly essence. [emphasis added]

This is difficult to believe: Browder could hardly have remained head of the Communist movement all through the thirties had he "always" felt so hostile to *Chocolate*. His "always" would seem to be a product of retrospective wisdom, perhaps of a desire to justify a past of which he was beginning to feel ashamed.

Chocolate has still another kind of relevance to the Browder case. It helps explain the curious lassitude, the utter absence of combative spirit, with which Browder met the attacks launched upon him by his former comrades.* In the same pamphlet explaining that he had "always" regarded the morality of *Chocolate* as reprehensible, Browder offered three reasons for his failure to fight in 1945:

> a) It would have involved the whole international leadership of Communism, with whose knowledge, consent and support I developed all my policies until 1945;
> b) I had discovered that the immediate support offered me among the American leaders was entirely unprincipled;
> c) I believed (mistakenly, as it turned out) that by permitting myself to be removed from the scene I would hasten the reconciliation of the American Communist Party on a sound basis, with a new leadership, if necessary, by means of help from the international movement.[11]

Of these explanations the last two are either naïve or disingenuous. It is the first reason that strikes to the heart of the matter. At the time of his expulsion Browder was still committed to the politics and morality of Stalinism.† If the hero of *Chocolate* had to die in the interests of his executioners, Browder had to maintain silence,

---

* In addition to the reason developed below, another point should be mentioned: Browder had lost the habit of speaking in his own right. A few years after his expulsion from the CP, he debated a socialist leader. After each rhetorical climax Browder would glance up at the audience as if waiting to hear the applause of the faithful followers—but the claque was no longer there, he was now alone, a mortal among mortals. For a man accustomed to the organized flattery of a political machine, the shock of having to stand on his own feet can prove temporarily paralyzing.

† A commitment that Browder would maintain for a number of years. In August, 1948, just before the fourteenth national convention of the CP, he sent a letter to Alexander Trachtenberg, head of the Party's Cadre and Review Commission, begging for readmission:

"Events in connection with Yugoslavia [the rise of the Titoist heresy] reveal serious dangers to the world movement. . . . Many, including myself, have hitherto had an inadequate understanding of these dangers. . . . Therefore I wish to end this situation quickly, *and by what means may be necessary.* I therefore ask you to obtain for me information of the conditions and procedure under which I may gain reinstatement" (emphasis added).

With a wonderful logic all its own, the CP convention unanimously decided that "the appeal by Browder for reinstatement is in keeping with his anti-Party activities."[12] Only after this decision did Browder begin to develop fundamental differences of outlook with the Communist movement.

listen to the abuse of comrades, and refrain from disrupting the party by a vigorous defense of his honor, all in the name of preserving the prestige of "the whole international leadership."

A man committed to the Zudin school of morality does not break free in a day.

2. Expelling Browder was a relatively easy and—for some party leaders—enjoyable task. Deciding upon policies to replace "Browderism" was somewhat more difficult. The party was now to veer "leftward," yet not in the manner of the late twenties or early thirties. Its "leftism" was to be directed primarily toward questions of foreign policy and, above all, toward trying to affect American strategy *vis-à-vis* the Soviet Union.

At the July, 1945, convention of the CP, the process of rewriting the history of the immediate past—indispensable to every Stalinist change of line—was hastily begun:

> The dominant sections of American finance capital supported the war . . . not because of hatred for fascism . . . but because it recognized in Hitler Germany a dangerous imperialist rival. . . .[13]

As relations between the West and Russia grew worse, the party began to discard its patriotic draperies; everything that had been said during the war years was now quietly dropped into the memory hole.*

* At no other point in its history did the CP so rigidly reflect the interests of Russian imperialism, and most of all in regard to the German problem.

Russian policy toward defeated Germany was simple: absorb as much of it as possible into a zone of occupation, reshape its industry to Russian needs, exact enormous reparations in capital and forced labor. A weak Germany, the Russians felt, would mean their triumph on the continent.

To justify this policy, V. J. Jerome, one of the CP theoreticians, improvised a theory of collective guilt that contained an element of inverted racism.

"Only in Germany [he wrote] the working class and the people had ears of stone for the clarion of liberation. . . . Hitler was about to fall, and the German masses rushed to man his last barricades! History is exacting retribution for centuries of submission to Prussianism, which has deformed the German people into arrogant robots of reaction. . . . Germany is a country that has not to its credit a single consummated revolution."

Such chauvinist ranting had a precise purpose: to justify the planned

The changes in Communist perspective took months to complete. President Truman, who upon taking office had been described
by the *Daily Worker* as "a tireless worker for progress," became in
July, 1945, an indecisive figure "*tending* to make certain concessions
. . . to the reactionaries." [emphasis added] A month after the
Duclos letter, however, it was still possible for Communists to speak
of General Eisenhower as "human, humane, humorous and heroic."

Nor were such inconsistencies the result of a "Browderite" hangover. In reality they had little to do with "Browderism," just as
"Browderism" had little to do with Browder. Party policy during the
war years had reflected fundamental Stalinist needs; now those needs
were *beginning* to change, and so too was party policy. But until the
deadlock of the cold war became a certainty, there was no reason for
the CP to embark upon a full "left" turn.

Directly after the foreign ministers of the "Big Five" met in
London in September, 1945, and quarreled over Italy, Trieste, the
east European satellites, and Iran, the CP hardened its line. "The
center of the reactionary forces in the world," wrote Adam Lapin,
a *Daily Worker* commentator, "today rests in the United States."
By the spring of 1946 President Truman, who a year earlier had
merely been "tending to make concessions to the reactionaries," was
denounced by Foster for having "abandoned . . . the vital policy of
friendly relations with the USSR." And no greater crime could man
commit.

By 1946 the American Communists made a startling "discovery"

---

deportation of labor from Germany to Russia.

"The vast areas plundered and destroyed by the fascist German armies
cannot be rebuilt without the *requisitioned* manpower from the destroyer
states."

Not only was slave labor necessary for Russia; it would prove "good" for
the German workers too:

"In the payment of reparations, especially in retributive labor abroad,
[the German people] will experience the regenerative values of constructive
labor" [14] (emphasis added).

Only a few people on the reactionary right, as well as some leftish
advisers of Secretary of the Treasury Morgenthau, spoke this political language. By 1945, however, the CP had begun to realize that unabashed
advocacy of slave labor might hurt its standing among liberal sympathizers.
A draft of the convention resolution proposing to "make Germany pay full
reparations in labor and in kind" was therefore changed in the final version
to "make Germany and Japan pay full reparation."

that would dominate their propaganda for the next decade, set the tone for their inner organizational life, and serve as their rallying cry against government attack: *the United States was on the road to fascism!* At a meeting of the CP National Committee in 1946, Eugene Dennis tried to give this notion a theoretical cast:

> . . . The next cyclical economic crisis . . . will enormously accentuate the dangers of fascism in the United States, which already today is the main center of world reaction. . . . The most reactionary monopolists [will] step up their efforts to organize a fascist movement with a mass base [and] they will also try to drive full speed ahead to prepare for and win a reactionary, pro-fascist victory in 1948.

It is clear from this last sentence that the party leadership was thinking—or claiming to think—of the rise of fascism in short-range terms. At the next meeting of the CP National Committee, in June, 1947, it went much farther. Foster said that "No other nation in history, not even Nazi Germany or militarist Japan, ever set for itself such all-inclusive imperialist goals" as the United States, and another party leader, Henry Winston, saw as imminent in this country "the state of affairs that existed in Japan and Hitler Germany . . . thought control, gestapo groups, the extension of the spy system within the labor movement."

By the fall of 1948, when the party held its fourteenth convention, fascism in America was declared a virtual *fait accompli:*

> With the introduction of the Mundt Bill, the development toward a police state approaches the stage of *qualitative change* [in the direction of fascism]. . . . The postwar fascization of the United States assumes the characteristic disguise of a defense against the mythical foreign and domestic "menace of communism."

Had the CP confined itself, both in 1948 and the following six or seven years, to deploring the state of civil liberties in the country, it would have been saying what a good many other and non-Communist Americans were saying. But the Communists had to cry fascism: politically, in order to justify their extreme hostility to every aspect of American foreign policy from the Truman Doctrine to the Marshall Plan; psychologically, to sustain the faltering comrades as they suffered attacks from the government, the unions, and almost every other institution in American life. The one thing the Communists could not admit, either in public or to themselves, was that it was they who were the main object of attack, and not the unions or the Negroes or the Jews. Their 1948 resolution declared the Taft-Hartley Act to be "fascist-inspired," asserted that "the Negro people are experiencing the most extreme, the most brutal manifestations of the growing fascist danger, especially in the South," and warned of "an alarming growth of anti-Semitism." [15] That none of these assertions was true did not deflect the Communist theoreticians from seeing fascism as an immediate factor in American life. For such party statements were written less as a means of analyzing or communicating with the outer world than as a device for rallying the besieged faithful.

Among those Communist militants who remained in the party during the late forties and early fifties the belief that fascism was close at hand constituted more than a theory: it quickly became part of a pervasive political mood that prevented them from comprehending or relating to postwar American life. Any particular criticism the CP made of "the McCarthy terror" might well be relevant, yet its total view involved both an extreme exaggeration of the extent of this terror and a crude simplification of what fascism meant. That its followers nonetheless found this total view persuasive is not hard to understand. The party *was* being deprived of political rights it had enjoyed without molestation for some years; American Communists *were* being subjected to harsh and systematic persecution. And since the party militants had been trained to regard themselves as the "vanguard of the working class," the best defenders of Negro rights, and the most determined opponents of anti-Semitism, it seemed plausible to them that attacks upon the CP were actual or potential outrages against labor, the Negroes, and the Jews. This assumption, in turn, led to a style of propaganda frequently bordering on the hysterical, as in the following excerpt from a radio broadcast by a party leader:

Our country is crawling with foreign agents, and they're all eating out of our withholding tax. Whenever a fascist or reactionary is voted out of office in Europe (and this sometimes does happen in spite of Wall Street dollars and bankers' bribes, in spite of State Department threats of starvation), whenever such a character is turned out of office, he sails for America—sure of a warm official welcome, wide publicity, and free food and drink.[16]

In its origins the line that America was approaching fascism reflected the need of Russia to revile its main enemy in the cold war. As applied by the party, this line was supposed to bind the ranks during a time of troubles. But in practice it forced the Communists in the trade unions into a hopelessly extremist position, thereby speeding the isolation and destruction of the party.

3. Directly after the war, approximately one-fourth of the total CIO membership was enrolled in unions controlled by the Communists. On the face of things, their power seemed greater than ever. In the United Electrical, Radio and Machine Workers union, with its 500,000 members, many top leaders were open CP members—William Sentner, Dave Davis, Ruth Young, Mercedes Reid—and the anti-Communist opposition was poorly led and badly disoriented. In the NMU, the Mine, Mill and Smelter Workers, the Transport Workers Union, the Communists seemed equally secure in their reign. Partly their strength within the CIO derived from years of hard and skillful work, but to a perhaps greater extent it was due to the willingness of Philip Murray and the official CIO leadership to accept the Stalinists as a legitimate wing of the labor movement. Not only did Murray make no effort to dislodge them from power; he actively discouraged those unionists, like Walter Reuther, who were trying to do so.

As they prepared for a new "left" turn, the Communists appeared confident that they could swing their unions along with them. But they had become a little dizzy with success, the corruptions of bureaucratism having eaten into their minds at least as much as into the minds of ordinary trade-union leaders; they failed to realize that a good share of their power rested on Murray's sufferance; and they did not adequately reckon the fact that even in those unions they controlled completely their support in the ranks was generally narrow and vulnerable. (In the whole of the maritime industry, for example, the 1945 party membership came to a mere 840.) What they had built up over a ten-year period could be wiped out from 1946 to 1949.

In later years the Communists would write that the destruction of their power within the CIO was due, in general, to the repressive atmosphere created by the cold war and, more particularly, to Murray's decision to fight the cold war within the union movement. There was of course some truth to this claim—the issues raised in the cold war being so fundamental and inescapable that they necessarily arose in every political or social institution. But it is important to notice that the first major defeat suffered by the Communists in the CIO had very little to do with the cold war and nothing whatever to do with Philip Murray. It came as the result of a genuine rank-and-file upsurge within the United Auto Workers, one of the most democratic and progressive unions in the country. All through the war years the Stalinists in the UAW had earned the contempt of militant members by their unconditional enmity to strikes and their persistent advocacy of "incentive pay." They had allied themselves with a mediocre leadership headed by R. J. Thomas, a "pork-chopper" more notable for his sense of pinochle than for his sense of world politics.* A group of socialistic and ex-Socialist UAW leaders, headed by Walter Reuther, quickly took the lead in articulating the discontent of the ranks; but had this discontent not already been there, they could not have made any significant progress.

In 1946 Reuther defeated Thomas for the UAW presidency; in 1947 the Reuther group took control of the union Executive Board. What made this event particularly significant was that the Communists were beaten in fair combat by a progressive and democratic

* A report by John Williamson to a 1948 meeting of the party's National Committee reveals how deeply and—from their point of view—disastrously the Communists had immersed themselves in the dubious politics of the group led by R. J. Thomas and two other UAW leaders, Richard Leonard and George Addes:

"In the UAW, for example, the Left Wing [i.e., the Communists] became so enmeshed in the Addes-Thomas-Leonard caucus—in its weaknesses, its isolation from the local unions, *its job corruption*, its factionalism—that the workers could not distinguish one group from the other. Even when the Left differentiated itself in the UAW as in its correct opposition to the factional degeneration—*the white chauvinism and subtle Red-baiting*—of the caucus mentioned, it limited its opposition to the specific local unions, instead of making it known to the UAW members as a whole" [17] (emphasis added).

group, which for the most part did not allow a necessary political campaign against the evils of Stalinist totalitarianism to degenerate into vulgar redbaiting. Not only did the rise of Reuther signal a change in the whole relationship of forces within the CIO by providing it with a gifted anti-Communist leader who could criticize the party from a sophisticated radical perspective and who had a grasp of political ideas quite exceptional in the trade-union movement; it showed that the Communists could be defeated without chicanery, without terror, without brutality—in a word, without resorting to their own methods.

In other CIO unions, however, the struggle against the CP was conducted on a far less democratic and principled basis. Union leaders whom the party had elevated from obscurity now turned against it, with a vicious sort of poetic justice, by employing the very techniques the Communists had taught them.

From its inception the National Maritime Union had been dominated by the Communists. Apart from its obvious strategic importance in American economic life, the maritime industry proved attractive to the party because its unique aspects facilitated access and manipulation. Large numbers of Negro and Puerto Rican workers, discriminated against on land, found at sea employment and equality of a sort. Men beset by wanderlust, men who could not abide the routines of factory work and family life, some who sought escape from personal misfortune and a few, perhaps, from the law— all went to sea. Into the NMU there poured thousands of alienated workers, naturally rebellious, not easily frightened by association with Communists, displaced while on land and badly treated while at sea. The party was quick to grasp that such elements might be peculiarly vulnerable to its appeal, and scores of YCL members fresh from school would "ship out," sometimes only once or twice, in order to get a union book. The ability to speak well and long counted for a great deal in a union where foreign-language workers comprised a large proportion of the membership; and the Communists could speak, sometimes well and always long. They knew how to inflame the resentments of men whose very occupation tended to cut them off from society; they had learned how to appeal to the special emotions of ethnic minorities; and they were skillful at arranging social affairs that would please footloose seamen in port.

In 1946 NMU President Joseph Curran, for years a close friend of the party, publicly broke with the Communists. Neither he nor anyone else has ever fully explained why he took this step. In part, it was surely the result of his native shrewdness: he saw that in the postwar years a union leader intimately connected with the CP could hardly expect a bright future. In part, it was due to a major Communist blunder. The party had decided to bring together all the maritime unions under a Committee for Maritime Unity, headed by Harry Bridges; but it had neglected to foresee that Curran would naturally regard this as a threat to his power on the east coast. When Bridges, in accord with the new "left" turn, pushed for a general strike in maritime, Curran decided that the time had come to abandon a leaky ship. He publicly attacked Bridges and the Committee for Maritime Unity—which meant to declare war on the Communists.

A ferocious struggle, marked by slander and blood, now convulsed the union for several years. Curran won his first important victory over the Communists at a special NMU convention in 1947 that lasted a full three weeks. Cleverly responsive to the moods of the maritime workers, Curran realized that he could defeat the Communists only if he attacked from the left, and so for a time he spoke in the accents of a radical union leader instinctively appalled by Stalinist methods. Disingenuous as this tactic might be, it worked. Here are some excerpts from the marathon speeches made by Curran, in which he can be seen skillfully tapping the latent and legitimate resentments felt by unionists against the CP:

In 1944, during the war period, Communist officials and members of our Union openly stated that the shipowners were our friends and could be worked with. Some of these officials and members brazenly . . . told our membership and the world that strikes had never gained anything for the workers. In this very hall, during the last Convention, CP members proposed that the wartime no-strike policy, which was necessary to assure deliveries of material to the battle fronts, should be continued after the war was over. These same Communist delegates had the colossal gall to even propose the elimination of our Strike Fund, as no longer necessary.

That Curran had also been saying some of the things he now accused the Communists of saying did not prevent his denunciation from being roughly effective. With the authority of an "insider," he spoke of the Communists' trade-union tactics:

> The record of membership meetings in New York shows that the Communists show up in force, including members working ashore whom they permit to retain their Union books. They come early and stay late. Their patrolmen are the ones to count the votes. Whenever one of their people is chairman, only Party members are recognized. . . . Their booing squads harass all non-Communist speakers. The meetings are filibustered until it is necessary to recess. . . .
>
> The following day they hold "continuation" meetings in the hall, during the morning or afternoon, when the majority of the membership is working. . . . At these "continuation meetings" the Communists, who always show up in force, jam through their disruptive policies.

Back and forth went the accusations and denunciations. Never noted for their restraint, the seamen fought it out with word and fist. Here is Curran again, as tough as those who made him tough:

> In the past, the Communists have refused to answer honest criticism or charges made against them. . . . [Boos]—(All right, Brothers, if you can't take it, go to sleep. Ignore it, if you can't take it. But I want to repeat that line again: "In the past, they have refused to answer honest criticism or charges made against them. . . .") [Applause]—They have always classified such criticism or charges . . . as "red baiting."
>
> This is the same method used by the scoundrels of the Black Legion and the Ku Klux Klan, who drape themselves in the American flag to cover up their fascist activities. [Commotion and cries of "Fascist."] [18]

Having broken the back of the Communist cell in the NMU, Curran proceeded to destroy several other opposition groups within the union. The next immediate victims were a number of NMU leaders—Charles Keith, Jack Lawrenson, Dave Drummond—who had worked with the CP for many years but by 1945 had abandoned it in order to join forces with Curran. Against these men and their followers, who wanted neither party domination nor personal dictatorship, Curran used threats, intimidation, and physical violence at union meetings.

The history of a man like Curran, both before and after his break with the party, reveals a great deal about the impact of Stalinism on the American labor movement. Because it spoke in the name of revolt while stressing the accents of power, the party attracted ambitious and authoritarian types. These men it serviced with a smattering of ideology (just enough to give them an advantage over routine unionists), a training in the techniques of manipulation, and a ruthless political machine. Having become union leaders through the help of the Communists, people like Curran and Michael Quill then sprang upon their mentors with an unrestrained violence, as if to show that those who abandon the party do not necessarily forget its teachings. Long after the CP had ceased to count as an organized force in the trade unions, its bitter heritage remained.

Like Curran, Michael Quill had worked for years with the Communists. And like Curran, he had proved to be a ready pupil. Where Curran favored violence, Quill preferred trickery. The methods he used in defeating the Communists within the Transport Workers Union were to be described with unusual candor by a New York labor journalist:

> For fourteen years Quill was known as "Red Mike"—so extreme in his championship of Communist causes that the party itself had to cool off his ardor. Today his is the lustiest voice in the anti-Communist chorus. A firm believer in the precept that the end justifies the means, he uses all the tricks he learned from the Communists to tear up their roots in American unions. . . .
>
> Quill accomplished the trick [of defeating the Communists in the Transport Workers Union] in nine months through a curious blend of tactics, borrowed from Barnum & Bailey and the NKVD. . . .
>
> He learned one day that Austin Hogan, president of the union's big New York local and a pillar of the pro-Communist forces, had sent telegrams to eighteen section chairmen summoning them to a meeting the next night to enlist their support

against Quill. He told a friend about the telegrams and the friend said:

"You'll go to the meeting, of course."

"Oh no, it won't be necessary," was the airy reply.

"Why not? Why should you give them a chance to get their poison across unchallenged?"

"Well, the fact is that there won't be any meeting. I've just sent off eighteen telegrams signed by Austin Hogan calling the meeting off." [19]

As the party had reaped, so had it sown.

4. In both the UAW and the NMU the Communists had been undone, though to varying degrees, by revolts from below. In the UAW these revolts had been represented by Reuther; in the NMU, exploited by Curran. But severe as the losses were, they did not yet destroy the fundamental position of the Communists within the CIO, for as long as Murray continued to tolerate them, they were likely to retain the bulk of their power. Murray was slow to move against the Communists for several reasons: he still remained subject to the spell of Lee Pressman; he looked with suspicion upon the socially conscious unionism of Reuther which, if the Communists were put out of the way, would inevitably become more influential; and he genuinely feared that a split with the Communists might wreck the CIO.

In turn, the Communists did everything they could to play upon Murray's fears of a split. They understood that as long as Murray, whom they labeled the "Center," hesitated to give battle to the "Left," there was no great reason to fear the "Right" led by Reuther.

But Murray's toleration of the Stalinists could not continue indefinitely. Each cold war bulletin, each step of the CP toward the "left," and each consequent worsening of relations within the CIO, made a showdown inevitable. As a believer in the "free enterprise" system, Murray had his ideological commitments, and at times they qualified his militancy or effectiveness as a trade-union leader; but they did not invariably determine his behavior; they were not so rigid or total as to prevent him from responding to the needs and pressures of the men he represented. By contrast, the Stalinists functioned within the labor movement as agents of a foreign state, their fundamental—though not always immediate—patterns of conduct being determined not by their relationship to the American workers but by their relationship to the Russian ruling group. Given this difference in the nature and direction of commitments, a clash between Murray and the Stalinists could no more be avoided than a clash between the United States and Russia.

At first Murray moved slowly. To appease the anti-Communists, he introduced a resolution at the 1946 CIO convention that mildly repudiated Communism and piously invoked the need for unity. How little this resolution actually meant was shown by the fact that everyone from Walter Reuther to Ben Gold voted for it.

Communist strategy was simple. The "Left" flattered Murray unceasingly, praising him as the indispensable leader who alone could hold together the divergent tendencies in the CIO and appealing to that unsophisticated side of him—the side that went back to early struggles in the mining towns—which believed that all good unionists could find a common basis of action through sheer good will. And within the steel union the 1,400 CP members were systematically docile, determined not to give Murray the faintest trouble.*

Until deep into 1947 the Communists kept trying to appease Murray. At a New York State CIO convention that year Communist delegates, following rigid instructions, voted for a resolution criticizing Russia's use of the veto in the UN. At the October convention of the national CIO, Communist delegates voted for a resolution endorsing the Marshall Plan. Such tactics, which did not deceive anti-Communists but did create uneasiness among party followers, suggest that in the trade unions the Foster leadership was, in effect, following a modified form of "Browderism."

By the end of 1947, however, it became clear that no amount of appeasement or conciliation could prevent the anti-Communists in

---

* A few years later, after Murray had begun to move against the Communists, the party's labor secretary rued the "great hesitations of the Left-Progressives in challenging some of the worst reactionaries in the steel workers union, on the ground that it would not be to Murray's liking, although this left a section of the steel workers at the mercy of reactionary Regional Directors." [20]

the CIO from launching an open attack. And as the cold war atmosphere grew more bitter and intense, Murray reluctantly moved closer to men like Walter Reuther and George Baldanzi of the Textile Workers Union.

Suddenly, as if in desperation, the CP sprang to the offensive. It chose to fight on three central questions: labor's response to the Taft-Hartley Act, the Marshall Plan, and the new third party that was being prepared.

In the December, 1947, issue of the party magazine, *Political Affairs,* this turn was publicly foreshadowed by a review of "errors" previously committed by Communists in the CIO:

It was a decisive weakness that dozens of progressive— especially Left Wing—delegates [at the 1947 CIO convention] did not take the floor to expose the lies of the Social Democrats and to take issue with President Murray.

A new and caustic note was sounded in regard to Murray:

He is a bundle of contradictions. At heart a bourgeois-re- formist believing in free enterprise, his ties with capitalist ideology and the pressure of the reactionary Catholic hierarchy lead him in the direction of collaboration with the entire Right forces.[21]

A few months later, at a meeting of the party's National Com- mittee, John Williamson announced that "the Left-Center coalition is no longer in existence," but that "whatever differences exist between Murray and the Social Democrats will have to be utilized to the fullest in the everyday work of the Left-Progressives." It was a vain hope. The differences between Murray and "the Social Democrats"—at least in regard to ridding the CIO of Communists— were now trivial. A year later Grant Oakes, the fellow-traveling president of the Farm Equipment Workers Union, was declaring Murray's leadership to be "as brutal as the lining up of the labor political front under Hitler in Germany," and the *Daily Worker* ran a screaming headline, "Steel Union Head in Plot with Klan." [22]

For the Communists there remained only one possibility of patching up relations with Murray, and this concerned the problem of how the unions were to react to the Taft-Hartley Act. An im-

portant provision of the act specified that if unions were to be
eligible for the services of the National Labor Relations Board their
officers would have to file affidavits swearing they were not Communists. Almost all American unions rose up against this provision
on the ground that it involved an unjustified discrimination; but
given the fact that the labor movement was disunited and prone to
jurisdictional raiding, most unions felt obliged to comply simply as
a means of self-protection. For it was obvious that if two unions
were competing for the support of workers in a plant, the one that
failed to file non-Communist affidavits would automatically suffer
defeat by being barred from the NLRB ballot.

Two kinds of unions refused to sign: first, those led by Communists, since the party felt that this might be an issue upon which
to rally popular support and since signing might subject its people
to charges of perjury; second, the mine and steel workers' unions,
which were so powerful that the loss of NLRB benefits would hardly
matter to them.

By fighting on this issue, the Communists badly miscalculated.
They exposed the unions under party control to a variety of raids
by other AFL and CIO units which had signed the affidavits, and
they seriously ruptured the relations between the party and those of
its members who were heads of unions and therefore had a stake in
their survival. What Lewis and Murray could do, the Communists
could not. In later years Rose Wortis, a party functionary specializ-
ing in labor work, reviewed the effects of Communist policy in
regard to the affidavits:

> When the most important trade unions agreed to sign the
> affidavit under protest and to work for its repeal, the unions under
> Left leadership persisted in the original policy [refusal to sign],
> which the workers could not understand and considered foolhardy.
> *This policy led to the removal or resignation of the Left leaders
> in the unions.* The policy was changed only after the Left lost
> leadership in many unions.[23] [emphasis added]

While accusing most unions of having "sold out" on Taft-
Hartley, the Communists launched an even more reckless campaign
to have the CIO repudiate the Marshall Plan. At the 1948 CIO
convention in Portland, Communist delegates fought and voted, for

the first time, against endorsement of the plan. The Portland convention met directly after the Berlin airlift, when the international atmosphere was charged with talk of war. In their objections to American foreign policy, the Communists made little impression upon the convention—but the convention had a telling effect upon the party. The "Left" bloc in the CIO now understood that it was slowly being crushed and that neither concessions nor trickery could save it. There was only one thing left: a desperate and hysterical counter-attack. Within the CIO, unions under CP control passed resolutions denouncing the Marshall Plan and attacking the Murray leadership. From without, Foster set the tone for a last-ditch fight:

> . . . The top labor leaders characteristically have adopted the Marshall Plan as their own, with the result that the American trade union movement save for its left Wing . . . now finds itself officially supporting a policy that could lead to world fascism and war. The Greens, the Murrays and Reuthers even outdo the employers in their red-baiting, militarist and anti-Soviet hysteria. . . .[24]

At least as ready as their enemy to believe in the imminence of war, the Communists saw their duty and—even at the sacrifice of their strength in the trade-union movement—proceeded to do it.

Little remained but the bitter formalities of a split. In May, 1949, the CIO Executive Board passed a motion that "All members of the Board who are unwilling to enforce the Constitution and carry out the instructions of the Convention . . . are called upon to resign." Four months later the United Electrical Workers, still the bulwark of Stalinism in the CIO, declared itself openly defiant. In November it was expelled and the CIO constitution was amended to permit the Executive Board, by a two-thirds vote, to remove from the CIO any union that consistently worked in behalf of "a totalitarian movement."

Charges were then brought against ten other unions; trial committees appointed; hearings held; and by March, 1950, every CP-dominated union in the CIO was expelled. Grave and knotty issues of union autonomy and democracy were involved in these proceedings—issues that might yet return to haunt the trade-union leadership. Was it right and proper for a trade-union federation to insist upon *political* discipline from its affiliates, as in effect the CIO did when it demanded that the Communist-led unions not express their disagreement with its "line" on the Marshall Plan? Was it right and proper for a union federation to insist that its affiliates could not endorse political candidates other than those it supported in a national election? Granting the desirability of eliminating Communist influence from the trade-union movement, one might still have argued that the mass expulsions not only were a poor way for achieving this end but constituted a threat to democratic values and procedures. But in the atmosphere of 1949 and 1950 not many people troubled to reflect upon such problems.

Meanwhile, because of their struggle against the CIO leadership and their refusal to sign non-Communist affidavits, most of the expelled unions were suffering heavy losses in membership. Mine, Mill and Smelter sank from 100,000 to 44,000 in the period from 1947 to 1949; the office workers' union from 45,000 to 12,000; the agricultural workers' union from 46,000 to 22,000. Only the UE continued to function as a significant union for two or three years—partly because of the ineptitude of the CIO leaders in the industry, partly because the Stalinists at the head of the UE, in order to maintain their contracts, were noticeably indulgent with management. By the mid-fifties, however, even the UE had been reduced to less than 80,000 members. Mine, Mill and Smelter retained a few contracts in the Midwest, but again by a policy that made it advantageous for management to deal with it. The Fur Workers Union, in which the power of the Communists had for years seemed unbreakable, was now torn apart by internal dissension, with party members rebelling against party leaders, important locals breaking away, and the leadership, after it had submitted to humiliating rites of "de-communization," surrendering its power by affiliating to the AFL Amalgamated Meat Cutters in 1955. Ben Gold, the Communist firebrand who had led the furriers through twenty-five years of battle, went back to work in a shop, perhaps in the hope of regaining followers, perhaps simply to end his days in quiet.

By the mid-fifties the Communists had been reduced to marginal status in the unions—a clump of harried party members here, a scattering of frightened sympathizers there. Those few unionists who remained loyal to the party, when they could find a moment of peace, kept asking themselves, what had gone wrong? Where had they made their mistakes? Could any portion of their once enormous power have been salvaged or was the "objective situation" too powerful to resist? Those who broke loose from Stalinist ideology were inclined to ask questions concerning far more serious matters than "mistakes" in strategy; questions that went to the very root of Communist intentions and behavior.

If in the mid-fifties the labor movement seemed peculiarly dull and heavy in its respectability, if it lacked the fighting élan and verve that had been characteristic of at least some American unions since the days of their inception, one reason—and by no means the least important—was that the Communists had seized and scattered so large a portion of its native left wing and rebellious spirit.

5. With a last frantic surge of energy, the Communists tried in 1948 to reenter American political life as a force that might affect, if not determine, crucial elements of foreign policy. They had no illusions that the presidential campaign for Henry Wallace, of which they were the dominant engineers, could possibly succeed; but they believed, plausibly enough, that if Wallace were to receive five million votes, this would constitute a significant check to the Truman foreign policy and, in particular, the Marshall Plan. From the point of view of international Stalinism, no objective could be more important.

When Jacques Duclos had written his letter cashiering Browder, the only non-Communist political figure in America for whom he found a kind word was Henry Wallace. "The former Vice President of the U.S.," noted Duclos, "said rightly that one cannot fight fascism abroad and tolerate [it] at home. . . ." [25] Surely it cannot have been this familiar sentiment that stirred Duclos to praise Wallace; what really impressed Duclos and those guiding his pen was that Wallace was becoming the dominant spokesman for that strand of American opinion which looked with distaste upon a "tough" foreign policy and wished, almost at any cost, to placate the Russians.

Quick to take its cue, the CP leadership declared in the summer of 1946 that

Recent developments [i.e., the beginning of the cold war]
make it incumbent upon us Communists more effectively to
promote the movement for a new people's party . . . to organize
in the 1946 election and immediately afterwards, a grass roots
political machinery and foundation for the new people's alignment. . . .

The job took somewhat longer than the party expected, but it
was done. A major, though hardly intentional, step toward the new
"people's party" occurred in September, 1946, when Wallace made
his Madison Square Garden speech announcing, in effect, his break
with the foreign policy of Secretary of State Byrnes. Because the
speech also contained a few criticisms of the Soviet Union, the
Daily Worker's first response was chilly; but the top CP leadership,
realizing that Wallace was stumbling toward a fundamental estrangement from the Truman administration, soon took a friendlier attitude. As Eugene Dennis wrote:

The *Daily Worker* editors were disoriented by the unjust and
harmful remarks by Wallace on the Soviet Union. . . . Because
of this, the comrades failed to grasp the fact that Wallace, in his
own way and within the limitations of his position, was challenging the main line of the Byrnes-Vandenberg policy and . . . the
"get tough with Russia" policy.[26]

At least from a Communist point of view, Dennis was entirely
right. What mattered to the Communists was not Wallace's opinion
of Soviet society but his proposals for a foreign policy *vis-à-vis* Soviet
society; what mattered to them was not his economic and labor
program (which they would soon label as "absurd on the face of it")
but his readiness to speak against the Marshall Plan. Shortly after
Dennis made this clear, a systematic campaign was begun, both by
the party and by the remnants of the Popular Front liberals, to
celebrate Wallace as the leader of the "progressive" and "peace"
forces in the United States.

It was a role for which Wallace was eminently qualified. He
was a nationally known figure, associated in the public mind with
the New Deal and Midwestern progressivism, the two political
traditions the Communists wanted most to exploit in 1948. In a

vague and troubled way, Wallace was an ambitious man, eager for power yet hesitant when it came to him, enveloped in a mist of progressivist rhetoric yet uncertain as to his own ends—exactly the kind of man who lent himself to manipulation by a determined minority group. Anxiously vibrating with good will, he lacked that shrewdness and decisiveness of mind which had made Franklin Roosevelt so masterful a politician—and this too opened Wallace to easy manipulation. Fearful of precise intellectual formulations and made uneasy by irreconcilable differences of political opinion, he brought together a home-brewed mysticism, a touch of the Popular Front *Schwärmerei* of the thirties, an unbelievable capacity for high-sounding and musty generalization, and a not uncynical opinion that if only enough friendly speeches (and political concessions) were offered to Stalin peace could be won for the world. When his rhetoric was stripped down to some sort of political meaning, it generally came to the proposal—a sort of "progressivist" imperialism —that the world be peaceably divided into two spheres of influence, with eastern Europe ceded to Russia and western Europe to the United States. And together with this went a readiness to believe the best about the worst aspects of the totalitarian world—indeed, there was something about Wallace that simply yearned to be deluded. Here are some of his choice declarations from the forties:

> Some in the United States believe that we have overemphasized political or Bill of Rights democracy. . . . Its extreme form leads to exploitation. Russia, perceiving some of the abuses of excessive political democracy, has placed strong emphasis on economic democracy. . . . Carried to an extreme, all power is centered in one man. . . . Somewhere there is a practical balance between economic and political democracy.

A man who could divide democracy in halves found it easy to propose that the world also be divided in half:

> Russian ideals of social and economic justice are going to govern nearly a third of the world. Our ideas of free enterprise will govern much of the rest. . . . By mutual agreement this competition should be put on a friendly basis, and the Russians should stop conniving against us in certain areas just as we should stop scheming against them in other parts of the world.

Wallace had interesting things to say about Russia itself:

> Had not Stalin carried through his ruthless purge of Nazi-Trotskyist conspirators, Adolf Hitler might have found it possible to conquer the world in years to follow.

And before going on a trip through Siberia:

> It is with great anticipation that I approach the Siberian experience. . . . Over 40,000,000 people have taken the place of the 7,000,000—mostly convicts—who miserably existed there under Imperial Russia. . . . I shall see the cities. I shall feel the grandeur that comes when men work wisely with nature. . . .
> It would be unfortunate for world peace if anything happens inside Russia to upset its system of government at the present time [1941].[27]

The sort of non-Communist mind—for Wallace was of course neither a Communist nor a fellow traveler—that could approach the locale of the Soviet slave camps expecting to vibrate with "the grandeur that comes when men work wisely with nature" is surely a unique product of the modern era. In his witty book on Wallace, Dwight Macdonald described this mind as a symptom of that moral callousness which so frequently attends liberal men of good will. "Wallace land," wrote Macdonald, "is the mental habitat of Henry Wallace plus a few hundred thousand regular readers of *The New Republic, The Nation* and *PM*. It is a region of perpetual fogs, caused by the warm winds of the liberal Gulf Stream coming in contact with the Soviet glacier." [28]

A slick enveloping operation began to close in upon Wallace. Sometimes, amid the mounting flattery of his admirers and the excitement of innumerable speeches and meetings, he seems to have felt a measure of uneasiness regarding the people who were running things but also to have refused—as a matter of principle, honor, or simple confusion—to investigate the matter. The Progressive Citizens of America, a new "liberal" group heavily infiltrated by fellow travelers, became the organizational fulcrum for the movement to project Wallace as the hero of the Common Man. Such old and experienced hands as Lee Pressman, John Abt, C. B. Baldwin,

Hannah Dorner, and Vito Marcantonio took control of one or another aspect of the drive to make Wallace a third-party candidate. And Henry—well, he went along.

In and near the CP, however, not everything was going smoothly. The top leadership had high hopes for the Wallace campaign, but the Communists in the CIO, already hard pressed in many ways, were frequently hesitant. At a private meeting of CP leaders and sympathetic unionists held in late December, 1947, the idea of a third party was received with considerable skepticism. Mike Quill objected violently that such a plan would split the CIO. Robert Thompson, the main party "rep," is then supposed to have replied that the left unions should endorse Wallace "even if it splits the CIO right down the middle." [29] As a result, a good many Communists in the unions quietly dropped out of the party, and others reluctantly joined the Wallace campaign only after heavy prodding from Foster, Dennis, and Williamson. The CP leadership, ruthlessly issuing orders and ultimatums, refused to admit that there were times when even the most devoted Communist at the head of a union could not do what it told him to. Thus the UE, while completely under party control, never formally endorsed Wallace— it was simply too risky in terms of both inner union and CIO politics. And in general, the absence of labor support proved a major weakness in the Progressive Party campaign.

As temporary recompense for their failure to win the unions to the Wallace movement, the Communists made some gains elsewhere. A sizable number of students were attracted to the new party, 500 enrolling in the Wallaceite student group at the University of Chicago, 600 at UC in Berkeley, and 500 at Brooklyn College. For a few months the Communist youth hoped to rebuild their shattered ranks by capitalizing on Wallace sentiment, but even when this sentiment was widespread it lacked the intensity and passion of the student radicalism of the thirties.

The Wallace movement also attracted a good many intellectuals and quasi-intellectuals, but on a basis significantly different from that of the thirties. A certain number of intellectuals were now sympathetic to the Soviet Union not because they thought it was a higher type of socialist democracy but because it was efficient, powerful and industrialized. Writers like Frederick Schuman were prepared to admit the most damning facts about Russia, and then to justify these facts in terms of *Realpolitik*. This new brand of fellow traveler, variously called totalitarian liberals, Stalinoids, and authoritarians of the left, has been well described by Dwight Macdonald:

> A "liberal" used to be someone who favored the spread of liberty: freedom of thought, more humane economic arrangements. . . . Today it has become one who favors the extension of governmental authority for reasons of efficiency. . . . The modern liberal generally calls himself a "progressive," a semantically interesting shift from a term which implies *values* to a term which implies *process*.
>
> The old liberals of the last century were dangerous men, devoted to high ideas and willing to challenge established institutions. . . . Later on, the passion and effectiveness shifted over to the Marxists and anarchists. . . . Of late years, a third type has become dominant: the liberal *realpolitiker*, the "social engineer" who Gets Things Done and thinks in terms of the efficient conduct of modern mass society. . . .
>
> The first type was principled and effective, the second principled and ineffective, the third is unprincipled and effective.

The kind of intellectuals and semi-intellectuals attracted to the Wallaceite movement would later be described in another context as people

> . . . who grew up under the influence of Stalinism and who have shaken off its formulas without abandoning its modes of thought. . . . For these people, the ideology of "left authoritarianism" provides an extremely comforting outlook. It no longer speaks to them in the name of liberty, mass spontaneity, the proletariat. . . . At the same time, it preserves and enlarges a cynical element of the traditional fellow-traveling outlook by connecting it with the most up-to-date and sophisticated theories of managerial and bureaucratic society: let the eggs be broken as they will, the omelette will still be made. It permits them to be indifferent to human values while retaining their faith in Dnieperstroy.[30]

Desirable as the Communists found it to attract some students and intellectuals to the Wallace movement, no genuine mass movement could be built with such limited groups. And the more the masses were absent, the more, necessarily, the Communists were present, running the Progressive Party organization, raising funds, and arranging its meetings.

By the time of the founding convention of the Progressive Party, held in Philadelphia during the last week of July, 1948, the Communists were in full organizational command.* Each important committee had its quota of old and reliable friends. Vito Marcantonio chaired the Rules Committee and was helped by Hugh Bryson, a party-lining trade unionist, and John Abt, a junior league version of Lee Pressman. The head of the Platform Committee was Rexford Tugwell, a veteran New Dealer and one of the few genuine liberals at the summit of the Wallace campaign, but he was flanked, surrounded, and squeezed by Lee Pressman, Harry Bridges, Julius Empsak, W. E. B. DuBois, Frederick Schuman, Grant Oakes, and Paul Robeson.

On the surface, the convention went smoothly enough, with fervent speeches for "peace" and entertainment from People's Songs Inc., including a special ditty called "Friendly Henry Wallace." Two political incidents proved especially revealing. When discussion on the Marshall Plan started, a delegate from Vermont introduced an amendment to the convention resolution stating that "It is not our intention to give blanket endorsement to the foreign policy of any nation." A hubbub broke out in the convention hall; Chairman Tugwell of the Platform Committee, though privately agreeing with the views of the gentleman from Vermont, thought the amendment unnecessary; and the party machine took care of the rest. No amendment.

At another point in the convention, a plank in the platform supporting the demands of the Macedonian people for a "unified homeland" was suddenly withdrawn. This traditional CP advocacy of Macedonian independence had, since its earlier insertion in the platform, taken on a new meaning. The Macedonians were now supporting Tito, the latest arch-heretic, and adoption of the plank

* But very self-conscious about it. Delegates were given blue, green, and white badges; only members of the press were allowed red ones. When Vito Marcantonio rose to speak, he began with a lusty "Com—" and then, in embarrassment, shifted to "Fellow Delegates." But no one grew angry about this sort of thing; as Americans like to say, it was all part of the game.

would have meant lining up with Yugoslavia against the Russians. The provision was therefore crudely stricken from copies of the platform given to the delegates.

An embarrassing moment followed, however, when a delegate from Minnesota rose to question the discrepancy. The leaders hastily gathered together on the stage, and Louis Adamic was assigned to "clarify" the reasons for the last-minute deletion. He might as well have been speaking in his native Serbian, for all the clarification he could give. But there were no further objections.

What the Progressive Party really signified was most sharply revealed in Wallace's acceptance speech. Speaking of the Berlin airlift he found it possible to remark: "We gave up Berlin politically and we can't lose anything by giving it up militarily in a search for peace." Later, during his campaign, Wallace would burst out: "Nazis are running our American government, so why should Russia make peace with them?" [31] It was the kind of talk that convinced Marcantonio, Abt, and Pressman they had done a good job.

But once the excitements of the convention died down,* the liberals felt decidedly unhappy. Tugwell admitted that behind the scenes "there had been a big row at Philadelphia" and added that

---

* The convention of the Young Progressives was, in some ways, still more curious: a blend of techniques from Madison Avenue, Nuremberg party congresses, Stalinist machine politics, and American hill-billy. We quote from a report of this convention:

"The opening session . . . met on the evening of Sunday, July 25. It opened with an invocation and the singing of the first two verses of the Star Spangled Banner. Then the lights went out . . . and an offstage voice addressed the audience for five minutes about the need for a new youth movement. Then, a spotlight focused on a girl who stepped to the stage to read the official Call to the Convention.

As she finished, the lights in the auditorium went on, and a man took the stage to ask for nominations for chairman of this opening session. He recognized someone already stationed at the microphone on the floor, who nominated Christine Walker. . . . She was the girl who had previously read the call to the convention. . . .

The lights were turned out. An offstage voice began to read an introduction for Senator Taylor [Wallace's running mate]. Suddenly lights went on, revealing Senator Taylor on stage. . . .

Senator Taylor spoke very briefly, and then demonstrated his political versatility by accompanying himself on the guitar while he sang a burlesque song parodying the "Isle of Capri." The burlesque verse was about a man who went swimming with a naked woman and, after an encounter with her husband, left his teeth on the Isle of Capri. [32]

"if the wrong people got control, old-fashioned progressives" would not feel at home in the Wallace movement. Asked if by "wrong people" he meant Communists, Tugwell answered, "I certainly don't know whether they are Communists, but they certainly act like Communists."

Wallace himself did not always seem to be at home in the Wallaceite movement. The fellow travelers managing his campaign put on a rather colorful performance, especially when they sent Wallace down South where he spoke courageously against Jim Crow. But on the issue of relations with the Communists he was pitifully confused. Months earlier, when asked by Congressman Sol Bloom how his attitude toward the Marshall Plan differed from that of the Communists, Wallace replied: "I am not familiar with the Communist approach and am unable to discuss it." When pressed, he could only say that he did "not follow the Communist literature." [33] In 1948 unfamiliarity with Communism hardly struck many Americans as a qualification for the presidency.

The CP itself had high hopes for the Wallace campaign. Its leaders wrote:

> The emergence of this new anti-monopoly, anti-fascist people's party has deepened the crisis in the Democratic Party and is leading to its disintegration.

And then to compound the deception or self-deception:

> The Wallace movement already has a broader working class base than had the LaFollette movement in 1924.[34]

Once the election was over, the Communists could not help being disappointed. Wallace had polled only a little more than a million votes—perhaps an encouraging beginning if the perspective had been slowly to build a new political movement, but bitterly inadequate as a means of changing the direction of American foreign policy. For a few years the Progressive Party lingered on, its liberals quietly drifting away, and its main function being to serve as a legal front for the harried Communists. When war broke out in Korea, Wallace declared that "I am on the side of my country and the UN," CP leader Gil Green denounced him for "shabby jingoism" and "abysmal ignorance," [35] Wallace resigned from the Progressive Party—and still another Stalinist adventure had come to an end.

6. Blows, desertions, defeats, persecutions—all came so rapidly during the late forties and early fifties that the party barely knew which way to turn. Once it grew clear that Communist influence in the CIO was at an end and that the Wallace campaign would not lead to a lasting alliance of "progressives," the party prepared to entrench itself for a long siege. Convinced that fascism was conquering the nation and plagued by platoons of secret agents sent into the party by the FBI, the leadership began to make serious preparations for going underground. By 1950-51, when the party membership had fallen below 40,000, the National Committee instructed local party bodies to send a third of their leading personnel into hiding, so that a reservoir of experienced comrades would be available for underground work. A large minority of the membership, estimated by some observers as about a third, was found to be deficient in the ideological fervor or personal hardihood needed for the coming days and was allowed to drift away. Inside the party Foster and his associates kept hammering on the need for a "hard core," a steeled remnant of Communist faithful who would be ready to withstand any attack.

During the late forties, however, some public activities, most of them in behalf of "peace," were still undertaken by the party. Considerable publicity was won by the Communists when, in the fall of 1949, a demonstration near Peekskill, New York, at which Paul Robeson spoke and sang, was assaulted by inflamed mobs. Communists and their sympathizers worked hard to collect signatures for the "Stockholm Peace Pledge"—two and a half million signatures were allegedly gathered in this country, though surely from people innocent of the petition's true sponsorship. In March, 1949, at a "Cultural and Scientific Conference for World Peace" held at the Waldorf in New York, the last major attempt was made to rally middle-class and intellectual sympathizers for a policy of "friendship" with the Soviet Union. The few thousand people who came to this conference were mostly fellow travelers from trade unions, front groups, and the mass communications industries (one of the few areas in American society where the party still had a certain following); very few genuinely distinguished intellectuals could now be tempted to such affairs. As a special treat, the conference presented the Russian composer Shostakovitch and the Russian writer Fadeyev, speaking as trustees of the faith from overseas—though Shostakovitch was clearly a hesitant and embarrassed man, and Fadeyev as clearly a commissar with fingers itching for a whip. On the whole, the conference proved a failure, for in the hostile atmosphere in which it met the participants could no longer gain the psychological satisfactions that had previously been yielded by such gatherings: they could not find the reassurance of massed numbers and swelling rhetoric, the pleasure of hearing confident and authoritative voices ring with affirmations of the line. After the Waldorf meeting no further attempts were made to set up a major cultural front, and the most the Communists could do in this field was to publish an uninfluential magazine, *Masses and Mainstream.*

Necessarily, the bulk of the party's energy was now spent in defense against the numerous attacks to which it was being subjected. These were the years that would later be called the "McCarthy era," and one need have no political sympathy for the Communists in order to feel that it was a disgraceful interval in American life. Of mob violence there was little. Like almost everything else in modern society, repression was becoming rationalized and impersonal, part of the bureaucratic process, a function of the state. Congressional "investigations" pilloried—all too often without humaneness or discrimination—both active Communists and people who had broken from the movement years before. Employees in the government, particularly those in the State Department, were harassed with humiliating questionnaires and investigations, the results of which proved what any sensible person knew all along: that the vast bulk of government employees was at least as moderate in its politics as the rest of the American population. Blacklists deprived leftist actors—often people who had thoughtlessly signed statements and petitions when the Popular Front was still popular—of their jobs on radio, television, and the stage. Hollywood was seized by a mood of panic for the wrong sins. Workers suspected of Communist sympathies occasionally met with violence in the factories, and sometimes with violence that had been condoned by the lower echelons of the trade-union leadership. Old lists of persons who had signed nominating petitions for the CP—petitions that merely made it possible for the party to appear on the ballot and did not necessarily signify political agreement—were scanned for the names of culprits. The Attorney General made public a list of "subversive organizations" without granting them a trial or a hearing; and soon this list, though presumably intended only for the use of government agencies in their hiring, became an unofficial—yet most effective because unofficial—black list used by many private institutions. Teachers were deprived of their jobs because of Communist membership or sympathy, regardless of their competence and often without any investigation as to whether they had actually tried to indoctrinate students. Repressive legislation—providing for internment camps in case of war, special registration for Communist "action" and "front" groups, and the deportation of foreign-born radicals—was passed in Congress under symmetrical sponsorship, first that of the reactionary Senator McCarran and then that of the liberal Senator Humphrey, a leader of the Americans for Democratic Action. Whatever was necessary or useful in the anti-Communist campaigns of this period—primarily the discovery of spies working for the Soviet Union—could have been handled by the usual law-enforcement agencies without public hysteria or infringement of civil liberties. But such a policy would have run counter to the public temper of the time.

It was an ugly moment in the history of the United States. Fascism did not come, as the Communists shouted, nor was there a "reign of terror," as Bertrand Russell wrote; but much was done and said in these years that should have brought shame and alarm to anyone concerned with freedom and civil liberties. The Palmer raids of the early twenties, though marked by greater violence and a more open manifestation of the vigilante spirit than the repressions of the late forties and early fifties, had quickly expended themselves and left only faint scars on the body of American society. By contrast, even after the Wisconsin Senator had ceased being a power in national life, some of the less blatant elements of McCarthyism were written into major legislation and tacitly accepted as part of the American political pattern.

The worst of it was that little of the Communist-hunting which filled the headlines week after week had anything to do with what was really troubling Americans. To outlaw the American arm of The Enemy, by now so withered and wretched an arm, signified little but a hidden fear among many of the men in power that The Enemy was beyond their reach and perhaps beyond anyone's. Unable to mobilize with political effectiveness against the true danger, which was abroad, the government turned with ferocity to the shadow of that danger, which was at home. Some of the hysteria attending Congressional investigations was clearly contrived, but most of it expressed the terrible frustration felt by many Americans, both in and out of government, before the successes of the Communists in Europe and Asia.

The main blows against the Communists were struck by the government in a series of trials charging party leaders with violation of the Smith Act. The first of these trials, which began in January, 1949, and lasted through October, was directed against the twelve members of the CP National Board (though Foster, because of a serious heart ailment, was never brought to court). They were charged with having conspired "with each other and with divers other persons . . . to organize as the Communist Party of the United States of America a society, group and assembly of persons who teach and advocate the overthrow and destruction of the Government of the United States by force and violence. . . ."[36]

So loosely worded was the Smith Act, and so loosely worded the indictment based upon it, that in the atmosphere of 1949 the conviction of the Communists was almost a foregone conclusion. Since the prosecution did not have to demonstrate the existence of any overt act, it contented itself with two main kinds of testimony: lengthy quotations from Marxist classics on "the road to power" and statements by ex-Communists and government informers that they had heard party leaders advocate the use of force and violence. Both of these kinds of testimony raised the most serious political and juridical problems. Could the writings of Marx and Lenin, open as they are to so many bewildering varieties of interpretation, be used decades after their first publication as legitimate evidence in a court of law? Did it then become illegal to publish and distribute *The Communist Manifesto* or *Left Wing Communism: An Infantile Disorder*—particularly if those who did so acknowledged intellectual sympathy with the content of these books? How much credence, as a rule, could be given to informers who had been sent into the party to find grounds for damaging it or who had broken from the party and then made a profession of testifying against it? How much credence could be given to an informer who testified, as did one at the trial of the national CP leaders, that he had heard a Communist organizer, Al Lannon, say at a party gathering that plans had been laid for the Russian army to invade the United States via Alaska? If such plans did exist, was it likely that the Russian army would have notified a CP organizer in Cumberland, Maryland? Very few people asked such questions in 1949, but they were questions that would remain to trouble the conscience of the country long after the Communist Party had ceased to matter.

What gave particular credence to the claim that the trial was primarily a punitive political measure arising from the cold war was its timing. The Smith Act had been passed in 1940, and if all that was necessary for convicting a Communist under its provisions was his presumed devotion to "Marxism-Leninism," such evidence had now been available for nine years—as available in 1943 as in 1949. The difference between 1943 and 1949 was a difference in politics.

The trial itself turned into a prolonged brawl, with the party leaders pursuing an extremely aggressive tactic meant to transform it into a political demonstration, and with Judge Medina allowing his hostility toward the defendants, at times a provocative and at other times a patronizing hostility, to reveal itself openly.

Once the national party leaders were convicted, the government followed with a series of prosecutions designed to cripple the secondary leadership in every important section of the country. Convictions were obtained with monotonous regularity. Dozens of party leaders were sent to jail; and the party itself was placed in the difficult position of being neither legal nor illegal, neither able to conduct its affairs as a public political movement nor forced to suspend its public operations. It was not officially killed, but neither was it allowed to live. And once the Korean war broke out—a war which the CP blamed entirely on "American imperialists"—the repressions against American Communists multiplied.

Shortly before a number of the convicted Communist leaders were to come before the Federal District Court in New York for sentencing, four top and four secondary leaders suddenly disappeared. This decision to flee and forfeit $80,000 in bail was made presumably in order to have these leaders available for the underground party apparatus. Among the party members the result was a kind of panic. Many of them had worked hard to raise bail—the CP claimed that more than a million dollars was raised for its defense activities—and the flight left them bewildered: how could they now return to their unions and communities to contend that the CP was a legitimate political party and the case against their leaders a frame-up? When party members asked for explanations of the flight, they were silenced by leaders who said that whatever the fugitives had done was for the good of the party and could not be discussed. More than any other single step taken during the years of Foster's leadership, this action lost the party sympathy among people who doubted the propriety or usefulness of the government prosecutions.

In such circumstances it is understandable that many party members, fearful for their jobs and wishing to protect their families, quietly dropped away. Nonetheless, there is good reason for supposing that if the party had not been harassed by government attack, it would have lost a large portion of its membership in any case. The full impact of Russian imperialism might then have registered upon the American comrades without the distracting rationale that persecutions in America required true believers to maintain solidarity. The rigidly sectarian policy of the Foster leadership might also have taken a large toll, particularly among Communist trade unionists, who could find no living space between the pressures of the CIO and the inflexible dogmatism of the CP leadership. As it was, the party lost heavily, but often for reasons having less to do with genuine intellectual disenchantment than with personal fear.

If the atmosphere of the nation made life difficult for the party militant, the atmosphere of the party compounded the difficulty. A regime of "war communism," blending panic and authoritarian decrees, quasi-military discipline and the assumption that the faintest deviation today meant desertion tomorrow, was instituted by the Foster leadership. Because everyone knew that the party was crawling with informers, some paid and others volunteer, the relationships among the members became poisoned with suspicion; and the tough policies of the leaders, though meant as a means of protecting the organization, actually contributed to this mood of pervasive mistrust. It would be hard to say which did more damage to the psychological security and intellectual morale of the average party member: the assaults of the government or the responses of the party leadership. Between the two, an unbearable tension was set up in the mind of the average comrade; for a year or two he might try to live with it; but then, unless he were one of the hardened veterans, he found himself, sometimes against his will, drifting away. What the atmosphere of the party was like during these years has been described by a not unsympathetic observer:

> The party's growing isolation did not go unremarked among its members. But any resistance to official dogma was met with repression. Dissenters were either "straightened out" by a process of verbal hammering—producing a sort of conviction-by-exhaustion—or expelled in a manner described by a New York party leader:
>
> "Each 'prosecutor' . . . knew there were a series of standard charges that had to be put into each case to make it stick: anti-leadership, undisciplined, anti-working class and, for the poor soul who would dare . . . argue his or her case, the cardinal crime of breaking the unity of the party. . . ."
>
> Party trade unionists, their ranks already decimated by Taft-Hartley oaths and screening programs, were expelled as "opportunists" if they were unwilling to crash head-on with labor's top leadership. White comrades were expelled for "white chauvinism," which could mean anything from disagreeing with the party's "Negro nation" line to holding a watermelon party; Negroes were expelled for "Uncle Tom-ism." . . .
>
> The deep and pervasive discontent [within the party] was never permitted to cohere into an articulate and perhaps saving opposition. In the face of overwhelming attack from without, few party leaders were willing to seek a showdown with Foster and the old guard. They kept their differences not only from the world at large, but from their own rank and file; the very existence of top-level dissent could only be inferred after lengthy research amid the close-printed jargon of "theoretical" articles. . . . Like cancer patients who fear the knife more than the disease, Communists would not name the thing that was killing them. . . .[37]

Yet nothing that any outside observer could say about the party in the years between 1945 and 1956 speaks as eloquently as the testimony of those members who, in the post-Stalin period, when for the first time it was possible to write with relative freedom in the party discussion bulletins and the *Daily Worker*, burst out in a torrent of long-suppressed rage and grief. Before this testimony the historian or critic can do little but withdraw into silence: it speaks for itself, with a revelatory power and a damning effect greater than those who offered it could possibly realize.

A party member writes about the Foster regime:

> . . . The worst features of our undemocratic practices which ultimately had to lead to one broken mass tie after another, to the resolution of internal differences by vilification, slander and expulsion, [were] the ideological purification processes which were literally *brainwashing*. . . .

A former local party leader apologizes in public print to those whom he had subjected to this process of "brainwashing":

> As a former Section Organizer of the party in Coney Island and Sea Gate, may I use this page [of the *Daily Worker*] to be critical and apologetic to the comrades and friends in that area.
>
> In the period when Pettis Perry's article "On Florida Vacations" [an attack upon middle-class white comrades] appeared in *Political Affairs,* I felt responsible to carry on the struggle against white chauvinism around this and several other questions. . . .
>
> I want to apologize to those former party members whom we "successfully" struggled with and to extend a hand to them to rejoin our party. I want particularly to most humbly apologize to Comrade A. G. who, in retrospect, was a victim of *an intensely bureaucratic gang-up.* . . .

Another party member berates the leadership along similar lines:

> I am shocked that the subject of unjust expulsions has been passed over so lightly as though it did not involve cruelty to human beings. . . .

Or is that you just don't care about those sincere socialist-minded people many of whose lives were shattered by separation from a movement in which they believed. . . . I am speaking directly to the leaders I knew, whose arrogance has committed so many injustices with an air of self-righteousness in the name of "inner-party struggle. . . ."

The leaders themselves, eating humble pie in sickening quantities, admit that the charges of undemocratic practices in the party during the cold-war years are essentially true. Here is the statement of a New York party committee:

> Even as we expounded the necessity for criticism and self-criticism, we brooked no criticism from within or without. We operated . . . more like a militant church than a political party. . . . As social conditions became less pressing, we became even more dogmatic, shrill and self-assertive. . . . As a result, we made ourselves vulnerable to government attack and facilitated our isolation.

These generalizations are given vivid embodiment in a discussion article by a maritime comrade:

> If we are ever to come out of the present state of affairs, one thing has got to be eliminated and that is the "cult of the family." There is a conglomeration of party leaders on all levels who have surrounded themselves with gracious admirers. These comrades are the perpetual full-timers who haven't worked a day in 17 years, or more, and who have made careers of being "professional revolutionists." They seldom express dissenting opinions but are the first to get up and throw bouquets at whatever report is on the floor for discussion. That family [of "professional revolutionists"] spreads from coast to coast and when they screw up in one area they are shifted to another and usually promoted to higher positions. Have they been elected by the membership? They are all things to all men. That nomad-like tribe of people without any roots, who act alike, have the same background, support each other and seem to be in perpetual leadership, must end!

Another party member puts the whole thing into a classical sentence:

We have never really been imbued with the democratic idea of listening to the majority.*

Still another party member spells out the meaning of such charges:

We have an organization which exalts the individual. We do not have any one comrade in such a position but our whole leadership has acted on the basis of the infallibility of the individual leader in an authoritative position. Comrades who have no knowledge of the relationship of forces within a trade union have made policies for those trade unions. The same has been true in many other organizations. Comrades who never went to a Parents Association meeting decide on the tactics to be used in fighting for the Powell Amendment. Women who live in a world of fantasy write at great length on how washing machines enslave the housewife. Journalists become experts on psychiatry. . . . (How many times has a Section Organizer acted as a marriage counsellor?) . . . This "cult of the individual" is written into our constitution: Article VII, Section VII which gives the national committee authority to make any decision on any question between conventions. . . . We have belittled the system of checks and balances in the U.S. constitution. I wish now we had learned more instead of scoffing. There are a few checks I'd like to use right now to balance some things out.

A Communist in cultural work describes the sterility of party efforts during the cold-war years:

* By the common testimony of scores of members there was precious little democracy in the party during the years from 1945 to 1956. By the testimony of the leaders there was precious little democracy during the years when Browder ruled. Thus, Roy Hudson, a member of the National Committee, speaking during the ceremonies of recantation that followed Browder's expulsion: "For years every instinct in me rebelled at certain methods of leadership. It seemed to me that in effect 'collective' work boiled down to everyone expressing what he had to say and *then Browder's word would be final*." The interesting question thus arises: even in terms of the Communist version of party history, how many years, perhaps decades, had it been since democracy existed within the movement?

More and more, we applied a political means test to all cultural work. Standards of beauty, taste, distinction and style became sloughed over or ignored. Disagreements, such as with V. J. Jerome's conclusion that the post-war screen depictions of the Negro constituted a "tactical concession . . . more dangerous because more subtle"—such disagreements were flatly rejected, labelled "anti-leadership" and pro-revisionist, and ordered withdrawn.

A former schoolteacher, "a victim of the witch-hunt in the New York school system," adds a critical word:

My immediate circle consists of teachers, artists, writers. Many of them were members of our organization at one time.

All of them are sympathetic to our cause, but were incapable of stomaching a blind, uncritical allegiance to the USSR. They resented the papal infallibility attributed to Stalin. They resented the attitude of many Communists that one becomes a Marxist simply by adopting the name and memorizing a few quotes from the Marxist classics.

Ten former members from Los Angeles add another stroke to this picture of the party regime:

While it has been mentioned in passing that incorrect expulsions took place during the Browder period *and after Duclos,* it is not generally known that amongst these were a whole New York branch, a whole San Francisco branch, numerous others in Los Angeles, San Diego, Denver, Philadelphia and many other cities. . . . Thousands dropped out because they were in agreement with those expelled. . . .

Particularly bitter are the few remaining Communists in the trade unions:

Certainly, no Communist can seriously believe that he could ever be effective if he continued to function in the same illegal and sometimes almost "conspiratorial" fashion. The Communist trade unionist has had to cope with this question for the past ten years and his only solution was to deny his association and forsake his friends. . . .   Many a known and respected Communist trade unionist felt the anguish that comes from being spurned, forsaken and isolated.

And finally a long quotation from a Communist trade unionist who writes with knowledge and authority:

> But when a position is adopted before the *majority of the rank and file* have been won to the support of this policy, particularly when it is against CIO policy . . . then we find ourselves where we were in the Left-led unions in the years 1946-1949.
>
> In one union, which had a long history of adopting positions without consulting the rank and file, and in most cases against their sentiments, a convention occurred in 1948. The struggle within the CIO, had hastened the development of a powerful Right-Center coalition of rank and file forces against the Left leadership.* The composition of the membership of this union . . . was most unfavorable for the projection of policies in conflict with the CIO. This had been made amply clear in membership sentiment expressed in many ways and forms prior to the convention. But the Left totally disregarded this. They recklessly projected policies on the Third Party, Marshall Plan and Taft Hartley that flew in the face of the sentiments of many of the delegates, and the vast majority of the membership. . . .
>
> The Union began to disintegrate before our eyes. Raids by other unions took advantage of and hastened this process. . . . Had the leadership of our party, in view of this and other similar situations, called a halt to these policies, and asked the rank and file to help find some badly needed answers, perhaps we might have avoided the almost total catastrophe which followed in most of the Left-led unions.

Why such a recourse to the rank and file of the party was out of the question is described in a later passage by the same writer:

> Firstly, the party membership was totally unable to participate in the formulation or correction of policy. . . . Policies were

* The writer is probably describing the situation in the United Electrical Workers.

handed down, not for discussion, not for debate, but for imple-
mentation. Leaders attending meetings of lower party bodies
"fought for the line." They did not come to listen to the voice,
opinion or suggestions of the rank and file.[38]

About such retrospective criticism, the authenticity of which is
beyond dispute, only one word need be said. Those members who in
1956 and 1957 still troubled to send articles to the discussion
bulletins or the *Daily Worker* were usually the ones who had
decided to remain in the party for a time. They consequently tended
to think of past policies as "mistakes"—not in the ritualistic sense
that had characterized previous changes of line, but in a genuine,
earnest, and confused way. What they did not yet see, however, was
that the Communist policy in the CIO, pressing against Murray on
the issue of the Marshall Plan, was not at all a "mistake" but a
necessary and organic part of Communist strategy at the time. The
dissenting members were still thinking in terms of individual
strategies and tactics, rather than of an assessment of the party as a
whole. But this in no way lessens the value of their heartsick
memoirs.

7. Psychologists and novelists have often described the shatter-
ing impact upon a religious person of a sudden loss of faith.
Few experiences can be as painful as the disintegration of a belief
or myth that has sustained and, in one way or another, given purpose
to life.

The Khrushchev "revelations" at the Twentieth Congress of the
Communist Party of Russia led to precisely such a painful experience
among many, perhaps the majority of, American Communists.
These people had defended the Moscow trials, the Hitler-Stalin
pact, the excommunication of Tito, every twist and turn of the party
line. They had rejected as slander the documented reports on slave
labor camps in the USSR. They had felt secure in the knowledge
that, even while a small and embattled minority, they represented
the cause of history, of truth, of humanity itself. And then came
the Khrushchev revelations, which in fact told little that any
sophisticated political person had not known for years but which

created the deepest trauma among thousands of American Communists.

For the first time, the official spokesmen of Communism themselves revealed that many innocent people had been tortured, that the plots had been invented, that slave camps did exist in Siberia, that Stalin had been a pathological terrorist—in short, that the very charges made for years by anti-Stalinists, particularly those of the left, were true. What could be rejected in the past as slander coming from adversaries and redbaiters could no longer be disbelieved when it came from the authorized spokesman of Russian Communism. In the eyes of a Communist, it was as if St. Paul, suddenly and without warning, had bitterly charged Christ with depravity and deceit. The very guardians of the faith, the living depositories of historical truth, now revealed that almost everything in which the comrades had believed was a sham. What else could an American Communist feel but deprived and rejected?

Yet this psychological explanation is clearly not sufficient. In other Communist parties there were also deep reactions to the Khrushchev speech, but in none—except perhaps the British—was there such an overflow of despair and pain. And for good reason. The French and Italian parties were mass organizations, which thousands of workers looked upon as the defenders of their immediate interest; these parties were deeply involved in practical day-to-day tasks, with ideology the concern of only a rather small number of quasi-intellectuals; the French and Italian Communist leaders had a material and social stake in preserving their organizations. In America, by contrast, the party had been reduced to a sect that had no significant relationship to either the labor movement or social life. Thrown back upon its own resources, without any compelling relationship to the social life of the country, the American party inevitably took matters of ideology with a greater and more literal seriousness than many of the European comrades. Since there was little occasion to engage in "works," all that remained was a justification by "faith." And now, that faith had been shattered at its very source. The French Communists could attempt to suppress their doubts by throwing themselves into union work, the Italian Communists by spreading propaganda among poor peasants in the south of Italy; but the American Communists had no means of escape, nothing in which to immerse themselves, no recourse but to stare with bewilderment at the shambles of their hope.

Not that all party members or leaders reacted in the same way. The responses varied from total repudiation of the Communist system to desperate efforts at salvaging it. (A fact, incidentally, that proves the absurdity of the thesis—see Chapter XI—that the Communist Party was simply a conspiratorial and "paramilitary" organization.) Once the Khrushchev revelations had flawed the basic doctrine, then the political, emotional, and moral differentiations among the American comrades—so long suppressed not only to the outside world but even to their own consciousness—burst forth with tremendous violence. A stream of heretical letters, articles, columns, pamphlets, and bulletins appeared. In the *Daily Worker* alone perhaps a thousand letters challenging, deploring, questioning, and castigating the party's past were printed.

> The American Communist Party [wrote one member] does not approach the American people with clean hands, as far as the Soviet Union is concerned. The American CP repeated as gospel truth which it sincerely believed, every lie told by the Soviet Union about its living standards, about Tito, about the Moscow Trials, about the electoral system, about the doctors' case, the stamping out of Jewish culture in Russia.[39]

Nor were such letters exceptional. It was as if all the dikes had burst, as if the long-suppressed reality about the Soviet Union which had been kept from consciousness by a kind of paratactical dissociation suddenly assailed the true believers. From the trivial to the basic, every dogma of the party—and sometimes, though not too frequently, its underlying moral assumptions—became the subject of debate. The very extent and intensity of this debate suggests the degree of repression that must have characterized the inner life of the party during the previous three decades. No democratic organization could possibly have experienced so explosive and violent an outburst as occurred in the Communist Party. To say, therefore, as some observers did, that the whole discussion might have been "arranged" in order to help the party over a difficult transition was simply to ignore the reality of what was happening. Whatever judgment one may make about the merit or intelligence of the 1956-57 discussions in the party, there can be no denying their reality and violence.

Even the most hardened functionaries, those who had not been personally moved by the Khrushchev revelations, realized that it was now impossible to suppress the ferment in the ranks. Some may have felt it was good politics to allow the members to blow off steam, others may simply have felt powerless; but whatever their motivations, most of the leaders did not try to prevent the orgy of self-criticism and self-castigation that took place in the party during the spring and summer of 1956.

By the fall it became possible to discern several tendencies within the leadership. William Z. Foster led a group of Communist Bourbons who felt that as little as possible should be made of Khrushchev's speech. "Now," wrote Foster, "upon the initiative of the leaders of the Communist Party of the Soviet Union, the Stalin undemocratic cult is being liquidated root and branch." And again: "Although the situation created by the Stalin revelations presented certain problems [sic!], no doubt the party could have overcome them without great difficulty, absorbing the immediate lesson from the Stalin exposure. . . ." To Foster and the small group clustered about him, nothing of fundamental importance, nothing to disturb them in their dogmatism, had happened in the Soviet Union. The real problem, as they saw it, was to combat the "rightist deviation" that had arisen in the American party: "If it were desired to liquidate our party, no more effective means could be found to this end than the current discrediting of the party and its leadership by ascribing to them endless 'errors,' many of which never happened." Beneath the irritated surface of Foster's prose there vibrates the commissar's impatience: what a pity that in America there is no possibility of using those summary methods for ending a discussion that have been so successful in the People's Democracies. "Such an exaggeration of mistakes as we have had in our party during recent months," he rightly remarked, "would not be tolerated in the Communist Party of the USSR, People's China, Italy etc." [40]

At the opposite pole from Foster stood a political tendency led by John Gates, editor of the *Daily Worker*. While the Foster group rested mainly upon old-time bureaucrats and a section of the Negro membership, the Gates tendency was strongest among the party intellectuals, the Jewish members, the secondary leaders, and the youth. Gates and his colleagues proposed sweeping changes in the party program, inner democratization, cooperation and perhaps eventual merger with Socialist organizations, open criticism of the Russian leadership, revisions of Marxism-Leninism. "The blind and uncritical attitude of the *Daily Worker* during the past years to the Soviet Union," wrote Joseph Clark, one of Gates' allies, "only did grave damage to our goals of promoting a socialist movement in this country." "This tragic situation," added Gates, "cannot be cured by a few patches here and there as we have been doing for many years. It can only be solved by drastic and basic changes. . . ." [41]

The Gates wing of the party was ready to acknowledge "mistakes" at every point in CP history. In the pages of the discussion bulletins and in open debate, Gates admitted that the whole anti-war line of the party during the Nazi-Soviet pact had been wrong, that the party had been amiss in not supporting the Trotskyists when the latter were being prosecuted under the Smith Act, that civil liberties should be extended in Russia, and that fundamental theories of Communism needed to be reexamined.

Gates and his colleagues—who included important party leaders in New York, California, and western Pennsylvania—went about as far in criticizing Communist doctrine as anyone still a Communist could go. But it is important to note that, at least until late 1957, these people remained Communists: they were still bound to the myth of Russia as a "socialist state," they still admired the Mao regime in China, they still claimed that the essential role of the party in America had been a constructive one.

It was this fact that proved a crucial handicap for the Gates group. Those party members who had really been shocked and wounded by the Khrushchev revelations and who might therefore be most sympathetic to the Gates position were now leaving the party in droves. Gates could have won and kept their support only if he had implied that his perspective was to split quickly from the party. But his perspective was to reform the party, not liquidate it; as he himself was to say, he remained a "party patriot." Hence his insoluble dilemma. Continued criticism of the Communist past, continued emphasis on the need for fresh thinking were imperative in order to repel the old-line Stalinists grouped around Foster; yet the more Gates and his friends offered criticism and admitted mistakes, the greater the number of party members who left in disgust.

On September 13, 1956, the National Committee of the CP adopted a draft resolution for submission to the party convention that was to be held in February, 1957. Foster and Benjamin Davis, Jr., accepted it with strong reservations, and Foster later changed his vote to outright opposition. Parts of this resolution consisted of routine Communist rationalizations for a change in line, but other parts were unprecedented in the past thirty years:

> Our party has also suffered from an oversimplified approach to and an uncritical acceptance of many views and ideas of Marxists in other countries. . . . The party must distinguish better between the additions to Marxist theory made by Lenin which are valid for all countries and those specific aspects of Lenin's writings which reflect exclusively certain unique features of the Russian Revolution or of Soviet society.

In regard to the Khrushchev speech, the resolution declared:

> The party also viewed uncritically developments in the Soviet Union. . . . It mistakenly thought that any public criticism of the views or policies of Marxist parties . . . would weaken the bonds of international working class solidarity. . . . The incorrectness of this view was highlighted by the revelations in Khrushchev's special report. . . . Because it held this view, the Communist Party of our country was entirely unprepared for and deeply shocked by the admissions of crimes, violations of socialist justice, mistreatment of certain national minorities. . . .

But then came the crucial sentence in which the party leadership, drawing back from its own boldness, indicated its continued tie with the Russian dictatorship:

> The courage shown [by Khrushchev] in making these disclosures and the profound process of self-correction begun some years

ago and sharply accelerated since the Twentieth Congress, are irrefutable evidence of the historic role and vitality of the social-ist system.[42]

More was still to come. In the early days of November, 1956, the party's National Committee condemned the Russian interven-tion during the Hungarian revolution:

> At the last moment, instead of meeting the legitimate griev-ances of the Hungarian working class and people, they [the Hun-garian Communists led by Gero and Kadar] again resorted to repression. Their calling in the Soviet troops stationed in Hun-gary to put down the popular demonstrations was a tragic error. . . . This dramatized the bankruptcy of a policy which was not based securely upon national needs. . . .

On November 5, when the early reports of the second Russian intervention in Hungary appeared, the *Daily Worker* wrote:

> The action of the Soviet troops in Hungary does not advance but retards the development of socialism because socialism cannot be imposed on a country by force. . . .[43]

This time, however, the *Daily Worker* editors, who formed the intellectual core of the Gates group, had gone too far. Insistence upon this view would probably have meant their expulsion from the party or a severe split. On November 19 the National Committee therefore adopted a compromise formula which straddled the issues: "We do not seek to justify the use of Soviet troops in Hungary's internal crisis on November 4. Neither do we join in the con-demnation of these actions. . . ." The overthrow of the Nagy gov-ernment was approved, however, as a step necessary "to head off the White Terror and . . . the danger of . . . an anti-Soviet, Horthy-like regime." The statement ended with the blunt admission: "On this there are different viewpoints in the national committee and in the party."

Trembling on the verge of a split which none of the factions yet wanted, the party leaders now tried to work out a temporary compromise. Benjamin Davis, Jr., wrote that the "second use of Soviet troops, after fascist elements had gained or were gaining the upper hand, was in my opinion a grim and painful necessity," while Gates continued both to criticize the Russians and to retain a belief in the most important elements of the Soviet myth.

A third faction now began to emerge under the leadership of the CP national secretary, Eugene Dennis. Though really lacking an independent view of its own, it tried to hold the balance between Foster and Gates, making some concessions to both while clinging to an orthodox Khrushchevite line and trying to keep control of the party machine within its hands.

When the party's much-advertised convention was finally held in February, 1957, it became clear that no faction held an absolute majority, though the Gates group, because it controlled the New York section of the party, was the largest of the three. But whenever the Gates people showed signs of assertiveness, Dennis would coalesce with Foster and thus leave the situation deliberately inconclusive. At the convention voting for a new National Committee, the Gates supporters won a majority; but the price for this was a sad political retreat, that is, a failure to fight on the two issues that were most deeply agitating the membership: Hungary and Soviet anti-Semitism.

In the last analysis, all of these maneuvers and conflicts were perhaps less important than the simple fact that members continued to abandon the party *en masse*. By June, 1957, the American Communist Party probably had no more than five or six thousand moderately active members.* In fact, the exodus was so rapid that shortly after the national convention the Gates group lost its stronghold, the New York branch of the party, simply because its supporters evaporated while the grim Fosterites hung on. It was clear that by choosing to remain in the CP Gates had lost his chance to hold

---

* In any case, party activity now came to very little. A veteran Communist, who had been in the party for twenty-one years, explained why he was leaving in 1957: "So you go out on a Sunday morning with the *Daily Worker*. Knock on a door, say you're selling a labor paper, they open up. When they see the name, you can hardly give it away. Say you're from the Communist Party and they probably don't even open the door. . . . In my party section we have 160 on the books. Seventy pay dues, maybe a couple of dozen come to meetings; we sit around and argue about Hungary and Leninism. What the hell else is there to do?" [44]

together the several thousand dissident Communists in a distinct political group.

Still another factor speeding the disintegration of the party was the tremendous shock which the revelation of Soviet anti-Semitism—so clearly shared and perpetuated by Khrushchev himself—had upon the Jewish members in New York and other large cities. The Communist Yiddish paper *Freiheit* printed sharp attacks not only on the past crimes of the Stalinist era, such as the mass extermination of Soviet Yiddish writers, but also upon Khrushchev himself. In November and December, 1956, the *Freiheit* printed a series of critical articles on the plight of the Russian Jews by a leading Canadian Communist, J. B. Salzburg. Among other things, Salzburg reported that Khrushchev had said that he agreed with Stalin's opposition to Jewish settlement in the Crimea because both of them—Stalin and Khrushchev—doubted the loyalty of the Jews during the war. With barely restrained bitterness, the *Freiheit* commented that while Khrushchev "was willing to grant that every people has its virtues and its faults, he saw only faults among the Jews." After such incidents, it hardly seemed possible that the party could retain any significant section of its Jewish membership.*

American Communism as an organized movement had reached the end of the road. The political fate of the Gates group—expulsion, quitting the CP or, most likely, a slow disintegration—might be of interest to those few people still concerned with Communist politics, but not a matter of public import. For all intents and purposes, as these lines are being written in late 1957, the American Communist Party is dead.†

* Not only Jewish Communists were affected. The following letter appeared in the *Daily Worker* on April 23, 1956:

"Your editorial 'Grievous Deeds,' rocked me like a ton of bricks. Recently I read in the *Daily Worker* a letter from a socialist that there was anti-Semitism in Russia. I was surprised that the *Daily* printed that letter because I just could not believe it. But when I read about the horrible deeds in the editorial my wife and I felt terrible.

"As Negro members of the movement for more than 20 years we always told our Negro and white friends with great pride how racial equality was established in the Soviet Union.

"Steel Worker from W. Pennsylvania"

† As this book was being prepared for the press, the disintegration of the Communist Party reached a climax. John Gates announced his resigna-

It is likely, of course, that as long as the world continues to be split into two major camps there will remain a small group of people in the United States, not important politically but perhaps influential in some intellectual circles, that will be committed to the Soviet myth and will continue to defend the Russian dictatorship as a "socialist state." It is even conceivable that in certain circumstances such an intellectual tendency could be of greater service to the Russians than the little sect of aging and isolated Communists.

At least half a million Americans passed through the ranks of the Communist movement, and countless thousands of others came under its influence. For nearly four decades the Communist Party exerted a profoundly destructive and corrupting influence upon American radicalism. In looking back upon its history—in remembering once more its underground adventures in the early twenties, its maneuvers in the farmer-labor movement a few years later, its dual unionism and social fascist theory during the Third Period, its Popular Front deceptions, its behavior during both phases of the Second World War—one is struck most of all by the enormous waste of potentially valuable human beings, men who had dreamed of a better world and had been ready to give their lives in order to realize it. Before this stark and tragic fact nothing that could happen in the party during the mid-fifties meant very much.

In early 1957 John Steuben, one of the old Communist leaders who had helped build the party among the steelworkers and in the industrial areas of Ohio, lay on his death bed, a forgotten and shattered man. Gasping for breath, he announced his break from the politics that had consumed his entire being and with a humility rare among former Communists said: "I want to live the rest of my life in agony and silence." It was the last word.

---

tion from the party; many of his followers had already dropped out; and the *Daily Worker,* which had for some months been in the hands of the Gates group, ceased publication. William Z. Foster, whose first principle of existence was loyalty to Moscow, had finally triumphed, but nothing remained to him except a scattering of hard-shelled believers.

Chapter XI. Toward a Theory of Stalinism

Since the destruction of Nazi Germany at the end of the Second World War, Stalinism has been the only political movement able to seize the initiative on a world scale. Winning control of vast populations and enormous land areas in both Europe and Asia, it succeeded in appropriating most of the social dynamism of the post-war world, so that both as a system of power and as an ideology it soon came to be a dominant problem of our time.

In this final chapter we propose to examine Stalinism as a political movement in the West. We shall not venture upon an extended discussion of the new form of society it has brought to Russia, and shall offer only a few comments on its special role in Asia. This limitation renders a complete analysis impossible, but it may well be that the time for such an analysis has not yet come.

One reason for placing particular stress upon the tentativeness of our study is that we are dealing with a fluid and unsettled problem: a problem that forms part of our immediate experience. Even as this book was being written, important developments were taking place inside Russia that would seem to point toward a "normalization" of totalitarian society. The lawless and often arbitrary terror which gripped Russia during the Stalin epoch has apparently been replaced by a latent terror, a terror-in-being. While the post-Stalin regime still commands the older mechanisms of repression, it seems determined to employ them, for the time at least, in a more orderly and restrained way.

We mention this matter not to discuss it in its own right but to indicate how thoroughly *problematic* our subject remains. Here we shall confine ourselves to discussing the nature of the Communist parties in the West during the Stalinist epoch.

From Lenin to Stalin: Revolution and Counter-Revolution.

1. In recent years it has become so fashionable to abandon the historical approach to social phenomena that a number

of writers have managed to construct a model of *the* Communist movement and ideology without troubling to consider that Communism, like all other political tendencies, has been in a constant process of change and that from the party of Lenin to the party of Stalin there is a fundamental disjuncture marked by a violent counter-revolution.[1] To say this is not to deny that certain features were held in common by the Communist movement of Lenin and the Communist movement of Stalin. But indiscriminately to mix quotations from Lenin's earlier writings with the recent pronouncements of Stalin and his successors is to obscure the complexity, the novelty, and the sheer deviousness of modern history. The Communist parties may, in the words of Maurice Thorez, always have been "not a party like the others," but the ways in which Lenin's party and Stalin's have been "not like the others" are crucially different.

"As the party bureaucracy increases," wrote Robert Michels in his classic study of early twentieth-century socialism, "two elements which constitute the essential pillars of every socialist conception undergo an inevitable weakening: an understanding of the wider and more ideal cultural aims of socialism, and an understanding of the international multiplicity of its manifestations. *Mechanism becomes an end in itself.*"[2] In these brilliant sentences Michels anticipated the basic curve of the historical development from the Leninist to the Stalinist movement.

From their very inception, most of the Western Communist parties labored under a severe handicap. Their leadership and following had generally come from the native radical movements, but the conditions under which the parties were formed made difficult a genuine response to the political needs of individual countries. The tempo of their formation, the rapid hardening of their doctrine, the frequently obtuse policies they tried to impose upon all other radicals —these derived from little more than a slavish enthusiasm for the model of revolution created by the Bolsheviks. And the weaker the roots of the nascent Communist parties in the social life of western Europe, the more uncritical this enthusiasm for all things Bolshevik was likely to be. Nonetheless, during the first years of their existence and particularly in such countries as Germany and France, the Communist parties were able to draw upon the resources of native radicalism and to provide discipline and coherence to its expression. It is true that the influence of the Russian leaders was enormous; but it was an influence based primarily on the prestige they had won as men "who knew how to make a revolution." Only rarely did it involve a mechanical imposition of their will upon the comrades in the West.

During the Leninist period—roughly from 1919 to 1923—the Communist movement attracted not only the more radical wing of the European working class but also some of the most brilliant intellectuals in Europe, a number of them figures of heroic cast and character. It was during this brief historical moment that Communism took on a genuinely tragic tone: these were the years when Eugene Levine, leader of the defeated soviet republic of Munich, could say to his judges, "I have known for a long time that we Communists are dead men on leave," and Raymond Lefèvre, leader of the French radical left, could chastise Renaudel, spokesman for the moderate Socialists, "You are too healthy, Renaudel, to understand France in her sickness."

Many of the leaders and most of the followers in the young Communist parties were devoted and selfless socialists. Whatever their mistakes or later corruptions, many of these men were infused with a profound idealism; in Kyo, the hero of Malraux's *Man's Fate,* and Pietro Spina, the hero of Silone's *Bread and Wine,* the early Communist leader was later to achieve a kind of tragic apotheosis. These were men who cut themselves off from the world in the hope they could thereby save it, who had abandoned personal desire and personal life to what they believed was the collective anticipation of the future of humanity. That such a surrender necessarily involved a dangerous and self-defeating fanaticism is, in retrospect, hardly debatable; but for a time they lived as selfless and autonomous men who felt that it was their fate to confront the most decisive moment in human history, a moment that demanded and deserved the fullest commitment.

Merely to compare such men with the mediocre time-servers who have since occupied the key posts of the Communist parties is to see how vast the historical change has been.* It is neither easy

* "The professional revolutionary of the 1920's either vanished of his own accord or else was 'liquidated'; he had become an anachronism, a mythical

nor rewarding to fix a precise date at which the Russian revolutionary dictatorship—Lenin himself, disturbed by its malformations, called it "a degenerate workers state"—was transformed into the totalitarianism of Stalin. This process of gradual counter-revolution began during or shortly after the Russian Revolution itself, in the inner life and structure of the Leninist regime; came to its decisive moment in the mid-twenties; and reached final expression in the mid-thirties, with the mass deportation of the peasants, the Moscow trials, and the blood purges. It was a counter-revolution that established a new kind of ruling class, one that neither owned nor could own property but instead controlled the state in whose legal custody property resided. Having consolidated its power, this new ruling class proceeded to exploit the opportunities for centralized economic planning that are peculiar to a nationalized economy; it undertook a "primitive accumulation" of capital so cruel and bloody as to make the earlier accumulation of bourgeois society seem, by comparison, a model of humaneness. The new society that crept into existence in Russia during the late twenties and early thirties was neither capitalist nor socialist, but an enemy of both. Resting upon the special interests of the technical intelligentsia, the political bureaucrats, the factory managers, the military officials, and above all, the party functionaries—elite categories easier to distinguish in analysis than to sort out in actuality—Stalinism developed an ethos, a system of rule, and a style of life uniquely its own.*

It is not our present task to inquire into the extent to which the Russia of Lenin must be held responsible for, or can be said to bear

---

figure. His place was taken . . . by a type which combined the cautious official, the astute parliamentarian, the genial orator, and the professional agitator. . . . During the period which Trotsky calls the 'period of domestication of international revolutionaries,' when Bukharin's quarrel with Stalin came to a head at the Sixth Congress of the Communist International, Bukharin read out a letter of Lenin's to Zinoniev and himself in which Lenin warned them if they began replacing independent and intelligent men in the International by docile imbeciles they would infallibly kill it." [3]

* " 'L'Etat, c'est moi' is almost a liberal formula by comparison with the actualities of Stalin's totalitarian regime. Louis XIV identified himself only with the State. The Popes of Rome identified themselves with both the State and the Church—but only during the epoch of temporal power. The totalitarian State goes far beyond Caesaro-Papism, for it has encompassed the entire economy of the country as well. Stalin can justly say, unlike the *Roi Soleil*, '*La Société, c'est moi*.' " [4]

the seeds of, the Russia of Stalin—except to remark that (1) the view which presents Lenin's Russia as a workers' democracy untainted by the later corruptions of Stalinism simply ignores the many respects in which Leninist Russia violated even its own formal claims as to what a workers' democracy should be, and (2) the view which takes Stalinism to be the legitimate heir of Leninism ignores those cataclysmic changes in the history of both Russia and international Communism without which neither the destruction of Leninism nor the triumph of Stalinism would have been possible. What is at fault in both of these simplistic theories is that neither permits the relation between Lenin's and Stalin's Russia to be examined in its fully problematic terms. Our own view, to merely state it, is that while Stalinism is a social and political phenomenon radically different from Leninism, it is nonetheless possible to find many of its sources in the theory and practice of Leninism.

In any case, what matters for our present purpose is that with the gradual counter-revolution in Russia during the twenties and thirties the Communist parties were transformed from groups of devoted revolutionaries enthusiastically uncritical of Leninism into agencies of a totalitarian state functioning through a skillful appropriation of the revolutionary tradition and vocabulary.* By the end of the twenties the transition to Stalinism was almost complete. The party line might still shift; in some countries the party might be little more than a parasitic sect feeding on the body of the labor movement, while in other countries it could seem the very fulcrum of historical change; yet the central traits of Stalinism were by now determined. Whether in the United States or India, Germany or Brazil, the Communist Party was invariably "a foreign national party," no longer representative of native radical opinion and no longer responsive to the interests, be they truly grasped or totally misconceived, of the native working class. Even as the parties con-

---

* "The Communist leadership . . . understood that to the Stalinist 'revolution from above' there corresponds a social stratum which organizes the planned society from the top downward—the technological intelligentsia. . . . In Marxian terms this signifies a change in the class structure of the party. Unquestionably the leaders are aware of it. Hence the peculiar moral climate of modern Communism, with its double standard of truth for the elect, its contempt for 'the masses,' and its elevation of the individual conscience to the position of public enemy number one." [5]

tinued to function within the political life of their respective countries, rarely could anything that happened within these countries
determine their fundamental conduct.

Berthold Brecht, one of the few great writers who remained
with the Stalinist movement to the end of his life, would later give
classical expression—frightful in its candor—to the ethos of the
party functionary:

> You are no longer yourself. . . . You are without a name,
> without a mother, blank sheets on which the Revolution will
> write its orders. . . . He who fights for Communism must be
> able to fight and to renounce fighting, to say the truth and not to
> say the truth, to be helpful and unhelpful, to keep a promise and
> to break a promise, to go into danger and to avoid danger, to be
> known and to be unknown. He who fights for Communism has
> of all the virtues only one: that he fights for Communism.

At the very time Brecht was composing this ode to the dehu-
manized agents of the party apparatus, Ernest Juenger, the gifted
ideologist of early Nazism, was praising the "heroic" representatives
of the new technological era, men whose heroism was to be defined
by their "color-blindness with regard to values." [6]

Mechanism had become an end in itself.

"Alienation" as a Key to Stalinism

2. Perhaps the most profound historical conception developed
by Karl Marx was that of "alienation." In his early philosophical essays and later in *Capital* Marx describes the process by
which men, in their effort to cast off the tyranny of nature, create
institutions and forms of production that seem to acquire an independent existence beyond the practical or cognitive grasp of their
creators. While actually the work of men, social institutions take
on a life of fantastic autonomy, as if they had been ordained by some
super-terrestrial force or were inherent in the nature of things, and
thereby enslave men to laws of their own. Like the fetishes of primitive society, they appear to shape human destiny even as, and perhaps because, they destroy human will. In the misty spheres of the

religious world, the products of the mind are elevated to a superior
reality of their own; in the practical spheres of bourgeois property
relations, commodities assume a similar fetishistic character.

> Every self-alienation of man from himself and from nature
> [wrote the young Marx] appears in the relationship by which he
> surrenders himself . . . to another man differentiated from him-
> self. Thus religious self-alienation necessarily appears in the
> relation of the layman to the priest. . . . In the practical world,
> self-alienation can only appear through the practical relation to
> another man. . . . The alienation of man . . . is first realized
> and expressed in the relation in which man stands to man.[7]

It is in similar terms that one can understand the relationship
between the Stalinist leaders and the radical workers and intellectuals. The movement born in the enthusiasm of the post-revolution-
ary period and proclaimed as the means for achieving the liberation
of humanity now became a fetish dominating the lives of men in
spiritual captivity.* Even as it reduced its members to the level of
malleable objects, the party appropriated the prerogatives of human
choice. If "religious self-alienation necessarily appears in the relation
of the layman to the priest," the self-alienation of the Stalinist movement appears in the relation between leaders and followers. In its
total and imperious discipline, in its assumption that at any given
moment the party dictum is entirely and necessarily correct, in its
identification of immediate advantage with the necessary "direction"
of History, the Stalinist party began to claim for itself a degree of
human allegiance that few previous institutions had dared or desired.
The values and motives which had brought the Communist movement into existence were now treated as if they were *things* entering into the calculations of the party, quite as raw materials enter
into the calculations of a speculator on the commodity exchange.

---

* Leninism had already tended to exalt the party as an entity superior to
individual judgment or criticism. Thus Trotsky, whose own youthful attacks
on the Leninist conception of the party he unfortunately ignored in his later
thinking, could write in 1923 that: "One can be right only with the party and
through the party, since history has created no other paths to the realization
of what is right. The English have a historical proverb: 'My country, right
or wrong.' With far greater historical right we can say: 'Right or not in
individual particular concrete questions, but it is my party.' "[8]

For if capitalism is dominated by the fetishism of commodities, Stalinism is haunted by the fetishism of the party: if the most powerful Marxist criticism of capitalist society is to be found in the concept of alienation, that criticism holds with even greater force and relevance in regard to the Stalinist movement.

The Conditions That Made Stalinism Possible

3. The bulk of this book has been devoted to tracing the history of the American Communist Party. But since genesis can never explain persistence, it is necessary to supplement historical narrative with a study of the structure and function of the Stalinist movement.*

Stalinism is a phenomenon *sui generis*. Every effort to describe it through terms and categories developed in the investigation of previous movements, while entirely necessary, runs the danger of missing its uniqueness. Comparisons with earlier historical events, particularly the much-abused analogy with the French Revolution

---

* Since, in developing our argument, we shall proceed from general statements to more restricted explanations of particular aspects of the Stalinist movement, it might prove helpful to the reader if the main steps in our analysis were sketched out in advance. Such a step-by-step analysis seems necessary here, since the complexity of our subject makes it impossible to be satisfied with the description of general characteristics that is often adequate for other topics.

We will first try to show why certain approaches to the problem of Stalinism, because of a tendency to oversimplification and premature generalization, have proved inadequate. We will then discuss why no explanation of Stalinism can afford to disregard the social conditions in which it appeared and why, at the same time, no explanation that is uniquely psychological can account for its many-sided character as a social movement. We will proceed to indicate why a simple economic explanation of the appeal of Stalinism fails to account for its differential impact among equally deprived groups. And then we shall introduce the concept of "relative deprivation" which, in our estimate, allows for a better understanding of the impact of Communism.

Moving from such questions as the impact of Stalinism and the varying susceptibilities to it, we will proceed to investigate the structure of the Stalinist party and the roles of the leaders and followers. We will here try to move away from stereotyped description of *the* Communist in order the better to understand the sharp divisions between leaders and militants. At this point we will attempt a socio-psychological typology of the leaders and the led. Finally, we will try to elucidate, in the last section of this chapter, the complex relation between Marxist ideology and Stalinist totalitarian practice.

and its aftermath, are likely to be as misleading as they are suggestive, for they involve an underestimation of the historical novelty of totalitarianism in general and Stalinism in particular.

"International Communism is a conspiracy." This formula contains an element of truth yet fails to explain the profound appeal Stalinism has had for millions of European workers and Asian peasants who have not shown the faintest conspiratorial inclinations.

"Communism is a mass totalitarian party." This formula provides a useful description but fails to consider the motives of those who turned to Stalinism because they were deeply repelled by the injustice of modern society and thirsted for a more fraternal order of life.

"Communism is a new secular religion in arms, a new Islam." [9] This formula, while pointing toward an important fact, also proves to be one-sided, since it fails to account for the cynical color blindness to values, the consciously manipulative behavior of the leading cadres in the Stalinist parties.

All of these statements suffer from incompleteness, an effort to enclose an enormously complex and protean movement in a monolithic formula. Stalinism was a totalitarian movement and a hidden conspiracy; a bureaucratic machine and a brotherhood of dedicated men—all of these *but none of them alone.* And it was all of them together in a particular context, so that each aspect of its existence, the most vicious and most "idealistic," was related to the condition of the society in which it appeared.

The year 1914 marks the beginning of the twentieth century and the beginning of the totalitarian age; it is one of those turning points at which history seems to draw a heavy line between all that has happened and all that is unforeseeable.

Since 1914 the fabric of Western society has been ripped apart; nations and individuals have repeatedly displayed what psychologists call "catastrophic reactions." [10] The survivors of the war, promised a world fit for heroes, discovered the world of bread lines and movies. Victorian amenity and compromise, the notion of gradual progress and civilized restraint seemed utterly irrelevant: men of all persuasions, or none at all, lived as intimately with desperation as their grandfathers had lived in the hope, and sometimes the reality, of comfort. In the years between wars the extreme course seemed indistinguishable from the sensible solution.

So familiar has this idea of crisis become that to repeat such facts may almost seem a lapse into rhetoric. An effort of the imagination is required to distinguish among the disasters of our century—to remember the breakdown of Western economy thirty years ago, the pauperization of large sections of the working class, the social and psychic strangulation of the middle class.

Lenin had called this the century of war and revolution, and the century had proved him a prophet. In the chaos that followed upon war, revolution, and depression, whole segments of the population were cut off from social life. Torn from their accustomed places, they set out in quest for a new order: intellectuals for ideas and values by which to live; workers for jobs and bread and values too; the middle class for a chance to remake everything as it had once been. In the very depths of our time, an apocalyptic hunger arose— it still exists, it still bursts forth—for "a second coming."

Only in the United States did a substantial part of the population retain an unqualified faith in a more or less established society. In Europe the conviction had become almost universal that nineteenth-century liberalism had turned senile. Prewar socialism had succumbed to the tribal nationalism of the First World War and to a policy of parliamentary compromise which seemed never to get to the roots of things. The old parties, still faithful to the tedious routines of parliamentary maneuver, could no longer provide rational or emotional sustenance. The need for change seeped into the consciousness of millions, and as the Nazis tapped the hysteria and sadism that swirled beneath this feeling, the Stalinists took over the revolutionary movement which in the early twenties had tried to give it coherent political form.

Communism and its cruel caricature, Stalinism, derived not from a psychological malaise unique to or predominant among its adherents* but from a general breakdown of society. Years earlier

* A recent study of the American CP claims that the majority of young Americans who joined it were prompted not by economic distress but by conflict with their family. Perhaps so; but it would be useful to know what relationship there might have been between these family conflicts and economic difficulties. In any case, the same results would very likely have

Marx had written, "Every human weakness binds men to the priest because it is the point where the priest can get access to the heart." [12] In our time every weakness of society binds certain men to Stalinism because it has discovered the point where those weaknesses cause the most pain.

In a time of permanent crisis Stalinism seemed to provide a faith, to cry forth a challenge and make possible an ideal. That its vision was defiled and its ideal corrupt mattered little to its followers since one condition for its strength was not only that there be a vision but that the vision be corrupt. Yet, in an era when traditional faiths were crumbling and extreme situations became the familiar texture of daily life, Stalinism attracted not only the worst but also the best. It was this "doubleness" of both its human appeal and its moral quality that proved to be its greatest source of strength.

Invariably the successes of Stalinism were symptomatic of the sickness of society. In a depersonalized world Stalinism was able to tap the residue of a yearning for communal fraternity, for a style of life concerned with the intrinsic rather than external characteristics of human beings.* As Ignazio Silone has said, the origin of Communist affiliation was often a search for comrades, men with whom one could live in fraternity:

> One fine Sunday some of us stopped going to Mass, not because Catholic dogma seemed to us, all of a sudden, false, but because the people who went began to bore us and we were drawn to the company of those who stayed away. . . . What characterized our revolt was the choice of comrades. Outside our village church stood the landless peasants. It was not their psychology we were drawn to; it was their plight.[14]

True tragedy, it has been argued, arises "when the idea of 'justice' appears to be leading to the destruction of higher values." [15] The tragedy of Stalinism arose when the quest for justice among its

---

been found in studies of people who joined the fascist movements or the primitivist religious sects; what needs to be explained is the *difference* in behavior caused by different political or social identifications.[11]

  * Louis Aragon, the French Communist poet, writes that party members like to refer to the party as "the family," and that this was particularly true during the underground days of the Resistance. In those days, he says, party comrades would be designated by familial names, such as cousin, uncle, etc.[13]

followers became indistinguishable from their loyalty to a profoundly unjust system of totalitarian domination. The dedicated Stalinist struggled against society with a clear conscience, believed himself a good man, and destroyed with neither compunction nor guilt. Had he been merely a self-interested conspirator he would hardly have mattered, except to the police; he was politically dangerous precisely because he saw himself as a spokesman for the truth.

Outside observers as well as some ex-Stalinists tend to picture the inner life of the party entirely in terms of manipulation, exploitation, and ruthless intrigue. All of these elements were clearly present, but if one saw nothing else there would follow a disastrous misunderstanding of Stalinism. Manipulation and intrigue were likely to remain hidden from the rank-and-filer, and life within the party could often be selfless and devoted. No politics has a monopoly on virtue, and no belief excludes the possibility of virtue.

Disillusioned former members, who are not always the most reliable witnesses, have testified to the boredom of party life; but even if entirely accurate, their testimony would not be decisive. For selflessness and boredom, even fraternity and boredom, are not necessarily in opposition: it was precisely the devotion of the active party member, his sense that together with his comrades he had begun to live a "new life," that enabled him to accept the boredom which may be inevitable in any organization.

That the Stalinist movement attracted many careerists and bureaucrats of dubious moral quality, that it always contained a predominance of unsavory types in its leadership, is hardly to be doubted; but it would be dangerous to draw conclusions about the ranks from facts about the leaders. Precisely because the Stalinist movement was always so hierarchical in structure, it could attract and exploit a wide range of personality types at the various levels of its work. As the Catholic Church could absorb an Ignazio of Loyola and a St. Francis, the refined intellectuality of the schoolmen and the spontaneous religious emotion of the peasant girl, so could the Communist parties accommodate the brutal callousness of the commissar and the sincere dedication of the rank-and-filer. What is more, the Stalinist movement could not have thrived without both of these types. A party of commissars alone could never have reached the passions of the poor; a genuinely idealistic party could never have accepted the task of defending and submitting to Russian totalitarianism.

The Psychological Approach to Stalinism

4. All efforts to explain Stalinism primarily through the categories of modern psychology are marred by a failure to understand the social context in which the movement arises. It is a failure similar to that which inheres in the effort to apply psychoanalysis to literature. When Ernest Jones sees in *Hamlet* the representation of an Oedipal conflict, one is led to insist that Hamlet happens to be a deposed prince, that Claudius rules the state and the state of Denmark is sick. The disease destroying Denmark can have neither an explanation nor a cure that is purely psychological.[16] Similarly, even if it be true that a large number of Stalinists are neurotic, it remains equally true that the schism of their souls, to borrow a phrase from Toynbee, cannot be understood apart from the schism in the body social.

That a good many of the people who joined the American Communist Party during the past thirty-five years were prompted to do so by psychological malaise seems a hypothesis for which considerable evidence is available.* Yet, this hypothesis granted, it needs to be asked why in all its history the Stalinist movement succeeded in attracting so tiny a proportion of the millions of neurotics available in the United States, or what it was in the particular character of Stalinism that won the allegiance of some neurotics but not others. And if, as many studies suggest, neurosis is distributed across the entire spectrum of American society, it would seem even more relevant to ask how or why our culture "produces" sickness.

To place major stress on the neurotic dispositions of those who became Stalinists is to succumb to the notion that Stalinism was primarily a sickness of the soul—a sickness of *other, special* souls—which neither drew from nor reflected upon society itself. And since those who see Stalinism primarily as an expression of neurosis are not, of course, likely to be Stalinists themselves, their diagnosis involves a parceling of souls that, verging on the sin of pride, can

* Cf. the rather conclusive data gathered by Gabriel Almond.[17]

provide them with considerable psychic reassurance. It is a theory that might be described as a self-comforting hypothesis.

But there is another, more important objection to the psychological approach to Stalinism. Those who explain the Stalinist appeal in terms of the anxiety of modern man—an anxiety said to be intensified by the loss of faith—not only fail to account for the strength of the Communist parties in non-Western parts of the world, where presumably the loss of faith has not been so great as in the West, but also employ categories so generalized and undifferentiated as to blur whatever in Stalinism is historically distinctive and unique. If psychological categories such as anxiety and insecurity are at the center of analysis, it becomes extremely difficult to explain why the pervasive yearning for authority that is said to be at work in our time leads some people to T. S. Eliot's Anglicanism and others to Father Divine's Messianism, some to fascism and others to Stalinism. And this is a question that psychology cannot answer so long as it remains within the limits of its own discipline.

Granted that a pervasive *anomie* and a breakdown in the normative structure of Western society are necessary conditions for the rise of Stalinism; they are not, however, sufficient conditions. No analysis of the character structure of party members can solve the problem raised by Stalinism as a mode of collective action. To do this, it is necessary to examine the specific social groupings in which Stalinism sinks its deepest roots and in which its appeal finds the most persistent response.

Economic Poverty and the Stalinist Appeal

5. The social alienation and political frustration upon which Stalinism thrives are obviously to be found throughout the world, but not with equally corrosive effects in all countries and not equally distributed among the various classes.

America suffered little during the First World War. The troubles of the depression were soon alleviated by New Deal measures and the soothing domestic effects of a permanent war economy. Compared to Europe and Asia, the United States remained relatively cushioned against the impact of total crisis, and Americans were hardly faced with those extreme situations and choices to which the rest of the world had grown accustomed. Though a mass movement in many European and Asian countries, Stalinism impinged upon little more than a few marginal strata in the United States.

Yet even in Europe and Asia, where the crisis was deep and unremitting, only certain groups proved susceptible to Stalinism. Further discriminations are necessary—particularly with regard to what in sociological jargon would be called the "differential impact" of Stalinism.

The appeal of Stalinism has often been explained in terms of economic deprivation. President Truman, in what he described as the struggle against "stomach communism," liberal proponents of Point Four, and other people who have taken a step or two toward political sophistication have habitually employed this argument. But unless severely modified and greatly complicated, it rests upon very little evidence. Many areas of the world in which poverty is most extreme have shown only the faintest susceptibility to Stalinism, while in such countries as England and the United States the Communist parties have gained most of their support from the less deprived sections of the population.

Not absolute deprivation but a sudden traumatic awareness of "relative deprivation" [18] seems to be a major immediate cause for the growth of Stalinism. When a social group compares its situation with that of other groups or has begun to reflect upon its real or imaginary past glory, then conditions are ripe for the party. Stalinism finds its greatest strength not in countries hopelessly sunk in misery but in countries where rapid and bewildering changes of social conditions assault the consciousness of people like a series of brutal shocks.

But when will a social group begin to compare its lot with that of other groups? In general, only when it no longer accepts implicitly the traditional "legitimation" for the *status quo*. So long as the binding ideology or mystique of a society continues to hold the allegiance of the masses, they will endure the grossest inequalities of wealth, status, and power. But once there occurs a breakdown of the traditional sanctions for regarding a society as if it were a "given" or ordained structure of existence—once people cease to look upon society as if it were a "natural" phenomenon—then a new standard of judgment seeps into the consciousness of the deprived groups and its members begin to feel a desire to compare their life with the life of those above and about them.

It follows that the role of those who deal professionally with the symbols of social legitimacy—the intellectuals and quasi-intellectuals—is crucially important. Given their peculiar sensitiveness to the hidden fissures of social instability and their trained receptivity to new ideological currents, they are likely to be among the first to criticize the accepted scheme of things. It is they who confront society with those nagging questions which do not yet threaten its existence but do undermine its self-regard. It is they who are the gatekeepers of society, strategically placed to facilitate or hinder the penetration of ideologies that might corrode traditional patterns of life.

In China, for example, the first appeal of Communism was not primarily to the peasants, wretched as their existence frequently was, but to lower middle-class elements in the cities, particularly to intellectuals and dispossessed intellectuals.[19] Cut loose from the moorings of traditional Chinese thought, the intellectuals were troubled by a sense of national humiliation; and because they lived in the cities and enjoyed a certain amount of social mobility, they were in a position to compare their fate with that of the Europeanized *comprador* class. Almost every class in China was socially deprived, but it was the intellectuals and a thin layer of the more skilled workers who were most "ready." Only after members of the alienated Chinese intelligentsia had gone to the countryside to spread Communist propaganda were the peasants raised to that level of awareness which made possible a comparison between their life and the life of other segments of Chinese society.

The political situation in the West, for all its obvious differences, can be explained in analogous terms. Since the early nineteenth century equalitarian ideologies have replaced earlier justifications for differences in rank and privilege. Whatever might be the reality of bourgeois society, it was probably the first in history that had to defend itself through an ideal of universal equality, the image of the "open society" in which every citizen can rise on the political and economic ladder. The bias of the state, the mythology of the age, the implicit valuations of religion have all sanctioned the goals of success. Yet large numbers of ambitious young men from the lower classes have found—this is one of the great themes of the nineteenth-century novel in Europe—that access to power, prestige, and wealth is severely limited. The expansion of opportunity in bourgeois society has seldom kept pace with its formal claims; and from this clash between reality and ideology, a clash that has inflamed the minds and embittered the hearts of millions, have come the violent social struggles of the past century.

Not absolute deprivation but the clash between a proclaimed ideal and the felt reality accounts for the growth of anti-capitalist sentiment in the West.[20] The absolute well-being of the workers in the West has increased during the past century, yet this has not prevented their *sense* of social disparity from becoming one of the overwhelming facts of twentieth-century European politics.*

If, as in France, a society proclaims its loyalty to the norms of Liberty, Fraternity, and Equality while the bulk of the working class remains a social pariah, this contrast between national ideology and class experience must lead to the most severe resentments and the deepest feelings of alienation among the workers. And if all the other parties are committed, or seem to be committed, to the defense of the *status quo,* it follows that Stalinism, with its claim to a total revolutionary solution, will reap the political profit.[21] †

* In speaking of the causes of the French Revolution, Carlyle makes a similar point: "Not *Hunger* alone produced even the French Revolution: no, but the feeling of the insupportable all-pervading *Falsehood* which had now embodied itself in Hunger, in universal material Scarcity and Nonentity, and thereby become indisputably false in the eyes of all" (Lecture VI, *Heroes, Hero-Worship and the Heroic in History*).

† But here a qualification is necessary. A major source of the strength of Stalinism has undoubtedly been its success in presenting itself as the legitimate heir of the European revolutionary and Marxist traditions. In the post-war years, however, the support that the French and Italian workers have given to Stalinism, though still resting upon a revolutionary tradition, particularly in so far as this tradition was reinforced during the anti-Nazi resistance, has also begun to take on a decidedly "conservative" character. The French and Italian workers who continue to vote for the CP and occasionally attend its rallies are thereby still registering their sense of social disaffection; but they may no longer be doing so out of an immediate revolutionary impulse. To vote for the CP in these countries means to continue a habit, just as for other European workers to vote for the Social Democrats means to continue a habit; it does not necessarily or always signify an act of revolutionary choice.

The "differential impact" of the Stalinist appeal in America can be similarly analyzed. Many students have noticed that a high proportion of the American party membership consisted of either first-generation immigrants or sons and daughters of such immigrants.[22] Why were they more susceptible than other strata of the population to the Stalinist appeal? A ready answer might be that newly arrived immigrants usually occupy the bottom of the American social pyramid and therefore experience considerable economic deprivation. But a moment's reflection would show that this is hardly an adequate explanation, for there are groups in American society, such as the Southern Negroes and poor whites, that have suffered even greater poverty than most immigrants yet have remained untouched by Stalinism. Again, the key variable would seem to be not absolute deprivation but a sense of social disparity.

Until recently the Southern poor constituted the backwash of the country, a group isolated from modern life, in, but hardly of, American society. The immigrant who settled in the big Eastern city, however, could not isolate himself from the main drift of our national life. If the first generation of immigrants tried to shield itself from American customs and values by erecting ghetto walls, their sons and daughters devoted themselves to tearing down these walls. Doing this meant participating in a society that stressed openness of opportunity and aspiration toward success. So that even if the Stalinist appeal might have been weak in the rural European countries from which many of the immigrants had come, it could quickly become effective once they entered an "open society" only to find that it was actually somewhat less than open. To turn to competitive values and then to be denied access to the means of competition—this was an experience that made second-generation immigrants particularly vulnerable to anti-capitalist doctrine.

But would not the discrepancy between proclaimed goals and realistic possibilities affect the working class as a whole? It depends upon which working class one has in mind. In western Europe, with its comparatively restricted social mobility, this was certainly true during the decades between, say, the First and the Second World War. But in the United States the workers of native or older immigrant families still enjoyed, during the years in which Stalinism arose, better prospects for social mobility than the workers of western

Europe had ever known. More important, as long as the living standards of the American workers were rising, they felt little impulse to concern themselves with the possibility that their "relative deprivation" may also have been increasing. It was only when a series of blows fell upon a social group—when, for example, urban immigrant workers suffered the handicap of being part of a minority ethnic group together with the frustration of being unable to live by the American values they had begun to accept—that anti-capitalist ideologies acquired a power of attraction.

The Party and Its Followers

6. What has been said thus far may seem to explain too much. And even if it does help account for the varying impact of anti-capitalist ideologies upon social groups, it does not yet explain the strength of the particular anti-capitalist ideology that is Stalinism. To do that, we shall have to glance at the relationship between the Stalinist movement and its followers.

The moral and psychological distance between the rank-and-file Stalinist and the earlier radical is enormous. What strikes one in reading the autobiographies and biographies of the early socialists— and in this respect the leaders were not very different from the followers—is the thoroughness with which they had absorbed the best and most vivid elements of nineteenth-century individualism. Though preaching a collectivist creed, they were far from colorless personalities: many of them were so intensely imbued with a concern for individual realization as to verge on eccentricity. Deep personal conviction, often achieved after a painful struggle of conscience but then clung to with an intensity proving that there *had* been a struggle, seems to have characterized a high proportion of the older radicals. Participation in "the movement" gave many of them a feeling of personal dignity as well as of communal strength, for they could learn to accept and transcend the frequent misery of their existence by binding themselves in a fraternal effort to remove it.

Nor need one idealize these early Socialists in order to stress the contrast with Stalinism. A good many of them must obviously have fallen short of the ideal type that has here been sketched.

What matters, however, is that autonomy and freedom of personality *was* the ideal, and that the early Socialist movement created conditions favorable to the growth of human personality. No achievement of early Socialism is more impressive or testifies more decisively to its affection for freedom than the way in which it helped a small but significant minority of the working class to absorb portions of serious culture and raise itself to a certain intellectual self-awareness.

By contrast, the Stalinist militant was usually characterized by a fear of independence. So completely did he identify himself with the Soviet Union and the Communist Party that the former, through a corrupt fantasy, became the emblem of the good society and the latter, through an abject surrender of the critical faculty, took on the aura of a chosen instrument of history. If he were truly one of the faithful, this identification reduced him to little more than a series of predictable and rigidly stereotyped responses: his personality became a function of his "belonging." * Nothing is more typical or tragic in our time than this surrender to an invisible yet absolute "We," this surrender which is a major source of the mystifications and terrorism characteristic of totalitarian movements.[24] Indeed, the politics of our century could be called the politics of the Counterfeit Collective.

A considerable proportion of the Stalinist militants harbored feelings of powerlessness and personal inadequacy which they tried to overcome by identifying with authorities who seemed potentially invincible and immediately omniscient.† Such persons could achieve a semblance of balance only by submitting themselves to authority. Yet this very sense of insignificance from which they

---

* The Freudian term "identification" cannot fully account for the differences between earlier radical and recent Stalinist personality types, for as Erich Fromm points out, the term has been applied to a variety of psychological mechanisms.[23] One kind of identification involves the loss of self through an immersion in an outer force or being; another involves a psychic aggrandizement, with the strength of the outer force or being appropriated to the self; and a third is based on equality and reciprocity. It is primarily the first and to a lesser extent the second that is found in the Stalinist movement.

† Cf. the findings of Gabriel Almond, who stresses however that the feeling of powerlessness seems more widespread among party members in the United States than among those in other countries.[25]

suffered was accompanied by a free-floating aggressiveness and *res-sentiment*.* Every threat to the self could be compensated and over-compensated by passive reliance on the strength of the leaders to whom they surrendered themselves.[26] The impoverished self sought security in the mystical body of the party, while the total belief in the authority of the party was linked with a readiness to attack all those outside of it, who, unless they were pliable "progressives" to be privately mocked for their naïveté, were by definition enemies. "The individual delegates, as it were, his power to the Party; and this proceeding recalls what Marx . . . described as 'alienation.' The individual worships his feeble power in the great power in which it reappears without its feebleness." [27]

But we must here distinguish between two kinds of power. The faithful Stalinist found enormous satisfaction in contemplating the physical power of the Soviet Union, and soon it became difficult, as indeed unnecessary, for him to distinguish between approval of Russia because she was right and adoration because she was strong. As he grew adept in Stalinist apologetics—which, it is important to note, were almost always a form of *self-persuasion*—he learned to convince himself that when the Soviet Union showed strength this was proof her policies were correct; that when she betrayed weak-ness this was proof she still stood on the side of the oppressed; that when she engaged in a cynical maneuver this was proof she com-manded the guile of those skilled in the struggle for power; and that when she was tricked by an enemy's still more cynical maneuver this was proof she possessed the innocence of those committed to an ideal. Judgment was not related to fact; fact was adapted to judgment. And in the end the Stalinist felt that he commanded the most important fact of all: the Soviet Union exists, the Soviet Union is powerful, and he, puny little party member, "shares" in its power.

But there is another kind of power which the Stalinists wor-shiped, and that was the power of systematized intellectual re-assurance. Many observers have been bewildered by the ability of hardened Communists to adapt themselves to the most dizzying

---

* We use this term as first advanced by the brilliant German writer Max Scheler to signify a type of hostility which arises out of diffuse feelings of hatred and envy, together with a sense of being unable to direct these actively against the hated objects.

turns of the "party line," a bewilderment which suggests they make the mistake of supposing that it was ideology as such which bound the members, whereas in reality it was *the organization as the faith made visible* which was the primary object of loyalty. A commitment to Marxism could never in itself provide total reassurance, since Marxism is a method that stresses the problematic nature of thought—indeed, anyone who conceives of it as a method (which the Stalinist obviously did not) cannot suppose it a mere strategy for reassurance. The Stalinist did not commit himself to the use of Marxism; he committed himself to the claims of the party that it "possessed" Marxism. His aspiration was not toward certainty of his own, for even that would imply a measure of personal autonomy, but toward the assurance that the party would always be there to relieve him of the doubts which it knew his fallibility would prompt him to have but which it also expected him to know it could always relieve.

The Stalinist has sometimes been described as *the man who knows,* but while this description holds for a sophisticated minority it seems more accurate to say that generally the Stalinist was *the man who knows Who knows.* His faith rested not so much in the total world-picture of Stalinism (for he was only too sensitive to the possibility that he might be in error or prove inadequate to the demands of world history) as in the certainty that the movement would sooner or later proclaim the correct line, which was all he knew or needed to know. And it was not so much this or the other leader in whom he placed his faith, for he had learned that those on high were as fallible as he and frequently even more vulnerable, but in the institution and the *idea* of leadership—which is one reason that the anonymous grayness of the party leadership, so disconcerting and bewildering to outsiders, could be so comforting to the faithful. It told them that they did not have to depend on mere human error: one leader has gone, another may go, a third may return, but the leadership remains.

Without accepting the notion that Stalinism was a "secular religion," it is clear that this kind of loyalty has many points of similarity to the faith of believers. Like religion, Stalinism provided a total explanation of the universe and set to rest those doubts and troubles which the unaided human intelligence can hardly avoid.

The process by which one became a devout Stalinist and, even more striking, by which one ceased to be a devout Stalinist has obvious parallels to religious conversion and the loss of faith; for it involved not merely a change of opinion or perspective but the assumption or loss of a "new being."

Are we here indulging in the kind of psychological speculation against which we warned earlier? We think not. The fact is that ego strength and weakness are grounded in historical contexts—they are social categories. To the extent that men are able to plan and determine their lives, to that extent are they likely to develop strength of ego. Men who are powerless, or feel themselves to be so, all too often overcome their anxieties not through autonomous cooperation but through a regressive identification with authorities, which, in turn, leads to further anxiety and still greater reliance on authority, and finally to what Franz Neumann has called "caesaristic identification." [28]

Thus, an essential condition for the growth of Stalinism was that it appear as a reaction to great defeats suffered by the European radical movements. *Stalinism was the movement that came afterward*—after the defeat and disillusion, after everything seemed lost yet the power of the Soviet Union remained. In Germany the Stalinist regime within the CP established itself only after the decisive defeats of radicalism in 1923; in Spain Stalinism became important only after the decline of the revolution; in Italy Stalinism achieved mass strength only after the working class had been demoralized by fascism. An apparent exception is France, where Stalinism emerged as a mass party during the Popular Front period; yet it should not be forgotten that this growth of influence paralleled a deep-rooted demoralization of French society in general and the French working class in particular. As Jules Monnerot has written:

> Where communism becomes strong it is at the expense of the working-class movement, which loses its autonomy to an external leadership. The conception of revolution as an eruption from the depths of the masses is replaced by a new and hybrid conception. What is now required is revolution to order, eruption by instalments, spontaneous effervescence controlled by written instructions.[29]

It might even be suggested that in those Western countries where Stalinism was strong the workers no longer acted as a coherent and self-disciplined class; there had begun that dissolution of all social groups into an atomized mass which is a condition for the rise of a totalitarian state. So long as Stalinism remained a movement that had not yet taken power, it had to try to keep the workers in an intermediary status between a conscious class and an amorphous mass. Were the workers to lose the characteristics of a class entirely, it might become hard to mobilize them for the political struggles of the Stalinist party; were they to gain a high degree of consciousness as a class, they might begin to break free from the Stalinist grasp.

Our detour into social psychology* permits us to qualify and make more specific some earlier observations. Alienating tendencies within capitalist society take on a particularly dangerous form among persons or groups that have lost or never possessed a sense of autonomy, and it is among such groups that the Stalinist appeal was strongest. In this age of crisis Stalinism attracted those who felt that the world must be changed but lacked the energy to change it through their own efforts and in a libertarian direction.

Nor is this mere assertion. All the available evidence suggests that the appeal of Stalinism was greatest among groups that suffered

---

* But doesn't the description of the past few pages hold for all totalitarian movements? Where are the critical points of difference between the Stalinist and Nazi movements? Adequate answers would require another book; here a few words will have to do.

Stalinism and Nazism are "symmetrical" phenomena, two kinds of totalitarianism; but it would be a serious mistake to ignore the distance between them.

The Stalinist tends to identify with the workings of an impersonal apparatus, the Nazi with the person of an exalted leader. The Stalinist movement claims to be the rightful heir of the Western Enlightenment, while the Nazis openly proclaim their contempt for Western thought. The Stalinist movement declares its commitment to rationality, while the Nazis celebrate the "depths" of irrationality. The Stalinists claim science, the Nazis surrender themselves to myth. The Stalinists have gone much further in the elaboration of a consistent ideology, while the Nazis have been able to develop little more than strands of ideology, each of which is often at odds with the other and most of which decline into demonology.

Finally, if one were to continue the comparison between the two movements, the difference in the societies they establish when in power would have to be specified in detail.

most severely from a sense of social dispossession and a loss of social perspective—that is, among groups in whom the ligatures of shared values were slackening. In Europe it was the unemployed, and particularly those among them who lost the hope of reentering the ranks of the active working force, that turned most readily to Stalinism. In periods of depression the unemployed are cut off from the normal processes and settings of social life: they subsist on the dole, go to the movies, scan the papers, sit in the parks, learn to get by on inadequate food. A gulf appears between those who have jobs and those who do not, between those who still retain a place in society and those who have lost it. Gradually the unemployed become declassed, forfeiting their sense of group identity and sinking to the level of raw material for totalitarian demagogues. As Franz Borkenau has written with regard to the pre-Nazi German Communist Party:

> Before the depression, at the height of the boom, the Communist Party had started to transform itself from a party of the workers into a party of the unemployed. By 1931 the process had taken on catastrophic dimensions. . . . And the unemployed the party won over were not occasionally unemployed. They had been unemployed for years . . . and it was very doubtful how far, in psychology and interests, they were still part of the working class.[30]

It is true, of course, that in some countries after the Second World War the Communists were able to win over the bulk of the employed working class—yet this fact does not controvert our point. In countries where the working class had attained a measure of strength and acceptance, such as the United States, England, and pre-Nazi Germany, the appeal of Stalinism had been greatest among marginal groups. In countries like France and Italy, however, the working class as a whole never felt itself to be fully part of the social life of the nation. The sense of being excluded, together with a series of previous political defeats, affected the French and Italian workers as a whole and thereby created conditions favorable to Stalinist penetration.*

* A recent Swedish study reports a very high correlation between "social isolation" and readiness to vote the Swedish CP ticket.[31]

Just as the appeal of Stalinism proved strongest among those sections of the working class that were or felt themselves to be socially dispossessed, so was it most successful among those intellectuals suffering from a sense of intellectual estrangement. It was almost always among the quasi-intellectuals, those lacking the possibility or capacity for serious work or those employed in the mass industries where the relationship to serious thought is parasitic, that Stalinism won adherents. Particularly after the mid-thirties, few intellectuals still in possession of their craft and able to employ it with a measure of independence and creativeness proved vulnerable to Stalinism for any length of time. Only during those moments of social crisis so extreme that they led to dislocations of entire peoples were any substantial number of serious intellectuals accessible to Stalinist appeals.

Neither economic poverty nor psychological insecurity—and not the two together—can alone account for the growth of Stalinism. The reality was more complex. Those groupings in whom the process of social atomization had gone farthest—the process by which the threads of communal solidarity and moral self-confidence gradually unravel—were the ones that provided the most fertile field for Stalinism. It is the *total quality* of social life that is decisive. The strength of Stalinism was in direct ratio to the weakness of society, its "health" a function of our sickness.

The Structure of the Stalinist Party

7. In some situations it is obviously useful, though never without risk, to speak of *the* Stalinist or *the* Catholic.* But once an effort is made to study the party organization more carefully, such generic categories must be abandoned. For between the rank-and-filer and the member of the Politbureau there is a difference at least as great as that between the communicant and the Cardinal.

The structure of the Stalinist party resembled an onion; but the onion can and should be peeled away, sector by sector. The sordid

---

* Still, it had better be stressed that when speaking of "the Stalinist" in the previous section of this chapter we have been referring mainly to the Stalinist militant, that is, the devoted and active party member.

power struggles among the leaders were part of the Communist Party, but so was the devotion of the nameless members who performed its routine chores; the NKVD and espionage networks were part of that complex social phenomenon known as Stalinism, but so were the inarticulate yearnings of the Asian peasants who, for the first time and even if only as pawns, came to a kind of historical consciousness through its activity and its prodding. To focus exclusively on any one of these aspects is to fail to see the Stalinist movement in its totality.

Especially is this true of the theories that present Stalinism as an armed secular religion. For some of its members Stalinism did indeed perform functions analogous to those performed by religion; and as long as we remember that we are speaking in metaphors it is sometimes useful to describe Stalinism as a kind of religion in which the realm of the sacred was transposed from the transcendent to the immanent, and the Historical Future acquired the same eschatological status that the Hereafter has for genuine otherworldly faiths. But there were also members of the Communist Party, both those at the inner core of leadership and those on the outer rim of proletarian following, who seemed but little touched by such quasi-religious impulses. The bureaucratic leaders saw themselves as technicians of the soul, overseers of stumbling humanity, members of an elite of *the knowing* who were endowed with a special historical clairvoyance and thereby entitled to manipulate, coerce, and when necessary terrorize the masses of the ignorant, in accordance with the decrees of History as revealed by the party.[32] The working-class members, however, often saw the party simply as a militant organization defending their rights. And while it is true that the party did have a high proportion of members who displayed an "authoritarian character," there are innumerable ways in which people of similar character can respond to ideas or political movements. Still more important is the fact that the *roles* people assume in the party— whether they are part of a trade-union "fraction" or of a secret apparatus in the government, whether they engage in open party activities or do clandestine work—also help shape their characters.

A major difficulty facing interpretations of Stalinism as a new religion is that membership in the Communist parties has always fluctuated very widely. Had Stalinism been essentially a quasi-religious movement, one might expect its membership to remain quite stable, since those who underwent a conversion would be likely to cling to their new faith with fanatical intensity. But while an inner ring of Stalinist militants did cleave to the party for long periods of time and with the devotion of true believers, the majority of members consisted of people who abandoned the party after a short stay.

In 1939 only 3 to 4 percent of the French Communist Party membership was reported to have belonged for more than six years, which suggests that the party was in a process of perpetual self-renewal. In 1937 it claimed 340,000 members as against 45,000 in February, 1934, which means that over 87 percent of its members in 1937 were of less than four years' standing. In December, 1944, the French party claimed 385,000 members and in December, 1945, over 1,000,000, which can only mean that at the latter date almost two out of three members had been in the party for less than one year. But of this total at least one out of four remained in the party for a very short time indeed, since by December, 1949, its membership had dropped to less than 800,000.[33]

The situation in the pre-Hitler German Communist Party was very much the same. Among the party members in 1927 only 27.79 percent dated their membership from the year 1920; in other words, within seven years almost three-quarters of the original membership had left or died. (These figures reveal, incidentally, how thorough is the change in composition from the pre-Stalinist to the Stalinist party.) In one region, Thuringia, for which breakdowns are available, some 10,000 members of the Independent Socialist Party had joined the CP in 1920; only 2,771 remained in the CP by 1927. In the Berlin party branch the rate of membership fluctuation was estimated at 40 percent during 1931. Even among the delegates to the Berlin District Congress in 1932, which would imply a selection of the most active members, 44 percent had belonged to the party for less than one year, a further 22 percent had belonged from one to three years, and only a little over 6 percent for more than ten years.[34]

Similarly with the American Communist Party. At the fourth national convention of the Workers (Communist) Party in August, 1925, National Secretary Charles Ruthenberg reported:

In the three and a half year period since the organization
of the Workers Party, we have admitted . . . more members
than we have in the party at the present time. At the time of
the organization of the party, some 10,000 members were affiliated
to it. Since that time . . . we have taken into the party over
20,000 new members. If we had all of these members, our party
would now have more than 30,000. The dues payment figures
for the past six months show an average of approximately 16,000
and we have therefore lost 14,000 members. . . .[35]

Nor did the picture change in later years. In 1928 the party had
between 9,000 and 10,000 members but during the preceding five
years more than 27,000 new members had been registered; in other
words, two-thirds of those who joined had left within five years.
From July, 1931, to December, 1933, the party recruited 43,426 new
members but the net increase was only 12,000, which means that it
lost about 70 percent of its total recruitment. Of the 12,000 members
in the American CP in April, 1932, only 3,000 had joined before
1930.[36] The membership figures for later years, when they are
available, show the same enormous turnover.

Such figures throw a certain doubt upon the interpretation of
Stalinism which makes it into a "New Islam," and they call into
question Sidney Hook's view of the Communist Party as a gigantic
conspiracy with most of its members active or potential conspirators.
For such theories imply that the party members were sharply cut off
from the rest of society, isolated from its main intellectual and moral
currents, and owing loyalty to no one but the Kremlin. While undoubtedly true for most of the devoted party militants, this cannot
be true, as the fluctuating membership figures indicate, for the
majority of party members—unless it be assumed that the Detroit
auto worker or New York schoolteacher who joined the party and
dropped out within a year or two could be transformed so quickly
into an expert spy or conspirator. Whatever may have been the case
for the leaders and devoted militants, the ordinary American Communist was not permanently cut off from society. A kind of metabo-
lism was at work by means of which "alienated" persons were
drawn into the party, only to leave it after a few years and return
to conventional life. Far from giving "the whole of their lives" to

Communism, most members were in a hurry to give up the party. Stalinism in America was able to attract a considerable number of followers during the past twenty-five years (one estimate, probably high, is that 750,000 people passed through the American CP since its formation[37]); but it also managed to repel the vast majority of them. The status of a "conspiracy" that is constantly creating masses of ex-conspirators surely would seem problematic.

A conspiracy—if that is the exact word for it—did and does exist in the form of an international espionage network maintained by the Russians. This network functioned within the Communist parties, though it probably did its most secretive and dangerous work outside the parties; it recruited agents from the parties, though it was capable of continuing to operate even when the parties were suddenly wiped out; but to identify the espionage system with the Stalinist movement as such, or to assume that party membership almost automatically transformed people into conspirators, is an error as dangerous as it is facile.

Party members stayed for short periods; they might be active for shorter periods; and a good many didn't even pay their dues regularly. Here is a complaint, which could be duplicated in any country, from the French Communist paper L'Humanité: "In some sections the money collected is only 60 percent of what it should be." "Ninety percent of our members," wrote a high official of the French party, "are new, and do not know, or inadequately know, not only the methods of working with the masses, but often and above all, the fundamental principles of party organization." [38]

Even while laying claim to Leninist principles of organization, the Stalinist parties embodied a quite different organizational practice. In their bulk they consisted not of a professional revolutionary elite but of transitory, ill-informed, and unreliable members. Only a thin layer of activists, seldom reaching more than 5 percent of the party membership, can be said to have had even a surface resemblance—and that more in the intensity of their devotion than the cast of their thought—to the Leninist type. Yet in emergencies the party leadership was forced to rely primarily upon these activists.*

---

* The initial impact of the party could sometimes be so great that members who had belonged only for a year or two would be entrusted with such responsible tasks as speaking for its point of view in a trade union, running

This relatively stable core may indeed have contained many whose adherence rested upon a total myth or secular religion—"cadre members" resembling in their behavior followers of a church militant. But between them and the unstable mass membership at the bottom of the party, as well as between them and the professional leaders at the top, there was an enormous distance. And even if he attended endless numbers of meetings, the average militant may never have met, or have known it if he did, those comrades who belonged to one of the secret apparatuses that cut across the party but functioned mainly outside of it.

That is why theories resting upon memories of former rank-and-filers prove of little value in understanding the functionaries and militants, while theories based on a study of the inner layers of the party are likely to be of little help in understanding the mass membership. When, for example, Ernst and Loth, in their study of American Communists, try to draw a collective portrait of "the Communist" from the reminiscences of a few ex-members, they neglect the fact that the party is a hierarchical structure in which the outlook of members on one level is quite different from that of members on another level. Strict internal hierarchy has been an invariable trait of Stalinist organization—for if an ultimate end of a totalitarian movement is to flatten society into a shapeless mass, it can do this only by maintaining a highly ordered internal structure.

Leadership, Faction, and Hierarchy

8. In an era when the systematic abuse of language has become an accepted technique of politics, the labels and programs of parties hide more than they reveal. Fascist totalitarians call themselves National Socialists, French conservatives pass as Radical Socialists, the Stalinists speak in the name of democracy. Given this mixture of inherited confusion and contrived mystifica-

---

for public office, and becoming a leader of a local party branch. But it seems most implausible that any but tested veterans of Communism would be assigned "delicate" tasks requiring secrecy and illegality.

The extent to which, and kinds of assignments for which, the mass membership could be drawn upon to swell the ranks of the militants was extremely limited—as, for that matter, was the number of militants able or willing to assume "underground" tasks.

tion, an analysis of formal programs, though still necessary, cannot be as conclusive in defining the nature of a movement as an analysis of its inner life and organizational structure. Not what it says about tomorrow but what it *is* today forms the crux of the matter.

There can be no better way of making this judgment than to study how an organization selects its leadership. In one "ideal type" of organization, leadership is chosen through a democratic competition in which the members more or less retain a decisive vote. Another kind follows the pattern made familiar by the army, where an elite commands positions of power and allocates shares of it to candidates who are judged by the completeness of their loyalty and their proficiency in carrying out assigned tasks.[39]

Despite the extent to which a centralist emphasis was imbedded in Bolshevik doctrine, the early Communist parties in the West were closer to the first of these models than to the second. To the degree that they ceased to be mere sects and became mass parties, the Western Communist parties moved away from the early Leninist scheme of a "vanguard" party composed of disciplined full-time revolutionists. Party members were sometimes able to choose—more often to topple—their leadership; they were always in a position to exert a certain check and control upon its policies. The parties were directed by large Central Committees which generally contained spokesmen for various shades of party opinion. And while these Central Committees necessarily had to delegate daily tasks and decisions to small subcommittees, they remained the centers of authority and prestige within the movement. The regions and districts into which the parties were divided chose their own committees. In large cities the active members were called together for frequent conferences, at which political orientation was voted upon.* Often enough the Russian influence was decisive, but the Russians could only try to persuade or apply pressure; they could not yet issue edicts. With each year, however—particularly as an increasing number of Communist officials were in the direct pay of Russian agencies abroad—the possibilities for applying pressure, and the readiness to do so, increased.

* It was at one of these conferences, Borkenau points out, that the Brandler leadership of the German CP was overthrown after the defeat of 1923.

By the mid-twenties a new organizational principle began to appear in the Communist movement, and within a few years it had crystallized into the typical Stalinist pattern. Unquestionably the strong centralist emphasis of the Lenin period facilitated this transition, especially as it provided handy catchwords and ingrained habits that could be put to new uses; but the direct and immediate cause was that the entire political-moral tone of the Communist movement was undergoing a cataclysmic change.

One of the factors that hastened the "Stalinization" of the parties was the appearance of numerous functionaries trained in the "Lenin School" in Moscow, which had first been established in 1926. Though often returning to work in their native countries, these functionaries were available for assignment in any part of the world; they had been purged of "national particularism" as they had been purged of critical independence. Some became public leaders, others disappeared into secret agencies, but all had in common that they were accountable not to the parties in which they functioned but to the Moscow "center," which could shift them at will and, as it turned out, controlled their very lives. The first full-scale examples of the new Stalinist type, these men no longer thought of themselves as revolutionary tribunes sprung up from the wrath of the people; they were obedient agents of an international machine, stripped of the desire for judgment or the capacity for private will.

The mere presence within each party of such a "parallel apparatus" exerting a decisive veto and not responsible to the members, would have been enough to destroy whatever vestige of democracy remained. But the formal structure of the parties was also significantly changed. Gradually the Central Committee became a ceremonial institution, its power being absorbed by a small Politbureau consisting of carefully screened functionaries who could not be suspected of any critical impulses. The idea that divergent political "tendencies" should be represented in the Central Committee along roughly proportionate lines became almost as great a heresy as the idea of permitting factions within the party at all. And at the same time the autonomy of lower-rung sections of the party was curtailed and finally abolished.

Though this organizational counter-revolution, which effectively deprived the membership of any possibility for determining the party's policies, was part of a gradual counter-revolution in the politics and spirit of the Communist movement, it soon acquired a momentum of its own. Rationales were discovered for what had at first been improvised maneuvers, and the new structural modes helped speed developments of which they had at first been mere reflections.

The major turning-point in the organizational history of the Communist movement was its decision to ban factions. What had been taken as an emergency measure at the Tenth Congress of the Russian party in 1921, though even then Lenin had said that he foresaw the reappearance of factions,[41] was now exalted into a basic principle of the monolithic Stalinist party. Not only was any member certain of immediate expulsion who presumed to organize a faction of the kind that had been common during the early twenties; the party was so organized as to make it impossible for any opposition tendency to win strength. The basic unit was now the local or factory "cell"; such units were bound into sections and the sections into districts, above all of which loomed the Central Committee in theory and the Politbureau in fact. Each lower echelon was supposed to elect representatives to the next higher one, but in practice elections became simple administrative formalities. In the absence of competing factions with distinct political platforms, whatever discussion of candidates did take place could only be ritualistic. Soon it became standard practice for the lower unit to accept a slate of officials prepared by the next higher body.

Such procedures obviously permit careful screening of independent or recalcitrant elements—elements that, to one or another extent, kept springing up in the parties throughout the late twenties and had to be eliminated before the control of the Stalinist hierarchy could be total. The secondary leadership, whose choice for and tenure of office was dependent on the will of the primary leadership, soon lost all possibility of independence. As an official American party manual puts it:

> Every elected party committee must report regularly on its activities to the party organization. It must give an account of its work. The lower party committees and all party members of the given party organization have the duty of carrying out the de-

cisions of the higher party committees and of the Communist International.[42]

Gradually the power of each committee was appropriated by "its" bureau, and the power of each bureau by "its" secretary, so that even as the façade of democratic forms remained and the mock ceremony of democratic procedures was solemnly adhered to, a relentless concentration of power took place. Elections became empty forms not merely because factions were prohibited or slates handed down from higher echelons but because the commonly accepted criteria for judging potential leaders were now primarily their Stalinist orthodoxy and then the estimate of their competence held by those who nominated them. In effect, elections to office became a form of promotion for faithful followers.[43]

Periodically the party would call upon its members for "discussion," and the leaders go through the stylized humiliation of "self-criticism," but these exercises had nothing to do with democratic give-and-take. They were simply a function of the power struggles within the Russian hierarchy or a means of finding scapegoats for failures in party work. The discussions that did take place had necessarily to be limited to peripheral matters (how best to carry out the party line) and lifeless reiterations of faith.

In the Stalinist party as it froze into shape during the late twenties and early thirties there was no possibility for political contact among the basic units of the organization. All relations were vertical. No channels for horizontal contact between the units were permitted. If, say, two units wanted to discuss a common divergence of opinion before a section meeting, there was no approved mechanism by which they could do so. Any political defiance that did appear in a local unit could easily be bottled up by the leadership and kept from spilling over into other units. And since each delegate of a lower unit was responsible not to those who had elected him but to the higher body that had nominated (i.e., selected) him, it became a common assumption that his duty was to keep his superiors informed of local disaffection. Under conditions in which parallel party units communicate only through a higher body, the limited freedom of discussion that might exist in a local branch could have little impact on the life of the party as a whole.*

Factional struggles could and did break out from time to time within the parties, as in France and Italy, but during the lifetime of Stalin these struggles had almost nothing in common with normal political disputes in which the membership is roused by contending factions and differences of opinion are publicly registered. They resembled, instead, the jockeying of cliques on top of a bureaucratic structure, each trying, half openly and half covertly, to edge the other out. Such struggles were always directed toward winning the favor of the highest authorities within the Stalinist world, that is, Moscow; they did not and could not involve any effort to stir the ranks to independent political motion, though the ranks might be used as a convenient tool in the competition of cliques for preferment. But in none of the factional struggles that broke out in the Stalinist parties—they were not, in any case, very numerous—was the membership appealed to for an independent and basic decision.

As the "Stalinization" of the Communist parties continued, all leaders were eliminated who could still distinguish between their loyalty to the Russian dictatorship and to the working class of their own country. A new kind of leader began to appear, the apparatus man whose chief talent was for the justification and carrying out of orders he might himself have had no part in drafting. The professional revolutionaries of an earlier period were, in Trotsky's phrase, "domesticated" and then destroyed. Their place was taken by cautious and shrewd careerists whose fundamental means of judging their success, as of prolonging their stay, in office was their standing in the eyes of Moscow.†

* A strikingly similar organizational structure dominated the empire of the Incas. The basic social unit consisted of ten householders under an official appointed from above; fifty householders were similarly grouped under a higher official; 100 householders under a member of the nobility; and so on, up to 40,000 households. Above these were four top officials and above them the Inca (Big Brother). Except for the very highest ranks, no relations were permitted between units or officials of similar standing; authority flowed vertically, downwards from level to level.

† These descriptions may require modification when Stalinist parties in power are being discussed. Their relations to Moscow varied from the complete subservience of certain Balkan leaders to the relative or apparent autonomy of the Chinese. But in these pages we are discussing only the parties that have not achieved power.

In any case: the real apex of the Stalinist pyramid was located outside the national parties altogether.

The Inner Core and the Outer Following

9. The idea that a man's worldly loyalty belongs to the nation, though an axiom of most modern politics, is a relatively modern one. Claims to exclusive national loyalty would have been unthinkable to the medieval mind, and even so recently as the nineteenth century Lord Acton could write without fear of disgrace:

> There is a moral and political country . . . distinct from the geographical which may possibly be in collision with it. The Frenchmen who bore arms against the Convention were as patriotic as the Englishmen who bore arms against King Charles, for they recognized a higher duty than that of obedience to the actual sovereign.[44]

Though the nineteenth century saw the birth of the First International and the successful adaptation to new conditions by that most powerful of international structures, the Catholic Church, it was nonetheless the century in which the claims of nationality thoroughly triumphed over all rival allegiances. Only in the late nineteenth and early twentieth centuries has this primacy of national consciousness been seriously challenged, first by the Marxist mass movements and later by the Stalinists. In the Marxist movements this challenge was justified by a vision of fraternal collaboration among the masses of the world, while in the Stalinist movement internationalism, though its vocabulary might be exploited, was replaced by a world-wide organization dependent upon a national imperialism. In both cases, however, there was a decisive break from the national consciousness that had been an integral part of traditional liberalism.

In all those countries where the parties had not yet taken power, the Stalinist militants considered themselves an unredeemed *irredenta,* an embattled minority temporarily separated from the true homeland but struggling to rejoin it. This total loyalty to the Soviet Union was perhaps the only point at which Stalinist theory and practice entirely converged. When Tito broke from the Russians, Vittorio Vidaldi, leader of the Trieste CP, expressed this outlook in an unusually clear and refreshing way:

> As a man who once belonged to the Communist movement [Tito] knew that *there is one basic law—that is our faith in the Soviet Union*. . . . He knew very well that in the struggle of our movement anyone who began to fight against its leadership inevitably joined our enemies.[45] [emphasis added]

That during the Stalinist era at least the first of Vidaldi's sentences was true, that the top leadership of all the Communist parties was composed of men whose total allegiance had been consigned to Russia, is by now so apparent there can hardly be any need to provide the all-too-familiar evidence. Nor does the obviousness of this statement diminish its importance. Nonetheless, it would be disastrous to draw rapid conclusions about the outlook of the rank and file from either the objective role of the party or the behavior of its leaders. In the various layers of the party hierarchy there were innumerable shades of attachment to, and detachment from, national consciousness—for there exist sentiments that no mere act of the will can eradicate. To suppose that the two million members of the Italian CP were conscious of having transferred their allegiance from Italy to Russia would be absurd; most of them were probably unaware that a problem of conflicting loyalties existed at all, and the rest succeeded in relegating it to a dim compartment of their minds. With many, it is also true, the sense of both national *and* international loyalty had decayed, so that identification with the Stalinist movement—and that often in a slack and passive way— replaced commitment to either the nation-state of liberalism or the international proletariat of Marxism.

It is similarly absurd to suppose that all members of the American CP shared the leadership's exclusive allegiance to the Soviet Union. During the late thirties, when the party won recruits through its Popular Front appeal, there were undoubtedly a considerable number who really believed that "Communism Is Twentieth Century Americanism," and most of these people must surely not have supposed that they were placing their loyalty to

Russia above their loyalty to America; in fact, it was in the very nature of Popular Frontism that it deliberately and with considerable success blurred such distinctions. During the "cold-war" decade after the Second World War, the American party, having been cut down to a hard core of faithful militants, very probably did contain a large percentage of members who, if pressed hard enough, might have said to themselves—though to no one else—that their primary loyalty was to Russia. But then this situation arose because the more cautious Stalinists, who under less difficult circumstances would have formed the outer layers of the party, had been frightened away.

Just as it was carefully structured into several organizational levels, so did the Stalinist movement function on several ideological levels. A rough but useful division can be made here between the esoteric or inner doctrine and the exoteric or public doctrine. In the esoteric doctrine, no matter what the party's public line might be at any given moment, allegiance to the Soviet Union remained the dominant note, the criterion by which everything else was judged. But this esoteric doctrine seldom percolated beyond the militants and sometimes not even beyond the second-rank functionaries.

The major function of this esoteric doctrine was not to advance or even explain the party line; it was to explain *why* for the moment the party needed to advance a given line, why it was necessary to do such "unpleasant" things as support the Stalin-Hitler pact or vote for bourgeois candidates in an American election. The esoteric doctrine told the true believer not merely or even primarily that the line was correct, nor did it invariably suggest that the line could be defended publicly in terms of its real motives or significance; what the esoteric doctrine told him was *why it was necessary*, by whatever means were available, to justify it in public. Almost always, this was communicated informally, by word of mouth or corridor gossip among the party veterans, and sometimes it trickled down to the ranks against the public (or even the sincere private) disclaimers of the leadership. When the American party, under Browder's guidance, declared its faith in the viability of American capitalism, many CP veterans were shocked. They soon told themselves and each other, however, that it was merely a temporary expedient. In a sense this was true enough—except that they failed to see that the party line, as publicly employed, could always be best understood as a temporary expedient. The esoteric doctrine served as a means of collective reassurance for the comrades disturbed by shifts in party program, particularly those who clung to the belief that the CP remained a revolutionary proletarian organization. While in no way challenging the authoritarian premises of the Stalinist movement, the esoteric doctrine allowed for a certain flexibility, a limited sort of communication from leaders to militants that could take place within the interstices of the party's formal structure. Given the hierarchical rigidity of Stalinism, this informal communication helped preserve a sense of participation and kinship among the more active members.

How useful the esoteric doctrine could be was proved in the French CP directly after the Second World War. At one point it seemed that if the party "took to the streets" it might be able to seize state power; yet the party leadership was faced with the delicate task of indicating to its more sophisticated followers, *without directly saying so,* that an important reason for working to prevent any revolutionary attempt was the fear that it might provoke the United States into a war for which the Soviet Union was not yet ready. The esoteric doctrine thus served to explain and rationalize the difficult position of an extra-parliamentary party which (a) had to avoid the appearance of having softened into a mere reformist party, since this could mean losing the support of many Frenchmen disillusioned with parliamentarism, while (b) not allowing its extra-parliamentary activity, from which it greatly profited, to reach the point of provoking a crisis of power. This meant, as the leaders of the French CP must have known, that they would gradually be dissipating the mass energies that were then at their disposal, for these energies could not remain static—they had either to be put to use or to suffer decline; but as good Stalinists, the French party leaders were ready to accept this loss of power at home in behalf of the over-all Russian strategy.

For the mass membership, however, it was the exoteric or public doctrine that mattered most. And while there was a constant stress upon the power and/or benevolence of the Soviet Union, a total and unqualified allegiance to the Russian leadership was generally not part of the public appeal. Depending on a given situation, the ordinary member might sincerely define himself as a social revolutionary, a militant trade unionist, a twentieth-century American—and while a large element of self-deception was no doubt involved in these roles, it would be a mistake simply to dismiss them as having no relation to reality.

Sidney Hook has written that "The Communist Party sees to it that all members are instructed about the purposes as soon as they join." If Professor Hook means that "all members are instructed" in the inner Stalinist doctrine, which can alone be the source of conspiratorial behavior, he is totally mistaken. If he means that all members are taught the public doctrine, he is partly mistaken. To claim, as he does, that membership in the Communist Party "is a form of *active cooperation and collaboration* in carrying out the purposes of a conspiratorial organization"[46] is first to ignore the hierarchical divisions in the Stalinist movement and second to overestimate its success in communicating to its members even the limited doctrine it wants them to have.*

In his careful study *The Appeals of Communism,* Gabriel Almond has shown that only 27 percent of those ex-Stalinists who responded to his questions had ever been exposed to the "classical" writings of Stalinism before or at the time of joining the party, and of the small proportion who *had* been exposed there were very few who absorbed these with any great attentiveness. More than half of his respondents saw the party, at the time they joined it, as a way of solving personal difficulties or attaining personal goals, and the number who felt this way rises to 73 percent among his American respondents. More than 30 percent of the Americans saw the party as an anti-authoritarian organization at the time they joined it, and thereby as a means of expressing their desire for social rebellion, while 39 percent saw it as a way of participating in a congenial group and thereby solving the problem of loneliness. Almost all the respondents, moreover, had thought of the party in terms that

---

* Together with the more sensational evidence of a Whittaker Chambers concerning the underground activities of Stalinism, one should also consider the statement of Mrs. Deborah Landy, a former party member whose son was temporarily denied a maritime commission in 1955 on the ground of "close association" with his mother. Before a Congressional investigating committee Mrs. Landy said: "I never intended to bring about a revolution. I never found Communism to be a conspiracy. Out here in the rural area [of New Jersey] it was more of a kaffee-klatch."[47]

brought together its public agitational themes: a movement against fascism, imperialism, and various types of discrimination. Still others saw it as a means of attaining trade-union objectives or general humanitarian goals.

Recent public opinion polls in France and Italy show similar results, sympathy for and adherence to the party being based on its agitational themes far more than its essential doctrine. Almond cites one poll in which 76 percent of the French Communist respondents justify their membership by references to their living conditions, while only a small minority offer doctrinal reasons for belonging to the party. And most striking of all, 65 percent of the Communist respondents thought that in a war between Russia and the United States, France should remain neutral—which suggests that the ingrained values of the Frenchman may still be deeper than the engrafted dogmas of the Stalinist.[48]

Many members, to be sure, did receive some indoctrination after joining the party, and the atmosphere of the movement itself communicated a political outlook in powerful if indirect ways; but the remarkable fact is that of Almond's sample 37 percent received no training in party doctrine while another 31 percent claimed to be self-taught. In other words, almost 70 percent had never been enrolled in party schools of any sort, and a high percentage of those who had enrolled generally left the party before the process of indoctrination could go very far.

Even members who remained in the party for longer periods of time were likely to perceive it in quite distinctive and idiosyncratic ways. Almond's hypothesis, that "what *is* said in the inner media of the movement and *not* said at the mass level of Communist communication is what has to be learned by the Communist neophyte if he is to move into the inner party," seems thoroughly sustained by his data; but the fact remains that the bulk of the members neither could nor did enter the "inner party" and hence never penetrated to full knowledge of the esoteric doctrine.

Once exposed to close observation and empirical test, the model of the party as a compact society of devoted conspirators falls to pieces. Far more useful in trying to understand the virtuosity of Stalinist organization and ideology is a complex model proposed by Jules Monnerot:

The originality of Communism consists in its being . . . a social fact *and* a secret society, a perpetually active electoral army *and* a *Freikorps* in the social struggle, a parliamentary party *and* an underworld *Bund*. It is a religion against religion, and an education for obscurantism. In being one thing it does not cease to be the other; it always has an ace up its sleeve because it is always playing two games at once.[49]

Two games? At the very least!

The Role of Ideology

10. A political party, wrote Edmund Burke at the dawn of the nation-state, "is a body of men united, for promoting by their joint endeavors the national interest, upon some particular principle in which they are all agreed." [50]

This description no longer holds fully for any political party, but least of all for Stalinism. And not merely because the Communist parties have no genuine stake in the national interest, but more important, because they are not united upon "some particular principle." The totalitarian party is "unprincipled" in the root sense of the term. All parties may violate their principles, yet the act of violation implies a certain recognition of norms. By contrast, the totalitarian party cannot, in any precise sense, be said to violate its principles: it can be described by its structure, its characteristics, its power goals, but not by any stable ideology or group of ideas. *The movement exists far less for the ideology than the ideology for the movement.**

Though the ideological spokesman of Stalinism advanced claims in regard to its ultimate ends that might seem similar to those of classical socialist thought, such pronouncements were manipulative, hortatory, and self-deceptive—generally a mixture of the three. For these statements of ultimate ends† had no controlling or restrain-

---

* In Ignazio Silone's novel *The Seed Beneath the Snow* a fascist orator, true in his comic fashion to the totalitarian ethos, asks the rhetorical question, Is the handkerchief for the nose or the nose for the handkerchief? and answers that every good fascist understands that the nose is for the handkerchief.

† Can totalitarian movements properly be said to have ultimate ends at all? It may be that this difficult question cannot yet be answered, but we shall touch upon it later.

ing influence on the actual behavior of the Stalinist movement; the claim it made to the heritage of socialism could not in itself lead to a softening of the cruelties in the Siberian labor camps, though a shrewd political expediency might. In the life of the totalitarian movement, the instrumental swallows up the ideological.

Or almost. For if the above is a usable description of the objective workings of the Stalinist movement, it is not sufficient for grasping the subjective processes of Stalinist thought. Many individual Stalinists were obviously entangled with ideology as no one else in our time has been. They felt that their version of "Marxism" provided them with omniscient knowledge of the course of History —knowledge so complete as to constitute a *possession* of History; that it made possible a finished program and a final answer; and that the decisions of the party were the means for realizing the decrees of History. Yet it is no contradiction to say that in a movement for which ideology had become a device there were many people whose submission to ideology was total, fanatical, and ruthless. On the contrary: the existence of such people was a precondition for such a movement.

Beliefs concerning the nature of History are here important insofar as they support the Stalinist myth, yet they cannot in themselves serve as guides to political or moral courses of action. History as such cannot provide values, though it may help and permit valuation. Moral and political principles, however, are based on choices among opposing possibilities; hence, an acceptance of or identification with the supposed decrees of History, simply because they are supposed decrees of History, is an amoral act, leading more often than not to colorblindness in the choice of values. It is here, in its reliance upon History, that Stalinism came closest to being an ideology. If, however, we mean by a genuine ideology a pattern of ideal norms that guide policy, something very different controlled the Stalinist movement. In the Communist parties ideologies were conceived as instruments of power, manipulable according to the needs of a given moment and very seldom serving as either check or standard for behavior.*

* The notion that the Stalinist leaders were fanatical ideologists who could not take a political step without measuring it against their dogmas seems to us an error. It is sometimes said, in defense of this notion, that in

Further qualifications are necessary, however, for in the relation between the Stalinist movement and the tradition of Marxism we face a highly complex and perhaps unprecedented problem. Stalinism, it is true, manipulated and exploited Marxist concepts and terms—but to say this is not yet fully to describe the relationship. Recognizing how deeply the Marxist mode of thought has seeped into the modern mind, the Stalinist movement stressed its claim to being the true receptacle of Marxism with a vigor second only to its claim to socialism and the tradition of the October Revolution. Particularly insofar as they were uncritically or even enthusiastically honored by most of its opponents, these claims constituted a major source of Stalinist power and prestige. Yet it would clearly have been impossible for the Stalinist movement to keep reiterating these claims without, in some way, coming to give them a certain credence itself.

Stalinism grew out of, even as it destroyed, a movement that had been deeply attached to the letter of Marxism. The older leaders of the Stalinist movement, who had once known what it meant to live in a non-totalitarian atmosphere, were trained in a school of exegetics that sharpened wits through prolonged polemics over the meaning of Marxist doctrine. In the world of their youth, a ready capacity to cite Marxist classics, and to cite them with some relevance, could bring prestige and political preferment. But the new Stalinist functionaries, those who were themselves products of Stalinism and had never lived in any other milieu, showed very little interest in Marxist or any other form of speculative thought. They no longer needed to engage in debates with brilliant opposition leaders, as Stalin had once done.

Priding themselves on being practical men, they attached very little prestige to intellectual work and betrayed no desire to emulate Stalin's pretensions as a political theoretician. They looked upon

those countries where Stalinist parties have taken power they have shown their ideological rigidity by risking the most severe opposition from the peasants rather than relax their insistence upon nationalization of the land. In fact, however, the Stalinists have shown a capacity for making temporary compromises with peasant ownership; and their general drive toward the abolition of private farms seems based far less on dogma than on the correct insight that as a ruling group which derives its power from total control of a statified economy they must regard *any* property-owning class as a potential threat.

Marxism as a vocabulary useful in controlling followers abroad, a group of symbols that helped cement social loyalty at home, and a body of dogmatics to be guarded by professional scholiasts, who in turn were themselves to be guarded. As Stalinism grew older, its relationship to Marxist doctrine became more manipulative, though seldom to the point of being entirely free of self-deception.

Fascinated as they now were by the mechanics of power, the Stalinist leaders, if they read Marxist works at all, were likely to turn to those dealing with political strategy and tactics rather than those concerned with ultimate goals or values. Lenin's *What Is to Be Done?* or *Left Wing Communism* might still be read by them with a certain interest, for while the topics of these pamphlets were not immediately relevant to the problems of Stalinism, they could be regarded as manuals of political warfare rich in suggestion to political strategists of almost any kind. By contrast, Marx's philosophical and economic studies were likely to be neglected by most Stalinist leaders—even though the need to validate their claim to the Marxist heritage, as well as to give themselves satisfactions akin to those felt by patrons of scholarship, prompted the Communist parties to publish these works.

Like one of the dark heretical cults of the Middle Ages which celebrated the devil through the ritual and imagery of Christ, Stalinism missed no occasion for proclaiming its Marxist orthodoxy. It defiled the intentions of Marx, his ethical passion and humanistic prophecy, but it clothed a rejection of his vision in the very language through which he had expressed it. Not for the first time in history, the vocabulary of a great thinker was turned against him, to corrupt his ideas and mock his values. Unlike other totalitarian and quasi-totalitarian movements, Stalinism was unable or unwilling to develop its own vocabulary, being an ideologically "dependent" system, an aftermath rather than a beginning.

But it would be an error to suppose that this dependence on the trappings of Marx's system was a mere useless survival. For many Stalinists it provided an indispensable means of reassurance: as long as the old words remained it was easier to evade the fact that new ideas had taken over. For the party, it facilitated the strategy of political access. The Stalinist claim to the Marxist tradition enabled it to compete for the allegiance of European workers who had been brought up in the Socialist movements, particularly those who were taught to suspect the Social Democratic parties as reformist. To have surrendered the signs and symbols it had appropriated from Marxism would have meant to face the enormously difficult task of trying to establish itself in the labor movement through a new vocabulary and what it would have had to acknowledge as a new set of ideas. Strategically, it proved far more advantageous to appear as the defender of orthodox Marxism even while ruthlessly emasculating it. The humanist elements in Marxism were discarded, the passion for man that animates Marx's writing was eliminated, and instead those aspects of Marx's thought were emphasized which might be said to be most tainted by the Hegelian *hubris* of claiming to know what the future *must* be.

So understood, Marxism could provide a feeling of having reached a "total view" which permits one to identify with History and act in accordance with its inner rhythm. The "essence" of History having been grasped, it then became possible to proclaim the primacy of *praxis*. From that point on, since there need be no further desire to question the underlying principle of social existence, strategy and tactics became all-important. The uncritical acceptance of a metaphysical assumption proved in practice to be a shield against any further assaults by metaphysical doubt or contemplative temptations. It was through works that the faith was to be manifested and tested. Theory, even while ritually celebrated, became an object of contempt.

This mixture of knowingness and a pragmatic rejection of abstract thought—a remarkable reflection, by the way, of the profoundly ambiguous feeling of the modern world toward the intellectual vocation—provided the Stalinist leaders and intellectuals with a sense of certainty in a time of doubt. And for the intellectuals it offered the sanction of doing, or seeming to do, something "real."

The elements in Marxism that have proved most attractive to the Stalinists were those most intimately tied to nineteenth-century progressivism, a mode of thought still powerful in the life of the European "left." Appearing before the world as fellow progressives —*fellow progressives in a hurry*—the Stalinists were able to utilize many aspects of the liberal tradition and to claim that far from being enemies of Western humanism—as, by contrast, many Nazi ideologues openly declared themselves—they were actually its true heirs.

Precisely to the extent that the left tradition in the West did adhere indiscriminately to a simple optimistic theory of progress, it became most vulnerable to Stalinist infiltration. For if all change tends to be impelled by the logic of History in a progressive direction, those who seemed to stand for the most change would also seem to be the greatest progressives. Put so crudely, the "progressivist" ideology comes close to intellectual caricature; but so, often enough, does political life itself. No Stalinoid intellectual in Paris would have been so unsophisticated as to accept the formula as we have reduced it here, but in the subtle writings of many a Stalinoid intellectual in Paris there was buried exactly this deification of "progress."

And precisely to the extent that modern progressivism committed itself to what might be called technological optimism—the notion that the growth of a society's productive forces automatically renders it "progressive"—did it, in turn, become most vulnerable to Stalinist influence. For the technological optimist, Dnieperstroy is an irrefutable argument.

Ideology in the Stalinist movement was both exalted and degraded as in no other movement, exalted in that it was constantly put to work and accorded formal honor, degraded in that it was never allowed any status in its own right but came to be regarded as a weapon in the struggle for power.

This relationship between Stalinism and its ideology followed from a fundamental attitude of totalitarian movements toward social and personal reality. The most terrifying assumption of the totalitarian mind is that, given the control of terror, anything is possible. In Orwell's 1894 and Milosz's *The Captive Mind* this idea is reiterated again and again, out of a despairing conviction that almost anyone can say the words but almost no one can apprehend their full significance. Given modern technology, total state control, the means of terror, and a rationalized contempt for moral values, you can do anything with men, anything with their minds, anything with words, anything with the past.

Reality is not something one recognizes or experiences; reality is something one manufactures, sometimes in anticipation, sometimes in retrospect. One day Beria is a hero of the Soviet Union, the next day a villain—which is neither so bad nor unusual. What is new is that by the third day *he does not exist*. His past has been destroyed, his name removed from the records. Many political movements have claimed to control the present, and others the future; totalitarianism was the first, however, which systematically proceeded to remake the past.

To do this, it was necessary to regard words and ideas as instrumentalities that could be put to any use. Nothing in thought or language need impose any limit. As Milosz wrote: "*What is not expressed does not exist*. Therefore if one forbids men to explore the depths of human nature, one destroys in them the urge to make such explorations; and the depths in themselves slowly become unreal." [51] And Orwell, in describing the totalitarian attitude to thought and language, pushed everything to an extreme which helped make the reality all the clearer:

> To know and not to know, to be conscious of complete truthfulness while telling carefully constructed lies, to hold simultaneously two opinions which cancelled out, knowing them to be contradictory and believing in both of them, to use logic, to repudiate morality while laying claim to it, to believe that democracy was impossible and that the Party was the guardian of democracy, to forget whatever it was necessary to forget, then to draw it back into memory again at the moment when it was needed, and then promptly to forget it again, and above all, to apply the same process to the process itself—this was the ultimate subtlety: consciously to induce unconsciousness, and then, once again, to become unconscious of the act of hypnosis you had just performed. Even to understand the word "doublethink" involved the use of doublethink.[52]

The Nature and Ends of Stalinism

11. What was fundamental to Stalinism was not an ideology but an objective: to extend the area of its control, hence the power of its organization, and to maximize the degree to which it could manipulate and disintegrate those parts of the world not yet under its control. "To the Communist, the map of the world is an organization chart." [53]

At its core, if not in its mass and peripheral membership, the Stalinist movement was a combat organization, and as in most combat organizations the leaders were so concerned with winning battles that they gave little or no thought to the ultimate human or moral consequences of winning battles. This is not to deny that some Stalinist leaders may at times have indulged themselves in daydreams about a better future for mankind once the battle was won, or that such dreams were extremely important to the life of the rank and file; it is only to suggest that the Stalinist leadership had arrived at so radical a disjunction between its presumed ideal and the practical activities of the movements it controlled that the ideal had lost its hold on everyday reality.

This process was frequently rationalized through the belief that the movement is constantly at war and that, in effect, it constantly will be. Theoretical allowance was made for the possibility of a total triumph of Stalinism on a world scale, but in the meantime every aspect of Stalinist behavior rested on the assumption that the struggle would continue through an indefinite future. This assumption, persuasive in that it did contain a fraction of the truth, provided the basic justification for everything in Stalinism which the outer world labeled as amoral and brutal but which the true believer felt to be a necessity of battle.

The Stalinist leader, and at times the Stalinist militant, might have seen himself as a chosen instrument of History, a Grand Inquisitor leading the passive proletarians to a golden Future, but beyond this he was not bound to any particular code of ideals. The "science" of power, the study of strategy and tactics in politics, took primacy over ideology.

For this reason it is impossible, and indeed pointless, to try to fit the Stalinist movement into the traditional categories of revolutionary or reformist parties. The divergence between revolutionary and reformist parties was not merely a tactical one, for it involved basic values in regard to the purposes as well as the means of action; and the discussions among Socialists on the permissibility or necessity of violence had focused not merely on the problem of effectiveness but also on moral justifications. In Bolshevism one can observe a dangerous disjunction between the ends sought and the means adopted, a tendency to suppose that the means stand in no need of short-run justification if once it is agreed that they serve the morally valid ends of revolutionary action. But in Stalinism this tendency was pushed to a terrible extreme, with the result that once sight had been lost of the ends, the primacy of revolutionary means had also been relinquished. As a result, the Stalinist party was neither revolutionary nor reformist, but was quite capable of assuming the guise of either.

Far from being committed, like Leninism, to the revolutionary mode of taking power, Stalinism could employ quite different strategies, ranging from infiltration of a government apparatus to exploiting the services of an invading Russian army. In recent years it often showed a decided repugnance to revolutionary tactics, fearing perhaps that spontaneous revolutionary activities might lead to the one condition most hateful to a bureaucratic elite—the loss of control. The only kind of revolution Stalinism wanted was a managed revolution.

Yet it was never to democracy that Stalinism was "converted," only to the belief that democratic regimes could be utilized much more easily than had once been believed. No political movement in modern times developed so elaborate a strategy for the penetration of every institution in bourgeois society, from parliaments to neighborhoods, from trade unions to academic societies. Stalinism could appear as the defender of democracy against fascism, the champion of workers' rights, or, for that matter, a loyal and patriotic ally of the secret police in its effort to ferret out subversive elements that hamper a war effort. The French CP, to cite an extreme instance of the flexibility of Stalinism, even tried to collaborate with the Nazi invaders during the time of the Hitler-Stalin pact; only after Hitler had broken the pact did it become active in the Resistance.[54]

While Stalinism appealed to Asian intellectuals as the only force capable of overcoming the humiliation of colonialism, it spoke to Western intellectuals as a movement capable of removing their sense of alienation and satisfying their desire for political power. To the workers in the Western countries it appealed in terms of the traditional categories of radicalism, and to the peasants of a country like France it spoke in the name of the national Jacobin tradition. No longer a class party making a class appeal, it was a party that aimed at attracting every stratum in modern society. Like all totalitarian movements, its temporary end might seem to have been the strengthening of the social groups it attracted; like all totalitarian movements, its final effect could only be to deprive them of their autonomy and flatten them to a speechless mass.

No fully developed or coherent ideology can be isolated as common to the appeals of Stalinism, but it is possible, perhaps, to note two underlying motifs or themes present in all Stalinist propaganda, the one "positive" and the other "negative":

a. No matter what its shifts of line or policy, Stalinism was always ready to make clear to its inner core, and sometimes to its mass following, that it stands as the proponent of total and ultimate measures, that it is committed to a decisive transvaluation of values, to a final *eschaton*. Seemingly endless as its adaptations to temporary needs might be, the Stalinist movement realized that a major source of its power lay in its appeal to the great hunger among modern men for a deep-going solution to social and moral problems, a change so thorough as to be, or seem, the equivalent of a rebirth.

b. Despite all its shifts in line and policy, Stalinism always rejected as incompatible with its very existence the idea that the masses of humanity can achieve their liberation through their own autonomous efforts. Autonomy and spontaneity of action it always looked upon as it deadliest enemy. Manipulation and terrorization from above were inherent in its outlook, its method, its tradition.

In the Stalinist demonology the outer, alien world was evil because uncontrolled. The progressive encroachment of Stalinist cadres upon all independent social forces, upon whatever was alive and free in modern society, was a major objective. Control as such, rather than a specific mode of achieving it or a specific ideological justification, lies at the heart of Stalinist intentions.

In Marx's system the idea of a society in which men finally come to dominate the forces of nature and organize fraternally in behalf of their common existence forms the underlying theme; in Stalinism this idea was transformed to mean that all human reality is to be at the mercy of a group of omnipotent and omniscient men of power. The idea of planning, once allied to the idea of rationality, assumed in the Stalinist ethos an independent and fetishistic role. By force and cunning, coercion and manipulation, the elite of the Polit Bureau and the chosen fortunate enough to circle it will

552   THE AMERICAN COMMUNIST PARTY

achieve control over the wavering, the misguided, the perplexed, and the timid—and will plan everything for everyone. The surgeons of politics, as they conceive themselves to be, men beyond good and evil, will operate upon the body of mankind as it lies etherized upon the table of History.

"The Communist Party is not a party like the others." Thorez was right. The party was not committed to a specific ideology; it was not responsive to the needs of a particular class outside of Russia; it was not a socialist party nor a radical nor a progressive nor a revolutionary nor a reformist party. It was a "foreign national party," dedicated to and controlled by the Russian ruling class. To the Russian leaders the whole of the unsubdued world must have appeared as a kind of flaw, a perpetual reminder of the imperfection and lack of completeness of their work.

But what, finally, was their work? Toward what end did they strive? Toward what end did they kill millions of people and each other? What was the ultimate purpose of Stalinism? The vision by which it lived? The kind of society it would have liked to see?

We are frank to acknowledge that in our estimate this question —for all the above questions really come to one—cannot yet be answered. "I understand HOW: I do not understand WHY," Winston Smith keeps repeating to himself in 1984. So it is with all of us in relation to totalitarianism. We can describe its methods, its assumptions, its strategy, its organization, its behavior; and if one description will not do, then another may. But the end toward which Stalinism moved, the kind of world it would have created if by some terrible miracle it had suddenly gained complete control of our planet, remains an enigma.

It may however be that—without trying to dismiss this residue of the unknown—our question is not a meaningful one. It may be that Stalinism, like all totalitarian movements in which terror and irrationality play so great a role, really had no ultimate end which could be related significantly to its activity. It may be that between its condition at a given moment and the possibility of its total triumph so many unpredictable factors would come into play— factors that could sharply alter its nature—that one cannot assign it an ultimate rationale in the way one can for slave society or feudalism or capitalism. What matters most is that the situation never be created in which the answer to this question can finally be known. Stalinism promised to satisfy the two basic needs of modern man: the economic and the spiritual. It laid claim to a world of planning and plenty, and it offered the vision of a life of community. It organized and legitimated a break from the *status quo*. It utilized the best impulses of modern man for the worst ends. But all of these things were possible only to the extent that people felt themselves weak and impotent, unable rationally to determine their own destinies. Stalinism could win the loyalty only of those who had not yet realized, as in Asia, or who had forgotten, as in Europe, that man can now make—or unmake—his own life.

Stalinism came into being as a caricature, a vast and terrible distortion, of the profound yearning of modern man for a new world and a better life. The power of the caricature should be sufficient testimony to the need for the genuine.

P.S.   The reader may have noticed that in the preceding pages of this chapter we have spoken, with a few exceptions, of Stalinism in the past tense. In using this tense it has not been our intention to suggest that Stalinism is now entirely a thing of the past and that it has been replaced by a new phase in the history of international Communism. Yet to have used the present tense might have suggested that we fail to recognize the important changes that have occurred. We shall have to content ourselves with the observation that to speak of a historical tendency as existing in the past does not necessarily imply that it is confined to the past.

Behind this problem of tenses there lies, of course, a complex dilemma likely to confront any analyst discussing Stalinism in our time. The character of the Communist movement has changed in important respects since the death of Stalin and the symbolic rejection of part of his inheritance at the Twentieth Congress of the Russian party. Yet, as the events in Hungary have proved, those who symbolically rejected part of Stalin's inheritance continued to react in an essentially Stalinist manner when confronted with crucial threats to their dominance.

Certain Communist parties can in 1957 no longer be said to be fully Stalinist parties, yet they are certainly very far from being anti-Stalinist. The various national parties have reacted in different ways to the toppling of the Stalin myth. In France the party has stubbornly resisted any changes whatever, while the American party has been wracked by factional disputes between true Stalinist believers and various kinds of "revisionists." Neither party presents the characteristics of a truly democratic organization, yet there can be no doubt that the public face of the American party has changed rather drastically. It seems highly probable, however, that at least with regard to the American party these changes are essentially symptoms of disintegration.

In any case, the answer to these problems, far from being a matter of mere analysis, will in large measure be determined by human activity, the political behavior of free men. The appropriateness of our use of tenses cannot, therefore, be entirely settled at the moment. Some years from now the reader who picks up this book will finally be able to judge.

December 1957

An Epilogue

In the three and a half years since this book was written, almost nothing has happened to the American Communist Party *as an institution* that would require a serious change in the estimate offered at the end of Chapter X. One or two reviewers chided us for seeming to write off American Communism prematurely; they failed to notice the distinction we made—one that has since become still more important—between the decline of the Communist Party and the survival of pro-Soviet sentiment. The party itself has staggered along, weakened by government attacks, major losses, and internal disputes, though by 1960 it had managed to consolidate itself as a monolithic and docile sect. But within these last few years there has also occurred a number of signficant political events that raise the possibility of a "progressive" political environment that might ease the isolation of the CP even if it does not bring it immediate organizational rewards. First, however, let us glance at the condition of the party itself.

About faction struggles in political movements at least one thing can be said with assurance: they are harder to stop than to start, for they have a way of persisting long after the causes for their appearance have come to seem unimportant or are forgotten. In the "left" movements, factionalism usually has some relation to a political problem and sometimes even to the problem ostensibly being fought over; but it also has roots that go far deeper than formal differences of political "line." It creates drama and tension within the organization as a surrogate for unfought battles outside. It thrives on frustration, disappointment, impotence. It feeds on emotions of dismay, particularly those felt by people who see themselves as attuned to the rhythms of history, yet deprived of the fruits of power. In the American Communist movement, factionalism has been especially severe because its leaders have always been disturbed by the contrast between the success of their cause in many other countries and its failure here—a contrast they cannot possibly admit may be due to the irrelevance of their program for American life and must therefore attribute to such subjective factors as their own inadequacies of leadership and political skill. And since these inadequacies have been real enough, there has always been an apparent plausibility in the exhibits of "self-criticism" that accompany changes in Communist strategy.

But there are two other and more immediately pressing reasons for the ferocity of the disputes besetting the party in the late 1950's. For about a quarter of a century now, since the later 1920's and interrupted only by the episode of Browder's expulsion, the CP has been an authoritarian organization, ruled by leaders (whether those recognized in public or those acting behind the scenes) who have commanded strict obedience. Inevitably, there have accumulated quantities of intellectual resentment and personal rancor. In a democratic organization such feelings might have been released gradually and normally, so that their force would be diminished; but nothing of the kind was possible in the CP. Here a district organizer who felt he had been given an onerous assignment often had to swallow his chagrin and keep silent; a party intellectual who had been snubbed by the functionaries often had to accept such treatment in the name of submitting to "proletarian leadership." But in the late 1950's, when every party member finally had a chance to release his aggressions, his complaints, and his doubts in an atmosphere of relative freedom, the factional struggle over political issues raised by the Khrushchev revelations and the Hungarian revolution took on a particularly feverish and often personal tone. William Z. Foster no doubt sincerely felt he was defending the true Soviet faith against renegades and backsliders, but he was also discharging a long-suppressed bitterness against those who in earlier years consigned him to honorary oblivion in the party structure. John Gates and Joseph Clark no doubt sincerely believed they were trying to wriggle out of Stalinist dogmatism, but they were also releasing a long-suppressed impatience with the arrogance and sheer thickheadedness of the more orthodox leaders. It was open season, and there was much to make up for.

At the time the faction struggle became most bitter—roughly between 1957 and 1959—a number of party leaders imprisoned under the Smith Act were being released from jail and allowed to return to political activity. These men had suffered; there could be

no doubt of that. They felt themselves to be the victims of Mc-
Carthyite hysteria and proto-fascism. They had proved themselves
by not succumbing to the blows of American imperialism. And now,
as they returned to the party, welcomed at special meetings and
given leading posts, they carried with them an aura of strength and
heroism. Almost to a man—with the exception of the aging theoretician Alexander Bittleman—they lined up solidly with Foster and
the orthodox pro-Soviet wing. They turned contemptuously against
the "revisionists," who in their eyes were buckling under the strains
of repression and isolation. Having upheld the honor of the party
in jail, they would not now permit its program to be adulterated
with "petty-bourgeois reformism." Robert Thompson, one of the
jailed leaders, was particularly notable for the harsh and jeering tone
he took against such "revisionists" as John Gates and Joseph Clark;
and in the rough-and-tumble of faction struggle it was hard for the
Gates faction, itself amorphous and on the verge of dissolution, to
cope with those leaders who spoke in the accents of martyrdom and
certainty.

How damaging the inner struggle was to the party any number
of documents make clear. In early 1957, a subcommittee of the CP
National Committee wrote: "One of the reasons many of us, leaders
and rank-and-file comrades, find it hard to keep their bearings today
is because they feel everything is lost." A secondary leader, writing
in the CP functionaries' journal *Political Affairs,* could say quite
frankly:

> Anyone who knows Detroit and Toledo, Youngstown and
> Pittsburgh, Chicago and Cleveland knows that in these and other
> towns and cities which constitute the heartland of America, you will
> find the wreckage of comrades, former comrades and Party clubs.

And Eugene Dennis, delivering his report as National Secretary at
the February, 1957 convention, bluntly said that the CP was suffering from "a bitter and divisive internal struggle, and is in danger of
being torn apart."

The political issues dividing the two groups—the orthodox
Communists led by Foster and the "revisionists" led by Gates—have
been discussed in Chapter X. Here it need only be remarked that
these political differences also had immediate organizational reper-

cussions, particularly since the Gates faction began to toy with a plan that would in effect have dissolved the party. The New York State Committee, controlled by Gates and his friends, had proposed that the CP be replaced by a vaguely leftist "educational" league, from whose title the word "Communist" would be dropped and in whose ranks, hopefully, there might be included a number of non-Communist leftists. It was a scheme born of desperation, of a feeling, as Foster correctly charged, that the CP was hopelessly compromised and had no future in America. And naturally the opponents of the idea, who won a majority of the National Committee when it came up for a vote, could rally against it the residual but therefore extremely intense emotions of party patriotism.

The Februrary, 1957 convention did not put an end to the faction fight, even though it made some pious gestures in that direction. The convention seemed to end with a formal victory for the Gates tendency but actually marked the beginning of its dispersal. For in a way Foster was right when he characterized the "revisionists" as people who were not really serious and would not know what to do with the party if they won control of it. No group suffering a basic intellectual crisis, even if the crisis stems from a sincere desire for political clarity, is likely to have the stamina for consolidating its faction victories. The "correct line" may be useful in a faction struggle, but an assurance of certainty is still more so. Struggling with their political doubts, the Gates people soon found themselves drifting out of the party or, if they remained nominal members, refusing to attend the incessant round of meetings at which they were subjected to rude attacks. The more support Gates won in the party, the more certain it became he would not be able to keep it.

An intellectual spokesman for the Fosterites, Hyman Lumer, has described the "revisionist" approach to Hungary—it could also apply ·o other matters—as a case of incipient liberalism:

> There are some . . . who have ceased to view historical developments in the light of the class struggle, and have substituted a bourgeois-liberal approach in which judgments are based on abstract, formal principles of morality and democracy . . . : Such individuals will draw different conclusions, even from the same facts, than those who approach them from a Marxist viewpoint.

No such problems, to be sure, troubled the minority of the party who followed Foster and who, through attrition, would become a majority. These people, who included the bulk of the old-time leaders, were driven by a passion for orthodoxy; they knew their first task was to cleanse the party of doubt, contemplation, open-mindedness, and similar evils. And they finally won—not merely because they had behind them the authority of the international Communist movement, but because they felt entirely sure of themselves and were ready to keep fighting as long as necessary. They enjoyed a tremendous advantage for political disputation: vindictiveness. And another asset: *Sitzfleisch*.

Steadily the Foster group chipped away here and assaulted there. Let the "revisionist" majority of a branch fade away, and the die-hards were ready to take over. Let the "revisionists" weary of the struggle, and the die-hards clung grimly to the field of battle. For them there was no life, no thought or possibility of a life, beyond the party; they were true believers, and they won.

An early move was a cautious offensive against the *Daily Worker*, most of whose writers were "revisionists." A party subcommittee chosen to examine the political worthiness of the paper offered a measure of praise and then proceeded to note dangerous concessions to liberalism. Concerning the recent Middle East crisis it reported:

> The *Daily* showed great sensitivity to the feelings of the Jewish people, though at least in the beginning not the same awareness of the need to keep in mind the feelings and sentiments of the Negro people. [The Negroes of Egypt?]

And then, pressing a bit harder:

> It is necessary to state that the Jewish masses here must be told the truth as regards the main forces and issues, the role of the Israeli government . . . [so as to bring] the correct line to the Jewish people, and not for capitulating to national feeling.

Which, in English, meant that the paper was charged with not following a sufficiently hostile attitude toward Israel.

There were other signs of a Fosterite offensive. Robert Thompson moved the attack on the "revisionists" to a level beyond comradely discussion when he accused them of being "wreckers" who wished to liquidate the party and join forces with Norman Thomas and other such enemies of the Soviet Union. Foster himself not only attacked the "revisionists," by now easy game, but also went after the political scalp of Eugene Dennis, who as National Secretary had been trying, in the name of party unity, to keep a delicate balance between the two contending groups and thereby create for himself an independent power:

> The uncertain line followed by Comrade Dennis [wrote Foster] has also done much to deepen and prolong the Party crisis. While he has opposed in writing some of the worst crudities of Comrade Gates, Dennis has never taken a firm stand against Revisionism, a course which has tended to appease and conciliate it.

This was a major step in a largely successful maneuver to prevent Dennis from establishing himself as an arbiter above the factions. And then, in a sentence that must have had a strong impact on the party faithful, Foster added: "The whole Communist world remarks this Revisionism in our party, but our leadership tries to deny or hide it."

Shortly after this article appeared in December, 1957, John Gates resigned from the party, soon to be followed by a scattering of his friends. The *Daily Worker* was suspended and replaced by a weekly paper, *The Worker,* now edited by a staunch Fosterite, James E. Jackson. When Gates resigned, the CP National Committee not only hurled at him the usual imprecations but put out a statement excommunicating the entire outlook he represented: "There is no place in the Party for a Gates or his ideology. The departure of such individuals will not injure but will strengthen the party." Through will and dialectic, defeat could be transmuted into victory.

The traditional Communist aura of unanimity would now be reestablished, and no longer could one find in the party press such disturbing signs of liberalism as reports of split votes in the National Committee. There remained, to be sure, a few stray dissidents, such as a group of Los Angeles Communists led by National Committee member Dorothy Healy, who refused to endorse Gates's politics yet hoped to retain a degree of open discussion in the party. Writing with a wistfulness that adds a rare human quality to Communist polemic, Miss Healy complained in the spring of 1958:

> There are some comrades who believe that a Socialist country cannot make mistakes in foreign policy, or that one can say so only after they are self-admitted. (As a matter of fact, even after the CPSU admits mistakes we have some comrades who consider it "anti-Soviet" to repeat the fact of the mistake or try to analyze it!)
>
> Perhaps the saddest line in Khrushchev's revelations . . . was that Stalin thought he acted in the interests of Socialism. I suppose each of us is positive in the "purity" of our intentions, and the fiendishness of the other's intent.

A true heresy because it undercut specific political issues to reach biases of value, this kind of statement could only stir the orthodox leaders to harsh anger:

> Dorothy Healy [replied James E. Jackson] contends for a Party of multiple ideologies in which agnosticism is enshrined as a primary virtue. . . . She invokes the words of great bourgeois libertarians—Milton, Jefferson, Mill—in defense of the equal rights of any system of ideas to be "let loose to play.". . . But we do not want to convert the Party into an ideological market-place . . .

Indeed not; and soon most of the Los Angeles dissidents were on their way. No obstacle remained to a total victory for the orthodox, and Eugene Dennis, preparing for the 17th National Convention in December, 1959, found himself obliged to conciliate the Fosterites by proclaiming the party's "firm adherence" to "Marxist-Leninist principles." Foster, quite energetic despite his advanced years and serious illness, now proposed the abolition of the "federalist" method of electing the National Committee that had been adopted at the previous convention and that gave the local districts a direct voice in choosing the Committee's members. His advice was taken.

Outwardly, the tone of American Communism became more aggressive. Herbert Aptheker, one of the few remaining Communist intellectuals, took over *Political Affairs* and began a running polemic against dissidents which expressed this new—or really, old—Communist spirit. His attack upon Howard Fast was typical:

> Renegades from Communism invariably ascribe their betrayal to superior morality. . . . They can no longer tolerate association with the cynicism and brutality and lack of sensitivity they suddenly discover to be characteristic of the Party . . . and forthwith one finds them demonstrating their finer sensibilities by appearances on TV where their craven fawning to the bourgeoisie is nauseating.

Only one exception needs to be noted to the re-established authoritarian harmony of the CP, a kind of tragicomic postscript to its whole history. In 1960, when Alexander Bittleman, the old Communist theoretician and faction hand, was released from prison, he wrote a series of articles for *The Worker* developing the theme that the welfare state had introduced important modifications in the nature of capitalist society and that the CP would suffer political death if it did not take these into account. For this "Browderite" deviation he was violently attacked by Foster—who knows what old scores were being settled here?—and expelled from the CP in December, 1960. The statement of expulsion is a masterwork of doublethink: "Bittleman has the right to express his views. . . . But such views must be in accord with Party principles."

Harried as it was by government prosecutions and factional distemper, the party could not really expect any serious organizational progress. A large portion of its energy was expended simply in holding together the branches, in reorganizing those which had suffered the loss of local leaders, and in persuading the membership there was still some point in coming to meetings, paying dues, and trying to sell *The Worker*. Of the few thousand remaining members, a good many were worn and shell-shocked political veterans, unable to imagine an existence outside the party but equally unable to adapt themselves to the new terms of that existence. The leaders prescribed the traditional cure of "mass work," but it was hard to administer the prescription and harder still to notice any results. Simply as an organization, the CP was so tightly coiled in its defensive posture, so caught up in the need to protect itself against government agents, so preoccupied with problems of internal security that it could hardly turn with any genuine fervor to public politics and trade-union work.

And the members were getting on. Nothing revealed the weakness of the party more than the fact that for the first time in decades it had no youth affiliate. Its handful of younger members tried for a time to work with the Trotskyist youth, but the results, from the CP point of view, were unfortunate: either the young comrades were contaminated by heresies or they found themselves entangled in a maze of sectarian discussion. Young people in America had little interest in politics, almost none in the Communist Party.

To anyone who had followed CP history, the leaders who took over the organization after the 17th National Convention—Benjamin Davis, Jr., Gus Hall, Elizabeth Gurley Flynn, James E. Jackson —were all familiar names, old-time party functionaries. There was one significant change in the leadership, apart from its now strongly Fosterite tinge. The main centers of "revisionism" had been the East and West Coast branches, while those in the Midwest remained comparatively orthodox. As a result, the new National Committee contained a heavy proportion of "practical party workers" from the Midwest, Communist organization men who would not be troubled by theoretic speculation; and of these Gus Hall, who was to become the General Secretary after the death of Eugene Dennis, was the prime example.

But in the main it was a reshuffling of old faces and old names. "For some two or three years," wrote Robert Thompson, "it has been fashionable in our party to bemoan the advancing age level of our membership." Fashionable or not, such complaints were true, and Thompson knew it. One sign of the advancing age level could be seen in 1960 when *Political Affairs* ran a survey of its readers to determine their attitudes to the magazine. A grand total of sixty-five comrades responded, and of these two-thirds were over forty and one-third over sixty.

An aging membership, shaken politically and bewildered organizationally—this was hardly the material from which to rebuild a Communist Party in a time of repression and hostility. Nevertheless, once the Fosterites gained control of the party and took over the national leadership, they did try to turn the CP outward, toward a modest quantity of "mass work."

One or two such efforts had already been made. In 1958 Elizabeth Gurley Flynn ran for the New York City Council on the Peoples Rights ticket in the Lower East Side, a neighborhood traditionally composed of Jewish workers but now containing many Negroes and Puerto Ricans. Miss Flynn received 710 votes, clear evidence of how feeble the party had become. Yet from the perspective of the New York CP leadership, which had had doubts as to the advisability of undertaking any campaign at all, there was some consolation in the fact that a few hundred party members from all over the city had been willing to risk public activity. And this was of some importance to the CP, since the leadership was trying to root out the "underground" psychology that had paralyzed the ranks since the late 1940's.

But the opportunities for public work were severely limited, not merely as a result of government harassment but also because of the party's own weakness and unpopularity. When the time came to consider a policy for the 1960 Presidential election, the CP lacked the resources even to think of running a candidate or campaign of its own, and it knew that in most states there was no chance whatever of getting on the ballot. It refused to endorse Kennedy, for it doubted that his views on the cold war were any more palatable than those of Nixon. At the same time, it was committed to working within the major parties, which in practice meant within the Democratic Party. Where it could discern a clear-cut difference between candidates, it also favored supporting those it regarded as lesser evils. Experienced politicos might appreciate the twists and turns of this position, but it was not likely to help the party break out of its isolation.

By the 17th National Convention the CP could claim "some inroads" among Puerto Ricans and Cubans living in the United States, but it had to admit a more significant fact: that it was largely cut off from the growing movement of Negro protest. Over the years the CP had made enormous efforts to root itself in the Negro communities, and in the thirties and forties had even met with some success. But now, at the very moment when the Southern Negroes were acting with such spectacular effect and when sympathetic responses could be heard from the North, the CP found itself unable to influence or even participate in this crucial development. The

Negro organizations had learned to be wary of comrades bearing gifts: the NAACP had profited from long experience, and the more militant CORE, which organized the Freedom Rides, was led by knowledgeable pacifists opposed to cooperating with Communists. Once the Freedom Rides began, a number of white and Negro Communists tried to work their way into the movement, but they were sharply repulsed and kept entirely away from the political and organizational direction of the Rides. The New York CP organized a series of meetings at which Gus Hall spoke to protest the arrest of Freedom Riders in the South; but more than that it could not do.

In the trade unions CP prospects were almost as bleak, though a few pockets of strength did survive, especially in those "left" unions that had been expelled from the CIO in 1949. In the other trade unions that had once contained strong party factions, little if anything remained. Faint remnants of CP influence might still be discernable in one or two locals of the garment and electrical workers unions. Here and there in the UAW party members and sympathizers remained active, providing "inside" material for the Michigan edition of *The Worker* and fostering an anti-Reuther "rank-and-file" committee in Detroit. But in the UAW as a whole, Communist influence was negligible and often served merely to discredit whatever genuine trade-union discontent might arise.

By the late fifties party supervision of work in the unions had become haphazard, and one of the goals of the reorganized leadership was to re-establish a functioning labor secretariat in the national headquarters. But again the problem was not primarily an organizational one. How difficult it was for Communists to work in the trade unions was admitted in an important document written in early 1961 by Robert Thompson:

> As a general fact it is impossible to be a publicly acknowledged Communist and retain a job in any sector of basic industry. A publicly declared Communist cannot hold a position in any important segment of the organized labor movement. In most cities and towns of basic industry the Party is for all practical intents and purposes illegalized.

Thompson then drew a key, if somewhat Aesopian, distinction between the party's "public role" and its "vanguard role," the first referring to such open activities as meetings, selling *The Worker*, etc., and the second to the clandestine work of individual Communists in the unions. The "public role," remarked Thompson, is not the entirety or even the most important part of the CP work, and efforts must be made so that "individual Communists participate effectively in every major economic, political and ideological struggle taking place in our country." The crucial word here is "individual," for it suggests that party members must learn to veil their affiliation and speak as good trade unionists or at most as "progressives," in the hope that their personal influence will eventually lead to strengthening the party itself.

An admittedly difficult task, it is one that the rank-and-file members cannot be blamed for finding difficult. In the last year or two the new leadership, speaking in the bluff tones of Gus Hall, has hectored the members to re-establish themselves in the unions and other mass organizations. At the 17th Convention, Hall found himself quoting from Dostoevsky's *Notes from the Underground* in order to describe certain moods of depression within the party:

> Some of our cadre . . . are afflicted by a disease one could designate as "negativism." This negativism or cynicism is not based on realities. . . . Your moods arise because you have permitted temporary subjective factors to overwhelm your better judgment. . . . Let me say that in reading the following quotation from Dostoevsky, I have nobody specifically in mind. But I do say that Dostoevsky describes the final product if negativism and cynicism is followed to its logical conclusion:
> "For all his intense sensibility he frankly considers himself a mouse and not a man. I grant you it is an intensely conscious mouse, but it is a mouse all the same. . . .
> "The unhappy mouse has already succeeded in piling up—in the form of questions and doubts—a large number of dirty tricks in addition to its original dirty trick; it has accumulated such a large number of insoluble questions round every one question that it is drowned in a sort of deadly brew, a stinking puddle made up of its own doubts. . . ."

It will be a long time, if ever, before the American Communists can regain the footing they once had in the trade-union and Negro movements. The objective handicaps are too severe, and neither skill nor sacrifice can overcome them. What little the party can do is propagandistic. It can continue to publish *The Worker,* for which it claims a circulation of 13,000 and has announced a change to semi-weekly appearance. It can help maintain the cultural magazine *Mainstream.* Its friends can continue to run the Liberty Book Club, which claims a membership of 7,000 and a total sale in the last decade of a million and a half books. But as it stands today, with its several thousand aging and tired members, the CP is little more than a shadow of its earlier self.

Recognition of a kind has, however, come to it. William Z. Foster, close to eighty and desperately ill, was flown in early 1961 to the Soviet Union to be cared for by Russian doctors, and there, as a reward for his services, was elected an "honorary professor" of the Moscow University. He died shortly thereafter.

If the future of the Communist Party seems dim, there have been some developments in the United States these past few years that should encourage those who believe the Soviet Union represents a force of historic progress. Among the disorganized but still numerous adherents of "the left," as also among a small number of college students, new political moods are discernible. These are not yet of special importance, but with time may become so.

The party finds itself in a vexing position. Its inner core remains static and immobilized, caught up in its political dilemmas. Yet the periphery of American Communism seems to have expanded somewhat, and more important, a political mood of a vaguely "progressive" kind is reappearing which may help the party survive, if not flourish. At first glance this mood bears some resemblance to the Popular Frontism of two decades ago; actually it is quite different. Here are some of its sources and components:

—a general weariness and disillusion regarding the cold war, together with the feeling that both sides, if not equally bad, are open to such severe criticism that they do not merit the support of independent liberals and radicals;

—a belief that the Soviet bloc has reached a point of stability or, as the matter is occasionally put, is "here to stay," so that all the talk about opposing (sometimes even about resisting) Communism is felt to be irresponsible or an invitation to atomic war;

—a discontent with American life that often takes the form of a

nonpolitical estrangement, a denunciation of American foreign policy as inept and reactionary, and a critical attitude less dependent on Marxist categories than on a distaste for American "materialism";
   —an indifference to abstract ideologies in general and the ideological claims of the two powers in particular;
   —a conviction that the big powers have become rigidly bureaucratic (or "square"), while the true sources of political vitality can be found only in certain underdeveloped countries where the national leaders still have style, initiative, and flavor.

Now these attitudes are obviously of unequal merit, and some of them conflict sharply with others, yet all contribute to the political mood we are trying to isolate. For involved here is not the formal coherence of a party line or ideology, but an emotional-intellectual groping, a search for a new style of political response. It is a mood that has little do with any interest in Communist ideas or Communist organization, yet is impatient with the claims—no matter who may make them—that the Communist movement is a major enemy of freedom. It is a mood that mixes cynicism about democracy with sharp critical insights into its failings in the United States, a mood that brings together a worship of power with a celebration of anarchic rebelliousness.

Where can such amorphous sentiments be found? Frequently, though least significantly, among certain old leftists. Also among "progressives" who do not consider themselves Marxists, a minority of pacifists, and vaguely radical students. And in such organizations as the Fair Play for Cuba Committee and the "peace" groups formed in a few cities as split-offs from SANE.

Old leftists still nostalgic about the hopes they once had for the Soviet Union now wish the past could be forgotten and Stalinism, perhaps vindicated as a cruel historic necessity, could be followed by an era of "liberalization." Certain "progressives" feel that the clash between the two major power blocs is a catastrophe in which they have no particular stake, that strong anti-Communism is unavoidably a veil for reaction, and that one must learn to live with the Communist states and parties. For some pacifists the threat of atomic war overshadows everything else, and they subordinate their sincere dislike of Communist authoritarianism to their wish to end the cold war, even if this means advocating policies that open them to the charge of "appeasement."

Such responses are familiar. What is new is the appearance of a younger group composed of students, intellectuals, and semi-intellectuals who endow these sentiments with a color distinctly their own. They have no particular attachment to Russia or Communism, but dislike intensely the idea of an anti-Communist "crusade." They are not very interested in distinguishing between kinds of anti-Communism, whether of the right or left. They cannot, of course, share the memories of people over forty, but they are singularly, even willfully, uninterested in what happened before World War II, and like all too many members of their generation, they suffer from an astonishing lack of the historical sense. They believe that the "old political quarrels" are largely meaningless and can dismiss as equally passé those who had the acumen to oppose the Moscow trials and those deluded or cynical enough to support them. They indulge themselves in the provincialism of their generation, which is a provincialism more of time than of space—as if nothing that happened before 1940 could possibly affect their lives. Yet despite all these traits, which in their sum are bound to stir the impatience of older people, they are right in feeling the need to avoid errors of the past; their mistake is in assuming that to do so they should also avoid a knowledge of the past.

When they turn to politics, they have little concern for clear or precise thought. What attracts them is the surface of vitality, the appearance of freshness, the gesture of drama. They care more for style than conviction, and incline more to outbursts of energy than sustained work. Several years ago such young people were likely to be attracted by Communist China, which then seemed bolder and less "Victorian" than Khrushchev's Russia. But the Mao regime proved too grim, too repressive, too dogmatic. Since then they have been searching for new models and heroes, usually in the underdeveloped countries. An intelligent labor leader like Tom Mboya of Kenya does not interest them nearly as much as did a demagogic orator like Patrice Lumumba of the Congo. The figure who has most won their imagination is Fidel Castro, who dared tweak Uncle Sam's nose, fought heroically, speaks rhetorically, and dresses spectacularly. Castro suggests to these young radicals the possibility of a politics that is not yet functionally rationalized, and meanwhile they have neglected to notice that it has become totalitarian. They have been drawn to figures like Lumumba and Castro out of a distaste for the mania for industrial production that the Soviet Union shares with the United States, but they fail to see that these leaders of underdeveloped countries, who seem attractive because they represent spontaneity and anarchic freedom, are themselves infused with precisely the same mania for industrial production.

Such moods among the young have been both encouraging and frustrating for the Communists. Encouraging, because for the first time in some years there is accessible to them a small milieu in which to function with at least some freedom. Frustrating, because they cannot really take organizational advantage of this fact. The old leftists are tired, the "progressives" too distant or cautious, the pacifists too sophisticated or suspicious. And the young radicals are too indifferent to traditional leftist politics even to consider the CP a serious option—for if they oppose efforts to persecute the Communists, they usually have no hesitation in brushing them aside.

All the CP can do, then, is to wait.

Whether it will be able or allowed to wait, is another matter. In June, 1961 the Supreme Court, by a five to four vote, held that the CP must register as a "Communist-action organization" under the provisions of the McCarran Internal Security Act of 1950. This Act requires that "Communist-action organizations" make public the names of their officers and members, as well as forfeit a variety of privileges. Failure to comply with the registration provisions is punishable by a five-year prison sentence and a fine of $10,000 for each day of refusal. When these provisions first came to President Truman, he wrote in a veto message that they "are not merely ineffective and unworkable. They represent a clear and present danger to our institutions." But so intense was the political hysteria that beset the United States in the 1950's that the McCarran bill became law over the President's veto. Now, after years of litigation, it has been upheld by the Supreme Court.

Directly after the Court decision, the National Committee of the CP declared it would not comply with the registration provisions, which, as it said, would "require the Party's officers to be informers for a police dragnet." Gus Hall added that "the Party's officers would spend the rest of their lives in jail rather than betray the trust of the membership by making members' names public." This decision was entirely predictable, for no one could suppose the CP leaders would accept a decision that not only brands their party but jeopardizes the livelihood and perhaps the safety of their followers. To try to force political enemies into such a dishonorable act is not exactly a cause for pride.

What the government will now do is not yet clear. If it cares to, it can prosecute every "known Communist" in the country, with the probable result that they will be sent to prison and the party driven underground. Such a course would not only do serious damage to the American tradition of political freedom, it would also gravely harm the international struggle against Communism. For it would allow the American Communists to present themselves as martyrs to the cause of civil liberties, and it would enable the Communist movement to use their suffering as an effective item of propaganda throughout the world.

One of the most loosely drawn and frenzied pieces of legislation ever passed by an American Congress, the McCarran Act reflects all too accurately the political atmosphere of the early 1950's. It now seems possible that we shall have a duplication of that atmosphere in the 1960's, for once again we are likely to encounter in our domestic political life that mood of frustration—that vexing awareness of how difficult it is to cope with the spread of Communism throughout the world—which leads people to strike out vindictively and irrelevantly against the Communists at home. Such a luxury is morally dubious and politically dangerous. The struggle against Communism has now become a world-wide political competition, and it can be won only through the name and substance of freedom. Both principle and expediency suggest that the American Communists, in the extremity of their self-exposure and defeat, be allowed to speak without interference or punishment—as exhibits of our confidence in the idea of a free society.

September 1961

Notes

In these notes, the following abbreviations are used:

DW   *Daily Worker*
NM   *New Masses*
PO   *Party Organizer*

Chapter I. Sources of American Radicalism

1. *Proceedings,* National Convention, Socialist Party, 1912, p. 4.
2. *Ibid.*
3. Cited in Lillian Symes and Travers Clement, *Rebel America,* New York, 1936, p. 214. The following few pages are indebted to Symes and Clement.
4. *International Socialist Review,* July, 1916.
5. See Daniel Bell, "Marxian Socialism in the United States," in Egbert *et al., Socialism and American Life,* Princeton, 1952, I, pp. 215-405.
6. See Floyd Dell, *Homecoming,* New York, 1933, p. 267.
7. See Ray Ginger, *The Bending Cross,* New Brunswick, 1949; Ira Kipnis, *The American Socialist Movement, 1879-1912,* New York, 1952, for treatments sympathetic to the left. Bell, *op. cit.;* James Oneal, *American Communism,* New York, 1947; Nathan Fine, *Labor and Farmer Parties in the United States,* New York, 1928, are all sympathetic to the right.
8. Quoted by Ginger, *op. cit.,* pp. 271-272.
9. Eugene V. Debs, "Danger Ahead," *International Socialist Review,* January, 1911.
10. Paul Brissenden, *The I.W.W., A*

Study in American Syndicalism, New York, 1920, p. 292.
11. William Haywood and Frank Bohn, *Industrial Unionism,* Chicago, 1911.
12. Eugene V. Debs, "Sound Socialist Tactics," *International Socialist Review,* February, 1912.
13. *Proceedings,* National Convention, Socialist Party, 1912.
14. Symes and Clement, *op. cit.,* p. 275.
15. *Bill Haywood's Book,* New York, 1929, p. 257.
16. Quoted in Alexander Trachtenberg, *American Socialists and the War* (pamphlet), New York, 1917.
17. The majority and both minority St. Louis resolutions appear in *Class Struggle,* July-August, 1917.
18. Cf. Louis Boudin, "The Emergency National Convention of the Socialist Party," *Class Struggle,* May-June, 1917.
19. Quoted in Trachtenberg, *op. cit.*
20. Quoted in Fine, *op. cit.,* p. 337.
21. Fine, *op. cit.,* p. 322.
22. *American Labor Yearbook, 1919-20,* New York, 1920, p. 81. For early accounts of the Peoples Councils, see *The Call,* June 1, 5, and 17, 1917; also *Class Struggle,* September-October, 1917.
23. Norman Thomas, *The Conscien-*

573

tious Objector in America, New York, 1923, p. 144.

24. *Writings and Speeches of Eugene Debs,* New York, 1948, p. 437.

25. See Oneal, *op. cit.,* p. 44; Benjamin Gitlow, *I Confess,* New York, 1940, p. 57.

26. Quoted in *Revolutionary Radicalism, Report of the Joint Legislative Committee Investigating Seditious Activities, Filed April 24, 1920, in the Senate of the State of New York,* I, p. 706. Also see *Revolutionary Age,* I,

17, and *Class Struggle,* May, 1919.

27. Quoted in *ibid.,* II, pp. 1899-1901.

28. Louis Fraina, *Revolutionary Socialism,* New York, 1918, p. 197.

29. Quoted in *Revolutionary Radicalism,* I, p. 558.

30. Bell, *op. cit.,* p. 323.

31. Quoted in *Revolutionary Radicalism,* I, p. 740.

32. Max Eastman, "The Chicago Conventions," *The Liberator,* October, 1919.

Chapter II. Underground Communism: Disorder and Early Sorrow

1. *Manifesto and Program* (CP) (pamphlet), Chicago, 1919; "Official Proceedings of CLP Convention," *Ohio Socialist,* September 17, 1919.

2. *Ohio Socialist,* September 17, 1919.

3. *Manifesto and Program,* p. 14.

4. Daniel Bell, "Marxian Socialism in the United States," in *Socialism and American Life,* ed. Donald Egbert *et al.,* Princeton, 1952, I, p. 334.

5. Cf. Richard Hofstadter, *The Age of Reform,* New York, 1955, pp. 237-239.

6. *The New Republic,* September 17, 1919.

7. Robert Morss Lovett, *All Our Years,* New York, 1948, pp. 154-155.

8. *The Nation,* August 16, 1919.

9. *Tulsa Daily World,* November 9, 1917, quoted in *The Liberator,* April, 1918.

10. *The New York Times,* August 22, 1922.

11. For a detailed and documented account see Robert K. Murray, *The Red Scare,* Minneapolis, 1955, esp. pp. 217-218.

12. "The Convention of the Communist Party," *The Communist* (CP), August, 1920.

13. Central Executive Committee of the Communist Party of America, "Rules for Underground Party Work," *The Communist International,* III, Nos. 16-17 (1921).

14. Cited in *The Toiler,* May 7, 1920; also Frankfurter, Chafee, Hale, Walsh, *et al., Report Upon the Illegal Practices of the Department of Justice* (pamphlet published by American Civil Liberties Union), May, 1920.

15. *People vs. Gitlow,* 195 App. Div. 773, 187 N.Y.S. 783 (1st Dept. 1921). (In Transcript of Record, pp. 65-66.)

16. *People vs. Ferguson,* 199 App. Div. 642, 192 N.Y.S. (1st Dept. 1922). (In Transcript of Record, p. 1036.)

17. *People vs. Lloyd,* 304 Ill. 23, 136 M.E. 505, pp. 1800-1805.

18. "Mass Strikes," *Class Struggle,* May, 1919.

19. "Rules for Underground Party Work," *The Communist Inter-*

national, III, Nos. 16-17 (1921), *op. cit.*

20. "Boycott the Elections," *The Communist* (CP), October 4, 1919.
21. "A Significant Letter," *The Communist* (CP), June 1, 1920.
22. *Stenographic Report of the "Trial" of L. C. Fraina* (CP) (pamphlet), 1920.
23. *Daily Worker*, December 19, 1925.
24. Bell, *op. cit.*, p. 334.
25. *Ohio Socialist*, October 29, 1919.
26. See "The Communist Party and the Communist Labor Party," *The Communist* (CP), September 27, 1919; *Ohio Socialist*, October 29, 1919; *The Communist* (CP), August 1, 1920.
27. See *The Communist* (CP), May 1, 1920; "Statement to the Membership," *ibid.*
28. Cited in *The Toiler*, June 25, 1920.
29. *Ibid.*
30. *Ibid.*
31. "Resolutions Adopted by the Second Convention of the Communist Party of America," *The Communist* (CP), August 1, 1920.
32. "The Communist International to the American Comrades," *The Communist International*, June-July, 1920.
33. "Activity of the Executive Committee of the Third International," *The Communist* (UCP), No. 11; "The Third International Has Acted," *The Communist* (UCP), No. 16. (No. 16 was the last issue of *The Communist* (UCP), probably appearing in May, 1921.)
34. "Program of the Communist Party of America," *The Communist* (official organ of CPA, uniting CP and UCP), July, 1921.

35. "Pre-Revolutionary Era," *Ohio Socialist*, October 29, 1919; "The Steel Strike," *The Communist* (CP), October 4, 1919.
36. "The Old Unionism," *The Communist* (CP), September 27, 1919.
37. "Arbitration," *The Communist* (CP), October 4, 1919.
38. "Program of United Communist Party," reprinted in *Revolutionary Radicalism*, I, pp. 1870-1891.
39. "Proclamation by the United Communist Party of America," *The Communist* (UCP), no. 7.
40. Jane Degras, *The Communist International 1919-1943*, Documents, 1919-1922, Vol. I, London, 1956, p. 73.
41. "The Communist International to the American Comrades," *The Communist International*, June-July, 1920; also *Revolutionary Radicalism*, *op. cit.*, pp. 1902-1908.
42. *The Toiler*, August 27, 1920.
43. William D. Haywood, "Revolutionary Problems in America"; V. Lossief, "Industrial Workers of the World"; A. Lozovsky, "The Labor Union in the Epoch of the Dictatorship of the Proletariat," all in *The Communist International*, III, Nos. 16-17.
44. Degras, "Extracts from a Letter from the ECCI to the Trade Unions of All Countries," *The Communist International*, 1919-1943, I, pp. 87-90.
45. From Stenographic Report of the Proceedings of the Second Congress, cited in *The Communist* (CP), November 1, 1920.
46. *The Communist* (CP), August 1, 1920.
47. *The Toiler*, November 6, 1920.
48. *The Communist* (CPA), May 1921.
49. *The Theses and Statutes of the Communist International* (CPA)

(pamphlet), New York, 1921.
50. "The Second U.C.P. Convention," *The Communist* (UCP), no. 13.
51. *James O'Neal vs. Robert Minor* (pamphlet), New York, 1921.
52. *Socialist World*, November 15, 1920.
53. "The Communist International to the American Socialists," *The Communist* (UCP), no. 10.
54. "The Open Communist Party— The Task of the Hour!" *The Workers Council*, October 15, 1921.
55. L. D. Trotsky, "Report on the World Economic Crises and the New Tasks of the International," *The First Five Years of the Comintern*, New York, 1945, I, p. 176; extract from the Theses on the Communist International and the

Red International of Labor Unions, adopted by the Third Congress, Degras, *The Communist International*, Documents, I, pp. 274-81.
56. *Program and Constitution* (pamphlet), Workers Party of America, New York, 1922.
57. "The UCP and the CP United," *The Communist* (CPA), July, 1921.
58. Benjamin Gitlow, *The Whole of Their Lives*, New York, 1948, pp. 62-63.
59. "Thesis on the Relation of Number One to Number Two," reprinted in Richard M. Whitney, *Reds in America*, New York, 1924, pp. 165-169.
60. "The UCP and the CP United," *The Communist* (CPA), July, 1921.

Chapter III. A Plunge into American Politics

1. "The Next Tasks of the Communist Party in America," reprinted in *People vs. Ruthenberg*, Transcript of the Record, Supreme Court of the United States, October Term, 1925, pp. 158-169.
2. Testimony of Jay Lovestone in *Ibid.*, p. 135.
3. *The Workers Challenge*, April 8, 1922.
4. Cited in Benjamin Gitlow, *I Confess*, New York, 1939, p. 133.
5. "The Next Tasks of the Communist Party," in *People vs. Ruthenberg, op. cit.*
6. "Thesis on the Relation of Number One to Number Two," reprinted in Whitney, *op. cit.*
7. *Story of Assault on Liberty in Michigan Red Raid Cases* (pamphlet), Chicago, 1923.
8. Jay Lovestone, *The Worker*, April 21, 1923.

9. Ella Reeve Bloor, *We Are Many*, New York, 1940, p. 189.
10. Comintern Communique reprinted in *The Worker*, February 24, 1923.
11. *Voice of Labor*, March 2, 1923.
12. John Pepper, *The Worker*, May 26, 1923.
13. "Resolution of the Adjustment Committee," reprinted in *People vs. Ruthenberg, op. cit.*, pp. 170-174.
14. *The Agricultural Crisis and Its Causes*, Report of the Joint Commission of Agricultural Inquiry, Part II, Government Printing Office, Washington, D. C., 1922, p. 7.
15. Selig Perlman and Philip Taft, *History of Labor in the United States, 1896-1932*, New York, 1935, IV, p. 491.
16. *Labor*, September 9, 1922.
17. John Pepper, *Underground Radicalism* (pamphlet), New York, 1923.

18. Cf. *The New Majority*, February 17, 1923.
19. *Advance*, March 3, 1922.
20. Quoted in Morris Hillquit, *Loose Leaves From a Busy Life*, New York, 1934, p. 312.
21. Jay Lovestone, *The Worker*, February 25, 1922.
22. See footnote 14, Leon Trotsky, *The First Five Years of the Communist International*, New York, 1945, I, p. 351.
23. Sigismund Kunfi, "A Meeting of the Soviet at Siofok," *Az Ember*, reprinted in appendices of Eleonor Malyusz, *Fugitive Bolsheviks*, London, 1931.
24. John Pepper, *For a Labor Party* (pamphlet), 3rd edition, Chicago, 1923, p. 19.
25. *Ibid.*, p. 57.
26. *The New Majority*, December 23, 1922.
27. *The Worker*, March 10, 1923.
28. Bell, *op. cit.*, p. 331.
29. *Labor Herald*, December, 1922.
30. "Manifesto of the Workers Party of America," *The Worker*, June 2, 1923.
31. John Pepper, *The Liberator*, July, 1923.
32. John Pepper, *The Worker*, July 7, 1923.
33. *The New Majority*, July 14, 1923.
34. *Ibid.*
35. *The New Majority*, May 24, 1924.
36. John Pepper, *The Liberator*, August, 1923.
37. John Pepper, *For a Labor Party*, pp. 74-75.
38. *The Second Year of the Workers Party*, Theses, Program, Resolutions, Chicago, 1924, p. 25.
39. *Ibid.*
40. Editorial, *Labor*, July 21, 1924.
41. *William F. Dunne's Speech* (pamphlet), Chicago, 1923.
42. William Z. Foster, *Labor Herald*, January, 1924.
43. For a detailed analysis of "August Thesis," see Max Shachtman, "The Problem of the Labor Party," *The New International*, March, 1935.
44. *From the Fourth to the Fifth World Congress*, Report of the Executive Committee of the Communist International, London, 1924, p. 79.
45. *The Second Year of the Workers Party of America*, p. 61.
46. Clarence Hathaway, *DW*, Dec. 22, 1924.
47. *Labor*, December 1, 1923.
48. John Pepper, *The Worker*, December 22, 1923.
49. John Pepper, *Liberator*, August, 1923.
50. Charles Ruthenberg, *DW*, March 31, 1924.
51. *The New York Times*, May 29, 1924; for background material on this letter, see Belle C. LaFollette and Fola LaFollette, *Robert M. LaFollette*, New York, 1953, II, pp. 1098-1105.
52. *Minnesota Union Advocate*, May 29, 1924.
53. Joseph Manley, *DW*, January 7, 1925.
54. *DW*, June 14, 1924.
55. *DW*, July 11, 1924.
56. *DW*, July 19, 1924.
57. Joseph Manley, *DW*, December 30, 1924.
58. William Z. Foster, *Workers Monthly*, November, 1924.
59. *DW*, December 3, 1924.
60. *DW*, November 7, 1924.

Chapter IV. The Party Becomes Stalinized

1. V. I. Lenin, *Works* (Russian Edition), XVIII, part I, p. 321; quoted in Leon Trotsky, *The Third International After Lenin*, New York, 1936, p. 14.
2. Max Shachtman, *The Struggle for the New Course*, New York, 1943, p. 131.
3. James P. Cannon, *Workers Monthly*, November, 1924.
4. *DW*, December 13, 1924.
5. Quoted in *The American Labor Yearbook 1926*, New York, 1926, p. 255.
6. Gitlow, *op. cit.*, p. 235.
7. *DW*, March 28, 1925.
8. *DW*, August 20, 1925.
9. *From the Third through the Fourth Convention of the Workers (Communist) Party of America*, Chicago, 1925, p. 19.
10. *Ibid.*
11. Max Bedacht, *The Menace of Opportunism* (pamphlet), Chicago, 1926.
12. Earl Browder, *Workers Monthly*, May, 1925.
13. Shachtman, Abern and Glotzer, *The Situation in the American Opposition* (mimeographed), n.d.
14. James P. Cannon, *The History of American Trotskyism*, New York, 1944, pp. 47-59.
15. Quoted in George Spiro, *Marxism and the Bolshevik State*, New York, 1951, p. 172.
16. Jay Lovestone, "Perspectives for Our Party," *The Communist*, June, 1927.
17. Bertram D. Wolfe, *The Trotsky Opposition* (pamphlet), New York, 1928.
18. "Resolution on the Report of the Political Committee," *The Communist*, July, 1928.
19. Quotes in this paragraph come from "The Right Danger in the American Party," platform of the United Opposition, submitted to the Sixth World Congress of the Comintern, reprinted in *The Militant*, November 15, 1928.
20. Jay Lovestone, "Some Issues in the Party Discussion," *The Communist*, January-February, 1929.
21. Bertram D. Wolfe, "The Right Danger in the Comintern," *The Communist*, December, 1928.
22. Bertram D. Wolfe, *The Trotsky Opposition*, *op. cit.*
23. Jay Lovestone, "Some Issues in the Party Discussion," *The Communist*, January-February, 1929.
24. Craig Thompson, "Moscow's Mouthpiece in New York," *Saturday Evening Post*, September 12, 1953.
25. *On the Road to Bolshevization* (pamphlet), New York, 1929.
26. Gitlow, *op. cit.*, p. 523.
27. L. D. Trotsky, *The Militant*, August 15, 1929.
28. Cited in "To All Members of the Communist Party of the United States," (from the ECCI), *DW*, May 20, 1929.
29. *Stalin's Speeches at the American Commission of the Communist Party* (pamphlet), New York, 1929.
30. Gitlow, *op. cit.*, p. 560.
31. Robert Minor, *Inprecorr*, 1929, no. 59, p. 1111.
32. Leon Platt, "The Struggle for the Comintern in America," *The Communist*, September, 1929.

Chapter V. Ultra-Leftism

1. William Z. Foster, *Acceptance Speech* (pamphlet), New York, 1928, p. 31.
2. Israel Amter, *DW*, June 11, 1928.
3. Scott Nearing, "The Political Outlook of the Workers (Communist) Party," *The Communist*, December, 1928.
4. Headline, *DW*, November 7, 1930; quoted by L. D. Trotsky, "The Third Period of the Comintern's Mistake," *The Militant*, February 15, 1930; *DW*, October 16, 1930.
5. Franz Borkenau, *The Communist International*, London, 1938, p. 332.
6. *Ibid.*, p. 339.
7. William Z. Foster, *History of the Communist Party of the U.S.*, New York, 1952, p. 266.
8. Borkenau, *op. cit.*, p. 338.
9. *Inprecorr*, October 9, 1924.
10. Foster, quoted in *Hearings Before a Special Committee to Investigate Communist Activities in the United States*, 1930, I, p. 348; ECCI quoted in C. L. R. James, *World Revolution*, New York, 1937, p. 311; "The Economic and Political Situation in the U.S. and the Tasks of the Communist Party," Central Committee resolution, CPUSA, *DW*, October 16, 1932.
11. Sidney Hook, "The Fallacy of the Theory of Social Fascism," *Modern Quarterly*, July, 1934.
12. Quoted in *ibid.*
13. Quoted in Alpha (L. D. Trotsky), "Radek's Novitiate: What Is Social Fascism?" *The Militant*, October 1, 1930.
14. This footnote includes all quotations in the five previous paragraphs: *Rote Fahne*, September 15, 1930, quoted in *Militant*, February 11, 1933; *Junge Garde*, late 1929, quoted in *Militant*, February 11, 1933; Ernst Thaelmann, "Some Mistakes in Our Work," *Communist International*, December 15, 1931; Piatnitsky quoted in C. L. R. James, *op. cit.*, p. 341; Willi Muenzenberg quoted in *Militant*, February 11, 1933; *Der Propagandist*, quoted in *Militant*, February 11, 1933; *DW*, February 8, 1933; *Rundschau*, No. 17, 1933, quoted in Borkenau, *op. cit.*, p. 378.
15. Earl Browder, *The Meaning of Social Fascism* (pamphlet), New York, 1933, p. 40; *DW*, December 19, 1929; *DW*, October 31, 1929; *DW*, October 24, 1929; *DW*, May 8, 1929; *DW*, June 19, 1929; *DW*, August 23, 1928; *DW*, November 13, 1928; *DW*, August 27, 1930.
16. *DW*, July 9, 1929; *DW*, January 23, 1928; *DW*, February 10, 1928; *ibid.*; *DW*, May 1, 1929; *DW*, May 3, 1929; *DW*, August 24, 1929.
17. *DW*, September 14 and 15, 1934.
18. *DW*, March 6, 1931; *DW*, March 12, 1931.
19. *DW*, January 11, 1932; *DW*, April 19, 1930.
20. Cf. Resolution, Central Committee, CP, *DW*, January 30, 1932.
21. *DW*, March 6, 1931; quoted in Phil Frankfeld, "The Crisis and the Strike Curve for 1930," *The Communist*, May, 1931; *DW*, October 21, 1933; Herbert Benjamin, "The Unemployed Movement in the U.S.," *The Communist*, June, 1935.
22. *DW*, August 6, 1928.
23. *DW*, July 16, 1930.

24. Jack Stachel, "Organizational Report to 6th Convention, CPUSA," *The Communist,* April, 1929; Earl Browder, "Report of the PC of the 12th CC Plenum of the CPUSA," *The Communist,* January, 1931.

25. *The Revolutionary Movement in the Colonies: Theses Adopted at the Sixth World Congress of the Communist International,* New York, 1929; Joseph Stalin, *Marxism and the Colonial Question,* New York, 1934.

26. "Resolution of the CI on the Negro Question in the United States," *The Communist Position on the Negro Question,* New York, 1930.

27. John Pepper, "American Negro Problems," *The Communist,* October, 1928; Harry Haywood, "The Theoretical Defenders of White Chauvinism in the Labor Movement," *The Communist,* June, 1931.

28. Clarence Hathaway, *DW,* April 15, 1931; William Weinstone, "The Economic Crisis in the U.S. and the Tasks of the CP," *Communist International,* February 15, 1930.

29. Wilson Record, *The Negro and the Communist Party,* Chapel Hill, 1951, p. 57. We are indebted to Mr. Wilson's full and informative account for some of the references in this section.

30. *Race Hatred on Trial: The Yokinen Case* (pamphlet), New York, 1931, *passim;* see also *New York Times,* February 28 and March 1, 1931.

31. Henry Lee Moon, *Balance of Power: The Negro Vote,* Garden City, 1948, pp. 129-130.

32. *DW,* June 17, 1931.

33. Robert Minor, "The Negro and His Judases," *The Communist,* July, 1931; James S. Allen, "The Scottsboro Struggle," *The Communist,* May, 1933.

34. T. Gussev, "The End of Capitalist Stabilization and the Basic Tasks of the British and American Sections of the Communist International," *Communist International,* October 15, 1932.

35. Earl Browder, letter to editor, *New York Times,* September 29, 1950.

36. This note includes all quotations in Section 6: "Toward Revolutionary Mass Work," Resolution, CC of CPUSA, 1932; *DW,* February 13, 1933; Earl Browder, *PO,* November, 1933; Browder, *DW,* January 28, 1933; *PO,* May-June, 1932; *NM,* February 20, 1934; *PO,* March, 1934; *PO,* August-September, 1934; Clarence Hathaway, "On the Use of Transmission Belts in Our Struggle for the Masses," *The Communist,* May, 1931; *DW,* May 8, 1934; *PO,* August, 1932; *PO,* February, 1932; *PO,* May-June, 1932; *PO,* September-October, 1934; Si Gerson, *DW,* February 27, 1930; *PO,* May-June, 1932; *PO,* March, 1935; *PO,* June, 1931; *PO,* October, 1934; *PO,* June, 1931; *DW,* May 6, 1929; *PO,* September-October, 1931; Report of National Organization Dept., 8th National Convention, CP, in *PO,* May-June, 1934; Will Herberg, "Outline for Speakers on Trotskyism" (mimeographed), 1929; *DW,* February 15, 1935; *DW,* December 11, 1929; Max Bedacht, *DW,* January 22, 1930; Beidel case report, *Militant,* August 5, 1933; on Radek, cf. James Casey, *The Crisis in the Communist Party,* New York, 1936; *Militant,* November 24, 1934; statistics on functionaries taken from "Chart D, Organizational Status of the

Party, Organizational Report, 8th CP Convention, 1934"; Moissaye Olgin, *DW*, November 25, 1935.

37. Earl Browder, "Why an Open Letter to Our Party Membership?" *The Communist*, August, 1933; Norman Thomas, quoted in *DW*, August 25, 1934; Clarence Hathaway, *DW*, May 30 and June 3, 1933.

38. Earl Browder, *DW*, July 8, 1933; *DW*, July 28, 1933; "Draft Reso-

lution, 8th Convention, CPUSA" (pamphlet), New York, 1934; Earl Browder, "Recent Political Developments and Some Problems of the United Front," *The Communist*, July, 1935.

39. James MacGregor Burns, *Roosevelt: The Lion and the Fox*, New York, 1956, pp. 198 and 193.

40. *DW*, November 23, 1933; *DW*, October 9, 1935.

Chapter VI. The Dual Unions: Heroism and Disaster

1. Cf. David Saposs, *Left Wing Unionism*, New York, 1926 and David M. Schneider, *The Workers (Communist) Party and American Trade Unions*, Baltimore, 1928.
2. William Z. Foster, *The Labor Herald*, September 1924.
3. William Z. Foster, *From Bryan to Stalin*, New York, 1937, p. 195.
4. *Program for Trade Union Educational League*, Third World Congress of the Red International of Labor Unions (pamphlet), Chicago, 1924, p. 55.
5. The facts are freely admitted in Foster's *From Bryan to Stalin*, a book published at a time when the CP line had veered sharply to the right so that it became permissible to discuss "sectarian errors" of the past.
6. Cf. Max Nomad, *Rebels and Renegades*, New York, 1932, pp. 359-360.
7. William Z. Foster, *Bankruptcy of the American Labor Movement*, New York, 1923.
8. William Z. Foster, *Misleaders of Labor*, New York, 1927, pp. 319-320.
9. Quoted in Nomad, *op. cit.*, p. 361. Nomad's lucid discussion of the struggle between Foster

and Haywood, pp. 360-362, is especially valuable.

10. *The Fourth National Convention*, Workers (Communist) Party, Chicago, 1925, p. 101.
11. Benjamin Gitlow, *I Confess*, New York, 1940, p. 363.
12. *Ibid.*
13. Albert Weisbord, *The Conquest of Power*, New York, 1937, II, p. 1115.
14. Gitlow, *op. cit.*, p. 366.
15. Cf. Mary Heaton Vorse, *The Passaic Textile Strike*, New York, 1927.
16. *The Christian Century*, August 5, 1926.
17. Gitlow, *op. cit.*, pp. 370-371.
18. *Ibid.*, p. 372 ff.
19. Cf. Paul Blanshard, "New Bedford Goes on Strike," *New Republic*, May 23, 1928; Robert Dunn and Jack Hardy, *Labor and Textiles*, New York, 1931, pp. 225-226; and for the contemporary Communist version, Albert Weisbord, "Some Aspects of the Situation in New Bedford," *The Communist*, July 1928.
20. For material on the following section, see Fred Beal, *Proletarian Journey*, New York, 1937, especially pp. 98-101; also J. B. S. Hardman, "Communism in

America," *New Republic*, September 3, 1930.

21. Cf. the invaluable study by Melech Epstein, *Jewish Labor in USA 1914-1952*, New York, 1953. Additional material is to be found in Benjamin Stolberg, *Tailor's Progress*, New York, 1944; Joel Seidman, *The Needle Trades*, New York, 1942 and David Schneider, *op. cit.*, Chapter VI. For a version sympathetic to the TUEL and TUUL, see Jack Hardy, *The Clothing Workers*, New York, 1935.

22. J. B. S. Hardman, "Ten Years of the Labor Movement," in *American Labor Dynamics*, edited by himself, New York, 1928, p. 29.

23. William F. Dunne, "The Left Wing at Two Conventions," *Workers Monthly*, February, 1926.

24. Accounts of the detailed factional alignments and of the key discussion at the decisive September 18 meeting differ somewhat. Compare Gitlow, *op. cit.*, pp. 361-362 and Epstein, *op. cit.*, pp. 145-146. There is agreement, however, on the essential point that the factional struggles within the party constituted the main reason for not settling the strike promptly.

25. In addition to Epstein, *op. cit.*, pp. 166-168, see Mathew Josephson, *Sidney Hillman*, New York, 1952.

26. Cf. Schneider, *op. cit.*, Chapter V; Epstein, *op. cit.*, pp. 168-177. For a pro-Communist version see Hardy, *op. cit.*, and William S. Foner, *The Furrier and Leather Workers Union*, New York, 1950.

27. C. S. Daugherty, *Labor Problems in American Industry*, New York, 1933, p. 356.

28. A. J. Muste, "Factions in Trade Unions," in J. B. S. Hardman, ed., *American Labor Dynamics*, New York, 1928, p. 346.

29. A. Lozovsky, "Results and Prospects of the United Front," *The Communist International*, March 15, 1928.

30. *Report of the Fourth Congress of the Red International of Trade Unions*, London, 1928, pp. 136-137.

31. *Theses and Resolutions, Third World Congress of the Communist International*, New York, 1921, p. 137.

32. Both statements quoted in J. B. S. Hardman, "Communism in America," *New Republic*, September 3, 1930.

33. For this "Resolution on Trade Union Work" as well as the positions of Foster and Cannon, see *The Communist*, July, 1928.

34. William Z. Foster, "Tasks and Lessons of the Miners' Struggle," *The Communist*, April, 1928.

35. In later years, when it was safe to criticize dual unionism, Foster repeatedly hinted at his disagreements with the 1928 decision. See his *From Bryan to Stalin*, p. 215 and his *History of the Communist Party of the USA*, New York, 1952, p. 258.

36. William Z. Foster, "The TUUL Convention," *The Communist*, September, 1929.

37. William Z. Foster, *Toward Soviet America*, New York, 1932, pp. 177-178.

38. Louis Stanley, "Communist Dual Unionism," *Labor Age*, October, 1929.

39. For these membership figures, see J. B. S. Hardman, "Communism in America," *New Republic*, September 3, 1930.

40. William Z. Foster, "Dilettantism in Strikes," *The Communist*, December, 1931.

41. *PO*, September-October, 1931.
42. Some of the background material is drawn from the excellent account by Tom Tippett, *When Southern Labor Stirs*, New York, 1931.
43. Quoted in Tippett, *ibid.*, p. 81.
44. Quoted in Paul Blanshard, "Communism in Southern Textile Mills," *The Nation*, April 24, 1929. Tippett, *op. cit.*, pp. 88-89, gives a slightly different but substantially similar version.
45. Beal, *op. cit.*, pp. 136-137.
46. *Ibid.*, pp. 139-140.
47. William F. Dunne, *Gastonia, Citadel of the Class Struggle in the New South* (pamphlet), New York, 1929.
48. *DW*, August 27, 1930.
49. W. J. Cash, *The Mind of the South*, New York, 1954, pp. 346-357.
50. For details on this and on the following paragraphs, see McAlister Coleman, *Men and Coal*, New York, 1943 and Saul Alinsky, *John L. Lewis*, New York, 1939.
51. See John Brophy, "Elements of a Progressive Union Policy," in *American Labor Dynamics, op. cit.*, pp. 186-191.
52. From an interview with Hapgood in Alinsky, *op. cit.*, p. 58.
53. Arne Swabeck, "The National Miners Union," *The Communist*, October, 1928.
54. William Z. Foster, *From Bryan to Stalin, op. cit.*, pp. 229-231.
55. *Labor Unity*, April 4, 1931.
56. *PO*, June-July, 1930.
57. *PO*, September-October, 1931; *PO*, November-December, 1932.
58. *PO*, August, 1932.
59. Kutnik, "The Revolutionary Trade Union Movement in the USA in the Condition of the New Deal of Trustified Capitalism," *Communist International*, September 20, 1934.
60. O. Piatnitsky, "Once More About Work in the Reformist and Fascist Unions," *Communist International*, January 15, 1934.
61. O. Piatnitsky, "Problems of the International Trade Union Movement," *Communist International*, November 20, 1934.
62. Jack Stachel, "Lessons of the Economic Struggles and the Work in the Trade Unions," *The Communist*, March, 1934.
63. Jack Stachel, "Our Trade Union Policy," *The Communist*, November, 1934.
64. Earl Browder, Speech at 13th Plenum of the ECCI, *The Communist International*, January 15, 1934.
65. Sam Darcy, "The Great West Coast Maritime Strike," *The Communist*, July, 1934.

Chapter VII. The Intellectuals Turn Left

1. Granville Hicks, "Communism and the American Intellectuals," in I. D. Talmadge, *Whose Revolution?* New York, 1941, p. 79.
2. Robert Morss Lovett, "Liberals and the Class War," *Modern Quarterly*, February, 1928.
3. John Dos Passos, "They Are Dead Now," *NM*, October, 1927.
4. Michael Gold, "Notes of the Month," *NM*, March, 1928.
5. Michael Gold, "Notes of the Month," *NM*, September, 1930.
6. Horace Gregory, review of M. Josephson, "Portrait of the Artist as an American," *NM*, August, 1930.
7. Herman Spector, review of A.

Kreymborg, "The Little World," *NM*, July, 1932.

8. A. B. Magil, "Mayakovsky," *NM*, June, 1930.

9. Newton Arvin, letter to editor, *NM*, December, 1930.

10. Advertisement for debate, *NM*, July, 1930.

11. "The Kharkov Conference of Revolutionary Writers," *NM*, February, 1931.

12. Edmund Wilson, *The Shores of Light*, New York, 1952, p. 498.

13. John Dos Passos, Granville Hicks, Sherwood Anderson, "Whither the American Writer," *Modern Quarterly*, Summer, 1932.

14. Sherwood Anderson, "A Writer's Notes," *NM*, August, 1932.

15. See Irving Howe, *Sherwood Anderson*, New York, 1951, p. 219.

16. V. J. Jerome, "Unmasking an American Revisionist of Marxism," *The Communist*, January, 1933.

17. Alfred Kazin, *On Native Grounds*, New York, 1942, p. 418.

18. Granville Hicks, "The Crisis in Criticism," *NM*, February, 1933; Isidor Schneider, "Of Love and Other Things," *NM*, July 7, 1936; Obed Brooks, review of M. Cowley, "After the Genteel Tradition," *NM*, August 17, 1937; A. B. Magil, review of G. Lumpkin, "To Make My Bread," *NM*, February, 1933; unsigned review of G. Stein, "Lectures in America," *NM*, April 9, 1935; Joseph Freeman, review of E. Rolfe, "To My Contemporaries," *NM*, March 10, 1936; V. J. Jerome, "Toward a Proletarian Novel," *NM*, August, 1932; Granville Hicks, review of F. Burke, "A Stone Came Rolling," *NM*, December 3, 1935; Robert Briffault, "The Marxist Founda-

tion of Humor," *NM*, July 9, 1935; E. B. Burgum, quoted in Kazin, *op. cit.*, pp. 418-419; Norman MacLeod, review of A. Halper, "On the Shore," *NM*. May 1, 1934; *NM* editorial, April 3, 1934; M. W. Mather, review of A. MacLeish, *Poems*, January 16, 1934; *NM* editorial, February 20, 1934; F. W. Dupee, "Stalinism and Hitlerism," *NM*, Jaunary 26, 1937.

19. Granville Hicks, "Communism and American Intellectuals," *op. cit.*, p. 84.

20. Michael Gold, "Why I Am a Communist," *NM*, September, 1932; Granville Hicks, "What Shall I Read?" *NM*, October 4, 1938; Clifton Fadiman, "How I Came to Communism," *NM*, September, 1932; John Howard Lawson, " 'Inner Conflict' and Proletarian Art," *NM*, April 17, 1934; Waldo Frank, Letter to editor, *New Republic*, February 27, 1935; Horace Gregory, "One Writer's Position," *NM*, February 12, 1935; Meridel Le Sueur, "The Fetish of Being Outside," *NM*, February 26, 1935; Isidor Schneider, *The Judas Time*, New York, 1946, p. 108.

21. Herbert Solow, "Minutiae of Left-Wing Literary History," *Partisan Review*, March, 1938.

22. Edmund Wilson, *The American Jitters*, New York, 1932, p. 22.

23. Philip Rahv, "The Literary Class War," *NM*, August, 1932.

24. "An Open Letter," *NM*, March 6, 1934.

25. William Phillips and Philip Rahv, "Recent Problems of Revolutionary Literature," in *Proletarian Literature in the United States*, Hicks, Gold, *et al.*, (eds.), New York, 1935, p. 368.

26. For a number of the ideas in the paragraphs that follow we are in-

debted to an unpublished manuscript by Granville Hicks which he was kind enough to place at our disposal.

27. Philip Rahv, "Proletarian Literature, a Political Autopsy," *Southern Review*, Winter, 1939.
28. James T. Farrell, *Literature and Morality*, New York, 1947, p. 160.
29. Michael Gold, *DW*, February 9, 1934.
30. Rahv, "Proletarian Literature, a Political Autopsy," *Southern Review*, Winter, 1939.
31. Michael Gold, *DW*, February 28, 1938.
32. Kazin, *op. cit.*, p. 420.
33. Granville Hicks, "The Failure of Left Criticism," *New Republic*, September 9, 1940.
34. Granville Hicks, letter to editor, *New Republic*, October 4, 1939.
35. All quotations from first American Writers Congress taken from Henry Hart, *American Writers Congress*, New York, 1935— Josephson, p. 38; Browder, p. 37;

the unionist, pp. 15-16; Conroy, p. 83.
36. Philip Rahv, "Two Writers Congresses," *Partisan Review*, February, 1940.
37. *Ibid.*
38. Dwight Macdonald, letter to editor, *The Nation*, June 19, 1937.
39. Henry Hart, *The Writer in a Changing World*, New York, 1937.
40. Murray Kempton, *Part of Our Time*, New York, 1955, p. 144.
41. "A Professor Joins the Communist Party," *NM*, October 5, 1937; "Browder and the Church," *NM*, August 2, 1938; also *NM*, 1937-38, *passim*.
42. Letter to editor, *The Nation*, August 26, 1939.
43. Michael Gold, "What Side Are You On?" *NM*, October 3, 1939.
44. Albert Maltz, "What Shall We Ask of Writers?" *NM*, February 12, 1946.
45. Howard Fast, "Art and Politics," *NM*, February 26, 1946.
46. Albert Maltz, "Looking Forward," *NM*, April 9, 1946.

Chapter VIII. The Popular Front: Success and Respectability

1. Borkenau, *op. cit.*, p. 387.
2. R. Palme Dutt, *Labour Monthly*, England, January, 1935.
3. *DW*, May 11, 1935.
4. Wilhelm Pieck, *Freedom, Peace and Bread* (pamphlet), New York, 1936.
5. Vaillant-Couturier, *L'Humanite*, June 7, 1936, quoted in C. L. R. James, *World Revolution*, p. 397; *Manchester Guardian*, September 6, 1936; Greek CP quote in *New York Post*, January 6, 1936; *Inprecorr*, August 22, 1936; *ibid.*, October 24, 1936.
6. Earl Browder, "Recent Political Developments and the United

Front," *The Communist*, July, 1935.
7. Thomas quoted in *DW*, December 14, 1935; *DW*, November 8, 1935; Thomas quoted in *DW*, December 12, 1935.
8. *DW*, November 29, 1935; *Which Road for American Workers?* (Thomas-Browder debate), New York, 1936.
9. *Proceedings, Ninth National Convention*, CP, New York, 1936.
10. *Ibid.*
11. *Proceedings, Tenth Convention*, New York State CP, 1938.
12. Alexander Bittleman, "Review of

the Month," *The Communist*, April, 1936.

13. *Proceedings*, Tenth Convention, New York State CP, 1938.

14. Earl Browder, *The Communists in the People's Front* (pamphlet), New York, 1937; Clarence Hathaway, "The People Versus the Supreme Court," *The Communist*, April, 1937.

15. Earl Browder, "Perspectives of the 1940 Election," *The Communist*, June, 1939; *DW*, August 22, 1939; E. Browder, *The Democratic Front* (pamphlet), New York, 1938.

16. J. Peters, *A Manual of Organization*, New York, 1935; *PO*, July-August, 1936; *PO*, January, 1936; *PO*, March, 1938; *PO*, July, 1937; *PO*, July-August, 1936; *PO*, January, 1936; *Proceedings*, New York State Convention, CP, 1938; *PO*, January, 1936; *PO*, January, 1937; *PO*, December, 1935; *PO*, March, 1936.

17. *PO*, August, 1938; *Proceedings*, New York State Convention, CP, 1938; *PO*, May, 1937; *DW*, October 13, 1938.

18. *Proceedings*, New York State Convention, CP, 1938; Young Communist League bulletin, University of Wisconsin, quoted in *Challenge of Youth*, June 1938; *Proceedings*, New York State Convention, CP, 1938.

19. *NM* editorial, April 21, 1936; Earl Browder, *The People's Front*, New York, 1938, p. 239; Louisiana CP quoted in *Socialist Appeal*, March 24, 1939; *DW*, October 5, 1936; Westbrook Pegler, *New York World Telegram*, July 2, 1936; *New York Post*, April 18, 1937.

20. Phil Frankfeld, "Work Among Catholics—A Key Question in Massachusetts," *The Communist*,

July, 1938; *ibid*; *PO*, May, 1938.

21. *Proceedings*, New York State Convention, CP, 1938.

22. *PO*, June, 1937; *Proceedings*, New York State Convention, CP, 1938; William Z. Foster, "The Communist Party and the Professionals," *The Communist*, September 1938; *PO*, May, 1937.

23. Bell, *op. cit.*, p. 359.

24. Earl Browder, *Communism in the United States*, New York, 1935, p. 53. For the first part of the section on the American League Against War and Facism we are indebted to an excellent study, Hillman Bishop's *The American League Against War and Fascism: A Study in Communist Tactics* (mimeographed), New York, 1937.

25. *DW*, October 2, 1933; Browder, *Communism in the United States*, p. 184.

26. *Workers Age*, October 15, 1934; *ibid*.

27. For membership figures see *NM*, January 21, 1936; *Fight* (official organ of the American League Against War and Fascism), February, 1939; Browder, *The Communists in the Peoples Front*; *PO*, July-August, 1936.

28. Quoted in *Militant*, January 11, 1936.

29. *Proceedings*, Third Congress Against War and Fascism, New York, 1936; *A Program Against War and Fascism* (pamphlet), New York, 1936.

30. *DW*, November 29, 1937.

31. Ickes quoted in *DW*, January 7, 1939; Jackson in *DW*, August 7, 1938.

32. *Fight*, February, 1939.

33. James Wechsler, "American Pacifism Seeks a Policy," *New Republic (NR)*, January 8, 1936; William P. Mangold, "Forming a Peoples Front," *NR*,

January 22, 1936; Robert Morss Lovett, "For Peace and Democracy," *NR*, December 15, 1937; Alson Smith, "Death of a League," *NR*, March 18, 1940.
34. *DW*, October 24, 1939.
35. Gunnar Myrdal, *An American Dilemma*, New York, 1944, p. 818.
36. The same point is made by Bell, *op. cit.*, p. 360.
37. Eleanor Roosevelt, *This I Remember*, New York, 1949, p. 200.
38. For the material in this paragraph we are indebted to Mr. George Rawick, who has made a special study of the subject and allowed us to examine his work on it.
39. Bell, *op. cit.*, p. 358.
40. *DW*, February 22, 1937; Carl Reeve, "Benjamin Franklin—Champion of Democracy," *The Communist*, July, 1939; *DW*, April 8, 1936; Browder, *Traitors in American History: Lessons of the Moscow Trials* (pamphlet), New York, 1938.
41. *DW*, October 19, 1938; *DW*, October 10, 1938; *DW*, December 17, 1938; *DW*, May 12, 1938; *DW*, November 15, 1938; *DW*, October 3, 1938 (on Martha Graham); *DW*, October 27, 1938.
42. *Plans and Results*, Bulletin of North American Committee to Aid Spanish Democracy, August 23, 1937; *Give a Party for the Party*, quoted in Eugene Lyons, *The Red Decade*, New York, 1937, p. 282.
43. *PO*, August 1934; *PO*, August, 1935.

44. Jack Stachel, "The Fight of the Steel Workers," *The Communist*, June, 1935.
45. Earl Browder, *The Results of the Election and the Peoples Front* (pamphlet), New York, 1936.
46. This paragraph has been adapted from Irving Howe and B. J. Widick, *The UAW and Walter Reuther*, New York, 1949, p. 51.
47. Quoted in Wellington Roe, *Juggernaut*, Philadelphia, 1948, p. 116.
48. Saul Alinsky, *John L. Lewis*, New York, 1949, p. 154.
49. Quoted in Richard Boyer and Herbert Morais, *Labor's Untold Story*, New York, 1955, pp. 318 and 325.
50. Murray Kempton, *Part of Our Time*, *op. cit.*, p. 71.
51. From *Report of the Special Congressional Committee on Un-American Activities*, January, 1939, pp. 52-54.
52. *PO*, April, 1938; *PO*, June, 1938; *PO*, April, 1938.
53. Clayton Fountain, *Union Guy*, New York, 1949, pp. 62-63.
54. From *Communist Domination of Unions and National Security*, Hearings Before a Subcommittee on Labor and Public Welfare, U. S. Senate, 1952, p. 204.
55. C. Wright Mills, *New Men of Power*, New York, 1948, p. 188.
56. Fountain, *op. cit.*, pp. 75-76.
57. Travers Clement, *Socialist Call*, June 11, 1938.
58. *Why Unions Voted Not to Participate in Harry Bridges' State Convention* (mimeographed pamphlet), Los Angeles, 1938.
59. *PO*, January-February, 1937.

Chapter IX. World War II: Are the Yanks Coming?

1. Earl Browder, *Fighting for Peace* (pamphlet), New York, 1939; Browder speech at Charlottesville, Va., quoted in *Socialist Call*, September 6, 1939.
2. Browder in *DW*, August 24,

1939; *DW*, August 25, 1939.
3. National Committee, CP, quoted in *DW*, September 5, 1939; *ibid;* *DW*, September 6, 1939; *DW*, September 7-30, 1939.
4. William Z. Foster, *The War Crisis, Questions and Answers* (pamphlet), New York, 1940; *Communist International*, February 1940.
5. Foster, *op. cit.*
6. Louis Budenz, *May Day 1940* (pamphlet), New York, 1940; Mike Quin, *The Yanks Are Not Coming* (pamphlet), San Francisco, 1940; Ann Rivington, *No Gold Stars For Us* (pamphlet), New York, 1940.
7. William Z. Foster, *Socialism, the Road to Peace, Prosperity and Freedom* (pamphlet), New York, 1941.
8. Statement, Political Committee, CP, *The Communist*, November, 1939; *DW*, September 5, 1940.
9. See *Socialist Call*, March 16, 1940, and April 27, 1940.
10. *DW*, April 1, 1940; *ibid.*
11. *World News and Views*, February 15, 1941; *DW*, July 10, 1941.
12. *DW*, September, 1939, *passim; DW*, April 11, 1940.
13. Earl Browder, *The Way Out*, New York, 1941, p. 148.
14. *DW*, May 9, 1941; *DW*, July 4, 1940; William Z. Foster, "The Trade Unions and the War," *The Communist*, October, 1940.
15. *DW*, June 17, 1941; *DW*, December 8, 1941.
16. V. J. Jerome, *Intellectuals and the War*, New York, 1940, pp. 12-13, 63; Michael Gold, *The Hollow Men*, New York, 1941, p. 67.
17. N. Chanin, *Jewish Daily Forward*, December 10, 1939.
18. *Yiddisher Kempfer*, November 3, 1939 and September 22, 1939.

19. L. Hendin, "The Crisis in the American Communist Movement," *Zukunft*, December, 1939.
20. *Yiddisher Kempfer*, November 3, 1939.
21. *Jewish Daily Forward*, December 19, 1939.
22. Roy Hudson, "For a Greater Vote and a Stronger Party," *The Communist*, August, 1940.
23. William Z. Foster, "Yankee Imperialism Grabs for the Western Hemisphere," *The Communist*, July, 1941; also editorial in same issue.
24. *DW*, June 26, 1941; *DW*, July 29, 1941.
25. *DW*, December 9, 1941.
26. John Gates, "The Army and the People," *The Communist*, November, 1941.
27. *DW*, November 24, 1941; *DW*, March 3, 1942.
28. *Business Week*, March 18, 1944.
29. *New York Post*, February 1, 1944.
30. Earl Browder, "The Strike Wave Conspiracy," *The Communist*, June 1943.
31. *DW*, April 26, 1943; *DW*, May 3, 1943; *DW*, May 8, 1943; *DW*, June 13, 1943; Earl Browder, "Hold the Home Front," *The Communist*, July, 1943. (For material in this section we are indebted to an excellent article by Joel Seidman, "Labor Policy of the Communist Party During World War II," *Industrial and Labor Relations Review*, October, 1950.)
32. Earl Browder, "The Strike Wave Conspiracy," *The Communist*, June, 1943; *ibid.*
33. George Morris, *The Trotskyite Fifth Column in the Labor Movement*, January, 1945.
34. Bridges, quoted in Albert Epstein and Nathaniel Goldfinger, "Communist Tactics in American

Unions" (mimeographed); *The
Pilot*, February 18, 1944.
35. Harry Henderson and Sam
Shaw, "Readin', Writin', and No
Strikin'," *Colliers*, April 21,
1945.
36. Roy Hudson, "Labor's Victory
Wage Policies," *Political Affairs*,
April, 1935.
37. Earl Browder, "Wage Policy in
War Production" (pamphlet),
New York, 1943; Bridges, quoted
in Epstein and Goldfinger, *op.
cit.*
38. *DW*, April 8, 1945; *ibid.*
39. Wilson Record, *The Negro and
the Communist Party*, Chapel
Hill, 1951, p. 222.
40. James W. Ford, "The Negro
People Unite for Victory," *The
Communist*, July, 1943.
41. *DW*, December 18 and 25,
1944.
42. Quoted in Herbert Hill, "The
Communist Party—Enemy of
Negro Equality," *The Crisis*,
July, 1951.
43. Cf. Herbert Hill, *op. cit.*; also
DW, April 8, 1945.
44. *DW*, February 2, 1942.
45. Townsend quoted in Herbert
Hill, *op. cit.*; Doxey Wilkerson,
"Speech on the Draft Resolution
of the National Board at the
Plenary Meeting of the National
Committee, CPA, June 18-20,
1945," *Political Affairs*, July,
1945.
46. *DW*, August 16, 1941; Israel
Amter, "Norman Thomas—A
Spearhead of Fascism," *The
Communist*, June, 1942.
47. John Williamson, "Lessons of the
Party Building Campaign," *The
Communist*, June, 1943.
48. *Ibid.*
49. Bella Dodd, *School of Darkness*,
New York, 1954, p. 138.
50. John Williamson, "Gearing Organizational Forms and Methods

to the War Effort," *The Communist*, July, 1943; *DW*, June
26, 1942; *DW*, March 23, 1943.
51. Max Weiss, "Toward a New
Anti-Fascist Youth Organization," *The Communist*, September, 1943.
52. John Williamson, "Strengthening Communist Collaboration in
National Unity," *The Communist*, September, 1942.
53. Earl Browder, "Hold the Home
Front," *The Communist*, July,
1943; Browder, *Victory and After*,
New York, 1942, pp. 112-113;
Browder, *Wage Policy in War
Production* (pamphlet), New
York, 1943.
54. Joe Curran, speech at Fifth National Convention of United
Office and Professional Workers
Union, quoted in *Socialist Call*,
September 15, 1944.
55. Earl Browder, *Victory and After*,
p. 83; Browder, *Teheran and
America* (pamphlet), New York,
1944; *ibid.*
56. Earl Browder, *Communism and
National Unity* (pamphlet),
New York, 1944; Browder,
"Teheran—History's Greatest
Turning Point," *The Communist*, January, 1944.
57. *DW*, July 6, 1943.
58. Browder, *Teheran and America.*
59. Robert Minor, *The Heritage of
the Communist Political Association*, New York, 1944.
60. Bella Dodd, *op. cit.*, pp. 162-163.
61. William Z. Foster, "Letter to
National Committee, Communist
Party," *Political Affairs*, July,
1945.
62. For most of the material in this
section on wartime American attitudes toward Soviet Russia we
are indebted to an excellent
article by Paul Willen, "Who
Collaborated With Russia," *An-
tioch Review*, September, 1954.

The following are additional references for quotations cited in this section: Meyer Schapiro, "Mission to Moscow," *Partisan Review*, May-June, 1943; Congressman Rankin quoted in *Labor Action*, March 13, 1944; Monsignor Sheen quoted in Richard E. Lauterbach, *These*

Are the Russians, New York, 1945, p. 248; Mrs. Bates-Batcheller quoted in Foster Rhea Dulles, *The Road to Teheran*, Princeton, 1944, p. 242.

63. Quoted in Dwight Macdonald, *Henry Wallace, The Man and the Myth*, New York, 1948, pp. 107-108.

Chapter X. The Cold War: Repression and Collapse

1. Moissaye Olgin, *That Man Browder* (pamphlet), New York, 1936; Joseph North, *The Case of Earl Browder* (pamphlet), New York, 1942; A. B. Magil, *America Needs Earl Browder* (pamphlet), New York, 1941.
2. Robert Minor, *The Heritage of the Communist Political Association* (pamphlet), New York, 1944.
3. *Ibid.*
4. *DW*, May 27, 1945.
5. Bella Dodd, *School of Darkness*, New York, 1954, p. 182.
6. Speeches by Thompson, Gurley Flynn, Dennis, Hudson, Childs, etc. in *Political Affairs*, July, 1945; Flynn's earlier eulogy of Browder in her pamphlet *Browder, The Man from Kansas*, New York, 1941; letters in *DW*, June 19 and 25, 1945.
7. Bella Dodd, *op cit.*, p. 187.
8. John Gates, *On Guard Against Browderism, Titoism, Trotskyism*, speech at 15th National Convention, CP, December 28-30, 1950; published as pamphlet, 1951.
9. Chick Mason, "Sources of the Present Dilemma," *Party Voice*, September, 1956.
10. Alexander Tarasov-Rodionov, *Chocolate*, London, 1933, p. 180.
11. Earl Browder, *Modern Resurrections and Miracles* (pamphlet), New York, 1950.
12. "The Convention Unanimously

Rejects Browder's Appeal," *Political Affairs*, September, 1948.
13. "The Present Situation and the Next Tasks," *Marxism-Leninism vs. Revisionism* (pamphlet), New York, 1945.
14. V. J. Jerome, *The Treatment of Defeated Germany* (pamphlet), New York, 1945.
15. Max Gordon, *DW*, April 14, 1945; "The Present Situation and the Next Tasks," *op. cit.*; *DW*, June 14, 1945; Adam Lapin, "Issues and Candidates in the New York Elections," *Political Affairs*, October, 1945; William Z. Foster, *Problems of Organized Labor Today* (pamphlet), New York, 1946; Eugene Dennis, Report to Plenary Meeting of National Committee, December 3-5, 1946, *Political Affairs*, January, 1947; William Z. Foster, "American Imperialism and the War Danger," *Political Affairs*, August, 1947; Henry Winston, "Not Against But With the Stream," *Political Affairs*, August, 1947; "Draft Resolution for the National Convention, C.P.U.S.A.," *Political Affairs*, June, 1948.
16. Lawrence Mahan, *Who Are the Foreign Agents?* (pamphlet), New York, 1948.
17. John Williamson, "Trade Union Problems and the Third Party," *Political Affairs*, March, 1948.

18. "Report of the President," *Proceedings of the Sixth National Convention* (National Maritime Union), New York, 1947, pp. 292-295.
19. A. H. Raskin, "Presenting the Phenomenon Called Quill," *New York Times Magazine*, March 5, 1950.
20. John Williamson, *Op. Cit.*
21. John Williamson, "The AF of L and CIO Conventions," *Political Affairs*, December, 1947.
22. John Williamson, "Trade Union Problems and the Third Party," *op. cit.;* Statement by Grant Oakes quoted in "CIO Policy Regarding Communist Party's Program of Disruption (Majority Report)," *Proceedings Twelfth Constitutional Convention* (UAW-CIO), 1949, p. 71; *DW* headline, cited by Walter Reuther, *ibid.*, p. 80.
23. Rose Wortis, *Discussion Bulletin*, November, 1956.
24. William Z. Foster, *The Twilight of World Capitalism*, New York, 1949, p. 69.
25. Jacques Duclos, "On the Dissolution of the Communist Party of the U.S.A.," *Marxism-Leninism vs. Revisionism, op. cit.*
26. Eugene Dennis, "Report to Plenary Meeting of National Community of C.P.U.S.A.," *Political Affairs*, January, 1947.
27. Quoted in Dwight Macdonald, *Henry Wallace, The Man and the Myth*, New York, 1948, p. 101; *The Herald Tribune,* September 13, 1946; quoted in Dwight Macdonald, *op. cit.*, p. 103; *The New York Times,* April 21, 1947.
28. Dwight Macdonald, *Henry Wallace*, p. 24.
29. Cf. Alfred Friendly, *The Washington Post,* May 2, 1948.
30. Dwight Macdonald, *Henry Wallace,* p. 36; Irving Howe and Lewis Coser, "Authoritarians of the Left," *Dissent,* Winter, 1955.
31. Quoted in *Henry Wallace, The Last Seven Months of His Campaign,* published by Americans for Democratic Action, 1948.
32. Report by Steve Muller of Students for Democratic Action, quoted in *ibid.*
33. *New York Times,* February 25, 1948.
34. "Draft Resolution for the National Convention, CPUSA," *Political Affairs,* June, 1948.
35. *DW,* July 18, 1950.
36. Quoted in Foster, *History of C.P.U.S.A.,* p. 509.
37. Robert Claiborne, "Twilight on the Left," *The Nation,* May 11, 1957.
38. Letter to *DW,* July 8, 1956; letter to *DW,* August 26, 1956; letter to *DW,* September 9, 1956; quoted in Claiborne, *ibid.;* A. Marine, "Don't Scuttle the Ship," *Party Voice,* November, 1956; E. S., "Toward a Socialist Democracy," *Party Voice,* October, 1956; Roy Hudson, Speech to National Committee, *Political Affairs,* July, 1945; Gene P., "Road to Socialism," *Party Voice,* October, 1956; letter to *DW,* March 29, 1956; letter to *DW,* June 11, 1956; unsigned, "Toward New Socialist Alliances," *Party Voice,* October, 1956; S., "Errors in Trade Union Activity," *Party Voice,* September, 1956.
39. L. W. M., "Our Attitude Towards the C.P.S.U.," *Party Voice,* December, 1956.
40. William Z. Foster, "On the Situation in the Communist Party," *Political Affairs,* October, 1956.
41. John Gates, "Time for a Change," *Political Affairs,* November, 1956.

42. *Draft Resolution for the 16th National Convention, CPUSA,* September 13, 1956, *Bulletin.*

43. *DW,* November 5, 1956.
44. Quoted in Claiborne, *op. cit.*

Chapter XI. Toward a Theory of Stalinism

1. See Nathan Leites, *A Study of Bolshevism,* Glencoe, Ill., 1954, and Philip Selznick, *The Organizational Weapon,* New York, 1952.
2. Robert Michels, *Political Parties,* Glencoe, Ill., 1949, p. 187.
3. Jules Monnerot, *Sociology and Psychology of Communism,* Boston, 1953, p. 187.
4. Leon Trotsky, *Stalin,* New York, 1941, p. 421.
5. G. L. Arnold, "Collectivism Reconsidered," *Dissent,* Fall, 1955.
6. Berthold Brecht "Die Massnahme," *Versuche 11-12,* Berlin, 1931, pp. 333-334; Ernst Juenger, *Der Arbeiter,* Hamburg, 1932.
7. Karl Marx, "Oekonomisch-philosophische Manuskripte," *Marx-Engels Gesamtausgabe,* III, Berlin, 1932.
8. Quoted in E. H. Carr, *A History of Soviet Russia,* IV, New York, 1951, pp. 363-364.
9. Sidney Hook, *Heresy Yes—Conspiracy No,* New York, 1953; Hannah Arendt, *The Origins of Totalitarianism,* New York, 1951; Monnerot, *op. cit.,* chap. 1.
10. Kurt Goldstein, *Human Nature in the Light of Psychopathology,* Cambridge, Mass., 1940.
11. Morris Ernst and D. G. Loth, *Report on the American Communist,* New York, 1952.
12. Marx, *op. cit.*
13. Louis Aragon, *L'Homme Communiste,* Paris, 1946.
14. Ignazio Silone, "The Choice of Comrades," *Dissent,* Winter, 1955.
15. Max Scheler, "On the Tragic," *Cross Currents,* Winter, 1954.

16. Cf. Francis Fergusson, *The Idea of the Theatre,* Princeton, N. J., 1949.
17. Gabriel Almond, *The Appeals of Communism,* Princeton, N. J., 1954.
18. This concept has been elaborated by Samuel Stouffer *et al.* in *The American Soldier,* I and II, Princeton, N. J., 1949.
19. Cf. Morris Watnick, "The Appeal of Communism to the Peoples of the Underdeveloped Areas," in Bendix and Lipset, *Class, Status and Power,* Glencoe, Ill., 1953.
20. Cf. Robert Merton, "Social Structure and Anomie," in his *Social Theory and Social Structure,* Glencoe, Ill., 1949.
21. Cf. Herbert Luethy, "Why Five Million Frenchmen Vote Communist," *Commentary,* September, 1951.
22. Ernst and Loth, *op. cit.;* Almond, *op. cit.,* pp. 201-202; also Francis X. Sutton, "The Radical Marxist," quoted by Almond, pp. 201-202.
23. Cf. Erich Fromm, "Sozialpsychologischer Teil," in *Autorität und Familie,* Max Horkheimer (ed.), Paris, 1936, p. 83.
24. *Ibid.* Also Fromm, *Escape from Freedom,* New York, 1941.
25. Almond, *op. cit.*
26. Theodore Adorno *et al., The Authoritarian Personality,* New York, 1950.
27. Monnerot, *op. cit.,* pp. 130-131.
28. Franz Neumann, "Anxiety in Politics," *Dissent,* Spring, 1955.
29. Monnerot, *op. cit.,* p. 94.
30. Franz Borkenau, *World Com-*

munism, New York, 1939, p. 364.

31. Sven Rydenfelt, *Kommunisme,* Lund, Sweden, 1954.
32. Monnerot, *op. cit.*
33. Maurice Duverger, *Political Parties,* New York, 1954, pp. 87-88.
34. Borkenau, *op. cit.,* pp. 369-370.
35. *The Fourth National Convention,* Workers (Communist) Party, Chicago, pp. 39-40.
36. *Inprecorr,* No. 74, 1929.
37. Ernst and Loth, *op. cit.*
38. J. M. Domenach, "The French Communist Party," in *Communism in Western Europe,* Mario Einaudi (ed.), Ithaca, N. Y., 1951, p. 101.
39. Cf. Max Weber, *The Theory of Social and Economic Organization,* New York, 1947, pp. 139-145, 245-250.
40. Borkenau, *op. cit.,* pp. 358-359.
41. Cf. V. I. Lenin, *Selected Works,* New York, 1937, IX, p. 129.
42. J. Peters, *The Communist Party*
—*A Manual of Organization,* New York, 1935.
43. Cf. Selznick, *op. cit.,* p. 31.
44. Lord Acton, "Nationality" in *Essays on Freedom and Power,* New York, 1955, p. 164.
45. *New York Times,* September 9, 1949.
46. Hook, *op. cit.,* p. 30.
47. *New York Times,* August 6, 1955.
48. Almond, *op. cit.,* pp. 100-109.
49. Monnerot, *op. cit.,* p. 117.
50. Edmund Burke, *Thoughts on the Cause of the Present Discontents,* Cambridge, England, 1930, p. 96.
51. Czeslaw Milosz, *The Captive Mind,* New York, 1953, p. 215.
52. George Orwell, *1984,* New York, 1949, p. 36.
53. Harold Rosenberg, "The Communist," *Commentary,* July, 1949.
54. Cf. Angelo Rossi, *A Communist Party in Action,* New Haven, 1949.

Index*

* Entries for the new material added to this revised edition (Epilogue) appear in an Index Addenda beginning on page 612.

Garment industry, sympathetic to CP, 241-251
Gastonia strike, 257-262
Gates, John, on military art, 408; on Browder, 448-449; and Khrushchev revelations, 493-494
Gaylord, W. R., 19
General Motors strikes, 370
Gerber, Julius, 37
German Communist Party, 527
German minorities, mistreatment of, in US, 24
Germany, revolution in (1918), 26; CP defeat in, 179; Nazi rise in, 184-185; CP and Social Democrats, 186; communists and Hitler's victory, 186; unemployed in, 195; intellectuals in, 297; invades Russia, 395, 405-407; Stalinism in, 522
Germer, Adolph, 371; convicted, 23
Gitlow, Benjamin, 34, 37, 45, 98; indicted (1919), 55; nominated for mayor, 90; on membership, 92; denounces LaFollette, 138; and 1924 election, 140; and Stalinization, 152; named secretary, 170; resists Stalin, 172, 173; and 1928 election, 175; and Botany Mills strike, 240-241
Gitlow trial, effect of, 55-57
Glassberg, Benjamin, 87
Gold, Ben, 251n, 371, 468; and Lore, 156; influence of, declines, 283
Gold, Mike, 399-400; and *New Masses*, 274-276; quoted, 293; and proletarian literature, 302, 304; on Stalin-Hitler pact, 316; on German invasion of Russia, 406
Goldberg, Millie, attacks Bridges, 384
Goldman, Emma, 51
Gompers, Sam, 10, 11; and TUEL, 236
Goose faction, 98
Gorman, Francis, 329
Government, communist cells in, 361
Graham, Martha, 365
Granger, Lester, 356
Great Britain, CP defeat in, 179; aid to, 395
Great Madness, The, 23
Great Tradition, The, 309

Greece, CP in, 325
Green, Gil, 446, 449, 451; denounces Wallace, 477
Green, P., 156-157; and Finnish Federation, 157-158
Green, William, 414; and Gastonia strike, 258
Gregory, Horace, 276, 282, 288; quoted, 293-294
Gross, Aaron, 251n
Gussev, T., 117, 156, 157; on Scottsboro case, 215-216

Halper, Albert, 287
Hammett, Dashiell, 315
Hapgood, Powers, 371; and UMW, 264-265
Hard, William, 47
Harding, President, grants amnesty, 60
Hardman, J. B., 105
Harlan County strike (1931), 266
Harriman, Job, 10
Harrison, Caleb, 89
Harrison, Charles Yale, 298
Hathaway, Clarence, 131, 209, 220, 330; on socialists, 231; convicted for libel, 400-401
Hayes, Max, 10, 351
Haywood, Bill, 13, 75; on class struggle, 16-17; convicted, 23
Haywood, Harry, on Negroes, 206
Heimwehr, in Austria, 181
Hellman, Lillian, 317
Hillman, Sidney, 251n; on party liners, 372
Hillquit, Morris, 2, 6, 10, 13, 33, 62, 246; on WW I, 19, 21; intellectual head of SP, 20; and People's Council, 21; and 1917 NY Mayoralty campaign, 24; defeated, 35
Hemingway, Ernest, 281, 312, 315
Henderson, Donald, 375
Herberg, Will, 198
Herbst, Josephine, novels of, 306
Heresy, 298
Herndon, Angelo, 356
Herron, Rev. George, 5
Hirshbein, Peretz, 402
Hiss, Alger, 434

Office of War Information, communists in, 434
Olgin, Moissaye, 105; and LaFollette campaign, 136; and Lore, 156; on Browder, 230, 340; on Jewish labor movement, 343
October Revolution, 25
O'Hare, Kate Richards, 35
One World, 432
O'Neal, James, 85
Opatashu, Joseph, 402
Orwell, George, on Spanish civil war, 366
Owens, Edgar, 58
Oxford Pledge, 202, 358

Pacific Maritime Federation, 371
Pacificism, early WW II, 392
Pacificists, treatment of, 24
Palestine, 343
Palmer, A. Mitchell, 50
Palmer raids, 50
Partisan Review, 301
Parity Commission, 156; choses Ruthenberg over Foster, 159-160
Party followers, 518-528
Party line, variations in, 310-318
Passaic (N.J.) strike, 239-243
Patterson, Joseph Medill, 5
Patterson, William L., 205
Peace groups, WW II, 393-395
Pearl Harbor, 407
Pegler, Westbrook, 410; on Browder, 341
People's Council for Democracy and Peace, 21-22
Pepper, John, 100, 115, 121; and LaFollette campaign, 136; on Negroes, 206
Perelman, S. J., 315
Pershing, George, and Gastonia strike, 258
Pesotta, Rose, 371
Phelps, J. G., 5
Phillips, David Graham, 3
Phillips, William, and proletarian literature, 303
Piatnitsky, denounces Trotsky, 185-186
Pieck, Wilhelm, 322
Platt, Leon, on Lovestone, 174

Plumb Plan, 111
PM, 427
Poetry, communism reflected in, 273-297
Pogany, Joseph. See John Pepper.
Poland, CP defeat in, 179; and WW II, 388
Polit Bureau, 229-230
Politics, domestic, CP interest in, 108
Pollitt, Harry, 170
Popular Front, period of, 313; in Europe, 318-325; and Spanish civil war, 320; in France, 320, 324; in US, 325-332; and Democratic party, 331-332; success of, 332; organizations comprising, 347; penetrates government, 360-363; cultural tactic, 363
Populism, 1
Porter, Katherine Anne, 274
Postwar capitalism, and Third Period, 178
"Potemkin village" rally, 139
Poverty, economic, and Stalinist growth, 513-518
Poyntz, Julia, Stuart, and Lore, 156
Pressman, Lee, 374, 396, 463, 472, 475
Prevey, Marguerite, 16
Pro Germanism (WW I), 19
Progressive International Committee, 263
Progressive movement, post WW I, 46; decline in, 49
Progressive Party (1948), Wallace a leader, 470-478; founding convention, 475
Prohibition, 175
Proletarian literature, 301-309
Proletarian Literature in the U.S., 303
Proletarian Party, 61
Propaganda, socialist, 2; in army and navy, 84

Quill, Michael, 371, 378; defeats communists in NMU, 463

Race relations, in CPUSA, 209
Radek, Karl, 78, 228

INDEX ADDENDA

Aptheker, Herbert, 561

Bittleman, Alexander, 557, 562
Browder, Earl, 556; and Bittleman, 562

Castro, Fidel, 569
Clark, Joseph, 556, 557
Communist China, 569
Communist Party, USA, decline of, 555; factional struggle in, 556–563; government prosecution of, 562, 570; "mass work" program, 562, 563; influences Puerto Ricans and Cubans, 564; loses with Negroes, 565; in trade unions, 565; propaganda efforts, 567; "progressives" in, 567; pacifism related to, 568; new adherents, 569; and McCarran Act, 570
CORE, 565

Daily Worker, and "revisionists," 559; suspended, 560
Davis, Benjamin, Jr., 563
Dennis, Eugene, quoted, 557; attacked by Foster, 560; yields, 561; death, 563
Dostoevsky, Fyodor, on "negativism," 566

Fair Play for Cuba Committee, 568
Fast, Howard, 562
Flynn, Elizabeth Gurley, 563, 564
Foster, William Z., as leader of orthodox Communists, 556–563; goes to Russia, dies, 567

Gates, John, "revisionist" leader, 556–560

Hall, Gus, 563; on Freedom Riders, 565; complains of negativism, 566; quoted on Supreme Court decision, 571
Healy, Dorothy, leads Los Angeles group, 560; quoted, 561
Hungarian revolution, 556; and "revisionists," 558

Jackson, James E., edits The Worker, 560; quoted, 561, 563

Khrushchev revelations, 556, 561

Liberty Book Club, 567
Lumer, Hyman, on "liberalism," 558
Lumumba, Patrice, 569

Mainstream, 567
Mboya, Tom, 569
McCarran Act, 570, 571
McCarthyism, 557

National Association for the Advancement of Colored People, 565

Political Affairs, quoted from, 557; Aptheker edits, 561; survey in, 563

SANE, 568

Thomas, Norman, 560
Thompson, Robert, as orthodox Communist leader, 557, 559; quoted, 563, 565, 566

Worker, The, replaces Daily Worker, 560; Bittleman in, 562; Michigan edition, 565; as propaganda, 566, 567

612